BONUS Mobile Versi

odes, more at BF4

Go to
www.primagames.com/BF4
and enter the code below

UNLOCK THIS GUIDE

Enter your code:

q9qn-duhk-c4bk-4rkg

Tutorial Videos
Tips and Videos from Professional Gamers
Sortable Charts • Weapons and Vehicles

GET YOUR BRONZE BATTLEPACK NOW!

Go to
www.primagames.com/BF4Battlepack
and enter the code below

UNLOCK THIS GUIDE

Enter your code:

5uut-8suw-3dur-v8ut

The Bronze Battlefield 4™ Battlepack contains combinations of camos, dog tags, knives, XP boosts, and more!

Access your guide from anywhere with an internet connection!

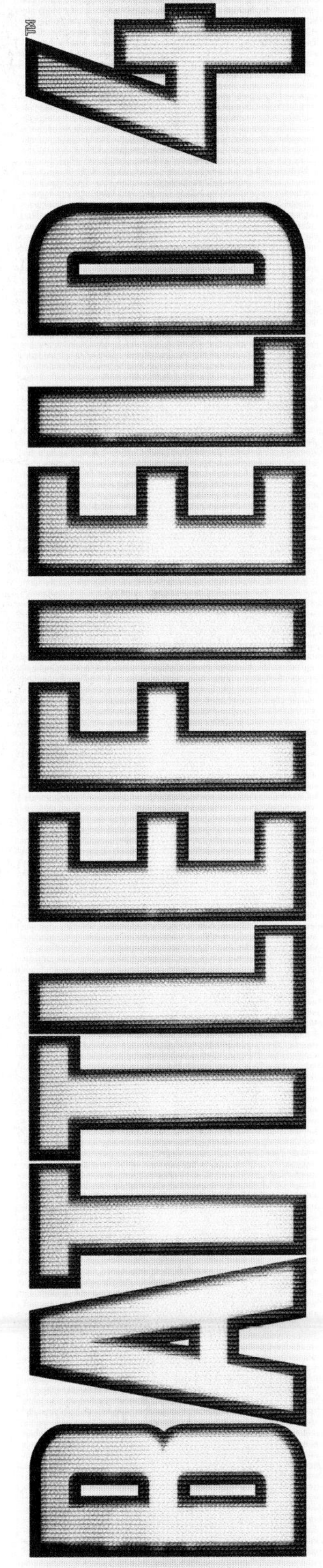

WRITTEN BY:

DAVID 'MABOOZA' KNIGHT

MICHAEL 'STRONGSIDE' CAVANAUGH

MICHAEL 'FLAMESWORD' CHAVES

MARCUS 'ELUMNITE' LOVEJOY

DAVID 'WALSHY' WALSH

CONTENTS

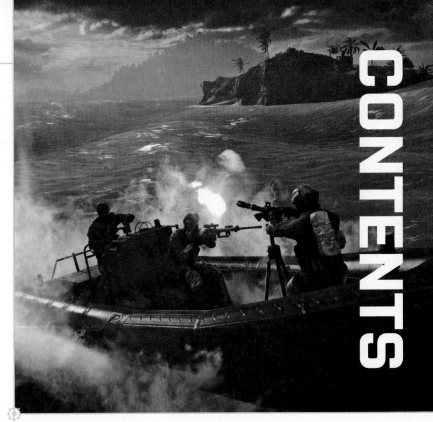

To learn more and watch instructional videos visit PrimaGames.com/BF4

MEET ALPHA SQUAD

MABOOZA

Name: David Knight

David is a veteran Prima Games author, writing more than 40 guides over the past decade. His love for all things *Battlefield* began in 2002, following the release of the *Battlefield 1942* Wake Island demo. When asked to write the guide for *Battlefield 1942*, he reveled in the opportunity to share his knowledge with other fans. Over the last 11 years, David has gone on to write guides for *Battlefield 2*, *Battlefield 2: Modern Combat*, *Battlefield 2142*, *Battlefield Bad Company 2*, and *Battlefield 3*. When he's not capping flags and arming M-COM stations, David enjoys target shooting and playing basketball.

BATTLEFIELD 4 FAVORITES

Map: Golmud Railway
Game Mode: Conquest Large
Class: Engineer
Weapon: SCAR-H SV
Gadgets: MBT LAW, M15 AT Mine
Grenade: M84 Flashbang
Field Upgrade: Anti-Tank

STRONGSIDE

Name: Michael Cavanaugh

Michael has extensive knowledge in competitive FPS gaming and has been competing for the past nine years. Known to pick up any game and become a master at it, Michael's dedication and drive are key factors behind his gaming success, winning several major professional tournaments in the last five years. Outside of FPS gaming, Cavanaugh enjoys rock climbing, wake boarding, skydiving and many other action sports. He is also an avid old-school gamer.

NOTABLE GAMING ACCOMPLISHMENTS

- 1st place in the worldwide tournament held by 343 Industries and Virgin Gaming's Infinity Challenge (Halo 4) winning a 2013 Halo Edition Ford F-150 Raptor
- 1st place MLG 2007 National Championship (Halo 2). Team did not lose a single game in the tournament
- 1st place BIC Pro FFA MLG 2011
- 16 1st place finishes at major national/worldwide tournaments
- 8 1st place finishes at MLG tournaments
- 30 top 4 finishes at major national/worldwide tournaments
- NBA player Gilbert Arenas sponsorship
- Invented the "StrongSide" move

BATTLEFIELD 4 FAVORITES

Map: Operation Locker and Flood Zone
Game Mode: Domination
Class: Recon
Weapon: SRR-61
Gadgets: Radio Beacon, T-UGS
Grenade: M67 Frag
Field Upgrade: Sniper

FLAMESWORD

Name: Michael Chaves

Michael "Flamesword" Chaves has been a professional gamer since 2009. A natural leader, Mike found success in 2008 when he created the prestigious *Halo* team "Status Quo"; a brand and team he wishes to expand into every FPS title. Always maintaining an active and healthy lifestyle; Mike enjoys bouldering, Crossfit, biking, and other action sports which keeps his reflexes and hand-eye coordination above the competition. Mike's story proves that a nice guy really can finish first—he believes in hard work and pursues excellence in everything he does.

NOTABLE GAMING ACCOMPLISHMENTS

- Sponsored by Red Bull
- Professional Player since 2009
- 3 1st place finishes
- 2011 MLG Dallas Championships (*Halo: Reach*)
- 2012 MLG Winter Championships (*Halo: Reach*)
- 2012 Arena Gaming Chicago (*Halo: Reach*)
- 6 Top 2 finishes at major tournaments
- 2010 MLG Dallas National Championships (*Halo 3*)
- 13 Top 4 finishes at major tournaments
- 20 Top 8 finishes at major tournaments
- Voted 2010 Strides Pros' Choice Award for Best Leader
- Voted 2011 Strides Pros' Choice Award for Best Strategist

BATTLEFIELD 4 FAVORITES

Map: Flood Zone
Game Mode: Domination
Class: Support
Weapon: M249
Gadgets: C4, Ammo Box
Grenade: M18 Smoke
Field Upgrade: Perimeter Defense

For *Battlefield 4* we have assembled a team of gamers with an eclectic mix of skills, backgrounds, and professional gaming experience. Together they have put hundreds of hours into *Battlefield 4* with the end goal of creating the most complete and comprehensive *Battlefield* guide to date. This is Alpha Squad.

ELUMNITE

Name: Marcus Lovejoy

Marcus has been a professional video gamer for five years, traveling around the US playing video games, and making money doing it. With faster reflexes than the average gamer, he's always been better at the FPS genre. Marcus' successes include winning many local tournaments and gaining sponsorships. He's even helped design a tournament controller from the ground up. When he's not gaming Marcus enjoys working out and watching anime.

BATTLEFIELD 4 FAVORITES

Map: Dawnbreaker
Game Mode: Conquest Small
Class: Assault
Weapon: ACE 21 CQB
Gadgets: Medic Bag, Defibrillator
Grenade: RGO Impact
Field Upgrade: Combat Medic

WALSHY

Name: David Walsh

A true veteran, David has been a professional gamer for nine years, winning more than 30 major tournaments over five different game titles. One of his biggest victories was winning GameStop's *Battlefield 2: Modern Combat* tournament in 2005 where he won a Dodge Charger SRT8. Outside of gaming David enjoys reading and traveling the world.

NOTABLE GAMING ACCOMPLISHMENTS

- 1st place in three MLG National Championships 2004, 2005, and 2007 (Halo 1 and Halo 2)
- 2nd place in two MLG National Championships 2006 and 2008 (Halo 2 and Halo 3)
- 30+ 1st place finishes at major national/worldwide tournaments
- 1st place at GameStop's Battlefield 2: Modern Combat tournament winning a Dodge Charger SRT8
- Was sponsored by multiple companies such as Red Bull, Gilbert Arenas, Old Spice, Stride Gum, and Sony Xperia
- Popularized the "Claw grip" as a way of holding the Xbox controller.

BATTLEFIELD 4 FAVORITES

Map: Siege of Shanghai
Game Mode: Rush
Class: Engineer
Weapon: AK 5C
Gadgets: RPG-7V2, Repair Tool
Grenade: M34 Incendiary
Field Upgrade: Mechanic

BATTLEFIELD BOOTCAMP

While the single-player campaign offers a great story and plenty of memorable moments, it's only one part of *Battlefield 4*. The multiplayer experience is the other part. Playing against others and working together as a team with members of your squad adds an entirely new dimension of intensity and fun. Plus, earning new ranks and unlocks is incredibly addictive, making hours melt away. So before jumping into a multiplayer match, make sure you've set aside plenty of free time. After all, who needs sleep?

To learn more and watch instructional videos visit PrimaGames.com/BF4

WHAT'S NEW?

If you're a grizzled *Battlefield* veteran, you can jump online now and feel right at home among the whizzing bullets and exploding shells. But before rushing into action, here's a quick summary of the some of the new features and gameplay mechanics. *Battlefield 4* builds on the successes of past installments while introducing entirely new features like Levolution, battle pickups, and Spectator Mode. These new features blend seamlessly with the tried and proven rock-paper-scissors balance fans have come to love, making *Battlefield 4* the deepest and most ambitious entry in the franchise's history.

LEVOLUTION

THE SKYSCRAPER TOPPLING IN SIEGE OF SHANGHAI IS A TRULY JAW-DROPPING LEVOLUTION MOMENT.

One of the most exciting and revolutionary features in *Battlefield 4* is Levolution, allowing players to alter their environment to gain a tactical advantage. Offering greater destructibility across the board, all maps have been designed from the ground up to feature epic-scale events, like a toppling skyscraper or crumbling dam. But Levolution offers much more than these memorable large-scale set pieces. Interacting with the environment goes even deeper, giving players the chance to perform smaller but equally effective actions—raise bollards, preventing enemy vehicles from passing, or cut power to a building, effectively blacking out rooms prior to an assault. The maps are no longer static, requiring a greater degree of flexibility on behalf of your squad and teammates. So before triggering an event, take into account the consequences of your actions—will it benefit your team?

COMMANDER MODE

AS YOUR TEAM'S COMMANDER, ISSUE ORDERS AND DEPLOY ASSETS TO GIVE YOUR TEAM THE UPPER HAND.

While Commander Mode isn't new, it's back and better than ever. When playing Conquest, Rush, or the new Obliteration mode, each team can benefit from the leadership of an attentive commander. In addition to issuing orders to squads, the commander has an array of assets at their fingertips, potentially shifting the balance of power and helping their team achieve victory. Need to locate enemies for your team? Deploy a UAV over a heated firefight to give your squads the upper hand. If a team is successful, the commander gains even more power, capable of deploying a Gunship overhead or calling in devastating Cruise Missile strikes. What's better, Commander Mode can be accessed from tablets, allowing you to connect to live games and lead your team to victory even when you're not in front of your PC or console.

FIVE-PLAYER SQUADS

NOW WITH A FIVE-PLAYER CAPACITY, SQUADS ARE MUCH MORE EFFECTIVE, WHETHER ATTACKING OR DEFENDING.

While it may seem like a subtle change, increasing squad capacity from four to five players has a big impact, particularly during close matches. Obviously, five-player squads bring much more firepower into any battle, making squads a more effective fighting unit. Experiment with different squad compositions depending on the tactical situation. Facing tons of enemy armor? Go with three engineers, one support, and one assault. Need to clear a building? Go with three assault, one support, and one recon. With five players, squads are much more effective at converting control points during Conquest too—the more players in the capture radius, the quicker the control point is converted. But since every squad member serves as a spawn point, having five players on the field greatly increases the survivability of the squad as whole, making it tougher for squads to be wiped.

FIELD UPGRADES

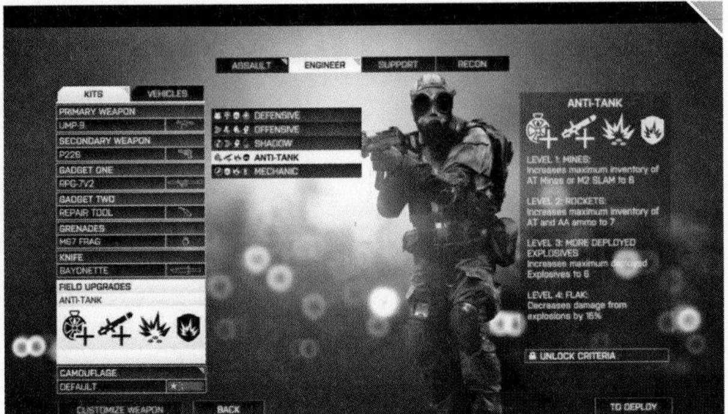

BEFORE DEPLOYING, CHOOSE A FIELD UPGRADE PATH FOR YOUR SOLDIER.

Remember the Field Upgrades from *Battlefield 2142*? Well, the concept has returned in *Battlefield 4*, providing individual rewards for squad-based teamplay. Field upgrades replace the specialization system from *Battlefield 3*, putting more emphasis on working together as a squad to gain unique perks, such as the ability to sprint faster or carry more grenades. Each class can select from four different Field Upgrade paths, each offering four upgrade levels. By default, each class has access to the Defensive and Shadow upgrade paths. But each class also has two other unique upgrade paths as well, like the assault class' Combat Medic and Grenadier upgrade paths. So go out of your way to heal, revive, repair, and resupply your squad members to progress through your chosen upgrade path. The more squad-based actions you perform, the faster you'll advance—if you reach the fourth level, you maintain all the upgrades in the path! However, if your squad is eliminated, you'll lose progress, potentially losing upgrades.

LEAN AND PEEK

THE ABILITY TO LEAN AROUND CORNERS IS A GAME CHANGER DURING CLOSE-QUARTER FIREFIGHTS.

Now when you approach cover with a compact weapon, you have the ability to lean around corners or peek over low cover. Simply move toward a corner and watch how your weapon is tilted, indicating you can lean out. Aim down sights to automatically lean out and aim around the corner. This allows you to engage targets while keeping the majority of your body behind cover, making you more difficult for opponents to hit. This mechanic works similar when crouching behind low objects—aim down sights to pop over the cover to take a shot. Both of these improvements make it easier (and safer) to engage opponents while utilizing cover. However, you can only lean or peek when using an assault rifle, PDW, carbine, shotgun, or pistol.

BATTLE PICKUPS

BATTLE PICKUPS, LIKE THE USAS-12 AUTO SHOTGUN LOADED WITH FRAG ROUNDS, CAN GIVE YOUR SQUAD A SERIOUS OFFENSIVE BOOST.

Battle pickups are unique, powerful weapons scattered across each map, like the one-shot kill M82A3 sniper rifle or the devastating M32 MGL semi-auto grenade launcher. These weapons can be equipped by any player lucky enough to grab one. But they're not necessarily hidden—look for the pistol icon on the HUD or minimap to find their spawn locations. Battle pickups function similar to vehicles—they spawn at predesignated spots on the map, allowing any player to pick them up. Due to their power, these weapons have very limited ammo, and they can't be replenished with an Ammo Box. So make each shot count. Don't be surprised if players flock around battle pickup spawn points, eager to grab a weapon or ambush those running for it.

NAVAL COMBAT

ARMED WITH A CANNON, MISSILES, AND TWO MINIGUNS, THE NEW ATTACK BOATS ARE A FORMIDABLE THREAT.

Naval combat has been part of the *Battlefield* franchise since *Battlefield 1942*, when destroyers, submarines, battleships, and even aircraft carriers roamed the seas of maps like Midway and Guadalcanal. Seaborne combat has returned in a big way with the introduction of attack boats in *Battlefield 4*. The new attacks boats perform like IFVs on the water, armed to the teeth with an array of weapons making them effective against virtually any threat, including aircraft. But the addition of attack boats isn't the only new feature. The physics of the water has received a major overhaul, producing real-time rolling waves, making for choppy seas. So when a storm rolls in, be prepared to be tossed around amidst the dynamic dune-like seascape while attempting to stay on course and on target. The game's netcode ensures the waves you encounter are the same exact ones seen by other players, allowing for balanced yet challenging engagements on the water. Don't get seasick.

GAME MODES

PREPARE YOURSELF FOR COMPLETE CHAOS IN THE NEW OBLITERATION MODE AS INFANTRY AND VEHICLES FIGHT FOR THE POSSESSION OF ONE BOMB.

Battlefield 4 features a total of eight game modes per map, bringing back favorites like Conquest Large/Small, Rush, Squad Deathmatch, and Team Deathmatch. Along with these classic game modes, DICE is featuring three new game modes. Obliteration is a unique tug-of-war style mode requiring teams to retrieve a randomly spawned bomb on the map and deliver it to an enemy bomb site—the first team to destroy all three of the opposing team's bomb sites wins the match. Domination is a small-scale infantry only Conquest-like match featuring three flags—you'll be familiar with this game mode if you played the *Close Quarters* expansion from *Battlefield 3*. Finally, Defuse is another infantry-only game mode requiring an attacking team to deliver a bomb to one of two bomb sites on the map. There are no respawns in Defuse, making it even more critical to clear corners and work together as a team.

SPECTATOR MODE

THE NEW SPECTATOR MODE GIVES YOU THE OPPORTUNITY TO OBSERVE THE BATTLEFIELD FROM ANY PERSPECTIVE.

With the introduction of Spectator Mode, players can now watch a live battle from virtually any angle or perspective. Whether watching from the Commander Mode-like table top view, first person, third person, or free cam, Spectator Mode presents a myriad of opportunities for casual and hardcore fans alike. The smooth camera movements and customizable interface are ideal for creating exciting, cinematic videos. Or if you're new to a particular map or game mode, enter Spectator Mode to get a better idea of how to play. Scouting a rival squad or team? Use Spectator Mode to study their tendencies and tactics before an upcoming match. This mode opens a world of possibilities for the *Battlefield* community, including the option of streaming matches online with broadcast-quality visuals.

GETTING STARTED

Are you new to *Battlefield*? If so, jumping into a well-established online community can be a bit intimidating. But there's really nothing to fear. Regardless of your experience or skill level, there is a role for everyone in *Battlefield*. In fact, this is one of the only online shooters where you can post a big score without even firing a single bullet. In this section we take a look at the basic gameplay mechanics as well as the different multiplayer game modes.

INTERFACE

The heads-up display, or HUD, is the way that vital information is displayed on your screen. None of the items on your HUD are there for aesthetics alone. They are there to help you accomplish your objectives and keep you alive. Here's a brief explanation of every major item on the HUD.

Reticle: The reticle is always located in the center of the HUD. The reticle is the aiming point for your selected weapon. To hit a target, place the reticle over it and fire. The reticle may change based on the weapon you're using—for example, shotguns have ring-shaped reticles. When firing at an enemy, watch for diagonal lines flashing around the perimeter of the reticle. This bloom animation means you're hitting the target. These hit indicators are especially useful when making long-range shots.

Minimap: Located in the bottom left corner of the screen, the minimap provides a top-down, 360-degree view of the environment through which you are moving. The minimap rotates as you change direction so that the top of the minimap is always the direction you are currently facing—make note of the compass headings on the perimeter of the map. In addition to showing the terrain, the minimap also shows the location of all detected enemies as red triangles or red vehicle icons. Teammates show up as blue icons, while squad members are green. Empty vehicles are represented by white icons, and battle pickups appear as white pistol icons. It is a good idea to constantly refer to the minimap to keep track of all detected enemies. Even if you can't see them visually, the minimap lets you know where they are located, whether behind a hill or inside a building. Finally, red and blue diamond icons show you the location of objectives—these same objective icons also appear on the HUD. The color of the ground on the minimap also has meaning. The shaded area behind the red line is out of bounds. If you move into this area, you have ten seconds to get back on the map or else you will die.

Game Mode Information: The icons and meters above the minimap relate to the current game mode. The diamond-shaped icons represent control points in Conquest mode and M-COM stations in Rush mode. The two meters below these icons track how many tickets each team has. Other game modes have slightly different configurations, but all have a ticket meter and a timer.

Objectives: The red- and blue-colored icons on the HUD represent objectives. Blue-colored icons are held by your team while red-colored icons are held by the opposing team. Beneath each of these icons is a number showing the distance to each objective in meters.

Health: By default your health is at 100%. But if you take damage, your health will drop—if it reaches 0%, you die. You can slowly regenerate health by staying behind cover and avoiding injury. But the fastest way to heal is with a Medic Bag dropped by an assault player. Stand (or lay) close to a Medic Bag to rapidly restore your health.

Ammo: Your ammo is represented by two numbers. The large number to the left is the number of rounds you currently have loaded in the weapon's magazine while the small number to the right is the amount of ammo available in unloaded magazines.

Grenades: The number in this box represents how many grenades you have. By default you can only carry one grenade. But the Grenade Boost Field Upgrade allows you to carry one additional grenade.

Fire Mode: Some weapons allow you to switch fire modes, choosing from single shot, automatic, and burst modes. The weapon's current fire mode is shown here.

Weapon/Gadget Cluster: The cluster of four icons at the bottom of the HUD represents gadgets and weapon interactions available in your loadout. Use the accompanying key or directional pad input shown next to each icon to select or toggle these specific options. The icons on the left and right represent your gadgets while the icons on the top and bottom represent interactions with your selected weapon—change fire modes, zero a scope, or toggle a light or laser sight on and off.

Kill Notifications: The text in the top right corner of the screen reports recent deaths, showing who killed who and with what weapon or vehicle.

Score Notification: Every time you earn points, text appears in the middle of the screen describing what action you're being rewarded for and how many points you gain.

Field Upgrade Meter: This meter represents progression in your chosen Field Upgrade path. Score squad-based actions to progress through the four levels of upgrades. But if your squad is eliminated, you'll lose progress.

Squad List: Shown in green text on the right side of the minimap, the squad list shows every member of your squad as well as the kit and specialization they currently have equipped. The squad leader appears at the top of the list with a star icon next to his or her name.

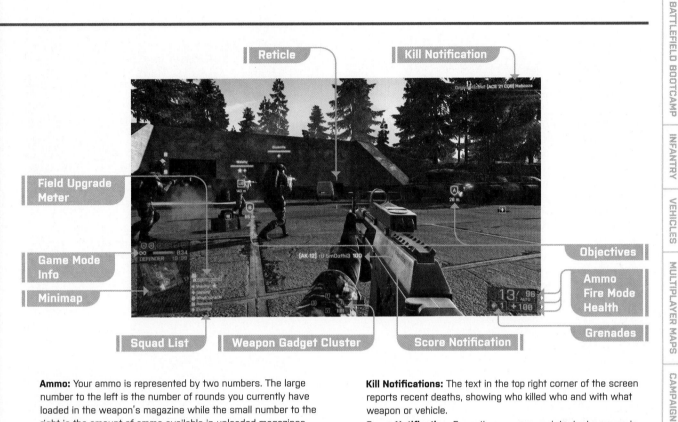

DEPLOY SCREEN

When you first join a game, the deploy screen is where it all begins. Before immediately jumping into the game, take a few seconds to choose your class and gear. It's possible to switch your primary weapon, sidearm, gadgets, and grenade from the deploy screen. But if you want to make more adjustments to your kit, choose the Customize option. This opens a new screen, allowing you to make even more tweaks to your loadout, including weapon attachments and camo. Once you're finished adjusting your loadout, return to the deploy screen and figure out where you want to join the fight. If you're in a squad, you can spawn on any living squad member. Or if a recon squad member has deployed a Radio Beacon, you can spawn at its location. Depending on the game mode, there are also bases, deployment areas, and control points you can spawn at. You can also spawn directly into the seat of a vacant vehicle belonging to your team. As you can see, the spawning options are numerous. In most instances you should spawn on or close to your squad so you can provide support. But if your squad is in a tense firefight, sometimes it's safest to spawn at a less dangerous location, otherwise you may get killed as soon as you spawn into the game—study the small video monitor in the bottom left corner of the deploy screen before spawning on a squad member. This live video feed allows you see if the selected squad member is under fire. When you've determined your spawn location, choose the Deploy option to enter the game.

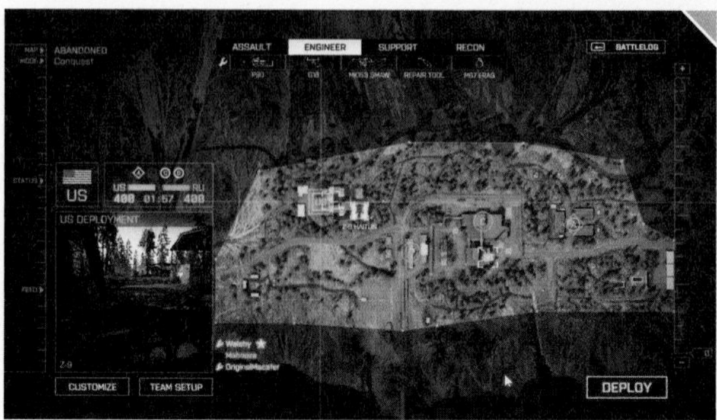

SPAWN DIRECTLY INTO VEHICLES OR ON YOUR SQUADMATES FROM THE DEPLOY SCREEN.

MOVEMENT

Congratulations, you've made it onto the battlefield. Now what? Moving your soldier around the battlefield is simple, especially if you've played the earlier installments or other first-person shooters. When standing, your soldier jogs at moderate pace, ideal for getting around areas where threats are minimal. While crouched, you move slower, and while prone your speed is literally reduced to a crawl. However, since you are lower, you make a smaller target for the enemy to hit and you can more easily duck behind cover. When advancing against an enemy position, it is best to move while crouched or prone, as it is harder for the enemy to detect you. Weapon accuracy is also increased while crouched or prone. So make a habit of dropping to a knee or down on your belly before firing a shot.

At times, it is better to move fast, by sprinting. You can't use weapons or gadgets while sprinting, but you are much more difficult for the enemy to hit. Sprint when you have to cross a dangerously open piece of ground, dashing from one position of cover to another. But never sprint in tight confined spaces where you're likely to encounter enemy troops. If you encounter an enemy at close range while sprinting, chances are you won't have time to stop, raise your weapon, and fire before your opponent does. So don't give in to the temptation to sprint. You're better off moving at a slower speed with your weapon raised and ready to fire.

IT'S EASY TO DROP OPPONENTS WHO ARE SPRINTING BECAUSE THEY DON'T HAVE THEIR WEAPON RAISED, GIVING THEM NO WAY TO RETALIATE.

SWIMMING

Given *Battlefield 4's* greater emphasis on naval combat, don't be surprised if you find yourself treading water, requiring you to swim. Swimming works just like moving on land, but at a significantly slower pace. But just like on land, you can sprint in the water—this is called sprint swim, causing your soldier to perform a quick freestyle stroke. Sprint swim is the fastest way to cross deep bodies of water—swim to shore as fast as possible and seek cover. And for the first time in *Battlefield*, you can now dive and swim underwater, using the water to conceal your movements—simply crouch while in deep water to dive beneath the surface. Swimming underwater is a good way to stay out of sight, but you're not invincible to incoming fire—bullets still penetrate the surface of the water and can injure or kill you. Furthermore, you can only hold your breath so long. If you remain underwater for an extended period of time, you'll begin losing health at a steady rate. Get to the surface before you drown! For the most part, it's best to avoid swimming when possible. While in the water your ability to defend yourself is greatly diminished, literally making you a sitting duck for enemy troops. While you're incapable of accessing your primary weapon or gadgets while swimming, you can equip your sidearm. Firing a pistol while swimming is highly inaccurate, but it's better than nothing.

WHILE SWIMMING, YOU CAN EQUIP YOUR SIDEARM AND SOME GADGETS, INCLUDING C4. DIVE BENEATH THE SURFACE TO CONCEAL YOUR MOVEMENTS.

▶ TIP

WHILE SWIMMING, THERE'S A CHANCE ENEMY WATERCRAFT MAY ATTEMPT TO RUN YOU DOWN. DIVING UNDERWATER CAN PREVENT YOU FROM GETTING TURNED INTO ROADKILL BY AN APPROACHING BOAT. WHILE SWIMMING UNDERWATER, INCOMING BULLETS STRIKE WITH REDUCED VELOCITY, INFLICTING LESS DAMAGE.

PARACHUTES

Whether jumping out of a damaged aircraft or hopping off a tall building, you can avoid making a crater into the ground by deploying your parachute. While in free fall, press the jump button/key once to open your parachute. You can steer the parachute with standard movement inputs. But unless parachuting from great heights, don't expect to travel great distances, as the descent is rapid. It's possible to fire your weapons during the descent, but your accuracy is greatly diminished unless using guided weapons like some of the engineer's rocket/missile launchers. If you're descending directly over an enemy position, consider dropping grenades or C4—just make sure they explode before you reach the ground. But the longer you're in the air, the more attention you're likely to attract. For this reason, free fall as long as possible and open the parachute just before you reach the ground. This is a great way to sneak into enemy-held territory.

GUIDED WEAPONS, LIKE THE STINGER AND JAVELIN, CAN BE DEPLOYED ACCURATELY WHILE DRIFTING TO THE GROUND IN A PARACHUTE.

▶ TIP

DURING CONQUEST MATCHES, IF YOUR TEAM HAS BEEN PUSHED BACK TO THEIR BASE, CONSIDER USING A JET OR HELICOPTER TO CONDUCT AIRBORNE ASSAULTS ON DISTANT CONTROL POINTS. SIMPLY FLY TOWARD THE CONTROL POINT, BAIL OUT, AND PARACHUTE TO THE GROUND, CONVERTING THE CONTROL POINT BEFORE THE ENEMY TEAM CAN RESPOND. THIS IS THE QUICKEST WAY TO STAGE BREAKOUT ATTACKS DURING SIEGES.

COMBAT FUNDAMENTALS

While moving about the battlefield is a major part of gameplay, the sole purpose of movement is to place you in a position where you can deploy your weapons, engaging and eliminating the enemy. And when it comes to weapons, *Battlefield 4* has you covered, offering a wide range of knives, firearms, grenades, and anti-vehicle options.

SPOTTING

Before attacking your first enemy, you must first learn how to spot them. When you have an enemy player or vehicle in your sight, press the spot button/key to highlight it for your team. This places a red icon on the HUD and minimap, showing your entire team where the enemy unit is located. Enemy infantry show up as red triangle icons while vehicles are represented by red vehicle icons. Targets only remain spotted for approximately five seconds, but that's usually more than enough time for your team to take notice of the threat. Also, once the icon disappears, you can spot the target again as long as you've maintained a line of sight. If a teammate kills the target you tagged, you earn a Spot Bonus worth 25 points. So consider playing as recon with a high-powered scope and simply spot enemy units for your team—you can also spot targets while using the recon's MAV, SOFLAM, or PLD. Even if you don't fire a shot, you can still rack up a decent score by spotting enemies for your team. Spotting is crucial for your team's aircraft, making it easier for pilots to perform air-to-ground attacks on infantry and vehicles. If nobody is spotting vehicles for your team's pilots, don't complain about a lack of close air support.

YOUR SOLDIER PHYSICALLY POINTS OUT ENEMIES WHEN SPOTTING, ALERTING SQUAD AND TEAMMATES OF A THREAT, VISIBLE ON THEIR HUDS AND MINIMAPS.

▶ CAUTION

WHILE SPOTTING ENEMIES IS A GOOD HABIT, SOMETIMES THIS EXTRA STEP CAN COST YOU, PARTICULARLY IN CLOSE-QUARTER ENGAGEMENTS. IF YOU'VE BEEN SEEN AND COME UNDER FIRE, FOCUS ON ELIMINATING THE THREAT OR TAKING COVER. IT'S ALWAYS BETTER TO STAY ALIVE.

MELEE COMBAT

Don't want to give away your position? Out of ammo? Consider taking out your unsuspecting opponent with a silent knife attack. The knife is a standard-issue weapon available to all players, regardless of their class or rank. But now you can choose what kind of knife your soldier wields—different knives have different attack animations. When approaching an enemy from behind, you can kill them instantly by attacking with the knife...assuming they don't counter it. But if you attack an enemy head-on, it takes at least two swipes with the knife to score a kill from the front. So if an enemy is looking in your direction, think twice before attempting a knife kill. Chances are they'll shoot you in the face before you can get within striking range. Instead, always look for opportunities to flank, sneaking up behind unsuspecting opponents and knifing them from behind. As in *Battlefield 2142* and every installment since, scoring knife kills earns you the victim's dog tags, providing you with a permanent trophy. But you only take your opponent's dog tags when attacking from behind or performing a counter. In addition to scoring stealthy kills, the knife is also great for slicing through chainlink fences and other light obstacles.

WHEN GETTING KNIFED FROM BEHIND, THE VICTIM HAS NO WAY TO COUNTER THE ATTACK.

COUNTER-KNIFE

Tired of getting knifed? With the new counter-knife gameplay mechanic, you now have the chance to turn the tables on your attacker—but it's not easy. Just before you're about to be knifed by an opponent from the front, immediately press the knife button/key to counter the attack and stab your opponent. You only need to press the knife button/key once at the right time to execute a counter-knife—repeatedly pressing the knife button/key won't help. Timing and quick reflexes are a must to perform a counter-knife, so don't be disappointed if you fail on your first attempt. A counter-knife cannot be countered by your opponent, ensuring your attacker's dog tags will be added to your collection.

ATTEMPTING TO KNIFE AN OPPONENT FROM THE FRONT GIVES THE INTENDED VICTIM THE OPPORTUNITY TO COUNTER.

FIREARMS

Battlefield 4 offers a wide range of firearms at your disposal. But it's up to you to pick the best weapon for the job, taking into account your chosen class and preferred style of play. But what's the difference between each weapon? Let's take a quick look at the types of firearms available.

Assault Rifles: Carried exclusively by the assault class, assault rifles are well-rounded full-auto weapons best deployed when engaging targets at intermediate ranges.

Personal Defense Weapons (PDWs): Now available solely to engineers, PDWs are compact, fully automatic weapons known for their high rate of fire, making them ideal during close-quarter engagements.

Light Machine Guns (LMGs): These bulky automatic weapons are lugged around by the support class, perfect for laying down high volumes of covering or suppressive fire.

Sniper Rifles: The recon class' bolt-action sniper rifles offer extreme power and precision, intended for long-range engagements—due to their low rate of fire, these are best deployed by marksman experts.

Designated Marksman Rifles (DMRs): Available to all classes, these semi-automatic rifles offer a great balance of precision and stopping power, putting them somewhere in between the assault rifles and bolt-action sniper rifles.

Carbines: Also available to all classes, carbines offer the versatility and functionality of an assault rifle in a smaller, compact frame, allowing them to perform admirably at both close and intermediate ranges.

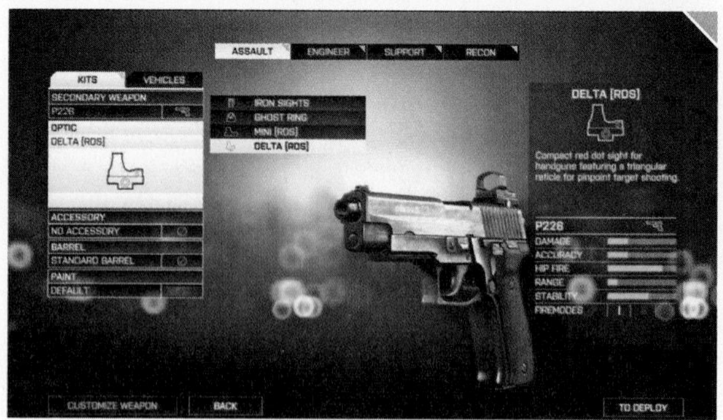

BEFORE DEPLOYING, CUSTOMIZE YOUR WEAPONS WITH OPTICS AND OTHER ATTACHMENTS, HELPING IMPROVE TARGET ACQUISITION AND PERFORMANCE.

Shotguns: These close-quarter beasts can be equipped by any class and can be loaded with a variety of ammo types including buckshot, frag rounds, and slugs.

Sidearms: Every soldier is equipped with a sidearm, serving as a backup to their primary weapon. Sidearms include a variety of pistols as well as the new Shorty 12G, a compact one-handed shotgun.

BASIC OPERATION

THE RETICLE'S HIT INDICATORS TELL YOU WHEN SHOTS ARE HITTING YOUR TARGET.

As mentioned earlier, the reticle in the center of the screen is your aiming point for using weapons. Most of the weapons you use are direct fire, meaning that the projectile you fire travels in a straight line from your weapon to the target. However, when engaging targets at long range, be prepared to aim high to compensate for bullet drop—gravity's pull on the bullet causes it to drop over distance. Using these weapons is simple. Place the reticle directly over the target and then squeeze the trigger. This is called firing from the hip. Firing from the hip isn't accurate, but it gets the job done at close range—attach a Laser Sight to your weapon to increase hip fire accuracy.

Most weapons in *Battlefield 4* have selectable fire modes, allowing you to choose from single-shot, burst, and automatic modes. For semi-automatic or single-shot weapons such as pistols, shotguns, and sniper rifles, each time you press the fire button/key, you fire a single round. However, for automatic weapons such as submachine guns, assault rifles, and light machine guns, they will continue to shoot as you hold down the fire button/key until they run out of ammo. So experiment with each weapon's fire modes in an effort to increase accuracy and reduce recoil.

RECOIL COMPENSATION

WHEN ENGAGING DISTANT OPPONENTS, FIRE IN SHORT BURSTS TO KEEP THE WEAPON ON-TARGET. ALLOW THE WEAPON TO SETTLE BEFORE FIRING A FOLLOW-UP BURST.

The first round you fire with any weapon exhibits the most recoil. As the muzzle climbs after the first shot, follow-up shots may miss the intended target completely. When firing automatic weapons, the longer the burst, the less accurate your fire. Therefore, to maintain greater accuracy and still put a lot of lead on-target, fire in short bursts. You are more likely to kill your target, especially at medium to long range, with a few accurate rounds rather than spraying an entire magazine over a wide area. If recoil is still a problem, consider switching to burst or single-shot mode. While attachments like the Compensator, Angled Grip, and Folding Grip help reduce recoil, they don't eliminate it entirely. As you get more comfortable with the weapons, compensate for muzzle climb by applying slight downward pressure, using either your mouse or controller's analog stick. This allows you to fight the recoil, helping keep the weapon on-target.

TIP

The accuracy of LMGs benefits greatly from the Bipod attachment. Bipods can be deployed while prone or next to a supportive piece of cover, like a planter, car or windowsill. Bipods help dampen recoil, making even prolonged automatic bursts significantly more accurate.

AIMING DOWN SIGHTS

When you fire a weapon using the reticle on the HUD to aim, you are firing from the hip. Hip fire is not accurate and should only be employed when engaging targets at close range. To increase your accuracy, press the zoom button/key to aim down the weapon's sights. This will bring up the ironsight view, where you are actually looking through the weapon's sight to aim. The butt of the weapon is brought up to your shoulder giving you greater stability and accuracy. If your weapon is equipped with an optic attachment, the zoom button/key will provide a view through the optic rather than ironsight. It is a good idea to get in the habit of pressing the zoom button to bring up your ironsight before firing. This not only is more accurate, but it also provides a zoomed-in view of the target. To further increase accuracy, crouch or drop prone and remain stationary while firing. When peering through high-powered scopes, there is noticeable sway, making it difficult to aim. You can temporarily reduce this sway by holding your breath—hold down the sprint button/key. But this only lasts for a few seconds. You can completely eliminate scope sway by using a Bipod.

YOUR WEAPON IS ALWAYS MUCH MORE ACCURATE WHEN AIMING THROUGH IRONSIGHTS OR AN OPTIC.

RELOADING

MAGAZINE-FED WEAPONS OFFER THE QUICKEST RELOAD TIMES. LEAVE A ROUND IN THE CHAMBER TO STREAMLINE THE PROCESS.

At some point you'll need to reload your weapon. While reloading, you're very vulnerable, so make an effort to find cover or have a squadmate watch your back. For most weapons, rounds are loaded in detachable box magazines that are then inserted into the firearm. The capacity of magazines differs greatly based on the type of weapon you're using—some sniper rifle magazines only hold five rounds while some LMG magazines can carry up to 200 rounds. It's best to reload your weapon after each major engagement, when you have a few rounds left in a magazine. This means a round is already chambered in the weapon, significantly reducing the duration of reload animation. If you fire a weapon until it runs dry, a reload animation automatically begins. But this time, the weapon's chamber is empty, requiring your soldier to load a fresh round after seating a new magazine. While this extra action may only take a second longer, one second can make all the difference during a heated firefight. But sometimes you can't avoid firing all the rounds in a magazine. If a threat is still active and your magazine is empty, instead of reloading your primary weapon, switch to your sidearm. It's always faster to draw your sidearm than it is to load a new magazine in your primary weapon—shots fired from a pistol may just be enough to eliminate your opponent. If you already began loading your primary weapon when you drew your sidearm, when you switch back to the primary weapon, the reload animation will continue where you left off instead of starting over from the beginning. This is called tiered reloading and is a welcome new feature in *Battlefield 4*.

Reloading should be a conscious decision and not a reaction. Many players get in the bad habit of reloading after each kill, leaving them open to retaliation by their victim's teammates—who are usually lurking around the next corner. So quickly analyze the situation before initiating a reload, ensuring you're in a relatively safe, covered location. Support troops carrying belt-fed LMGs have the most difficult time reloading, as the process can take up to seven seconds—these players should find a good hiding spot before beginning this lengthy animation. Pump shotguns and some semi-auto shotguns are a bit tricky too, requiring soldiers to load one shell at a time. Load these shotguns frequently, inserting new shells at your earliest convenience until the weapon is full.

▶ CAUTION

In Hardcore mode, think twice before reloading a magazine still holding live rounds. Any rounds remaining in the magazine are lost for good, providing a heightened sense of realism to this challenging mode. If you're not careful, you'll run out of ammo fast, requiring frequent resupply from a support teammate carrying an Ammo Bag or Ammo Pack.

ATTACHMENTS

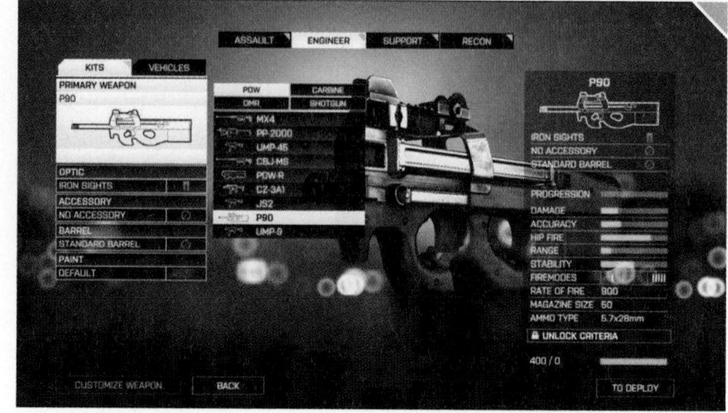

NEWLY UNLOCKED WEAPONS HAVE NO ATTACHMENTS AVAILABLE—YOU MUST EARN THEM BY SCORING KILLS.

All firearms can be equipped with a variety of attachments, allowing you customize your weapon to meet the demands of any tactical situation. By default, most weapons have no attachments available—you must earn them. New attachments are unlocked at regular ten-kill intervals while using a particular weapon. For example, scoring your first ten kills with the ACE 23 assault rifle earns you the Reflex (RDS) optic. The next ten kills earn you the Laser Sight accessory, and so on. Once an attachment has been unlocked, you can equip it by choosing the Customize option from the deploy screen, followed by the Customize Weapon button. Most firearms have five customization slots—here's a brief rundown of the most common options:

Optic: Here you can choose from three categories of optics from close-range red dot sights to long-range, high-magnification ballistic scopes.

Accessory: Choose from a variety of laser sights and lights for your weapon. The new Canted Ironsight is also available in this category.

Barrel: Swap out your weapon's barrel for a Heavy Barrel or attach a Muzzle Brake, Flash Hider, or Suppressor.

Underbarrel: The Bipod and grips available here help dampen recoil, making the weapon easier to control. Assault rifles can also be equipped with the underbarrel M26 Shotgun or M320 Grenade Launcher.

Paint: Select a camo pattern for your weapon to help blend in with your environment.

As you unlock more and more attachments for your weapons, experiment with different configurations until you find one that best matches your style of play. Like weapons, attachments are largely subjective. So don't be afraid to try out new configurations, taking into account the type of weapon you're customizing—a favorite configuration for an assault rifle might not feel the same when applied to a carbine or DMR. This is why it's important to keep experimenting.

▶ NOTE

Attachments unlocked for one weapon cannot be applied to another. Each weapon has its own unlock progression of available attachments. For more information on attachments, reference the Weapons section in the next chapter.

GRENADES

Battlefield 4 introduces an entirely new array of grenade types, allowing you to further customize your loadout to meet the needs of your squad and team. Let's take a quick look at what grenades are available.

Hand Flare: Deploy a bright red flare for lighting up dark areas or marking areas of tactical importance.

M18 Smoke: Releases a cloud of thick smoke that obstructs vision.

M34 Incendiary: Explodes with a cloud of fire, damaging any targets in the area of effect.

M67 Frag: Explodes on a timer.

M84 Flashbang: Explodes with a blinding flash.

RGO Impact: Explodes directly on impact with any surface.

V40 Mini: A smaller grenade with less explosive force, but a larger quantity is allowed to be carried and it can be thrown farther.

THE NEW M34 INCENDIARY GRENADE IS GREAT FOR DEFENDING CHOKEPOINTS SUCH AS DOORWAYS, HALLS, AND STAIRWELLS.

Although these grenades perform different functions, they're all deployed by throwing them. Use your weapon's reticle on the HUD to best judge where you want to throw a grenade. One press of the grenade button/key causes the grenade to be thrown, shown as a orange flashing icon on the HUD. But grenades have limited range, so you may need to aim high to get them near your intended target—the farther your target, the higher you should aim your throw. With the exception of the RGO Impact, grenades have a short fuse, detonating within five seconds of being thrown. As a result, you can bounce grenades around corners or roll them down inclines. Like your own grenades, enemy grenades show up as flashing orange icons on the HUD. So if you see one of these flashing icons nearby, sprint in the opposite direction before it explodes.

▶ NOTE

Unless playing on Hardcore mode, your grenades do not harm teammates. However, they can still harm you. So be extra careful, particularly when tossing the RGO Impact Grenade.

GRENADE LAUNCHERS

Hand grenades aren't the only option. Grenades can also be launched from the assault kit's M320 Grenade Launcher or the M32 MGL battle pickup. Like the hand grenades, a variety of M320 ammo is available for this launcher. Unlike a bullet or rocket, which travels in a straight line, launched grenades travel in a parabolic arc due to their lower speed and the effect of gravity. Therefore, the farther away you are from the target, the higher you need to aim. That is why the reticle for a grenade launcher's ironsight has several horizontal line aiming points. For a short-range shot, use the top line. The farther away your target, use the lower lines. By using a lower aiming point, you are essentially aiming the weapon up higher to lob the grenade towards the target. With the exception of the M320 LVG, all launched grenades explode on impact, much like a rocket or missile. So take this into account, particularly when launching grenades at nearby targets—the splash damage of a M320 HE round may injure or kill you.

GRENADE LAUNCHERS ARE HANDY FOR BREACHING WALLS, ALLOWING YOUR SQUAD TO PERFORM DYNAMIC ENTRIES.

ANTI-VEHICLE WEAPONS

The battlefield is a dangerous place for infantry, made even more deadly by the presence of enemy ground, naval, and air vehicles—small arms fire do little to deter these threats. Some soldiers can carry specialized weapons designed to damage and destroy these vehicles. The engineer is the master of these weapons, capable of equipping anti-tank weapons like the RPG-7V2, SMAW, SRAW, LAW, and Javelin. All of these rocket- and missile-based weapons are capable of targeting enemy vehicles through direct fire, laser designation, or their own on-board guidance systems. The engineer can also knock aircraft out of the sky using shoulder-fired surface-to-air missiles like the Stinger or IGLA. But there are passive options too, like the engineer's M15 AT Mine and M2 SLAM—place these explosives in high traffic areas frequented by enemy ground vehicles. The engineer isn't the only one capable of deploying explosives. Both the support and recon class are capable of carrying remotely detonated C4, ideal for turning any vehicle into a flaming wreck. So even when you're on foot, you're not totally defenseless against vehicles. Still, minimize your exposure to vehicles as much as possible—even when carrying these powerful weapons, you're still outgunned.

THE M15 AT MINES, CARRIED BY THE ENGINEER, ARE ONE OF THE MOST EFFECTIVE WAYS TO KNOCK OUT A TANK.

▶ NOTE

In addition to carrying C4, both the support and recon class can now deploy Claymores, perfect for setting booby traps for enemy infantry.

VEHICLES

Battlefield has always prided itself in providing a rock-paper-scissor balance to vehicle combat, meaning there's no one vehicle that can truly dominate. Each vehicle has always had strengths and a weaknesses, and that tradition continues with *Battlefield 4*. As the driver or pilot of a vehicle, it's up to you to exploit each vehicle's strengths while guarding its weaknesses. No matter what vehicle you're in, there's always a host of threats you need to prepare for. For example, if driving a tank, you can blast most ground vehicles with impunity, but still need to watch out for attack helicopters, jets, and engineers. Of course, skill and an attentive crew can help overcome a vehicle's weaknesses—such as an engineer hopping out of a tank to conduct repairs while the driver continues to fight. A crew that communicates and works together can be a formidable threat on the battlefield, sometimes turning the tide in a close match.

TANK BATTLES ARE STILL A HIGHLIGHT OF ANY MATCH. REMEMBER, KEEP YOUR THICK FRONT ARMOR FACING THE ENEMY AT ALL TIMES.

TRANSPORTATION

THE SCOUT AND TRANSPORT HELICOPTERS ARE THE QUICKEST WAY TO MOVE TROOPS AROUND THE BATTLEFIELD.

The maps in *Battlefield 4* are massive—it can take several minutes to cross them on foot. Therefore, use vehicles to get around whenever possible, making an effort to pick up teammates along the way. There are several types of vehicles in the game, yet they all are driven with similar controls. All vehicles have more than one seat. When you get into an vacant vehicle, you are placed in the driver's seat by default. However, you can move to another position inside the vehicle with the press of a button/key, cycling through all seats. The driver has control of a vehicle's movement and, in the tanks, IFVs, and attack boats, also controls the vehicle's turret-mounted primary weapon. Most vehicles even have gunner and passenger positions, allowing teammates to man other vehicle-mounted weapons. At the start of a match, make sure all crew positions are filled before leaving a base or deployment area—leaving teammates stranded back at your base won't help your team win.

DAMAGE: CRITICAL HITS

SOME GUIDED WEAPONS, LIKE THE JAVELIN AND MBT LAW, ARE DESIGNED TO SCORE TOP HITS ON TANKS, RESULTING IN CRITICAL HITS.

In *Battlefield 3*, vehicle damage was completely overhauled. With *Battlefield 4*, vehicle damage is being adjusted once again with the introduction of critical hits. When a vehicle takes damage, there's a chance the attacking weapon has scored a critical hit. Critical hits take into account damage, the angle of attack, and which area of the vehicle has been hit—hits to a tank's weak rear or top armor are more likely to result in critical hits. When a vehicle suffers a critical hit, it becomes immobilized, causing it to move slow or become unresponsive—this can be deadly when flying a jet or helicopter. But unlike in *Battlefield 3*, this immobilization is only temporary, lasting a few seconds. At this point vehicle crew members have a choice: do they stay with the immobilized vehicle and try to score more kills or do they bail out and attempt to find cover before their ride suffers more damage and explodes? An experienced crew can stay with the vehicle and fight their way out of trouble until the vehicle becomes responsive. Compared to *Battlefield 3*, the temporary immobilization state provides greater incentive for staying with your vehicle.

TIP

WHILE MOST VEHICLES MUST BE DISABLED BEFORE THEY'RE DESTROYED, THERE ARE EXCEPTIONS TO THE RULE. C4 AND MINES CAN DESTROY MOST GROUND VEHICLES INSTANTANEOUSLY. AND IF YOU'RE LUCKY ENOUGH, YOU CAN EXPLODE A HELICOPTER OR JET WITH A TANK ROUND OR A SINGLE ROCKET FIRED FROM ONE OF THE ENGINEER'S ANTI-TANK WEAPONS.

VEHICLE AMMO

CONSERVE YOUR AMMO WHEN OPERATING VEHICLES. WHILE AMMO REPLENISHES OVER TIME, EXCESSIVE USE OF THE VEHICLE'S PRIMARY WEAPON CAN LEAVE YOU VULNERABLE.

In the most recent iterations of *Battlefield*, vehicles had unlimited ammo, making them extremely powerful. But that has changed in *Battlefield 4*, limiting infinite ammo to secondary weapons like machine guns. This means drivers and pilots must be more selective when firing their primary weapons. But ammo doesn't disappear forever. Similar to health, ammo regenerates over time. Furthermore, vehicles can be replenished through supply drops initiated by the team's commander. Initially, tank drivers are most likely to feel the pinch—running out of ammo in the middle of a tank duel can be deadly...and somewhat embarrassing. But limiting vehicle ammo promotes greater skill and discipline in such engagements, requiring deeper tactical planning. So before engaging an enemy vehicle, make sure you have enough ammo to finish it off.

NOTE

FOR MORE INFORMATION ON VEHICLES, INCLUDING STATS AND TACTICS, REFERENCE THE VEHICLES CHAPTER.

KILL CAM

Every time you die, you get a brief glimpse of your killer through the kill cam. This screen appears briefly immediately after your death, providing a shot of the player who killed you as well as their name, rank, health, dog tags, kit, weapon, and attachments. It may seem like a frivolous feature, but the kill cam has larger implications for how the game is played. Snipers can't camp one spot and kill from an undisclosed location throughout the entire match. Through the kill cam, victims can see approximately where an enemy player is camping and enact revenge once they respawn. So make a habit of moving frequently, or else you're likely to face one of your angry victims sneaking up behind you with a knife.

SQUAD PLAY

If you've played past installments of *Battlefield*, you know the benefits of joining a squad. A squad is a five-player unit that can communicate with each other over headsets. Being able to talk to the other players in your squad allows you to discuss each situation and respond as a single unified fighting force. Beyond the obvious tactical advantages, being in a squad allows you to earn the squad bonus points, boosting your score and fast-tracking promotions. But if you're new to *Battlefield* and the squad system, let's take a look at how they work.

JOINING A SQUAD

DON'T WANDER TOO FAR FROM YOUR SQUADMATES. THEY ARE IDENTIFIABLE BY THEIR GREEN NAME TAGS, ALWAYS VISIBLE ON THE HUD.

At the start of any match, while the map is loading, you're asked if you want to join a squad. Always choose yes. In this instance, you'll be automatically assigned a squad randomly. Chances are your new squadmates are complete strangers, so say hi and ask what kit they could use before spawning into the game. If you prefer playing with friends, you can create a squad from your friend's list before even joining a game. You don't need five players to form a squad, so feel free to join a game once you have at least one friend on your side. However, if you have less than five players in your squad, the extra slots could be filled by strangers. Once formed, squads can be locked, preventing others from joining without an invite.

SQUAD SPAWN

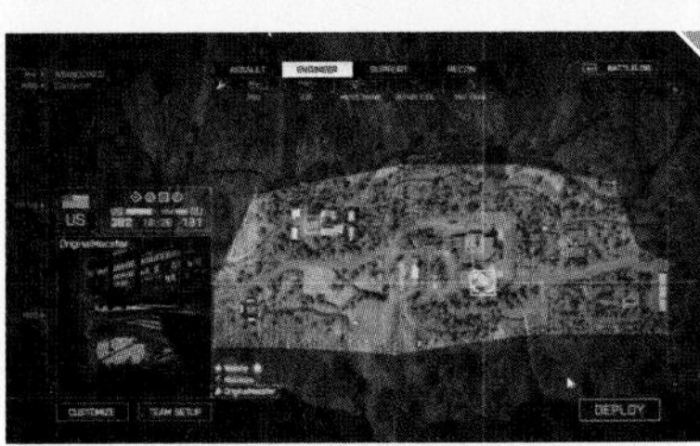

SPAWN DIRECTLY ON YOUR SQUADMATES FROM THE DEPLOY SCREEN TO MAINTAIN A COHESIVE UNIT.

One of the huge benefits of playing in a squad is the ability to spawn on any squadmate. In the deploy screen you can see a number of spawning options, including your team's base and vehicles. If you don't want to spawn at one of those static locations, spawn on one of your squad members, represented by a green icon on the deploy screen. As you select their icon, the camera view in the left corner of the deploy screen switches to the selected squad member's perspective. Before spawning on a squad member, make sure they're in a safe location. The last thing you want to do is spawn in the middle of an enemy kill zone. You can also spawn on any squad member who is in a vehicle with unoccupied seats. The Radio Beacons from *Battlefield 3* are back, deployed by recon troops. Radio Beacons can be placed almost anywhere on the map and serve as forward spawn points for your squad. This is a great way for attackers to maintain a presence close to an objective, especially during Rush matches. But don't let enemies see where your Radio Beacon is placed, otherwise they may camp nearby and pick off your squadmates as they enter the game.

SQUAD LEADER

Each squad has one squad leader tasked with issuing attack and defend orders. The first player to form a squad is the squad leader. When you've been selected as the squad leader, a message appears on the screen informing you of your new job. Your name also appears at the top of the squad list on the left side of the HUD, marked with a star icon. Serving as squad leader, you can better direct your squad by placing attack or defend orders on objectives. Once an order has been placed at a location, any kills that occur within a wide radius of the given order results in points for both you and your squad. It's a simple mechanic, but it's a great way to keep your squad focused on one objective.

USE SQUAD ORDERS TO KEEP EVERYONE FOCUSED ON THE SAME OBJECTIVE. SQUADMATES EARN BONUS POINTS FOR FOLLOWING ORDERS.

TEAMWORK

Once in the game, you can identify your squadmates by the green name tags above their heads accompanied by their kit icon—they also show up as green triangles on the minimap. Other teammates have blue name tags above their head while enemies appear as red. Stay close to your squad so you can support one another. But don't cluster around each other too tightly or else all five of you can be eliminated by an explosive attack. Instead, try to stay within each others' line of sight. By simply communicating and working together you can gain a huge advantage over your opponents, especially those that wander off by themselves.

In addition to talking to each other over your headsets, use the target spotting system to tag enemies and issue attack/defend orders. Only the squad leader can issue orders so watch for blinking boxes around objectives like M-COM stations and control points. If no order has been issued, ask your squad leader to place an order on an objective. Kills performed within close proximity of an objective marked with an attack/defend order results in a squad order bonus, worth 50 additional points. So if you're the squad leader, don't forget to issue orders to help your squad's scores, otherwise you're just leaving points on the table.

IN SQUAD DEATHMATCH, STAY CLOSE TO YOUR SQUADMATES AT ALL TIMES SO YOU CAN SUPPORT EACH OTHER—ALL OTHER SQUADS WILL BE GUNNING FOR YOU.

PERSISTENCE SYSTEM

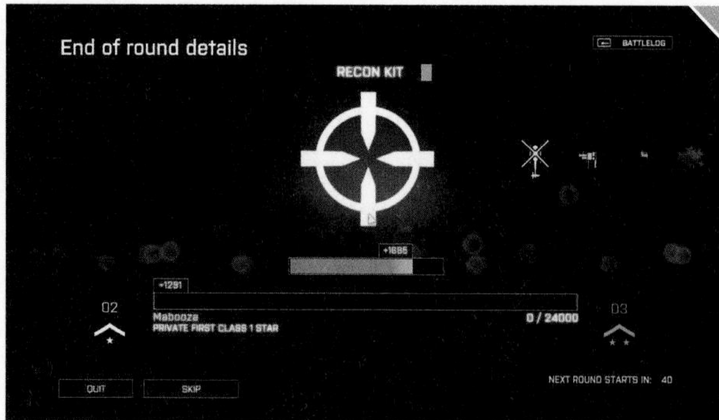

STAY TUNED FOLLOWING EACH MATCH FOR A SUMMARY OF YOUR PROGRESS, INCLUDING A BREAKDOWN OF UNLOCKS AND AWARDS.

Every action performed in a multiplayer match earns you points. Various actions, kills, assists, resupplies, assignments, and much more count towards your progression and earns you statistics over the course of your career. The better you perform, the faster you move up the ranks, and as you move up the ranks, you gain access to new weapons and gadgets. So at the end of a round, check out your overall performance in the end of round screens. These screens show your current rank as well as your progress toward achieving the next rank. It also has statistical breakdowns of your score, showing how many points were earned with each kit, vehicles, and awards. Speaking of awards, any dog tags, medals, or ribbons earned during the round are shown in the Unlocks and Awards sections. The kits screen shows how much progress you've made toward unlocking new equipment for each kit. Finally, the Scoreboard is displayed, showing where you ranked among teammates and opponents.

PERSISTENCE AND AWARDS

IMAGE	NAME	DESCRIPTION
	Ribbons	You earn a ribbon when you accomplish an in-game objective, such as getting a certain number of Kill Assists or Headshots. Ribbons are earned on a per-match basis and can be received multiple times.
	Medals	You are awarded with a medal once you have collected a certain amount of ribbons of the same type. Medals represent milestones for good performance and can be earned multiple times.
	Dog Tags	Every player in *Battlefield 4* has a pair of dog tags. The standard dog tag has your name written on it. The advanced dog tag features an etching and a statistic, such as your headshot count. You can collect the dog tags of other players by knifing them.
	Service Stars	A service star is awarded for completing a Tour of Duty for every weapon, lethal gadget, vehicle class, soldier class, and game mode. The stars vary depending on class and difficulty. Each service star can be obtained 100 times.
	Assignments	There are three difficulty levels of assignments in *Battlefield 4*: Basic, Advanced, and Expert. As you progress through different ranks, new assignments will be unlocked. Fulfilling the assignments unlocks dog tags, weapon paint, and more.
	Battlepacks	Battlepacks contain random combinations of new camo, dog tags, knives, XP boosts, and more. These items are designed to add customization options and give you some personalization on the battlefield. Battlepacks are earned through progression or promotion. There are six types of Battlepacks: standard, advanced, superior, distinguished, special, and premium.

BATTLEFIELD COMPENDIUM

NOTE

For complete information on the game's scoring system, ranks, and awards, flip to the Battlefield Compendium chapter at the back of the guide. There you'll find scoring details for each action as well as criteria for earning every rank, medal, ribbon, and dog tag. You'll also find the criteria for completing each assignment and acquiring every achievement and trophy.

MULTIPLAYER TACTICS

Tactics is the combining of maneuvers and firepower to achieve an objective. Both movement and weapons have already been covered, so this section focuses on using the two together in an effort to gain an advantage over your opponents.

PLAN AHEAD

WHEN ATTACKING IN DEFUSE, MAKE SURE YOUR TEAM HAS A SOLID PLAN IN PLACE BEFORE CARRYING THE BOMB TOWARD ONE OF THE OBJECTIVES.

There is an old saying that those who fail to plan, plan to fail. You need to come up with a plan before the bullets start flying. The best place to start is to look at your game mode's objectives, since those determine victory or defeat. While killing the enemy is always a goal, it is often a means to an end. Instead, focus on the objectives. Do you have to destroy a target, defend a position, or just get to a certain point on the map?

Once you know what you must do, look at the map and examine the terrain. Where are you located? Where is the objective? How will you get there? Are there any vehicles you can use? These are all questions you need to ask yourself. Once you have determined how to get to the target, you must then consider how to accomplish your orders. Will you need to get in close to plant an explosive charge on the target? If so, how will you secure the perimeter? Finally, you need to take into account your opposition. What does the enemy have and where are they located? Usually you will not know that type of information until you get in close to the target and can see the enemy with your own eyes. Therefore, planning continues on the fly as you learn new information about enemy positions and actions.

To learn more and watch instructional videos visit PrimaGames.com/BF4

COVER

USING THE NEW LEAN MECHANIC, YOU CAN PEEK AROUND CORNERS, LIMITING YOUR EXPOSURE TO INCOMING FIRE.

Combat is very dangerous. Bullets and other deadly projectiles fly through the air and can kill you outright if they make contact. The concept of cover is to place something solid between you and the enemy that will stop those projectiles and keep you safe. The multiplayer maps are filled with objects that you can use as cover—buildings, walls, trees, rocks, earthen mounds, and so on. Some types of cover will stop small arms fire such as rifle bullets, but not stop the heavier weapons. Walls will stop machine gun fire, but not rockets or tank rounds. Therefore, pick cover that will protect you from the current threat—objects constructed from wood or flimsy sheet metal won't stop a bullet.

Cover should become ingrained in your combat thinking. In addition to looking for enemies, you also need to be looking for cover. During a firefight, always stay behind cover. The only reason you leave cover is to move to another position with cover. If the cover is low, you may need to crouch down or drop prone to get behind it, standing only to fire over it. When moving from cover to cover, sprint to get there quicker. If carrying a compact weapon, you can now lean around corners, allowing you to peek out and return fire while keeping most of your body behind cover.

While you want to stay behind cover, you also want to try to deny the benefit of cover to your enemies. Destroying their cover is a way to do that. Another way is to reduce the effect of their cover by moving to hit them from a direction for which they have no cover. This is called flanking. For example, if an enemy is taking cover behind a wall, move around to the side of the wall so that the wall is no longer between you and your target. Or, if you have an explosive weapon, you can simply blow a hole in the wall, taking your target out in the process.

DESTRUCTIBLE ENVIRONMENTS

THE POWERFUL IEDS ON GOLMUD RAILWAY COMPLETELY DEMOLISH STRUCTURES AND ANYTHING ELSE IN THEIR WIDE BLAST RADIUS.

One of the awesome features in *Battlefield 4* is that many of the structures and objects can be damaged or outright destroyed. This presents a large range of possibilities and opportunities that will affect the tactics you use. For example, if the enemy is holed up in a house and taking shots at you from the windows, you could try to throw a grenade through the window or rush into the house via the doorway and clear the threat out with close-range combat. However, with destruction as an option, you can launch a rocket at a wall of the structure and blow a hole in it. If an enemy was on the other side of the wall, that threat might be killed. Otherwise, you can then use direct fire to kill the enemy, since you destroyed the wall providing cover.

Often structures can funnel you into a kill zone the enemy has set up. But you can blast your way through walls or other objects and come at the enemies from different directions that they might not expect. While this may seem to favor the attacker, the defender can also use this as an advantage. Destroy potential cover the attacker may use to approach your position. Call in artillery or mortar strikes on groves of trees or shoot out wooden fences to deny the enemy a place to hide. As a result, you can create your own kill zones of open land that the enemy must traverse—all the while under the fire of your weapons.

TIP

Some structures that take heavy damage can completely collapse, killing everyone inside. Target a building's exterior walls until you hear a series of creaking and moaning sounds, indicating an imminent collapse. This can be a fun (yet inefficient) way to take out a pesky sniper hiding in an attic or upper floor. Obviously, if you find yourself in a creaking and moaning building, get out fast!

CLOSE-QUARTER COMBAT

SHOTGUNS AND PDWS ARE THE PREFERRED WEAPONS FOR CLOSE-QUARTER ENCOUNTERS.

In close quarters, such as in a town or even within a building, you don't have a lot of time to aim before shooting. However, at such short ranges, accuracy is not really a factor. Instead, you need a weapon that puts out a lot of firepower with some spread so you are more likely to get a hit while moving. Shotguns and PDWs are great for close-quarter combat. Your minimap is also an important tool, especially if teammates have spotted targets. Since you can see where enemies are located, use this info to set up shots while strafing around corners. Your weapon will already be aimed at the target as it appears on the minimap, which saves you just enough time to have the advantage and make the kill rather than be killed. Don't forget to use grenades, which can be thrown around corners or over walls to hit enemies who think they are safe behind cover.

TIP

Have you just run out of ammo in the middle of a close-quarter duel? It's much faster to draw your pistol than to reload your main weapon. Or if your opponent is reloading too, rush in for a melee kill.

LONG-RANGE COMBAT

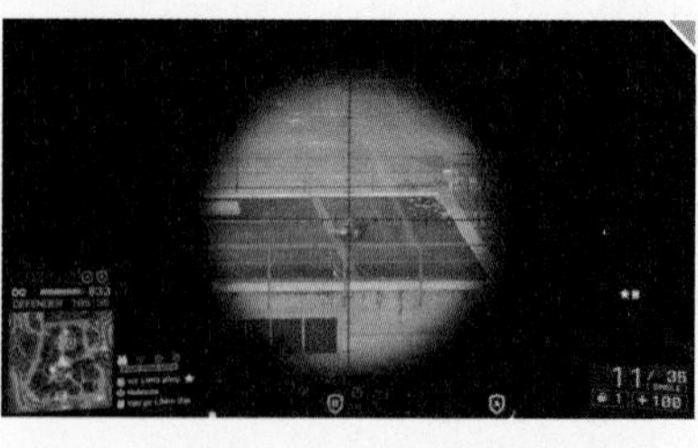

WATCH FOR THE GLINT OF HIGH-POWERED SCOPES. BUT IF YOU CAN SEE THEM, CHANCES ARE THEY CAN SEE YOU.

If possible, it is best to try to attack the enemy at long range before they're even aware of your presence. While sniper rifles work great for this type of combat, you can even use assault rifles, light machine guns, or rocket launchers to hit targets at long range. The key to winning at long range is to take your time. Drop prone, stay still, and use ironsights or scopes to increase your magnification and accuracy. As always, make sure you have some good cover in case the enemy decides to shoot back—if you can see them, they can see you. Also remember to fire in short bursts to ensure that more of your bullets hit the target. High-powered scopes (6X and higher) can now be zeroed for accurate targets beyond 100 meters. Scopes can be zeroed for 0, 200, 300, 400, 500, and 1,000 meters. Use a Range Finder to determine the distance to your target, then make adjustments on your high-powered optic to set the range. By zeroing a scope properly, you no longer have to account for bullet drop. Simply place the crosshairs over your target and squeeze the trigger.

ENGAGING VEHICLES

WHEN POSSIBLE, USE A WEAPON WITH LASER-GUIDED CAPABILITY TO DAMAGE AND DESTROY ENEMY VEHICLES FROM LONG RANGE. OF COURSE, YOU'LL NEED A TEAMMATE TO PAINT THE TARGET WITH A SOFLAM OR PLD.

Attacking vehicles is dangerous—especially when you are a soldier on foot. However, modern infantry have a lot of firepower they can use to disable and destroy vehicles. This role usually falls to the engineer, who carries anti-tank weapons and mines. It takes only a single rocket to immobilize most light vehicles. However, tanks and IFVs require at least two rocket hits to disable, and even more to destroy. Always try to attack tanks from the rear, where their armor is the weakest. Rocket launchers are most effective, but grenade launchers can work in a pinch too, assuming the vehicle is already heavily damaged. Of course, the best way to kill a tank is with another tank.

Even if you don't have those powerful weapons or gadgets, you can still damage light vehicles with small arms fire. The gunners on the light vehicles are completely exposed—shoot them and the vehicles lose their firepower. For those who are really daring, engineers can place mines in the path of moving vehicles. C4 (now carried by the support and recon class) is also very effective against vehicles, but you have to get very close to slap on a charge.

GAME MODES

There are a total of seven game modes spread across ten different maps, offering plenty of variety for all. Most of the game modes are familiar classics, but the addition of Obliteration, Defuse, and Domination adds some variety to the mix.

CONQUEST LARGE/SMALL

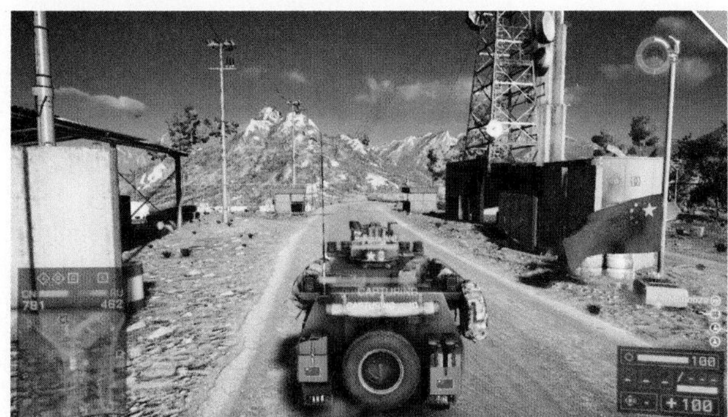

CONQUEST IS ALL ABOUT CAPTURING CONTROL POINTS (FLAGS) AND DEFENDING THEM. IF YOU WANT TO WIN, DON'T FORGET THE DEFEND PART.

This classic *Battlefield* game mode is back, requiring your team to dominate the area of operations by capturing control points and holding them. Simply stand next to a flagpole at a control point to raise your team's flag—the more teammates there are in the flag's capture radius, the faster the flag is raised. Once captured, some control points provide vehicles and stationary weapons, so leave some personnel back to defend these locations. Both teams have a limited number of reinforcements known as tickets. The ticket count for both teams appears just above the minimap—the team who runs out of tickets first loses the match. You can drain the enemy ticket count by holding more than half of the control points on the map. So if there are four control points, all you need to do is hold three to initiate a ticket drain. Capture a majority of the control points early on and stay put, forcing the enemy to attack your defended positions.

RECOMMENDED PLAYERS: 64 (24 ON XBOX 360 AND PS3)

Goal:

- Conquest is all about territory control.
- Win by draining enemy tickets to zero.

Rules:

- Capture and hold flags to drain enemy tickets.
- Killing enemies also drains tickets (1 per kill).
- Each team has an uncapturable home base where most of the team's vehicles spawn.
- Can spawn on any flag under your control, including your home base.
- Spawns also available on squadmates, certain vehicles, and Radio Beacons.

NOTE

Conquest Large is only available on the PC, Xbox One, and PS4.

RUSH

WHEN ATTACKING, WORK TOGETHER WITH YOUR SQUAD TO RUSH M-COM STATIONS—HAVE A TEAMMATE PROVIDE COVER WHILE YOU SET THE CHARGE.

RECOMMENDED PLAYERS: 32 (24 ON XBOX 360 AND PS3)

Goal:

- Attackers win by blowing up all the defenders' bases or zones.
- Defenders win by draining attackers' tickets to zero.

Rules:

- There are two M-COM stations per zone that the attackers need to arm.
- Defenders can disarm armed M-COM stations (which can then be re-armed).
- Defenders have unlimited spawns.
- Attackers' respawn cost 1 ticket per soldier.
- Deployment areas (and vehicle setups) shift as the game advances through zones.
- Can spawn in current deployment zone or on squad members, certain vehicles, and Radio Beacons.

In this game mode, one team is the attacker while the other is the defender. On the map there are several bases controlled by the defender. The attacker's objective is to destroy the two M-COM stations at each zone. Once both stations have been destroyed, that base is considered destroyed and the defender receives a new zone to defend with two more M-COM stations. The attacker has a limited number of tickets at the beginning of a match, shown just above the minimap. Whenever an attacking soldier dies, it costs a ticket for the soldier to respawn on the map. Once the tickets run out, the attackers can't spawn new soldiers back onto the map, giving the defenders a win. However, once the attacker destroys both M-COM stations in a zone, the team gets more tickets as well as a new set of vehicles. The defenders do not have to worry about tickets—they have an unlimited number of respawns. The defender wins by eliminating all attackers and reducing their tickets before they can destroy all the M-COM stations on the map.

▶ NOTE

M-COM stations can't be destroyed by explosive weapons or falling debris from collapsed buildings. Therefore soldiers must approach each objective and physically plant a charge on it—stand next to an M-COM station and hold down the interact button/key to arm or disarm a charge.

OBLITERATION

RETRIEVING AND TRANSPORTING THE BOMB IN OBLITERATION REQUIRES A COORDINATED EFFORT BY YOUR WHOLE TEAM—VEHICLES ARE A MUST!

RECOMMENDED PLAYERS: 32 (24 ON XBOX 360 AND PS3)

Goal:

- Win by destroying the enemy's three targets (using bomb spawned on map) or reducing enemy tickets to zero.

Rules:

- Bomb spawns in the bomb spawn zone.
- Bomb can be picked up by either team.
- Only one bomb in play at any given time.
- Bomb can be transported in vehicles.
- Detonate bomb on enemy target to blow it up (-1 ticket for enemy team and the target is removed).
- Can spawn at home base, on squad members, on certain vehicles, on Radio Beacons, and at forward base (inside bomb spawn zone).

Obliteration is an all-new game mode requiring each team to destroy three targets belonging to the opposing team. This is a very chaotic game mode because all players are focused on one objective: obtaining and transporting the bomb to one of the targets. The bomb is visible at all times, both on the HUD and minimap, allowing all players to vector in on its location. The addition of vehicles to this mode adds an extra layer of intensity and tactical gameplay. Teams are most successful when grabbing the bomb and immediately transition to a vehicle (like a Quad Bike or helicopter) for transport. Carrying the bomb on foot is a likely death sentence. Once a bomb carrier has reached an enemy target, the bomb can be planted, similar to setting a charge on an M-COM station in Rush. However, the bomb detonates much faster, killing anyone in its large blast radius. The game is over when all three of a team's targets are destroyed or when one team runs out of tickets. Given the competitive nature of this game mode, don't be surprised if no targets are destroyed during a match.

▶ NOTE

In Obliteration, if a bomb carrier is killed while swimming in deep water, don't worry—the bomb floats, and can be retrieved by another swimmer.

DEFUSE

SLOW DOWN AND WATCH YOUR CORNERS. YOU CAN ONLY BE REVIVED ONCE AND THERE ARE NO RESPAWNS IN DEFUSE.

RECOMMENDED PLAYERS: 10

Goal:

- Attackers win by killing the enemy team or blowing up one of the two enemy targets.
- Defenders win by killing the enemy team or disarming the bomb.

Rules:

- Infantry only.
- Designed for two teams of five.
- Attackers attempt to transport bomb to A or B target and blow it up.
- Defenders can disarm the bomb.
- Take turns playing as attacker and defender.
- Points tallied and winner announced after two sets.
- No respawns. One Defibrillator revive per player. Spectate after death.

Defuse is a significant departure from the large-scale battles of Conquest and Rush. The game mode is designed as a compact infantry conflict between two opposing squads. Both teams take turns playing as the attacker and defender—the attackers must destroy one of two targets (marked A and B) while the defenders must prevent these targets from being destroyed. At the start of the round, an attacker must pick up a bomb and serve as the bomb carrier. If the bomb carrier is killed, the bomb can be picked up by another attacker—defenders can't pick up the bomb, but they can camp a dropped bomb, preventing the attackers from retrieving it and carrying it to a target. But if the attackers get through, they can plant the bomb at one of two targets. At this point the attackers must keep an eye the bomb until it detonates, preventing the defenders from disarming it. Unlike all other game modes, there are no respawns in Defuse, ramping up the tension. But each player can be revived once with an assault soldier's Defibrillator. If you die and aren't revived, you must wait until the next round starts before you can get back into the game—but you can watch the remainder of the match from a third-person perspective, following other players on your team. With no respawns, teammates must work together, moving and clearing areas methodically to avoid getting wiped out.

DOMINATION

PREPARE FOR SOME CLOSE-QUARTER, IN-YOUR-FACE BATTLES IN THIS COMPACT, INFANTRY-ONLY GAME MODE.

RECOMMENDED PLAYERS: 20

Goal:

- Similar to Conquest, players fight for control over three flags.
- If a team controls a majority (two or more) of the flags, the opposing team begins to bleed tickets.
- Win by draining enemy tickets to zero.

Rules:

- Infantry only.
- Designed for ten vs. ten, but can support up to 16 vs. 16 on PC, Xbox One, and PS4.
- Three neutral flags.
- Random spawning and squad spawning allowed.
- One to three battle pickups per map with additional respawn time (60 seconds).

Domination made its debut in the *Close Quarters* expansion for *Battlefield 3*. Think of this as a very compact, small-scale version of Conquest with no vehicles. There are always three flags on the map, and they capture much faster than they do in Conquest. As a result, defense is just as important as offense, since enemy troops can steal a flag away from your team within a few seconds. Both teams should strive to capture and hold a minimum of two flags to initiate a drain on the opposing team's ticket count. The addition of battle pickups on the map adds a unique element to these matches, often drawing players to other areas of the map. But don't let battle pickups become a distraction. While a battle pickup can offer more firepower, it's more important to stay focused on capturing and holding flags. Since squad spawning is supported, do your best to stay close to your squadmates. These are matches where its beneficial to move around as a squad, leveraging the squad's combined firepower to overwhelm enemies.

SQUAD DEATHMATCH

PAY CLOSE ATTENTION TO WHEN AND WHERE THE IFV SPAWNS. ACQUIRING THIS VEHICLE (AND KEEPING IT REPAIRED) IS OFTEN THE KEY TO VICTORY.

RECOMMENDED PLAYERS: 20

Goal:

- The squad that reaches the kill limit wins.

Rules:

- Infantry only except for an IFV that spawns and respawns at one of four locations around the map.
- All other squads are your enemy.
- Each kill counts toward the squad total.
- Can respawn at a computer-selected spot anywhere on the map, on squad members, or a Radio Beacon.

In this mode there are four five-player squads each representing a different team: A, B, C, and D. The team that scores 50 kills first wins—the score is listed on the left side of the screen above the minimap. To make things more interesting, each Squad Deathmatch map contains one Infantry Fighting Vehicle (IFV), spawning in four possible locations. Whoever can take control of this vehicle gains a huge advantage in firepower. But while manning the vehicle, be aware that there are three other squads gunning for you. As you can imagine, this is a very fast-paced game mode best played with good squadmates you can rely on to watch your back. Stay together, and stay alive!

TEAM DEATHMATCH

TAKE ADVANTAGE OF BATTLE PICKUPS, LIKE THE M32 MGL SEMI-AUTO GRENADE LAUNCHER.

RECOMMENDED PLAYERS: 20

Goal:

- The team that first reaches the kill limit wins.

Rules:

- Infantry only.
- Each kill counts towards the team total.
- Can respawn at a computer-selected spot anywhere on the map or on a Radio Beacon.

Team Deathmatch is a no-holds-barred infantry-only battle in a confined area. The two teams struggle to score the most kills to win the match. Each kill is counted, so take down your enemies to increase your team's score, represented by the numbers and status bars above the minimap. It's your choice whether to stick with your team or to go on a solo hunt. But be warned, the tempo is high and enemies can pop up from behind almost any corner. Monitor the scoring status bars to see how the fight is going, and make tactical adjustments as necessary. For example, if both teams are close to scoring the requisite points necessary for a win, play is safe to avoid giving the enemy team the kills they need.

TIP

The Recon kit's T-UGS and Motion Sensor gadgets are very useful in Team Deathmatch, helping reveal the locations of enemy troops.

HARDCORE MODE

Hardcore Mode is back, available on all game modes. This server-side setting removes most of the HUD elements, including the minimap and reticle. Therefore you must aim using your weapon's ironsights or optic. Friendly fire is turned on, so watch your fire around teammates, especially when using explosive weapons. All weapons inflict more damage, making for a hyper-realistic *Battlefield* experience designed specifically for experts.

BATTLEFIELD ESPORTS: Q&A WITH STRONGSIDE

With the introduction of Defuse and Domination, *Battlefield* is making its first major push into the world of professional gaming, also known as eSports. So what is eSports and what does it mean for *Battlefield*? Who better to ask than pro gaming veteran Michael "StrongSide" Cavanaugh.

What do you think about the addition of the eSports game modes Domination and Defuse?

Nothing compares to the fast-paced action that Domination and Defuse provide. I can't wait to see the potential these game modes have for competitive tournament play in the future. Besides competitive play, these game modes are perfect for when you want to play with a smaller team because every decision you make will have much bigger impact on the team. My favorite addition is Domination because it's squad vs. squad, so there is always something going on. There is never a dull moment in Domination. If you're looking for a challenge, you can catch me in the Domination game mode!

Obviously in a game like* Battlefield*, you need teammates you can trust. What do you look for when selecting teammates prior to a tournament?

When I look for a teammate, that person should be a player who is dedicated and has an incredible amount of will to win. A teammate needs to be able to communicate well and work together with others. So having someone who can take constructive criticism and give constructive criticism is a great way to build communication. You want a teammate who is positive regardless of the score and someone you enjoy gaming with.

In team-based games, communication is key. How do you rally your troops and keep them focused on the objective?

In every game mode, our team needs to have a beginning strategy and overall game plan to win. I like to go over strategies and call outs so we all have the same game plan in mind and everyone knows what is expected of them. It is much harder to win when a team runs around the map and has no set goal planned.

Leading up to a tournament, how much time do you spend practicing with your team?

Before a tournament I'll spend anywhere from 8-14 hours a day practicing. But I make it a point to take some time for myself and my personal life because I have to have a balanced life. You'll burn yourself out if you don't take the time to relax and do the things you enjoy.

When it comes time to compete, how do you deal with the pressure of tournament play? Is it ever difficult to focus on the game?

Every player has their own way of dealing with pressure. I don't think about anything else but staying focused on my game. I enjoy having people watch me play, so that has never been an added pressure. Pressure and challenges are just opportunities for me to rise.

"Pressure and challenges are just opportunities for me to rise."

"You want a teammate who is positive regardless of the score and someone you enjoy gaming with."

What advice could you give to gamers seeking to make the transition into professional gaming?

To become a high-level player, you have to try your hardest every game. If you fail, you have to take the opportunity to learn from your mistakes and improve it. Your stats and wins may not go up every match you play; the exact opposite can occur while learning new routes, strategies, and skill sets. To be one of the best you need to try new things, so take on new roles like being the aggressor or being the sniper. You may not be great at every role at first, but it takes time to be a well-rounded player. The game and the players are constantly evolving; that is why you should be learning something new every day. I excelled in many video games I played because I always focused on what I could do better. When I would lose, I would watch my opponents, learned what they did, and mimicked them or learn to counter their play style. I always try to evaluate my decisions and think of what I could have done different or better with what is in front of me. This prepared me to recognize recurring situations and make better choices instead of repeating the same costly mistakes. Most of all have fun!

EXTENDED PLAY

With the additions of Commander Mode, Spectator Mode and an improved Battlelog, there's more to do in *Battlefield* than ever before—and you don't even have to be in front of your PC or console to take part. Whether taking command of your team and leading them to victory, or simply watching a battle unfold from the sidelines, these features offer more ways to experience and make new *Battlefield* moments.

COMMANDER MODE

ZOOMING IN GIVES YOU A BETTER PERSPECTIVE OF THE ACTION ON THE GROUND AND ALLOWS YOU TO DEPLOY ASSETS WITH GREATER PRECISION.

First introduced in *Battlefield 2*, Commander Mode is finally back and better than ever. While playing Conquest, Rush, or Obliteration, any player above rank 10 can apply to become their team's commander. From the team setup screen, select Take Command to become your team's commander. Commanders are assigned on a first-come-first-serve basis. However, if you connect to the server as a commander, you will have a small window of opportunity where you can apply before other players. While playing as the commander, your soldier no longer occupies a slot on your team, nor are you physically present anywhere on the map. Instead, you occupy an overhead view of the entire map, allowing you to watch your teammates take on enemy forces below. Zoom in from overhead to watch individual firefights, or zoom out to get a broader perspective of the battle. Commander Mode is filled with tools and perspectives designed to give your team the upper hand. But it's up to you to put these tools to proper use.

INTERFACE

Asset Overview: The Asset Overview displays all assets that are available on a map, and distinguishes between those you currently have access to and those you can gain access to. It also displays the amount of time left until you can deploy an asset. Most assets have to cool down before they can be used again.

Squad Asset Bar: When the squads under your command work together, they are awarded squad scores. All your squads' scores contribute to your Squad Asset Bar, with which you can award your squads with assets. When a squad asset is deployed, the Squad Asset Bar is drained. The amount drained depends on the value of the deployed asset.

Game Mode Info: This feature provides you with information about the status of the round, including the status of objectives and ticket counts for both teams.

Live Camera Feed: Live Camera Feed shows you a view of an area. Selecting a squad leader will give you a first-person view. Selecting an objective shows you a top-down view of the objective and surrounding area. Select a Cruise Missile for a perspective from its onboard nose camera. Or select a UAV or Gunship to show a view of the area they're circling.

Squad Status: If you select a squad leader, his squad mates will appear in green. Selecting a squad leader also displays any orders given to the squad as a green line. If you give the squad leader an order, it is displayed as a dotted line, and if the order is accepted it turns into a full line. An accepted commander order replaces any prior squad leader order.

Asset Selection: Deploy commander assets by selecting any point of the map. This brings up a branching menu of options, allowing you to deploy assets or issue orders.

COMMANDER ASSETS

The commander's primary role is to support their team. This is accomplished through the deployment of assets and the issuing of orders. Let's take a quick look at all of the options available at each commander's fingertips.

ASSET BREAKDOWN

ICON	NAME	DESCRIPTION
DEFAULT ASSETS		
	Scan UAV	Deploy an Unmanned Aerial Vehicle (UAV), which spots enemies in the area.
	EMP UAV	Deploy an Electromagnetic Pulse (EMP) UAV, which hides activity in the area from the enemy commander; can disable incoming Cruise Missile.
	High Value Target	Marks an enemy that has a high kill-streak as a High Value Target (HVT). The enemy is spotted for allied soldiers.
	Early Warning	Warn allied soldiers in the area of incoming danger, like an incoming Cruise Missile.
	Order	Give an order to a squad leader to either attack or defend an objective.
SQUAD ASSETS		
	Promote Squad	Promote selected squad. Squad members gain next Field Upgrade in selected path.
	Supply Drop	Deploy a crate via parachute that automatically heals and gives ammo to nearby soldiers. Allied soldiers can also switch their kit by interacting with the crate.
	Rapid Deploy	Reduces selected squad's deploy time.
	Vehicle Drop	Map-sensitive parachute vehicle drop—PWC or Quad Bike.
OBJECTIVE ASSETS		
	Infantry Scan	Spot all enemy infantry.
	Vehicle Scan	Spot all enemy vehicles.
	Cruise Missile	Launch a Cruise Missile at an area, destroying all enemies within a large blast radius.
	Gunship	When the Gunship is deployed, it will circle the location that it is tied to. Your team can spawn in the Gunship and parachute from it. The Gunship is also equipped with various powerful weapons that allies can use.

TIP

The Gunship is equipped with 105mm, 40mm, and 25mm cannons. Use these devastating weapons to rain down fire on your opponents. Maintaining control of this powerful asset should be a critical element of your team's overall strategy.

COMMANDER TACTICS

- When playing Commander Mode, you're essentially trying to outsmart and out-strategize the opposing commander while leading your team to victory. Of course, your effectiveness largely depends on your team's progress on the ground. So issue orders to your squads to keep them focused on objectives and reward them with squad assets like Rapid Deploy, Supply Drop, and Vehicle Drop.
- The Cruise Missile and Gunship assets are only available in Conquest and are tied to a specific control point—it's always the Cruise Missile or the Gunship, as these powerful assets are never available on the same map. Both of these offensive assets are capable of turning the tide in a close match, so make sure your squads capture and defend the control point responsible for producing these powerful weapons.
- All orders issued by the commander are relayed through squad leaders—the commander does not have direct contact with all soldiers on the ground. With a top-down overview of the entire battle, the commander has a better perspective on what's happening on the battlefield. Use this information to issue squad orders, sending your squads to capture and hold control points and other critical locations. Squad leaders don't have to follow a commander's order, but they're rewarded with points if they do.
- When ordering squads around the map, do your best to keep them in particular zones. This works best during Conquest matches. Simply assign one squad to each control point. For the duration of the match it's each squad's job to attack and defend that same control point. If manpower allows, assign two squads to hotly contested control points. By sticking to this plan, your team stands a good chance of winning. But it's up to your squads to remain disciplined, even if it means defending a rear location that sees little action.
- When you're not busy managing your squads, gather intelligence by using the Scan UAV, Infantry Scan, and Vehicle Scan assets. All of these reconnaissance-based assets reveal the locations of enemy troops and vehicles, instantly relaying information to your squads' HUDs and minimaps. Giving your squads the ability to spot enemy units makes a huge difference on the ground. But these assets can be thwarted if the opposing commander plays a EMP UAV, making a small portion of the map dark, despite your recon efforts.
- The Supply Drop asset comes in handy for resupplying friendly troops. But as in *Battlefield 2*, this asset can also be used offensively. Locate an enemy sniper or other stationary soldier and drop one of these crates on top of them. The crate drops from the sky silently, giving your victim no warning of their imminent demise.
- When an enemy soldier is on a kill streak, mark them with the High Value Target (HVT) asset. This marks the enemy on your squads' minimaps as well as spots the HVT on everyone's HUD. With every squad member gunning for the HVT, the HVT's kill streak is likely to come to an end.
- The EMP UAV interferes with the minimaps and HUDs of enemy troops operating beneath it. But this powerful asset can also prevent an enemy Cruise Missile from reaching its target. When you spot an Cruise Missile on the map, deploy a EMP UAV at its target site to prevent it from detonating.

NOTE

If the commander does a poor job, and you are a squad leader, you can disapprove of the commander via the Team Setup screen—go to Options/Team Setup/Toggle Rating. If the majority of squad leaders disapproves of the commander, a mutiny will start. If a mutiny is taking place, the commander will be kicked out within a short amount of time unless the majority of squad leaders toggles the rating back to "Approve". A mutiny cannot be started against a player who recently became commander.

SPECTATOR MODE

SPECTATOR MODE'S FREE CAM OPTION ALLOWS SPECTATORS TO WATCH THE BATTLE FROM ANY ANGLE THEY CHOOSE.

Spectator Mode is completely new to *Battlefield 4*, offering players the opportunity to simply watch a match unfold. Each server supports up to four spectators per match—like playing as commander, joining as a spectator does not count against the server's maximum player count. Once in Spectator Mode you have four camera perspectives to choose from. The Table Top view looks similar to Commander Mode, giving you a broad view of the map, complete with the ability to zoom all the way in and watch pitched battles from a satellite-like perspective. With the First Person camera, you can switch to the perspective of any player on the map, seeing exactly what they see in real-time. The Third Person perspective puts you behind any player on the map, along with a player card that shows their current weapon, attachments, health, and ammo. Finally there's the Free Cam, tied to no single perspective. Instead, you can simply fly around the battle and choose any perspective you like—this is perfect for those seeking to make videos. Whichever perspective you choose, Spectator Mode offers a unique way to experience Battlefield. Consider sitting in on some matches and watch how others play—you may learn something new.

▶ NOTE

THERE ARE A NUMBER OF SPECTATOR MODE DISPLAY OPTIONS THAT CAN BE TOGGLED ON AND OFF, INCLUDING THE ABILITY TO HIDE CERTAIN HUD ELEMENTS. YOU CAN EVEN TURN EVERYTHING OFF, FOR A PRISTINE, INTERFACE-FREE VIEW OF THE BATTLE.

BATTLELOG

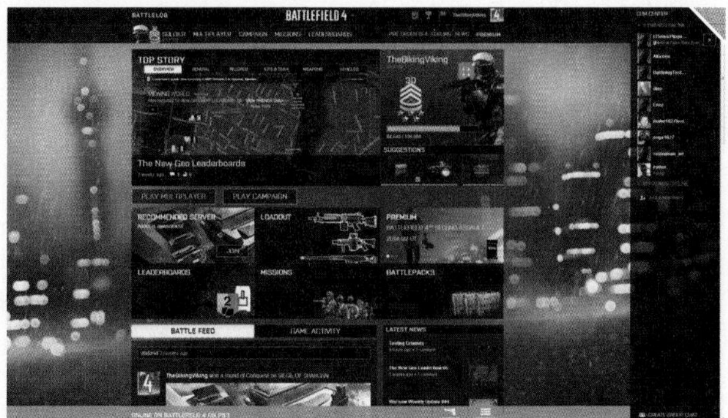

BATTLELOG IS THE GO-TO PLACE TO KEEP IN TOUCH WITH FRIENDS, COMPARE STATS, AND ADJUST YOUR LOADOUTS.

Battlelog.com extends your *Battlefield 4* experience by enhancing your gameplay, tracking your progression throughout your multiplayer career, and allowing you compete with millions of *Battlefield* players all around the world. Battlelog is available in-game, on the web, and through tablet and smartphone apps. Battlelog can track all rounds you have played, your unlocks, stats, awards, assignments, and much more. You can complete missions and compete with your friends to see who the best tank driver is, or use the Geo Leaderboards to compete against people in your city or country. Or customize your loadout and find a server in the Server Browser that is right for you.

You can always bring up Battlelog in-game too. You can check your stats, your friends' stats, see how your suggested or tracked unlocks are progressing, create and join missions, see how you are doing in the Geo Leaderboards, and much more.

MOBILE ACCESS

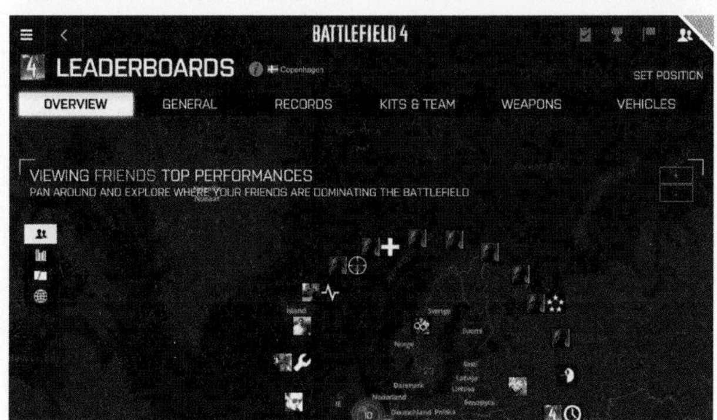

WHILE ON YOUR TABLET OR PHONE, STAY UP-TO-DATE WITH WHAT'S HAPPENING ONLINE. WHO ARE THE BEST PLAYERS IN YOUR CITY, COUNTRY, OR CONTINENT?

Battlelog is available on iPhone and iPad, as well Android phones and tablets running Android 4.0 or higher. You can find and download the free Battlelog app from the relevant store for your device. Launch the app and log in with your Origin account, e-mail address, or by using the QR Code from the in-game Battlelog. With the Battlelog app, you can access most of the features available from Battlelog.com and take it with you on the go.

Battlelog can also act as a companion while you play. Access BattleScreen to have a full screen mini-map from the game shown on your device (tablets and PC only), or customize your loadout and have it synced directly to the game. You can also find friends or new servers from your phone or tablet, and instantly switch to another game server.

PLAYER EMBLEMS

The emblem is a feature that gives you an additional identity marker. The emblem is displayed on vehicles, weapons, and characters. Create your unique emblem with the Emblem Editor on Battlelog.com. You can create several emblems and then choose between them before entering a server.

COMMUNITY

The *Battlefield* community is very active, and always a good source of information for game news, software updates, patch notes, and even unorthodox tactics. Here's a few good sources to check out for the latest *Battlefield* news:

BATTLEFIELD BLOG

BLOGS.BATTLEFIELD.EA.COM

This is the official blog maintained by employees of DICE. Go here for all the latest information on the game straight from the developers.

OFFICIAL BATTLEFIELD TWITTER

@BATTLEFIELD

Get the latest tweets from the game's developers.

PRIMAGAMES.COM

PRIMAGAMES.COM/BF4

Check back with the Prima team for blogs and videos, offering even more insight on classes, weapons, vehicles, and evolving tactics.

INFANTRY

To learn more and watch video on classes visit PrimaGames.com/BF4

CLASSES

Succeeding during multiplayer often comes down to choosing the right tools for the job. That's where the classes (also known as troop kits) come in to play. Before spawning into a game, you're prompted to choose which class you wish to play as. If you're a team player, your choice should be based on what is needed as opposed to which kit you want to play as. For example, if your base is being overrun by enemy tanks, choose the engineer kit and use rockets or mines to eliminate the threats. Although there are only four troop kits to choose from, the customization options are the most elaborate of any *Battlefield* game to date, allowing you to mix and match weapons, gadgets, and Field Upgrades to create a completely unique kit that compliments your style of play and meets the demands of any tactical situation.

FIELD UPGRADES

BEFORE DEPLOYING, BE SURE TO SELECT A FIELD UPGRADE FOR YOUR SOLDIER. EACH CLASS HAS FIVE UPGRADE PATHS TO CHOOSE FROM.

The specializations from *Battlefield 3* have been replaced with Field Upgrades, a concept first introduced in *Battlefield 2142*. Field Upgrades reward players with individual perks for performing squad-based actions, such as revives, repairs, and resupplies. Your progress through your chosen Field Upgrade path can be monitored on the meter just above the squad list on the left side of the HUD. Each Field Upgrade path has four levels of upgrades. Each time you perform an action that assists your squad, the Field Upgrade meter fills from left to right. New upgrades are awarded as the meter fills, allowing you to take advantage of all four upgrades once the meter is completely filled. However, every time your squad is wiped, progress on the Field Upgrade meter is lost, potentially leading to the loss of previously attained upgrades. By default, the Defensive and Shadow Field Upgrade paths are available to all players. But the Offensive and eight class-specific upgrade paths must be unlocked. Here's a quick look at the universal upgrades available to all classes. For information on the class-specific upgrades, reference the following sections covering the four classes.

UNIVERSAL FIELD UPGRADES

LEVEL	ICON	NAME	DESCRIPTION
DEFENSIVE			
1		Armor	Reduces incoming damage to the chest by 10%.
2		Cover	Decreases amount of incoming suppression by 50%
3		Flak	Decreases damage from explosions by 15%.
4		Quick Regen	Decreases time before Out of Combat heal by 20%.
OFFENSIVE			
1		Sprint	Increases maximum Sprint Speed by 10%.
2		Ammo	Increases maximum inventory of bullets by 50%.
3		Grenades	Increases maximum inventory of hand grenades by 1.
4		Reduced Fall	Increases height you can fall without taking damage.
SHADOW			
1		Quick Unspot	Reduces time you are spotted by two seconds.
2		Sprint	Increases maximum Sprint Speed by 10%.
3		Reduced Fall	Increases height you can fall without taking damage.
4		Stealth	Undetected by Motion Sensors except when sprinting.

NOTE

The Shadow Field Upgrade was designed by the *Battlefield* community prior to the game's launch.

ASSAULT

US ASSAULT

RU ASSAULT

CN ASSAULT

STARTING LOADOUT

PRIMARY WEAPON	AK-12		GRENADE	M67 FRAG		GADGET 2	M320 HE	
SIDEARM	P226		GADGET 1	FIRST AID PACK		KNIFE	BAYONETTE	

STRENGTHS: **WELL-ROUNDED KIT; HEAL/REVIVE TEAMMATES** WEAKNESSES: **WEAK ANTI-VEHICLE CAPABILITY**

When you're not sure which class to choose, you can't go wrong with assault. The assault rifles associated with this kit are excellent at any range, with great damage output and impressive rates of fire. Each assault rifle can also be equipped with an underslung M320 40mm grenade launcher, great for blasting infantry, light-skinned vehicles, and even structures—keep playing as the assault class to unlock new types of ammo for your M320. The M26 MASS shotgun is another weapon unique to the assault class, capable of firing a variety of devastating rounds, including slugs. Beyond its impressive offensive capabilities, the assault class is responsible for healing injured teammates with their First Aid Pack and reviving downed teammates with the Defibrillator. The Defibrillator isn't immediately available, so keep playing as the assault class to unlock it—it's the first item unlocked and can make a world of difference during close matches. Keep playing as assault to unlock the familiar Medic Bag for greater healing efficiency.

UNLOCK PROGRESSION

UNLOCK	NAME	IMAGE	SCORE
1	Defibrillator		11,000
2	M26 MASS		22,000
3	Offensive Field Upgrade		33,000
4	M320 SMK		44,000
5	M26 DART		55,000

UNLOCK	NAME	IMAGE	ASSAULT SCORE
6	Combat Medic Field Upgrade		66,000
7	M320 DART		77,000
8	M26 Slug		89,000
9	Medic Bag		100,000

UNLOCK	NAME	IMAGE	ASSAULT SCORE
10	M26 Frag		110,000
11	M320 FB		122,000
12	Grenadier Field Upgrade		133,000
13	M320 LVG		140,000

GADGETS

FIRST AID PACK

Unlock: Assault Kit Start

Description: Single-use Medic Pack that slowly heals a single soldier to full health.

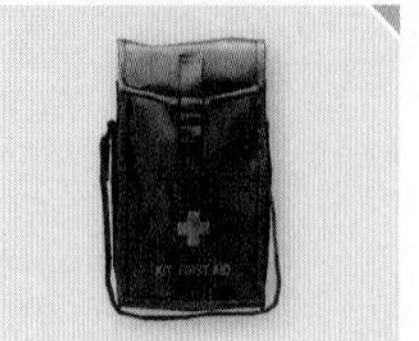

FIELD NOTES

The familiar Medic Bag doesn't unlock until later. For beginning assault soldiers, the First Aid Pack is the only option available when it comes to healing themselves and teammates. When tossed on the ground, any injured soldier can pick up a First Aid Pack by simply walking over it. Once retrieved from the ground, the First Aid Pack immediately begins healing, eventually restoring the soldier to full health. Since the First Aid Pack is picked up, the injured soldier can continue moving about the battlefield while continually gaining health. By contrast, soldiers gathered around a Medic Bag must remain stationary until they reach full health. So if you're on the move, the First Aid Pack has its benefits. It can also be tossed greater distances, ideal for dispensing medical supplies to distant teammates if you are pinned behind cover.

DEFIBRILLATOR

Unlock: 11,000 Assault Score

Description: Automated External Defibrillator (AED) revives downed teammates and electrocutes enemies. Charging the paddles will revive teammates with increased health. Needs to recharge after multiple quick uses.

FIELD NOTES

The Defibrillator has undergone some changes since *Battlefield 3*. For one, you only have a maximum of three charges available at any given time, requiring you to think carefully before each use. Using one quick charge on a downed teammate will revive them, but with only 20% health. Hold down the trigger to give the Defibrillator full power before deploying, to revive a teammate with 100% health—a full charge is also necessary to score a kill with the Defibrillator. Once all three charges have been expended, the Defibrillator must recharge before it can be used again—charges are replenished one at a time over the course of a few seconds. So instead of carrying around a dead Defibrillator, switch back to your weapon and get back to the fight. After approximately 15 seconds, your Defibrillator is ready for use, loaded with three fresh charges, allowing you to revive teammates or zap unsuspecting enemy troops. Defibrillator kills are still as satisfying (and hilarious) as they've always been.

M320 GRENADE LAUNCHER

Unlock: Assault Kit Start

Description: The M320 grenade launcher allows a large variety of ammunition to be used with the weapon, including fragmentation, flechette, and smoke rounds.

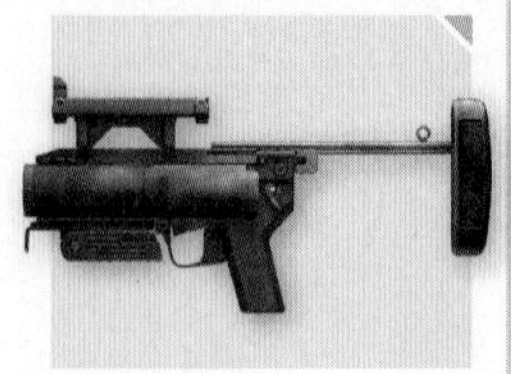

M320 AMMO

NAME	IMAGE	DESCRIPTION	UNLOCK
M320 HE		High Explosive 40mm grenade with a small blast radius for engaging grouped infantry and light vehicles.	Assault Kit Start
M320 SMK		A 40mm grenade that creates a blinding cloud of white smoke on impact, which also blocks spotting.	44,000 Assault Score
M320 DART		Flechettes packed in a 40mm cartridge that effectively transforms the launcher into a shotgun.	77,000 Assault Score
M320 FB		Flashbang 40mm grenade with a suppressive flash to temporarily blind enemies in close quarters.	122,000 Assault Score
M320 LVG		A 40mm grenade that bounces before exploding on a timer.	140,000 Assault Score

FIELD NOTES

The M320 grenade launcher fires 40mm rounds and can be carried as a separate gadget or attached on an assault rifle's Underslung Rail. In any case, the weapon is deployed in a similar fashion, utilizing a series of horizontal notches visible on the ironsights—or horizontal lines superimposed on the HUD when firing from the Underslung Rail. These horizontal marks help determine barrel elevation prior to firing. Unlike traditional firearms, the M320 is an indirect fire weapon, meaning rounds are lobbed toward distant targets, flying an arc-like trajectory—aim high to hit distant targets. As a result, the weapon isn't very accurate beyond 100 meters. However, with practice, the M320 is a very formidable weapons platform capable of firing a variety of ammo, allowing for greater tactical flexibility. HE (High Explosive) is the first ammo type available. But as your assault score increases, you'll unlock more ammo types including smoke, flechettes, Flashbangs, and bouncy LVG rounds. Smoke rounds are particularly useful for concealment when cover is sparse and your squad must advance over open terrain. Use the flechette-filled DART rounds to engage opponents behind light cover. The FB (Flashbang) rounds come in handy prior to storming a room filled with opponents, temporarily blinding them. Or use the LVG rounds to bounce timed, explosive rounds around corners or through windows.

M26 MASS

Unlock: 22,000 Assault Score

Description: Compact shotgun capable of being mounted below the barrel of select assault rifles. Loaded with standard buckshot with high damage but no penetration. The M26 can also accept different ammo types including flechette, slug, and frag rounds.

M26 AMMO

NAME	IMAGE	DESCRIPTION	UNLOCK
M26 DART		Loaded with flechette rounds that reduce damage but increase range and penetration.	55,000 Assault Score
M26 Slug		Loaded with metallic slugs for increased efficiency at longer ranges.	89,000 Assault Score
M26 Frag		Loaded with explosive frag ammunition for increased suppressing power.	111,000 Assault Score

FIELD NOTES

When it comes to close-quarter engagements, the M26 Modular Accessory Shotgun System (MASS) is an excellent backup to any assault rifle. Designed as a lightweight alternative to larger, more cumbersome breaching shotguns, the 12-gauge M26 can be fitted beneath most assault rifles, attached on an Underslung Rail. This unique shotgun is fed from a five-round box magazine and must be manually loaded after each shot by operating the oversized bolt handle on the shooter's left side. As a result, the rate of fire is quite slow, particularly when compared with standard pump and semi-auto shotguns. But the weapon doesn't disappoint at close range, whether loaded with standard buckshot, flechette rounds, slugs, or frag rounds—new rounds are unlocked as your assault score increases. The DART ammo contains several metal flechettes, ideal for ripping through light cover, like wood. Slug rounds significantly increase the weapon's effective range, and hit hard. Frag rounds are great for suppressing enemies and blowing away solid cover, but don't expect to do too much damage to your opponents. So consider equipping the M26 whenever you need a little extra firepower. But remember, this weapon occupies a gadget slot, limiting your revive and healing capabilities.

NOTE

The M320 grenade launcher and M26 MASS cannot be equipped simultaneously. Choose one or the other.

MEDIC BAG

Unlock: 100,000 Assault Score

Description: Stationary persistent Medic Bag. Soldiers nearby will slowly heal to full health, even in combat.

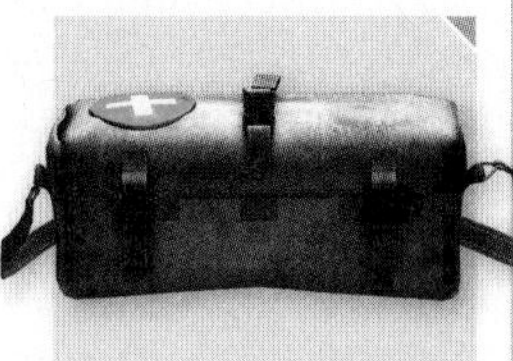

Medic Bags function similar to the support kit's Ammo Box, only they replenish health instead of ammo. Simply drop these on the ground near wounded teammates to heal them. The longer you (or an injured teammate) stand next to a Medic Bag, the more health they'll receive. The Medic Bag has a small healing radius, requiring players to stand very close to it. Healing team and squadmates earns you a healing bonus. Critically injured teammates have a white cross icon flashing above their head—the same icon appears on the minimap. These icons are only visible to friendly assault players so look for them to locate and heal teammates before they die. All players (including enemies) have a life meter below their name, allowing you to see exactly how much health they have. So even if a teammate isn't critical, offer them a Medic Bag to fully replenish their health. Unlike the First Aid Pack, the Medic Bag can heal multiple teammates at once, making it far more effective when it comes to scoring Heal points. However, players must stay within the Medic Bag's healing radius, potentially making them vulnerable if the Medic Bag is deployed in a dangerous location. So pay close attention to where you drop these—you don't want teammates rushing out into incoming fire just to access your Medic Bag in the middle of a street.

ASSAULT: SCORING OPPORTUNITIES

ACTION	POINTS	DESCRIPTION
Heal	10	Heal points are awarded for every 20% health healed on a friendly.
Squad Heal	15	Heal a squadmate.
Revive	100	Revive a teammate.
Squad Revive	125	Revive a squadmate.

UNIQUE FIELD UPGRADES

LEVEL	ICON	NAME	DESCRIPTION
COMBAT MEDIC			
1		Medkit Upgrade	Increases maximum deployed Medic Bags and First Aid Packs by 1.
2		Sprint	Increases maximum Sprint Speed by 10%.
3		Defib Upgrade	Increases charge up speed of the Defibrillator by 100%.
4		Medical Unit	Occupied vehicles will slowly heal nearby soldiers.

LEVEL	ICON	NAME	DESCRIPTION
GRENADIER			
1		Grenades	Increases maximum inventory of hand grenades by 1.
2		Sprint	Increases maximum Sprint Speed by 10%.
3		40mm Grenades	Increases maximum inventory of 40mm grenades by 3.
4		Flak	Decreases damage from explosions by 15%.

ASSAULT TACTICS

- The assault class is ideal for beginners. If you're new to the game, join a squad as assault and assist your squadmates by tossing out First Aid Packs and performing revives with the Defibrillator. Even if you never fire a shot, simply keeping your squad alive and healthy will make a difference. Once it's available, choose the Combat Medic Field Upgrade path to increase the efficiency of your Defibrillator, First Aid Packs, and Medic Bags.
- Always drop Medic Bags behind cover, where teammates can heal without coming under direct enemy fire. First Aid Packs have the added benefit of allowing teammates to heal while on the move.
- Most of the kit's assault rifles are fully automatic. But go easy on the trigger when firing automatically, as the rifle's recoil can pull your aim skyward. Instead, tap the trigger, firing in short bursts, to keep the weapon on target. Many of the assault rifles have single-shot and burst fire modes you can select if recoil becomes a problem.
- Pestered by an enemy firing from a window? Using the M320, launch a grenade just below the window to take out the entire wall and the shooter standing behind it. The Grenadier Field Upgrade path is recommended when equipping the M320. The 40mm Grenades upgrade within this path increases the number of M320 grenades you can carry by three.
- Grenades cause very little damage to heavy vehicles like tanks and IFVs. Don't bother attacking these vehicles unless you see fire and smoke pouring out, indicating heavy damage. If you do attack a heavy vehicle, always strive to hit their weak rear or top armor to maximize damage.
- Once you unlock the M320's smoke ammo, use it to cover your squad's advances or obscure defensive positions. Smoke causes no damage, but it can greatly increase the survivability of your teammates by hindering the enemy's vision—if they can't see you, they'll have a hard time hitting you.
- When selecting the M26 MASS, attach the Underslung Rail to your assault rifle to mount the compact shotgun beneath. This allows you to quickly switch between your assault rifle and M26 MASS, ideal when transitioning between open and close-quarter environments. The M26 DART and M26 Frag rounds are particularly effective when going door to door and clearing rooms.
- Assault troops can earn a ton of points by simply healing and reviving teammates. Drop Medic Bags near injured teammates to earn Heal and Squad Heal points. Also, keep an eye open for downed teammates lying on the ground. Zap them with the Defibrillator to score Revive and Squad Revive points. Healing and reviving can be a full-time job, particularly when defending on Rush maps.
- Revived teammates don't have to respawn, and thus don't use up the team's precious tickets. Conserving tickets in this manner can give your team a huge advantage in tightly contested Conquest matches, so keep those shock paddles buzzing. As veterans know, the Defibrillator can also be used to kill opponents with consistently hilarious results. But the Defibrillator must be fully charged to deliver a lethal zap.
- Did an assault teammate just die in front of you? You can save him, even if you're not playing as the assault class. Grab his kit, then equip the Defibrillator to revive your teammate before his body disappears. Any kit can be grabbed off a dead enemy or teammate. This is a good way to test weapons and equipment you haven't unlocked yet.

PRO TIP: STRONGSIDE

When playing as the assault class my main mission is to keep my team alive. I like to run near my squad and if the opportunity is open I'll be right there to use the Defibrillator to keep our tickets higher than the other team. I'm also constantly throwing down Medic Bags whenever I see my teammates need health.

PRO TIP: FLAMESWORD

Staying true to its class name, a great assault player engages in constant firefights while putting pressure on the opposing team. When I am playing with this class, I like to combine the M320 FB with Smoke Grenades. I like throwing Smoke Grenades in closed-off areas followed by a round from the M320 FB to blind the opponents, allowing my squad to move in and clear out the area.

PRO TIP: ELUMNITE

When playing as the assault class I drop Medic Bags and use the Defibrillator to bring teammates back onto the battlefield. I like to be the game changer and equip a M320 HE to blow holes in the sides of buildings, creating more opportunities for my team to flank.

PRO TIP: WALSHY

When playing assault, I know I am going to be on the front line of combat so I always prepare accordingly by having a mid/close-range weapon. My favorite gadget is the First Aid Pack because it allows you to heal up the fastest and get back in the fight right away.

ENGINEER

US ENGINEER

RU ENGINEER

CN ENGINEER

STARTING LOADOUT

PRIMARY WEAPON	MX4	GRENADE	M67 FRAG	GADGET 2	MBT LAW
SIDEARM	P226	GADGET 1	REPAIR TOOL	KNIFE	BAYONETTE

STRENGTHS: **ANTI-VEHICLE SPECIALIST; VEHICLE REPAIR**

WEAKNESSES: **LIMITED ANTI-INFANTRY CAPABILITY**

Engineers are great at taking out vehicles as well as fixing them. Out of the gate, the engineer is equipped with the MBT LAW rocket launcher. Use this weapon, and the kit's vast arsenal of other launchers, to take out enemy vehicles, including heavily armored tanks, IFVs, and even aircraft—the FIM-92 Stinger and SA-18 IGLA shoulder-fired anti-aircraft missiles are perfect for shooting down helicopters and jets. While the engineer is strong against vehicles, the kit's PDWs are a bit underpowered, particularly at long range. So when you're not facing tons of vehicles, consider choosing a different kit with better performance against infantry. Alternatively, equip your engineer with a carbine or DMR for better performance at range. In addition to demolishing vehicles, the engineer can also repair them with the Repair Tool. Repairing manned friendly vehicles can earn you Repair points, a great way to supplement your score. Try to use the vehicle you're repairing as cover to avoid getting picked off by enemies. Or send an EOD Bot in to handle dangerous repair, armament, and disarmament jobs. The engineer is essential to any squad, so take the time to learn this class.

UNLOCK PROGRESSION

UNLOCK	NAME	IMAGE	SCORE
1	FIM-92 Stinger		18,000
2	AK 5C		36,000
3	M15 AT Mine		55,000
4	Offensive Field Upgrade		73,000
5	RPG-7V2		109,000

UNLOCK	NAME	IMAGE	ASSAULT SCORE
6	SA-18 IGLA		127,000
7	Mechanic Field Upgrade		146,000
8	M2 SLAM		164,000
9	EOD Bot		182,000

UNLOCK	NAME	IMAGE	ASSAULT SCORE
10	MK153 SMAW		200,000
11	Anti-Tank Field Upgrade		218,000
12	FGM-148 Javelin		236,000
13	FGM-172 SRAW		250,000

GADGETS

REPAIR TOOL

Unlock: Engineer Kit Start
Description: Handheld oxy-fuel welding and cutting torch that repairs friendly vehicles and damages enemy vehicles and infantry.

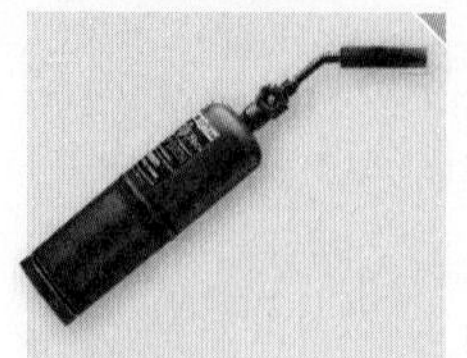

FIELD NOTES

The engineer kit's Repair Tool is the only way to repair disabled vehicles. To deploy, simply stand next to a damaged vehicle (while aiming at it) and hold down the trigger. Watch the circular meter in the center of the HUD fill in a clockwise fashion. Once the meter is filled completely, the vehicle is fully repaired. You're vulnerable while using this tool, so make sure you have adequate cover. During tank duels, stand behind a friendly tank and repair it as it takes damage. Repairing vehicles manned by a team or squadmate earns you Repair points—a great way to boost your score while playing as an engineer. The Repair Tool can also be turned against enemies—torching an occupied enemy vehicle causes it to lose health rapidly. But be careful when using the Repair Tool on an enemy vehicle. If the vehicle's health is completely depleted, the vehicle will explode, killing you. In addition to damaging enemy vehicles, the repair tool is also lethal against enemy infantry. All it takes is a quick hit with this torch to send your opponent back to the deployment screen.

FIM-92 STINGER

Unlock: 18,000 Engineer Score
Description: An anti-air missile with a focused targeting system for locking on to and guiding the missile towards long-range targets.

FIELD NOTES

With helicopters and jets firing rockets and missiles from above, the battlefield is a dangerous place for troops on the ground. Fortunately, engineers have a powerful way to counter these airborne threats. Simply aim the missile at an enemy jet or helicopter and wait for a red diamond-shaped icon to surround the aircraft while peering through the weapon's sight. When the word "SHOOT" appears above the diamond icon, the missile has attained a lock and is ready to fire. At this point the missile automatically tracks the targeted aircraft and slams into it, dealing heavy damage. But before spending an entire round looking skyward, make sure a teammate is watching your back. While peering through the Stinger's sight, you're extremely vulnerable to sneaky knife attacks. It's also a good idea to be near a support teammate so you can resupply from an Ammo Box.

MBT LAW

Unlock: Engineer Kit Start
Description: A guided homing missile weapon for taking out enemy land vehicles. Achieve and maintain lock-on until the missile reaches its target.

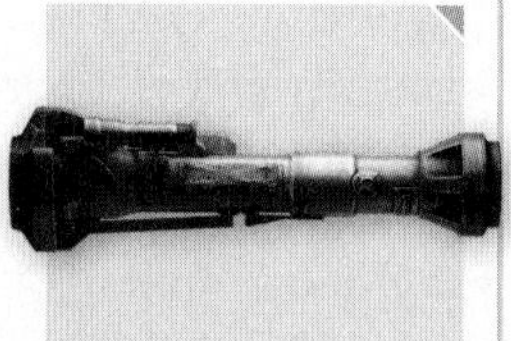

FIELD NOTES

All engineers begin their tank-busting career with the MBT LAW, equipped with an onboard tracking system. Take aim through the weapon's optic, keeping the target centered in the middle of the reticle. Fire the missile and watch it zoom toward your target. As the missile approaches the target, it suddenly climbs before crashing down on top of it. This is ideal for scoring critical hits on a tank's weak top armor. While your target is disabled, quickly fire a follow-up shot. While the MBT LAW's homing missile is a welcome feature, it doesn't have the same power as some of the other launchers, like the RPG-7V2, requiring more hits to inflict serious damage. If you want to fire the MBT LAW without exposing yourself, consider engaging laser-designated targets. This allows you to stay and engage distant targets without exposing yourself to retaliatory fire.

M15 AT MINE

Unlock: 55,000 Engineer Score
Description: A heavy explosive that is triggered when an enemy vehicle rolls over it.

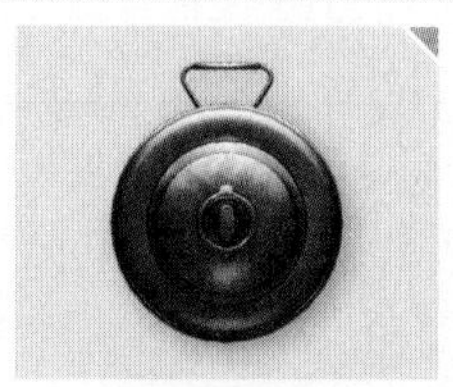

FIELD NOTES

This is a powerful anti-tank mine, effective against any ground vehicle. It takes two of these mines to take out a tank, but a single mine is powerful enough to instantly disable all other vehicles. Scatter these around high-traffic areas such as control points or M-COM stations. Chokepoints like bridges or narrow urban streets are also good ambush spots. Enemy mines can be destroyed with explosives, such as grenades or tank rounds—any mine can also be picked up by engineers. Although they're only triggered by enemy vehicles rolling over them, an anti-tank mine can still be lethal to all nearby infantry given its large blast radius. So keep your distance, or else you may be killed by your own detonating mine. Even after you die, the mines you've placed on the map remain for several minutes.

RPG-7V2

Unlock: 109,000 Engineer Score
Description: Powerful rocket-propelled anti-vehicle launcher capable of disabling even heavily armored vehicles from the sides and rear. Capable of locking on to laser-designated targets.

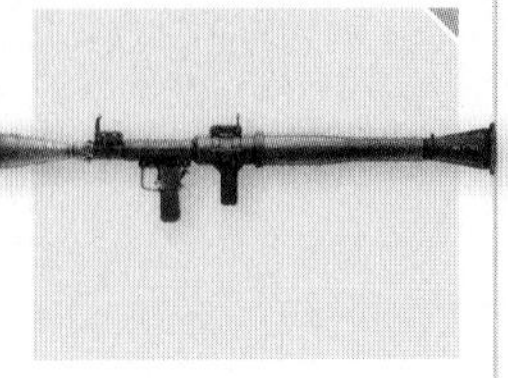

FIELD NOTES

The RPG-7V2 is an extremely powerful anti-tank weapon. Unlike most AT weapons, this rocket launcher has no optical sighting system. Instead you must use the rudimentary ironsights to aim the weapon prior to launch. Aim high when firing at distant infantry or vehicles because the rocket tends to drop when traveling great distances. Despite its somewhat crude targeting mechanism, the RPG-7V2 is capable of locking on to laser-designated targets as well. When you spot a bright red diamond icon on the HUD, an enemy vehicle (or stationary weapon) has been painted by a teammate. Aim at the diamond icon while peering through the RPG-7V2's ironsights to acquire a lock. When the word "SHOOT" appears above the diamond icon, the target is locked—this is your cue to fire. Once launched, the rocket automatically homes in on the painted target, scoring a hit. Given the RPG-7V2's limited accuracy, firing at laser-designated targets is recommended, particularly when engaging moving or distant threats.

M2 SLAM

Unlock: 164,000 Engineer Score
Description: Selectable Lightweight Attack Munition (SLAM) usable as either an off-route anti-tank mine or a traditional land mine. Blast damage is less than the M15, but is still capable of a critical hit on heavily armored vehicles.

FIELD NOTES

These small mines don't pack the same punch as the M15 AT Mines, making them far less effective against tanks and IFVs. But one M2 SLAM still contains enough explosive power to temporarily disable light vehicles and Armored Fighting Vehicles like the SPM-3 and MRAP. Still, you'll want to scatter several of these mines at narrow chokepoints to guarantee optimal damage—it takes three M2 SLAMs to take out a tank or IFV. Given their small size, these mines are also much tougher to spot, particularly if concealed within grass. Once deployed, any engineer can pick up an M2 SLAM.

SA-18 IGLA

Unlock: 127,000 Engineer Score
Description: Equipped with anti-air rockets and a targeting system with a wider field, the user can easily acquire a lock and then maintain it while guiding the missile towards its target.

FIELD NOTES

The IGLA is a shoulder-fired anti-aircraft missile system. It functions much like the Stinger, but requires the shooter to maintain a lock on the target until the missile strikes. Begin by tracking an air target through the IGLA's aiming optic. If the target is within the weapon's range (approximately 550 meters), a red diamond icon appears around the enemy aircraft surrounded by red brackets. When the brackets converge and form a crosshair icon within the diamond, and the word "SHOOT" appears, a lock has been achieved and the missile can be fired. However, after launch, keep aiming at the enemy aircraft to maintain a lock. If the lock is lost, the missile will veer off-course and miss the target. The IGLA is most effective against high-flying jets, helicopters, and the commander-deployed Gunship. It's much more difficult to maintain a lock on low-flying aircraft, as trees, buildings, and other objects can be used by skilled pilots to break the weapon's lock.

EOD BOT

Unlock: 182,000 Engineer Score
Description: Remote-controlled Explosive Ordnance Disposal robot, which can repair friendly vehicles, sabotage enemy assets, disarm explosives, and arm or disarm Rush objectives.

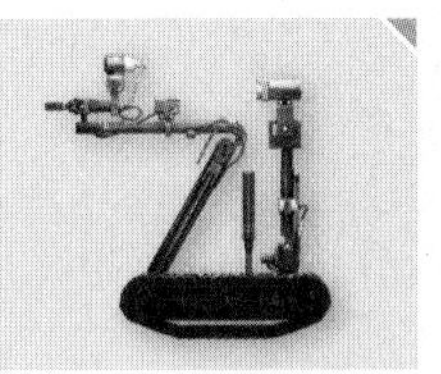

FIELD NOTES

When you don't want to expose yourself to incoming fire, send an EOD Bot to do the dangerous work. However, before you deploy an EOD Bot, find a very good hiding spot. While controlling this robot you're completely vulnerable to attacks, so drop prone behind some cover to make yourself as invisible as possible. Once the EOD Bot is deployed, the camera switches to the robot's vantage point, a black-and-white camera view. The EOD Bot controls just like a vehicle. Drive next to a friendly vehicle and repair. Or drive next to an enemy vehicle and damage it with the EOD Bot's own Repair Tool. The EOD Bot is most effective in Rush matches where it can be used to arm and disarm charges on M-COM stations. But don't expect your new friend to go unnoticed by enemies. Although this little robot can absorb some damage, it won't last long when exposed to high concentrations of enemy fire. The EOD Bot can kill enemy infantry with its Repair Tool, but it's much easier to simply run them over. Scoring a road kill with an EOD Bot is sure to be the highlight of any match.

MK153 SMAW

Unlock: 200,000 Engineer Score
Description: High-speed, low-drag anti-vehicle launcher with flatter trajectory but lower damage than the RPG-7V2. Most effective against the sides and rear of armored targets. Capable of locking on to laser-designated targets.

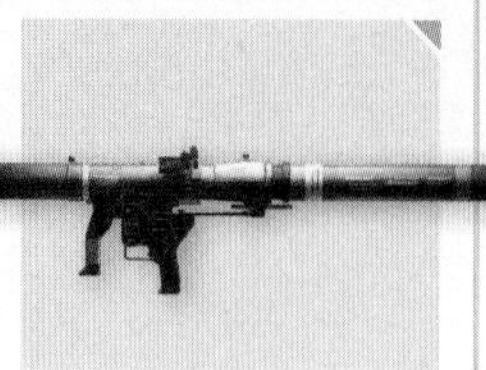

FIELD NOTES

The Shoulder-launched Multipurpose Assault Weapon (SMAW) fires an 83mm High Explosive Dual Purpose (HEDP) rocket ideal for targeting tanks, IFVs, and light vehicles. The rocket's high speed translates into better accuracy than the RPG-7V2, particularly when firing at distant targets. This means you don't have to aim as high. In addition to firing in its unguided mode, the SMAW can also lock on to laser-designated targets. But if teaming up with a recon player equipped with a PLD or SOFLAM, consider going with the RPG-7V2 over the SMAW. The RPG-7V2 inflicts considerably more damage than the SMAW, and laser-designation practically guarantees a hit, despite the projectile's relatively slow speed. But if you don't have the benefit of engaging painted targets, the SMAW comes out on top thanks in large part to its unguided accuracy.

FGM-148 JAVELIN

Unlock: 236,000 Engineer Score
Description: Guided anti-tank missile launcher that locks on to land vehicles. Warhead does medium damage to armor from any angle of attack. Launcher must maintain lock until the missile hits the target.

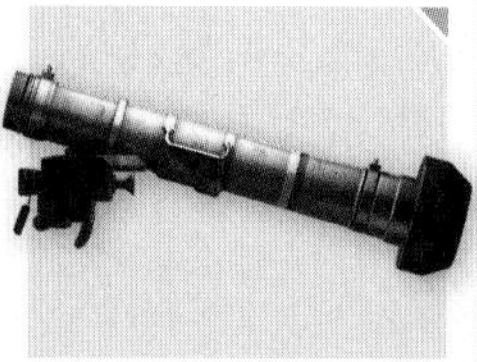

FIELD NOTES

Firing a 127mm High Explosive Anti-Tank (HEAT) missile, the Javelin takes tank killing to whole new level. The weapon is aimed through a small TV screen that totally blocks all peripheral vision, so make sure a buddy is watching your back while aiming this weapon system. When you place the green crosshair over a vehicle, a red diamond appears and a beeping sound is heard. When a set of red crosshairs fill the diamond icon and the beeps transition into a solid high-pitched tone, the missile has acquired a lock on the targeted vehicle. Fire the missile, but keep aiming to maintain the lock—if the lock is lost, the missile will fly off-course. When launched, the missile flies straight up then comes crashing down on the target, ideal for scoring critical top hits on tanks and IFVs. However, tanks can break locks by deploying IR Smoke. So consider waiting for a tank to use their smoke before firing a missile. The Javelin can also hit laser-designated targets, allowing you to fire the weapon from behind cover, limiting your exposure. When engaging a laser-designated target, you don't need to keep aiming—as long as the target is painted, the missile will find its mark without your assistance.

FGM-172 SRAW

Unlock: 250,000 Engineer Score
Description: Wire-guided anti-tank missile launcher. Can be manually guided to the target as long as the launcher is in aimed mode. Capable of locking on to laser-designated targets.

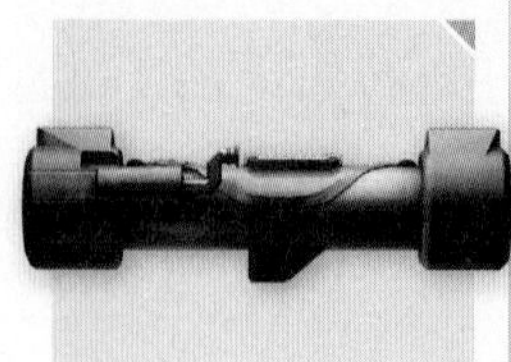

FIELD NOTES

Veterans of *Battlefield 2* are very familiar with the wire-guided Short-Range Assault Weapon (SRAW). Unlike the other anti-tank weapons in the engineer's arsenal, this weapon is manually guided. Directional inputs provided by the shooter are fed to the missile in-flight via a thin wire connected to the launcher. The ability to provide course corrections while the missile is in flight makes the SRAW the most accurate anti-vehicle weapon, ideal for hitting moving targets. However, while guiding the missile to a target, you're vulnerable, particularly given the weapon's narrow field of view, blocking all peripheral vision. Another drawback is the weapon's relatively weak explosive payload—even when scoring critical top hits, it can take more than four SRAW missiles to knock out a single tank. Like other anti-vehicle weapons, the SRAW can also lock on to laser-designated targets. But when engaging painted tanks and IFVs, all other anti-vehicle weapons inflict more damage than the SRAW. As a result, this weapon is best deployed against fast-moving light vehicles and other soft targets when laser designation is not available.

ENGINEER: SCORING OPPORTUNITIES

ACTION	POINTS	DESCRIPTION
Repair	10	Repair a teammate's vehicle. Repair points are given for every 10% of vehicle damage repaired.
Squad Repair	15	Repair a squadmate's vehicle. Repair points are given for every 10% of vehicle damage repaired.

UNIQUE FIELD UPGRADES

LEVEL	ICON	NAME	DESCRIPTION
MECHANIC			
1		Fast Repair	Increases speed and sabotage of repairs by 35%.
2		Flak	Decreases damage from explosions by 15%.
3		Cover	Decreases amount of incoming suppression by 50%.
4		Repair Unit	Occupied vehicles will slowly repair nearby vehicles.
ANTI-TANK			
1		Mines	Increases maximum inventory of AT Mines or M2 SLAM to 6.
2		Rockets	Increases maximum inventory of AT and AA ammo to 7.
3		More Deployed Explosives	Increases maximum deployed explosives to 6.
4		Flak	Decreases damage from explosions by 15%.

ENGINEER TACTICS

- The PDWs associated with this kit are excellent during close-quarter fire fights thanks to their blazing rates of fire and high hip fire accuracy. Consider equipping a Laser Sight to these weapons in an effort to blind your opponents, giving you a slight advantage in dark environments. A Laser Sight also improves the PDW's hip fire accuracy.
- If the PDWs don't have the range you seek, consider switching to a carbine or DMR. The engineer unlocks the first carbine, the AK 5C, soon after acquiring the FIM-92 Stinger. Carbines offer greater accuracy and damage output at intermediate range.
- Make friends with the support class. You'll need Ammo Boxes dropped at your feet if you want to keep firing rockets and missiles. Given the greater emphasis on laser-designation, a recon squadmate equipped with a SOFLAM or PLD is also essential.
- If you have plans for driving or riding in a tank or IFV, bring along a Repair Tool. As the vehicle takes damage, hop out and repair while your crewmate continues fighting. But when you exit, be careful to use your damaged vehicle for cover to avoid falling victim to incoming fire.
- When serving aboard a vehicle, consider choosing the Mechanic Field Upgrade path. The upgrades in this path increase your efficiency when repairing. If you reach the end of the path you can take advantage of the Repair Unit upgrade. When driving (or riding) in a vehicle, this upgrade emits a repair radius, automatically repairing nearby friendly vehicles. Two tanks driven by engineers with this upgrade are a force to be reckoned with, allowing the tanks to repair each other when side-by-side.
- The engineer's Stinger and IGLA help even the playing field when enemy jets and helicopters are present. But you must maintain line-of-sight with the target to achieve a missile lock. If your target flies behind a hill or line of trees before a lock is achieved, the missile cannot be fired. The missile cannot be dumb-fired at any other targets either. So don't bother equipping these missiles unless there's plenty of air traffic.
- Never attack tanks or IFVs head-on with a rocket launcher. For one, the driver will probably see you and return fire, sending you back to the deploy screen. Second, the front armor on these vehicles is very thick, reducing the effectiveness of your weapon's warhead. Instead, try to hit the vehicle from the side or rear, where you're less likely to be spotted. Furthermore, the side armor is weaker than the front and the rear and top armor is weakest of all, ensuring your rocket inflicts maximum damage.
- Try to hit tanks and IFVs at perpendicular angles when attacking with the rocket and missile launchers. Glancing shots may deflect, inflicting considerably less damage. A rocket striking armor at a perpendicular angle ensures maximum penetration by the warhead's shaped charge. The vertical surfaces covering the wheels and treads on the side are good targets, as is the engine compartment at the back of each vehicle, and the weak top armor. Hitting any of these areas at a perpendicular angle increases the likelihood of scoring a critical hit, temporarily immobilizing the vehicle.
- Anti-tank mines, like the M15 AT Mine and M2 SLAMS, are extremely powerful explosives capable of instantly disabling any ground vehicle. Consider deploying mines when defending a static position with predictable avenues of attack, such as bridges.
- If defending a static position, such as in Rush, consider opting for the Anti-Tank Field Upgrade path. This significantly increases the number of mines and rockets you can carry and deploy.

PRO TIP: STRONGSIDE

This is the most important class when playing on vehicle-heavy maps. I like to run with one or two engineers in my squad and gang up on all the enemy vehicles throughout the map. Doing this will ensure you have the advantage against the enemy vehicles. In Rush, the EOD Bot is extremely useful and fun. The EOD Bot is extremely fast and if you can master driving it you'll be able to pull off some incredible plays. My favorite thing to do is sneak by enemy defenses and arm M-COM stations with the EOD Bot before the enemy knows what happened.

PRO TIP: FLAMESWORD

This class is one of the most important classes in the game. The RPG-7V2 plays a big role in destroying vehicles. I especially enjoy using the RPG-7V2 to clear out squads hiding behind cover or in buildings—the impact of the rocket will destroy anything in its path, either killing the enemy or destroying their cover.

PRO TIP: ELUMNITE

When playing as the engineer class I like to keep it basic and use the RPG-7V2 for some quick explosive action. I find myself using this just for the great mix of indoor/outdoor combat availability. Whether engaging infantry in buildings, or IFVs and tanks out in the open, this high-damage rocket launcher is ideal for taking out opponents nice and fast.

PRO TIP: WALSHY

When playing as an engineer I am focused on one thing—vehicles. Whether it is destroying enemy vehicles or repairing my team's vehicles, I always make sure to have both options available to me by equipping the Repair Tool and my favorite rocket launcher, the Javelin.

SUPPORT

US SUPPORT

RU SUPPORT

CN SUPPORT

STARTING LOADOUT

PRIMARY WEAPON	U-100 MK5		**GRENADE**	M67 FRAG		**GADGET 2**	XM25 AIRBURST
SIDEARM	P226		**GADGET 1**	AMMO PACK		**KNIFE**	BAYONETTE

STRENGTHS: **SOLID ANTI-INFANTRY KIT; AMMO RESUPPLY**

WEAKNESSES: **LIMITED ANTI-ARMOR CAPABILITY**

The support class is responsible for handing out ammo and laying down suppressive fire. These guys carry the massive light machine guns, capable of laying down high volumes of sustained fire, great for suppressing enemy infantry. The support class also has access to some of the most devastating weapons in the game including C4, Claymores, the M224 Mortar, and the new XM25 grenade launcher. When they're not busy scoring kills, support troops should supply teammates using the Ammo Pack or Ammo Box. The new Ammo Pack gives soldiers the ability to resupply while on the move—but these packs only contain bullets. The Ammo Box dispenses ammunition, grenades, and other munitions to all within a small radius. You earn a Resupply bonus whenever a teammate retrieves ammo from an Ammo Pack or Ammo Box, so don't be stingy with these things. Scatter them around your teammates to boost your score. Support players are also effective at taking out enemy vehicles with C4, either through direct application or through the creation of car bombs. So if you're not satisfied laying down suppressive fire from a distance, take the fight to close range and do some damage with your explosives. But such attacks are extremely dangerous, so you better have an assault buddy nearby to revive you.

UNLOCK PROGRESSION

UNLOCK	NAME	IMAGE	SCORE
1	M18 Claymore		17,000
2	QBS-09		52,000
3	Offensive Field Upgrade		70,000
4	Ammo Box		87,000

UNLOCK	NAME	IMAGE	ASSAULT SCORE
5	Indirect Fire Field Upgrade		105,000
6	XM25 Smoke		122,000
7	M224 Mortar		139,000
8	MP-APS		157,000

UNLOCK	NAME	IMAGE	ASSAULT SCORE
9	Perimeter Defense Field Upgrade		174,000
10	XM25 DART		190,000
11	C4 Explosive		210,000

GADGETS

AMMO PACK

Unlock: Support Kit Start
Description: Single-use Ammo Pack that resupplies a small amount of bullets to a single soldier on the move.

FIELD NOTES

The new Ammo Pack is available to the support class from the very beginning, offering a rudimentary method of resupplying friendly troops. This gadget functions much like the First Aid Pack carried by the assault class. When an Ammo Pack is tossed on the ground, any friendly soldier can pick it up by simply running over it. Once retrieved, the Ammo Pack automatically replenishes some of the soldier's rounds. But it's important to note that Ammo Packs only contain bullets. Grenades, rockets, missiles, mines, and other munitions must be retrieved from an Ammo Box or a Supply Crate dropped by the commander. In this sense, the Ammo Pack is rather limited. But until you unlock the Ammo Box, this is the only way to go. And unlike the Ammo Box, the Ammo Pack allows soldiers to resupply while on the move—they don't need to gather around an Ammo Box or Supply Crate while resupplying.

M18 CLAYMORE

Unlock: 17,000 Support Score
Description: Anti-personnel mine that launches three trip wires shortly after being deployed. Breaking a wire will detonate the mine. A mine with no trip wires is unable to detonate and should be redeployed.

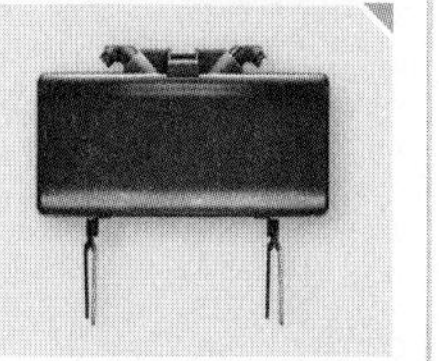

FIELD NOTES

Adding to the support kit's deadly arsenal is the M18 Claymore anti-personnel mine. Unlike traditional land mines, the Claymore is a directional mine, spraying shrapnel in the direction it's facing upon detonation. So think carefully before dropping one of these. What direction is your enemy likely to approach from? Once you figured out where you want to place this mine, orient yourself in the proper direction before dropping the Claymore. Claymores are triggered by enemies running into one of the three trip wires. You can avoid triggering a Claymore by simply avoiding these trip wires. But it's much safer to take a Claymore out from a distance by tossing a grenade at it or shooting it with an explosive weapon such as a rocket or grenade launcher. The support class can carry two Claymores at a time, but more can be retrieved from the support kit's own Ammo Box. Like C4, Claymores are great for defending flags in Conquest and M-COM stations in Rush. Unlike C4, these weapons trigger on their own, so you don't have to constantly babysit them, waiting for an enemy to enter the kill zone.

XM25

Unlock: Support Kit Start
Description: A 25mm semi-automatic grenade launcher fed by a five-round box magazine. Aiming down the sights at cover will lock in that distance, allowing the grenade to explode in the air three meters past the cover.

XM25 AMMO

NAME	IMAGE	DESCRIPTION	UNLOCK
XM25 Airburst		Fires 25mm grenades that can explode mid-flight, creating an airburst effect to eliminate targets behind cover.	Support Kit Start
XM25 Smoke		Fires 25mm grenades that can explode mid-flight, creating an airburst smoke effect to block sight and spotting.	122,000 Support Score
XM25 DART		Fires a 25mm cartridge packed with penetrating flechettes that effectively transform the launcher into a semiautomatic shotgun.	190,000 Support Score

FIELD NOTES

Compared to the assault class' M320 40mm grenade launcher, the XM25 benefits from a number of improvements, including greater accuracy and range. The weapon is equipped with an infrared optic utilizing an integrated Range Finder. When peering through this optic, the range to target is shown on the right while the detonation range of the loaded ammo is shown on the left. All rounds are triggered to detonate three meters beyond the target, so keep this in mind when aiming with Airburst rounds. The idea is to detonate the round just above a piece of cover where enemy troops are hiding, raining down shrapnel from above. After setting the range, aim just a bit over the cover and fire to hit enemies on the other side. The Airburst round is most effective against infantry and does virtually no damage to vehicles. Even then, the Airburst round has a fairly limited blast radius—you're more likely to injure and suppress enemies than you are to kill them outright with a single round. So rapidly fire multiple rounds to produce lethal results. In addition to the standard Airburst round, the XM25 can also be loaded with Smoke and DART ammunition. Smoke ammo give the weapon the ability to accurately and rapidly dispense smokescreens, ideal for concealing the movements of your squad—this is far more effective than the slow-firing M320. Or load the XM25 with DART ammo to turn the weapon into a devastating close-range shotgun. When firing DART rounds, it's recommended to fire from the hip, using the ring-shaped reticle on the HUD to aim.

AMMO BOX

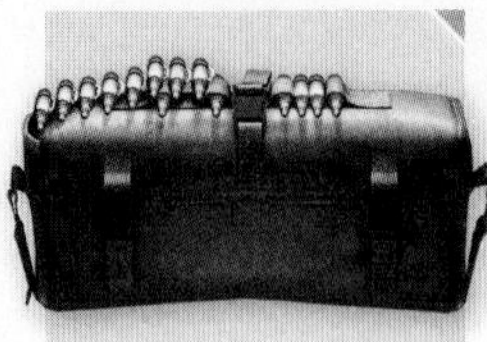

Unlock: 87,000 Support Score
Description: A crate filled with ammunition. All comrades nearby will start having their ammo cache restored for all their weapons and gadgets.

FIELD NOTES

The Ammo Box is a significant improvement over the standard-issue Ammo Pack. For one, the Ammo Box contains ammo for all weapon types. Simply stand next to one of these boxes for a few seconds to replenish the ammo for all of your weapons, including grenades and rockets. When playing as support, drop these boxes around clusters of teammates—each time someone retrieves ammo from a pack you earn a Resupply bonus. This is a great way to supplement your score while supporting your teammates and squadmates. If a teammate or squadmate is low on ammo, an icon depicting three bullets appears above their head. Get them some ammo fast! By default you can only drop one Ammo Box at a time, but with the Ammo Bag Upgrade (from the Indirect Fire Field Upgrade path) you can deploy up to two Ammo Boxes at a time, greatly increasing your resupply score. For best results, drop these boxes in areas where multiple teammates are pinned or defending chokepoints.

M224 MORTAR

Unlock: 139,000 Support Score
Description: Remote-controlled 60mm mortar that fires high explosive rounds using a terrain grid targeting system. Shells travel a ballistic path and may hit objects between the launcher and the intended target. Rapid fire is very inaccurate; single shells have great precision.

FIELD NOTES

One of the most unique weapons introduced in *Battlefield 3* was the support kit's M224 Mortar. The M224 has undergone some changes in *Battlefield 4*. For one, it can be deployed and operated remotely from a safe distance, protecting the operator from counter-mortar fire and knife attacks. The mortar is also equipped with a TV-like monitor offering a top-down view of the map, allowing for more precise targeting. When you first select the weapon, you must find a flat piece of terrain to deploy it. Once deployed, the weapon can rotate 360 degrees; consider placing it between two objectives for optimal coverage. Once you've found a good spot set it down and walk away, finding a good hiding spot before operating the weapon remotely. You can then access the mortar from any point on battlefield via a handheld tablet. At this point the map view appears on the tablet's screen, allowing you to see friendly (blue) and enemy (red) units spotted by your teammates. The white crosshair icon placed over the minimap shows you where you're aiming the mortar. Simply place the crosshair over an enemy target and fire—the white ring-shaped icons show the blast radius of each impacting shell. Don't expect to score tons of kills with this weapon, but it's great for softening up enemy positions prior to or during an assault on a fixed position. When you're finished firing, don't forget to retrieve the mortar before moving on.

MP-APS

Unlock: 157,000 Support Score
Description: Man-Portable Active Protection System that detonates incoming explosive rockets and shells from both infantry and vehicles before they can hit their targets. Will not stop normal bullets or hand-thrown grenades. Can destroy multiple incoming threats in a 180-degree arc, but must recharge between uses.

FIELD NOTES

The tripod-mounted MP-APS is an interesting addition to support class gadgets, offering protection against incoming missiles and rockets. Before deploying this device, take into account where incoming rockets and missiles are likely to come from. Once you have a location selected, place the gadget on the ground while facing in the direction of the likely threat. Soon after it's placed, the MP-APS must warm-up before scanning for incoming missiles in a 180-degree arc. The green-lit area on the ground, around the base of the MP-APS, represents the safe zone—stand here to avoid getting injured by incoming rockets and missiles. When a rocket or missile passes within a few meters of the MP-APS, the projectile is automatically detonated. The MP-APS must recharge periodically, leaving the shielded area vulnerable for a few seconds. But once recharged, the MP-APS resumes intercepting incoming rockets and missiles. The MP-APS is equipped with a camera that can be accessed remotely via a handheld tablet. The camera can be rotated and used to spot enemy units. Using the MP-APS as a security camera may not sound too fun, but it can be very useful in high-traffic areas. Given its limited defensive arc, the MP-APS is best deployed directly in front of stationary tanks or IFVs, serving as a protective shield. It can also be effective in hallways or other cramped interiors where incoming rockets are a constant threat. But if an MP-APS becomes too troublesome, it can be taken out with grenades or small-arms fire.

C4 EXPLOSIVE

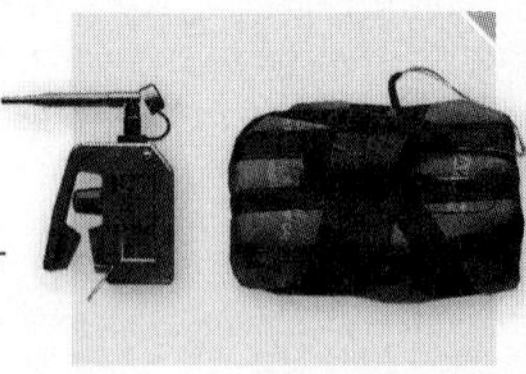

Unlock: 210,000 Support Score
Description: Plastic explosives that stick to most surfaces. Capable of a Mobility Kill on vehicles, and the remote detonator allows for traps and ambushes.

FIELD NOTES

As the last unlock available in the support class progression, you'll need to work hard to get C4. Initially, up to three explosive charges can be placed at a time and detonated simultaneously with a remote detonator. However, the support class can replenish their C4 using an Ammo Box, allowing them to set elaborate C4 deathtraps involving more than three simultaneously detonated charges. Explosives are great for taking out vehicles. Simply stick a couple of charges on the back of a tank and step back a safe distance to watch the fireworks. When attacking vehicles, no matter the size, always plant at least two charges. One C4 charge will only disable a vehicle temporarily—it takes at least two to instantly destroy it. Charges can also be used as booby traps, placed around critical high-traffic areas like control points or M-COM stations—but it's up to you to detonate them when there's enemies nearby. When defending in Rush, Obliteration, or Defuse matches, use the alarm sound of an armed objective to alert you to nearby enemies—detonate your charges before they can move away from the kill zone.

SUPPORT: SCORING OPPORTUNITIES

ACTION	POINTS	DESCRIPTION
Resupply	10	Resupply a teammate.
Squad Resupply	15	Resupply a squadmate.

UNIQUE FIELD UPGRADES

INDIRECT FIRE

LEVEL	ICON	NAME	DESCRIPTION
1		Ammo Bag Upgrade	Increases maximum deployed Ammo Boxes and Ammo Packs by 1.
2		Ammo	Increases maximum inventory of bullets by 50%.
3		Indirect Fire	Increases maximum M224 and XM25 ammo.
4		Resupply Unit	Occupied vehicles will slowly resupply nearby soldiers.

PERIMETER DEFENSE

LEVEL	ICON	NAME	DESCRIPTION
1		Ammo	Increases maximum inventory of bullets by 50%.
2		Suppression	Increases amount of outgoing suppression by 50%.
3		Claymores	Increases maximum inventory of Claymores to 3.
4		MP-APS Upgrade	Increases time MP-APS can detect incoming explosives.

SUPPORT TACTICS

- The support class plays a pivotal role in any squad. When playing as support, lay down covering fire while the rest of your squad advances. Even if you can't see the enemy, fire rounds in the area around them to keep their heads down. The support kit's light machine guns have a greater suppressive effect than most firearms, causing your suppressed opponents to suffer from blurred vision and poor accuracy. If your teammates kill an enemy you suppressed, you get a Suppression Assist bonus.
- The LMGs are notorious for harsh recoil, decreasing accuracy. When possible, deploy the LMG's Bipod—all LMGs are equipped with a Bipod by default. The Bipod is automatically deployed when aiming down sights while prone or next to a supportive piece of cover. Once deployed, the Bipod reduces recoil, making the LMG extremely accurate, even when firing prolonged automatic bursts. This is how suppressive weapons are meant to function!
- Sometimes you need something a little smaller than a bulky LMG. Consider equipping your support soldier with a carbine, DMR, or shotgun. The carbines and shotguns are good options when your squad is always on the move or operating in close quarters. The QBS-09 shotgun is the second unlock for the support class, making the weapon available to all classes.
- The belt-fed light machine guns take a long time to reload, so make sure a teammate has your back while you load fresh rounds into your weapon. At the very least, find an isolated piece of cover before initiating a reload. The magazine-fed weapons have much faster reload times.
- The Indirect Fire Field Upgrade path is recommended for support players seeking to score big Resupply points. The fourth and final upgrade in this path is Resupply Unit. When this upgrade is achieved, a support soldier riding in a vehicle emits a resupply radius, effectively turning the vehicle into a giant Ammo Box, capable of resupplying all friendly soldiers nearby.
- Use the light machine guns to target light vehicles like the Quad Bikes, PWCs, and VDV Buggies. The occupants of these vehicles are completely exposed, making it easy to score a few kills with a prolonged burst. You may even disable the vehicle. These rapid-firing weapons are also great for shooting down MAVs that are deployed by enemy recon troops.
- The support kit should never run out of ammo, so don't forget to toss an Ammo Box at your feet if you're running low on ammo, grenades, C4, or Claymores. Also, make sure the recon and engineer players on your team have plenty of ammo. Sniper rifles and rocket launchers run dry quickly, so supplying these players with their own Ammo Box can become quite lucrative in terms of scoring Resupply points.
- When attacking an objective in Rush, Obliteration, or Defuse, plant three C4 charges around the objective before arming the objective itself. Then seek cover at a distance and set off the charges as your opponents rush in to disarm the objective. Not only does this prevent the objective from being disarmed, it also nets you some easy kills.
- The M224 Mortar is only effective if your team spots targets, otherwise you'll be firing blind, with no enemy icons appearing on the weapon's minimap. The recon kit's T-UGS Motion Sensor can automatically place targets on the minimap as well. But even when you have enemy icons to shoot at, don't expect to score tons of kills. Like the light machine guns, the mortar is a great suppressive weapon. You're more likely to suppress and injure enemies with this weapon than kill them.
- When defending a fixed position, select the Perimeter Defense Field Upgrade path. The Suppression upgrade greatly increases the amount of outgoing suppression you inflict, made even more effective when firing LMGs. As you progress through this path, you can carry more Claymores and increase the effectiveness of the MP-APS gadget.

PRO TIP: STRONGSIDE

With this class, I lay down steel for my team with the massive amounts of bullets in my LMG's magazine. I'm also always using the Ammo Box to keep my team packed with ammunition. Placing Claymores strategically in high-traffic areas or near objectives is also a favorite activity—I try to place the Claymore in a darker spot if possible, making it less visible for the enemy to see its trip wires.

PRO TIP: ELUMNITE

This class is one of my top picks for the sole reason of their Ammo Boxes. I never worry about running out of ammo. I just lay fire down on any enemies in my path, while refilling my teammates' weapons as well. I'll stick close to my engineer teammates to keep them stocked up on rocket ammo too.

PRO TIP: FLAMESWORD

This is my favorite class to use in the game because of its versatility. The various amounts of LMGs to choose from allow you to provide long-distance suppressive fire and excel in close range when hip firing due to its large magazine. And who could forget the C4? I love running around like a ninja, sneaking behind vehicles and snipers, planting C4, and watching them go BOOM.

PRO TIP: WALSHY

Staying true to its class name, a great support player is always there to back up a squad and can be one of the most dangerous mid/close range classes in the game if equipped with the right tools. Since the support class has C4 to effectively deal with vehicles and high-capacity LMGs for laying down suppressive fire, I argue that support is the most versatile mid/close range class in the game.

RECON

US RECON

RU RECON

CN RECON

STARTING LOADOUT

PRIMARY WEAPON	CS-LR4	**GRENADE**	M67 FRAG	**GADGET 2**	C4 EXPLOSIVE
SIDEARM	P226	**GADGET 1**	PLD	**KNIFE**	BAYONETTE

STRENGTHS: **LONG-RANGE/SPOTTING SPECIALIST** WEAKNESSES: **SLOW-FIRING; LIMITED ANTI-VEHICLE CAPABILITY**

The recon class is much more than just a sniper. New equipment like C4 and Claymores give the class more offensive tools than ever before, allowing the recon player to fill more than just a supporting role. But traditionalists need not worry, as the recon class still maintains sniper files and a whole host of reconnaissance-based equipment including the new PLD and the beloved Motion Sensors from *Battlefield: Bad Company 2*. Using these and other gadgets, it's up to the recon class to spot targets for infantry and vehicles, informing teammates of enemy movement and designating targets for laser-guided munitions. But this doesn't mean recon troops still can't crack skulls at long range. The sniper rifles offered by this kit require the greatest amount of skill and patience of any weapon type, best reserved for players willing to put in the practice to master them. Unless you score headshots every time, it will take at least two hits to down an opponent with these powerful weapons. But with the ability to attach a Range Finder and zero scopes, expect greater accuracy and lethality out of the recon class.

UNLOCK PROGRESSION

UNLOCK	NAME	IMAGE	SCORE
1	Motion Sensor		16,000
2	RFB		48,000
3	Offensive Field Upgrade		64,000
4	Radio Beacon		80,000

UNLOCK	NAME	IMAGE	ASSAULT SCORE
5	Spec Ops Field Upgrade		96,000
6	T-UGS		112,000
7	SOFLAM		128,000
8	Sniper Field Upgrade		144,000

UNLOCK	NAME	IMAGE	ASSAULT SCORE
9	MAV		160,000
10	M18 Claymore		180,000

GADGETS

PLD

Unlock: Recon Kit Start

Description: Portable Laser Designator that laser paints targets while lock is maintained. The designator enables friendlies with missile systems to lock on to the targeted vehicles.

FIELD NOTES

The handheld PLD makes laser-designating targets easier than ever. Simply aim through the device's infrared optic and place the red reticle over an enemy vehicle or stationary weapon. As a lock is acquiring, a flashing white diamond icon appears over the target, surrounded by white brackets. A lock is achieved when the diamond icon stops flashing and turns red, accompanied by the word "SHOOT." At this point the target is designated, allowing friendly units to shoot it with laser-guided munitions. However, the target only remains painted while the PLD is actively aimed and maintains a line of sight—this makes the operator vulnerable to retaliatory attacks. If the PLD is put away or if the target moves behind cover, the lock is lost. So it's important to find a concealed, elevated position from which to designate targets. Now that the engineer's anti-vehicle weapons all have laser-guidance capability, there's a greater emphasis on laser designation. Work together with the engineers in your squad to score critical hits on enemy vehicles.

MOTION SENSOR

Unlock: 16,000 Recon Score

Description: Thrown Motion Sensor, which detects enemy movement in a 25-meter radius and reports it to your team's minimap for up to 24 seconds after deployment.

FIELD NOTES

The Motion Sensor is back! A favorite recon gadget from *Battlefield: Bad Company 2*, the Motion Sensor functions similar to the T-UGS, but is far less cumbersome and quicker to deploy while on the move. These grenade-sized devices mark all enemy units within their detection radius, showing up as red icons on the minimaps of all your teammates. Knowing exactly where enemies are hiding gives your team a huge advantage when clearing buildings and other confined spaces. Simply toss a Motion Sensor in the direction of your enemies to monitor their movements and use this intel to get the jump on them. And the Motion Sensor does not distinguish contacts on different elevations—toss a Motion Sensor onto the first floor of a building to see all enemies on the second floor or in the basement. Motion Sensors only operate for 24 seconds, so it may be necessary to deploy more during prolonged firefights. Fortunately, Motion Sensors can be replenished from a support soldier's Ammo Box or the commander's Supply Crate.

C4 EXPLOSIVE

Unlock: Recon Kit Start

Description: Plastic explosives that stick to most surfaces. Capable of a Mobility Kill on vehicles, and the remote detonator allows for traps and ambushes.

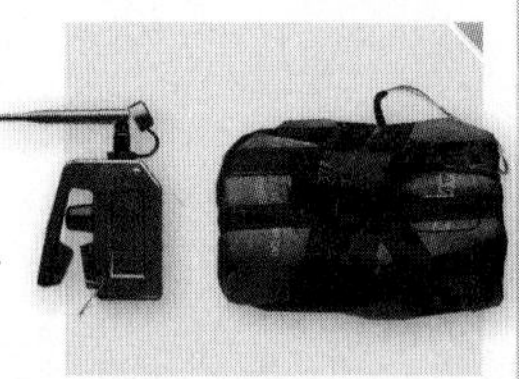

FIELD NOTES

Once the domain solely of the support class, the recon class gets C4 too—and the recon kit gets it from the very start. The addition of C4 allows the recon class to deal with vehicles more directly as well as set up devastating booby traps. Initially, up to three explosive charges can be placed at a time and detonated simultaneously with a remote detonator. Explosives are great for taking out vehicles. Simply stick a couple of charges on the back of a tank and step back a safe distance to watch the fireworks. When attacking vehicles, no matter the size, always plant at least two charges. One C4 charge will only disable a vehicle temporarily—it takes at least two to instantly destroy it. Charges can also be used as booby traps, placed around critical high-traffic areas like control points or objectives—but it's up to you to detonate them when there's enemies nearby. When defending in Rush, Obliteration, or Defuse matches, use the alarm sound of an armed objective to alert you to nearby enemies—detonate your charges before they can move away from the kill zone.

RADIO BEACON

Unlock: 80,000 Recon Score

Description: Portable Spawn Beacon that creates an additional spawn position for a squad. Only functional as a member of a squad. When deployed with a clear view of the sky in open environments it will function as a Paradrop Beacon.

FIELD NOTES

The Radio Beacon from *Battlefield 3* makes its return, and it functions the same way. Use this device as a forward spawn point, ideal for getting your squad back into the action. This is particularly helpful for attackers during Rush matches, allowing squads to spawn close to the objectives. The Radio Beacon can be placed on any flat surface. However, pay close attention to where you're placing it. You don't want to place it anywhere enemy troops can easily spot, otherwise your spawning squadmates may be killed before they get a chance to defend themselves. For best results, place it within a structure or within an area without a clear view of the sky. If not, your squadmates will come soaring down to the battlefield in parachutes, making them vulnerable to incoming fire. The Radio Beacon emits a constant beeping sound. Enemies can use this distinct sound to home in on the device and either destroy it or camp it. If your Radio Beacon is being camped, immediately notify your squad, warning them not to spawn on it. You can retrieve the Radio Beacon by interacting with it. Alternatively, it can be destroyed with explosives or disabled with the MAV's jamming feature.

T-UGS

Unlock: 112,000 Recon Score
Description: Tactical Unattended Ground Sensor (T-UGS), which detects enemy movement in 25-meter radius and reports it to your team's minimap.

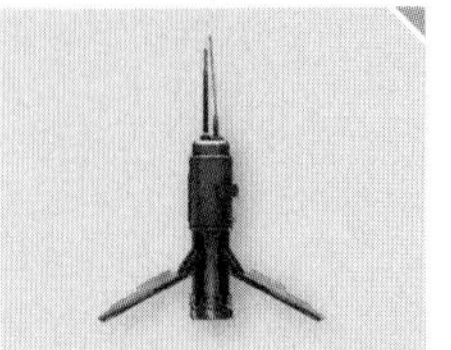

FIELD NOTES

Like the hand-tossed Motion Sensors, the T-UGS offer an alternative way to keep tabs on enemy movements. This is particularly effective when defending fixed positions, such as around flags in Conquest or near M-COM stations in Rush matches. To deploy this device, you must find a piece of even terrain—it cannot be deployed on rocks or steep slopes. Since the device is visible, try to place it in high grass or vegetation to better conceal it from enemy troops. Once deployed, enemy units that move within the 25-meter detection radius of the T-UGS show up on each teammate's minimap, ideal for guiding units toward hostile intruders. However, enemies can avoid detection by crawling. Like the Radio Beacon, the T-UGS makes a beeping sound, potentially warning enemies of its presence. If you find an enemy T-UGS, you can destroy it with explosives or jam it with a MAV, rendering it inoperable. Unlike the smaller Motion Sensors, a T-UGS can be deployed indefinitely, remaining in the same spot until it's destroyed or until its operator dies.

MAV

Unlock: 160,000 Recon Score
Description: Micro Air Vehicle (MAV) used to remotely fly behind enemy lines to spot incoming threats or destroy deployed enemy gadgets. Includes a Motion Sensor with a 35-meter radius; active only when the vehicle is remotely controlled.

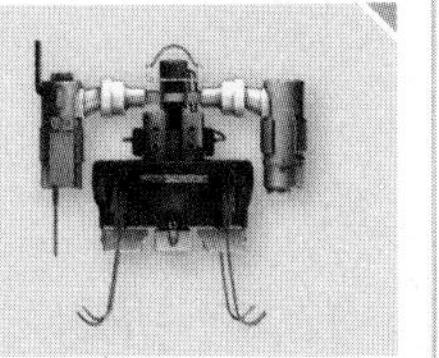

FIELD NOTES

The MAV is a small, unmanned reconnaissance drone deployed by the recon class. While operating the MAV you're vulnerable to attack, so only deploy this device when you're in a relatively secure area. You must also find a relatively flat piece of terrain from which the MAV can take off. Once activated, the view switches to the MAV's camera, allowing you to control the small vehicle remotely from a handheld tablet. Equipped with an infrared camera, the MAV makes it easy to spot enemy troops and vehicles by highlighting their heat signatures, appearing as bright white on the black-and-white screen. Using the spotting function, call out the positions of enemies for your teammates. The MAV also has the ability to disable enemy Radio Beacons, T-UGS, SOFLAMs, and EOD Bots with its electronic jamming function. But the MAV is very fragile and susceptible to small arms fire. So either keep it high above the battlefield or use trees and hills to mask its location. If you're good, you can even score a Road Kill with a MAV by flying low and crashing into enemy infantry at high speed.

SOFLAM

Unlock: 128,000 Recon Score
Description: Special Operations Forces Laser Marker (SOFLAM) that automatically laser paints enemy vehicles when deployed in a stationary position. Capable of remote operation, the SOFLAM enables friendlies with missile systems to lock on to the targeted vehicles.

FIELD NOTES

The SOFLAM is a laser target designator, much like the PLD. This tripod-mounted device is used to target vehicles for laser-guided munitions fired by engineers IFVs, tanks, helicopters, and jets. Once a target is painted with a laser, teammates equipped with laser-guided weapons get a red diamond indicator on their HUD. At that point, all they have to do is fire and the shell or missile automatically zeroes in on the target and scores a hit. While operating the device, you can pan and zoom in on targets at will. If you leave the SOFLAM behind, it can still acquire targets on its own, but only within a limited viewing arc. So if you leave the SOFLAM behind, point it down a street or other narrow passage that is frequented by enemy vehicles. Unlike the PLD, the SOFLAM doesn't need constant monitoring. Instead, you can place it, move out, and check up on it from the handheld tablet. While accessing the SOFLAM's camera system, you can also spot targets. Like all equipment, SOFLAMs can be destroyed with explosives or fried by an enemy MAV's EMP attack.

M18 CLAYMORE

Unlock: 180,000 Recon Score
Description: Anti-personnel mine that launches three trip wires shortly after being deployed. Breaking a wire will detonate the mine. A mine with no trip wires is unable to detonate and should be redeployed.

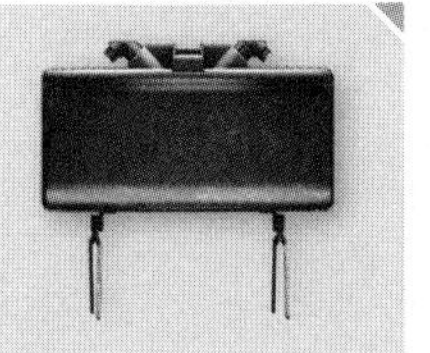

FIELD NOTES

Finally, the recon class gets the Claymore back, ideal for establishing a defensive perimeter while sniping. This gives recon players piece of mind while sniping, allowing them to focus on zeroing their scope instead of worrying about an enemy sneaking up behind them with a knife. Unlike traditional land mines, the Claymore is a directional mine, spraying shrapnel in the direction it's facing upon detonation. So think carefully before dropping one of these. What direction is your enemy likely to approach from? Once you figured out where you want to place this mine, orient yourself in the proper direction before dropping the Claymore. Claymores are triggered by enemies running into one of the three trip wires. You can avoid triggering a Claymore by simply avoiding these trip wires, but it's much safer to take a Claymore out from a distance by tossing a grenade at it or shooting it with an explosive weapon such as a rocket or grenade launcher. The recon class can carry two Claymores at a time, but more can be retrieved from the support kit's Ammo Box. Like C4, Claymores are great for defending flags in Conquest and M-COM stations in Rush. Unlike C4, these weapons trigger on their own, so you don't have to constantly babysit them, waiting for an enemy to enter the kill zone.

RECON: SCORING OPPORTUNITIES

ACTION	POINTS	DESCRIPTION
Marksman Bonus	50+	Score a headshot with a sniper rifle at a distance greater than 50 meters. Score is distance to the target.
Motion Sensor Assist	10	An enemy was killed while in your MAV/T-UGS/Motion Sensor's range.
Radio Beacon Spawn	25	Squad member spawns on your Radio Beacon.
Target Vehicle Marked	25	Lock on to an enemy vehicle with the PLD or SOFLAM.
Target Vehicle Hit	50	Target painted with the PLD or SOFLAM is hit by laser-guided weapon.
Target Vehicle Destroyed	100	Target painted with the PLD or SOFLAM is destroyed by laser-guided weapon.

UNIQUE FIELD UPGRADES

LEVEL	ICON	NAME	DESCRIPTION
SPEC OPS			
1		Stealth	Undetected by Motion Sensors except when sprinting.
2		C4 Explosives	Increases maximum inventory of C4 Explosives to 6.
3		Motion Sensors	Increases maximum inventory of Motion Sensors to 5. Increases range of T-UGS and MAV by 40%.
4		Quick Unspot	Reduces time you are spotted by two seconds.

LEVEL	ICON	NAME	DESCRIPTION
SNIPER			
1		Hold Breath	Increases time you can steady your scope by 100%.
2		Cover	Decreases amount of incoming suppression by 50%.
3		Quick Unspot	Reduces time you are spotted by two seconds.
4		Advanced Spot	Increases time your targets are spotted by 45%.

RECON TACTICS

- The introduction of scope zeroing and the Range Finder marks a new era for the sniper rifles. Use the Range Finder to determine the range to target, then adjust your scope to compensate for range. Once properly zeroed, you can aim directly at your target instead of aiming high. As long as the scope is properly zeroed, the round will go exactly where the scope's crosshairs are placed.
- High-powered scopes (6X or higher) can be zeroed for 0, 200, 300, 400, 500, and 1,000 meters. But these scopes still exhibit noticeable scope glint, potentially giving away your position when aiming through the scope. So avoid scanning for targets through the scope until you're ready to engage.
- Equip the Bipod as soon as you unlock it for your selected sniper rifle. Like holding your breath, the Bipod stabilizes the rifle, eliminating all lateral and horizontal scope drift. This makes it much easier to engage targets, especially at long range. The Straight Pull auxiliary attachment allows you to view through scope while loading a new round, allowing you to keep the target centered while operating the rifle's bolt. Both the Bipod and Straight Pull bolt are great additions, but they can't be used together; choose one.
- Gravity greatly affects the trajectory of your bullets when sniping, causing each round to drop over distance. If you're not using a high-powered scope (4X or lower), which can't be zeroed, be ready to compensate for range by aiming high, just above the target's head. Use your scope's vertical crosshair line to gauge proper barrel elevation before gently squeezing the trigger. Sometimes low-powered scopes are easier to use. Plus, they don't produce scope glint, allowing you to remain concealed. Still, after scoring a kill or two, move to a new location—the kill cam gives away your sniping spot, so don't wait around for reprisals.
- Choose your sniping location carefully, paying close attention to how you appear to enemy snipers. To avoid presenting your enemies with a clearly defined silhouette, avoid sniping from rooftops and the crests of hills. Instead, snipe from lower elevations, using bushes and other objects behind you to break up your visible outline. If you must snipe from a high elevation, make sure you have adequate cover and concealment, as you're likely to draw plenty of attention in such a predictable spot. And always drop prone. This not only reduces your chances of being spotted, but it also increases accuracy and stability.
- If sniping is your thing, choose the Sniper Field Upgrade Path. The upgrades in this path greatly increase your efficiency and prowess as a top-notch marksman. The Hold Breath upgrade allows you to steady your aim longer, while the Quick Unspot upgrade reduces the amount of time you're spotted by enemy troops.
- You'll never capture a flag or destroy an objective by sniping. The powerful sniper rifles make the recon class extremely popular, but a well-rounded squad should never have more than one sniper. While the recon class is great for long-range combat, the other classes are better suited for taking and holding ground.
- The recon kit isn't restricted to using just sniper rifles. Consider equipping a shotgun or carbine for better close-quarter performance. This is a great way to boost your recon score if your sniping skills are lacking. The semi-automatic DMRs are also open to the recon class, combining stopping power with a faster rate of fire. The RFB DMR is the recon kit's second unlock, making the weapon available to all classes. If you prefer keeping a sniper rifle, always switch to your pistol before moving around for quicker close-range target acquisition and rate of fire.
- If playing in a match with friendly jets and helicopters, take it upon yourself to serve as the team's spotter. Using the high-powered scopes attached to the sniper rifles, it's easy to zoom in on distant enemy troops and vehicles and spot them for your teammates. The MAV and SOFLAM are equally effective for spotting and designating targets for destruction. Due to their high speeds, aircraft have a tough time identifying ground targets. Spotting enemies greatly enhances their ability to identify and target enemy units.
- Now that the recon class has the ability to equip C4 and a carbine, consider recreating the spec ops class from *Battlefield 2*. Add Motion Sensors for a highly mobile and offensive-minded loadout, perfect for slipping behind enemy lines and conducting surprise attacks. The Spec Ops Field Upgrade path is highly recommended when choosing this loadout.

PRO TIP: STRONGSIDE

When playing as recon I find elevated positions overlooking the area my team is trying to infiltrate. I'll snipe as many players as I can and spot every enemy I see to aid my team. On a close-quarter map, I'll carry a shotgun and place T-UGS around the objective or high-traffic areas to alert my team and myself exactly where the enemy is, giving my team a huge advantage.

PRO TIP: ELUMNITE

When playing as the recon class, I like to find a safe place to set up and use a MAV to scout around and locate enemy vehicles. I can fly deep behind enemy lines and relay to my team where the enemy is and what vehicles they're using. I also like frying their deployed gadgets using the MAV's jamming feature. When that's done I go back to some sniping goodness.

PRO TIP: FLAMESWORD

The recon class in *Battlefield 4* has been buffed and now allows players to either snipe or get into small- to medium-range battles due to the different weapons you can equip. I love equipping Radio Beacons; they play a huge role in any gametype. I like to set these in areas the enemy can't see and then run away from them. I make a distraction so my downed teammates can spawn on the beacon and flank the enemy.

PRO TIP: WALSHY

Equipped with a sniper rifle, a good recon player can only dominate the long-range battles. But a great recon player is able to spot enemies and even do damage in close quarters. I love throwing Motion Sensors toward control points before my team advances in, revealing exactly where the enemy is hiding.

WEAPONS

Just like selecting a class, choosing the right weapons is all about finding the right tool for the job. In *Battlefield 4*, there are more weapons than ever, including assault rifles, PDWs, LMGs, sniper rifles, carbines, DMRs, shotguns, and pistols. Plus, every weapon has its own unlock progression, allowing you to equip new accessories such as optics, grips, and barrel attachments. Weapons are unlocked a little differently now. Instead of being tied to ranks and class progression, weapon unlocks are now tied to weapon type. For example, the more you use assault rifles, the higher your assault rifle score, leading to more assault rifle unlocks. Unlock progression works the same way for all other weapon types—the more you use a particular weapon type, the more weapons you'll unlock within that category. No two weapons are exactly the same, so get to know them and select ones that best fit your style of play.

WEAPON CUSTOMIZATION

While veteran *Battlefield* players are accustomed to tweaking their weapons, there has never been so many weapon customization options available as there are in *Battlefield 4*. Each weapon now has up to five customization slots, allowing a deeper level of fine-tuning. To customize your weapon from the deploy screen, choose the Customize option and then select Customize Weapon. Here you can choose from optics, accessories, barrel attachments, underbarrel equipment, and even paint schemes. But what does each attachment do? The following table lists every attachment, offering a brief description of how it impacts the performance of your weapon. Or simply study the stat bars on the right side of the customization screen—these bars grow and shrink as you select different attachments, offering immediate analysis of each item's impact on your weapon's performance.

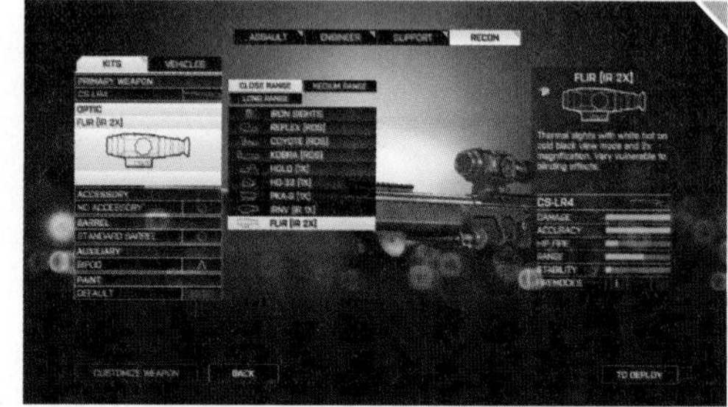

STUDY THE WEAPON'S STAT BARS ON THE RIGHT AS YOU SELECT DIFFERENT ATTACHMENTS TO UNDERSTAND HOW EACH ONE AFFECTS PERFORMANCE.

OPTICS

IMAGE / NAME	DESCRIPTION	OPTIC VIEW
CLOSE RANGE		
Reflex (RDS)	American red dot sight with a sharp reticle and a clear sight picture for rapid target acquisition and tracking.	
Coyote (RDS)	A Chinese red dot sight for easier tracking of targets through a wide angle aperture.	
KOBRA (RDS)	Russian reflex sight with a T cross reticle that keeps the point of aim clearer than other red dot sights.	
HOLO (1X)	Open sight picture for close- to mid-range engagements. The reticle features a ballistic circle and dot configuration.	
HD-33 (1X)	Optimized for close to mid range target acquirement with an open circle and dot reticle for easy tracking of targets.	
PKA-S (1X)	Russian advanced holographic sight featuring a circle and dot reticle for easier aiming.	
IRNV (IR 1X)*	Infrared Enhanced Night Vision sights with no magnification for low and no light situations. Very vulnerable to blinding effects.	
FLIR (IR 2X)*	Thermal sights with white hot on cold black view mode and 2x magnification. Very vulnerable to blinding effects.	

IMAGE / NAME	DESCRIPTION	OPTIC VIEW
MEDIUM RANGE		
 M145 (3.4X)	Optimized for mid-to long-range engagements. Most commonly found on M240 and M249 LMG weapons.	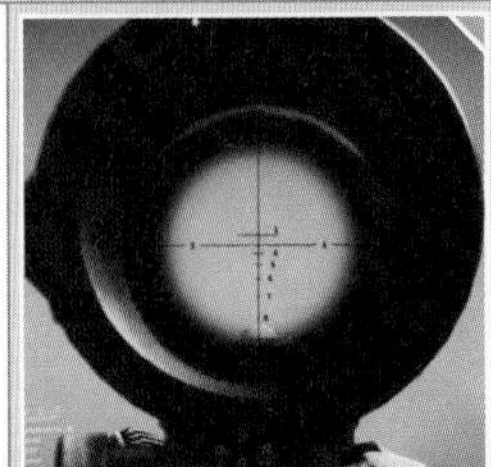 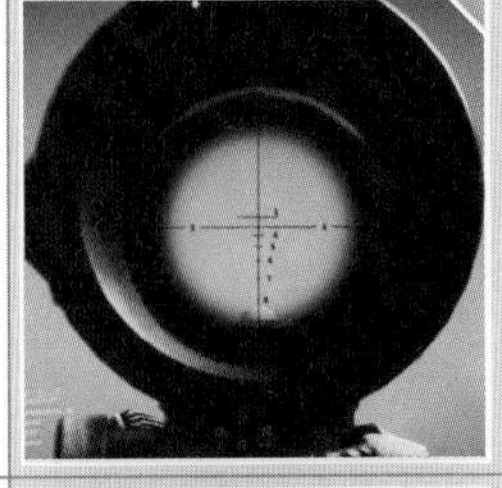
 PRISMA (3.4X)	3.4X magnification with a cross and dot reticle. Best used in mid-to long-range fights.	  
 PK-A (3.4X)	3.4x scope with a traditional Russian chevron reticle design typically found on assault rifles and carbines.	 
 ACOG (4X)	Advanced Combat Optic Gunsight medium speed and medium range scope which magnifies at 4x.	  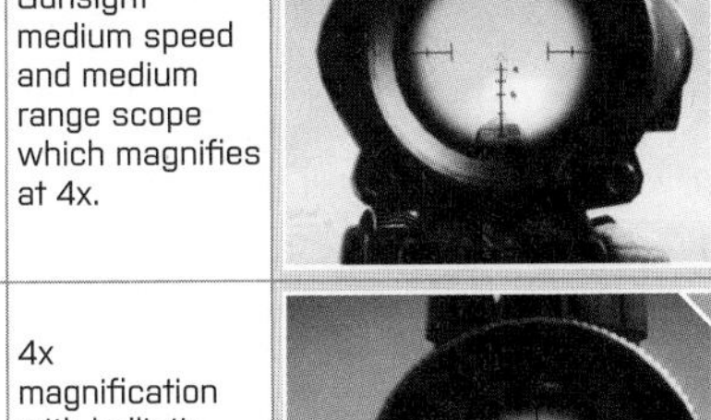
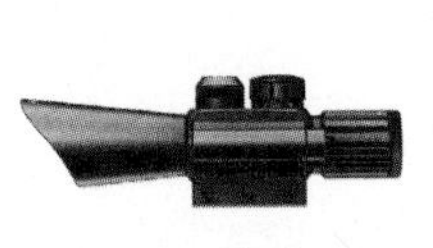 JGM-4 (4X)	4x magnification with ballistic reticle to more easily calculate bullet drop across medium to long distances.	
 PSO-1 (4X)	Standard Issue Russian medium speed, medium range scope with a 4x magnification.	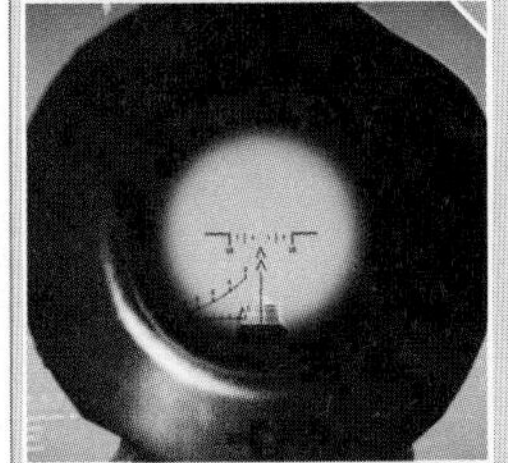
LONG RANGE		
 CL6X (6X)	A high magnification standard issue 6x Chinese scope for taking out targets at moderate distances.	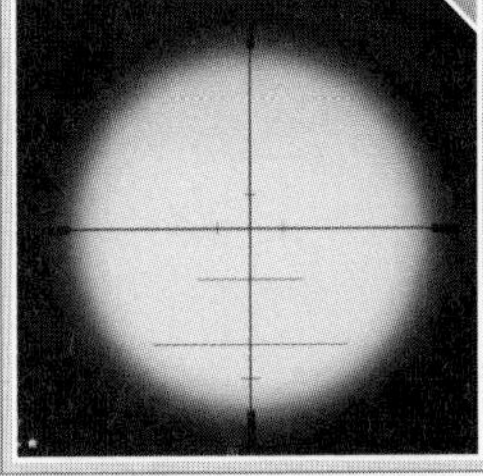
 PKS-07 (7X)	7x high magnification Russian standard issue marksman scope for engaging targets over long distances.	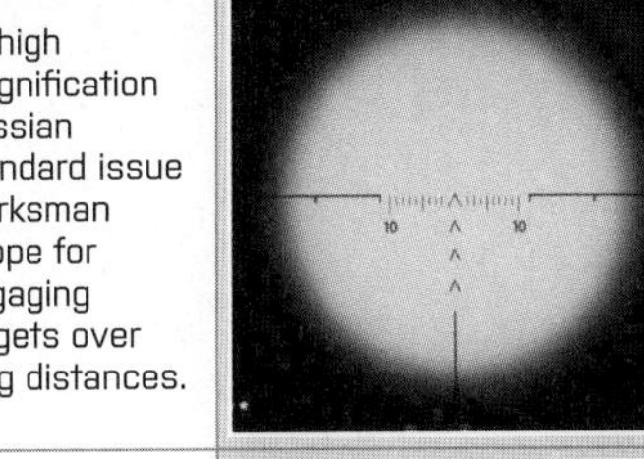
 Rifle Scope (8X)	Western standard issue 8x magnification rifle scope with ballistic drop reticle to aid in long range fire.	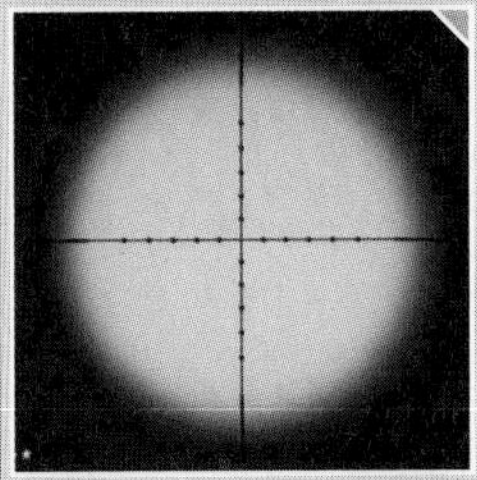
 Hunter (20X)*	High magnification 20x scope for accurate target shooting in long range combat situations.	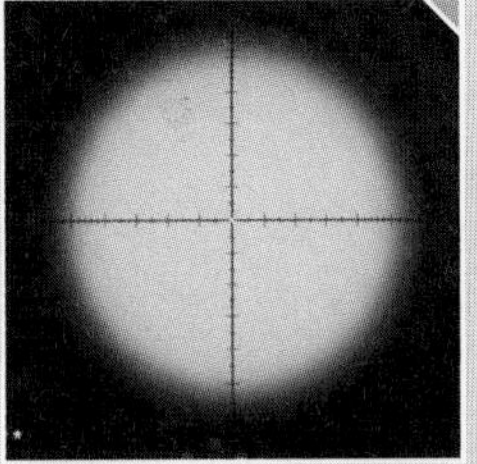
 Ballistic (40X)	A very high-powered scope with a serious 40x magnification for taking out targets at the most extreme distances.	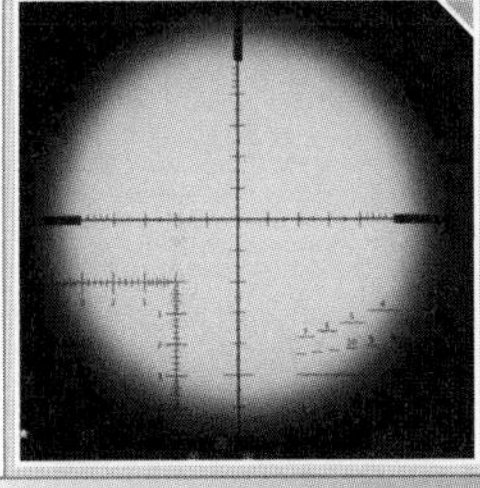
PISTOL		
 Ghost Ring	Replaces the standard ironsights with a set of rapid acquisition rear ring and front post sights for a clear sight picture.	
 Mini (RDS)	American compact red dot sight designed to be mounted on pistols. Makes target acquisition and tracking easier.	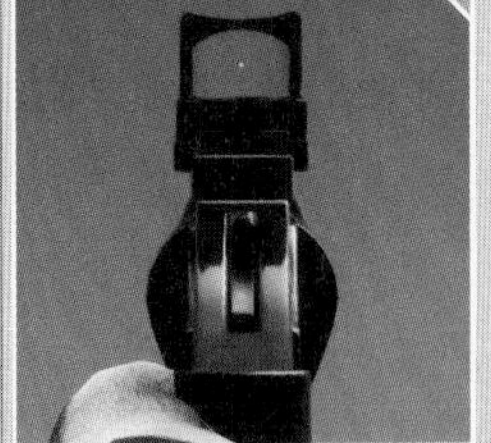
 Delta (RDS)	Compact red dot sight for handguns featuring a triangular reticle for pinpoint target shooting.	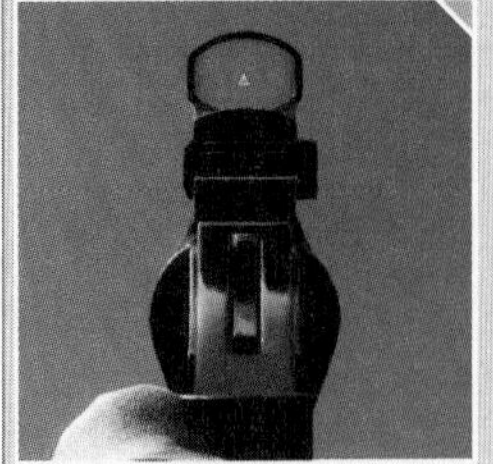

* = only available in Battle Pack

ATTACHMENTS

IMAGE	NAME	DESCRIPTION
ACCESSORIES		
	Canted ironsights	ironsights canted at a 45 degree angle for quick target acquisition at close range, even when using a scope.
	Flashlight	Lights up dark corners and disorients nearby enemies. Especially blinding against IRNV and FLIR sight equipment.
	Tactical Light*	Light activated automatically when you aim your weapon. Especially blinding against IRNV and FLIR sight equipment.
	Laser Sight	Bright red laser sight improves Hip Fire via a 25% reduction in the hip fire penalty. Can blind enemies at moderate ranges.
	Tri Beam Laser*	Triple Beam laser sight that provides the normal benefits of a laser sight, but with three individual dots for rapid sight acquisition.
	Green Laser Sight*	High intensity, high visibility green laser sight improves Hip Fire via a 25% reduction in the hip fire penalty. Can blind enemies at moderate ranges.
	Laser/Light Combo*	Toggle between a blinding flashlight or Hip Fire-improving laser sight depending on your situation. Cannot be toggled off.
	Variable Zoom (14X)	Adds another toggleable 14x magnification mode to any high-powered scope.
	Range Finder	Laser range finder that displays the distance to the target as well as the current zero distance on the weapon. No beam can be detected from this laser.
	Magnifier (2X)	Adds a toggleable 2x zoom to any red dot and holographic sights to allow shooters to adapt to different engagement ranges in the field.

IMAGE	NAME	DESCRIPTION
BARREL		
	Muzzle Brake	Improves Stability by reducing muzzle climb by 25%, but adds a 30% penalty to the Accuracy of automatic fire.
	Compensator	Improves Stability by reducing muzzle drift by 25%, but adds a 30% penalty to the Accuracy of automatic fire.
	Flash Hider*	Eliminates the flash generated by firing the weapon without the bullet speed penalty of a full-fledged silencer.
	Heavy Barrel	Heavy cold hammer forged barrel to improve aimed fire Accuracy by 50% at the cost of 50% muzzle climb, a penalty to Stability.
	Suppressor	Western silencer that increases stealth by hiding your muzzle report and position on the minimap. Reduces bullet velocity and increases bullet drop.
	LS06 Suppressor	Chinese silencer that increases stealth by hiding your muzzle report and position on the minimap. Reduces bullet velocity and increases bullet drop.
	PBS-4 Suppressor	Russian silencer that increases stealth by hiding your muzzle report and position on the minimap. Reduces bullet velocity and increases bullet drop.
	R2 Suppressor*	Western compact silencer that increases stealth by hiding your muzzle report and position on the minimap. Reduces bullet velocity and increases bullet drop.
	QSW-06 Suppressor	Chinese pistol silencer that increases stealth by hiding your muzzle report and position on the minimap. Reduces bullet velocity and increases bullet drop.
	TGPA-5 Suppressor	Russian pistol silencer that increases stealth by hiding your muzzle report and position on the minimap. Reduces bullet velocity and increases bullet drop.

IMAGE	NAME	DESCRIPTION
SHOTGUN BARREL		
	Duckbill	Flattens the normal spread of pellets horizontally, making shot spread in a flat line towards targets.
	Full Choke	Significantly tightens the shot spread for improved Accuracy, but has penalities for Stability and Hip Fire as well. Not recommended with Slugs.
	Modified Choke	Moderately tightens the shot spread for improved Accuracy, but has penalities for Stability and Hip Fire as well. Not recommended with Slugs.
SNIPER RIFLE AUXILIARY		
	Bipod	Enables you to enter Supported Shooting when prone and on most covers. Improves Stability and Accuracy when deployed.
	Straight Pull	Removes the need to zoom out between shots, allowing for rapid follow-up shots.
UNDERBARREL		
	Underslung Rail	Used to attach the M320 Grenade Launcher or the M26 Shotgun making switching to these gadgets faster.
	Bipod	Enables you to enter Supported Shooting when prone and on most covers. Improves Stability and Accuracy when deployed.
	Ergo Grip	An ergonomic grip to help steady your weapon in run and gun situations. Improves Hip Fire by reducing the penalty added for shooting on the move by 50%.
	Angled Grip	A modern grip that aims to improve firearm ergonomics and control. Improves Stability by reducing first shot recoil by 33%.
	Stubby Grip	Shortened foregrip provides a good middle ground between ergonomics and weapon control. Improves Accuracy by reducing the automatic fire penalty by 15%.

IMAGE	NAME	DESCRIPTION
	Vertical Grip*	Traditional foregrip to help steady your weapon in run and gun situations. Improves Hip Fire by reducing the penalty added for shooting on the move by 50%.
	Folding Grip*	Customized folding foregrip to improve the ergonomic application of firepower. Improves Stability by reducing first shot recoil by 33%.
	Potato Grip*	Rounded foregrip named for its obvious visual similarity to the classic spud. Improves Accuracy by reducing the automatic fire penalty by 15%. Do not eat.
SHOTGUN AMMO		
	12G Buckshot	A swarm of deadly pellets best used against a single unarmored target at close range.
	12G Dart	Fires multiple tungsten alloy darts instead of shot which yield higher penetration and range at the loss of close range stopping power.
	12G Frag	12 gauge explosive FRAG ammunition for increased suppressing power.
	12G Slug	Plastic saboted slug designed engage the rifling in the shotgun barrel. Provides increased Accuracy and vastly improved Range by the use of a single projectile.

* = only available in Battle Pack

WEAPON STATS: A WORD FROM DICE

A weapon's performance is broken up by five different statistics: damage, accuracy, hip fire, range, and stability. What do all these stats mean? Who better to ask than the developers themselves. Here's how DICE defines each statistic.

Damage: The maximum damage the weapon can output at close range.

Accuracy: High values mean less spread in zoom, making the shots more accurate.

Hip Fire: High values mean less spread in hip fire, making accurate fire on the move easier.

Range: How far the weapon maintains its damage. Higher values mean higher damage at longer range.

Stability: How easy the weapon is to control during rapid and automatic fire. Higher values make it easier to control.

ASSAULT RIFLES

Assault rifles are the most versatile primary weapon available, useful in a variety of situations. All assault rifles can be equipped with a M320 Grenade Launcher, offering even more firepower capable of knocking down walls and damaging light-skinned vehicles. An underslung M26 MASS Shotgun attachment is also available. These rifles can only be accessed by the assault kit. Continue playing as the assault kit to boost your assault score, leading to more assault rifle unlocks.

ASSAULT RIFLE UNLOCK PROGRESSION

IMAGE	NAME	SCORE
	AK-12	0
	SCAR-H	1,000
	M416	2,000
	SAR-21	3,000
	AEK-971	4,000
	FAMAS	5,000
	AUG A3	6,000
	M16A3	7,000
	CZ-805	8,000
	QBZ-95-1	N/A*
	ACE 23	N/A**

* = unlocked in campaign
** = unlocked by completing Assault Combat Expert Assignment

FUNDAMENTALS

- THE ASSAULT RIFLES CAN ONLY BE EQUIPPED BY THE ASSAULT CLASS. ALTHOUGH LENGTHY, THEY'RE STILL COMPACT ENOUGH TO PEEK AROUND CORNERS.
- ASSAULT RIFLES INFLICT THE MOST DAMAGE WITHIN 50 METERS, BUT REMAIN ACCURATE WELL BEYOND 100 METERS.
- CONSIDER EQUIPPING A 4X OPTIC ALONG WITH CANTED IRONSIGHTS, GIVING YOUR RIFLE GREATER VERSATILITY WHEN ENGAGING OPPONENTS AT VARIOUS RANGES.
- IF RECOIL IS A PROBLEM, TRY THE WEAPON'S SEMI-AUTO SETTING. IF ISSUES PERSIST, ATTACH AN ANGLED GRIP AND COMPENSATOR.
- MOST ASSAULT RIFLES CAN ACCOMMODATE THE M320 GRENADE LAUNCHER OR M26 MASS SHOTGUN WHEN THE UNDERSLUNG RAIL IS ATTACHED.

ASSAULT RIFLE SERVICE STAR

You earn an Assault Rifle Service Star for every 100 kills you score with each assault rifle.

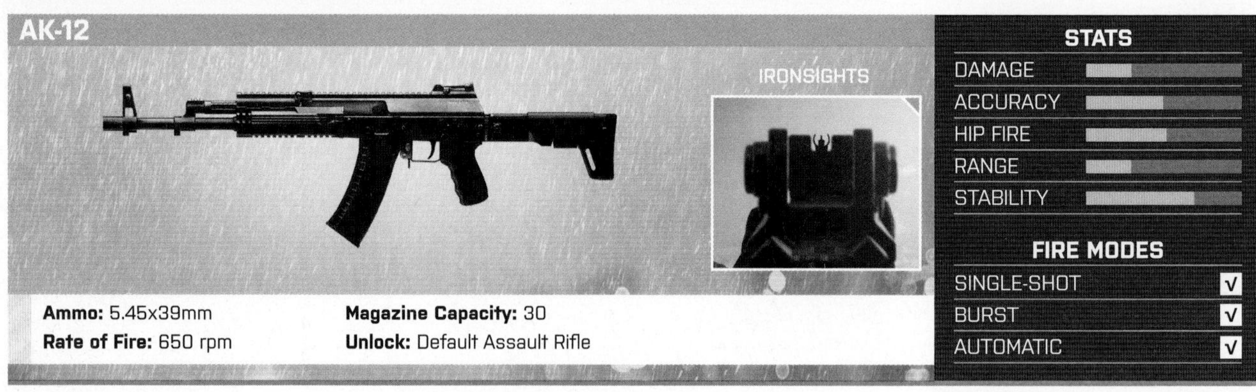

AK-12
IRONSIGHTS
STATS
DAMAGE
ACCURACY
HIP FIRE
RANGE
STABILITY
FIRE MODES
SINGLE-SHOT √
BURST √
AUTOMATIC √
Ammo: 5.45x39mm
Rate of Fire: 650 rpm
Magazine Capacity: 30
Unlock: Default Assault Rifle

The AK-12 is the latest assault rifle fielded by the Russian Army. Based largely on the AK-74's design, the AK-12 features several exterior modifications including the integration of attachment rails, an adjustable buttstock, and a ambidextrous magazine release. As the first assault rifle available, it comes equipped with an Underslung Rail, KOBRA (RDS) optic, a Laser sight, and Ergo Grip.

UNLOCK PROGRESSION

IMAGE	ATTACHMENT	SLOT	KILLS
	Underslung Rail	Underbarrel	0
	KOBRA (RDS)	Optic (Close Range)	0
	Laser Sight	Accessory	0
	Ergo Grip	Underbarrel	0
	Muzzle Brake	Barrel	10
	PSO-1 (4X)	Optic (Medium Range)	20
	Canted ironsights	Accessory	30
	Angled Grip	Underbarrel	40
	Heavy Barrel	Barrel	50
	PK-A (3.4X)	Optic (Medium Range)	60
	Flashlight	Accessory	70
	Bipod	Underbarrel	80
	Compensator	Barrel	90
	PKA-S (1X)	Optic (Close Range)	100
	Magnifier (2X)	Accessory	110
	Stubby Grip	Underbarrel	120
	PBS-4 Suppressor	Barrel	130

SCAR-H

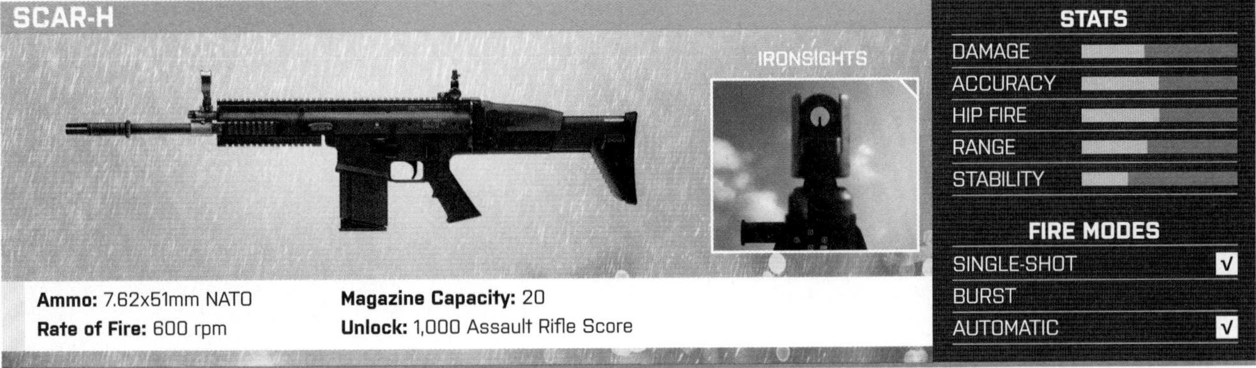

Ammo: 7.62x51mm NATO
Rate of Fire: 600 rpm
Magazine Capacity: 20
Unlock: 1,000 Assault Rifle Score

STATS

DAMAGE
ACCURACY
HIP FIRE
RANGE
STABILITY

FIRE MODES

SINGLE-SHOT	√
BURST	
AUTOMATIC	√

Developed for the US SOCOM, the SCAR is a modular series of weapons available in multiple interchangeable calibers, barrel lengths, and configurations. This particular model has been configured as the heavy SCAR-H variant with a long barrel and chambered for the hard hitting 7.62mm NATO round.

UNLOCK PROGRESSION

IMAGE	ATTACHMENT	SLOT	KILLS
	Underslung Rail	Underbarrel	0
	Reflex (RDS)	Optic (Close Range)	10
	Laser Sight	Accessory	20
	Ergo Grip	Underbarrel	30
	Muzzle Brake	Barrel	40
	ACOG (4X)	Optic (Medium Range)	50
	Canted ironsights	Accessory	60
	Angled Grip	Underbarrel	70
	Heavy Barrel	Barrel	80
	M145 (3.4X)	Optic (Medium Range)	90
	Flashlight	Accessory	100
	Bipod	Underbarrel	110
	Compensator	Barrel	120
	HOLO (1X)	Optic (Close Range)	130
	Magnifier (2X)	Accessory	140
	Stubby Grip	Underbarrel	150
	Suppressor	Barrel	160

M416

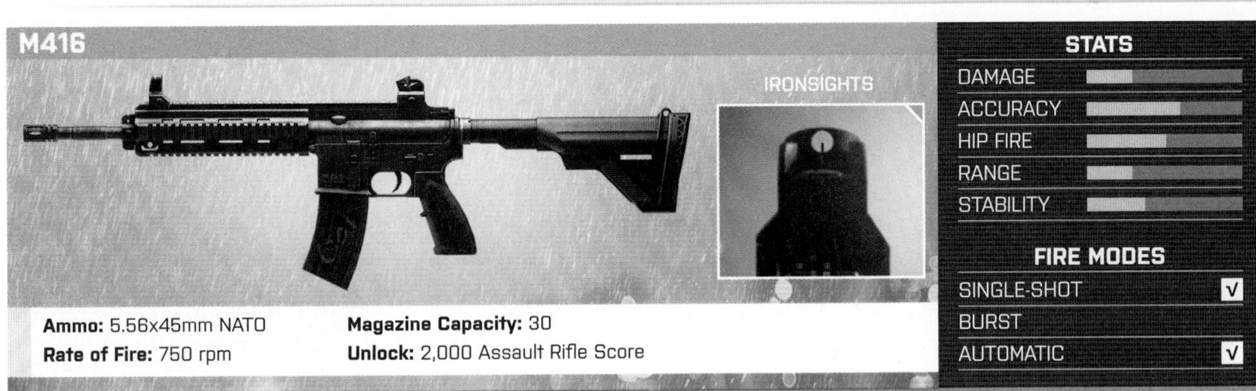

Ammo: 5.56x45mm NATO
Rate of Fire: 750 rpm
Magazine Capacity: 30
Unlock: 2,000 Assault Rifle Score

STATS

DAMAGE
ACCURACY
HIP FIRE
RANGE
STABILITY

FIRE MODES

SINGLE-SHOT	√
BURST	
AUTOMATIC	√

The M416 was developed by a famous German weapons manufacturer as a more reliable version of the classic M16. The weapon is essentially a fusion of the M16 and the G36 Assault Rifles. The M416 is reliable and accurate, with a moderate recoil and rate of fire that makes for an effective all-around weapon.

UNLOCK PROGRESSION

IMAGE	ATTACHMENT	SLOT	KILLS
	Underslung Rail	Underbarrel	0
	Reflex (RDS)	Optic (Close Range)	10
	Laser Sight	Accessory	20
	Ergo Grip	Underbarrel	30
	Muzzle Brake	Barrel	40
	ACOG (4X)	Optic (Medium Range)	50
	Canted ironsights	Accessory	60
	Angled Grip	Underbarrel	70
	Heavy Barrel	Barrel	80
	M145 (3.4X)	Optic (Medium Range)	90
	Flashlight	Accessory	100
	Bipod	Underbarrel	110
	Compensator	Barrel	120
	HOLO (1X)	Optic (Close Range)	130
	Magnifier (2X)	Accessory	140
	Stubby Grip	Underbarrel	150
	Suppressor	Barrel	160

SAR-21

STATS

- DAMAGE
- ACCURACY
- HIP FIRE
- RANGE
- STABILITY

FIRE MODES

SINGLE-SHOT	√
BURST	
AUTOMATIC	√

Ammo: 5.56x45mm NATO
Magazine Capacity: 30
Rate of Fire: 600 rpm
Unlock: 3,000 Assault Rifle Score

The SAR-21 is manufactured in Singapore and has been fielded by the Singapore Armed Forces since 1999. Chambered in the universal 5.56x45mm NATO round, the SAR-21's bullpup design makes is easy to maneuver in tight quarters, making it particularly effective during urban deployments. It also exhibits light recoil, making the rifle easy to control.

UNLOCK PROGRESSION

IMAGE	ATTACHMENT	SLOT	KILLS
	Underslung Rail	Underbarrel	0
	Coyote (RDS)	Optic (Close Range)	10
	Laser Sight	Accessory	20
	Ergo Grip	Underbarrel	30
	Muzzle Brake	Barrel	40
	JGM-4 (4X)	Optic (Medium Range)	50
	Canted ironsights	Accessory	60
	Angled Grip	Underbarrel	70
	Heavy Barrel	Barrel	80
	PRISMA (3.4X)	Optic (Medium Range)	90
	Flashlight	Accessory	100
	Bipod	Underbarrel	110
	Compensator	Barrel	120
	HD-33 (1X)	Optic (Close Range)	130
	Magnifier (2X)	Accessory	140
	Stubby Grip	Underbarrel	150
	LS06 Suppressor	Barrel	160

AEK-971

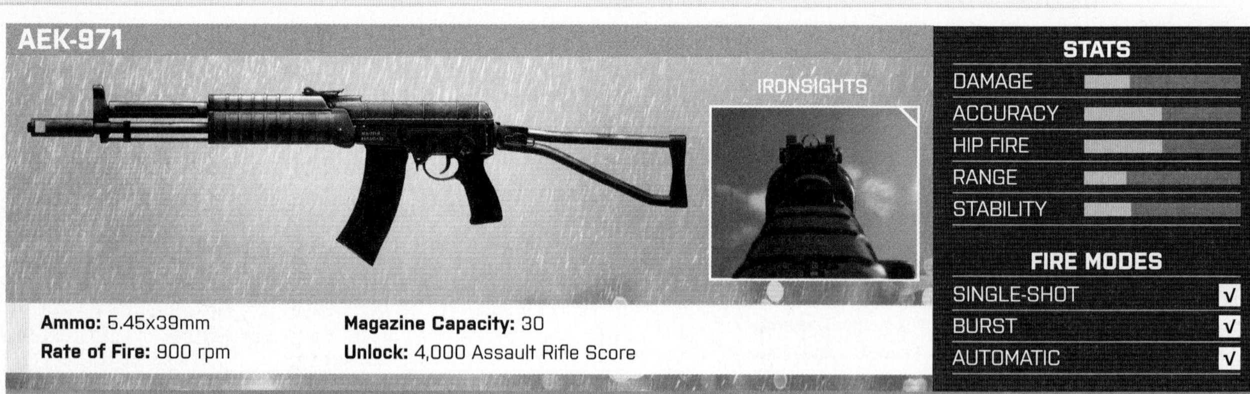

STATS

- DAMAGE
- ACCURACY
- HIP FIRE
- RANGE
- STABILITY

FIRE MODES

SINGLE-SHOT	√
BURST	√
AUTOMATIC	√

Ammo: 5.45x39mm
Magazine Capacity: 30
Rate of Fire: 900 rpm
Unlock: 4,000 Assault Rifle Score

The AEK-971 was developed as a possible successor to the AK-74 series of assault rifles and features a unique recoil reduction system. The AEK-971's high rate of fire makes it excellent in close quarters but difficult to control. Shooters should switch to semi-automatic or 3-round burst for longer ranges.

UNLOCK PROGRESSION

IMAGE	ATTACHMENT	SLOT	KILLS
	Underslung Rail	Underbarrel	0
	KOBRA (RDS)	Optic (Close Range)	10
	Laser Sight	Accessory	20
	Ergo Grip	Underbarrel	30
	Muzzle Brake	Barrel	40
	PSO-1 (4X)	Optic (Medium Range)	50
	Canted ironsights	Accessory	60
	Angled Grip	Underbarrel	70
	Heavy Barrel	Barrel	80
	PK-A (3.4X)	Optic (Medium Range)	90
	Flashlight	Accessory	100
	Bipod	Underbarrel	110
	Compensator	Barrel	120
	PKA-S (1X)	Optic (Close Range)	130
	Magnifier (2X)	Accessory	140
	Stubby Grip	Underbarrel	150
	PBS-4 Suppressor	Barrel	160

FAMAS

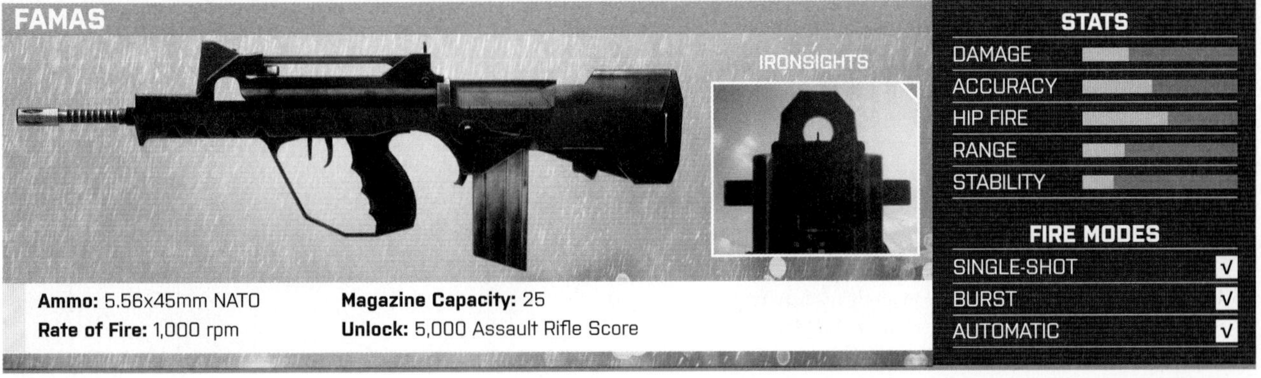

Ammo: 5.56x45mm NATO
Rate of Fire: 1,000 rpm
Magazine Capacity: 25
Unlock: 5,000 Assault Rifle Score

STATS	
DAMAGE	
ACCURACY	
HIP FIRE	
RANGE	
STABILITY	

FIRE MODES	
SINGLE-SHOT	√
BURST	√
AUTOMATIC	√

The FAMAS is the standard-issue assault rifle of the French military. It is chambered in the 5.56mm NATO round and features a compact, bullpup configuration ideal for operating in close-quarters environments. The rifle has a blazing rate of fire, resulting in harsh recoil. An Angled Grip and Compensator can help mitigate muzzle climb, making it easier to keep the weapon on-target.

UNLOCK PROGRESSION

IMAGE	ATTACHMENT	SLOT	KILLS
	Underslung Rail	Underbarrel	0
	Reflex (RDS)	Optic (Close Range)	10
	Laser Sight	Accessory	20
	Ergo Grip	Underbarrel	30
	Muzzle Brake	Barrel	40
	ACOG (4X)	Optic (Medium Range)	50
	Canted ironsights	Accessory	60
	Angled Grip	Underbarrel	70
	Heavy Barrel	Barrel	80
	M145 (3.4X)	Optic (Medium Range)	90
	Flashlight	Accessory	100
	Bipod	Underbarrel	110
	Compensator	Barrel	120
	HOLO (1X)	Optic (Close Range)	130
	Magnifier (2X)	Accessory	140
	Stubby Grip	Underbarrel	150
	Suppressor	Barrel	160

AUG A3

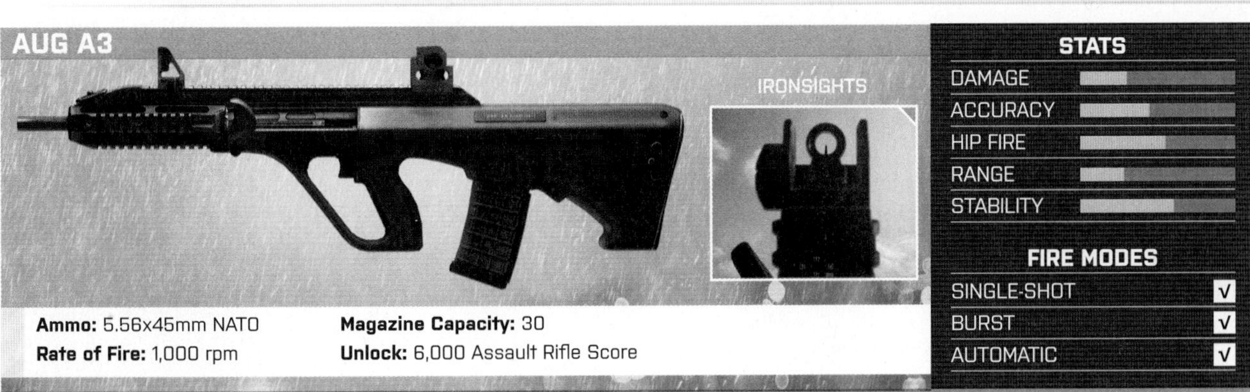

Ammo: 5.56x45mm NATO
Rate of Fire: 1,000 rpm
Magazine Capacity: 30
Unlock: 6,000 Assault Rifle Score

STATS	
DAMAGE	
ACCURACY	
HIP FIRE	
RANGE	
STABILITY	

FIRE MODES	
SINGLE-SHOT	√
BURST	√
AUTOMATIC	√

This 5.56 bullpup design was developed in the 1970s and features high modularity while being fully ambidextrous. Since its adoption as the standard rifle of the Austrian army in 1977, it has seen great success as an export, with a high number of global users praising its ruggedness and excellent handling.

UNLOCK PROGRESSION

IMAGE	ATTACHMENT	SLOT	KILLS
	Underslung Rail	Underbarrel	0
	Reflex (RDS)	Optic (Close Range)	10
	Laser Sight	Accessory	20
	Ergo Grip	Underbarrel	30
	Muzzle Brake	Barrel	40
	ACOG (4X)	Optic (Medium Range)	50
	Canted ironsights	Accessory	60
	Angled Grip	Underbarrel	70
	Heavy Barrel	Barrel	80
	M145 (3.4X)	Optic (Medium Range)	90
	Flashlight	Accessory	100
	Bipod	Underbarrel	110
	Compensator	Barrel	120
	HOLO (1X)	Optic (Close Range)	130
	Magnifier (2X)	Accessory	140
	Stubby Grip	Underbarrel	150
	Suppressor	Barrel	160

M16A3

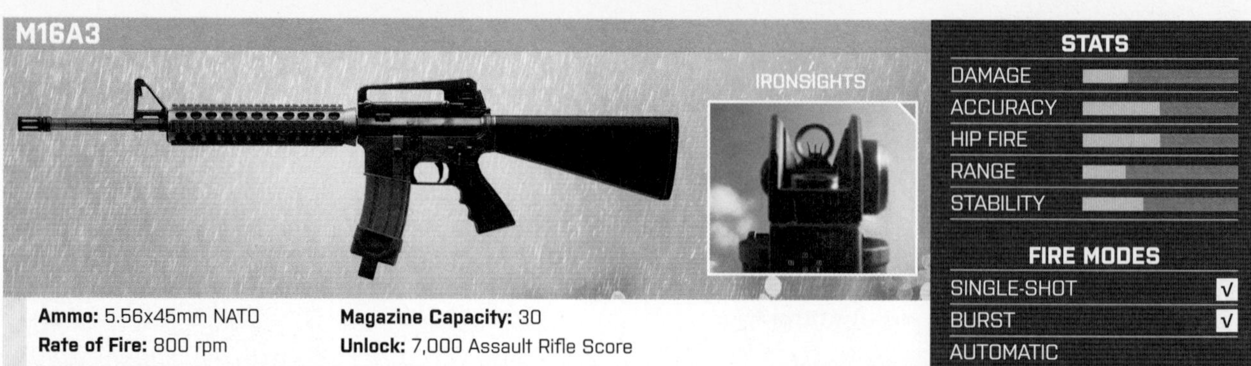

Ammo: 5.56x45mm NATO

Rate of Fire: 800 rpm

Magazine Capacity: 30

Unlock: 7,000 Assault Rifle Score

The third generation M16 has been upgraded with a RIS (Rail Interface System) for mounting accessories and is capable of burst and semi-automatic fire. Available to front line units engaged in urban combat, the M16A3's low recoil makes it capable all-around weapon.

UNLOCK PROGRESSION

IMAGE	ATTACHMENT	SLOT	KILLS
	Underslung Rail	Underbarrel	0
	Reflex (RDS)	Optic (Close Range)	10
	Laser Sight	Accessory	20
	Ergo Grip	Underbarrel	30
	Muzzle Brake	Barrel	40
	ACOG (4X)	Optic (Medium Range)	50
	Canted ironsights	Accessory	60
	Angled Grip	Underbarrel	70
	Heavy Barrel	Barrel	80
	M145 (3.4X)	Optic (Medium Range)	90
	Flashlight	Accessory	100
	Bipod	Underbarrel	110
	Compensator	Barrel	120
	HOLO (1X)	Optic (Close Range)	130
	Magnifier (2X)	Accessory	140
	Stubby Grip	Underbarrel	150
	Suppressor	Barrel	160

CZ-805

Ammo: 5.56x45mm NATO

Rate of Fire: 700 rpm

Magazine Capacity: 30

Unlock: 8,000 Assault Rifle Score

This Czech-manufactured assault rifle was selected to replace the aging Sa vz. 58 by the Czech Armed Forces in 2010. Chambered in the 5.56mm NATO round, the CZ-805 is constructed from durable, lightweight alloy and polymer components and features three selectable fire modes, including a two-round burst.

UNLOCK PROGRESSION

IMAGE	ATTACHMENT	SLOT	KILLS
	Underslung Rail	Underbarrel	0
	KOBRA (RDS)	Optic (Close Range)	10
	Laser Sight	Accessory	20
	Ergo Grip	Underbarrel	30
	Muzzle Brake	Barrel	40
	PSO-1 (4X)	Optic (Medium Range)	50
	Canted ironsights	Accessory	60
	Angled Grip	Underbarrel	70
	Heavy Barrel	Barrel	80
	PK-A (3.4X)	Optic (Medium Range)	90
	Flashlight	Accessory	100
	Bipod	Underbarrel	110
	Compensator	Barrel	120
	PKA-S (1X)	Optic (Close Range)	130
	Magnifier (2X)	Accessory	140
	Stubby Grip	Underbarrel	150
	PBS-4 Suppressor	Barrel	160

QBZ-95-1

STATS

DAMAGE
ACCURACY
HIP FIRE
RANGE
STABILITY

FIRE MODES

SINGLE-SHOT	√
BURST	√
AUTOMATIC	√

Ammo: 5.8x42mm DAP-87
Rate of Fire: 650 rpm
Magazine Capacity: 30
Unlock: Campaign Unlock

This modified variant of the widely deployed Chinese QBZ-95 is chambered to accommodate the heavy DAP-87 round. The rifle also features several exterior alterations to improve operations and ergonomics. Like other bullpup-configured assault rifles, the QBZ-95-1's compact size makes it ideally suited for operation in close-quarter environments.

UNLOCK PROGRESSION

IMAGE	ATTACHMENT	SLOT	KILLS
	Underslung Rail	Underbarrel	0
	Coyote (RDS)	Optic (Close Range)	10
	Laser Sight	Accessory	20
	Ergo Grip	Underbarrel	30
	Muzzle Brake	Barrel	40
	JGM-4 (4X)	Optic (Medium Range)	50
	Canted ironsights	Accessory	60
	Angled Grip	Underbarrel	70
	Heavy Barrel	Barrel	80
	PRISMA (3.4X)	Optic (Medium Range)	90
	Flashlight	Accessory	100
	Bipod	Underbarrel	110
	Compensator	Barrel	120
	HD-33 (1X)	Optic (Close Range)	130
	Magnifier (2X)	Accessory	140
	Stubby Grip	Underbarrel	150
	LS06 Suppressor	Barrel	160

ACE 23

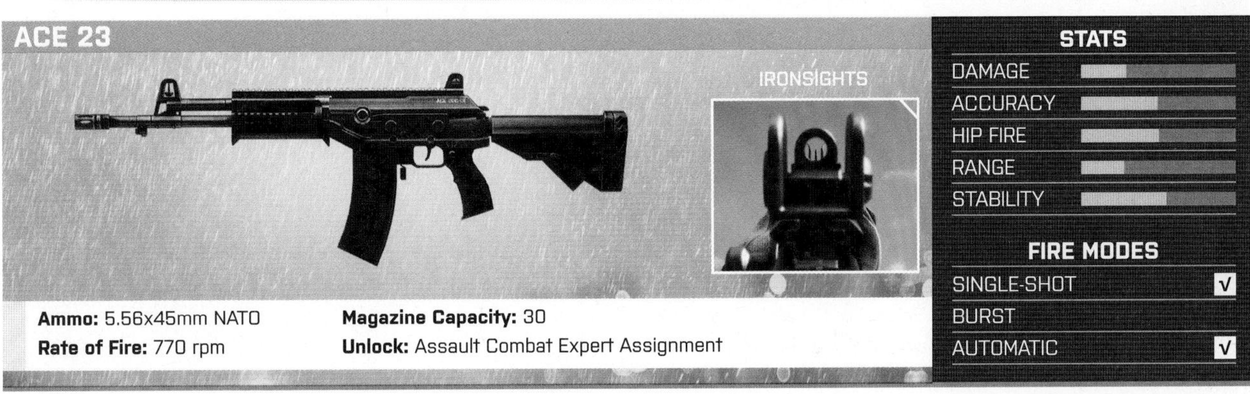

STATS

DAMAGE
ACCURACY
HIP FIRE
RANGE
STABILITY

FIRE MODES

SINGLE-SHOT	√
BURST	
AUTOMATIC	√

Ammo: 5.56x45mm NATO
Rate of Fire: 770 rpm
Magazine Capacity: 30
Unlock: Assault Combat Expert Assignment

The ACE 23 is just one variant of the ACE family of firearms, fielded by military and police forces throughout Central and South America. Constructed of durable composite materials, the ACE 23 offers a good balance of accuracy and stability, making it a well-rounded assault rifle with various customization options.

UNLOCK PROGRESSION

IMAGE	ATTACHMENT	SLOT	KILLS
	Underslung Rail	Underbarrel	0
	Coyote (RDS)	Optic (Close Range)	10
	Laser Sight	Accessory	20
	Ergo Grip	Underbarrel	30
	Muzzle Brake	Barrel	40
	JGM-4 (4X)	Optic (Medium Range)	50
	Canted ironsights	Accessory	60
	Angled Grip	Underbarrel	70
	Heavy Barrel	Barrel	80
	PRISMA (3.4X)	Optic (Medium Range)	90
	Flashlight	Accessory	100
	Bipod	Underbarrel	110
	Compensator	Barrel	120
	HD-33 (1X)	Optic (Close Range)	130
	Magnifier (2X)	Accessory	140
	Stubby Grip	Underbarrel	150
	LS06 Suppressor	Barrel	160

PERSONAL DEFENSE WEAPONS (PDWS)

In *Battlefield 4*, the PDWs are now available only to the engineer class. These compact and lightweight weapons are best deployed in close quarters due to their short range. But what they lack in accuracy and damage output, they make up for in rate of fire. So consider choosing one of these weapons when tasked with assaulting or defending a building interior or other confined space.

PDW UNLOCK PROGRESSION

IMAGE	NAME	SCORE	IMAGE	NAME	SCORE	IMAGE	NAME	SCORE
	MX4	0		CBJ-MS	3,000		JS2	6,000
	PP-2000	1,000		PDW-R	4,000		P90	N/A*
	UMP-45	2,000		CZ-3A1	5,000		UMP-9	N/A**

* = unlocked in campaign ** = unlocked by completing Combat Expert Assignment

FUNDAMENTALS

- THE PDWS ARE NOW ONLY AVAILABLE TO THE ENGINEER CLASS.
- DESIGNED FOR CLOSE-QUARTER COMBAT, THE PDWS ARE MOST EFFECTIVE WITHIN 50 METERS...AND COMPLETELY UNRELIABLE BEYOND 50 METERS.
- PDWS HAVE EXTREMELY HIGH HIP FIRE ACCURACY. ATTACH A LASER SIGHT TO INCREASE THEIR HIP FIRE POTENTIAL... AND BLIND YOUR OPPONENTS.
- DUE TO THEIR COMPACT SIZE AND SHORT BARREL LENGTH, PDWS ARE RAISED QUICKLY WHEN AIMING DOWN SIGHTS.
- WHILE CARRYING A PDW, PEEK AROUND CORNERS OR OVER LOW COVER TO ENGAGE THREATS WITHOUT EXPOSING YOURSELF.

PDW SERVICE STAR

You earn a PDW Service Star for every 100 kills you score with each PDW.

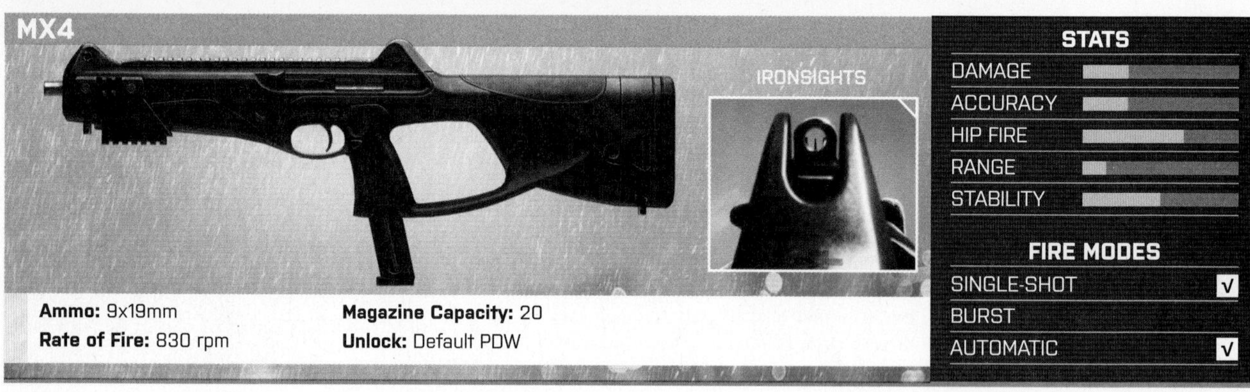

Ammo: 9x19mm
Rate of Fire: 830 rpm
Magazine Capacity: 20
Unlock: Default PDW

Sporting a compact, sleek design, the Italian-manufactured MX4 is seen by many militaries and police agencies as a possible replacement for the legendary MP5. The weapon is fed by a 30-round box magazine inserted through the pistol grip and has garnered a solid reputation among its adopters as a reliable and highly maneuverable PDW. It comes equipped with a Reflex (RDS) optic, a Laser Sight, and Ergo Grip.

UNLOCK PROGRESSION

IMAGE	ATTACHMENT	SLOT	KILLS
	Reflex (RDS)	Optic (Close Range)	0
	Laser Sight	Accessory	0
	Ergo Grip	Underbarrel	0
	Compensator	Barrel	10
	M145 (3.4X)	Optic (Medium Range)	20
	Flashlight	Accessory	30
	Angled Grip	Underbarrel	40
	Muzzle Brake	Barrel	50
	HOLO (1X)	Optic (Close Range)	60
	Stubby Grip	Underbarrel	70
	Suppressor	Barrel	80
	ACOG (4X)	Optic (Medium Range)	90
	Canted ironsights	Accessory	100
	Heavy Barrel	Barrel	110

PP-2000

Ammo: 9x19mm
Rate of Fire: 650 rpm
Magazine Capacity: 44
Unlock: 1,000 PDW Score

STATS	
DAMAGE	
ACCURACY	
HIP FIRE	
RANGE	
STABILITY	

FIRE MODES	
SINGLE-SHOT	√
BURST	
AUTOMATIC	√

Though chambered in the standard 9x19mm caliber, the PP-2000 is designed to use Russian overpressure rounds at high velocity to penetrate body armor. The high muzzle velocity of the PP-2000 gives it a flatter trajectory than other 9mm weapons. Equipped with a 44-round magazine, the PP-2000 functions admirably in a CQB assault role.

UNLOCK PROGRESSION

IMAGE	ATTACHMENT	SLOT	KILLS
	KOBRA (RDS)	Optic (Close Range)	10
	Laser Sight	Accessory	20
	Ergo Grip	Underbarrel	30
	Compensator	Barrel	40
	PK-A (3.4X)	Optic (Medium Range)	50
	Flashlight	Accessory	60
	Angled Grip	Underbarrel	70
	Muzzle Brake	Barrel	80
	PKA-S (1X)	Optic (Close Range)	90
	Stubby Grip	Underbarrel	100
	PBS-4 Suppressor	Barrel	110
	PSO-1 (4X)	Optic (Medium Range)	120
	Canted ironsights	Accessory	130
	Heavy Barrel	Barrel	140

UMP-45

Ammo: .45 ACP
Rate of Fire: 600 rpm
Magazine Capacity: 25
Unlock: 2,000 PDW Score

STATS	
DAMAGE	
ACCURACY	
HIP FIRE	
RANGE	
STABILITY	

FIRE MODES	
SINGLE-SHOT	√
BURST	√
AUTOMATIC	√

German built, the UMP-45 is a fully automatic PDW noted for its versatility and optimal mobility. Essentially an improved version of the MP5, the UMP-45 is functionally similar but substantially cheaper to manufacture and includes several modern upgrades such as the top and forward accessory rail. But the weapon's harsh recoil can take some getting used to.

UNLOCK PROGRESSION

IMAGE	ATTACHMENT	SLOT	KILLS
	Reflex (RDS)	Optic (Close Range)	10
	Laser Sight	Accessory	20
	Ergo Grip	Underbarrel	30
	Compensator	Barrel	40
	M145 (3.4X)	Optic (Medium Range)	50
	Flashlight	Accessory	60
	Angled Grip	Underbarrel	70
	Muzzle Brake	Barrel	80
	HOLO (1X)	Optic (Close Range)	90
	Stubby Grip	Underbarrel	100
	Suppressor	Barrel	110
	ACOG (4X)	Optic (Medium Range)	120
	Canted ironsights	Accessory	130
	Heavy Barrel	Barrel	140

CBJ-MS

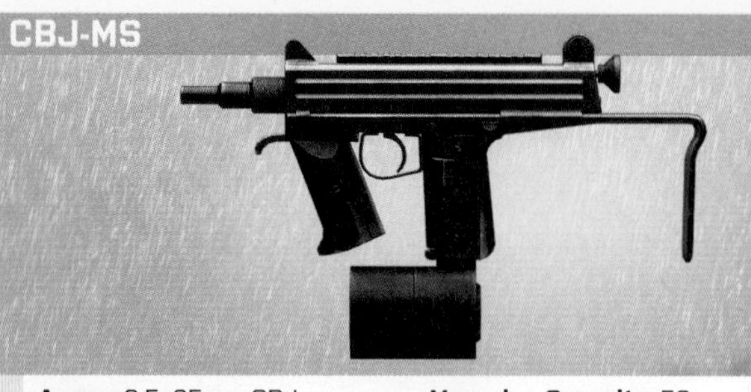

IRONSIGHTS

Ammo: 6.5x25mm CBJ
Rate of Fire: 700 rpm
Magazine Capacity: 50
Unlock: 3,000 PDW Score

STATS

DAMAGE
ACCURACY
HIP FIRE
RANGE
STABILITY

FIRE MODES

SINGLE-SHOT	√
BURST	√
AUTOMATIC	√

The Swedish-designed CBJ-MS is a ultra-compact PDW fed by a 50-round drum magazine inserted through the weapon's pistol grip. This weapon fires the new high-velocity 6.5x25mm CBJ round designed to penetrate body armor. Whether aiming down sights or firing from the hip, the CBJ-MS is a force to be reckoned with during close-quarter engagements.

UNLOCK PROGRESSION

IMAGE	ATTACHMENT	SLOT	KILLS
	Reflex (RDS)	Optic (Close Range)	10
	Laser Sight	Accessory	20
	Ergo Grip	Underbarrel	30
	Compensator	Barrel	40
	M145 (3.4X)	Optic (Medium Range)	50
	Flashlight	Accessory	60
	Angled Grip	Underbarrel	70
	Muzzle Brake	Barrel	80
	HOLO (1X)	Optic (Close Range)	90
	Stubby Grip	Underbarrel	100
	Suppressor	Barrel	110
	ACOG (4X)	Optic (Medium Range)	120
	Canted ironsights	Accessory	130
	Heavy Barrel	Barrel	140

PDW-R

IRONSIGHTS

Ammo: 5.56x45mm NATO
Rate of Fire: 750 rpm
Magazine Capacity: 30
Unlock: 4,000 PDW Score

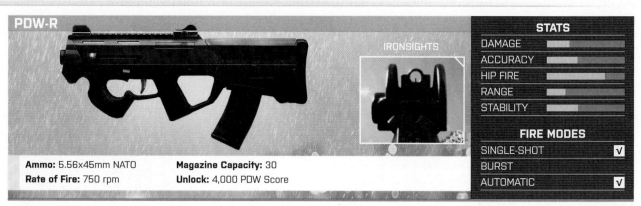

STATS

DAMAGE
ACCURACY
HIP FIRE
RANGE
STABILITY

FIRE MODES

SINGLE-SHOT	√
BURST	
AUTOMATIC	√

Developed as a Personal Defense Weapon, the PDW-R differs from most other PDW concepts by utilizing the standard 5.56mm NATO rounds of the M16 or M4. This allows the PDW-R to share magazines and supply lines with standard troops while its short length and bullpup configuration allow the PDW-R to be easily operated in CQB. Though it lacks the accuracy of a rifle, the PDW-R has a greater punch at longer ranges than other PDWs.

UNLOCK PROGRESSION

IMAGE	ATTACHMENT	SLOT	KILLS
	Reflex (RDS)	Optic (Close Range)	10
	Laser Sight	Accessory	20
	Ergo Grip	Underbarrel	30
	Compensator	Barrel	40
	M145 (3.4X)	Optic (Medium Range)	50
	Flashlight	Accessory	60
	Angled Grip	Underbarrel	70
	Muzzle Brake	Barrel	80
	HOLO (1X)	Optic (Close Range)	90
	Stubby Grip	Underbarrel	100
	Suppressor	Barrel	110
	ACOG (4X)	Optic (Medium Range)	120
	Canted ironsights	Accessory	130
	Heavy Barrel	Barrel	140

CZ-3A1

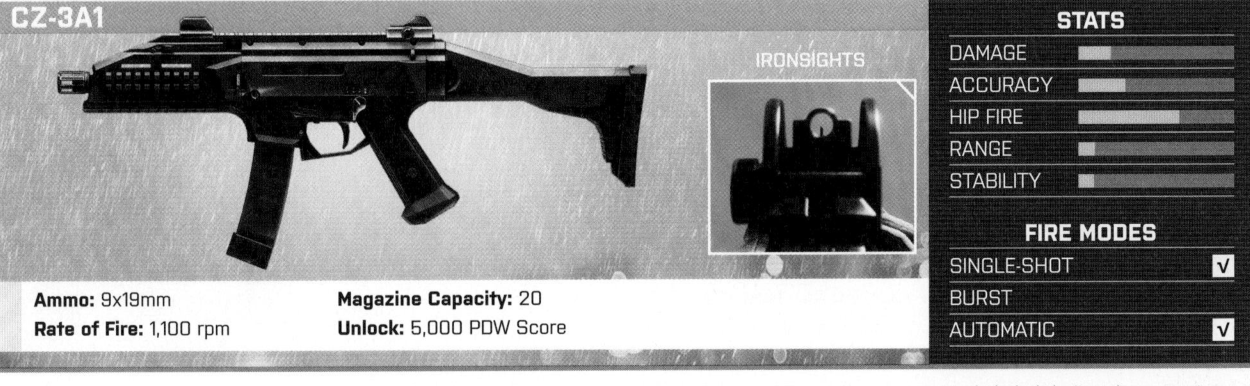

Ammo: 9x19mm
Rate of Fire: 1,100 rpm
Magazine Capacity: 20
Unlock: 5,000 PDW Score

STATS

DAMAGE, ACCURACY, HIP FIRE, RANGE, STABILITY

FIRE MODES

SINGLE-SHOT	√
BURST	
AUTOMATIC	√

Also known as the Scorpion, this Czech-designed PDW features an extremely high rate of fire, making it extremely lethal during close-quarter engagements. However, the blazing rate of fire comes at the cost of stability, exhibiting excessive recoil during prolonged auto bursts. When accuracy counts, switch to the weapon's burst setting. Attaching an Angled Grip and Compensator can also help reduce recoil.

UNLOCK PROGRESSION

IMAGE	ATTACHMENT	SLOT	KILLS
	KOBRA (RDS)	Optic (Close Range)	10
	Laser Sight	Accessory	20
	Ergo Grip	Underbarrel	30
	Compensator	Barrel	40
	PK-A (3.4X)	Optic (Medium Range)	50
	Flashlight	Accessory	60
	Angled Grip	Underbarrel	70
	Muzzle Brake	Barrel	80
	PKA-S (1X)	Optic (Close Range)	90
	Stubby Grip	Underbarrel	100
	PBS-4 Suppressor	Barrel	110
	PSO-1 (4X)	Optic (Medium Range)	120
	Canted ironsights	Accessory	130
	Heavy Barrel	Barrel	140

JS2

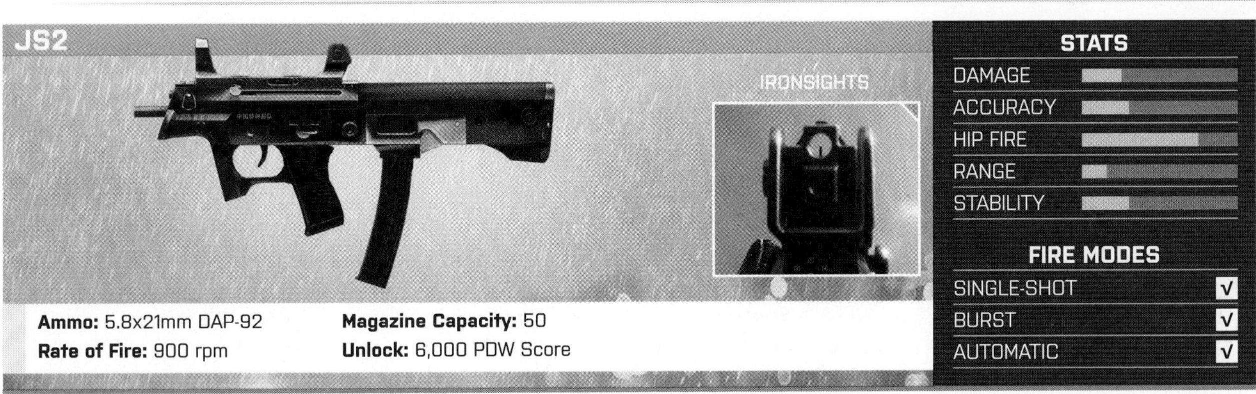

Ammo: 5.8x21mm DAP-92
Rate of Fire: 900 rpm
Magazine Capacity: 50
Unlock: 6,000 PDW Score

STATS

DAMAGE, ACCURACY, HIP FIRE, RANGE, STABILITY

FIRE MODES

SINGLE-SHOT	√
BURST	√
AUTOMATIC	√

The Chinese JS2 PDW is highly maneuverable PDW thanks to its bullpup configuration. This makes it easy to round corners and sweep rooms during house-to-house urban fighting. Consider equipping it with a Laser Sight to boost its already impressive hip fire accuracy. The JS2's generous 50-round magazine is always a welcome feature during intense fire fights.

UNLOCK PROGRESSION

IMAGE	ATTACHMENT	SLOT	KILLS
	Coyote (RDS)	Optic (Close Range)	10
	Laser Sight	Accessory	20
	Ergo Grip	Underbarrel	30
	Compensator	Barrel	40
	PRISMA (3.4X)	Optic (Medium Range)	50
	Flashlight	Accessory	60
	Angled Grip	Underbarrel	70
	Muzzle Brake	Barrel	80
	HD-33 (1X)	Optic (Close Range)	90
	Stubby Grip	Underbarrel	100
	LS06 Suppressor	Barrel	110
	JGM-4 (4X)	Optic (Medium Range)	120
	Canted ironsights	Accessory	130
	Heavy Barrel	Barrel	140

P90

IRONSIGHTS

Ammo: 5.7x28mm
Rate of Fire: 900 rpm
Magazine Capacity: 50
Unlock: Campaign Unlock

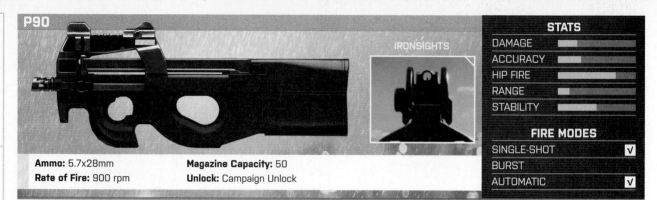

STATS

DAMAGE
ACCURACY
HIP FIRE
RANGE
STABILITY

FIRE MODES

SINGLE-SHOT	V
BURST	
AUTOMATIC	V

Developed in Belgium as a PDW for vehicle crews, Special Forces, and Counter-Terrorist groups, the P90 is a compact and capable weapon system. The three forward rails allow an operator to mount a wide variety accessories and the 5.7x28mm armor piercing ammunition is fired at nearly rifle velocity. Standard with a 50-round magazine, the P90 is capable as an offensive CQB weapon for highly mobile personnel.

UNLOCK PROGRESSION

IMAGE	ATTACHMENT	SLOT	KILLS
	Reflex (RDS)	Optic (Close Range)	10
	Laser Sight	Accessory	20
	Ergo Grip	Underbarrel	30
	Compensator	Barrel	40
	M145 (3.4X)	Optic (Medium Range)	50
	Flashlight	Accessory	60
	Angled Grip	Underbarrel	70
	Muzzle Brake	Barrel	80
	HOLO (1X)	Optic (Close Range)	90
	Stubby Grip	Underbarrel	100
	Suppressor	Barrel	110
	ACOG (4X)	Optic (Medium Range)	120
	Canted ironsights	Accessory	130
	Heavy Barrel	Barrel	140

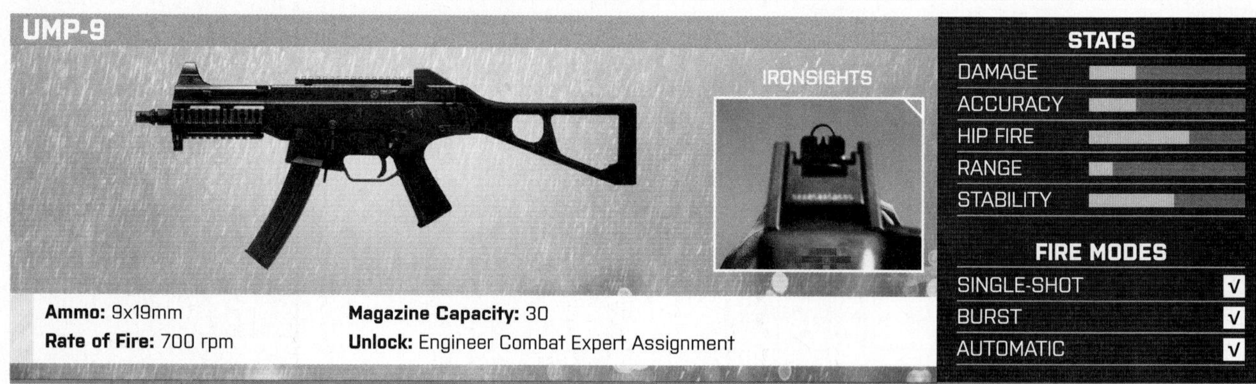

UMP-9

IRONSIGHTS

Ammo: 9x19mm
Rate of Fire: 700 rpm
Magazine Capacity: 30
Unlock: Engineer Combat Expert Assignment

STATS

DAMAGE
ACCURACY
HIP FIRE
RANGE
STABILITY

FIRE MODES

SINGLE-SHOT	V
BURST	V
AUTOMATIC	V

The UMP-9 utilizes the same frame and overall construction as the UMP-45, but is chambered for the smaller 9x19mm cartridge. As a result, the UMP-9 has a larger magazine capability and reduced recoil. However, the 9mm round has less stopping power than .45 ACP round, requiring more hits to produce lethal results. But this is somewhat offset by the weapon's higher rate of fire.

UNLOCK PROGRESSION

IMAGE	ATTACHMENT	SLOT	KILLS
	Reflex (RDS)	Optic (Close Range)	10
	Laser Sight	Accessory	20
	Ergo Grip	Underbarrel	30
	Compensator	Barrel	40
	M145 (3.4X)	Optic (Medium Range)	50
	Flashlight	Accessory	60
	Angled Grip	Underbarrel	70
	Muzzle Brake	Barrel	80
	HOLO (1X)	Optic (Close Range)	90
	Stubby Grip	Underbarrel	100
	Suppressor	Barrel	110
	ACOG (4X)	Optic (Medium Range)	120
	Canted ironsights	Accessory	130
	Heavy Barrel	Barrel	140

LIGHT MACHINE GUNS (LMGS)

When it comes to laying down high volumes of fire, few weapons are as effective as the light machine guns. Thanks to their large magazine capacities and high rates of fire, these hulking weapons can fire long bursts of automatic fire, sending your opponents diving for cover. This is the support kit's primary weapon, ideal for suppressing opponents. Continue playing as the support class to unlock new light machine guns. All light machine guns come equipped with a Bipod for greater stability while firing automatic bursts.

LMG UNLOCK PROGRESSION

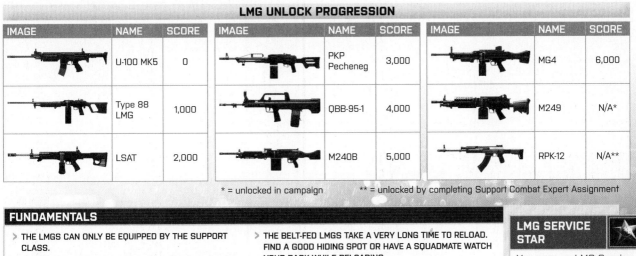

IMAGE	NAME	SCORE
	U-100 MK5	0
	Type 88 LMG	1,000
	LSAT	2,000

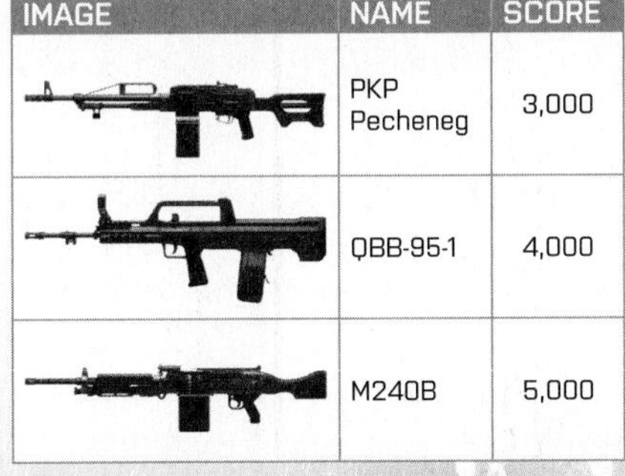

IMAGE	NAME	SCORE
	PKP Pecheneg	3,000
	QBB-95-1	4,000
	M240B	5,000

IMAGE	NAME	SCORE
	MG4	6,000
	M249	N/A*
	RPK-12	N/A**

* = unlocked in campaign ** = unlocked by completing Support Combat Expert Assignment

FUNDAMENTALS

- THE LMGS CAN ONLY BE EQUIPPED BY THE SUPPORT CLASS.
- ALTHOUGH CAPABLE OF HIGH RATES OF SUSTAINED FIRE, LMGS DEAL THE MOST DAMAGE WITHIN 50 METERS.
- WHENEVER POSSIBLE, DEPLOY THE LMG'S BIPOD FOR GREATER ACCURACY AND STABILITY.
- THE BELT-FED LMGS TAKE A VERY LONG TIME TO RELOAD. FIND A GOOD HIDING SPOT OR HAVE A SQUADMATE WATCH YOUR BACK WHILE RELOADING.
- DUE TO THEIR CUMBERSOME SIZE, YOU CAN'T PEEK AROUND COVER WHILE CARRYING AN LMG.

LMG SERVICE STAR

You earn an LMG Service Star for every 100 kills you score with each light machine gun.

U-100 MK5

STATS

- DAMAGE
- ACCURACY
- HIP FIRE
- RANGE
- STABILITY

FIRE MODES

SINGLE-SHOT	✓
BURST	✓
AUTOMATIC	✓

Ammo: 5.56x45mm NATO
Rate of Fire: 590 rpm
Magazine Capacity: 45
Unlock: Default LMG

The MK5 is the latest variant of the U-100 line of light machine guns. Produced in Singapore and deployed by armed forces throughout the world, this variant is equipped with attachment rails and a 45-round box magazine. As the first LMG available, it comes equipped with a Bipod, HD-33 (1X) optic, a Magnifier (2X), and Muzzle Brake.

UNLOCK PROGRESSION

IMAGE	ATTACHMENT	SLOT	KILLS
	Bipod (Default)	Underbarrel	0
	HD-33 (1X)	Optic (Close Range)	0
	Magnifier (2X)	Accessory	0
	Muzzle Brake	Barrel	0
	Stubby Grip	Underbarrel	10
	PRISMA (3.4X)	Optic (Medium Range)	20
	Laser Sight	Accessory	30
	Compensator	Barrel	40
	Coyote (RDS)	Optic (Close Range)	50
	Flashlight	Accessory	60
	Ergo Grip	Underbarrel	70
	LS06 Suppressor	Barrel	80
	JGM-4 (4X)	Optic (Medium Range)	90
	Angled Grip	Underbarrel	100
	Heavy Barrel	Barrel	110

TYPE 88 LMG

Ammo: 5.8x42mm
Rate of Fire: 700 rpm
Magazine Capacity: 100
Unlock: 1,000 LMG Score

STATS

DAMAGE
ACCURACY
HIP FIRE
RANGE
STABILITY

FIRE MODES

SINGLE-SHOT
BURST
AUTOMATIC ✓

The Chinese belt-fed Type 88 LMG has only recently entered wide service with the People's Liberation Army. The Type 88 LMG fires a special heavy DAP-87 version of the Chinese 5.8x42mm round and is equipped by default with a Bipod for supported shooting.

UNLOCK PROGRESSION

IMAGE	ATTACHMENT	SLOT	KILLS
	Bipod (Default)	Underbarrel	0
	HD-33 (1X)	Optic (Close Range)	10
	Magnifier (2X)	Accessory	20
	Muzzle Brake	Barrel	30
	Stubby Grip	Underbarrel	40
	PRISMA (3.4X)	Optic (Medium Range)	50
	Laser Sight	Accessory	60
	Compensator	Barrel	70
	Coyote (RDS)	Optic (Close Range)	80
	Flashlight	Accessory	90
	Ergo Grip	Underbarrel	100
	LS06 Suppressor	Barrel	110
	JGM-4 (4X)	Optic (Medium Range)	120
	Angled Grip	Underbarrel	130
	Heavy Barrel	Barrel	140

LSAT

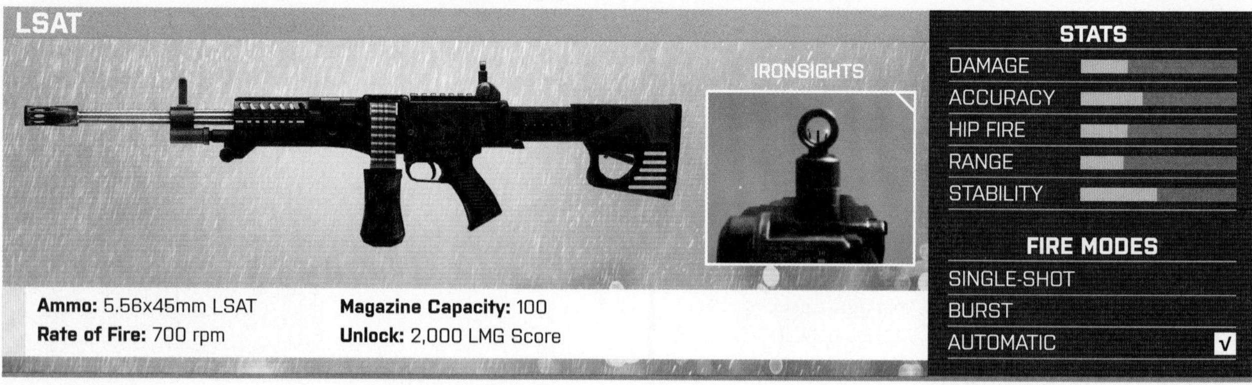

Ammo: 5.56x45mm LSAT
Rate of Fire: 700 rpm
Magazine Capacity: 100
Unlock: 2,000 LMG Score

STATS

DAMAGE
ACCURACY
HIP FIRE
RANGE
STABILITY

FIRE MODES

SINGLE-SHOT
BURST
AUTOMATIC ✓

This US JSSAP prototype is intended to significantly reduce the weight associated with small arms and their ammunition. Using a High Ignition Temperature Propellant, this prototype light machine gun features belt-fed caseless ammunition. Should the program be successful, this weapon system could become a great improvement over the heavier and more cumbersome squad automatic weapons currently in use.

UNLOCK PROGRESSION

IMAGE	ATTACHMENT	SLOT	KILLS
	Bipod (Default)	Underbarrel	0
	HOLO (1X)	Optic (Close Range)	10
	Magnifier (2X)	Accessory	20
	Muzzle Brake	Barrel	30
	Stubby Grip	Underbarrel	40
	M145 (3.4X)	Optic (Medium Range)	50
	Laser Sight	Accessory	60
	Compensator	Barrel	70
	Reflex (RDS)	Optic (Close Range)	80
	Flashlight	Accessory	90
	Ergo Grip	Underbarrel	100
	Suppressor	Barrel	110
	ACOG (4X)	Optic (Medium Range)	120
	Angled Grip	Underbarrel	130
	Heavy Barrel	Barrel	140

PKP PECHENEG

Ammo: 7.62x54mm R
Rate of Fire: 600 rpm
Magazine Capacity: 100
Unlock: 3,000 LMG Score

STATS	
DAMAGE	
ACCURACY	
HIP FIRE	
RANGE	
STABILITY	

FIRE MODES	
SINGLE-SHOT	
BURST	
AUTOMATIC	✓

Another modernization of a traditional Russian weapon, the PKP Pecheneg replaces the PKM machine gun in service with Spetsnaz units. Firing a heavier round than the RPK-74M, the Pecheneg is able to supply greater suppressive fire thanks to its increased power and belt feed. The Pecheneg comes equipped by default with a Bipod for supported shooting.

UNLOCK PROGRESSION

IMAGE	ATTACHMENT	SLOT	KILLS
	Bipod (Default)	Underbarrel	0
	PKA-S (1X)	Optic (Close Range)	10
	Magnifier (2X)	Accessory	20
	Muzzle Brake	Barrel	30
	Stubby Grip	Underbarrel	40
	PK-A (3.4X)	Optic (Medium Range)	50
	Laser Sight	Accessory	60
	Compensator	Barrel	70
	KOBRA (RDS)	Optic (Close Range)	80
	Flashlight	Accessory	90
	Ergo Grip	Underbarrel	100
	PBS-4 Suppressor	Barrel	110
	PSO-1 (4X)	Optic (Medium Range)	120
	Angled Grip	Underbarrel	130
	Heavy Barrel	Barrel	140

QBB-95-1

Ammo: 5.8x42mm DAP-87
Rate of Fire: 650 rpm
Magazine Capacity: 75
Unlock: 4,000 LMG Score

STATS	
DAMAGE	
ACCURACY	
HIP FIRE	
RANGE	
STABILITY	

FIRE MODES	
SINGLE-SHOT	✓
BURST	
AUTOMATIC	✓

The Chinese QBB-95-1 is the most recent variant deployed as a squad automatic weapon for the People's Liberation Army. Along with new ergonomic features on the exterior, the LMG's barrel and firing mechanics have been upgraded to accommodate the heavier DAP-87 round. This variant is also equipped with a 75-round drum magazine and a Bipod for supported shooting.

UNLOCK PROGRESSION

IMAGE	ATTACHMENT	SLOT	KILLS
	Bipod (Default)	Underbarrel	0
	HD-33 (1X)	Optic (Close Range)	10
	Magnifier (2X)	Accessory	20
	Muzzle Brake	Barrel	30
	Stubby Grip	Underbarrel	40
	PRISMA (3.4X)	Optic (Medium Range)	50
	Laser Sight	Accessory	60
	Compensator	Barrel	70
	Coyote (RDS)	Optic (Close Range)	80
	Flashlight	Accessory	90
	Ergo Grip	Underbarrel	100
	LS06 Suppressor	Barrel	110
	JGM-4 (4X)	Optic (Medium Range)	120
	Angled Grip	Underbarrel	130
	Heavy Barrel	Barrel	140

M240B

Ammo: 7.62x51mm NATO
Rate of Fire: 650 rpm
Magazine Capacity: 100
Unlock: 5,000 LMG Score

The M240B was first developed in Belgium and adopted by the USMC in 1991. The M60 was replaced first by the M240G, and subsequently by the M240B, which provides commonality between the Marines and the US Army. Firing the heavier 7.62mm NATO round, the M240B has greater power than the M249 and is equipped with a Bipod for supported shooting.

UNLOCK PROGRESSION

IMAGE	ATTACHMENT	SLOT	KILLS
	Bipod (Default)	Underbarrel	0
	HOLO (1X)	Optic (Close Range)	10
	Magnifier (2X)	Accessory	20
	Muzzle Brake	Barrel	30
	Stubby Grip	Underbarrel	40
	M145 (3.4X)	Optic (Medium Range)	50
	Laser Sight	Accessory	60
	Compensator	Barrel	70
	Reflex (RDS)	Optic (Close Range)	80
	Flashlight	Accessory	90
	Ergo Grip	Underbarrel	100
	Suppressor	Barrel	110
	ACOG (4X)	Optic (Medium Range)	120
	Angled Grip	Underbarrel	130
	Heavy Barrel	Barrel	140

MG4

Ammo: 5.56x45mm NATO
Rate of Fire: 800 rpm
Magazine Capacity: 100
Unlock: 6,000 LMG Score

Selected by the German Bundeswehr as the replacement for the 7.62mm MG3, the aptly named MG4 is a belt-fed general purpose machine gun chambered in the smaller 5.56mm NATO round. This makes the weapon lighter and relatively easy to operate, putting it on par with M249. By default, the MG4 is equipped with a Bipod for supported shooting.

UNLOCK PROGRESSION

IMAGE	ATTACHMENT	SLOT	KILLS
	Bipod (Default)	Underbarrel	0
	HOLO (1X)	Optic (Close Range)	10
	Magnifier (2X)	Accessory	20
	Muzzle Brake	Barrel	30
	Stubby Grip	Underbarrel	40
	M145 (3.4X)	Optic (Medium Range)	50
	Laser Sight	Accessory	60
	Compensator	Barrel	70
	Reflex (RDS)	Optic (Close Range)	80
	Flashlight	Accessory	90
	Ergo Grip	Underbarrel	100
	Suppressor	Barrel	110
	ACOG (4X)	Optic (Medium Range)	120
	Angled Grip	Underbarrel	130
	Heavy Barrel	Barrel	140

M249

STATS

DAMAGE
ACCURACY
HIP FIRE
RANGE
STABILITY

FIRE MODES

SINGLE-SHOT	
BURST	
AUTOMATIC	✓

Ammo: 5.56x45mm NATO
Rate of Fire: 800 rpm
Magazine Capacity: 200
Unlock: Campaign Unlock

Adapted from the Belgian, the M249 was modified to conform to the United States design requirements. The M249 has seen action in every major conflict since the 1989 invasion of Panama and has earned a reputation as a reliable weapon. A single M249 can supply suppressive fire equivalent to 15 riflemen. The M249 comes equipped with a Bipod for supported shooting.

UNLOCK PROGRESSION

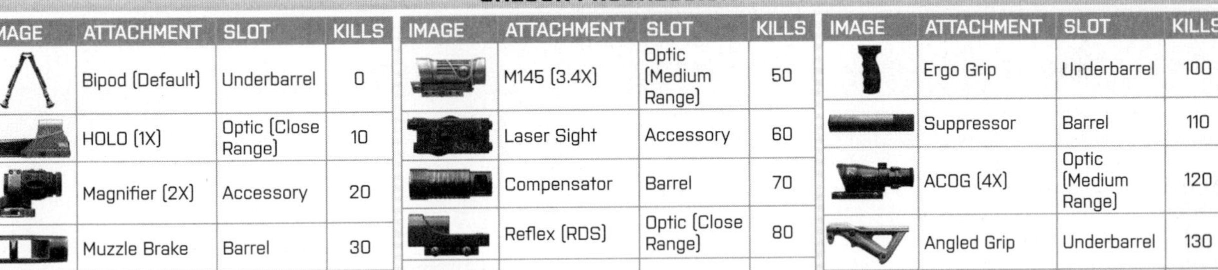

IMAGE	ATTACHMENT	SLOT	KILLS
	Bipod (Default)	Underbarrel	0
	HOLO (1X)	Optic (Close Range)	10
	Magnifier (2X)	Accessory	20
	Muzzle Brake	Barrel	30
	Stubby Grip	Underbarrel	40
	M145 (3.4X)	Optic (Medium Range)	50
	Laser Sight	Accessory	60
	Compensator	Barrel	70
	Reflex (RDS)	Optic (Close Range)	80
	Flashlight	Accessory	90
	Ergo Grip	Underbarrel	100
	Suppressor	Barrel	110
	ACOG (4X)	Optic (Medium Range)	120
	Angled Grip	Underbarrel	130
	Heavy Barrel	Barrel	140

RPK-12

STATS

DAMAGE
ACCURACY
HIP FIRE
RANGE
STABILITY

FIRE MODES

SINGLE-SHOT	✓
BURST	
AUTOMATIC	✓

Ammo: 5.45x39mm WP
Rate of Fire: 600 rpm
Magazine Capacity: 60
Unlock: Support Combat Expert Assignment

A derivative of the RPK-74, the RPK-12's heritage dates back to the late 1950s. But there's nothing old fashioned about this weapon. Constructed from durable, lightweight composite materials, the RPK-12 is a magazine-fed LMG that functions much like an assault rifle. When holding a fixed position, deploy its Bipod for greater accuracy and stability.

UNLOCK PROGRESSION

IMAGE	ATTACHMENT	SLOT	KILLS
	Bipod (Default)	Underbarrel	0
	PKA-S (1X)	Optic (Close Range)	10
	Magnifier (2X)	Accessory	20
	Muzzle Brake	Barrel	30
	Stubby Grip	Underbarrel	40
	PK-A (3.4X)	Optic (Medium Range)	50
	Laser Sight	Accessory	60
	Compensator	Barrel	70
	KOBRA (RDS)	Optic (Close Range)	80
	Flashlight	Accessory	90
	Ergo Grip	Underbarrel	100
	PBS-4 Suppressor	Barrel	110
	PSO-1 (4X)	Optic (Medium Range)	120
	Angled Grip	Underbarrel	130
	Heavy Barrel	Barrel	140

SNIPER RIFLES

If you prefer engaging enemies at extreme distances, the sniper rifles are the choice for you. These are the most powerful and accurate weapons available, but they also require the most skill and patience to master, given their slow rate of fire and lengthy reload speeds. Sniper rifles are only available to the recon kit.

SNIPER RIFLE UNLOCK PROGRESSION

IMAGE	NAME	SCORE	IMAGE	NAME	SCORE	IMAGE	NAME	SCORE
	CS-LR4	0		SV-98	3,000		M98B	6,000
	M40A5	1,000		JNG-90	4,000		SRR-61	7,000
	Scout Elite	2,000		338-Recon	5,000		FY-JS	N/A*

* = unlocked by completing Recon Combat Expert Assignment

FUNDAMENTALS

- SNIPER RIFLES REMAIN THE DOMAIN OF THE RECON CLASS, CAPABLE OF 2-SHOT KILLS TO THE BODY OR ONE-SHOT KILLS TO THE HEAD.
- THESE RIFLES HAVE THE LONGEST EFFECTIVE RANGE, DISHING OUT OPTIMAL DAMAGE WELL BEYOND 100 METERS.
- DUE TO THEIR CUMBERSOME SIZE, YOU CAN'T PEEK AROUND CORNERS WHILE HOLDING A SNIPER RIFLE.
- EQUIP THE STRAIGHT PULL AUXILIARY ATTACHMENT TO MAINTAIN LINE OF SIGHT WITH YOUR TARGET WHILE OPERATING THE WEAPON'S BOLT.
- THE RANGE FINDER TAKES ALL GUESSWORK OUT OF ZEROING YOUR SCOPE. ATTACH IT AS SOON AS IT'S AVAILABLE.

SNIPER RIFLE SERVICE STAR

You earn a Sniper Rifle Service Star for every 100 kills you score with each sniper rifle.

CS_LR4

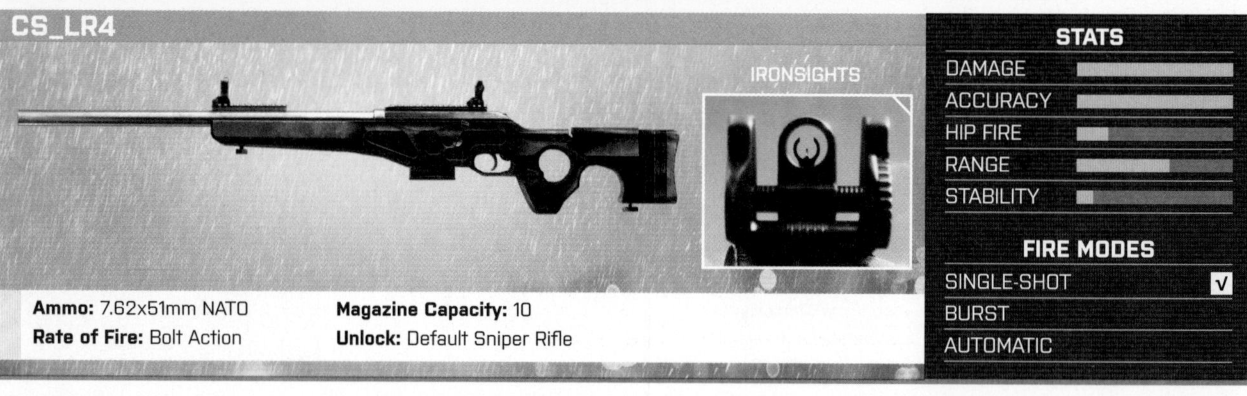

Ammo: 7.62x51mm NATO
Rate of Fire: Bolt Action
Magazine Capacity: 10
Unlock: Default Sniper Rifle

STATS	
DAMAGE	
ACCURACY	
HIP FIRE	
RANGE	
STABILITY	

FIRE MODES	
SINGLE-SHOT	✓
BURST	
AUTOMATIC	

This highly ergonomic Chinese bolt action sniper rifle features a composite thumb-hole stock with an adjustable cheek piece. As the first sniper rifle available, the weapon comes equipped with the CL6X (6X) optic, the Variable Zoom (14X), and a Bipod. These attachments should help any shooter get acquainted with the fundamentals of sniping and scope zeroing. Another all around weapon, as the starting weapon it's easy to master with a good muzzle velocity and a medium bolt action speed.

UNLOCK PROGRESSION

IMAGE	ATTACHMENT	SLOT	KILLS
	CL6X (6X)	Optic (Long Range)	0
	Variable Zoom (14X)	Accessory	0
	Bipod	Auxiliary	0
	JGM-4 (4X)	Optic (Medium Range)	10
	Canted ironsights	Accessory	20
	Straight Pull	Auxiliary	30
	Coyote (RDS)	Optic (Close Range)	40
	Laser Sight	Accessory	50
	LS06 Suppressor	Barrel	60
	PRISMA (3.4X)	Optic (Medium Range)	70
	Flashlight	Accessory	80
	Muzzle Brake	Barrel	90
	HD-33 (1X)	Optic (Close Range)	100
	Ballistic (40X)	Optic (Long Range)	110
	Range Finder	Accessory	120

M40A5

IRONSIGHTS

STATS

DAMAGE
ACCURACY
HIP FIRE
RANGE
STABILITY

FIRE MODES

SINGLE-SHOT ✓
BURST
AUTOMATIC

Ammo: 7.62x51mm NATO
Rate of Fire: Bolt Action
Magazine Capacity: 10
Unlock: 1,000 Sniper Rifle Score

Developed around the bolt-action of a proven American hunting rifle, the M40A5 has been upgraded with a lightened fiberglass stock, a detachable magazine, and the provisions for mounting various attachments. An incredibly accurate rifle, the M40A5 currently serves as the primary Sniper Rifle for the USMC. The M40A5 is by default equipped with a Rifle Scope (8x). This weapon is slightly faster to fire multiple rounds, with a quick bolt action. However, it has lower muzzle velocity making long range shots more difficult.

UNLOCK PROGRESSION

IMAGE	ATTACHMENT	SLOT	KILLS
	Rifle Scope (8X)	Optic (Long Range)	0
	Variable Zoom (14X)	Accessory	10
	Bipod	Auxiliary	20
	ACOG (4X)	Optic (Medium Range)	30
	Canted ironsights	Accessory	40
	Straight Pull	Auxiliary	50
	Reflex (RDS)	Optic (Close Range)	60
	Laser Sight	Accessory	70
	Suppressor	Barrel	80
	M145 (3.4X)	Optic (Medium Range)	90
	Flashlight	Accessory	100
	Muzzle Brake	Barrel	110
	HOLO (1X)	Optic (Close Range)	120
	Ballistic (40X)	Optic (Long Range)	130
	Range Finder	Accessory	140

SCOUT ELITE

Ammo: 5.56x45mm NATO
Rate of Fire: Bolt Action
Magazine Capacity: 10
Unlock: 2,000 Sniper Rifle Score

Developed in Austria, the Scout Elite has gained favor among SWAT and counter-terrorist teams throughout the world thanks to its accuracy and relative compact size. But a shorter barrel length and smaller cartridge translates into less stopping power and shorter effective range than its counterparts. By default the rifle comes equipped with a Rifle Scope (8X). The Scout Elite makes up for its small round count and low range by being the very fastest weapon rate of fire sniper rifle, with a high muzzle velocity and mobility.

UNLOCK PROGRESSION

IMAGE	ATTACHMENT	SLOT	KILLS
	Rifle Scope (8X)	Optic (Long Range)	0
	Variable Zoom (14X)	Accessory	10
	Bipod	Auxiliary	20
	ACOG (4X)	Optic (Medium Range)	30
	Canted ironsights	Accessory	40
	Straight Pull	Auxiliary	50
	Reflex (RDS)	Optic (Close Range)	60
	Laser Sight	Accessory	70
	Suppressor	Barrel	80
	M145 (3.4X)	Optic (Medium Range)	90
	Flashlight	Accessory	100
	Muzzle Brake	Barrel	110
	HOLO (1X)	Optic (Close Range)	120
	Ballistic (40X)	Optic (Long Range)	130
	Range Finder	Accessory	140

SV-98

Ammo: 7.62x54mm
Rate of Fire: Bolt Action
Magazine Capacity: 10
Unlock: 3,000 Sniper Rifle Score

STATS

DAMAGE
ACCURACY
HIP FIRE
RANGE
STABILITY

FIRE MODES

SINGLE-SHOT	√
BURST	
AUTOMATIC	

Similar to its Western counterparts, the SV-98 began life as a proven bolt-action sporting rifle. The SV-98 is equipped with a 10-round detachable box magazine, several attachment points, and backup ironsights. The SV-98 is standardly equipped with a PKS-07 (7x) for very long-range shooting. A good all around weapon, the SV98 has good muzzle velocity and a medium speed bolt action.

UNLOCK PROGRESSION

IMAGE	ATTACHMENT	SLOT	KILLS
	PKS-07 (7X)	Optic (Long Range)	0
	Variable Zoom (14X)	Accessory	10
	Bipod	Auxiliary	20
	PSO-1 (4X)	Optic (Medium Range)	30
	Canted ironsights	Accessory	40
	Straight Pull	Auxiliary	50
	KOBRA (RDS)	Optic (Close Range)	60
	Laser Sight	Accessory	70
	PBS-4 Suppressor	Barrel	80
	PK-A (3.4X)	Optic (Medium Range)	90
	Flashlight	Accessory	100
	Muzzle Brake	Barrel	110
	PKA-S (1X)	Optic (Close Range)	120
	Ballistic (40X)	Optic (Long Range)	130
	Range Finder	Accessory	140

JNG-90

Ammo: 7.62x51mm NATO
Rate of Fire: Bolt Action
Magazine Capacity: 10
Unlock: 4,000 Sniper Rifle Score

STATS

DAMAGE
ACCURACY
HIP FIRE
RANGE
STABILITY

FIRE MODES

SINGLE-SHOT	√
BURST	
AUTOMATIC	

Easily identified by its massive muzzle brake, the JNG-90 serves as the standard sniper rifle of the Turkish army. This modern rifle has integral rail systems and many other accessory options, making it adaptable to shifting situations. It provides the shooter great stopping power, as well as sub minute of angle accuracy. This weapon has the best bullet speed of all the 7.62mm rifles, but it has the slowest bolt action speed of the group as well.

UNLOCK PROGRESSION

IMAGE	ATTACHMENT	SLOT	KILLS
	PKS-07 (7X)	Optic (Long Range)	0
	Variable Zoom (14X)	Accessory	10
	Bipod	Auxiliary	20
	PSO-1 (4X)	Optic (Medium Range)	30
	Canted ironsights	Accessory	40
	Straight Pull	Auxiliary	50
	KOBRA (RDS)	Optic (Close Range)	60
	Laser Sight	Accessory	70
	PBS-4 Suppressor	Barrel	80
	PK-A (3.4X)	Optic (Medium Range)	90
	Flashlight	Accessory	100
	Muzzle Brake	Barrel	110
	PKA-S (1X)	Optic (Close Range)	120
	Ballistic (40X)	Optic (Long Range)	130
	Range Finder	Accessory	140

338-RECON

Ammo: .338 Magnum
Rate of Fire: Bolt Action
Magazine Capacity: 5
Unlock: 5,000 Sniper Rifle Score

Firing the high-velocity .338 Magnum round, the 338-Recon delivers devastating stopping power with pinpoint accuracy. While its bullpup design is unusual for a sniper rifle, its precision and relative compact size have made the 338-Recon a favorite among US SOCOM units. The rifle comes equipped with a Rifle Scope (8X). When compared to the M98B this weapon is more mobile, and has a faster bolt action than the M98B, but a lower muzzle velocity.

UNLOCK PROGRESSION

IMAGE	ATTACHMENT	SLOT	KILLS
	Rifle Scope (8X)	Optic (Long Range)	0
	Variable Zoom (14X)	Accessory	10
	Bipod	Auxiliary	20
	ACOG (4X)	Optic (Medium Range)	30
	Canted ironsights	Accessory	40
	Straight Pull	Auxiliary	50
	Reflex (RDS)	Optic (Close Range)	60
	Laser Sight	Accessory	70
	Suppressor	Barrel	80
	M145 (3.4X)	Optic (Medium Range)	90
	Flashlight	Accessory	100
	Muzzle Brake	Barrel	110
	HOLO (1X)	Optic (Close Range)	120
	Ballistic (40X)	Optic (Long Range)	130
	Range Finder	Accessory	140

M98B

Ammo: .338 Magnum
Rate of Fire: Bolt Action
Magazine Capacity: 10
Unlock: 6,000 Sniper Rifle Score

A precision tactical rifle, the M98B was uniquely developed from the ground up as a bolt-action sniper rifle. Firing the .338 Magnum round from a detachable box magazine, the M98B is capable of impressive accuracy and great stopping power even at extreme ranges. The M98B is currently being evaluated by US SOCOM in a modified form. The M98B comes equipped with a Rifle Scope (8x). A great long range rifle due to the high damage of the round, but the bolt action is the slowest of all rifles.

UNLOCK PROGRESSION

IMAGE	ATTACHMENT	SLOT	KILLS
	Rifle Scope (8X)	Optic (Long Range)	0
	Variable Zoom (14X)	Accessory	10
	Bipod	Auxiliary	20
	ACOG (4X)	Optic (Medium Range)	30
	Canted ironsights	Accessory	40
	Straight Pull	Auxiliary	50
	Reflex (RDS)	Optic (Close Range)	60
	Laser Sight	Accessory	70
	Suppressor	Barrel	80
	M145 (3.4X)	Optic (Medium Range)	90
	Flashlight	Accessory	100
	Muzzle Brake	Barrel	110
	HOLO (1X)	Optic (Close Range)	120
	Ballistic (40X)	Optic (Long Range)	130
	Range Finder	Accessory	140

SRR-61

Ammo: .408 CT
Rate of Fire: Bolt Action
Magazine Capacity: 7
Unlock: 7,000 Sniper Rifle Score

STATS

DAMAGE
ACCURACY
HIP FIRE
RANGE
STABILITY

FIRE MODES

SINGLE-SHOT	√
BURST	
AUTOMATIC	

Firing the specialized .408 CT round, the SRR-61 is capable of lethal precision well beyond 1,000 meters. By default the rifle comes equipped with a Rifle Scope (8x). But SRR-61 doesn't realize its full potential until equipped with Ballistic (40X) scope and a Range Finder, allowing it to take down threats at extreme ranges. Very similar to the M98B, but with a higher velocity bullet this is the best long range rifle. It has a similar slow bolt action and a lower magazine size than the M98B.

UNLOCK PROGRESSION

IMAGE	ATTACHMENT	SLOT	KILLS
	Rifle Scope (8X)	Optic (Long Range)	0
	Variable Zoom (14X)	Accessory	10
	Bipod	Auxiliary	20
	ACOG (4X)	Optic (Medium Range)	30
	Canted ironsights	Accessory	40
	Straight Pull	Auxiliary	50
	Reflex (RDS)	Optic (Close Range)	60
	Laser Sight	Accessory	70
	Suppressor	Barrel	80
	M145 (3.4X)	Optic (Medium Range)	90
	Flashlight	Accessory	100
	Muzzle Brake	Barrel	110
	HOLO (1X)	Optic (Close Range)	120
	Ballistic (40X)	Optic (Long Range)	130
	Range Finder	Accessory	140

FY-JS

Ammo: 5.8x42mm DBP-10
Rate of Fire: Bolt Action
Magazine Capacity: 10
Unlock: Recon Combat Expert Assignment

STATS

DAMAGE
ACCURACY
HIP FIRE
RANGE
STABILITY

FIRE MODES

SINGLE-SHOT	√
BURST	
AUTOMATIC	

The Chinese FY-JS shares much in common with the Scout Elite, offering great accuracy but less stopping power and a reduced effective range than many of the other sniper rifles. This makes it most effective when sniping within relatively confined locations. The included CL6X (6X) scope is decent, but consider going with the JGM-4 (4X) scope when operating in urban environments. This weapon is very fast to chamber rounds, but the smaller bullets it fires does less damage at long range. It is are also very mobile, being better to shoot from the hip, and faster to be accurate when zoomed.

UNLOCK PROGRESSION

IMAGE	ATTACHMENT	SLOT	KILLS
	CL6X (6X)	Optic (Long Range)	0
	Variable Zoom (14X)	Accessory	10
	Bipod	Auxiliary	20
	JGM-4 (4X)	Optic (Medium Range)	30
	Canted ironsights	Accessory	40
	Straight Pull	Auxiliary	50
	Coyote (RDS)	Optic (Close Range)	60
	Laser Sight	Accessory	70
	LS06 Suppressor	Barrel	80
	PRISMA (3.4X)	Optic (Medium Range)	90
	Flashlight	Accessory	100
	Muzzle Brake	Barrel	110
	HD-33 (1X)	Optic (Close Range)	120
	Ballistic (40X)	Optic (Long Range)	130
	Range Finder	Accessory	140

CARBINES

Carbines bridge the gap between assault rifles and PDWs, ideal for a variety of combat situations. Their compact design makes them easy to maneuver in tight quarters. The shorter barrel length means less muzzle velocity, accuracy, and range than their assault rifle counterparts. But they still have the stopping power to take down opponents quickly. The best part—carbines are now available to all classes, allowing for greater versatility among the kits.

CARBINE UNLOCK PROGRESSION

IMAGE	NAME	SCORE
	AK5-C	0*
	ACW-R	1,000
	SG553	2,000
	AKU-12	3,000
	A-91	4,000
	ACE 52 CQB	5,000
	G36C	6,000
	M4A1	7,000
	ACE 21 CQB	8,000
	Type-95B-1	9,000

* = engineer class unlock

FUNDAMENTALS

- THE CARBINES ARE AVAILABLE TO ALL CLASSES AND BEST DEPLOYED AT CLOSE-TO-INTERMEDIATE RANGES; SMALL ENOUGH TO PEEK AROUND CORNERS.
- ALTHOUGH SIMILAR, CARBINES HAVE LESS STOPPING POWER THAN ASSAULT RIFLES, ESPECIALLY BEYOND 50 METERS.
- THE 1X OPTICS ARE MORE THAN SUFFICIENT WHEN OPERATING A CARBINE, PARTICULARLY WHEN EQUIPPED WITH THE MAGNIFIER (2X) ACCESSORY.
- IF YOU NEED GREATER PRECISION OUT OF YOUR CARBINE, ATTACH A HEAVY BARREL. JUST BE READY TO COMPENSATE FOR THE HEAVIER RECOIL.
- THE RECON CLASS GAINS GREATER FLEXIBILITY WHEN EQUIPPING A CARBINE. ATTACH A SUPPRESSOR FOR A STEALTHY LOADOUT.

CARBINE SERVICE STAR

You earn a Carbine Service Star for every 100 kills you score with each carbine.

AK5-C

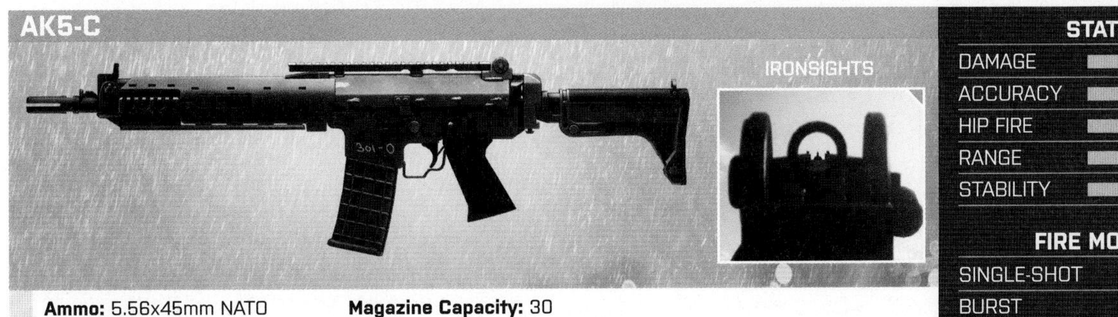

STATS

DAMAGE
ACCURACY
HIP FIRE
RANGE
STABILITY

FIRE MODES

SINGLE-SHOT	✓
BURST	
AUTOMATIC	✓

Ammo: 5.56x45mm NATO
Rate of Fire: 700 rpm
Magazine Capacity: 30
Unlock: 36,000 Engineer Score

The AK5-C is the carbine variant of the AK5 assault rifle deployed by Swedish Armed Forces. Along with a reduced barrel length and overall weight, the AK5-C also benefits from the addition of attachment rails, an adjustable buttstock, and several ergonomic features designed to enhance ease of use and weapon maneuverability in close quarters.

UNLOCK PROGRESSION

IMAGE	ATTACHMENT	SLOT	KILLS
	Reflex (RDS)	Optic (Close Range)	10
	Laser Sight	Accessory	20
	Ergo Grip	Underbarrel	30
	Muzzle Brake	Barrel	40
	HOLO (1X)	Optic (Medium Range)	50
	Magnifier (2X)	Accessory	60
	Stubby Grip	Underbarrel	70
	Suppressor	Barrel	80
	M145 (3.4X)	Optic (Medium Range)	90
	Canted Ironsights	Accessory	100
	Angled Grip	Underbarrel	110
	Heavy Barrel	Barrel	120
	ACOG (4X)	Optic (Medium Range)	130
	Flashlight	Accessory	140
	Bipod	Underbarrel	150
	Compensator	Barrel	160

ACW-R

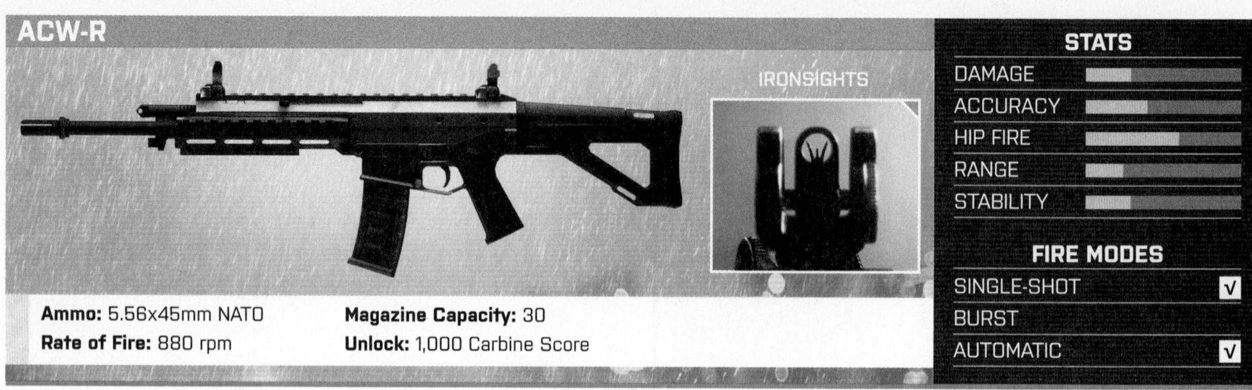

Ammo: 5.56x45mm NATO
Rate of Fire: 880 rpm
Magazine Capacity: 30
Unlock: 1,000 Carbine Score

This adaptive combat rifle features a number of recent rifle designs and acts as a lightweight, feature heavy, rifle platform. Built to endure rough weather conditions and capable of utilizing standard STANAG magazines, this rifle is equipped to fill many of the roles required by both military and law enforcement uses.

UNLOCK PROGRESSION

IMAGE	ATTACHMENT	SLOT	KILLS
	Reflex (RDS)	Optic (Close Range)	10
	Laser Sight	Accessory	20
	Ergo Grip	Underbarrel	30
	Muzzle Brake	Barrel	40
	HOLO (1X)	Optic (Medium Range)	50
	Magnifier (2X)	Accessory	60
	Stubby Grip	Underbarrel	70
	Suppressor	Barrel	80
	M145 (3.4X)	Optic (Medium Range)	90
	Canted Ironsights	Accessory	100
	Angled Grip	Underbarrel	110
	Heavy Barrel	Barrel	120
	ACOG (4X)	Optic (Medium Range)	130
	Flashlight	Accessory	140
	Bipod	Underbarrel	150
	Compensator	Barrel	160

SG553

Ammo: 5.56x45mm NATO
Rate of Fire: 830 rpm
Magazine Capacity: 30
Unlock: 2,000 Carbine Score

A carbine variant of the Swiss Army's standard SG550 rifle, the SG553 improves over its predecessor, the well-known SG552, by including integrated rails for mounting accessories. A carbine with excellent ergonomics, the SG553 is capable of automatic, three-round burst, and semi-automatic fire and is an excellent close-range weapon.

UNLOCK PROGRESSION

IMAGE	ATTACHMENT	SLOT	KILLS
	Reflex (RDS)	Optic (Close Range)	10
	Laser Sight	Accessory	20
	Ergo Grip	Underbarrel	30
	Muzzle Brake	Barrel	40
	HOLO (1X)	Optic (Medium Range)	50
	Magnifier (2X)	Accessory	60
	Stubby Grip	Underbarrel	70
	Suppressor	Barrel	80
	M145 (3.4X)	Optic (Medium Range)	90
	Canted Ironsights	Accessory	100
	Angled Grip	Underbarrel	110
	Heavy Barrel	Barrel	120
	ACOG (4X)	Optic (Medium Range)	130
	Flashlight	Accessory	140
	Bipod	Underbarrel	150
	Compensator	Barrel	160

AKU-12

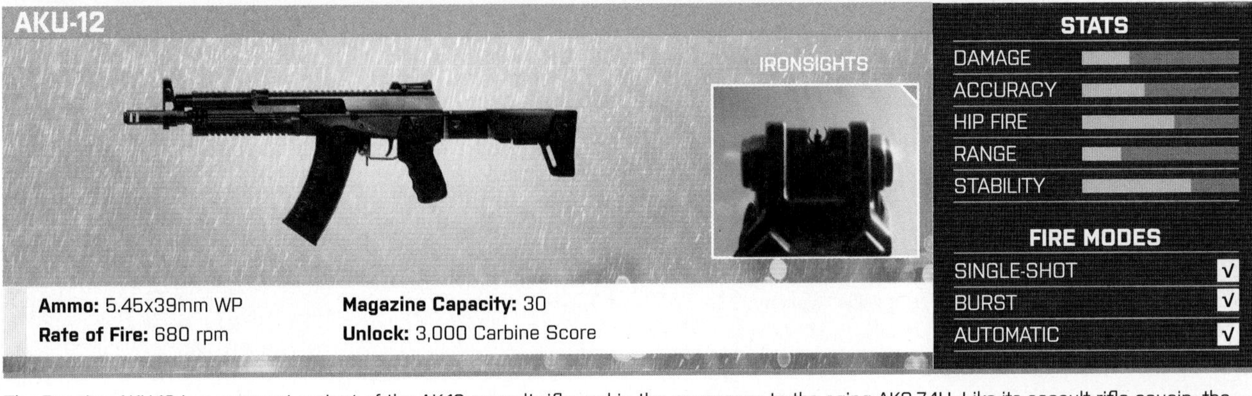

STATS

- DAMAGE
- ACCURACY
- HIP FIRE
- RANGE
- STABILITY

FIRE MODES

- SINGLE-SHOT ✓
- BURST ✓
- AUTOMATIC ✓

Ammo: 5.45x39mm WP
Rate of Fire: 680 rpm
Magazine Capacity: 30
Unlock: 3,000 Carbine Score

The Russian AKU-12 is a compact variant of the AK-12 assault rifle and is the successor to the aging AKS-74U. Like its assault rifle cousin, the AKU-12 benefits from lightweight composite construction and a host of improvements, including a folding buttstock, integrated rail systems, and dampened recoil.

UNLOCK PROGRESSION

IMAGE	ATTACHMENT	SLOT	KILLS
	KOBRA (RDS)	Optic (Close Range)	10
	Laser Sight	Accessory	20
	Ergo Grip	Underbarrel	30
	Muzzle Brake	Barrel	40
	PKA-S (1X)	Optic (Medium Range)	50
	Magnifier (2X)	Accessory	60
	Stubby Grip	Underbarrel	70
	PBS-4 Suppressor	Barrel	80
	PK-A (3.4X)	Optic (Medium Range)	90
	Canted Ironsights	Accessory	100
	Angled Grip	Underbarrel	110
	Heavy Barrel	Barrel	120
	PSO-1 (4X)	Optic (Medium Range)	130
	Flashlight	Accessory	140
	Bipod	Underbarrel	150
	Compensator	Barrel	160

A-91

STATS

- DAMAGE
- ACCURACY
- HIP FIRE
- RANGE
- STABILITY

FIRE MODES

- SINGLE-SHOT ✓
- BURST
- AUTOMATIC ✓

Ammo: 5.45x39mm WP
Rate of Fire: 800 rpm
Magazine Capacity: 30
Unlock: 4,000 Carbine Score

An unusual weapon, even by Russian standards, the A-91 is a bullpup carbine chambered in the 5.56mm WP round instead of a standard NATO caliber. Made from polymers, it features a forward shell ejection system that keeps shells well clear of the shooter's face upon ejection.

UNLOCK PROGRESSION

IMAGE	ATTACHMENT	SLOT	KILLS
	KOBRA (RDS)	Optic (Close Range)	10
	Laser Sight	Accessory	20
	Ergo Grip	Underbarrel	30
	Muzzle Brake	Barrel	40
	PKA-S (1X)	Optic (Medium Range)	50
	Magnifier (2X)	Accessory	60
	Stubby Grip	Underbarrel	70
	PBS-4 Suppressor	Barrel	80
	PK-A (3.4X)	Optic (Medium Range)	90
	Canted Ironsights	Accessory	100
	Angled Grip	Underbarrel	110
	Heavy Barrel	Barrel	120
	PSO-1 (4X)	Optic (Medium Range)	130
	Flashlight	Accessory	140
	Bipod	Underbarrel	150
	Compensator	Barrel	160

ACE 52 CQB

IRONSIGHTS

Ammo: 7.62x51mm NATO
Rate of Fire: 650 rpm
Magazine Capacity: 25
Unlock: 5,000 Carbine Score

STATS

DAMAGE
ACCURACY
HIP FIRE
RANGE
STABILITY

FIRE MODES

SINGLE-SHOT	√
BURST	
AUTOMATIC	√

Yet another firearm from the ACE family, the ACE 52 CQB is a shortened version, but fires the 7.62mm NATO round, giving the weapon plenty of stopping power. But the larger, heavier round translates into heavier recoil and a reduced magazine capacity. Attach an Angled Grip and Compensator to help bring the weapon under control.

UNLOCK PROGRESSION

IMAGE	ATTACHMENT	SLOT	KILLS
	Coyote (RDS)	Optic (Close Range)	10
	Laser Sight	Accessory	20
	Ergo Grip	Underbarrel	30
	Muzzle Brake	Barrel	40
	HD-33 (1X)	Optic (Medium Range)	50
	Magnifier (2X)	Accessory	60
	Stubby Grip	Underbarrel	70
	LS06 Suppressor	Barrel	80
	PRISMA (3.4X)	Optic (Medium Range)	90
	Canted Ironsights	Accessory	100
	Angled Grip	Underbarrel	110
	Heavy Barrel	Barrel	120
	JGM-4 (4X)	Optic (Medium Range)	130
	Flashlight	Accessory	140
	Bipod	Underbarrel	150
	Compensator	Barrel	160

G36C

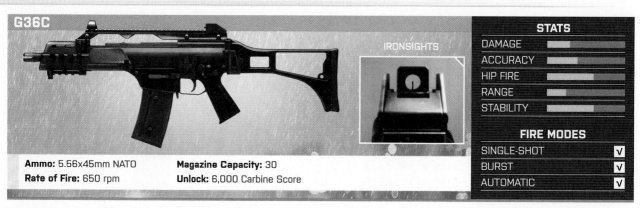

IRONSIGHTS

Ammo: 5.56x45mm NATO
Rate of Fire: 650 rpm
Magazine Capacity: 30
Unlock: 6,000 Carbine Score

STATS

DAMAGE
ACCURACY
HIP FIRE
RANGE
STABILITY

FIRE MODES

SINGLE-SHOT	√
BURST	√
AUTOMATIC	√

A compact version of the German Army's full-size G36 rifle, the G36C is equipped with a number of rails for accessories and a set of backup ironsights, instead of the integrated optics and carry handle of the G36. Its great ergonomics and short length make it excellent in short-range encounters. The G36C also includes a two-round burst mode.

UNLOCK PROGRESSION

IMAGE	ATTACHMENT	SLOT	KILLS
	Reflex (RDS)	Optic (Close Range)	10
	Laser Sight	Accessory	20
	Ergo Grip	Underbarrel	30
	Muzzle Brake	Barrel	40
	HOLO (1X)	Optic (Medium Range)	50
	Magnifier (2X)	Accessory	60
	Stubby Grip	Underbarrel	70
	Suppressor	Barrel	80
	M145 (3.4X)	Optic (Medium Range)	90
	Canted Ironsights	Accessory	100
	Angled Grip	Underbarrel	110
	Heavy Barrel	Barrel	120
	ACOG (4X)	Optic (Medium Range)	130
	Flashlight	Accessory	140
	Bipod	Underbarrel	150
	Compensator	Barrel	160

M4

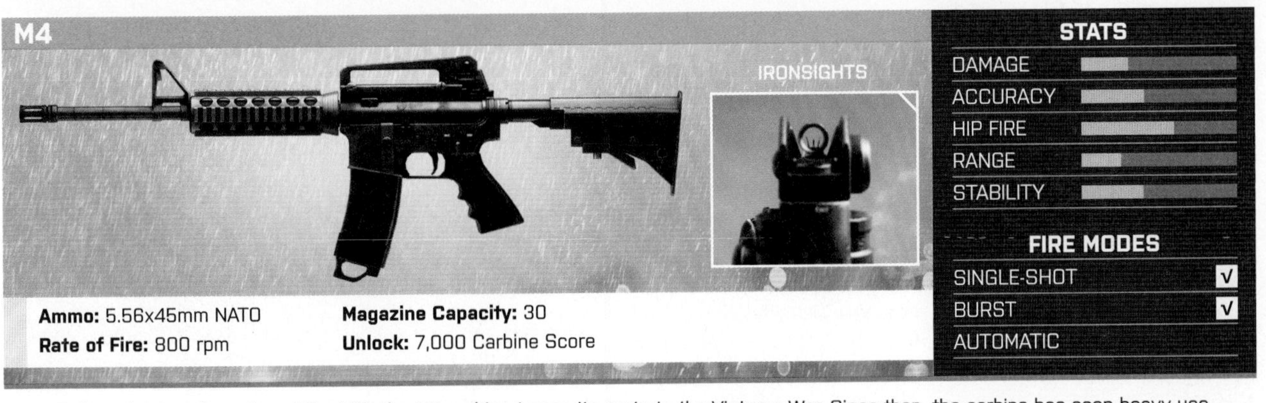

Ammo: 5.56x45mm NATO
Rate of Fire: 800 rpm
Magazine Capacity: 30
Unlock: 7,000 Carbine Score

Essentially a shortened version of the M16, the M4 carbine traces its roots to the Vietnam War. Since then, the carbine has seen heavy use at the frontlines of Iraq and Afghanistan in close quarters and urban environments. The M4 is only capable of semi-auto and burst fire. It also features a quad rail, useful for equipping a large number of accessories.

UNLOCK PROGRESSION

IMAGE	ATTACHMENT	SLOT	KILLS
	Reflex (RDS)	Optic (Close Range)	10
	Laser Sight	Accessory	20
	Ergo Grip	Underbarrel	30
	Muzzle Brake	Barrel	40
	HOLO (1X)	Optic (Medium Range)	50
	Magnifier (2X)	Accessory	60
	Stubby Grip	Underbarrel	70
	Suppressor	Barrel	80
	M145 (3.4X)	Optic (Medium Range)	90
	Canted Ironsights	Accessory	100
	Angled Grip	Underbarrel	110
	Heavy Barrel	Barrel	120
	ACOG (4X)	Optic (Medium Range)	130
	Flashlight	Accessory	140
	Bipod	Underbarrel	150
	Compensator	Barrel	160

ACE 21 CQB

Ammo: 5.56x45mm NATO
Rate of Fire: 770 rpm
Magazine Capacity: 35
Unlock: 8,000 Carbine Score

The ACE 21 is the smaller cousin to the ACE 52 CQB. Chambered in the smaller, lighter 5.56mm NATO round, the weapon offers greater stability due to reduced recoil, despite a higher rate of fire. But this comes at a cost of less stopping power, requiring more hits on-target to neutralize a threat.

UNLOCK PROGRESSION

IMAGE	ATTACHMENT	SLOT	KILLS
	Coyote (RDS)	Optic (Close Range)	10
	Laser Sight	Accessory	20
	Ergo Grip	Underbarrel	30
	Muzzle Brake	Barrel	40
	HD-33 (1X)	Optic (Medium Range)	50
	Magnifier (2X)	Accessory	60
	Stubby Grip	Underbarrel	70
	LS06 Suppressor	Barrel	80
	PRISMA (3.4X)	Optic (Medium Range)	90
	Canted Ironsights	Accessory	100
	Angled Grip	Underbarrel	110
	Heavy Barrel	Barrel	120
	JGM-4 (4X)	Optic (Medium Range)	130
	Flashlight	Accessory	140
	Bipod	Underbarrel	150
	Compensator	Barrel	160

TYPE-95B-1

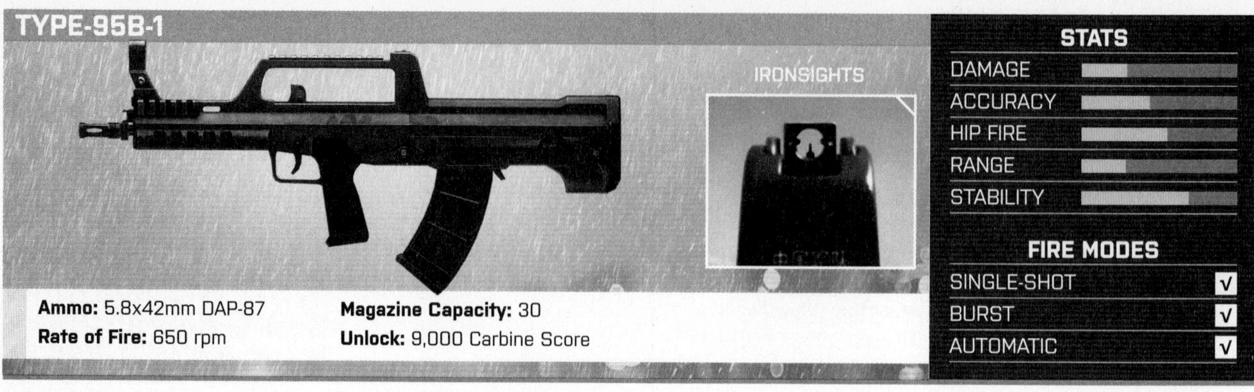

The Chinese Type-95B-1 is the carbine variant of the standard-issue QBZ-95 rifle deployed by the People's Liberation Army. Benefitting from a shortened barrel and bullpup configuration, this carbine is very effective in close-quarter environments, whether aiming down sights or firing from the hip. Improve its close-quarter performance by attaching a Laser Sight and Compensator.

UNLOCK PROGRESSION

IMAGE	ATTACHMENT	SLOT	KILLS
	Coyote (RDS)	Optic (Close Range)	10
	Laser Sight	Accessory	20
	Ergo Grip	Underbarrel	30
	Muzzle Brake	Barrel	40
	HD-33 (1X)	Optic (Medium Range)	50
	Magnifier (2X)	Accessory	60
	Stubby Grip	Underbarrel	70
	LS06 Suppressor	Barrel	80
	PRISMA (3.4X)	Optic (Medium Range)	90
	Canted Ironsights	Accessory	100
	Angled Grip	Underbarrel	110
	Heavy Barrel	Barrel	120
	JGM-4 (4X)	Optic (Medium Range)	130
	Flashlight	Accessory	140
	Bipod	Underbarrel	150
	Compensator	Barrel	160

DESIGNATED MARKSMAN RIFLES (DMRS)

The new DMRs, available to all classes, bridge the gap between assault rifles and sniper rifles, offering impressive stopping power while maintaining respectable rates of fire and reload times. These semi-automatic rifles are best deployed when engaging targets at intermediate to long ranges. Their size makes them somewhat cumbersome when operating in close quarters, so consider switching to a sidearm when entering structures and other confined spaces.

DMR UNLOCK PROGRESSION

IMAGE	NAME	SCORE
	RFB	0*
	MK11 MOD 0	1,000
	SKS	2,000
	SVD-12	3,000
	QBU-88	4,000
	M39 EMR	5,000
	ACE 53 SV	6,000
	SCAR-H SV	7,000

* = recon class unlock

FUNDAMENTALS

- THE DMRS ARE AVAILABLE TO ALL CLASSES, GIVING ALL SOLDIERS SOME SERIOUS FIREPOWER.
- DMRS INFLICT OPTIMAL DAMAGE WITHIN 70 METERS, BUT ARE ACCURATE WELL BEYOND 100 METERS.
- A 4X OPTIC SUPPLEMENTED BY CANTED IRONSIGHTS GIVES YOUR DMR THE ABILITY TO ENGAGE TARGETS AT ALL RANGES.
- DUE TO THEIR LENGTH, DMRS ARE A BIT TOO CUMBERSOME FOR CLOSE-QUARTER ENGAGEMENTS; YOU CAN'T PEEK AROUND CORNERS.
- ALTHOUGH SLOW FIRING, IT ONLY TAKES 2-3 HITS TO DROP AN OPPONENT WITH A DMR.

DMR SERVICE STAR

You earn a DMR Service Star for every 100 kills you score with each DMR.

RFB

STATS	
DAMAGE	
ACCURACY	
HIP FIRE	
RANGE	
STABILITY	

FIRE MODES	
SINGLE-SHOT	√
BURST	
AUTOMATIC	

Ammo: 7.62x51mm NATO
Rate of Fire: Semi-Auto
Magazine Capacity: 20
Unlock: 48,000 Recon Score

The Rifle Forward-Ejection Bullpup (RFB) is a modern, composite-constructed DMR. Given its impressive stopping power, the RFB is surprisingly maneuverable in confined spaces thanks to its bullpup configuration. But it also performs admirably at intermediate range, particularly when equipped with the ACOG (4X) or M145 (3.4X) optics.

UNLOCK PROGRESSION

IMAGE	ATTACHMENT	SLOT	KILLS
	ACOG (4X)	Optic (Medium Range)	10
	Canted Ironsights	Accessory	20
	Angled Grip	Underbarrel	30
	Heavy Barrel	Barrel	40
	Reflex (RDS)	Optic (Close Range)	50
	Laser Sight	Accessory	60
	Ergo Grip	Underbarrel	70
	Suppressor	Barrel	80
	HOLO (1X)	Optic (Medium Range)	90
	Magnifier (2X)	Accessory	100
	Stubby Grip	Underbarrel	110
	Muzzle Brake	Barrel	120
	M145 (3.4X)	Optic (Medium Range)	130
	Flashlight	Accessory	140
	Bipod	Underbarrel	150
	Compensator	Barrel	160

MK11 MOD 0

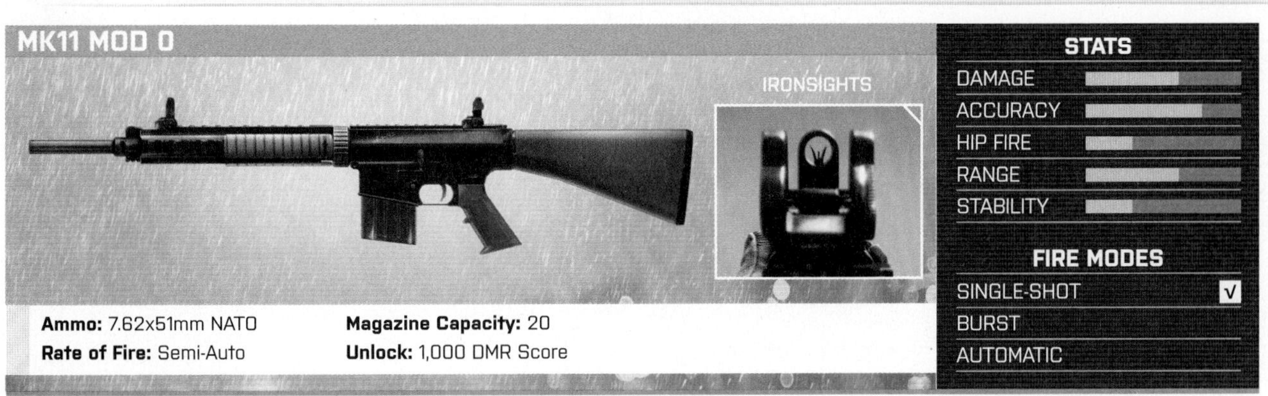

STATS	
DAMAGE	
ACCURACY	
HIP FIRE	
RANGE	
STABILITY	

FIRE MODES	
SINGLE-SHOT	√
BURST	
AUTOMATIC	

Ammo: 7.62x51mm NATO
Rate of Fire: Semi-Auto
Magazine Capacity: 20
Unlock: 1,000 DMR Score

Essentially an M16 chambered for the heavy 7.62mm NATO round, the Mk 11 MOD 0 features a longer, heavier, free-floating barrel and enhanced rail system for applying multiple attachments. Everything about the Mk 11 MOD 0 is designed to enhance accuracy and provide a squad long-range, accurate, semi-automatic fire.

UNLOCK PROGRESSION

IMAGE	ATTACHMENT	SLOT	KILLS
	ACOG (4X)	Optic (Medium Range)	10
	Canted Ironsights	Accessory	20
	Angled Grip	Underbarrel	30
	Heavy Barrel	Barrel	40
	Reflex (RDS)	Optic (Close Range)	50
	Laser Sight	Accessory	60
	Ergo Grip	Underbarrel	70
	Suppressor	Barrel	80
	HOLO (1X)	Optic (Medium Range)	90
	Magnifier (2X)	Accessory	100
	Stubby Grip	Underbarrel	110
	Muzzle Brake	Barrel	120
	M145 (3.4X)	Optic (Medium Range)	130
	Flashlight	Accessory	140
	Bipod	Underbarrel	150
	Compensator	Barrel	160

SKS

Ammo: 7.62x39mm WP
Rate of Fire: Semi-Auto
Magazine Capacity: 20
Unlock: 2,000 DMR Score

Millions of SKS rifles were produced originally for the Soviet Army in 1945 and in China as the Type 56. The SKS is a popular rifle with civilian shooters, and can still be found in a number of arsenals around the world. A number of aftermarket upgrades are available for the SKS; this model is equipped with a synthetic stock and detachable 20-round magazine.

UNLOCK PROGRESSION

IMAGE	ATTACHMENT	SLOT	KILLS
	PSO-1 (4X)	Optic (Medium Range)	10
	Canted Ironsights	Accessory	20
	Angled Grip	Underbarrel	30
	Heavy Barrel	Barrel	40
	KOBRA (RDS)	Optic (Close Range)	50
	Laser Sight	Accessory	60
	Ergo Grip	Underbarrel	70
	PBS-4 Suppressor	Barrel	80
	PKA-S (1X)	Optic (Medium Range)	90
	Magnifier (2X)	Accessory	100
	Stubby Grip	Underbarrel	110
	Muzzle Brake	Barrel	120
	PK-A (3.4X)	Optic (Medium Range)	130
	Flashlight	Accessory	140
	Bipod	Underbarrel	150
	Compensator	Barrel	160

SVD-12

Ammo: 7.62x54mm R
Rate of Fire: Semi-Auto
Magazine Capacity: 15
Unlock: 3,000 DMR Score

The Russian SVD-12 is a modern update of the legendary Dragunov sniper rifle, originally developed in the 1960s. Gone is the wooden stock, in favor of a lighter, composite stock with an integrated rail system. But the rifle still retains its hard-hitting reputation, firing the 7.62x54mm R round, resulting in impressive stopping power and long-range performance.

UNLOCK PROGRESSION

IMAGE	ATTACHMENT	SLOT	KILLS
	PSO-1 (4X)	Optic (Medium Range)	10
	Canted Ironsights	Accessory	20
	Angled Grip	Underbarrel	30
	Heavy Barrel	Barrel	40
	KOBRA (RDS)	Optic (Close Range)	50
	Laser Sight	Accessory	60
	Ergo Grip	Underbarrel	70
	PBS-4 Suppressor	Barrel	80
	PKA-S (1X)	Optic (Medium Range)	90
	Magnifier (2X)	Accessory	100
	Stubby Grip	Underbarrel	110
	Muzzle Brake	Barrel	120
	PK-A (3.4X)	Optic (Medium Range)	130
	Flashlight	Accessory	140
	Bipod	Underbarrel	150
	Compensator	Barrel	160

QBU-88

Ammo: 5.8x42mm DAP-87
Rate of Fire: Semi-Auto
Magazine Capacity: 10
Unlock: 4,000 DMR Score

STATS

DAMAGE
ACCURACY
HIP FIRE
RANGE
STABILITY

FIRE MODES

SINGLE-SHOT	√
BURST	
AUTOMATIC	

The Chinese QBU-88 entered service in 1997 as the People's Liberation Army's designated marksman rifle. It is a relatively compact DMR, utilizing a bullpup configuration and chambered to accommodate the heavy DAP-87 round. The weapon is most effective at intermediate ranges, particularly when equipped with the JFM-4 (4X) scope.

UNLOCK PROGRESSION

IMAGE	ATTACHMENT	SLOT	KILLS
	JGM-4 (4X)	Optic (Medium Range)	10
	Canted Ironsights	Accessory	20
	Angled Grip	Underbarrel	30
	Heavy Barrel	Barrel	40
	Coyote (RDS)	Optic (Close Range)	50
	Laser Sight	Accessory	60
	Ergo Grip	Underbarrel	70
	LS06 Suppressor	Barrel	80
	HD-33 (1X)	Optic (Medium Range)	90
	Magnifier (2X)	Accessory	100
	Stubby Grip	Underbarrel	110
	Muzzle Brake	Barrel	120
	PRISMA (3.4X)	Optic (Medium Range)	130
	Flashlight	Accessory	140
	Bipod	Underbarrel	150
	Compensator	Barrel	160

M39 EMR

Ammo: 7.62x51mm NATO
Rate of Fire: Semi-Auto
Magazine Capacity: 20
Unlock: 5,000 DMR Score

STATS

DAMAGE
ACCURACY
HIP FIRE
RANGE
STABILITY

FIRE MODES

SINGLE-SHOT	√
BURST	
AUTOMATIC	

The M39 Enhanced Marksman Rifle (EMR) is a highly modernized M14 designed to be utilized by USMC-designated marksmen. Issued with match-grade 7.62mm NATO long-range ammunition, the M39 is significantly lighter and more accurate than the original M14. The M39 is limited to semi-automatic fire, but supports a number of accessories.

UNLOCK PROGRESSION

IMAGE	ATTACHMENT	SLOT	KILLS
	ACOG (4X)	Optic (Medium Range)	10
	Canted Ironsights	Accessory	20
	Angled Grip	Underbarrel	30
	Heavy Barrel	Barrel	40
	Reflex (RDS)	Optic (Close Range)	50
	Laser Sight	Accessory	60
	Ergo Grip	Underbarrel	70
	Suppressor	Barrel	80
	HOLO (1X)	Optic (Medium Range)	90
	Magnifier (2X)	Accessory	100
	Stubby Grip	Underbarrel	110
	Muzzle Brake	Barrel	120
	M145 (3.4X)	Optic (Medium Range)	130
	Flashlight	Accessory	140
	Bipod	Underbarrel	150
	Compensator	Barrel	160

ACE 53 SV

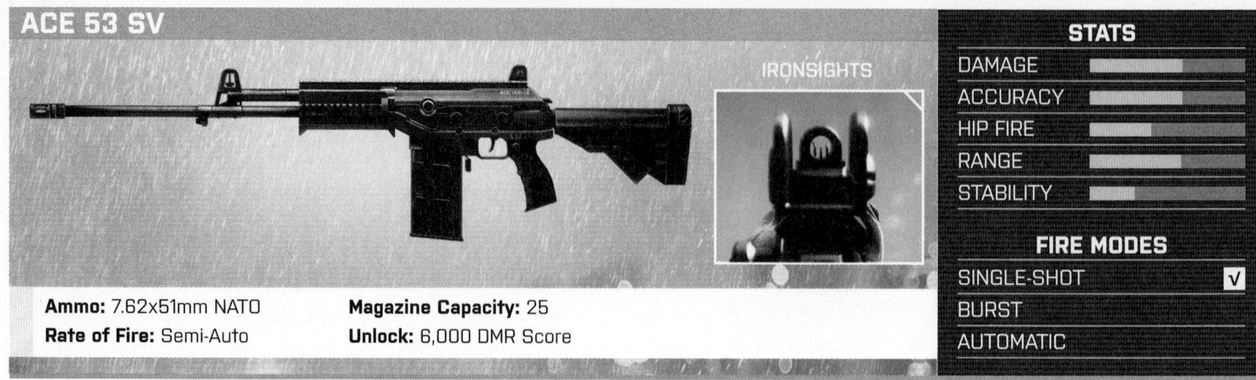

Ammo: 7.62x51mm NATO
Rate of Fire: Semi-Auto
Magazine Capacity: 25
Unlock: 6,000 DMR Score

The ACE 53 SV features the same basic appearance and functionality as other firearms in the ACE line. However, this DMR is equipped with a longer barrel and fires heavy 7.62mm NATO rounds, resulting in greater stopping power and accuracy at range. The end result is a well-balanced DMR with somewhat excessive recoil.

UNLOCK PROGRESSION

IMAGE	ATTACHMENT	SLOT	KILLS
	JGM-4 (4X)	Optic (Medium Range)	10
	Canted Ironsights	Accessory	20
	Angled Grip	Underbarrel	30
	Heavy Barrel	Barrel	40
	Coyote (RDS)	Optic (Close Range)	50
	Laser Sight	Accessory	60
	Ergo Grip	Underbarrel	70
	LS06 Suppressor	Barrel	80
	HD-33 (1X)	Optic (Medium Range)	90
	Magnifier (2X)	Accessory	100
	Stubby Grip	Underbarrel	110
	Muzzle Brake	Barrel	120
	PRISMA (3.4X)	Optic (Medium Range)	130
	Flashlight	Accessory	140
	Bipod	Underbarrel	150
	Compensator	Barrel	160

SCAR-H SV

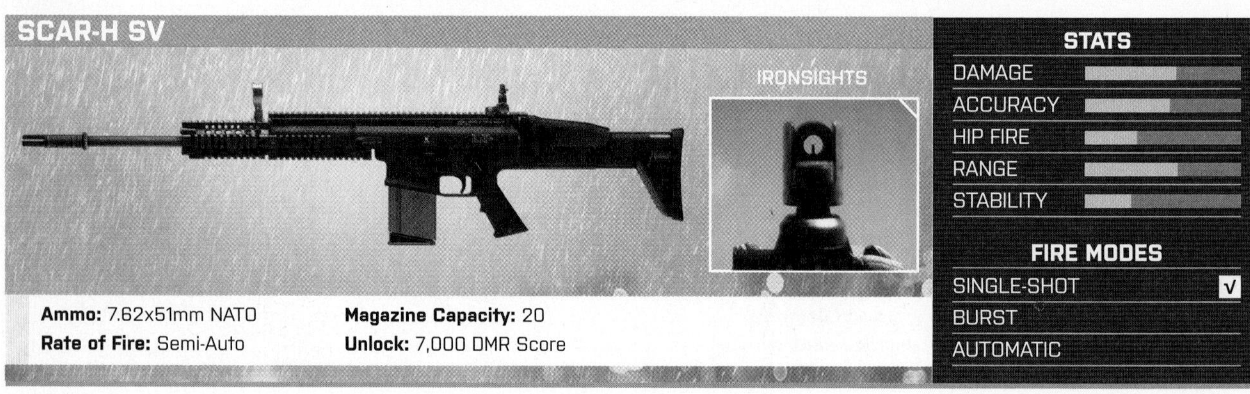

Ammo: 7.62x51mm NATO
Rate of Fire: Semi-Auto
Magazine Capacity: 20
Unlock: 7,000 DMR Score

Built on the versatile SCAR platform, the SCAR-H SV is not much different than the SCAR-H assault rifle, with both rifles firing the hard-hitting 7.62mmm NATO round. However, the SCAR-H SV features a longer barrel offering increased muzzle velocity, translating into greater effective range and stopping power.

UNLOCK PROGRESSION

IMAGE	ATTACHMENT	SLOT	KILLS
	ACOG (4X)	Optic (Medium Range)	10
	Canted Ironsights	Accessory	20
	Angled Grip	Underbarrel	30
	Heavy Barrel	Barrel	40
	Reflex (RDS)	Optic (Close Range)	50
	Laser Sight	Accessory	60
	Ergo Grip	Underbarrel	70
	Suppressor	Barrel	80
	HOLO (1X)	Optic (Medium Range)	90
	Magnifier (2X)	Accessory	100
	Stubby Grip	Underbarrel	110
	Muzzle Brake	Barrel	120
	M145 (3.4X)	Optic (Medium Range)	130
	Flashlight	Accessory	140
	Bipod	Underbarrel	150
	Compensator	Barrel	160

SHOTGUNS

Nobody misses with a shotgun. Although these weapons lack the accuracy and finesse of the other weapons, their brutal power is a worthwhile trade-off. At close range, these weapons are unmatched, capable of killing with one shot. Like the carbines, shotguns can be equipped by every kit, giving each class the ability to dominate in close quarters.

SHOTGUN UNLOCK PROGRESSION

IMAGE	NAME	SCORE
	QBS-09	0*
	870MCS	1,000
	M1014	2,000
	HAWK 12G	3,000
	SAIGA 12K	4,000
	SPAS-12	5,000
	UTS-15	6,000
	DBV-12	7,000

* = support class unlock

FUNDAMENTALS

- LIKE THE CARBINES AND DMRS, THE SHOTGUNS CAN BE EQUIPPED BY ANY CLASS.
- DESIGNED FOR EXTREME CLOSE-QUARTER COMBAT, SHOTGUNS ARE MOST EFFECTIVE WITHIN 10-15 METERS.
- STANDARD 12G BUCKSHOT OFFERS THE MOST DAMAGE OUTPUT AT CLOSE RANGE, OFTEN KILLING WITH ONE SHOT.
- ATTACH A FULL CHOKE BARREL ATTACHMENT TO NARROW THE SHOTGUN'S SPREAD, PERFECT FOR MAXIMIZING DAMAGE AGAINST INDIVIDUAL TARGETS.
- THE PUMP ACTION SHOTGUNS MUST BE LOADED ONE SHELL AT A TIME. TOP OFF THE WEAPON AFTER EACH ENGAGEMENT TO AVOID LENGTHY RELOAD TIMES.

SHOTGUN SERVICE STAR

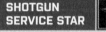

You earn a Shotgun Service Star for every 100 kills you score with each shotgun.

QBS-09

Ammo: 12 Gauge
Rate of Fire: Semi-Auto
Magazine Capacity: 6
Unlock: 52,000 Support Score

STATS

DAMAGE
ACCURACY
HIP FIRE
RANGE
STABILITY

FIRE MODES

SINGLE-SHOT	✓
BURST	
AUTOMATIC	

This Chinese semi-auto, gas-operated shotgun entered service with the People's Liberation Army in 2009 and is constructed from lightweight polymers and alloys. A spring-buffered, retractable buttstock absorbs recoil, helping mitigate muzzle climb. Loaded with 12G Buckshot by default, the QBS-09 delivers devastating stopping power at close range.

UNLOCK PROGRESSION

IMAGE	ATTACHMENT	SLOT	KILLS
	Duckbill	Barrel	10
	Coyote (RDS)	Optic (Close Range)	20
	Laser Sight	Accessory	30
	Modified Choke	Barrel	40
	JGM-4 (4X)	Optic (Medium Range)	50
	Canted Ironsights	Accessory	60
	Muzzle Brake	Barrel	70
	12G Slug	Ammo	80
	HD-33 (1X)	Optic (Medium Range)	90
	Magnifier (2X)	Accessory	100
	Full Choke	Barrel	110
	12G Dart	Ammo	120
	PRISMA (3.4X)	Optic (Medium Range)	130
	Compensator	Barrel	140
	Flashlight	Accessory	150
	12G Frag	Ammo	160

870MCS

STATS: DAMAGE, ACCURACY, HIP FIRE, RANGE, STABILITY

FIRE MODES

SINGLE-SHOT	√
BURST	
AUTOMATIC	

Ammo: 12 Gauge
Rate of Fire: Pump Action
Magazine Capacity: 8
Unlock: 1,000 Shotgun Score

The 870 Modular Combat Shotgun is an American-made pump-action shotgun that has been used by Special Forces units for decades. In urban environments, the 870MCS is especially effective due to its high stopping power at close range. The ability to load different types of shells makes the 870MCS able to adapt to a wide variety of situations, while a narrow choke gives the weapon slightly more range than other shotguns.

UNLOCK PROGRESSION

IMAGE	ATTACHMENT	SLOT	KILLS
	Duckbill	Barrel	10
	Reflex (RDS)	Optic (Close Range)	20
	Laser Sight	Accessory	30
	Modified Choke	Barrel	40
	ACOG (4X)	Optic (Medium Range)	50
	Canted Ironsights	Accessory	60
	Muzzle Brake	Barrel	70
	12G Slug	Ammo	80
	HOLO (1X)	Optic (Medium Range)	90
	Magnifier (2X)	Accessory	100
	Full Choke	Barrel	110
	12G Dart	Ammo	120
	M145 (3.4X)	Optic (Medium Range)	130
	Compensator	Barrel	140
	Flashlight	Accessory	150
	12G Frag	Ammo	160

M1014

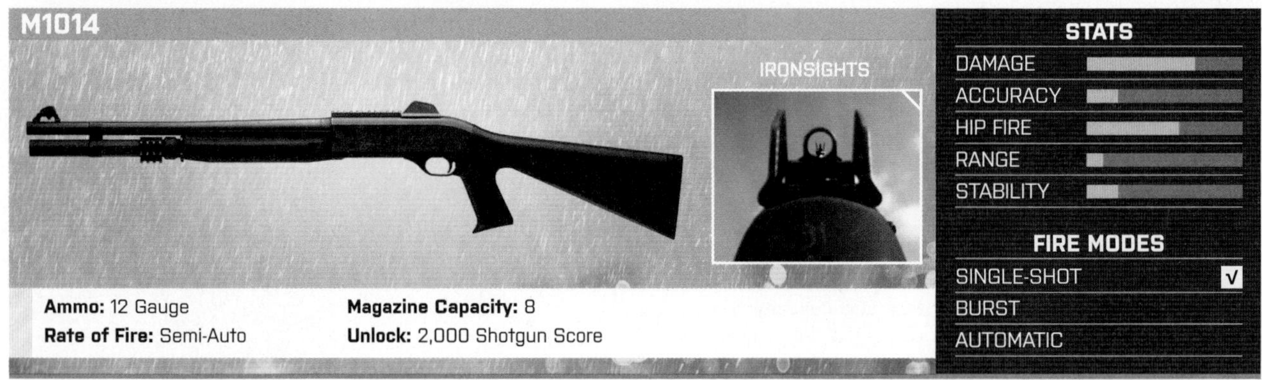

STATS: DAMAGE, ACCURACY, HIP FIRE, RANGE, STABILITY

FIRE MODES

SINGLE-SHOT	√
BURST	
AUTOMATIC	

Ammo: 12 Gauge
Rate of Fire: Semi-Auto
Magazine Capacity: 8
Unlock: 2,000 Shotgun Score

An Italian semi-automatic shotgun, delivered to USMC in 1999, the M1014 fires 12-gauge rounds without the need for the pump action seen on the M870. A reliable and versatile weapon, the M1014 is also equipped with a rail for the mounting of various accessories and an open choke that results in wide pellet spread.

UNLOCK PROGRESSION

IMAGE	ATTACHMENT	SLOT	KILLS
	Duckbill	Barrel	10
	Reflex (RDS)	Optic (Close Range)	20
	Laser Sight	Accessory	30
	Modified Choke	Barrel	40
	ACOG (4X)	Optic (Medium Range)	50
	Canted Ironsights	Accessory	60
	Muzzle Brake	Barrel	70
	12G Slug	Ammo	80
	HOLO (1X)	Optic (Medium Range)	90
	Magnifier (2X)	Accessory	100
	Full Choke	Barrel	110
	12G Dart	Ammo	120
	M145 (3.4X)	Optic (Medium Range)	130
	Compensator	Barrel	140
	Flashlight	Accessory	150
	12G Frag	Ammo	160

HAWK 12G

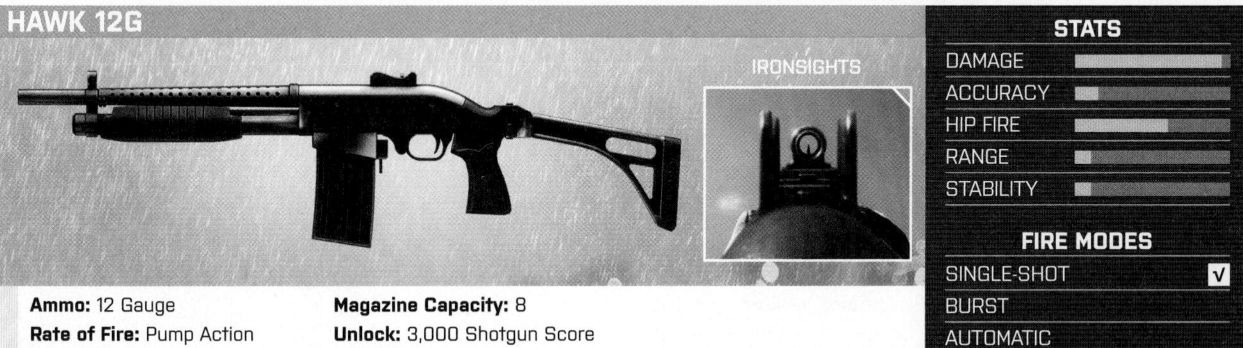

STATS

DAMAGE
ACCURACY
HIP FIRE
RANGE
STABILITY

FIRE MODES

SINGLE-SHOT	V
BURST	
AUTOMATIC	

Ammo: 12 Gauge
Rate of Fire: Pump Action
Magazine Capacity: 8
Unlock: 3,000 Shotgun Score

The Chinese Hawk 12G is a combat pump action shotgun with a detachable box magazine capable of holding six shells. While the design is largely based on the 870MCS, the detachable magazine is a true game changer, allowing for quicker reloads than its American counterpart. This makes the Hawk 12G very effective during chaotic close-quarter firefights, when there's no time to load one shell at a time.

UNLOCK PROGRESSION

IMAGE	ATTACHMENT	SLOT	KILLS
	Duckbill	Barrel	10
	Coyote (RDS)	Optic (Close Range)	20
	Laser Sight	Accessory	30
	Modified Choke	Barrel	40
	JGM-4 (4X)	Optic (Medium Range)	50
	Canted Ironsights	Accessory	60
	Muzzle Brake	Barrel	70
	12G Slug	Ammo	80
	HD-33 (1X)	Optic (Medium Range)	90
	Magnifier (2X)	Accessory	100
	Full Choke	Barrel	110
	12G Dart	Ammo	120
	PRISMA (3.4X)	Optic (Medium Range)	130
	Compensator	Barrel	140
	Flashlight	Accessory	150
	12G Frag	Ammo	160

SAIGA 12K

STATS

DAMAGE
ACCURACY
HIP FIRE
RANGE
STABILITY

FIRE MODES

SINGLE-SHOT	V
BURST	
AUTOMATIC	

Ammo: 12 Gauge
Rate of Fire: Semi-Auto
Magazine Capacity: 9
Unlock: 4,000 Shotgun Score

This Russian-made magazine-fed 12-gauge shotgun is based on the proven AK-47 action and equipped with a folding stock. It is reliable, fast to reload, and capable of mounting a variety of accessories. The Saiga 12K is popular with Russian police and security services, and it is an effective close combat weapon with a wide pellet spread.

UNLOCK PROGRESSION

IMAGE	ATTACHMENT	SLOT	KILLS
	Duckbill	Barrel	10
	KOBRA (RDS)	Optic (Close Range)	20
	Laser Sight	Accessory	30
	Stubby Grip	Underbarrel	40
	Modified Choke	Barrel	50
	PSO-1 (4X)	Optic (Medium Range)	60
	Canted Ironsights	Accessory	70
	Angled Grip	Underbarrel	80
	12G Slug	Ammo	90
	PKA-S (1X)	Optic (Medium Range)	100
	Magnifier (2X)	Accessory	110
	Full Choke	Barrel	120
	12G Dart	Ammo	130
	PK-A (3.4X)	Optic (Medium Range)	140
	Ergo Grip	Underbarrel	150
	Flashlight	Accessory	160
	12G Frag	Ammo	170

SPAS-12

IRONSIGHTS

STATS

DAMAGE
ACCURACY
HIP FIRE
RANGE
STABILITY

FIRE MODES

SINGLE-SHOT	√
BURST	
AUTOMATIC	

Ammo: 12 Gauge
Rate of Fire: Pump Action
Magazine Capacity: 9
Unlock: 5,000 Shotgun Score

This Italian-smade iconic shotgun has seen great success since its introduction on the market during the 1980s. It has become popular in many countries thanks to its capacity to handle a great variety of shell types. Its unique magazine design further simplifies the use of varied ammunition, allowing the SPAS-12 to remain in high regard with police and military units worldwide.

UNLOCK PROGRESSION

IMAGE	ATTACHMENT	SLOT	KILLS
	Duckbill	Barrel	10
	Reflex (RDS)	Optic (Close Range)	20
	Laser Sight	Accessory	30
	Modified Choke	Barrel	40
	ACOG (4X)	Optic (Medium Range)	50
	Canted Ironsights	Accessory	60
	Muzzle Brake	Barrel	70
	12G Slug	Ammo	80
	HOLO (1X)	Optic (Medium Range)	90
	Magnifier (2X)	Accessory	100
	Full Choke	Barrel	110
	12G Dart	Ammo	120
	M145 (3.4X)	Optic (Medium Range)	130
	Compensator	Barrel	140
	Flashlight	Accessory	150
	12G Frag	Ammo	160

UTS-15

IRONSIGHTS

STATS

DAMAGE
ACCURACY
HIP FIRE
RANGE
STABILITY

FIRE MODES

SINGLE-SHOT	√
BURST	
AUTOMATIC	

Ammo: 12 Gauge
Rate of Fire: Pump Action
Magazine Capacity: 15
Unlock: 6,000 Shotgun Score

This unorthodox pump-action shotgun features two side-by-side tubular magazines located just above the barrel. Loading ports on the side of the weapon allow the shotgun to be loaded manually and topped off after each engagement. But the large-magazine capacity and compact size of the UTS-15 is offset by its lack of stopping power, particularly when compared to the other pump-action shotguns.

UNLOCK PROGRESSION

IMAGE	ATTACHMENT	SLOT	KILLS
	Duckbill	Barrel	10
	Reflex (RDS)	Optic (Close Range)	20
	Laser Sight	Accessory	30
	Modified Choke	Barrel	40
	ACOG (4X)	Optic (Medium Range)	50
	Canted Ironsights	Accessory	60
	Muzzle Brake	Barrel	70
	12G Slug	Ammo	80
	HOLO (1X)	Optic (Medium Range)	90
	Magnifier (2X)	Accessory	100
	Full Choke	Barrel	110
	12G Dart	Ammo	120
	M145 (3.4X)	Optic (Medium Range)	130
	Compensator	Barrel	140
	Flashlight	Accessory	150
	12G Frag	Ammo	160

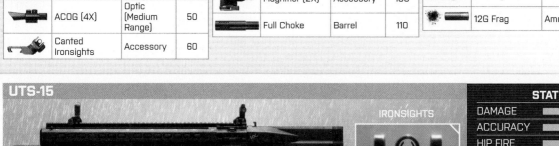

DBV-12

IRONSIGHTS

STATS	
DAMAGE	
ACCURACY	
HIP FIRE	
RANGE	
STABILITY	

FIRE MODES	
SINGLE-SHOT	✓
BURST	
AUTOMATIC	

Ammo: 12 Gauge
Rate of Fire: Semi-Auto
Magazine Capacity: 10
Unlock: 7,000 Shotgun Score

Like the Saiga 12K, the Russian DBV-12 shares many similarities with the legendary AK-47, giving it the feel of an assault rifle. Loaded with a 10-round magazine, the DBV-12 is quick to reload, making it very effective during close-quarter fire-fights. But like most semi-auto shotguns, the DBV-12 lacks the stopping power of its pump-action counterparts.

UNLOCK PROGRESSION

IMAGE	ATTACHMENT	SLOT	KILLS
	Duckbill	Barrel	10
	KOBRA (RDS)	Optic (Close Range)	20
	Laser Sight	Accessory	30
	Stubby Grip	Underbarrel	40
	Modified Choke	Barrel	50
	PSO-1 (4X)	Optic (Medium Range)	60
	Canted Ironsights	Accessory	70
	Angled Grip	Underbarrel	80
	12G Slug	Ammo	90
	PKA-S (1X)	Optic (Medium Range)	100
	Magnifier (2X)	Accessory	110
	Full Choke	Barrel	120
	12G Dart	Ammo	130
	PK-A (3.4X)	Optic (Medium Range)	140
	Ergo Grip	Underbarrel	150
	Flashlight	Accessory	160
	12G Frag	Ammo	170

SIDEARMS

Don't write off these sidearms as mere peashooters. The pistols pack a serious punch and can save your life during desperate close-quarter duels—remember, it's faster to draw your pistol than it is to load a fresh magazine in your primary weapon. The pistols can be equipped by any kit, filling the sidearm slot in the loadout screen.

SIDEARM UNLOCK PROGRESSION

IMAGE	NAME	SCORE
	P226	0
	M9	1,000
	QSZ-92	2,000
	MP443	3,000
	Shorty 12G	4,000
	G18	5,000
	FN57	6,000
	M1911	7,000
	93R	8,000
	CZ-75	9,000
	.44 Magnum	10,000
	Compact 45	11,000
	M412 REX	N/A*

* = unlocked in campaign

FUNDAMENTALS

- SIDEARMS ARE EQUIPPED BY ALL CLASSES. BY DEFAULT, ALL CLASSES BEGIN WITH THE P226.
- THE PISTOLS ARE MOST EFFECTIVE WITHIN 50 METERS—DON'T FIRE THE SHORTY 12G UNTIL YOU'RE WITHIN 5 METERS OF YOUR TARGET.
- THE SEMI-AUTOMATIC PISTOLS HAVE THE LEAST RECOIL, MAKING IT EASIER TO ACCURATELY FIRE FOLLOW-UP SHOTS.
- WHILE THE SIDEARMS HAVE EXCELLENT HIP FIRE ACCURACY, THEY'RE EVEN MORE EFFECTIVE WHEN EQUIPPED WITH A LASER SIGHT.
- THE SHORTY 12G, .44 MAGNUM, AND M412 REX PROVIDE HIGH DAMAGE OUTPUT. BUT THEIR HARSH RECOIL AND SMALL MAGAZINE CAPACITIES ARE SERIOUS DRAWBACKS.

HANDGUN SERVICE STAR

You earn a Handgun Service Star for every 100 kills you score with each handgun.

P226

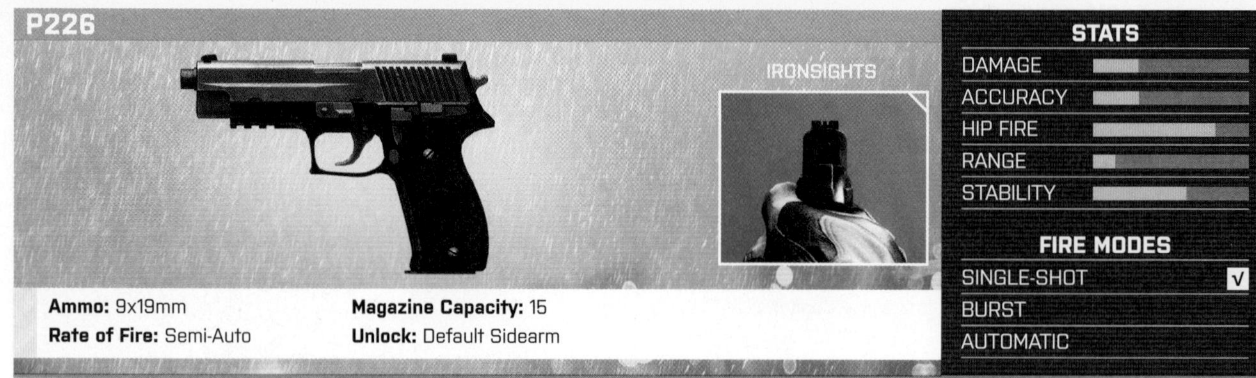

Ammo: 9x19mm
Rate of Fire: Semi-Auto
Magazine Capacity: 15
Unlock: Default Sidearm

STATS

DAMAGE
ACCURACY
HIP FIRE
RANGE
STABILITY

FIRE MODES

SINGLE-SHOT	V
BURST	
AUTOMATIC	

The Swiss P226 was originally designed as a replacement for the US military's aging M1911, but lost out to the M9 during the 1984 trials. Despite this setback, the P226 has gone on to build a solid reputation among armed forces and police agencies around the world, lauded for its reliability and ease of use. It has also been adopted by several Special Forces units, including the US Navy SEALs.

UNLOCK PROGRESSION

IMAGE	ATTACHMENT	SLOT	KILLS
	Flashlight	Accessory	10
	Muzzle Brake	Barrel	20
	Ghost Ring	Optic	30
	Compensator	Barrel	40
	Mini (RDS)	Optic	50
	Laser Sight	Accessory	60
	Suppressor	Barrel	70
	Delta (RDS)	Optic	80
	Heavy Barrel	Barrel	90

M9

Ammo: 9x19mm
Rate of Fire: Semi-Auto
Magazine Capacity: 15
Unlock: 1,000 Sidearm Score

STATS

DAMAGE
ACCURACY
HIP FIRE
RANGE
STABILITY

FIRE MODES

SINGLE-SHOT	V
BURST	
AUTOMATIC	

The M9 was selected as the primary sidearm of the entire United States military in 1985. Developed in Italy, the M9 was selected in a series of often disputed trials, only narrowly beating out other contenders, including the P226, because of its high quality and low price. The M9 is the primary sidearm of the USMC.

UNLOCK PROGRESSION

IMAGE	ATTACHMENT	SLOT	KILLS
	Flashlight	Accessory	10
	Muzzle Brake	Barrel	20
	Ghost Ring	Optic	30
	Compensator	Barrel	40
	Mini (RDS)	Optic	50
	Laser Sight	Accessory	60
	Suppressor	Barrel	70
	Delta (RDS)	Optic	80
	Heavy Barrel	Barrel	90

QSZ-92

STATS: DAMAGE, ACCURACY, HIP FIRE, RANGE, STABILITY

FIRE MODES

SINGLE-SHOT	√
BURST	
AUTOMATIC	

Ammo: 5.8x21mm DAP-92
Rate of Fire: Semi-Auto
Magazine Capacity: 20
Unlock: 2,000 Sidearm Score

Designed in the mid-1990s, the Chinese QSZ-92 pistol is also known as the Type 92 handgun. The pistol fires the special 5.8x21mm DAP-92 round, designed to pierce body armor while providing the same stopping power as a 9mm round. This 5.8mm variant of the QSZ-92 is largely issued to officers within the People's Liberation Army. It has also been exported to the armed forces of Bangladesh.

UNLOCK PROGRESSION

IMAGE	ATTACHMENT	SLOT	KILLS
	Flashlight	Accessory	10
	Muzzle Brake	Barrel	20
	Ghost Ring	Optic	30
	Compensator	Barrel	40
	Mini (RDS)	Optic	50
	Laser Sight	Accessory	60
	QSW-06 Suppressor	Barrel	70
	Delta (RDS)	Optic	80
	Heavy Barrel	Barrel	90

MP443

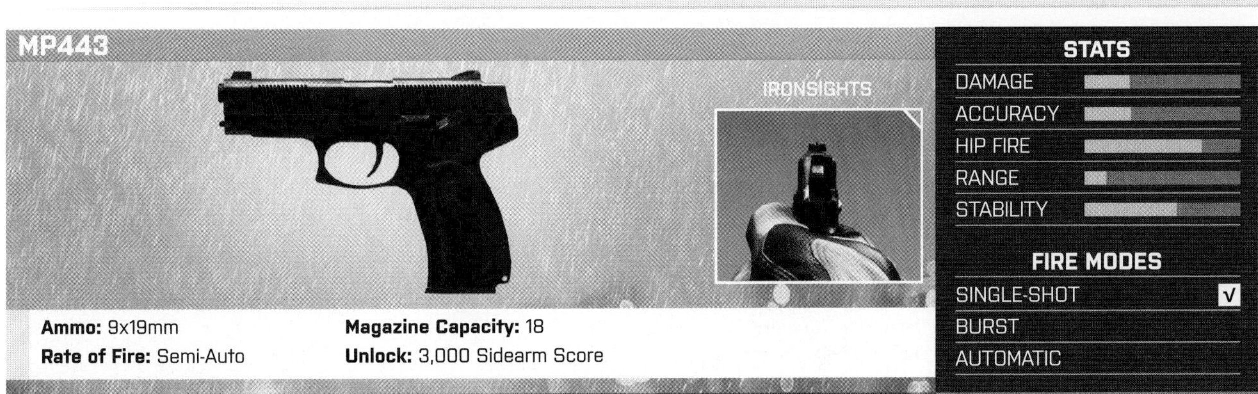

STATS: DAMAGE, ACCURACY, HIP FIRE, RANGE, STABILITY

FIRE MODES

SINGLE-SHOT	√
BURST	
AUTOMATIC	

Ammo: 9x19mm
Rate of Fire: Semi-Auto
Magazine Capacity: 18
Unlock: 3,000 Sidearm Score

Designed to replace the dated PMM pistol, the MP443 pistol was developed in 1993 and fires high-powered armor-piercing 9mm Russian rounds. The pistol is a combined construction of polymers and steel and has been adopted by select Special Forces units in the Russian military.

UNLOCK PROGRESSION

IMAGE	ATTACHMENT	SLOT	KILLS
	Flashlight	Accessory	10
	Muzzle Brake	Barrel	20
	Ghost Ring	Optic	30
	Compensator	Barrel	40
	Mini (RDS)	Optic	50
	Laser Sight	Accessory	60
	TGPA-5 Suppressor	Barrel	70
	Delta (RDS)	Optic	80
	Heavy Barrel	Barrel	90

SHORTY 12G

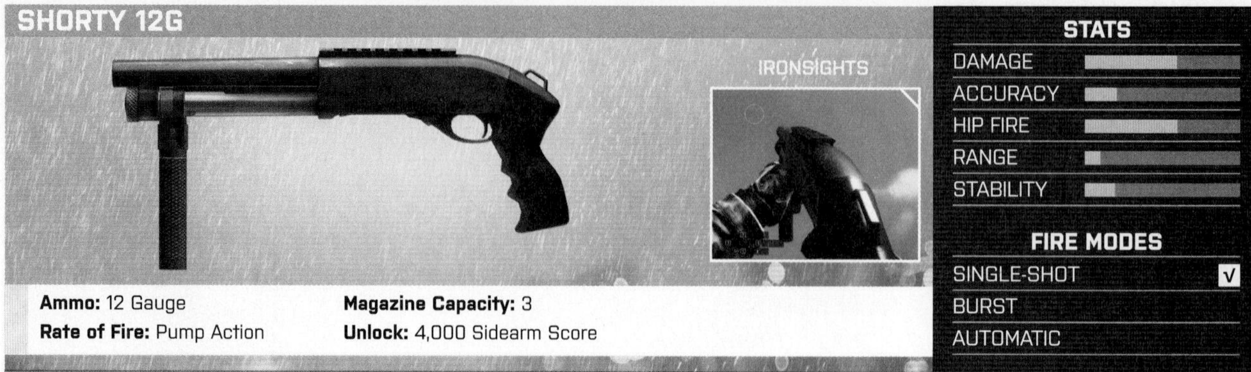

Ammo: 12 Gauge
Rate of Fire: Pump Action
Magazine Capacity: 3
Unlock: 4,000 Sidearm Score

STATS

DAMAGE
ACCURACY
HIP FIRE
RANGE
STABILITY

FIRE MODES

SINGLE-SHOT	√
BURST	
AUTOMATIC	

The American-designed Shorty 12G is essentially a miniaturized version of a pump action-shotgun. Due to its compact size, it can be deployed as a sidearm, offering much higher damage output than its pistol counterparts. Firing 12-buckshot and only capable of holding three shells in its tubular magazine, the Shorty 12G is best deployed during extreme, point-blank engagements.

UNLOCK PROGRESSION

IMAGE	ATTACHMENT	SLOT	KILLS
	Flashlight	Accessory	10
	Muzzle Brake	Barrel	20
	Ghost Ring	Optic	30
	Compensator	Barrel	40
	Mini (RDS)	Optic	50
	Laser Sight	Accessory	60
	Duckbill	Barrel	70
	Delta (RDS)	Optic	80

G18

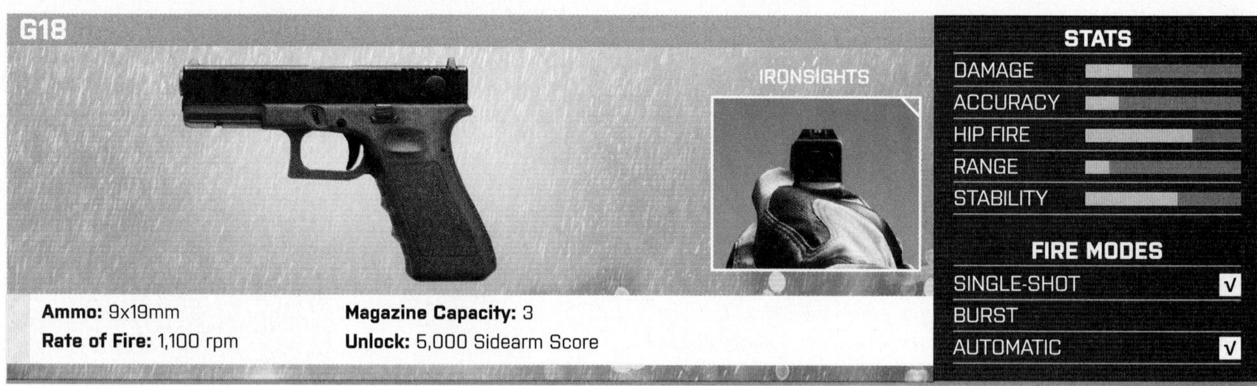

Ammo: 9x19mm
Rate of Fire: 1,100 rpm
Magazine Capacity: 3
Unlock: 5,000 Sidearm Score

STATS

DAMAGE
ACCURACY
HIP FIRE
RANGE
STABILITY

FIRE MODES

SINGLE-SHOT	√
BURST	
AUTOMATIC	√

Essentially an automatic version of the G17, the G18 was developed for the Austrian EKO Cobra counter-terrorist force. Classified as a machine pistol, the G18 has been equipped with a number of modifications to allow greater control over its very rapid fire. Regardless, the G18 in automatic is incredibly difficult to fire effectively at anything other than extremely short ranges.

UNLOCK PROGRESSION

IMAGE	ATTACHMENT	SLOT	KILLS
	Flashlight	Accessory	10
	Muzzle Brake	Barrel	20
	Ghost Ring	Optic	30
	Compensator	Barrel	40
	Mini (RDS)	Optic	50
	Laser Sight	Accessory	60
	Suppressor	Barrel	70
	Delta (RDS)	Optic	80
	Heavy Barrel	Barrel	90

FN57

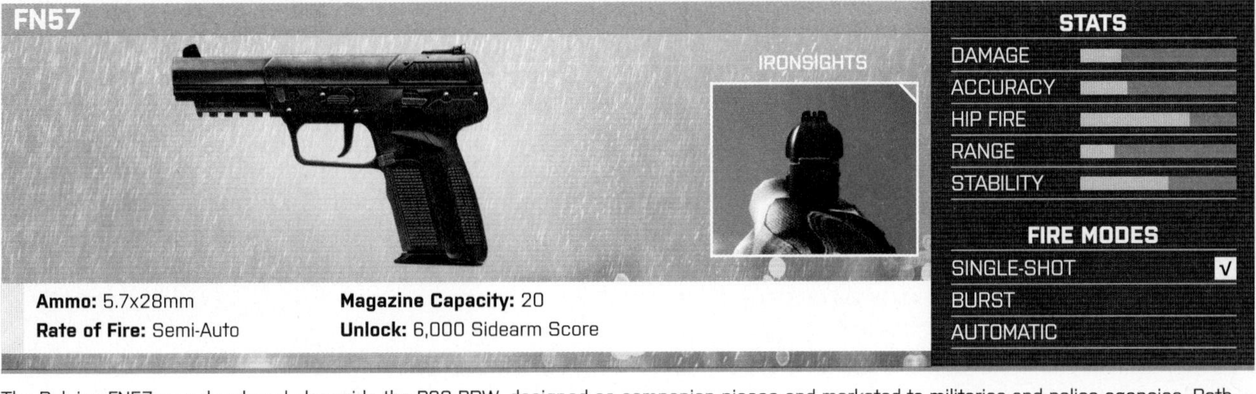

STATS	
DAMAGE	
ACCURACY	
HIP FIRE	
RANGE	
STABILITY	

FIRE MODES	
SINGLE-SHOT	√
BURST	
AUTOMATIC	

Ammo: 5.7x28mm
Rate of Fire: Semi-Auto
Magazine Capacity: 20
Unlock: 6,000 Sidearm Score

The Belgian FN57 was developed alongside the P90 PDW, designed as companion pieces and marketed to militaries and police agencies. Both weapons fire the same proprietary 5.7x28mm round, designed to have a greater range and higher velocity than the larger 9mm round. The smaller round also allows for a larger magazine capacity, always a welcome feature during fire fights.

UNLOCK PROGRESSION

IMAGE	ATTACHMENT	SLOT	KILLS
	Flashlight	Accessory	10
	Muzzle Brake	Barrel	20
	Ghost Ring	Optic	30
	Compensator	Barrel	40
	Mini (RDS)	Optic	50
	Laser Sight	Accessory	60
	Suppressor	Barrel	70
	Delta (RDS)	Optic	80
	Heavy Barrel	Barrel	90

M1911

STATS	
DAMAGE	
ACCURACY	
HIP FIRE	
RANGE	
STABILITY	

FIRE MODES	
SINGLE-SHOT	√
BURST	
AUTOMATIC	

Ammo: .45 ACP
Rate of Fire: Semi-Auto
Magazine Capacity: 8
Unlock: 7,000 Sidearm Score

The M1911 is one of the most popular pistols in the world. Adopted in 1911 for the US armed forces, the M1911 served as the primary sidearm until 1985. Many clones and copies of the M1911 exist, and the internal action is used in nearly all modern pistols. Modernized and updated versions of the M1911 are still in use by MEU(SOC) US Marine Corps Special Forces.

UNLOCK PROGRESSION

IMAGE	ATTACHMENT	SLOT	KILLS
	Flashlight	Accessory	10
	Muzzle Brake	Barrel	20
	Ghost Ring	Optic	30
	Compensator	Barrel	40
	Mini (RDS)	Optic	50
	Laser Sight	Accessory	60
	Suppressor	Barrel	70
	Delta (RDS)	Optic	80
	Heavy Barrel	Barrel	90

93R

Ammo: 9x19mm
Rate of Fire: 1,100 rpm
Magazine Capacity: 20
Unlock: 8,000 Sidearm Score

STATS

DAMAGE
ACCURACY
HIP FIRE
RANGE
STABILITY

FIRE MODES

SINGLE-SHOT	√
BURST	√
AUTOMATIC	

A modified version of the M9 pistol, the 93R is able to fire in three-round bursts. The 93R is equipped with a forward folding fore grip and an extended barrel, which is ported to reduce recoil. Trained shooters are able to fire busts in rapid succession, and the pistol is typically seen in service only with elite special purpose units.

UNLOCK PROGRESSION

IMAGE	ATTACHMENT	SLOT	KILLS
	Flashlight	Accessory	10
	Muzzle Brake	Barrel	20
	Ghost Ring	Optic	30
	Compensator	Barrel	40
	Mini (RDS)	Optic	50
	Laser Sight	Accessory	60
	Suppressor	Barrel	70
	Delta (RDS)	Optic	80
	Heavy Barrel	Barrel	90

CZ-75

Ammo: .40 SW
Rate of Fire: Semi-Auto
Magazine Capacity: 12
Unlock: 9,000 Sidearm Score

STATS

DAMAGE
ACCURACY
HIP FIRE
RANGE
STABILITY

FIRE MODES

SINGLE-SHOT	√
BURST	
AUTOMATIC	

Developed in the 1970s, this innovative Czech pistol was one of the first handguns to utilize a staggered magazine feed configuration, allowing for greater capacity. This variant of the CZ-75 is chambered in .40 SW, giving slightly more stopping power than its 9mm counterparts. But the larger round results in a smaller magazine capacity too.

UNLOCK PROGRESSION

IMAGE	ATTACHMENT	SLOT	KILLS
	Flashlight	Accessory	10
	Muzzle Brake	Barrel	20
	Ghost Ring	Optic	30
	Compensator	Barrel	40
	Mini (RDS)	Optic	50
	Laser Sight	Accessory	60
	TGPA-5 Suppressor	Barrel	70
	Delta (RDS)	Optic	80
	Heavy Barrel	Barrel	90

.44 MAGNUM

A .44 Magnum, the most powerful handgun in the world, this particular model features a ported barrel, a compact frame for easy carry, and of course, a round that will blow your head clean off. The .44 Magnum is the most powerful available sidearm, but the recoil and weight of the weapon makes fast follow-up shots extremely difficult.

UNLOCK PROGRESSION

IMAGE	ATTACHMENT	SLOT	KILLS
	Flashlight	Accessory	10
	Muzzle Brake	Barrel	20
	Ghost Ring	Optic	30
	Compensator	Barrel	40
	Mini (RDS)	Optic	50
	Laser Sight	Accessory	60
	Suppressor	Barrel	70
	Delta (RDS)	Optic	80
	Heavy Barrel	Barrel	90

COMPACT 45

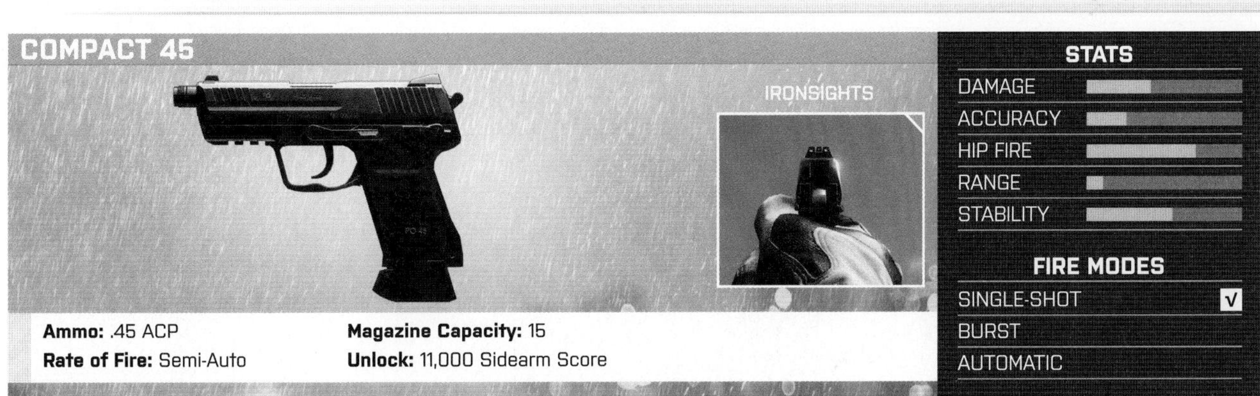

Chambered in the powerful .45 ACP round, the German-developed Compact 45 is the smaller variant of a pistol originally designed to replace the US armed forces' M9. Given the larger round, the 45 Compact exhibits impressive stopping power and surprisingly manageable recoil, putting it in the same territory as the M1911, albeit with a larger magazine capacity.

UNLOCK PROGRESSION

IMAGE	ATTACHMENT	SLOT	KILLS
	Flashlight	Accessory	10
	Muzzle Brake	Barrel	20
	Ghost Ring	Optic	30
	Compensator	Barrel	40
	Mini (RDS)	Optic	50
	Laser Sight	Accessory	60
	Suppressor	Barrel	70
	Delta (RDS)	Optic	80
	Heavy Barrel	Barrel	90

M412 REX

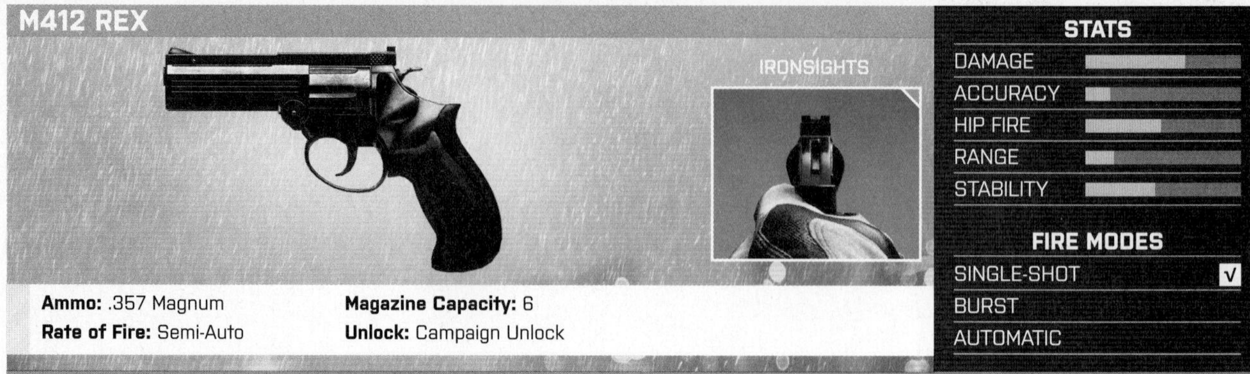

Ammo: .357 Magnum | **Magazine Capacity:** 6
Rate of Fire: Semi-Auto | **Unlock:** Campaign Unlock

Developed for export in Russia (REX stands for Revolver for Export), the M412 is a compact .357 Magnum handgun with an interesting tilt open and auto extraction design. While not as powerful as the .44 Magnum, the .357 Magnum round from the M412 offers excellent stopping power and the compact package offers a slightly higher rate of accurate fire.

UNLOCK PROGRESSION

IMAGE	ATTACHMENT	SLOT	KILLS
	Flashlight	Accessory	10
	Muzzle Brake	Barrel	20
	Ghost Ring	Optic	30
	Compensator	Barrel	40
	Mini (RDS)	Optic	50
	Laser Sight	Accessory	60
	TGPA-5 Suppressor	Barrel	70
	Delta (RDS)	Optic	80
	Heavy Barrel	Barrel	90

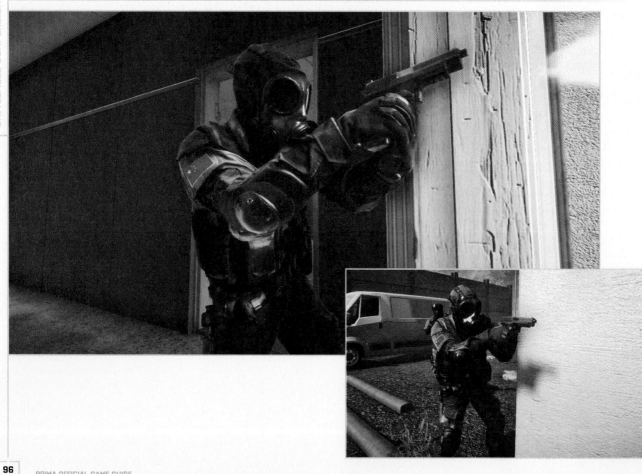

GRENADES

In *Battlefield 4* there are now several types of hand-thrown grenades available while customizing your soldier's loadout. By default, all classes begin with the M67 Frag grenade. But more grenade types are unlocked throughout your multiplayer career—the more frequently you score with grenades, the more you unlock. You can only carry one or two grenades at a time, depending on which one is equipped in your loadout. But the Grenades Field Upgrade allows you to carry one extra.

UNLOCK PROGRESSION

IMAGE	NAME	SCORE	IMAGE	NAME	SCORE	IMAGE	NAME	SCORE	IMAGE	NAME	SCORE
	M67 Frag	Default		RGO Impact	2,000		M18 Smoke	4,000		Hand Flare	6,000
	V40 Mini	1,000		M34 Incendiary	3,000		M84 Flashbang	5,000			

M67 FRAG

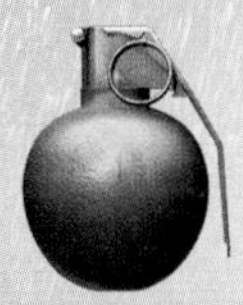

Description: Standard timed fuse hand grenade with all around performance and balanced range and damage.

Unlock: Default

The M67 Frag is a standard-issue fragmentation grenade, available to all classes at the start of your multiplayer career. The M67 is most effective against infantry, but they can also inflict minor damage against light-skinned vehicles—just don't try taking out a tank with them. The M67 doesn't explode on impact. Instead, they tend to roll around until the timed fuse triggers the explosion. So keep this in mind when tossing an M67—they will bounce off surfaces and roll down slopes. Make a habit of tossing this grenade in buildings prior to entering, especially if you suspect an enemy presence.

V40 MINI

Description: Mini hand grenade that can be thrown farther than the standard M67 but with reduced blast yield. Three of these grenades can be carried.

Unlock: 1,000 Grenade Score

The V40 Mini performs just like the M67 Frag, utilizing a similar time-delay fuse. But their smaller size allows you to carry three V40 Minis instead of only one—achieve the Grenades Field Upgrade to carry four. While more grenades is always a good thing, the explosive payload of each device is reduced, resulting in a smaller blast radius than their bigger M67 cousin. However, these miniature grenades can be lobbed greater distances, perfect for suppressing distant opponents.

RGO IMPACT

Description: Russian RGO Impact grenade that explodes shortly after impacting a surface. A smaller grenade with a lower blast yield, two of these grenades can be carried at one time.

Unlock: 2,000 Grenade Score

Unlike standard hand grenades, the RGO Impact Grenade explodes upon striking any surface, giving opponents no time to run away. Given the grenade's significantly smaller blast radius, it requires greater precision on behalf of the thrower to place these as close to the intended target as possible—for best results, throw it directly at your target. Be extremely careful when deploying these grenades in close quarters. Any contact the grenade makes during flight will cause it to detonate, potentially injuring or killing you.

M34 INCENDIARY

Description: Incendiary hand grenade that creates a cloud of intense burning particles for a short duration. Particles stick to soldiers and will continue to burn outside the original fire.

Unlock: 3,000 Grenade Score

Designed primarily as a signaling device, these nasty grenades emit a shower of red-hot white phosphorous, injuring (and potentially killing) anyone unlucky enough to be caught within its wide and persistent blast radius. During combat, the M34 is best deployed in tight chokepoints such as hallways, doorways, and stairwells, effectively halting the advance of enemy troops. The device continues emitting white phosphorus for approximately 3-4 seconds, leaving behind a thick cloud of black smoke that lingers for several seconds longer. Don't expect to score many kills with this grenade, as victims can often step outside its blast radius before suffering lethal injuries. Instead, use it primarily as a deterrent when defending chokepoints.

M18 SMOKE

Description: Timed fuse hand-thrown grenade that creates a blinding cloud of white smoke that also blocks spotting.

Unlock: 4,000 Grenade Score

Previously, smoke could only be deployed by the assault and support classes. But now, through the addition of the M18 Smoke Grenade, all classes can deploy smoke screens, ideal for concealing squad movements when there is a lack of cover. Smoke remains essential in Rush, while arming and disarming M-COM stations. But smoke is also vital in the new Obliteration and Defuse game modes, offering concealment while retrieving the bomb or when arming and disarming objectives. Or use smoke offensively to disorient opponents while picking them off through the IRNV (IR 1X) or FLIR (IR 2X) optics.

M84 FLASHBANG

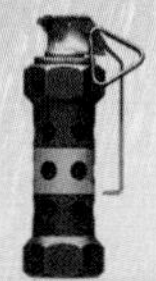

Description: Hand grenade with a suppressive Flashbang effect to temporarily blind enemies in close quarters.

Unlock: 5,000 Grenade Score

The M84 Flashbang is a popular tactical aid deployed by SWAT and hostage rescue teams, serving as a deterrent while clearing rooms and performing dynamic entries in close-quarter environments. In some respects, the Flashbang is more effective than its more lethal counterparts, blinding opponents for approximately three seconds, leaving them vulnerable. The duration an opponent is blinded varies depending on their proximity to device when it detonates. The direction an opponent is facing is also significant—if an opponent's back is turned, they won't be blinded as long. Toss Flashbangs into rooms occupied by opponents just prior to rushing in and mowing down the opposition—this is an easy (but somewhat cheap) way to score knife kills too.

HAND FLARE

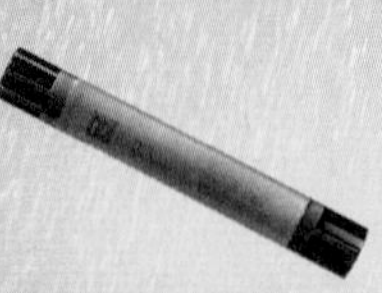

Description: Emergency Red Flare that burns to light up dark space and provides a small blinding effect.

Unlock: 6,000 Grenade Score

The least intimidating of the grenades, this standard Hand Flare can serve a variety of purposes on the battlefield. When operating in dark environments, use it to light up rooms or blind opponents, particularly those equipped with infrared optics. Or if your squad is pinned, toss it toward enemies to get the attention of teammates. The Hand Flare is highly visible over great distances, including from the air. Use the Hand Flare to designate strafing zones for friendly jets and helicopters.

KNIVES

Knife combat has evolved in *Battlefield 4* with the introduction of counters and more elaborate melee animations. But the core mechanics remain the same. For best results, always sneak up on your opponent from behind, taking them by surprise. When knifing from behind, your opponent has no opportunity to counter, allowing you to score the kill and secure their dog tags. Or if you like living on the edge, rush directly toward your opponent and attempt a frontal melee attack. Frontal knife attacks give your opponent the opportunity to counter, potentially leading to the loss of your own dog tags.

KNIVES

IMAGE	NAME	DESCRIPTION	UNLOCK
	Bayonette	Standard-issue USMC M9 bayonet for melee combat. Use it in melee combat to steal enemy dog tags.	Default
	ACB-90	Battlefield Veteran knife with added gut-hook to take out an enemy in melee and steal their dog tags.	Battlefield Veterans Only

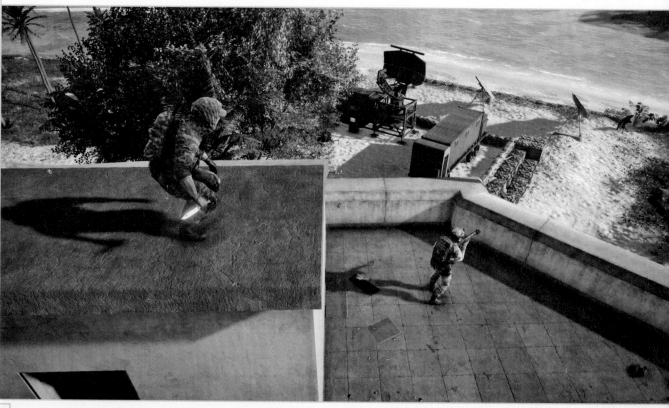

BATTLE PICKUPS

New to *Battlefield 4*, Battle Pickups are unique weapons found scattered about the battlefield, giving soldiers the chance to dish out some impressive firepower. Battle Pickups are marked on the HUD and minimap by a white pistol icon. Interact with a Battle Pickup to retrieve it from the ground and then operate it like any other firearm. Battle Pickups have very limited ammo and they can't be resupplied by Ammo Packs or Ammo Boxes. So take the time to make each shot count.

BATTLE PICKUPS

IMAGE	NAME	DESCRIPTION
	HVM-2	A shoulder-launched anti-vehicle missile system with its own guidance system, useful against air, ground, and naval units.
	M136 CS	A shoulder-launched anti-vehicle missile system with its own guidance system, useful against air, ground, and naval units.
	M32 MGL	A semi-automatic grenade launcher capable of firing six high-explosive grenades in quick succession.
	AMR-2	A one-shot kill sniper rifle equipped with a long-range optic.
	AMR-2 CQB	A one-shot kill sniper rifle equipped with a close range optic.
	AMR-2 MID	A one-shot kill sniper rifle equipped with a medium-range optic.
	M82A3	A one-shot kill sniper rifle equipped with a long-range optic.
	M82A3 CQB	A one-shot kill sniper rifle equipped with a close-range optic.
	M82A3 MID	A one-shot kill sniper rifle equipped with a medium-range optic.
	USAS-12	A fully automatic shotgun loaded with frag rounds, ideal for suppressing opponents and destroying cover.
	USAS-12 FLIR	A fully automatic shotgun loaded with frag rounds, ideal for suppressing opponents and destroying cover. Equipped with a FLIR optic for low-light amplification.

BATTLE PICKUP SERVICE STAR

A Battle Pickup service star is awarded for every 100 kills you score with each weapon. All kills scored with he AMR-2, M82A3, and USAS-12 variants count toward the same service star.

VEHICLES

LAND, AIR AND SEA

One of the highlights of any *Battlefield* game are the vehicles. Nothing can be more entertaining than hopping into a tank and cruising across the landscape, laying waste to both enemy vehicles and structures alike. *Battlefield 4* continues this rich tradition, allowing you to hop aboard boats, tanks, helicopters, and jets, to quickly move across the battlefield with speed and devastating firepower.

VEHICLE CUSTOMIZATION

In *Battlefield 4*, most of the vehicles can be customized utilizing unlockable upgrades, optics, countermeasures, and even weapons. The more you use a vehicle from a particular class, the more points you earn, unlocking new equipment at regular intervals in a linear progression. Once an unlock is awarded, you can assign it through the same loadout screen you use to customize the soldier classes. Most vehicles have five assignable slots: two weapon slots, one optic slot, one upgrade slot, and one countermeasure slot. IFVs, tanks, and attack helicopters gain additional slots for their gunners. Upgrades and optics are passive and require no action to take advantage of their benefits. Meanwhile, countermeasures and weapons require some interaction on the part of the driver or pilot to deploy. So as you progress through your multiplayer career, you will have to make some tough decisions as to what unlocks you wish to equip. Some unlocks improve offensive capabilities while others impact survivability. Experiment with the different options until you find a combination that best suits the tactical situation and your style of play. The unlock progression for each vehicle type is provided in this chapter, listing the point requirements to unlock each as well as a brief description of every weapon, optic, upgrade, and countermeasure. In addition to equipping vehicles with new gear, you can also alter their appearance by selecting different camo patterns through the paint slot. There are no unlocks available for light vehicles, armored transports, mobile artillery, and transport helicopters.

ATTACK HELICOPTERS HAVE THE MOST CUSTOMIZATION OPTIONS, ALLOWING FOR A WIDE RANGE OF POSSIBLE LOADOUTS.

To learn more and watch video on vehicles visit PrimaGames.com/BF4

LIGHT VEHICLES

The light vehicles are the fastest vehicles in the game, useful for rushing control points and other objectives at the start of a battle. But their light armor and exposed positions make them death traps if driven into heavy action. Most explosive munitions can disable these vehicles with one hit, potentially killing the driver and passengers. Their greatest defensive asset is their speed and off-road capability. To ensure survival, use these vehicles to traverse terrain on a map's periphery, but stay away from heated battles near control points and M-COM stations. Although these vehicles can attain high speeds on roads, most roads are traveled by larger and more deadly vehicles like tanks and IFVs. So stay off-road and out of sight. Such tactics are essential when staging raids on distant enemy-held control points or objectives. There are no vehicle unlocks or loadout options associated with the light vehicles.

QUAD BIKE

Nationality: All
Description: Fast unarmored, all-terrain transport vehicle with two seats.

VEHICLE PERFORMANCE

SPEED
ARMOR
FIREPOWER

VEHICLE OCCUPANCY

SEAT	POSITION	WEAPON	AMMO
1	Driver	None	—
2	Passenger	Troop Kit	—

FIELD NOTES

The Quad Bike is the fastest ground vehicle available, making it ideal for zipping across the battlefield at high speed while avoiding the slower, heavily armored vehicles. The driver has no access to weapons, but the passenger riding on the back can equip all weapons in their troop kit. But at high speed, firing from the back of a fast-moving Quad Bike is highly inaccurate—unless firing a guided weapon like the Javelin.

M1161 ITV

Nationality: US
Description: Used by the USMC starting in 2009, the M1161 ITV is the only transport vehicle that fits in the V-22 Osprey.

VEHICLE PERFORMANCE

SPEED
ARMOR
FIREPOWER

VEHICLE OCCUPANCY

SEAT	POSITION	WEAPON	AMMO
1	Driver	None	—
2	Gunner	HMG .50Cal	Infinite
3	Passenger	Troop Kit	—

FIELD NOTES

The M1161 ITV is fast and maneuverable, but the open-cockpit design leaves the driver and passengers vulnerable to incoming small arms fire. Never drive this vehicle into the middle of an intense fire fight. Instead, use it for quick raids on distant control points.

VDV BUGGY

Nationality: RU
Description: Russian Paratrooper light buggy.

VEHICLE PERFORMANCE

SPEED
ARMOR
FIREPOWER

VEHICLE OCCUPANCY

SEAT	POSITION	WEAPON	AMMO
1	Driver	None	—
2	Gunner	12.7mm HMG	Infinite
3	Passenger	Troop Kit	—

FIELD NOTES

Like the US M1161 ITV, the VDV Buggy is a fast attack vehicle ideal for launching sneaky flanking attacks on lightly defended enemy positions. Due to the lack of armor, take extra steps to keep this vehicle out of the line of fire. While the machine gun turret is great for suppressing enemy infantry, the gunner position is completely exposed.

LYT2021

Nationality: CN
Description: A Chinese fast attack vehicle deployed by PLA forces.

VEHICLE PERFORMANCE

SPEED
ARMOR
FIREPOWER

VEHICLE OCCUPANCY

SEAT	POSITION	WEAPON	AMMO
1	Driver	None	—
2	Gunner	12.7mm HMG	Infinite
3	Passenger	Troop Kit	—

FIELD NOTES

Closely resembling the Russian VDV Buggy, the Chinese LYT2021 is a fast attack vehicle with a wide wheel base, giving it greater stability when traveling off-road. Like its American and Russian counterparts, the vehicle is equipped with a machine gun turret. This machine gun is effective against other light vehicles and helicopters.

PWC

Nationality: All

Description: Unarmed rapid insertion Personal Watercraft (PWC). Seats two for high-speed amphibious landings.

VEHICLE PERFORMANCE

SPEED

ARMOR

FIREPOWER

VEHICLE OCCUPANCY

SEAT	POSITION	WEAPON	AMMO
1	Driver	None	—
2	Passenger	Troop Kit	—

FIELD NOTES

The PWC is like the water version of the Quad Bike, capable of rapidly transporting two soldiers across a body of water. Both the driver and passenger are completely exposed, so avoid using this vehicle during frontal assaults. Also, avoid beaching the craft unless you have no intent of using it again.

RHIB

Nationality: All

Description: The Rigid-Hull Inflatable Boat (RHIB) is an excellent vehicle for transport on the water.

VEHICLE PERFORMANCE

SPEED

ARMOR

FIREPOWER

VEHICLE OCCUPANCY

SEAT	POSITION	WEAPON	AMMO
1	Driver	None	—
2	Gunner	7.62mm Minigun	Infinite
3	Passenger	Troop Kit	—
4	Passenger	Troop Kit	—

FIELD NOTES

Mounted with a powerful minigun on the front, the RHIB is not just a transport, but also a fierce weapon for changing the tide of battle. The rapid-firing minigun can make quick work of infantry, light vehicles, and even aircraft. But the gunner is exposed, along with the driver and passengers. So it's best to keep moving when using the RHIB in an offensive role.

LIGHT VEHICLE TACTICS

- The roof-mounted machine guns found on the fast attack vehicles are excellent anti-aircraft guns. Fire a steady burst of automatic fire at enemy helicopters to make them spin out of control. You can even pick off opponents riding in the back of transport helicopters by firing into the rear passenger compartment.
- Think twice before loading your squad into one of these vehicles. All it takes is one hit from a tank or rocket launcher to disable your ride, potentially killing a large number of your squad members. If the vehicle becomes disabled, bail out and seek cover before the flaming wreck explodes. An engineer equipped with a Repair Tool can conduct repairs from one of the passenger positions, negating the need to bail out.
- Given their speed, the light vehicles are great for scoring road kills. Simply drive directly toward enemy troops at high speed and run them down before they can dash out of your way. Just hope they don't fire a rocket in your direction before you make contact.
- Passengers in the Growler ITV and VDV Buggy can fire the weapons from their troop kits. But accurately targeting enemies out of a moving vehicle is tough. It's often better to save your ammo for when the vehicle reaches its destination.
- At the start of a battle, don't drive off in one of these vehicles until a few teammates hop inside. On most maps, these vehicles serve as your team's primary means of transportation. Stranding teammates at your base won't win you any fans. However, your squadmates can spawn into the vehicle if there are open seats.
- Quad Bikes make excellent car bombs. Stick two or three C4 charges to the front of a Quad Bike and then drive it into the side or rear of an enemy tank or IFV. While traveling at high speed, jump off the Quad Bike approximately 15 meters before impacting the enemy vehicle. The Quad Bike will continue traveling in a straight line toward the enemy vehicle. When the abandoned, explosive-packed Quad Bike makes contact, detonate the C4 to score an unorthodox vehicle kill.
- It's possible to accurately fire guided anti-vehicle weapons like the Javelin, IGLA, or Stinger from the passenger positions of the light vehicles. The addition of these weapon systems can make light vehicles a formidable threat on a battlefield filled with tanks and aircraft.

- At the start of a battle, don't drive off in one of these vehicles until it's completely filled, either with squad members or teammates. On most maps, these vehicles serve as your team's primary means of transportation. Stranding teammates at your base won't win you any fans. However, your squadmates can spawn into the vehicle if there is an available seat.
- Quad Bikes can perform amazing jumps. Look for ramps or other sloped terrain to send this vehicle flying through the air.
- PWCs are the fastest vehicles on the water, making them perfect for surprising enemy attack boats. Sneak up behind an enemy attack boat and have a support or recon passenger toss C4 charges onto the deck before speeding away and detonating the explosives. Sure, it's a dangerous maneuver, but it's very rewarding when it works.

ARMORED TRANSPORTS

These heavily armored transports are slower than the light vehicles, but offer much more protection for their crews—small arms fire bounces off every surface, including the windows. Each vehicle is also equipped with a roof-mounted heavy machine gun turret controlled by a gunner, who operates the weapon remotely from within the vehicle. This allows the gunner to accurately engage hostile infantry without worrying about getting picked off by sharpshooters. While the armor on these vehicles is resistant to small arms fire, explosive weapons can temporarily disable or outright destroy them. A single hit by a rocket or tank round isn't enough to destroy an armored fighting vehicle. But successive hits by multiple explosive munitions can inflict lethal damage—get ready to bail out if one of these vehicles becomes disabled.

MRAP

Nationality: US

Description: Entering service in 2007, the Mine-Resistant Ambush Protected (MRAP) vehicle was designed to withstand powerful IED attacks.

VEHICLE PERFORMANCE

SPEED

ARMOR

FIREPOWER

VEHICLE OCCUPANCY

SEAT	POSITION	WEAPON	AMMO
1	Driver	None	—
2	Gunner	HMG .50Cal	Infinite
3	Passenger	None	—
4	Passenger	None	—

FIELD NOTES

The MRAP is a highly armored vehicle best deployed as a troop transport. Despite its sluggish acceleration, the MRAP is capable of impressive speeds once it gets moving. However, due to its weight, the vehicle takes a while to stop and is less than agile when attempting to make sharp turns. Therefore watch your speeds in areas where enemy mines may be present, otherwise you won't be able to avoid them.

SPM-3

Nationality: RU

Description: The latest variant in a line of Russian-designed armored cars with improved ballistic protection.

VEHICLE PERFORMANCE

SPEED

ARMOR

FIREPOWER

VEHICLE OCCUPANCY

SEAT	POSITION	WEAPON	AMMO
1	Driver	None	—
2	Gunner	12.7mm HMG	Infinite
3	Passenger	None	—
4	Passenger	None	—

FIELD NOTES

The rugged SPM-3 is a bit smaller than the American MRAP, making it easier to conceal behind low hills and other pieces of cover. But it still exhibits similar characteristics when on the move, including sluggish acceleration and labored steering. When not ferrying troops around, consider using it as a stand-off weapon, hammering distant enemy positions with its heavy machine gun.

ZFB-05

Nationality: CN

Description: The Chinese ZFB-05 entered service in 2008 and has served a variety of roles, including UN peacekeeping.

VEHICLE PERFORMANCE

SPEED

ARMOR

FIREPOWER

VEHICLE OCCUPANCY

SEAT	POSITION	WEAPON	AMMO
1	Driver	None	—
2	Gunner	12.7mm HMG	Infinite
3	Passenger	None	—
4	Passenger	None	—

FIELD NOTES

Functioning almost identically to its American and Russian counterpart, the ZFB-05 has unique angular features, making it difficult to score perpendicular hits with rockets. But these features have little impact over how much damage the vehicle can absorb, as one hit is usually enough to temporarily disable it.

ARMORED TRANSPORT VEHICLE TACTICS

- Despite their intimidating appearance, these armored vehicles aren't designed for frontline combat. Like the light vehicles, they're best deployed as troop transports, carrying infantry from one objective to the next while avoiding encounters with tanks and IFVs.
- When driving an armored transport, be ready for enemy ambushes. Although armored, running over mines and getting rocked by other explosive weapons can turn these vehicles into deathtraps. As a result, avoid high-traffic areas and chokepoints, particularly in urban environments. Instead, take the long way around and deliver your passengers to their destination without incident.
- The roof-mounted heavy machine guns on these vehicles are perfect for pinning down enemy infantry or damaging light vehicles, including helicopters and jets. Since the gunner position is completely armored, retaliatory attacks are less of a concern. Plus, the machine gun's view can be zoomed, ideal for engaging distant targets with surprising accuracy. But the rapid-firing weapon is likely to gain the attention of enemy engineers and pilots. So keep the vehicle on the move to avoid becoming a sitting duck for incoming rockets and other explosive attacks.
- When struck with explosive weapons, the side and rear doors of these vehicles can detach, leaving the driver and passengers exposed to small arms fire and other lethal attacks—fire a rocket or grenade inside the vehicle to kill all occupants. Once doors have been blown off, they cannot be replaced, even if the vehicle is completely repaired. In such instances, it's best to hop out and find a new ride.
- Unlike the light vehicles, passengers within the armored transport cannot equip their weapons and gadgets. Therefore if one of these vehicles is damaged, an engineer must exit and conduct repairs from the exterior.

INFANTRY FIGHTING VEHICLES (IFVS)

The Infantry Fighting Vehicles are the most versatile vehicles in the game, sometimes referred to as light tanks. They lack the heavy armor of tanks, but still have plenty of firepower. Their main weapon is an auto cannon, which fires high explosive rounds in quick succession as long as you hold down the fire button. But the auto cannon can only fire six rounds before a new rack must be loaded, resulting in a brief interruption. The IFVs also have a machine gun turret—the driver controls the auto cannon while the gunner controls the machine gun. There are also four passenger seats equipped with port- and starboard-mounted machine guns, making it ideal for hauling around your entire squad.

IFV UPGRADES

IMAGE	NAME	SLOT	UNLOCK POINTS	DESCRIPTION
DEFAULT UPGRADES				
	25mm Explosive Shell	Primary Weapon	—	Fires a 25mm explosive shell effective against infantry and light armor.
	Coaxial LMG	Secondary Weapon	—	Attaches a 7.62mm light machine gun to the main cannon for enhanced anti-infantry capability.
	IR Smoke	Countermeasure	—	Launches puffs of IR-deflecting metal shards that break lock-ons and spoof incoming missiles.
	Zoom Optics	Optics	—	A basic optic enhancement that provides a magnification of 3X when activated.
	Maintenance	Upgrade	—	Recovery from damage and critical hits starts sooner.
	Gunner Zoom	Gunner Optics	—	Zooms the view to more easily spot and take out targets at greater distance.
	Gunner Belt Feeder	Gunner Upgrade	—	An enhanced mechanism that makes reloading faster.
UNLOCKABLE UPGRADES				
	Thermal Camo	Upgrade	3,000	Special plating that increases the time it takes for enemy targeting systems to lock on to you.
	TOW Missile	Secondary Weapon	6,000	A wire-guided anti-tank missile that deals a large amount of damage to heavily armored targets and infantry within the blast radius.
	Gunner Proximity Scan	Gunner Upgrade	9,000	Scans the area around the vehicle and reveals enemy movement on the minimap.
	IRNV Optics	Optics	11,000	Enhanced infrared night vision that will make heat signatures easily distinguishable at close to medium ranges.
	APFSDS-T Shell	Primary Weapon	14,000	A shell without an explosive payload that travels at an increased velocity compared to other shells of the same caliber.
	Smokescreen	Countermeasure	17,000	Releases a thick cloud of smoke that visually obstructs the vehicle and makes it impossible for incoming missiles to achieve precise critically damaging shots.
	Gunner IRNV	Gunner Optics	20,000	Enhanced infrared night vision that will make heat signatures easily distinguishable at close to medium ranges.
	Autoloader	Upgrade	23,000	An enhanced mechanism that makes reloading faster.
	Thermal Optics	Optics	26,000	A black and white night vision system that shows heat signatures across all ranges.
	Gunner SOFLAM	Gunner Upgrade	29,000	Paints a target, allowing it to be locked on to by missile weapons that respond to laser designation.
	Canister Shell	Primary Weapon	32,000	Fires a 25mm canister of tungsten balls. Very effective for eliminating enemy infantry.
	Fire Extinguisher	Countermeasure	34,000	Can only be deployed when the vehicle is in a critically damaged state. It will put out any fires, bring the vehicle back to a functional state, and let the vehicle start recovering from sustained damage.
	Reactive Armor	Upgrade	37,000	Reactive armor absorbs some of the shock from incoming attacks, requiring hits to deal higher damage to count as critical.
	Gunner Thermal	Gunner Optics	40,000	A black and white night vision system that shows heat signatures across all ranges.
	Zuni Rockets	Secondary Weapon	43,000	Fires anti-infantry rockets also capable of taking out light armor.
	Gunner Incendiary	Gunner Upgrade	46,000	Releases a cloud of incendiary smoke that damages all soldiers in its area of effect.
	Active Protection	Countermeasure	50,000	When this system is activated, it will sense incoming missile and rocket threats and detonate them before they reach the vehicle. The system will enter a cooldown state after a threat has been neutralized or no threats have been detected for a short time.

LAV-25

Nationality: US

Description: The LAV-25 is an eight-wheeled amphibious infantry fighting vehicle (IFV) used by the USMC.

VEHICLE PERFORMANCE

SPEED

ARMOR

FIREPOWER

VEHICLE OCCUPANCY

SEAT	POSITION	WEAPON	AMMO
1	Driver	25mm Auto Cannon	36
2	Gunner	HMG .50Cal	Infinite
3	Passenger	Machine Gun	Infinite
4	Passenger	Machine Gun	Infinite
5	Passenger	Machine Gun	Infinite
6	Passenger	Machine Gun	Infinite

FIELD NOTES

Sporting thick armor and bristling with weapons, the LAV-25 is the ideal troop transport for the US team. While the vehicle is very effective against enemy infantry, it is vulnerable to attacks by tanks, helicopters, and jets. So if such threats are in the area, consider dropping off your passengers as soon as possible.

BTR-90

Nationality: RU

Description: Presented publicly for the first time in 1994, the amphibious BTR-90 is the Russian Army's next generation armored personnel carrier.

VEHICLE PERFORMANCE

SPEED

ARMOR

FIREPOWER

VEHICLE OCCUPANCY

SEAT	POSITION	WEAPON	AMMO
1	Driver	30mm Auto Cannon	36
2	Gunner	12.7mm HMG	Infinite
3	Passenger	Machine Gun	Infinite
4	Passenger	Machine Gun	Infinite
5	Passenger	Machine Gun	Infinite
6	Passenger	Machine Gun	Infinite

FIELD NOTES

The BTR-90 is a Russian Infantry Fighting Vehicle (IFV) sporting a powerful 30mm auto cannon as well as a turret-mounted heavy machine gun. The cannon can fire six high-explosive rounds in quick succession. The BTR-90 benefits from the same upgrades as the other IFVs, so don't forget to customize the vehicle's loadout prior to deploying.

ZBD-09

Nationality: CN

Description: The ZBD-09 is an amphibious eight-wheeled IFV that made its debut for the PLA in 2009.

VEHICLE PERFORMANCE

SPEED

ARMOR

FIREPOWER

VEHICLE OCCUPANCY

SEAT	POSITION	WEAPON	AMMO
1	Driver	30mm Auto Cannon	36
2	Gunner	12.7mm HMG	Infinite
3	Passenger	Machine Gun	Infinite
4	Passenger	Machine Gun	Infinite
5	Passenger	Machine Gun	Infinite
6	Passenger	Machine Gun	Infinite

FIELD NOTES

The ZBD-09 performs identically to its American and Russian counterparts. While the IFV excels as an armored troop transport, its impressive armament makes it a formidable weapons platform. Keep the vehicle back from the action and hammer enemy emplacements with the auto cannon and heavy machine gun. Avoid confined areas where the ZBD-09 can be hit with rockets and C4.

AAV-7A1 AMTRAC

Nationality: US
Description: The AAV-7A1 is the current amphibious troop transport of the USMC.

VEHICLE PERFORMANCE

SPEED
ARMOR
FIREPOWER

VEHICLE OCCUPANCY

SEAT	POSITION	WEAPON	AMMO
1	Driver	None	—
2	Gunner	LMG/Grenade Launcher	Infinite/27
3	Passenger	None	—
4	Passenger	None	—
5	Passenger	None	—
6	Passenger	None	—

FIELD NOTES

Technically the AMTRAC is not an IFV, so it does not benefit from the unlocks associated with the vehicle class. However, it performs just like an IFV, capable of carrying six players. It also serves as a mobile spawn point. Park this vehicle anywhere, and as long as seats are available, any teammate can spawn directly into the AMTRAC. The gunner position's grenade launcher and light machine gun give this slow transport some much-needed firepower.

IFV TACTICS

- The IFVs are well-armed, but they're not designed to take on tanks. However, there are several upgrades you can equip to give an IFV a fighting chance in a tank battle. For one, equip it with the Reactive Armor upgrade—this increases the amount of damage the vehicle can take. The armor-piercing APFSDS-T Shell and TOW Missile are other worthwhile upgrades, giving the IFV better offensive performance against tanks. Finally, equip the Active Protection countermeasure to intercept any incoming rockets or missiles fired by other units. These upgrades may not be enough to win a duel against a tank, but at least you'll inflict some heavy damage before it's time to abandon your IFV.
- The LAV-25, BTR-90, and ZBD-09 are wheeled vehicles. As a result, driving them is more like maneuvering a car than a tank. This means you need to drive either forward or backward to turn—and these vehicles have a huge turning radius. Vehicles with treads, like tanks and the AMTRAC, can rotate in place, making much easier to maneuver in close quarters. So when driving the wheeled IFVs, give yourself plenty of space before attempting a U-turn. It's faster to throw the vehicle into reverse when attempting a hasty retreat.
- The auto cannon and machine gun turrets on these vehicles are devastating against infantry. To better spot infantry at range, equip IRNV or Thermal Optics. These optics highlight a target's heat signature, making them much easier to spot, even if concealed by smoke or shadows.
- Never charge into a group of enemy infantry. IFVs are well-armored, but they can't withstand more than two or three rocket hits, not to mention mines. Instead, hold back and engage infantry from a safe distance, where they can't sneak up behind you. Equip the Proximity Scan upgrade to keep an eye on your vehicle's surroundings—nearby enemies appear on the minimap, serving as a welcome heads-up. Deploy the Incendiary countermeasure if C4-toting enemies get too close for comfort.
- The new Zuni Rockets are a secondary weapon, fired by the driver. These rockets are best equipped when playing on infantry-heavy maps or during Squad Deathmatch. These rockets perform similar to those fired by the attack helicopters. But they're more effective against infantry and light vehicles than they are against tanks and other IFVs.
- All the IFVs are amphibious, allowing them to travel across deep bodies water. Use this to your advantage by staging attacks from unpredictable directions. This is a great way to take enemies by surprise. But these vehicles move very slow while in the water, so watch out for helicopters, jets, and attack boats.
- When engaging an IFV, try to maneuver so you can score a side or rear hit, where the vehicle's armor is thinnest. Top hits are also very effective, making laser-guided weapons a serious threat. When driving one of these vehicles, be mindful of these weaknesses and try to keep the vehicle's front armor facing the enemy at all times. To avoid hits by laser-guided weapons, equip the Thermal Camo upgrade and Active Protection countermeasure.
- With six seats, the IFV is an ideal squad transport. Be careful when transporting your entire squad in an IFV. Driving over a cluster of mines could send your whole squad back to the deploy screen.
- Like recon troops, the IFV can laser-designate enemy vehicles when using the gunner's SOFLAM upgrade. So once you've unlocked this upgrade, keep your IFV back from the action and paint enemy vehicles with the SOFLAM's laser. A red diamond icon appears on the HUD when an enemy target has been designated.
- Completely different tactics apply when driving the AMTRAC. This slow troop transport only has a grenade launcher and light machine gun for defense, making it vulnerable against tanks and other heavy vehicles. When using this vehicle as a forward spawn point, park it in a relatively safe location that's still close to the action. This is very effective when attacking M-COM stations during Rush matches, allowing the attacking team to maintain a presence close to the objectives.

PRO TIP: STRONGSIDE

The IFVs will be your go-to vehicle for transporting squadmates and killing enemy infantry. Six soldiers fit in these vehicles, so be sure to catch a ride any time it spawns on the map. These vehicles are capable of maneuvering through water, making them very adept for all kinds of battle. Drive-by shooting is recommended—if the driver stays still too long enemies can easily hit you with rockets or run up and plant C4. Be cautious—if an enemy is staying back and drawing you in, it could mean mines are planted nearby.

MAIN BATTLE TANKS (MBTS)

While tanks are still at the top of the food chain during ground combat, they're far from invincible. Missiles fired by infantry, helicopters, and jets pose a big threat, as do other tanks. A tank's side, top, and rear armor are the weakest points. For this reason, keep the front armor facing a threat at all times, especially when engaging other tanks. The rounds fired by a tank's main gun travel in an arc-like trajectory. So compensate for range by elevating the barrel and aiming above your target. Use the horizontal lines on the tank's HUD to determine the proper elevation setting to score a hit.

MBT UPGRADES

IMAGE	NAME	SLOT	UNLOCK POINTS	DESCRIPTION
DEFAULT UPGRADES				
	AP Shell	Primary Weapon	—	A 120mm shell dealing high damage to light, medium, and heavy armor.
	Coaxial LMG	Secondary Weapon	—	Attaches a 7.62mm light machine gun to the main cannon for enhanced anti-infantry capability.
	IR Smoke	Countermeasure	—	Launches puffs of IR-deflecting metal shards that break lock-ons and spoof incoming missiles.
	Zoom Optics	Vehicle Optics	—	Zooms the view to more easily spot and take out targets at greater distance.
	Maintenance	Upgrade	—	Recovery from damage and critical hits starts sooner.
	Gunner Zoom	Gunner Optics	—	Zooms the view to more easily spot and take out targets at greater distance.
	Gunner Belt Feeder	Gunner Upgrade	—	An enhanced mechanism that makes reloading faster.
UNLOCKABLE UPGRADES				
	Thermal Camo	Upgrade	4,000	Special plating that increases the time it takes for enemy targeting systems to lock on to you.
	Guided Shell	Secondary Weapon	8,000	A powerful missile that locks on to ground vehicles. Once lock-on is achieved, the user has to maintain it until the missile has reached its target. If lock-on is lost, it can be re-acquired and the target can still be taken out. Can also lock on to laser-designated targets.
	Gunner Proximity Scan	Gunner Upgrade	11,000	Scans the area around the vehicle and reveals enemy movement on the minimap.
	IRNV Optics	Vehicle Optics	15,000	Enhanced infrared night vision that will make heat signatures easily distinguishable at close to medium ranges.
	HE Shell	Primary Weapon	19,000	A shaped charge fired from the tank's main cannon. Travels at a lower speed but deals heavy damage when used against armored targets.
	Smokescreen	Countermeasure	23,000	Releases a thick cloud of smoke that visually obstructs the vehicle and makes it impossible for incoming missiles to achieve precise, critically damaging shots.
	Autoloader	Upgrade	27,000	An enhanced mechanism that makes reloading faster.
	Gunner IRNV	Gunner Optics	30,000	Enhanced infrared night vision that will make heat signatures easily distinguishable at close to medium ranges.
	Coaxial HMG	Secondary Weapon	34,000	Attaches a .50 caliber machine gun to the turret for eliminating infantry and light armor.
	Thermal Optics	Vehicle Optics	38,000	A black and white night vision system that shows heat signatures across all ranges.
	Canister Shell	Secondary Weapon	42,000	Fires a 120mm canister of deadly tungsten pellets for eliminating enemy infantry.
	Fire Extinguisher	Countermeasure	46,000	Can only be deployed when the vehicle is in a critically damaged state. It will put out any fires, bring the vehicle back to a functional state, and let the vehicle start recovering from sustained damage.
	Gunner SOFLAM	Gunner Upgrade	49,000	Paints a target, allowing it to be locked on to by missile weapons that respond to laser designation.
	Reactive Armor	Upgrade	53,000	Reactive armor absorbs some of the shock from incoming attacks, requiring hits to deal higher damage to count as critical.

MBT UPGRADES, CONTINUED

IMAGE	NAME	SLOT	UNLOCK POINTS	DESCRIPTION
	STAFF Shell	Secondary Weapon	57,000	A 120mm shell with a smart warhead that will identify enemy targets and explode above them for a critical hit. Can also lock on to laser-designated targets.
	Gunner Thermal	Gunner Optics	61,000	A black and white night vision system that shows heat signatures across all ranges.
	Sabot Shell	Primary Weapon	64,000	A shell without an explosive payload that travels at an increased velocity compared to other shells of the same caliber.
	Gunner Incendiary	Gunner Upgrade	68,000	Releases a cloud of incendiary smoke damaging all soldiers in its area of effect.
	Active Protection	Countermeasure	72,000	When this system is activated, it will sense incoming missile and rocket threats and detonate them before they reach the vehicle. The system will enter a cooldown state after a threat has been neutralized or no threats have been detected for a short time.

M1 ABRAMS

Nationality: US

Description: The M1 Abrams is the principal battle tank of the USMC.

VEHICLE PERFORMANCE

SPEED

ARMOR

FIREPOWER

VEHICLE OCCUPANCY

SEAT	POSITION	WEAPON	AMMO
1	Driver	120mm Cannon	5
2	Gunner	HMG .50Cal	Infinite

FIELD NOTES

Powered by a turbine engine, the M1 Abrams sounds more like a jet than a tank, producing a distinct whining sound. The green horizontal lines in the center of the tank's HUD can be used to gauge barrel elevation when firing at distant targets. But hitting targets at extreme ranges requires more guess work, as there are no lines to reference. Fire a shot, watch where it lands, and then either elevate or lower the barrel to zero-in on your target.

T-90A

Nationality: RU

Description: The T-90A is derived from the T-72, and is the most modern tank in service with the Russian Ground Forces and Naval Infantry.

VEHICLE PERFORMANCE

SPEED

ARMOR

FIREPOWER

VEHICLE OCCUPANCY

SEAT	POSITION	WEAPON	AMMO
1	Driver	125mm Cannon	5
2	Gunner	12.7mm Machine Gun	Infinite

FIELD NOTES

The T-90A is well balanced when countering the US M1 Abrams or Chinese Type 99 MBT, but its HUD offers a bit more help when engaging targets at long range. Use the green vertical line beneath the tank's center crosshairs to better gauge barrel elevation. The horizontal notches on this line can be used as reference points when firing the main gun—if the first notch was too low, elevate your aim to the second notch, and so on.

TYPE 99 MBT

Nationality: CN

Description: The Type 99 is a third generation Main Battle Tank (MBT) fielded by the Chinese People's Liberation Army.

VEHICLE PERFORMANCE

SPEED

ARMOR

FIREPOWER

VEHICLE OCCUPANCY

SEAT	POSITION	WEAPON	AMMO
1	Driver	125mm Cannon	5
2	Gunner	12.7mm Machine Gun	Infinite

FIELD NOTES

The Type 99 MBT performs much like its American and Russian counterparts, sporting a sleek, modern design along with substantial firepower and thick armor. When driving the vehicle, a simple crosshair reticle appears at the center of the HUD, offering a point of reference when aiming the tank's 125mm cannon. While the simple reticle is effective at close ranges, elevate your aim when engaging targets at medium to long range.

MBT TACTICS

- Tanks are designed for one purpose: killing other tanks. Statistically, the M1 Abrams, the T-90A, and Type 99 MBT are identical, providing an even playing field for both drivers during tank duels. But there are a few tactics you can use to gain the upper hand. For one, try to maneuver so you can target the enemy tank's weak side or rear armor. Likewise, rotate your tank so both the chassis and turret are facing the enemy tank's main gun. This allows the thick front armor to absorb the majority of the damage. The Autoloader and Reactive Armor upgrades can also make a huge difference in a tank duel.
- Due to the new ammo system applied to vehicles, the tanks can only fire five shells in rapid succession. Ammo slowly replenishes over time, but you'll need to constantly monitor the tank's ammo count, displayed in the bottom right corner of the HUD. Don't pick a fight with another tank until you have the maximum five rounds ready to fire.
- Since ammo is now limited, make use of the secondary weapons to keep your tank in the fight, even when the primary weapon is out of ammo. The Coaxial LMG and Coaxial HMG are machine guns that have unlimited ammo and are perfect for mowing down infantry and damaging light vehicles. Canister Shell effectively turns the tank's cannon into a massive shotgun, firing pellets over a wide area and perfect for wiping out infantry or damaging vehicles—try hitting low-flying helicopters and jets with the Canister Shell.
- The new STAFF Shell fills the secondary weapon slot, but offers great tank-killing potential. The shell is equipped with a smart warhead designed to score top hits on enemy vehicles. One hit from a STAFF Shell has the ability to temporarily disable an enemy tank or IFV, making it extremely vulnerable to follow-up shots. When closing in for the kill, use a shell fired from the primary weapon, such as the AP, HE, or Sabot Shell.
- Tanks are best deployed as stand-off weapons. Use the power and range of the cannon to engage enemy vehicles at long range. This is easiest when firing the Guided Shell weapon unlock. These shells are capable of locking on to laser-designated targets painted by a recon soldier's SOFLAM or PLD. A tank can designate its own targets too, using the Gunner SOFLAM upgrade. Any vehicle can be designated with a laser, including aircraft. This Guided Shell is very effective in taking down enemy jets and helicopters, assuming a lock can be maintained.
- Never go hunting for infantry in a tank, especially in urban environments. If you spot enemy infantry on the periphery, immediately back up while firing before one of them can toss a mine or C4 in your direction. The Gunner Proximity Scan upgrade is ideal for detecting enemies approaching your vehicle—they show up as red icons on the minimap.
- Consider playing as an engineer when driving a tank. As you take damage, retreat, hop out, and use the Repair Tool to fix your ride. Better yet, have your engineer gunner get out and repair while you continue firing the main gun. This tactic gives you a huge advantage during tank duels and is the only way to keep a disabled tank in the fight.
- Helicopters and jets are a tank's worst enemy. However, the machine gun turret is completely capable of damaging these airborne threats. But when counterattacking, stay on the move to prevent giving your opponent an easy target to strafe. Use the IR Smoke or Smokescreen countermeasures to conceal your position and break the locks of laser-guided munitions.
- The tank's last countermeasure unlock is Active Protection. This functions just like the MP-APS carried by the support class, automatically destroying incoming rockets and missiles. This device is a game changer when facing incoming rockets and laser-guided munitions fired by enemy engineers and vehicles. But Active Protection enters a cooldown state after destroying each incoming projectile, leaving your tank vulnerable for a few seconds. Reactive Armor serves as a good backup, absorbing damage until Active Protection is back online. But you'll still want a friendly engineer (or EOD Bot) nearby to conduct repairs if your tank is overwhelmed by incoming fire.
- The driver's seat of a tank offers poor visibility. Unless a teammate is manning the machine gun turret and actively scanning the perimeter for threats, switch to an external view when driving a tank through city streets. This allows you to spot enemy troops attempting to sneak up on your tank—support troops can ruin your day by sticking C4 to the back of your ride.

PRO TIP: FLAMESWORD

TANKS ARE DESIGNED FOR ONE PURPOSE: TO FORCE THE OPPONENT INTO CHAOS. YOUR BEST OPTION IS TO PARK THE TANK A DISTANCE FROM YOUR OPPONENT AND FIRE SHELLS FROM YOUR MAIN CANNON AT OPPONENTS, ALLOWING YOUR INFANTRY PLAYERS TO MOVE IN. THE GUNNER SHOULD FOCUS ON MOWING DOWN ENEMY INFANTRY AND REPAIRING THE VEHICLE AS NEEDED. TANKS ARE EQUIPPED WITH TOUGH ARMOR, SO DON'T BE AFRAID TO CHARGE INTO AN AREA IF A SITUATION IS DIRE—SUCH DISTRACTIONS MAY BE ENOUGH TO ALLOW YOUR TEAM'S INFANTRY TO SET A CHARGE ON AN OBJECTIVE.

MOBILE AA

Despite their rugged armored appearance, these vehicles aren't intended for toe-to-toe slugfests with enemy tanks. In fact, their armor isn't much stronger than an IFVs. But these vehicles are designed for the sole purpose of shooting down enemy aircraft. Move them to strategically advantageous locations to provide your forces protection from air strikes. The auto cannons on these vehicles are great for shredding helicopters and jets alike. But these weapons can also be very effective when targeting infantry and light vehicles. Mobile AA vehicles are rare, so take steps to protect them by keeping them repaired at all times.

MOBILE AA UPGRADES

IMAGE	NAME	SLOT	UNLOCK POINTS	DESCRIPTION
DEFAULT UPGRADES				
	20mm Cannon	Primary Weapon	—	Fires 20mm bullets at an extremely high rate of fire for eliminating airborne targets.
	Heatseekers	Secondary Weapon	—	Once locked on, these surface-to-air missiles will guide themselves towards their target.
	IR Smoke	Countermeasure	—	Fires canisters of vaporized brass and graphite particles, which interferes with the tracking of hostile missiles and laser designations.
	Zoom Optics	Optics	—	Zooms the view to more easily spot and take out targets at greater distance.
	Maintenance	Upgrade	—	Recovery from damage and critical hits starts sooner.
UNLOCKABLE UPGRADES				
	Thermal Camo	Upgrade	1,000	Special plating that increases the time that it takes for targeting systems to lock on to the vehicle.
	IRNV Optics	Optics	2,000	Enhanced infrared night vision that will make heat signatures easily distinguishable at close to medium ranges.
	Autoloader	Upgrade	3,000	An enhanced mechanism that reduces the time taken to reload.
	Passive Radar	Secondary Weapon	4,000	Surface-to-air homing missile system that requires the lock to be maintained all the way to the target.
	Proximity Scan	Upgrade	5,000	Scans the area surrounding the vehicle, revealing enemy movement on the minimap.
	Smokescreen	Countermeasure	6,000	Releases a thick cloud of smoke that surrounds the vehicle, impairing target acquisition and making it impossible for incoming missiles to achieve precise, critically damaging shots.
	30mm Cannon	Primary Weapon	7,000	Fires 30mm anti-air shells at a moderately high rate of fire.
	Thermal Optics	Optics	8,000	A black and white night vision system that shows heat signatures across all ranges.
	Reactive Armor	Upgrade	9,000	Reactive armor absorbs some of the shock from incoming attacks, requiring hits to deal higher damage to count as critical.
	Fire Extinguisher	Countermeasure	10,000	Can only be deployed when the vehicle is in a critically damaged state. It will put out any fires, bring the vehicle back to a functional state, and let the vehicle start recovering from sustained damage.
	Zuni Rockets	Secondary Weapon	11,000	Fires anti-infantry rockets also capable of taking out light armor.
	Air Radar	Upgrade	12,000	Replaces the minimap with a radar display, highlighting airborne targets in a large radius around the aircraft.
	Active Radar	Secondary Weapon	13,000	Once fired, these missiles will locate and track toward the nearest airborne target and explode within close proximity.
	Active Protection	Countermeasure	14,000	When this system is activated, it will sense incoming missile and rocket threats and detonate them before they reach the vehicle. The system will enter a cooldown state after a threat has been neutralized or no threats have been detected for a short time.

LAV-AD

Nationality: US

Description: The LAV-AD includes the Avenger anti-air system on a LAV-25 chassis.

VEHICLE PERFORMANCE

SPEED

ARMOR

FIREPOWER

VEHICLE OCCUPANCY

SEAT	POSITION	WEAPON	AMMO
1	Driver	20mm AA Cannon	Infinite

FIELD NOTES

The LAV-AD looks just like the LAV-25, but it performs quite differently. For one, it only has a driver seat and cannot be used to transport troops. But the five-barreled 20mm cannon attached to its turret is great for tearing apart enemy helicopters and jets. The weapon is equally devastating against infantry and light vehicles. It can even damage tanks.

9K22 TUNGUSKA-M

Nationality: RU

Description: Mobile surface-to-air gun and missile system in service since 1982. Developed in response to range shortcomings in the ZU-23 Shilka design.

VEHICLE PERFORMANCE

SPEED

ARMOR

FIREPOWER

VEHICLE OCCUPANCY

SEAT	POSITION	WEAPON	AMMO
1	Driver	Dual 20mm AA Cannons	Infinite

FIELD NOTES

Offensively, the Tunguska performs identically to the LAV-AD and Type 95 AA, ideal for ripping apart aircraft, light vehicles, and infantry with its rapid-firing 20mm cannons. However, this hulking tracked vehicle is a bit more sluggish than its wheeled counterpart, but has increased maneuverability in tight spaces, capable of rotating in place.

TYPE 95 AA

Nationality: CN

Description: The Type 95 AA is a self-propelled anti-aircraft vehicle that entered PLA service in 1999.

VEHICLE PERFORMANCE

SPEED

ARMOR

FIREPOWER

VEHICLE OCCUPANCY

SEAT	POSITION	WEAPON	AMMO
1	Driver	Quad 20mm AA Cannons	Infinite

FIELD NOTES

The Chinese Type 95 AA is virtually identical to the Russian Tunguska-M in both appearance and functionality. Like its Russian counterpart, the Type 95 AA is a tracked vehicle that maneuvers just like a tank. Although it's a bit slow, the Type 95 AA is surprisingly maneuverable in tight spaces. Rotate the vehicle as necessary, absorbing incoming fire with its thick front armor.

MOBILE AA TACTICS

- Before moving out, analyze your team's air defenses and move the vehicle to an area where it can protect your team. Make an effort to park it in a well-protected area that is out of sight from advancing enemy tanks and infantry. While scanning the skies for targets, it's easy to lose sight of the battle happening around you, so be aware of approaching infantry and vehicles. The Proximity Scan upgrade serves as a good early detection system, identifying nearby enemies on the minimap.
- Instead of constantly rotating the turret to look for targets, rely on the minimap to spot enemy jets and helicopters. If spotted by teammates, these threats appear as red icons on the minimap. So rotate the turret in the direction of these icons, then scan the sky for the target—if still spotted, a red icon appears above the aircraft, making it easy to track. The Air Radar upgrade automatically marks the positions of all enemy aircraft on the minimap, making it much easier to track air targets.
- The mobile AA vehicles have unlimited ammo, but the cannons tend to overheat when fired for long, uninterrupted bursts. To prevent overheating, fire in bursts that last no longer than four seconds. A quick pause in firing allows the guns to cool down.
- When attacking one of these vehicles, try to hit them from the side, top, or rear, where their armor is weakest. Although they fill a very specialized role, these vehicles have thick armor capable of withstanding heavy damage. Tanks and IFVs are best suited for taking out these vehicles.
- These vehicles have several weapon unlocks, allowing you to customize them for different situations. The Heatseekers are the default secondary weapon, perfect for targeting enemy aircraft—these missiles are fire and forget, automatically tracking an aircraft's heat source. The Passive Radar anti-air missiles are unlocked later, but require a constant lock throughout the missile's flight to the target—use these when you have a clear view of the sky, with few obstructions. Active Radar missiles are easier to use. Simply fire them and let them track down any air target on their own, ideal when fighting on maps with plenty of air traffic.
- When locking on to an aircraft with missiles, the pilot you're tracking is made aware of the missile lock and may deploy IR Flares or other countermeasures in an effort to break the lock. So consider waiting for the pilot to dump their flares before reacquiring a lock and firing a missile. If the lock is achieved quickly, the pilot won't have a chance to deploy a second set of flares.
- In addition to shooting down jets and helicopters, the mobile AA vehicles are devastating against infantry and light vehicles. Adding Zuni Rockets as a secondary weapon makes these vehicles even more intimidating. The Zuni Rockets are capable of rapid fire, perfect for targeting infantry and ripping into light vehicles. But these rockets are less effective when targeting tanks and IFVs. Still, they give the mobile AA vehicle some much-needed offensive capability against their ground-based predators.

PRO TIP: STRONGSIDE

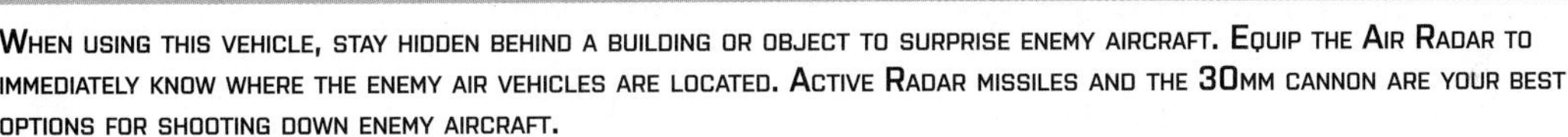

WHEN USING THIS VEHICLE, STAY HIDDEN BEHIND A BUILDING OR OBJECT TO SURPRISE ENEMY AIRCRAFT. EQUIP THE AIR RADAR TO IMMEDIATELY KNOW WHERE THE ENEMY AIR VEHICLES ARE LOCATED. ACTIVE RADAR MISSILES AND THE 30MM CANNON ARE YOUR BEST OPTIONS FOR SHOOTING DOWN ENEMY AIRCRAFT.

MOBILE ARTILLERY

The M142 mobile artillery unit, available to all nationalities, launches volleys of high-explosive rockets over great distances, giving each team the ability to bombard targets from across the map. The M142 is capable of launching up to six rockets in quick succession. Since *Battlefield 3: Armored Kill*, the targeting system for this vehicle has been upgraded, making them much more precise and deadly. From the gunner position, use the video display to target different locations on the map—simply place the white reticle over your target and fire. After firing six rockets, the vehicle automatically begins the long reload process. During this time the vehicle is completely defenseless. At close range, mobile artillery units are vulnerable to attacks by infantry, tanks, and aircraft. So keep these units back from the front lines where they're less likely to be harassed by enemies.

M142

Nationality: All

Description: Mobile rocket artillery used by the USMC and Fire Brigade.

VEHICLE PERFORMANCE

SPEED

ARMOR

FIREPOWER

VEHICLE OCCUPANCY

SEAT	POSITION	WEAPON	AMMO
1	Driver	None	—
2	Gunner	227mm Rockets	6

FIELD NOTES

The hulking M142 is approximately the size of a bus, so don't expect to get anywhere fast in this vehicle. Fortunately, it's best deployed behind the front lines, so its sluggish acceleration and wide turn radius shouldn't be much of a drawback. While the outer skin of the vehicle can repel small arms fire, the driver and gunner can be shot through the narrow front and side windows.

MOBILE ARTILLERY TACTICS

- Despite their impressive display, the standard rockets fired by the mobile artillery units don't cause much splash damage. It practically takes a direct hit to significantly damage an armored vehicle like a tank or IFV. But the impact of multiple rockets in a small area can have a significant psychological effect on infantry, causing them to scramble for cover. So even if you don't score too many kills with these vehicles, they play a big role in suppressing enemy troops during attacks on control points and other objectives. They're also great for leveling small buildings, denying cover to the enemy.
- The targeting system of the M142 functions just like the support soldier's M224 Mortar. Scroll across the map view on the TV screen while scanning for targets on the map. This map looks just like the minimap, showing the locations of objectives and friendly units. However, only spotted enemies will appear on this map, so make sure your teammates are spotting enemy infantry and vehicles—otherwise you'll be firing blind.
- The rockets have an effective range of approximately 650 meters when the rocket tubes are raised to their maximum angle and when the vehicle is parked on even terrain. However, you can get a bit more distance from the rockets by parking the unit on an elevated slope. This allows you fire the rockets at a steeper trajectory, resulting in greater range.
- Make a habit of parking these vehicles in remote areas of the map where they're less likely to be disturbed by enemies traveling between control points or other high-traffic areas. However, once you start firing rockets, your position will be easy to spot. So make a habit of moving the vehicle after you've fired a volley of rockets. Staying in one position too long can make you an easy target for enemy aircraft and counter-artillery bombardments.
- When encountering enemy vehicles at close range, these vehicles are defenseless. It's often better to retreat or hop out and fight on foot than it is to try and engage and win a fight with a tank or IFV at close range. However, if you manage to score a hit with one of the M142 rockets, you may have a chance to survive the encounter.

ATTACK BOATS

The attack boats are new to *Battlefield 4*, taking naval combat to a whole new level. These sleek and fast boats are essentially IFVs on the water, equipped with a pilot-operated auto cannon turret—this turret also supports secondary weapons like the default TOW Missile. But unlike the IFVs, the attack boats are also fitted with port and starboard miniguns, operated by crewmates. The miniguns are deadly implements in their own right, capable of shredding infantry, light vehicles, and even aircraft. For a boat, these watercraft can also absorb some heavy damage. If the boat is nearly destroyed, crew can escape in one of two PWCs, towed behind each attack boat. Riding a PWC to shore sure beats swimming.

ATTACK BOAT UPGRADES

IMAGE	NAME	SLOT	UNLOCK POINTS	DESCRIPTION
DEFAULT UPGRADES				
	25mm Cannon	Primary Weapon	—	Explosive shells that deal heavy damage against infantry and light armor.
	TOW Missile	Secondary Weapon	—	A user-guided anti-tank missile that deals huge damage to heavily armored targets and infantry inside the blast radius.
	IR Smoke	Countermeasure	—	Launches puffs of IR-deflecting metal shards that break lock-ons and spoof incoming missiles.
	Zoom Optics	Optics	—	Zooms the view to more easily spot and take out targets at greater distance.
	Maintenance	Upgrade	—	Recovery from damage and critical hits starts sooner.
UNLOCKABLE UPGRADES				
	Thermal Camo	Upgrade	4,000	Special plating that increases the time it takes for enemy targeting systems to lock on to you.
	Passive Radar	Secondary Weapon	8,000	Surface-to-air missiles that require the user to maintain a lock on the target. If the lock-on is lost, it can be reacquired and the missiles might still reach their target.
	Smokescreen	Countermeasure	12,000	Releases a thick cloud of smoke that visually obstructs the vehicle and makes it impossible for incoming missiles to achieve precise, critically damaging shots.
	Proximity Scan	Upgrade	16,000	Scans the area around the vehicle and reveals enemy movement on the minimap.
	IRNV Optics	Optics	19,000	Enhanced infrared night vision that will make heat signatures easily distinguishable at close to medium ranges.
	30mm Cannon	Primary Weapon	23,000	Fires 30mm shells with a bigger explosive payload for increased damage against infantry and armor, but at the expense of decreased ammo capacity.
	Belt Feeder	Upgrade	27,000	An enhanced mechanism that reduces the time taken to reload.

ATTACK BOAT UPGRADES, CONTINUED

IMAGE	NAME	SLOT	UNLOCK POINTS	DESCRIPTION
	Laser Guided	Secondary Weapon	31,000	A powerful missile that locks on to ground vehicles. Once lock-on is achieved the user has to maintain it until the missile has reached its target. If lock-on is lost, it can be re-acquired and the target can still be taken out.
	Air Radar	Upgrade	35,000	Replaces the minimap with a radar display showing airborne targets in a large radius around the aircraft.
	Zuni Rockets	Secondary Weapon	39,000	Fires anti-infantry rockets also capable of taking out light armor.
	Fire Extinguisher	Countermeasure	43,000	Can only be deployed when the vehicle is in a critically damaged state. It will put out any fires, bring the vehicle back to a functional state, and let the vehicle start recovering from sustained damage.
	Burst Cannon	Primary Weapon	47,000	Fires a ten-round burst of 25mm shells for devastating effect against aircraft and other light armored vehicles.
	Thermal Optics	Optics	51,000	A black and white night vision system that shows heat signatures across all ranges.
	TV-Guided Missile	Secondary Weapon	54,000	A missile controlled by the user via remote camera. Effective against armored targets.
	Active Protection	Countermeasure	60,000	When this system is activated, it will sense incoming missile and rocket threats and detonate them before they reach the vehicle. The system will enter a cooldown state after a threat has been neutralized or no threats have been detected for a short time.

RCB-90

Nationality: US

Description: The RCB-90 is the US variant of an attack boat originally produced for the Swedish Navy.

VEHICLE PERFORMANCE

SPEED

ARMOR

FIREPOWER

VEHICLE OCCUPANCY

SEAT	POSITION	WEAPON	AMMO
1	Pilot	25mm Cannon	90
2	Gunner	7.62mm Minigun	Infinite
3	Gunner	7.62mm Minigun	Infinite
4	Passenger	Troop Kit	—

FIELD NOTES

Bristling with powerful weapons, the RCB-90 is a fast and agile watercraft best deployed as an offshore weapons platform in support of amphibious landings. These boats are often deployed from aircraft carriers, serving as the US team's base. But in rare occasions these vehicles spawn at control points during Conquest matches.

DV-15

Nationality: RU/CN

Description: The French-developed DV-15 attack boat can operate in shallow water, making it perfect for coastal patrol duty.

VEHICLE PERFORMANCE

SPEED

ARMOR

FIREPOWER

VEHICLE OCCUPANCY

SEAT	POSITION	WEAPON	AMMO
1	Pilot	25mm Cannon	90
2	Gunner	7.62mm Minigun	Infinite
3	Gunner	7.62mm Minigun	Infinite
4	Passenger	Troop Kit	—

FIELD NOTES

The DV-15 is used by both Russian and Chinese forces and is equipped with the same weapon loadout as the American RCB-90. Like its American counterpart, this is a very versatile watercraft capable of taking on ground vehicles as well as helicopters and jets. These usually deploy at Chinese and Russian bases—don't leave them there. Get this boat on the water and rack up some kills.

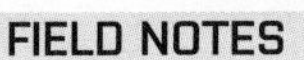

ATTACK BOAT TACTICS

> Traditionally, watercraft have served mostly as transports, ferrying troops across large bodies of water. The attack boats change all of that. Think of them more as a tank or IFV, using them to hunt down enemy vehicles and infantry. But be careful when operating in shallow water near shore—unintentionally beaching one of these vehicles is a terrible waste.

> The attack boat's default weaponry is impressive enough. But consider customizing the boat's weapon loadout to transform it into a serious anti-air threat. Equip Passive Radar missiles, Burst Cannon, Air Radar, and Active Protection, then hunt down enemy jets and helicopters.

> When not attacking aircraft, use the attack boat in a supportive role, assisting infantry and ground units. The Zuni Rockets are ideal for attacking infantry while the Laser Guided missile and TV-Guided Missile are very effective against enemy vehicles, including other attack boats.

> With so many weapons to choose from, it's tempting to anchor an attack boat off-shore and bombard enemy positions from a distance. But it's important to keep moving, making the boat a more difficult target to hit. If you stay in one spot too long, enemy infantry might swim out to challenge you. Although uncommon, recon and support troops can dive beneath the surface and attach C4 to the bottom of the boat.

> Soldiers riding in the fourth position, at the back of the boat, may feel like they're missing out on all the fun. But an engineer posted in this position can make a big difference. Weapons and gadgets from the soldier's troop kit can be accessed from this position, allowing engineers to conduct repairs with their Repair Tool while still aboard the boat. Engineers can also fire guided weapons like the IGLA, Stinger, or Javelin, giving the attack boat an even greater offensive punch.

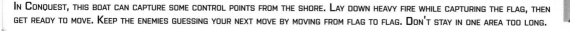

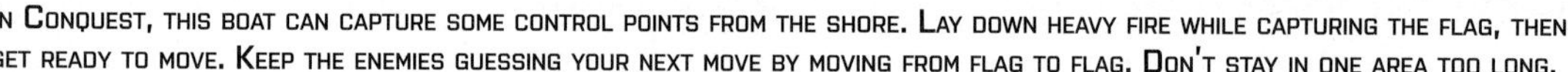

In Conquest, this boat can capture some control points from the shore. Lay down heavy fire while capturing the flag, then get ready to move. Keep the enemies guessing your next move by moving from flag to flag. Don't stay in one area too long.

TRANSPORT HELICOPTERS

Each transport helicopter is capable of holding five players, making them ideal for transporting squads to any spot on the battlefield. During Conquest matches, these large choppers are the best way to capture neutral control points at the start of a battle. But the transport helicopter's impressive troop capacity is also its weakness, and may result in a big score for a fighter pilot or any other unit armed with heat-seeking missiles. To avoid such threats, fly low and fast, using trees, hills, and buildings to mask your movements. As long as you avoid line-of-sight with your enemies, they can't attain a lock and fire a missile. There are no vehicle unlocks or loadout options for transport helicopters.

UH-1Y VENOM

Nationality: US

Description: Newest modern version of the "Twin Huey" helicopters used by the USMC since the 1970s. This new variant was introduced in 2008.

VEHICLE PERFORMANCE

SPEED

ARMOR

FIREPOWER

VEHICLE OCCUPANCY

SEAT	POSITION	WEAPON	AMMO
1	Pilot	None	—
2	Gunner	Minigun	Infinite
3	Gunner	Minigun	Infinite
4	Passenger	Troop Kit	—
5	Passenger	Troop Kit	—

FIELD NOTES

The Venom is the US team's fastest high-capacity troop transport. It is also armed with port and starboard mounted miniguns. The miniguns have a blazing rate of the fire, ideal for engaging troops and light vehicles. With sustained fire, they can even damage armored vehicles such as tanks and IFVs.

KA-60 KASATKA

Nationality: RU

Description: New utility helicopter from Kamov entering service with the Russian Air Force to replace the aging Mi-8.

VEHICLE PERFORMANCE

SPEED

ARMOR

FIREPOWER

VEHICLE OCCUPANCY

SEAT	POSITION	WEAPON	AMMO
1	Pilot	None	—
2	Gunner	Minigun	Infinite
3	Gunner	Minigun	Infinite
4	Passenger	Troop Kit	—
5	Passenger	Troop Kit	—

FIELD NOTES

The KA-60 performs much like the US team's Venom, but the pilot sits on the starboard side. This can be a bit disorienting at first, compared to piloting the other choppers where the pilot either sits in the middle or on the port side. So when maneuvering the chopper at low altitude, be mindful of the port side to avoid clipping trees, towers, and other objects.

Z-9 HAITUN

Nationality: CN

Description: Based on a French design, the Chinese Z-9 Haitun was first deployed by the PLA in 1994, serving primarily as a troop transport.

VEHICLE PERFORMANCE

SPEED

ARMOR

FIREPOWER

VEHICLE OCCUPANCY

SEAT	POSITION	WEAPON	AMMO
1	Pilot	None	—
2	Gunner	Minigun	Infinite
3	Gunner	Minigun	Infinite
4	Passenger	Troop Kit	—
5	Passenger	Troop Kit	—

FIELD NOTES

The pilot in the Z-9 sits on the port side. This makes piloting the Z-9 just like flying the US team's Venom. This helicopter is almost always deployed at bases, serving as the perfect transport for quickly moving a squad to distant objectives. Fly low and get troops on the ground as quickly as possible.

TRANSPORT HELICOPTER TACTICS

- Unless you have experience flying helicopters, don't try to fly a transport helicopter filled with teammates. This is the wrong time to take a flying lesson—go practice on the Test Range until you're ready. This will allow you to experiment with taking off, flying, and landing. Don't pilot one of these helicopters in a match until you can easily land on a rooftop.
- It takes a few seconds for a transport helicopter's rotor to spin up before take-off. So after securing an enemy base in Rush matches, watch for enemies lurking about during these vulnerable seconds as you can die fast if you get hit with a rocket or tank round. Also, take steps to ensure the enemy doesn't steal your choppers.
- The transport helicopters can be used to quickly capture control points during Conquest matches—hover over the flag to convert it. The more players on board, the faster it will be captured. However, watch out for defenders below. A hovering chopper makes a juicy target. It's much safer to drop troops via parachute onto a control point.
- Use the miniguns to blow apart light cover offered by walls and rooftops. This is a great way to expose objectives located inside small structures during Rush and Obliteration matches.
- The miniguns are capable of high rates of fire, but they have a tendency to overheat, rendering them inoperable for a few seconds. So lay off the trigger occasionally to allow the barrels a chance to cool down. For a better view of distant targets, use the minigun's zoom function.
- When piloting a transport helicopter, orbit around a contentious point so the gunners on the port and starboard sides can provide supporting fire with the miniguns. While orbiting around one location, usually only one gunner has the best view. Consider switching directions so both gunners get a chance to lay down some fire. A transport helicopter spitting out thousands of rounds is likely to draw attention, so be prepared to escape to a safe distance if you detect a missile lock. Drop altitude fast in an attempt to break line-of-sight with a missile before it is launched.

- Soldiers riding in the fourth and fifth positions can access their weapons and gadgets. This gives engineers the ability to repair the helicopter while it's in flight—they can also fire guided weapons like the Stinger, SRAW, or Javelin. Support and recon players can toss C4 charges down onto the battlefield, blowing up unsuspecting enemies.

PRO TIP: STRONGSIDE

Transport helicopters aren't meant for heavy combat, but are equipped with miniguns on both sides, perfect for targeting and suppressing enemy infantry. Recon troops will likely want to hitch a ride—drop them on rooftops to give them a good vantage point. Flying fast and staying low to the ground is vital, reducing the helicopter's risk of being shot down by rockets and missiles. Large maps are great for the transport helicopter, picking up and dropping off teammates at contested locations around the map.

SCOUT HELICOPTERS

The scout helicopters bridge the gap between the attack helicopters and the transport helicopters. Initially the scout helicopters only have light armament in the form of gun pod-mounted miniguns, ideal for strafing infantry and light vehicles. But new and more powerful weapons can be equipped as well, turning these small, agile helicopters into formidable weapons platforms. Heatseekers and Laser Guided missiles give these helicopters a more active role in shooting down enemy aircraft and destroying enemy armor. But with three passenger seats, the scout helicopter is best utilized as a quick way to move troops around the battlefield.

SCOUT HELICOPTER UPGRADES

IMAGE	NAME	SLOT	UNLOCK POINTS	DESCRIPTION
DEFAULT UPGRADES				
	7.62mm Miniguns	Primary Weapon	—	Very high rate of fire machine guns for use against infantry, light armor, and other aircraft.
	IR Flares	Countermeasure	—	Infrared flare launchers that, when deployed, spoof incoming missiles and break lock-ons.
	Gyro Stabilizer	Upgrade	—	A system that tries to maximize maneuverability until automatic repairs can be started. Is automatically activated when the aircraft receives a critical hit.
UNLOCKABLE UPGRADES				
	Stealth Coating	Upgrade	7,000	Special plating that increases the time it takes for enemy targeting systems to lock on to you.
	Heatseekers	Secondary Weapon	13,000	Once locked on, these heat-seeking missiles will guide themselves towards their target.
	Proximity Scan	Upgrade	20,000	Scans the area around the vehicle and reveals enemy movement on the minimap.
	Fire Extinguisher	Countermeasure	27,000	Can only be deployed when the vehicle is in a critically damaged state. It will put out any fires, bring the vehicle back to a functional state, and let the vehicle start recovering from sustained damage.
	25mm Cannons	Primary Weapon	33,000	Fires 25mm explosive shells effective against light and medium armor as well as infantry.
	Belt Feeder	Upgrade	40,000	An enhanced mechanism that makes reloading faster.
	ECM Jammer	Countermeasure	47,000	When activated, this system will prevent targeting systems from locking on to you and will spoof any incoming missiles for a short while before it needs to be reloaded.
	Air Radar	Upgrade	53,000	Replaces the minimap with a radar display, showing airborne targets in a large radius around the aircraft.
	Laser Guided	Secondary Weapon	60,000	A powerful missile that locks on to ground vehicles. Once lock-on is achieved, the user has to maintain it until the missile has reached its target. If lock-on is lost it can be re-acquired and the target can still be taken out. Can also lock on to laser-designated targets.

AH-6J LITTLE BIRD

Nationality: US
Description: Improved attack version of the MH-6.

VEHICLE PERFORMANCE

SPEED
ARMOR
FIREPOWER

VEHICLE OCCUPANCY

SEAT	POSITION	WEAPON	AMMO
1	Pilot	7.62mm Miniguns	Infinite
2	Passenger	Troop Kit	—
3	Passenger	Troop Kit	—
4	Passenger	None	—

FIELD NOTES

When piloting the Little Bird, be mindful of your passengers in the second and third positions riding on the helicopter's landing skids. These passengers are completely exposed to incoming fire. So fly low and fast to prevent these troops from being hit. Consider dropping these passenger off before performing any strafing runs.

Z-11W

Nationality: RU/CN
Description: Armed military version of the Z-11 Chinese light utility helicopter.

VEHICLE PERFORMANCE

SPEED
ARMOR
FIREPOWER

VEHICLE OCCUPANCY

SEAT	POSITION	WEAPON	AMMO
1	Pilot	7.62mm Miniguns	Infinite
2	Passenger	Troop Kit	—
3	Passenger	Troop Kit	—
4	Passenger	None	—

FIELD NOTES

Deployed by both Russian and Chinese forces, the Z-11W is slightly larger than the Little Bird, but it still possesses the same speed and maneuverability. In this chopper the passengers in the second and third positions ride within the cargo compartment in the back. This gives them a bit more protection from incoming fire than riding on the landing skid.

SCOUT HELICOPTER TACTICS

- Don't learn to fly with the scout helicopters. They may be a bit too fast and maneuverable for new pilots. Instead, it's recommended to wait until you have a few hours of practice in the transport helicopters before taking to the skies in these speedy choppers.
- Like all aircraft, the scout helicopters are now equipped with IR Flares by default, giving even new pilots the opportunity to evade incoming missiles. Applying the Stealth Coating upgrade is also recommended, making the chopper more difficult to lock on to.
- On some maps, the scout helicopters are the fastest way to transport troops, so don't take off until every seat is full. Instead of landing, fly over your destination so you passengers can bail out and parachute down to the ground. This is the best way to quickly secure control points during Conquest matches. For more precise troop insertions, these helicopters are small and agile enough to land on rooftops or other elevated positions usually inaccessible to infantry. Consider dropping recon troops on high perches so they can monitor the battlefield from above.
- The crosshair-like reticle in the center of the pilot's HUD is the aiming point for the chopper's miniguns. The miniguns are fixed and always fire straight ahead. This requires you to dip the nose of the chopper while engaging targets on the ground. When pitching the nose down, the chopper will lose altitude. Applying full rotor speed can reduce the speed of descent, but you will still need to pitch the nose of the chopper up to avoid crashing. So when performing strafing runs, don't get greedy. Fire a quick burst and then pull away before you crash.
- The miniguns are best deployed against infantry and light vehicles. But with sustained accurate fire, they can damage armored vehicles too, including IFVs and tanks. As usual, try to hit these vehicles from the side or rear to inflict the most damage. For even more damage against armored vehicles, equip the punishing 25mm cannons.
- Once the Laser Guided missile is unlocked, a scout helicopter becomes a self-sufficient tank killer. It's up to the pilot to both designate the target and fire the missile. Start by orienting the chopper within line-of-sight of an enemy vehicle to automatically attain a lock. At this point a Guided missile can be fired, automatically homing in on the laser.

- Given their speed and maneuverability, the scout helicopters serve as great air-to-air weapons platforms when armed with the Heatseekers unlock. When an enemy aircraft is within view, instead of chasing it, simply rotate the chopper so you're always facing the target. This gives the missile enough time to lock on. While carrying these missiles, the pilot can still switch back to the gun pods for strafing runs. Available from the start, there's no reason not to have the Heatseekers assigned to the secondary weapon slot. But when the Laser Guided missile is unlocked, you'll have to make a choice between the two.
- Soldiers sitting in the second and third positions can access their weapons and gadgets. This allows engineers equipped with a Repair Tool to fix the chopper while it's in flight—this is an awesome way to score some easy Repair points. Weapons can also be deployed from these two positions. But firing from a fast-moving chopper is difficult unless you're launching guided weapons like the Stinger, IGLA, or Javelin. Still, dropping C4 out of the chopper is always fun too.

PRO TIP: ELUMNITE

Quick and versatile, the scout helicopters are great for moving troops to the front lines. Its mobility allows you to pick up soldiers back at base and transport them around the map. The chopper's stable control allows you to hover efficiently while covering teammates in tight spaces. Equip the Fire Extinguisher countermeasure so you can quickly recover from heavy damage.

ATTACK HELICOPTERS

The attack helicopters are the most devastating vehicles in the game, but only when manned by a capable pilot and gunner. A two-man crew is essential for each attack helicopter to live up to its deadly potential. The pilot can fire the chopper's unguided rockets, ideal for taking out tanks and other ground vehicles. But it's the gunner who benefits from the awesome firepower provided by the chin-mounted turret. Like the auto cannons found on the IFVs, the cannons on attack helicopters fire small explosive rounds. The gunner can use this weapon to rack up dozens of infantry kills. Despite their impressive offensive capability, attack helicopters are vulnerable to heavy machine gun fire, rockets, and guided missiles fired by engineers or other aircraft. But with some fancy flying, and the aid of countermeasures and upgrades, it's possible to minimize the danger posed by these threats. Unlike other vehicles, attack helicopters have six loadout slots—three for the pilot and three for the gunner. This allows an experienced crew to become more powerful with each attained unlock.

ATTACK HELICOPTER UPGRADES

IMAGE	NAME	SLOT	UNLOCK POINTS	DESCRIPTION
DEFAULT UPGRADES				
	Hydra Rockets	Primary Weapon	—	A versatile rocket pod system capable of eliminating infantry as well as light, medium, and heavy armor.
	Heatseekers	Secondary Weapon	—	Once locked on, these heat-seeking missiles will guide themselves towards their target.
	IR Flares	Countermeasure	—	Infrared flare launchers that, when deployed, disrupt incoming missiles and breaks lock-ons.
	Gyro Stabilizer	Upgrade	—	A system that tries to maximize maneuverability until automatic repairs can be started. Is automatically activated when the aircraft receives a critical hit.
	Gunner Zoom	Gunner Optics	—	Zooms the view to more easily spot and take out targets at greater distance.
	Gunner Belt Feeder	Gunner Upgrade	—	An enhanced mechanism that makes reloading faster.
UNLOCKABLE UPGRADES				
	Stealth Coating	Upgrade	5,000	Special plating that increases the time it takes for enemy targeting systems to lock on to you.
	Gunner Proximity Scan	Gunner Upgrade	10,000	Scans the area around the vehicle and reveals enemy movement on the minimap.
	Fire Extinguisher	Countermeasure	15,000	Can only be deployed when the vehicle is in a critically damaged state. It will put out any fires, bring the vehicle back to a functional state, and let the vehicle start recovering from sustained damage.
	Gunner IRNV	Gunner Optics	20,000	Enhanced infrared night vision that will make heat signatures easily distinguishable at close to medium ranges.
	Zuni Rockets	Primary Weapon	25,000	Slow but powerful anti-infantry rockets.
	ECM Jammer	Countermeasure	30,000	When activated, this countermeasure will prevent targeting systems from locking on to you and will disrupt any incoming missiles for a short time before it needs to be reloaded.

ATTACK HELICOPTER UPGRADES, CONTINUED

IMAGE	NAME	SLOT	UNLOCK POINTS	DESCRIPTION
	Laser Guided	Gunner Secondary Weapon	35,000	A powerful missile that locks on to ground vehicles. Once lock-on is achieved, the user has to maintain it until the missile has reached its target. If lock-on is lost, it can be re-acquired and the target can still be taken out. Can also lock on to laser-designated targets.
	Air Radar	Upgrade	40,000	Replaces the minimap with a radar display showing airborne targets in a large radius around the aircraft.
	Gunner Thermal Optics	Gunner Optics	45,000	A black and white night vision system that shows heat signatures across all ranges.
	TOW Missile	Secondary Weapon	50,000	A user-guided anti-tank missile that deals huge damage to heavily armored targets and infantry inside the blast radius.
	TV-Guided Missile	Gunner Secondary Weapon	55,000	A missile controlled by the user via remote camera. Effective against armored targets.
	Smart Rockets	Primary Weapon	60,000	A rocket system with built-in guidance that will track towards the nearest armored target after being fired.

AH-1Z VIPER

Nationality: US

Description: The AH-1Z Viper (also called "SuperCobra" or "Zulu Cobra") is a twin-engine helicopter based on the AH-1W.

VEHICLE PERFORMANCE

SPEED

ARMOR

FIREPOWER

VEHICLE OCCUPANCY

SEAT	POSITION	WEAPON	AMMO
1	Driver	Hydra Rockets	28
2	Gunner	20mm Cannon	Infinite

FIELD NOTES

When piloting the Viper, use the I-shaped reticle in the middle of the HUD to aim your rockets. You can fire up to 14 rockets in one salvo, but then the rockets must reload. Likewise, the gunner can only fire 30 cannon rounds in quick succession before the weapon must be reloaded. The time it takes to reload these weapons can be reduced by applying Autoloader to both the pilot and gunner upgrade slots.

MI-28 HAVOC

Nationality: RU

Description: The Mil Mi-28 (NATO reporting name "Havoc") is a Russian all-weather day-night two-seat anti-armor attack helicopter.

VEHICLE PERFORMANCE

SPEED

ARMOR

FIREPOWER

VEHICLE OCCUPANCY

SEAT	POSITION	WEAPON	AMMO
1	Driver	Hydra Rockets	28
2	Gunner	30mm Chain Gun	Infinite

FIELD NOTES

The Havoc performs identically to the US team's Viper, even utilizing the same HUD layout. In the default configuration, the pilot can fire rockets while the gunner controls the chin-mounted Chain Gun. Both weapons are effective against infantry as well as light and armored vehicles. When not firing, the gunner position is great for spotting targets, particularly when the Zoom Optics or Thermal Optics gadgets are selected.

Z-10W

Nationality: CN

Description: The Chinese Z-10W entered service in 2010 and is deployed primarily in an anti-tank role by the PLA.

VEHICLE PERFORMANCE

SPEED

ARMOR

FIREPOWER

VEHICLE OCCUPANCY

SEAT	POSITION	WEAPON	AMMO
1	Driver	Hydra Rockets	28
2	Gunner	30mm Chain Gun	Infinite

FIELD NOTES

The Z-10W's angular features give it a stealthy, modern appearance. But despite the chopper's futuristic design, it performs identically to its American and Russian counterparts. The pilot's view in the Z-10W is partially obscured by the compact canopy design. This reduces visibility significantly. So when you're not actively targeting enemies, fly from the third-person perspective to avoid collisions.

ATTACK HELICOPTER TACTICS

- If you're planning to fly an attack helicopter, discuss loadouts with your gunner before deploying into the game. Mix up your primary and secondary weapon loadouts to maximize the effectiveness of this powerful vehicle.
- With the new vehicle damage system, critical hits can prove fatal to helicopters unless you have the Gyro Stabilizer upgrade equipped. If you stay away from enemy fire for a few seconds, your chopper will automatically return to full health. However, if your helicopter catches fire, there are only two ways to repair it. You can land and have an engineer use their Repair Tool or you can use the Fire Extinguisher countermeasure to put out the flames.
- Heatseekers are the default secondary weapon for the attack helicopter's pilot. This gives the attack helicopter the ability to shoot down enemy aircraft. Heatseekers can only lock on to enemy aircraft in flight. Once a lock is achieved, fire the missile and watch it streak toward the target.
- IR Flares are also standard equipment in attack helicopters. Apply Stealth Coating to greatly increase your chances of survival. Both upgrades make it difficult for heat-seeking missiles to achieve a lock. If you don't have these upgrades equipped, stay low to the ground, utilizing nap-of-the-earth (NOE) flight to put objects such as hills and trees between your chopper and hostile missile launchers. By breaking line-of-sight with a guided missile, you can prevent a lock prior to launch.
- The chin turrets on the attack helicopters are absolutely devastating against infantry. So when piloting these choppers, try to give your gunner a stable firing platform to increase the weapon's accuracy. Instead of dipping the chopper's nose forward, fly laterally, keeping the nose pointed toward the enemy. Strafing left and right keeps the chopper moving while allowing your gunner to accurately engage enemy ground targets.
- The Laser Guided missile is very effective and can acquire a lock on its own. Once a target is painted, the missile can be fired. However, the pilot must keep the chopper in a position where it can maintain a line-of-sight with the target. Alternatively, the missile can lock on to targets designated by SOFLAMs and PLDs.
- The gunner's TV-Guided missile is manually guided. When fired, the missile's perspective fills the screen, allowing the gunner to fly the missile into any target. Countermeasures don't work against these missiles, allowing the gunner to score some devastating hits on even the most prepared tank drivers. For best results, try to hit the top or rear armor of tanks and IFVs to score critical hits.
- As soon as it's available, choose the Fire Extinguisher as your countermeasure. If your chopper ever becomes disabled, it's incredibly difficult to control, potentially leading to a crash. But if you immediately deploy the Fire Extinguisher, the controls are immediately restored. Still, you may want to seek cover while the helicopter regenerates health.

PRO TIP: ELUMNITE

As always, watch your air space. When attacking, keep the chopper's nose facing your target as long as possible to unleash a volley of heavy fire. The attack helicopter is meant for quick, heavy, and suppressive attacks. Attack often to ease pressure in a location for your team's infantry. But make sure you have a Fire Extinguisher countermeasure equipped to recover from the heavy damage you're likely to take.

STEALTH JETS

Jets have been divided into two different categories in *Battlefield 4*: stealth jets and attack jets. The new stealth jets are the fastest vehicles in the game and designated as air superiority fighters. Along with other aircraft, these jets can travel a significant distance outside the map's combat zone. This is useful when engaged in a dogfight with an enemy pilot. But eventually a jet must turn around to avoid flying off the map. If your jet is heavily damaged, make sure you're within the map's combat zone before bailing out. Initially each stealth jet is equipped with a cannon, Heatseekers, IR Flares, and Stealth Coating, providing a respectable loadout for pilots seeking to test their air combat skills. But as you score more points with the stealth jets, more upgrades become available including more powerful cannons and missiles.

STEALTH JET UPGRADES

IMAGE	NAME	SLOT	UNLOCK POINTS	DESCRIPTION
DEFAULT UPGRADES				
	20mm Cannon	Primary Weapon	—	A high rate of fire Chain Gun capable of incapacitating light armor and other aircraft.
	Heatseekers	Secondary Weapon	—	Once locked on, these heat-seeking missiles will guide themselves toward their target.
	IR Flares	Countermeasure	—	Infrared flare launchers that, when deployed, spoof incoming missiles and break lock-ons.
	Stealth Coating	Upgrade	—	Special plating that increases the time it takes for enemy targeting systems to lock on to you.
UNLOCKABLE UPGRADES				
	Belt Feeder	Upgrade	5,000	An enhanced mechanism that makes reloading faster.
	Passive Radar	Secondary Weapon	10,000	Air-to-air missiles that require the user to maintain lock-on to the target. If the lock-on is lost, it can be re-acquired and the missiles can still reach their target.
	Proximity Scan	Upgrade	14,000	Scans the area around the vehicle and reveals enemy movement on the minimap.
	25mm Cannon	Primary Weapon	19,000	A powerful 25mm Chain Gun with medium rate of fire, damaging against other aircraft and light armor.
	ECM Jammer	Countermeasure	24,000	When activated, this system will prevent targeting systems from locking on to you and will spoof any incoming missiles for a short while before it needs to be reloaded.
	Laser Guided	Secondary Weapon	29,000	A powerful missile that locks on to ground vehicles. Once lock-on is achieved, the user has to maintain it until the missile has reached its target. If lock-on is lost it can be re-acquired and the target can still be taken out. Can also lock on to laser-designated targets.
	Fire Extinguisher	Countermeasure	34,000	Can only be deployed when the vehicle is in a critically damaged state. It will put out any fires, bring the vehicle back to a functional state, and let the vehicle start recovering from sustained damage.
	30mm Cannon	Primary Weapon	38,000	A 30mm cannon with lower rate of fire but increased damage against aircraft and light armor.
	Gyro Stabilizer	Upgrade	43,000	An automatic system that helps to stabilize the vehicle after receiving a critical hit.
	Active Radar	Secondary Weapon	50,000	Once fired, these missiles will locate and track toward the nearest airborne target and explode within close proximity.

F-35

Nationality: US

Description: The F-35 is a multi-role aircraft designed for the USMC as a replacement for the AV-8B Harrier.

VEHICLE PERFORMANCE

SPEED

ARMOR

FIREPOWER

VEHICLE OCCUPANCY

SEAT	POSITION	WEAPON	AMMO
1	Pilot	20mm Cannon	Infinite

FIELD NOTES

The Vertical Take-Off and Landing (VTOL) functionality of the F-35 makes it the most unique jet in the game. By throttling down, the jet enters VTOL mode, allowing it to both land and take off vertically. But the VTOL function can also come in handy during combat. While dogfighting, VTOL mode can be activated sporadically to rapidly decrease air speed, allowing for tighter turns.

SU-50

Nationality: RU

Description: Designed as a successor to the MiG-29 and Su-27, the SU-50 is Russia's latest frontline fighter jet.

VEHICLE PERFORMANCE

SPEED

ARMOR

FIREPOWER

VEHICLE OCCUPANCY

SEAT	POSITION	WEAPON	AMMO
1	Pilot	20mm Cannon	Infinite

FIELD NOTES

Although lacking the VTOL features of the F-35, the SU-50 is a very nimble, responsive jet. The aircraft is equipped with a powerful afterburner, allowing for quick acceleration. But the SU-50 also benefits from stability at low speeds, ideal for pulling tight turns during dogfights or lining up accurate strafing runs.

J-20

Nationality: CN

Description: The J-20 is China's first stealth jet, incorporating an angular design and a pair of canards positioned behind the cockpit.

VEHICLE PERFORMANCE

SPEED

ARMOR

FIREPOWER

VEHICLE OCCUPANCY

SEAT	POSITION	WEAPON	AMMO
1	Pilot	20mm Cannon	Infinite

FIELD NOTES

Beyond its unusual design, the next most striking thing about the J-20 is its frameless canopy. The bubble-like canopy provides the pilot excellent visibility, with no obstructions. This makes it much easier to spot and track air targets, crucial during chaotic dogfights.

STEALTH JET TACTICS

- There's no need to camp runways waiting for jets to spawn at your base. You can spawn directly into a waiting jet (or helicopter) from the deploy screen. Simply choose the name of a jet from the list of available spawn points to hop in the pilot's seat.
- Pay close attention to the floating circle icon in the center of the jet's HUD. This is the angle of attack indicator, representing the true direction your aircraft is travelling. If the icon is firmly in the center of the HUD, you are travelling straight ahead. However, if the icon drifts to the bottom of the HUD, you're experiencing a stall. Immediately apply throttle and gently lift the nose of the aircraft to increase lift before you crash.
- All stealth jets are equipped with afterburners. Press and hold the sprint key/button to activate the afterburners, producing a sudden increase in speed. Apply afterburners when taking off or when trying to prevent a stall. Do not use the afterburner when attempting to make tight turns. This increases the turn radius of the aircraft, putting you at a disadvantage during dogfights. Instead, decrease throttle during tight turns to reduce the aircraft's turn radius.
- All stealth jets are equipped with Air Radar by default—you don't even have to equip it. This feature replaces the minimap with a radar screen, showing all objectives on the ground as well as all enemy aircraft, appearing as red icons. Keep an eye on this radar to monitor the enemy aircraft, particularly jets sneaking up behind you.
- Due to the stealth jets' high speed, it's difficult to lock on to a slow chopper with Heatseekers. Your jet will often zoom past the helicopter before it can acquire a lock. Therefore, consider using the cannon when engaging enemy choppers. This requires more skill, but if your aim is true, the enemy helicopter is toast. The cannon is also a good option when dogfighting enemy jets, because IR Flares can't fool this weapon. Equip the powerful 25mm and 30mm cannons as soon as they're unlocked to dish out even more damage.
- All stealth jets come equipped with IR Flares by default. These countermeasures some in handy for breaking locks and evading incoming missiles. The ECM Jammer is equally effective. But all countermeasures take several seconds to recharge, leaving your jet vulnerable to attack. Either fly out of the danger zone or decrease your altitude, using hills and treetops to mask your movements until your countermeasure of choice is ready.

PRO TIP: ELUMNITE

With a stealth jet, make your way to the edge of the combat zone and then quickly turn around and head back towards the map's center. This will give you a great sight of the enemy jets. Equip an ECM Jammer to give you a few extra seconds to make a getaway from incoming missiles. Tall buildings can be your friend if maneuvered around them correctly; use them to break missile locks. The Laser Guided missile gives the stealth jet some air-to-ground capability, aiding in the destruction of enemy tanks and other vehicles.

ATTACK JETS

Compared to the sleek and futuristic stealth jets, these aircraft aren't much to look at. But each of these Cold War-era attack jets has a proven track record. Although they're capable of serving an air-to-air role, these jets were designed to provide close air support, tearing apart tanks and other armored vehicles with their powerful cannons and hard-hitting air-to-ground rockets, missiles, and bombs. By default, each attack jet comes equipped with a 30mm cannon, Laser Guided missiles, and IR Flares, giving them the ability to make their presence felt on the ground. So instead of chasing down enemy jets and helicopters, get busy helping your squad and teammates knock out tanks and other high-value targets.

ATTACK JET UPGRADES

IMAGE	NAME	SLOT	UNLOCK POINTS	DESCRIPTION
DEFAULT UPGRADES				
	30mm Cannon	Primary Weapon	N/A	A heavy 30mm Gattling cannon, effective against heavily armored targets.
	Laser Guided	Secondary Weapon	N/A	A powerful missile that locks on to ground vehicles. Once lock-on is achieved, the user has to maintain it until the missile has reached its target. If lock-on is lost it can be re-acquired and the target can still be taken out.
	IR Flares	Countermeasure	N/A	Infrared flare launchers that, when deployed, spoof incoming missiles and break lock-ons.
	Belt Feeder	Upgrade	N/A	An enhanced mechanism that makes reloading faster.
UNLOCKABLE UPGRADES				
	Stealth Coating	Upgrade	5,000	Special plating that increases the time it takes for enemy targeting systems to lock on to you.
	Heatseekers	Secondary Weapon	11,000	Air-to-air missiles that require the user to maintain lock on the target. If the lock-on is lost, it can be reacquired and the missiles might still reach their target.
	Proximity Scan	Upgrade	16,000	Scans the area around the vehicle and reveals enemy movement on the minimap.
	Hydra Rockets	Secondary Weapon	21,000	A rocket pod system for taking out targets without the need to lock-on or laser designate.

ATTACK JET UPGRADES, CONTINUED

IMAGE	NAME	SLOT	UNLOCK POINTS	DESCRIPTION
	ECM Jammer	Countermeasure	27,000	When activated, this system will prevent targeting systems from locking on to you and will spoof any incoming missiles for a short while before it needs to be reloaded.
	Fire Extinguisher	Countermeasure	32,000	Can only be deployed when the vehicle is in a critically damaged state. It will put out any fires, bring the vehicle back to a functional state, and let the vehicle start recovering from sustained damage.
	TV-Guided Missile	Secondary Weapon	37,000	A missile controlled by the user via remote camera. Effective against armored targets.
	Gyro Stabilizer	Upgrade	43,000	A system that tries to maximize maneuverability until automatic repairs can be started. Is automatically activated when the aircraft receives a critical hit.
	JDAM Bomb	Secondary Weapon	50,000	A powerful bomb that can also be dropped onto a laser-designated target.

A-10 WARTHOG

Nationality: US

Description: Designed for a USAF requirement to provide Close Air Support (CAS) of ground forces by attacking ground targets with limited AA capability.

VEHICLE PERFORMANCE

SPEED

ARMOR

FIREPOWER

VEHICLE OCCUPANCY

SEAT	POSITION	WEAPON	AMMO
1	Pilot	30mm Cannon	Infinite

FIELD NOTES

Designed as a tank killer, the A-10 excels in a ground attack role. Its massive 30mm cannon can pierce the thick armor of tanks and IFVs, disabling them with a single strafing pass. The aircraft benefits from a relatively low stall speed, allowing you to reduce speed during strafing runs, giving you more time to fire the cannon or rockets.

SU-25TM FROGFOOT

Nationality: RU

Description: Soviet-designed Close Air Support (CAS) plane designated "Frogfoot" by NATO.

VEHICLE PERFORMANCE

SPEED

ARMOR

FIREPOWER

VEHICLE OCCUPANCY

SEAT	POSITION	WEAPON	AMMO
1	Pilot	30mm Cannon	Infinite

FIELD NOTES

Like the A-10, the Russian SU-25TM is best deployed as a ground attack aircraft. However, with the addition of the Heatseekers, the aircraft can also serve as a fighter. While banking, apply the air brake to perform tight turns. But don't forget to apply throttle after the turn to prevent stalling.

Q-5 FANTAN

Nationality: CN

Description: Based on the MiG-19, the Q-5 was developed in the 1960s to fill a close air support role for the PLA.

VEHICLE PERFORMANCE

SPEED
ARMOR
FIREPOWER

VEHICLE OCCUPANCY

SEAT	POSITION	WEAPON	AMMO
1	Pilot	30mm Cannon	Infinite

FIELD NOTES

The Q-5 is an old attack jet, and it flies like one. Visibility from the cockpit is extremely limited, so consider flying from the third person perspective—this makes it much easier to spot ground targets. But despite this drawback, the Q-5 performs well as a ground-attack aircraft, benefiting from a low stall speed.

ATTACK JET TACTICS

- Despite their relative slow speed, attack jets travel so quickly that it's difficult for them to identify ground targets without assistance. Teammates on the ground or in slower-moving helicopters can greatly aid jets by spotting ground targets such as tanks and IFVs. This temporarily marks targets on the HUD, making it much easier for jets to set up strafing runs. Recon troops equipped with SOFLAMs or PLDs are equally important when firing the Laser Guided missile.
- Getting struck by missiles can result in a critical hit, causing the aircraft to lose control. To prevent this, apply the Gyro Stabilizer upgrade and the Fire Extinguisher countermeasure. Together, these loadout options will increase your survivability when nursing a crippled attack jet back to full health.
- Be careful when aiming the Laser Guided missile. When equipped, the screen switches to the view of a belly-mounted camera—at this point you have no control of the jet. So make sure you fly high and level above the battlefield before accessing this weapon. While in the weapon's view, you can pan and tilt the camera slightly. Place the reticle over an enemy target and wait for a lock to be acquired. Once locked, the missile can be fired. But you must maintain the lock until the missile reaches the target. This is a lot to manage while attempting to fly a jet. It's much easier to have teammates on the ground paint targets for you using a SOFLAM or PLD. Stay in contact with squadmates on the ground to set up some memorable coordinated attacks.
- When aligning your aircraft prior to a strafing run, use the strafe controls to apply left and right rudder. Performing these slight lateral adjustments makes it much easier to align your jet with the target. After making a strafing pass, continue flying straight for a couple of seconds, then perform a half-loop. If you made no lateral adjustments, you'll still be lined up with your target, assuming it hasn't moved.
- The Hydra Rockets function just like the rockets fired by the attack helicopters. When selected, an I-shaped reticle appears at the center of the HUD. Use this reticle to aim the rockets during strafing runs. You can fire up to 14 rockets per salvo at which point the weapon must reload. So when making a pass, simply hold down the trigger to fire all 14 rockets. By the time you circle around for another pass, a new salvo of rockets should be ready to fire. The Belt Feeder upgrade significantly reduces the reload time.
- The powerful JDAM Bomb is most effective when dropped on a laser-designated target. But this requires the assistance of teammates equipped with SOFLAMs or PLDs. It's also possible to drop the JDAM Bomb manually, but this takes some practice.

PRO TIP: ELUMNITE

With an attack jet, mobility is slightly lowered and you'll need to have the enemy in your sights as long as possible. The ECM Jammer is the best countermeasure for these aircraft, allowing you to evade incoming missiles while remaining focused on ground targets. The 30mm cannon rips tanks into shreds when your sights are properly aligned during strafing runs.

GUNSHIP

Originally introduced in *Battlefield 3: Armored Kill*, the Gunship is back, rewarding one team with a powerful airborne weapons platform. In some Conquest matches there is one control point associated with the Gunship. Once captured, the control point grants the controlling team's commander the ability to deploy the Gunship—your team must have a commander to gain access to this aircraft. But once deployed, the commander does not control the Gunship—that's up to the team. Spawn directly into the Gunship from the deployment screen to take a seat onboard. Unlike other aircraft, there is no pilot position in the Gunship. Instead, the aircraft orbits around the map on its own with three crew positions accessible from the spawn screen. Each gunner position is equipped with a port-mounted cannon. The 105mm cannon is essentially a tank gun mounted on the side of the aircraft, perfect for scoring critical top hits on tanks and IFVs. The 40mm cannon performs much like the auto cannons on the IFVs, firing up to 12 rounds in rapid succession before undergoing a brief reload phase. The 25mm cannon functions like a minigun, spitting out tons of rounds—it has infinite ammo but can overheat, so fire in short, controlled bursts. In addition to serving as an awesome ground-attack aircraft, the Gunship is also a mobile spawn point, capable of dropping troops over the battlefield along its circular flight path.

GUNSHIP

Nationality: All
Description: Heavily armored ground-attack vehicle with three mounted cannons.

VEHICLE PERFORMANCE

SPEED
ARMOR
FIREPOWER

VEHICLE OCCUPANCY

SEAT	POSITION	WEAPON	AMMO
1	Gunner	105mm Cannon	5
2	Gunner	40mm Cannon	24
3	Gunner	25mm Cannon	Infinite
4	Passenger	Troop Kit	—

FIELD NOTES

This converted cargo aircraft is equipped with three powerful cannons capable of tearing apart any ground vehicle. But this slow-moving aircraft is an easy target for enemy aircraft and anti-aircraft units on the ground. Fortunately, the Gunship can take heavy damage before falling out of the sky. The automatic IR Flares help defend the Gunship against enemy aircraft and incoming missiles.

GUNSHIP TACTICS

- Before using the Gunship Paradrop option to deploy, monitor the Gunship's position on the spawn screen's map. Don't jump out of the plane until the Gunship is flying next to your intended destination. This will allow you to drop close to your target and perform a low-altitude deployment of your parachute. Free fall as long as possible to avoid becoming an easy target for enemy troops on the ground. The longer you drift in your parachute, the more likely you are to be spotted and hunted down.
- What the Gunship's minigun-like 25mm cannon lacks in stopping power, it makes up for in volume and rate of fire. A steady barrage of 25mm rounds can disable and eventually destroy a tank. But this weapon is much more effective against infantry and light vehicles. It can even tear apart lower-flying helicopters and jets. For a closer view of the target, activate the zoom function for 3X magnification.
- The 40mm cannon offers a good balance between rate of fire and damage output. While this weapon can eventually take out armored vehicles, like tanks and IFVs, it's much more effective against light vehicles. All it takes is a few rounds from this weapon to disable and eventually destroy a light vehicle. It's also very deadly against infantry. Use the 3X zoom magnification to get a closer view of your targets.
- Due to the Gunship's constant movement, accurately firing the 105mm cannon can be a little tricky. For starters, don't fight the controls. Instead, aim ahead of your target and let the Gunship's movement do the rest. As the reticle passes over the target, fire. Watch your point of impact on the ground, and adjust your aim before firing a follow-up shot. Like the 25mm cannon, this weapon is also equipped with a 3X zoom magnification option, offering a slightly more detailed view of the target. The camera's default infrared display also makes it easy to spot the heat signatures of enemy vehicles and troops—look for the bright, white dots.
- The Gunship's IR Flares are deployed automatically whenever an enemy missile locks on to the aircraft. The flare deployment lasts several seconds, preventing any new locks from being acquired. But the Gunship is left vulnerable after flare deployment—it takes several seconds for the flares to reload. During this reload phase, the Gunship can be hit with any guided missile. When targeting the Gunship, wait for it to jettison its flares, then attack.
- The Gunship can sustain heavy damage, but it cannot be repaired. Unlike other vehicles, the aircraft's health does not regenerate on its own either. Since all damage is permanent, take extra steps to keep the Gunship airborne. Use jets and helicopters to ward off enemy aircraft attacking the Gunship. Keep a close eye on the Gunship's health and be ready to bail out before it reaches 1%. When the Gunship's health reaches zero, the aircraft simply explodes, giving you no time to bail out.

STATIONARY WEAPONS

When the weapons you're carrying aren't enough to hold back enemy infantry and vehicles, look for stationary weapons to gain some extra firepower. Machine guns, anti-tank missile launchers, and anti-air guns are available on most multiplayer maps. These weapons are fixed and can't be relocated, but each can rotate. Simply stand next to one of these weapons and interact with it to take control. All stationary weapons have unlimited ammo. But like vehicles, they can be locked on to by laser-guided weapons.

.50CAL HEAVY MACHINE GUN

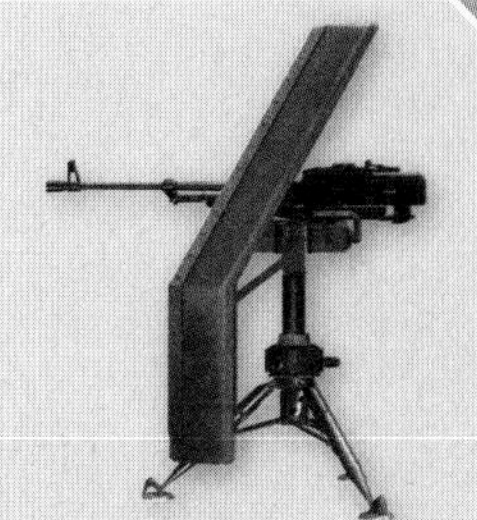

These heavy machine guns are usually found in defensive positions, mounted behind sandbags. The thick plate of armor surrounding the gun serves as a ballistic shield, protecting the operator from small arms fire. This shield can withstand hits from the most powerful sniper rifles, including shots to the view slit, covered with ballistic glass. However, there is one weak spot in this shield—aim for the small gap where the gun protrudes from the armor plating. Threading rounds through this small opening will hit the gunner in the torso. These powerful machine guns are effective against infantry, light vehicles, and helicopters. But don't bother shooting at tanks or IFVs—you'll just agitate the crew as your bullets bounce off the vehicle's armor. While these gun emplacements are resistant to small arms fire, explosive weapons have no problem knocking them out.

ANTI-TANK LAUNCHERS

The US M220 TOW, Russian 9M133 Kornet, and Chinese HJ-8 look similar and function identically. These launchers fire a wire-guided anti-tank missile capable of inflicting heavy damage to any vehicle it strikes. Once launched, the missile must be guided manually into the target. This leaves the operator vulnerable to attack while operating the weapon system. So make sure a squad or teammate has your back while using this weapon. When engaging tanks or other armored vehicles, don't attack their front armor. Not only does this inflict minimal damage, but the tank crew is likely to spot the launch of the missile, resulting in a quick retaliation. Instead, try to hit the side or rear armor of a tank where you can inflict more damage and stand a better chance of remaining undetected.

ANTI-AIRCRAFT TURRETS

Unlike the defensive anti-air guns in *Battlefield 3*, the new AA turrets are automated, engaging spotted enemy aircraft on their own. These weapons are usually found at bases and deployment areas, helping protect spawned vehicles from strafing runs by enemy pilots. So if piloting a jet or helicopter, stay clear of your enemy's base. Each turret's cannon is similar to the ones attached to the mobile AA vehicles, capable of intense rapid fire. The range of these turrets is quite limited, but you'll feel their wrath if you fly too close for comfort—a short burst from these weapons can easily disable a jet or helicopter.

MULTIPLAYER MAPS

To watch the major Levolution moments for each map visit PrimaGames.com/BF4

ALPHA SQUAD: IMPRESSIONS

MABOOZA

Form a purely aesthetic perspective, Dawnbreaker is absolutely stunning, with rays of sunlight peeking through the rows of skyscrapers. But don't get caught sightseeing. This is a relative compact urban environment, easily traversed by both infantry and vehicles. With all the cover and accessible building interiors, you may want to consider moving around on foot. Just make sure you have a few engineers in your squad to deal with the large number of enemy ground and air vehicles you're likely to encounter.

STRONGSIDE

When first playing on this map I thought the features were incredible. Playing in the shadowy night makes this map come to life. I love to sneak through the alleyways and buildings on this map. You'll also find me using the recon class, sniping away from the rooftops.

WALSHY

The urban combat on this map has no match. Whether you are trying to fly through the narrow airspace between the buildings or trying to sneak around on foot, every location you go in Dawnbreaker has intense battles waiting for you as you try to outsmart the opponent at every turn.

FLAMESWORD

Playing this map for the first time was very exciting. I enjoyed moving throughout various buildings to find elevators that led to the top of the building. I set up shop and spotted enemies. If trouble came to me I would BASE jump off the building and make my getaway.

ELUMNITE

Dawnbreaker has a great mix of indoor vs. outdoor battles, and I like to utilize a generator in the small office in Rush on Zone 2 near M-COM Station B to engulf myself in darkness, impairing enemy vision. Levolution on this map is also crazy, turning the central avenue into a raging underground battlefield.

DAWNBREAKER

DAWNBREAKER

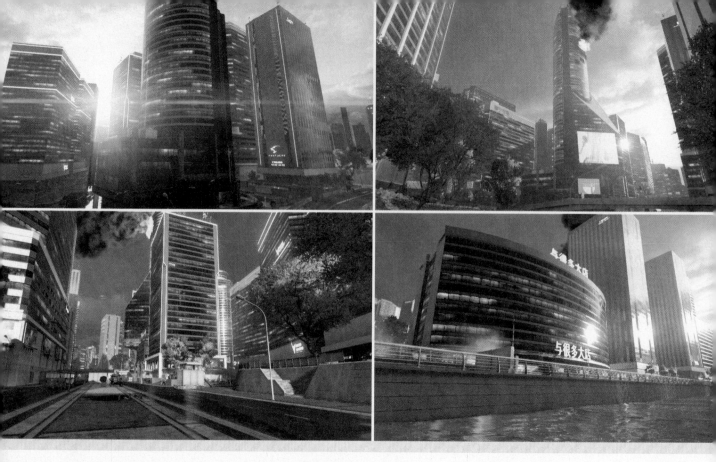

LEVOLUTION MOMENTS

WHAT IS IT?

Building pressure in a subterranean gas pipe causes an explosion, damaging the central avenue and collapsing the Bridge.

HOW IS IT TRIGGERED?

Increase pressure on both sides of avenue by operating two valves beneath the street. Pressure can be increased and decreased by interacting with these two valves. The explosion occurs shortly after pressure is maximized on both sides.

HOW IS GAMEPLAY IMPACTED?

The central avenue is filled with debris and a trench-like fissure opens up along the median, providing cover and concealment for infantry advances. The collapsed Bridge and other debris make vehicle movement difficult along the avenue.

CONQUEST LARGE

RECOMMENDED SQUAD COMPOSITION:

In this battle, the US and CN team engage in firefights in the dark as the night has covered the city. There are a total of five control point on this map: Bus Terminal (A), Plaza (B), Bridge (C), Hospital (D), and Embassy (E). The US team's best strategy will be to capture the Bus Terminal (A), Plaza (B), and the Bridge (C). The CN team's safest and best strategy will be capturing the Embassy (E), the Hospital (D), and the Bridge (C). The Bridge (C) will be the focal point of this map as the controlling team is rewarded a Gunship for their commander to call. Both teams have a few helicopters and jets at hand. This map will test the best pilots as there are many buildings you will need to maneuver through in order to make an impact in the game. These buildings are accessible through elevators and should be used to snipe from; the sniper will also be able to spot enemies, revealing them on teammates' minimap. Be sure to take advantage of the light vehicles that spawn. This map is large, so you don't want to be caught running the entire game. This map only requires you to capture three control points in order to slowly bleed the opponent's tickets, so stay on defense and hold down the fort.

US BASE

- The US base is located in the northeastern tip of the map and is quite a distance to nearest control point. Be sure to make full use of the vehicles and catch a ride with a squadmate. This saves you travel time and lets you get right into the action.
- The US team has a variety of ground vehicles and two helicopters: one attack helicopter and one scout helicopter. These vehicles will greatly aid you when capturing the Bridge (C), which unlocks the Gunship for the commander of the team.
- The closest control points to the US base are the Bus Terminal (A) and Plaza (B). The US team's best strategy is to control these two with another control point in order to begin draining the enemy's tickets.
- A squad should take half of the light vehicles and immediately head towards the Bus Terminal (A). This control point shouldn't be tough to capture off the beginning of the game as the opposing team will surely be capturing the objectives closest to their base. Once captured, the squad should take the light vehicles and head towards the Bridge (C) from the south side, catching the enemy off guard and leading to an easier capture.
- Squads should enter the tanks and light vehicles and head for the Plaza (B). Once captured, they can begin moving towards the Bridge (C) and begin firing rounds to distract the enemy. When performed successfully, the squad on the Quad Bikes can come in from the rear and begin capturing the Bridge (C) while the enemy is distracted.

BASE ASSETS

NAME	Quad Bike	MRAP	M1 Abrams	LAV-AD	AH-6J Little Bird	AH-1Z Viper	F-35
QUANTITY	4	2	2	1	1	1	2

CN BASE

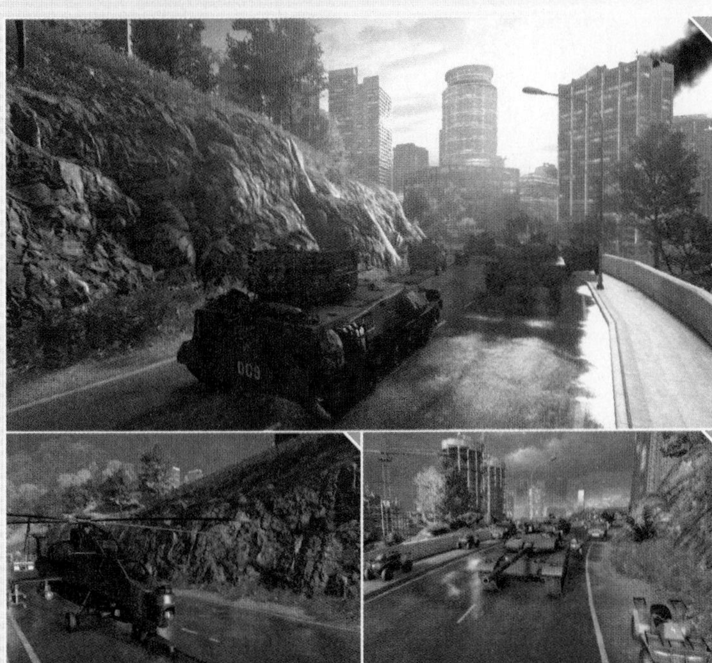

- The CN base is located to the southwest side of this city. Both you and the enemy US team have multiple vehicles at the start. Be prepared for vehicle-on-vehicle combat during these early skirmishes.
- At the start, be sure to send your light vehicles fully loaded up the dirt path to the northeast. This way you can beat your enemies to the Bridge (C) and secure this control point for your commander to utilize the Gunship and cause some damage from above.
- When pushing towards the Bridge (C) with vehicles, avoid taking the high road. If you take cover from below you will avoid all the aircraft, and enemy engineers will have a more difficult shot.
- This map will be won when your squad mainly focuses on Plaza (B), Bridge (C), and Hospital (D) because of the commander abilities that these control points unlock.
- Aircraft need a very skilled pilot to navigate the narrow areas between these skyscrapers. If you are new to flying, don't start your practice on this map.

BASE ASSETS

NAME	Quad Bike	ZFB-05	Type 99 MBT	Type 95 AA	Z-11W	Z-10W	J-20
QUANTITY	4	2	2	1	1	1	2

A: BUS TERMINAL

- The Bus Terminal (A) is located southwest of the US base. This control point is located at a bus hub and has several buses outside on the streets.
- Capturing this point allows the controlling team to get access to two Quad Bikes.
- Players can go prone inside the multiple buses around and wait for enemies to neutralize the objective. At that exact moment, exit the bus and ambush the enemies inside the station.
- This control point is out of the way for the CN team and should not be approached unless the opportunity presents itself in the late game.
- The Bus Terminal (A) provides great cover when inside. When defending, bobby trap doorways with C4 and Claymores. Squads should gear up for close-quarter combat.

CONTROL POINT ASSETS

US CONTROL	CN CONTROL
Quad Bike (2)	Quad Bike (2)

B: PLAZA

- This flag is located on the north side of the map next to an imperial guardian lion statue.
- When controlling this objective you gain control of a IFV and a Quad Bike. Use the IFV to defend this area. Use the Quad Bike to make your way to a nearby flag.
- North of the flag you'll find a balcony that oversees the entire control point. Move from the east and west on the balcony to check for enemies on the roads from the south, east, and west. Use the railing partition for cover. This position is great for taking out incoming enemy infantry.
- The second level in the tall building southwest of the objective is a good position to control as it oversees the objective towards the north. Use this area to check for enemies, then make your way onto the glass and metal floors outside the windows to the northeast to capture the control point. Place T-UGS inside this building to watch for sneaky enemy infantry.
- In this building you'll find an elevator in the second level that will take you to the roof. Place a T-UGS and Radio Beacon here. Parachute down and get back into the action.

CONTROL POINT ASSETS

US CONTROL	CN CONTROL
Quad Bike (1)	Quad Bike (1)
LAV-25 (1)	ZBD-09 (1)

C: BRIDGE

- This objective is located in the center of the map and surrounded by all of the other control points.
- Controlling this flag nets both teams an extra Quad Bike.
- This control point grants a Gunship to the commander of the team who captures this objective. This Gunship is very powerful; teams will need to make it a mission to capture this point.
- When attacking, have a scout helicopter drop engineers and support troops near the Bridge (C).
- After the Levolution is triggered, the Bridge (C) will be completely destroyed. This will make the area more open, making it easier to control.

PRO TIP: WALSHY

PLAYING AS AN ENGINEER ON THIS MAP IS A MUST. I RACK UP MASSIVE AMOUNTS OF POINTS BY CAMPING OUTSIDE THE BRIDGE (C) TO TAKE OUT ENEMY VEHICLES WITH MY ROCKETS AND HELP OUT MY TEAM BY REPAIRING ANY DAMAGED FRIENDLY VEHICLE THAT COMES IN MY AREA.

CONTROL POINT ASSETS

US CONTROL	CN CONTROL
Quad Bike (1)	Quad Bike (1)

D: HOSPITAL

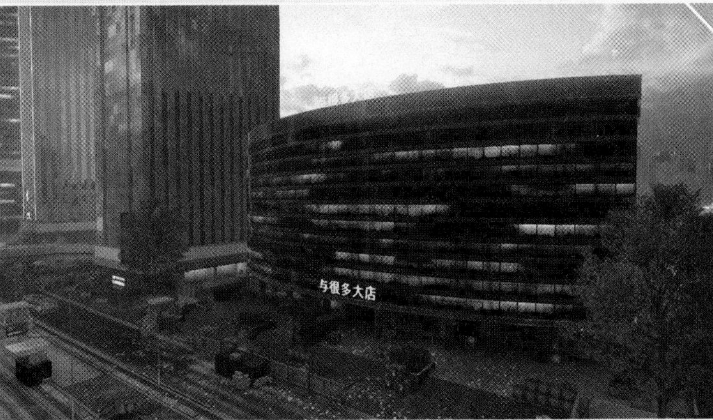

- Located in the southern part of the map, the Hospital (D) has a cluster of crates and boxes that surround the flag.
- There is one IFV and one Quad Bike that spawns here for the team that captures this objective.
- Inside the Hospital (D) there are two shutters that block up the windows when activated. There will be only one way inside, and that's through the front entrance, making it easier to defend.
- Attackers can use Motion Sensors to locate the defenders hiding inside the Hospital (D) building. This makes clearing the objective easier.
- Squads composed of engineers will prove useful at this objective for both attacking and defending. If you are trying to recapture this objective be sure to have rockets to take out any vehicles guarding the flag.

CONTROL POINT ASSETS

US CONTROL	CN CONTROL
Quad Bike (1)	Quad Bike (1)
LAV-25 (1)	ZBD-09 (1)

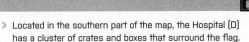

E: EMBASSY

- This flag is located at the western side of the city and is connected to the surrounding areas by a two-lane winding road.
- When defending this flag, with only one main route for land vehicles to enter this area, your biggest threat will be infantry storming the control point from virtually every direction.
- When attacking this flag, you have to fully clear out the second floor of this building, otherwise the enemy team will continuously spawn their team until your squad is overwhelmed.
- When attacking, if you want to get the high ground advantage on this area, have one of your helicopters drop you off on the roof, which is accessible only by air, and contest the control point from above.
- Once you capture this flag, you receive two Quad Bikes to allow you to travel quickly to your next points. Ideally you do not want to wait around this objective—you want to capture it and quickly head back to the center of the map where all the action is at.

CONTROL POINT ASSETS

US CONTROL	CN CONTROL
Quad Bike (2)	Quad Bike (2)

CONQUEST SMALL

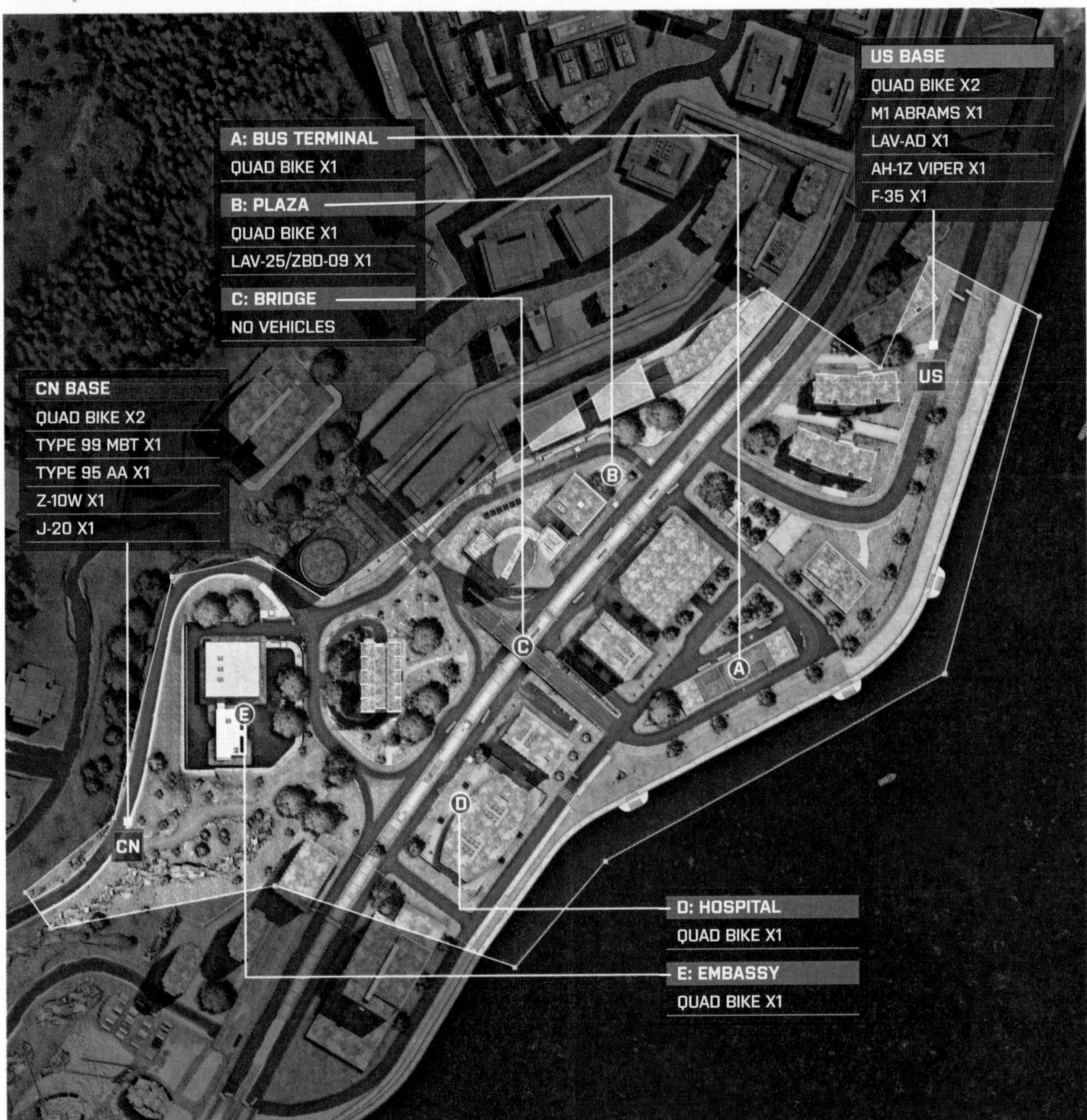

RECOMMENDED SQUAD COMPOSITION:

The Conquest Small and Conquest Large maps are identical in Dawnbreaker, with the same control point layout. The only differences between these game modes are the number of vehicles and number of players allowed on the map. In this battle, the US and CN team engage in firefights in the dark as the night has covered the city. There are a total of five control points on this map: Bus Terminal (A), Plaza (B), Bridge (C), Hospital (D), and Embassy (E). The US team's best strategy is to capture the Bus Terminal (A), Plaza (B), and Bridge (C). The CN team's safest and best strategy is capturing the Embassy (E), Hospital (D), and Bridge (C). The Bridge (C) will be the focal point of this map as the controlling team is rewarded a Gunship for their commander to call. Both teams have a few helicopters and jets at hand; this map will test the best pilots as there are many buildings you will need to maneuver through in order to make an impact in the game. These buildings are accessible through elevators and should be used to snipe from; the sniper will also be able to spot enemies, revealing them on teammates' minimap. Be sure to take advantage of the light vehicles that spawn. This map is large, so you don't want to be caught running the entire game. This map only requires you to capture three control points in order to slowly bleed the opponent's tickets, so stay on the defense and hold down the fort.

US BASE

- The US base is located in the northeastern tip of the map and is quite a distance to nearest control point. Be sure to make full use of the vehicles and catch a ride with a squadmate. This saves you travel time and lets you get right into the action.
- The US team has a variety of ground vehicles and air vehicles. These vehicles will greatly aid you when capturing the Bridge (C), which unlocks the Gunship for the commander of the team.
- The closest control points to the US base are the Bus Terminal (A) and Plaza (B). The US team's best strategy is to control these two, along with another control point, in order to begin draining the enemy's tickets.
- A squad should take half of the light vehicles and immediately head towards the Bus Terminal (A). This control point shouldn't be tough to capture off the beginning of the game as the opposing team will surely be capturing the objectives closest to their base. Once captured, the squad should take the Quad Bikes and head towards the Bridge (C) from the south side, catching the enemy off guard and leading to an easier capture.
- Squads should enter the tank and Quad Bikes and head for the Plaza (B). Once captured, they can begin moving towards the Bridge (C) and begin firing rounds to distract the enemy. When performed successfully, the squad on the Quad Bikes can come in from the rear and begin capturing the Bridge (C) while the enemy is distracted.

BASE ASSETS

NAME	Quad Bike	M1 Abrams	LAV-AD	AH-1Z Viper	F-35
QUANTITY	2	1	1	1	1

CN BASE

- The CN base is located to the southwest side of this city. Both you and the enemy US team have a handful of vehicles at the start. Prepare for vehicle-on-vehicle combat during these early skirmishes. Be sure to focus on the enemy's tank before they can take out your Type 99 MBT.
- At the start, be sure to send your light vehicles fully loaded up the dirt path to the northeast. This way you can beat your enemies to the Bridge (C) and secure this control point for your commander to utilize the Gunship and cause some damage from above.
- When pushing towards Bridge (C) with vehicles, avoid taking the high road. If you take cover from below, you will avoid all the aircraft and enemy engineers will have a more difficult shot.
- This map will be won when your squad mainly focuses on the Plaza (B), Bridge (C), and Hospital (D) because of the commander abilities that these control points unlock.
- Aircraft need a very skilled pilot to navigate the narrow areas between these skyscrapers. If you are new to flying, don't start your practice on this map.

BASE ASSETS

NAME	Quad Bike	Type 99 MBT	Type 95 AA	Z-10W	J-20
QUANTITY	2	1	1	1	1

A: BUS TERMINAL

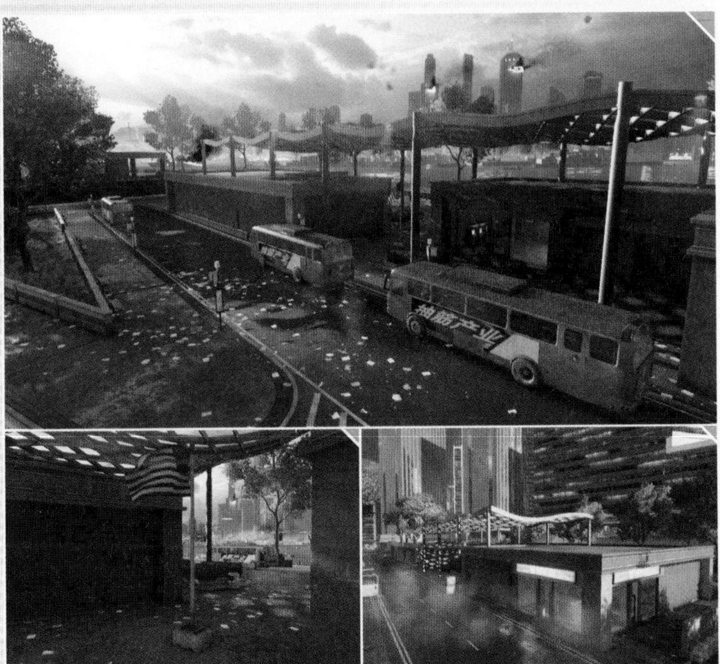

- The Bus Terminal (A) is located southwest of the US base. This control point is located at a bus hub and has several buses outside on the streets.
- Capturing these points allows the controlling team to get access to a Quad Bike.
- Players can go prone inside the multiple buses around and wait for enemies to neutralize the objective. At that exact moment, exit the bus and ambush the enemies inside the station.
- This control point is out of the way for the CN team and should not be approached unless the opportunity presents itself late in the game.
- The Bus Terminal (A) provides great cover when inside. When defending, booby trap the doorways with C4 and Claymores. Squads should gear up for close-quarter combat.

CONTROL POINT ASSETS

US CONTROL	CN CONTROL
Quad Bike (1)	Quad Bike (1)

B: PLAZA

- This flag is located on the north side of the map next to an imperial guardian lion statue.
- When controlling this objective, you gain control of a Quad Bike. Use the Quad Bike to make your way to a nearby flag quickly.
- North of the flag you'll find a balcony that oversees the entire control point. Move from the east and west on the balcony to check for enemies on the roads from the south, east, and west. Use the railing partition for cover. This position is great for taking out incoming enemy infantry.
- The second level in the tall building southwest of the objective is a good position to come through as it oversees the objective towards the north. Use this area to check for enemies, then make your way onto the glass and metal floors outside the windows to the northeast to capture the control point. Place T-UGS inside this building to watch for sneaky enemy infantry.
- In this building, you'll find an elevator in the second level that will take you to the roof. Place a T-UGS and Radio Beacon here. Parachute down and get back into the action.

CONTROL POINT ASSETS

US CONTROL	CN CONTROL
Quad Bike (1)	Quad Bike (1)

C: BRIDGE

> This objective is located in the center of the map and enclosed by all of the other control points.
> No vehicles spawn at this location. Use the surrounding objects and for cover and to stay hidden when enemies are approaching.
> This control point grants a Gunship to the commander of the team who captures this objective. This Gunship is very powerful; teams will need to make it a mission to capture this point.
> When attacking, have a scout helicopter drop engineers and support classes near the Bridge (C). You will want to locate and destroy the Mobile Artillery Vehicle quickly as this vehicle can do heavy damage to your team.
> After the Levolution is triggered, the Bridge (C) is completely destroyed. This will make the area more open, making it easier to control.

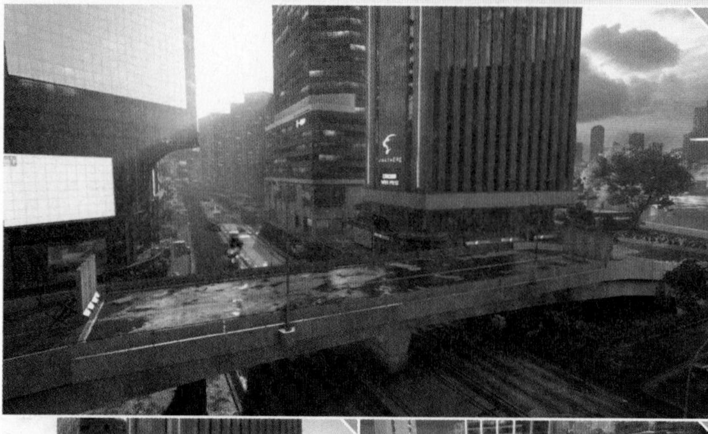

D: HOSPITAL

> Located in the southern part of the map, the Hospital (D) has a cluster of crates and boxes that surround the flag.
> One Quad Bike spawns here for the team that captures this objective. Use this to quickly make your way towards nearby flags.
> Inside the Hospital (D), there are two shutters that block up the windows when activated. There will be only one way inside, and that's through the front entrance, making it easier to defend.
> Attackers can use Motion Sensors to locate the defenders hiding inside the Hospital (D) building. This makes clearing the objective easier.
> Squads composed of engineers will prove useful at this objective for both attacking and defending. If you are trying to recapture this objective, be sure to have rockets to take out any vehicles guarding the flag.

CONTROL POINT ASSETS

US CONTROL	CN CONTROL
Quad Bike (1)	Quad Bike (1)

E: EMBASSY

- This flag is located at the western side of the city and is connected to the surrounding areas by a two-lane winding road.
- When defending this flag, with only one main route for land vehicles to enter this area, your biggest threat is infantry storming the control point from virtually every direction.
- When attacking this flag, you have to fully clear out the second floor of this building, otherwise the enemy team will continuously spawn their team until your squad is overwhelmed.
- When attacking, if you want to get the high ground advantage on this area, have one of your helicopters drop you off on the roof, which is accessible only by air, and contest the control point from above.
- Once you capture this flag, you receive a single light vehicle to help you travel to the next points. Ideally you do not want to wait around this objective—you want to capture it and quickly head back to the center of the map where all the action is at.

CONTROL POINT ASSETS

US CONTROL	CN CONTROL
Quad Bike (1)	Quad Bike (1)

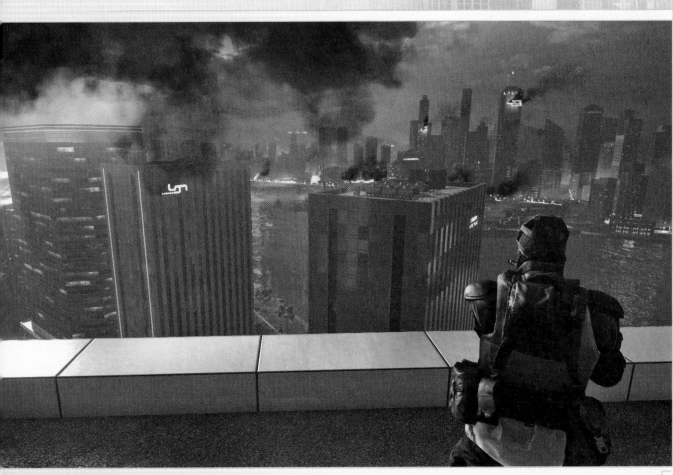

RUSH

The outskirts of Shanghai hold the battle between the US and CN team. The US team will attempt to push the CN team back through a total of four zones with two M-COM stations in each zone. The US team starts north of the first zone located in the Bus Terminal. The US team has an IFV or two through the first three zones. Be sure to have an engineer on deck to repair the damages when needed as the IFV will be very useful in defeating the CN team. The CN team has no vehicles when defending the Bus Terminal, but don't be too worried if you are playing on the defending team. Each area has an M-COM station in an enclosed in a building, allowing to defenders to equip shotguns and excel in close-quarter combat, making the attacker's vehicles useless. The last zone is pushed back to the Embassy where the CN team has one last chance to make a stand. Being on either the US or CN team, be prepared for an intense urban firefight during the nighttime.

ZONE 1: BUS TERMINAL

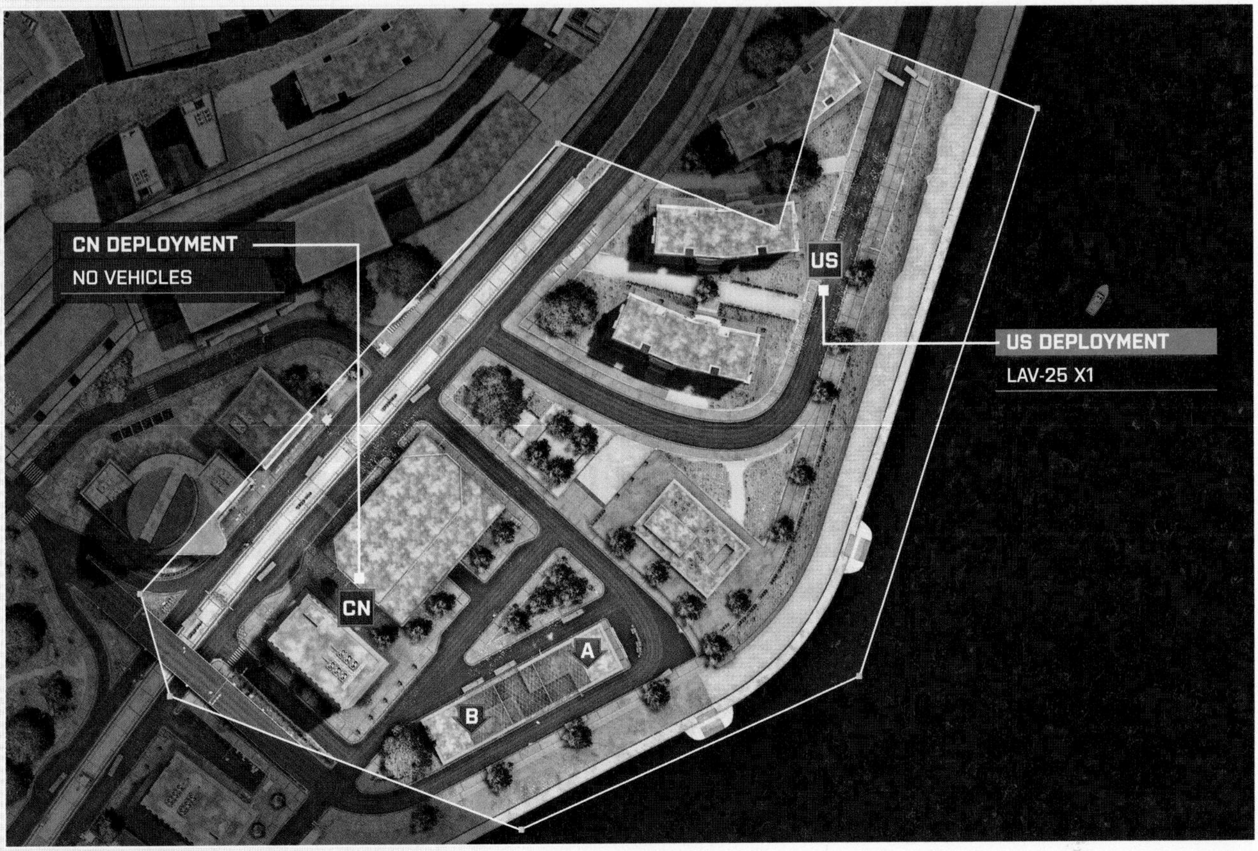

CN DEPLOYMENT
NO VEHICLES

US DEPLOYMENT
LAV-25 X1

US
CN
A
B

US DEPLOYMENT

RECOMMENDED SQUAD COMPOSITION:

- This deployment is located to the northeast of the M-COM stations. You have a direct path by foot to an overlook of the building that houses the objectives.
- Be aware of the three .50Cals and HJ-8 Launcher that are placed along the road. These should be easy kills if you have an engineer shoot a rocket near the base of any of these stationary weapons.
- You only have one IFV at the back of your base on this zone. Swing around to the southernmost road to avoid the HJ-8 Launcher that is located directly north of M-COM Station B.
- The enemy does not have any vehicles in the zone. Use your IFV with care and continue to repair it and pick off enemies as you slowly move up the southern road.
- Make sure your squad has a good balance of every class. You will need your recon and engineer players to sit back and take out threats such as enemy snipers and .50Cals. Your assault and support players are going to be on the front line storming the buildings until you can arm both M-COM stations.

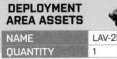

DEPLOYMENT AREA ASSETS

NAME	LAV-25
QUANTITY	1

CN DEPLOYMENT

RECOMMENDED SQUAD COMPOSITION:

- The CN deployment area starts out southwest of the US deployment. The M-COM stations are placed southeast from the CN deployment.
- The CN deployment area deploys with one LAV-25, so have a few squad members as engineers to even the playing field against the vehicle.
- Off the spawn, rush southeast towards M-COM Station A to set up your defenses before the attacking team can reach this objective. Place a T-UGS within this close-quarter building at M-COM Station A and equip a shotgun. Walls cannot be destroyed at this building, so you only need to watch the entrances.
- Send a squad towards M-COM Station B as well and watch for enemies pushing from the northeast side of the map.
- Equip players in the many .50Cals sitting around the objectives to set up a solid defense before the attackers push towards the objectives.

M-COM STATION A

- M-COM Station A is located inside the Bus Terminal in a small room.
- This area is also surrounded by .50Cals and concrete walls with sandbags on them. With no vehicles in Zone 1 for the CN team, be sure to use these stationary turrets when guarding the M-COM stations.
- Defenders have to really work together to protect M-COM Station A and should locate a safe place to drop a Radio Beacon to the east of the objectives. This will make it so your team is spawning near the objectives in two different locations.
- Defenders should have assault classes and hide inside of the building holding M-COM Station A. Equip a shotgun; due to the close-quarter action, this gun will be at its best when used.
- When attacking, round up a few assault, engineer, and support classes in a LAV-25 and make your way south towards M-COM Station A. Have a second squad with a recon class take the far southeast route and place a Radio Beacon next to the building that resembles a restaurant.

M-COM STATION B

- M-COM Station B is located inside the ticket center of the Bus Terminal south of the CN deployment.
- There are a handful of stationary weapons around the Bus Terminal. These are effective in keeping the attackers at bay.
- When defending, there are plenty of rooms around the object. Have squads split up from room to room and prepare to ambush the enemy when they walk through the entrances.
- Attackers will find Smoke Grenades and Flashbangs to be super effective. Defenders are bunkered up in the rooms of the Bus Terminal; these grenades will decrease their vision and disorient their senses. Attackers can then move in and clear the room.

PRO TIP: FLAMESWORD

When I am playing on the attacking team during Rush, I love playing as the assault class during Zone 1. Both M-COM stations are in the Bus Terminal area, which consists of many close-quarter rooms. I enjoy having Flashbangs and the M320 SMK grenade launcher equipped. These weapons help me punish the defenders camping in the corners of the room.

ZONE 2: BRIDGE

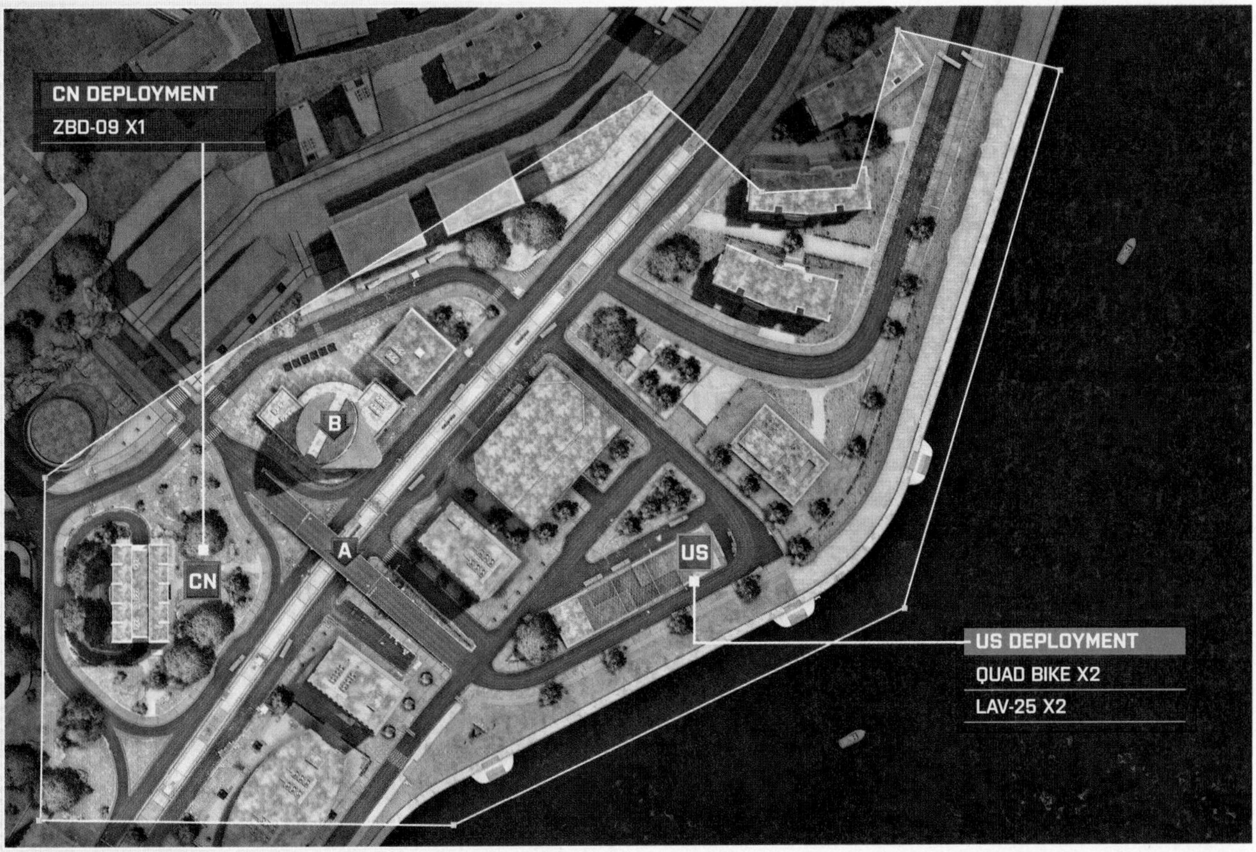

CN DEPLOYMENT
ZBD-09 X1

B
A
CN
US

US DEPLOYMENT
QUAD BIKE X2
LAV-25 X2

US DEPLOYMENT

RECOMMENDED SQUAD COMPOSITION:

- The US now spawns to the southeast of the new M-COM stations. Also, you have more vehicles at your disposal. Make use of the two LAV-25s that spawn towards the back of the eastern road and the four Quad Bikes that spawn directly on the US deployment area.
- The enemy has two HJ-8 Launchers located on top of the Bridge. These rocket launchers have a 360-degree turn radius, so there is no way to completely surprise them. However, your best angle of attack is to take the northernmost road around M-COM Station B, and from here you will have a clear shot to take out their stationary weapons.
- The stationary weapons are not the only threat in this zone—the enemy now has a ZBD-09 for their own counter-infantry measures. Have at least two engineers in your squad to help eliminate the enemy IFV and repair the damage that your LAV-25s take.
- When pushing M-COM Station B, be prepared to fight in this close-quarter combat area with your favorite shotgun.
- When attacking M-COM Station A, this area is wide open with numerous areas from the southwest for the enemy to pick you off as your try to arm this objective. Push past the Bridge to clear these enemies out before going for M-COM Station A.

DEPLOYMENT AREA ASSETS

NAME	Quad Bike	LAV-25
QUANTITY	2	2

CN DEPLOYMENT

RECOMMENDED SQUAD COMPOSITION:

- After losing Zone 1, the CN deployment now sits on the southwest side of the objectives.
- Spawning at this deployment area, you'll find a ZBD-09 to counter the CN team's two LAV-25s. Have your squad play as a few engineers to stop the enemy vehicles in their tracks.
- Send a squad immediately towards M-COM Station B to set up your defenses inside the building containing the objective. This is another close-quarter area, so be sure to equip your shotgun and let the shells unload. Use the many objects and structures within the building for cover.
- M-COM Station A is located underneath the Bridge in a fairly open area. This objective can only be seen from southeast of the station. You'll want to cover this objective, making sure enemies are not able to reach the objective since it has so much cover.
- Inside the building holding M-COM Station B, there is a switch above the objective. Shoot this switch to turn off the lights within the building, which lasts for approximately thirty seconds. Scatter Claymores throughout the darkness in an attempt to score some sneaky kills.

DEPLOYMENT AREA ASSETS

NAME	ZBD-09
QUANTITY	1

M-COM STATION A

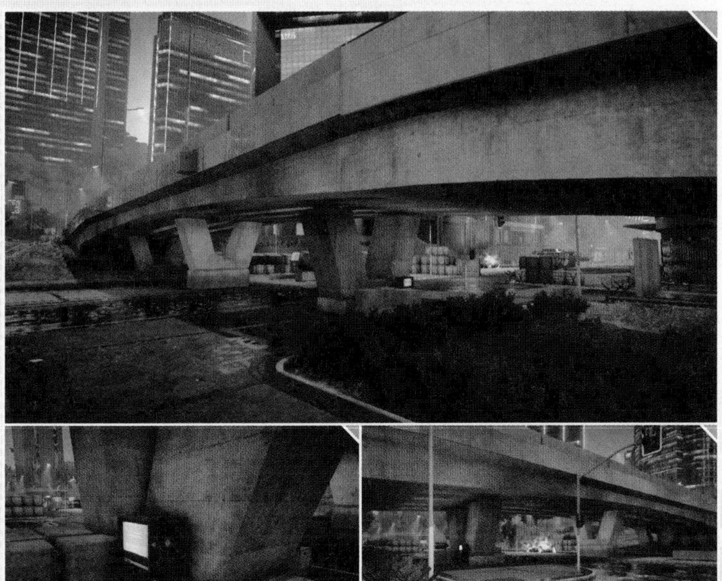

- M-COM Station A is located just underneath the Bridge. There is a bus and a few crates that would serve as cover around this point.
- When attacking, send a recon member to the building west of the US deployment. Choose the recon class and make your way to the balcony. At this position you'll provide great cover for your teammates attempting to arm the objective.
- Defenders can lay some T-UGS around the M-COM station just in case some enemies slip by, in which case they will be picked up on the team's minimap.
- The attacking squad should have assault and support classes; take control of any areas where snipers may be posted before moving near the M-COM station.

M-COM STATION B

- This M-COM station sits far back in the Plaza.
- Due to the distance from the US deployment to the objective, the defending team has plenty of time to set up a perimeter. A recon player can take the elevator to the roof of the Plaza and snipe incoming attackers.
- When defending or attacking, recon players will play a huge role. These players can drop their MAVs and fly them around while spotting members of the opposing team.
- Defenders need to take advantage of the circuit board above the objective. First plant C4 and Claymores around the Plaza's entrances and then shoot the circuit board. Shooting this circuit board will cause the lights to go out for roughly 30 seconds. The attackers won't know what they are walking in to.
- This objective promotes close-quarter combat as players will move from office to office. When attacking, prepare to use Smoke Grenades and shotguns to take out the camping defenders.

ZONE 3: HOSPITAL

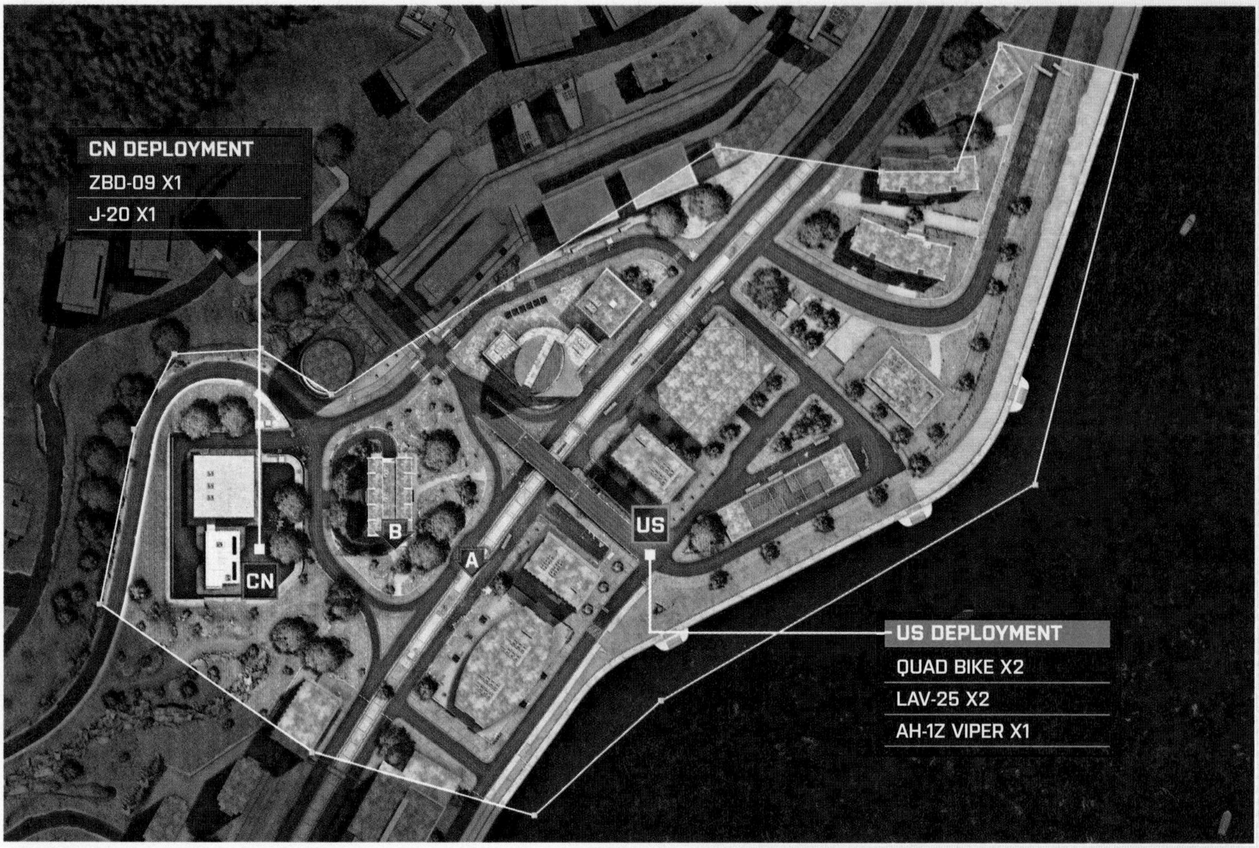

CN DEPLOYMENT
ZBD-09 X1
J-20 X1

B
A
US
CN

US DEPLOYMENT
QUAD BIKE X2
LAV-25 X2
AH-1Z VIPER X1

US DEPLOYMENT

RECOMMENDED SQUAD COMPOSITION:

- The US deployment spawns to the east of the M-COM stations with several vehicles, including an attack helicopter.
- Beware of the J-20 stealth jet the enemy now has. Have your engineers equipped with Stingers and IGLAs to take care of this aircraft before it inflicts too much damage.
- M-COM Station B is heavily fortified with stationary weapons surrounding it. Go for this objective first while the enemy is split up and focused on both M-COM stations. M-COM Station A is much easier to arm, being underground with fewer angles to attack for the defenders.
- Take your LAV-25s to the north end of M-COM Station B where you are less likely to be ambushed. Have a teammate lower the bollards so you can safely drive your LAV-25 inside the garage.
- Make sure your squad consists of engineers and mid-range anti-infantry when attacking M-COM Station B. Your squad should consist of close range and a recon member when attacking M-COM Station A.

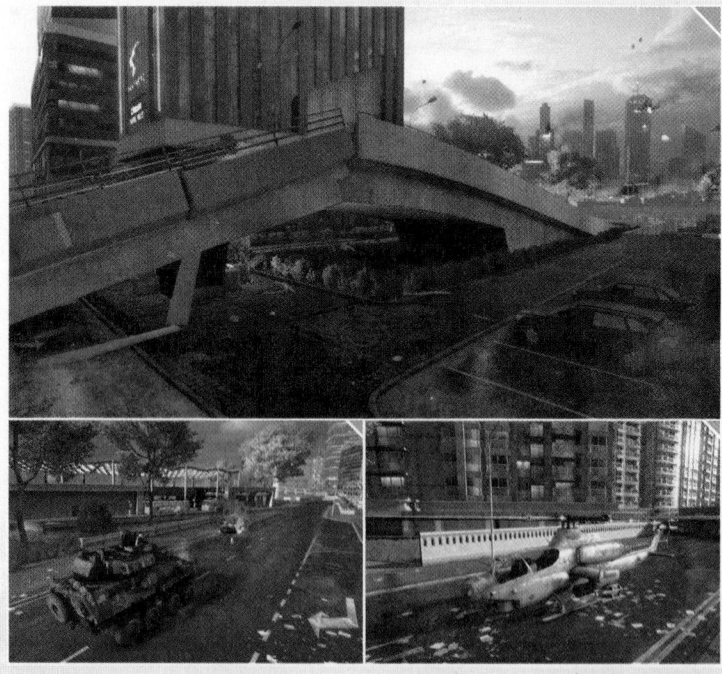

DEPLOYMENT AREA ASSETS			
NAME	Quad Bike	LAV-25	AH-1Z Viper
QUANTITY	2	2	1

CN DEPLOYMENT

RECOMMENDED SQUAD COMPOSITION:

- The CN deployment is now located west of the objective and spawns an ZBD-09 and J-20. The US deployment spawns two LAV-25s and an attack helicopter.
- When defending M-COM Station B, raise the bollards to stop enemy vehicles from entering.
- Initially make your way to M-COM Station B to set up your defenses inside the lower level of the garage.
- With how dark it is around M-COM Station A, lay Claymores all over to pick up a few enemies rushing to arm the objective.

PRO TIP: STRONGSIDE

SELECT THE RECON CLASS AND HEAD UP THE ELEVATOR LOCATED IN THE BUILDING HOLDING M-COM STATION B. AT THE TOP OF THE BUILDING YOU'LL HAVE A BIRD'S EYE VIEW OVER EVERY PLAYER HEADING TOWARDS M-COM STATIONS A AND B. YOU ARE ABLE TO SEE M-COM STATION A CLEARLY AND SNIPE ANY ENEMY WHO ATTEMPTS TO ARM THE M-COM STATION. PLACE A T-UGS ON THE ROOF NEAR THE ELEVATOR TO BE WARNED OF INCOMING ENEMIES.

DEPLOYMENT AREA ASSETS

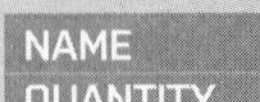

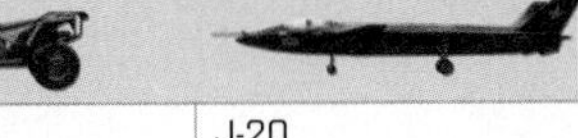

NAME	ZBD-09	J-20
QUANTITY	1	1

M-COM STATION A

- M-COM Station A is located underneath the damaged street. There are a few long, dark tunnels that all connect to each other leading to the objective.
- The CN team has two vehicles that spawn at this zone and can be used to defend the area: a stealth jet and a ZBD-09.
- Defenders can lay Claymores all around the dark areas in the tunnels. This will take out flanking attackers and protect the objective.
- Attackers will want engineers equipped with a Stinger or IGLA to take out the opposing team's jet. This allows the US team's scout helicopter to move in and provide air support while dropping squadmates in the area.

M-COM STATION B

- M-COM Station B is located in the parking garage adjacent to the Hospital.
- Inside the parking garage are interactive control panels that raise and lower a set of bollards. When raised, these bollards prevent ground vehicles from entering.
- The parking garage has an elevator that leads to the roof of the building. Attackers should sneak in and place a Radio Beacon at the top to give your team closer spawns and allow you to get more attempts at the objective.
- In the south entrance of the parking garage, a staircase leads to an underground tunnel towards M-COM Station A. This allows defenders to help protect both objectives as they can run back and forth.
- In the south entrance, defenders can man the stationary weapons to assist in destroying the US team's IFVs.

PRO TIP: ELUMNITE

WHEN DEFENDING, USING THE J-20 IS A GREAT OPTION AS THE US TEAM WON'T HAVE ANY JETS TO COUNTER YOU WITH. RULE THE SKY WITH THIS STEALTH JET AND PICK OFF ANY ATTACK HELICOPTERS AND LAND VEHICLES YOU SEE. MANEUVERING AROUND BUILDINGS WILL HELP YOU AVOID ANY MISSILES THAT LOCK ON TO YOU. PLUS WITH THE ADDITION OF FLARES, YOU ALMOST NEVER SHOULD GET SHOT DOWN.

ZONE 4: EMBASSY

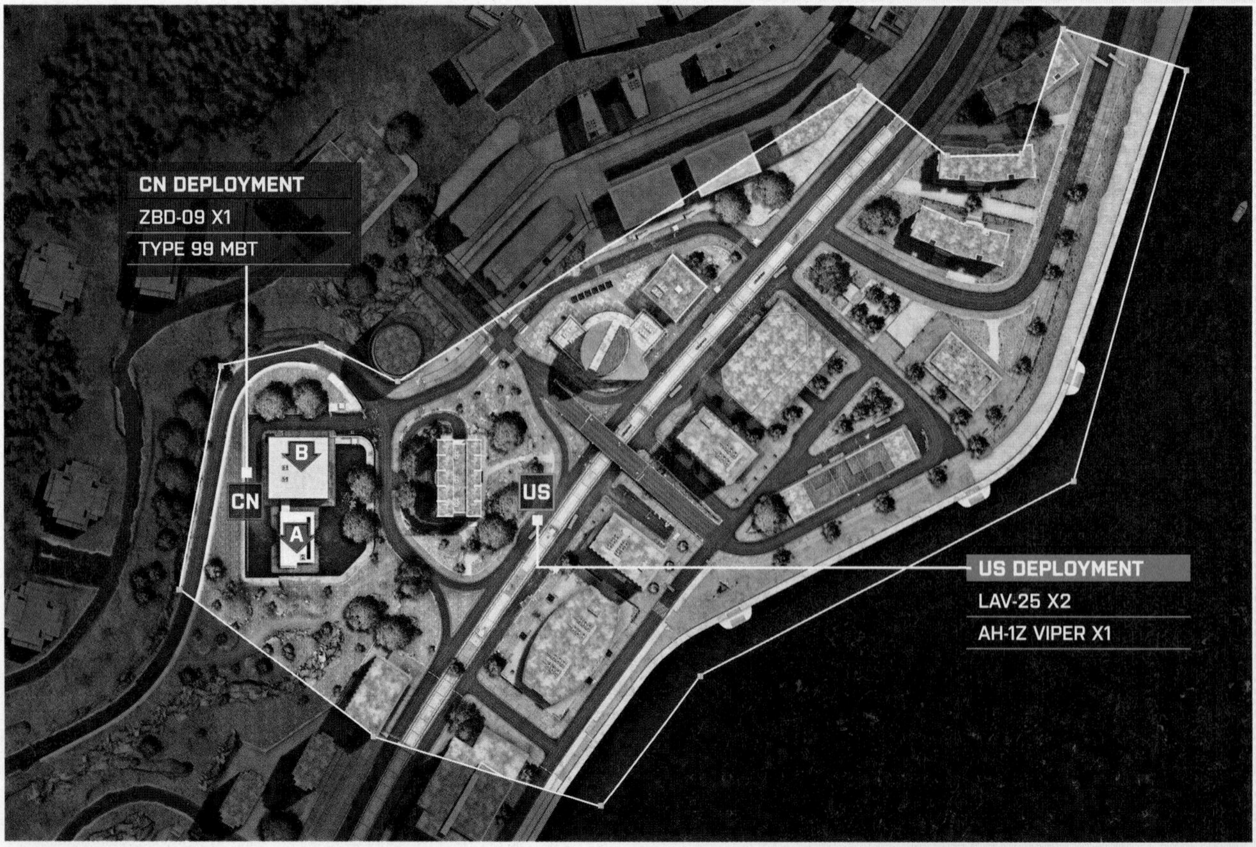

US DEPLOYMENT

RECOMMENDED SQUAD COMPOSITION:

- The US deployment is located to the east of the M-COM stations, which are placed inside the Embassy.
- When attacking the Embassy, there is only one main route for land vehicles to enter this area. You need teammates to push in from multiple directions to distract defenders while your LAV-25s enter from the northwest.
- The defending CN team has a ZBD-09 and a Type 99 MBT. Be sure to have multiple engineers ready to take out the Type 99 MBT before it dominates your LAV-25s.
- Lay down a T-UGS before heading up the stairwells underneath M-COM Station A. This will reveal when enemies are waiting for you so you can have the upper hand.
- Try to arm M-COM Station A first, since this area is the most difficult to get control of. From here, finishing the game by arming M-COM Station B will be simple since you have the building under full control.

DEPLOYMENT AREA ASSETS

NAME	LAV-25	AH-1Z Viper
QUANTITY	2	1

CN DEPLOYMENT

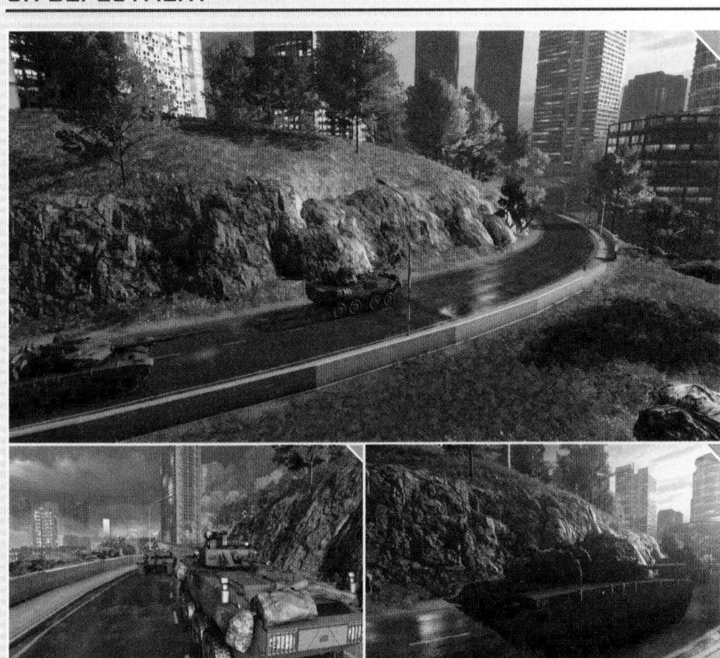

RECOMMENDED SQUAD COMPOSITION: 

- In Zone 4, the CN deployment is moved to southwest of the objectives.
- At this deployment area, a ZBD-09 and a Type 99 MBT spawn here. Use these to stop enemies from making their way into the buildings containing the objectives.
- Place a Radio Beacon on the north balcony of the building containing M-COM Station A. If your squad is taken out, you'll still be given a good spawn near the objective to stop the arm.
- Place T-UGS in both of the buildings containing the objectives. For this close-quarter area you'll want to know what your enemy is doing every second.
- You'll have some time to set up your defenses, so get into a good position with cover and watch the area towards the US deployment. It will take US enemies a bit of time to make their way towards the Embassy, but be patient.

DEPLOYMENT AREA ASSETS

NAME	ZBD-09	Type 99 MBT
QUANTITY	1	1

M-COM STATION A

- M-COM Station A is located towards the west part of the map and is on the second floor of the building.
- The CN team has an MBT that will be used to cover the whole building and take out any ground units trying to sneak inside.
- Watching the staircases is the most effective way to protect M-COM Station A. Defending support players should station themselves at the top of both stairs and kill any attacker that approaches.
- Attackers will push their way through in the IFVs transporting engineers who are ready to take out any tanks outside the Embassy.
- The attack helicopter will drop some players off on the roof of the buildings and place a Radio Beacon there. Then, while the other attackers are distracting the defenders, the roof squad will make their move on the M-COM station, catching the CN team by surprise.

M-COM STATION B

- M-COM Station B is located within the Embassy security room. The security room has cameras watching the activity of an aircraft carrier.
- The Embassy has stationary weapons that assist in preventing the attackers from reaching the objective.
- Defenders can plant the entire room with Claymores as they watch from the top of the stairs. Be sure to move in after the Claymores go to ensure every attacker was wiped out.
- Defenders can plant T-UGS in the two bathrooms to detect any nearby enemies. This will allow you to assist in defending M-COM Station A as they are only a few meters away.
- Attackers will have to flood the Embassy from multiple entrances in order to arm. Be sure to have a recon player plant hidden Radio Beacons behind the Embassy to allow constant squad spawns, which will assure the arming of M-COM Station B.

OBLITERATION

RECOMMENDED SQUAD COMPOSITION:

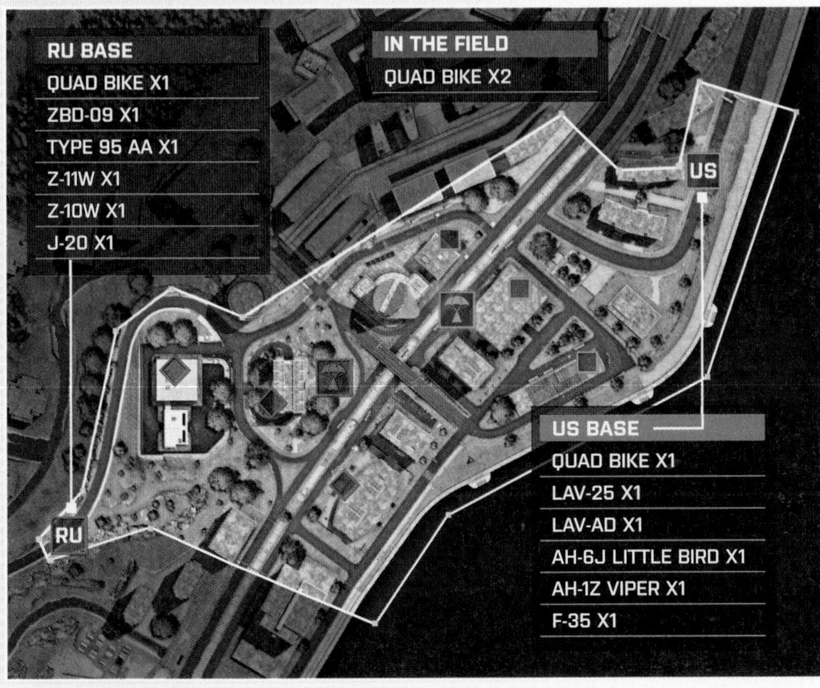

- The US team must defend the targets between the Plaza and the Bus Terminal.
- The CN team guards the targets between the Embassy and the Hospital.
- The bomb is located around the conference room of the building near the Plaza.
- Pilots will enjoy this map as they can maneuver around the tall buildings and use them as cover. The attack helicopters can use these buildings to flank the opponents and lay down some heavy artillery.
- Using the parachute deployment, recon players can reach the top of many buildings that provide amazing sniping angles.

DEFUSE

RECOMMENDED SQUAD COMPOSITION:

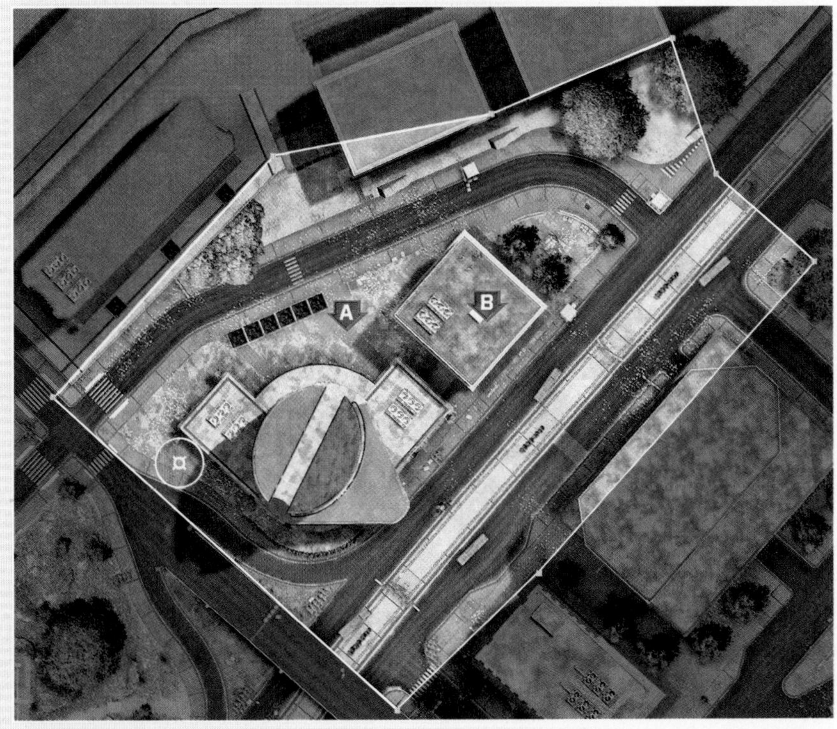

- This epic battle is held around the building adjacent to the Plaza, where the US team spawns near the west entrance and the CN team can be found on the northeast entrance.
- Laptop A is located in the courtyard between the two connected buildings. There are many items that can be used for cover, including a bus players can hide in.
- Laptop B is found just outside of the elevator that leads to the roof of the building adjacent to the Plaza. Beware of defenders hiding inside of the elevator.
- The defending CN team can take the elevator to get to the roof of the building and jump to a lower roof that will allow them to completely lock down Laptop A. The only risk is that you will not be able to watch the other objective, so plan accordingly with how many people go to the top.
- The US team should focus on staying inside the building as the defenders gain early access to the roof. Bring Flashbangs and punish the CN team for leaving only a few people down low to watch Laptop B.

DOMINATION

RECOMMENDED SQUAD COMPOSITION:

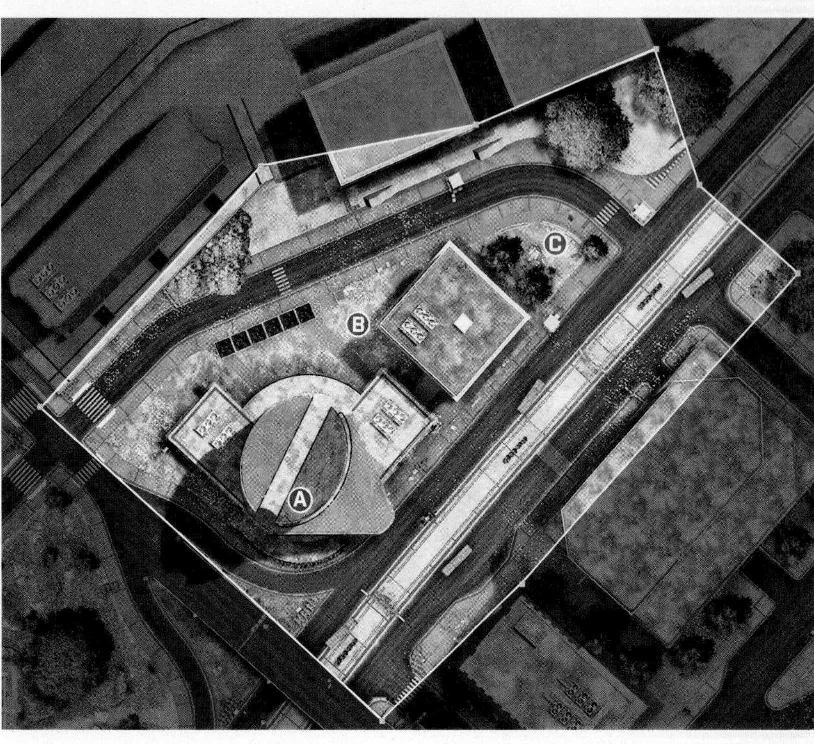

- The three control points on this map are the Meeting Room (A), Plaza (B), and Statue (C).
- After capturing the Plaza (B), plant C4 around crates to get easy kills as opponents try to recapture this flag.
- The elevator near the Statue (C) leads to the roof, which lets you clearly watch over the Plaza (B) and the Statue (C). This strategy allows you to safely guard the control points from a distance.
- The roof of the building near the Statue (C) lets you move around at a fast pace, allowing you to respond to squad commands.
- When defending, throw Motion Sensors so you know where enemies are coming from at all times.

SQUAD DEATHMATCH

RECOMMENDED SQUAD COMPOSITION:

- Squads battle each other around the Plaza on this map.
- The interior of the building is a power position throughout the game. Moving from the back to the front, your squad will witness all the action going on outside, allowing you to clean up some easy kills since your opponents are distracted.
- When inside the building be sure to equip close-quarter weapons as you are fighting in confined halls and rooms. Shotguns are suggested as you can hide in the small storage rooms to surprise your enemy.
- Inside the building near the front entrance is a circuit board that you can shoot; this will cause all the lights inside to go off. Equip an IRNV scope to excel during this darkened firefight.
- Be sure to stay close to your squad. Moving near each other will allow you to react to one another's call outs. As most of the action will occur around the building; you want to be able to shoot the same targets and revive a squadmate if downed.

TEAM DEATHMATCH

RECOMMENDED SQUAD COMPOSITION:

- Prepare yourself for all kind of fights on this map, including close-quarter, outside firefights, and rooftop battles.
- When fighting inside of the building next to the Plaza, there are fire extinguishers that produce a smoke screen for cover when shot. Drop prone and gun down opponents as they run by.
- There is a circuit box that shuts off the power for some time when shot. Equip the IRNV to excel in these areas with the lights out.
- There are glass overhangs that make new paths inside of the building when you destroy the steel pillar holding the overhang. Use these if the opposing team is defending the inside of the building.
- There is an elevator that leads to the top of the building; from here you can jump to one of the lower buildings. The lower buildings provide a superior angle as you can hide from incoming fire.

ALPHA SQUAD: IMPRESSIONS

MABOOZA

Whether the map is flooded or not, I hate finding myself on the ground level, where I'm usually spotted and immediately picked off by opponents on higher ground. I prefer patrolling the rooftops with an assault rifle or carbine, where at least I have a fighting chance to survive encounters with the enemy.

STRONGSIDE

The Levolution on this map is incredible. It changes the entire environment into a water world. Once Levolution is activated you'll find me cruising on a PWC around the map and in the alleyways between the buildings. But watch out—I'll be sure to sneak up behind you using the stairways beneath the Rooftop Garden and Shanty Town!

WALSHY

I really enjoy the rooftop battles on this map. To me it is the most exciting and fun mid- to close-range battles in the entire game. Whether you love being sneaky and flanking around or you like to eliminate the element of surprise and attack from the air, there are so many options to take over and fight for the rooftops.

FLAMESWORD

As soon as I started running around this map, the first thing that popped in my head was parkour! This map has so many rooftops and ledges that allow for some risk-taking jumps. Being a specialist in close quarters pays its dues on this map.

ELUMNITE

Transporting on this map is my forte by grabbing the Z-9 Haitun or UH1Y Venom and getting a few teammates back into the battle by dropping them off on some of the rooftops. This is something I like to do after the map is flooded, as it helps my team move from place to place more efficiently.

FLOOD ZONE

FLOOD ZONE

LEVOLUTION MOMENTS

WHAT IS IT?

A levee breaks, which is holding back a large mass of water. The water floods in over the map, creating a new environment of gameplay on the ground level.

HOW IS IT TRIGGERED?

Take down the levee with vehicle missiles, RPGs, SMAWs, C4, grenades, or any explosive weapon. Look for the cracks and hit that spot repeatedly.

HOW IS GAMEPLAY IMPACTED?

Water level is raised significantly so infantry has to swim, land vehicles are replaced with boats, a battle pickup is disabled, some routes are opened up, and other routes are closed.

CONQUEST LARGE

RECOMMENDED SQUAD COMPOSITION:

This larger variant of Conquest throws two more control points into the mix of the game: Shanty Town (C) located just a hair south of Rooftop Garden (B) and the Gas Station (D), which is even more south from the above two control points. The safest strategy for the US team is to control Garage (A), Rooftop Garden (B), Shanty Town (C), and possibly Gas Station (D) if the CN team is being pushed back easily. Another strategy for the US team, albeit more risky, is to control Garage (A), Gas Station (D), and the Park (E). These control points spawn extra vehicles, which make defending and moving around the map easier. The CN team should focus on controlling the Park (E), Shanty Town (C), Rooftop Garden (B), and possibly Gas Station (D) if the US team isn't able to advance. The CN team can try the risky strategy above as well, but be warned! If the levee is destroyed, water fills up the entire map making these vehicles disappear. If the levee is destroyed, both teams should focus on having control of Rooftop Garden (B) and Shanty Town (C) to have more vantage points. Once the map is flooded, there will be more players swimming, so it is easy pickings for the team controlling the high ground. The strategy of controlling the Garage (A), Gas Station (D), and Park (E) can still work; the map being filled with water makes defending the Garage (A) and Gas Station (D) even easier. This risky strategy does have a huge benefit. If the opposing team tries to retreat to recapture the control point closest to their base, it leaves an opening to capture the Rooftop Garden (B) or Shanty Town (C).

US BASE

PRO TIP: FLAMESWORD

ALPHA SQUAD'S SQUAD LEADER SHOULD DRIVE THE **AMTRAC** WHILE BRAVO SQUAD FILLS THE REST OF THE SEATS. HAVE BRAVO SQUAD JUMP OUT AT GAS STATION (D) AND THEN ALPHA SQUAD CAN SPAWN IN VEHICLE. THIS IS AN EASY WAY TO TAKE ADVANTAGE OF THE SQUAD AND VEHICLE SPAWN SYSTEM.

- The US base is located on the west side of the map. There are many vehicles that spawn off the start of the game, so the initial push will be very important. A few players should immediately go on foot towards the Garage (A) for an easy capture, seeing as it is closest to the US base.
- Two air vehicles are at the base: the AH-6J Little Bird and UH1Y-Venom. The UH1Y-Venom should be filled up with five players and head straight towards the Rooftop Garden (B) and Shanty Town (C). The rooftops will play a huge role in the game, so take control quickly. The pilot of the AH-6J Little Bird should continue east past the Rooftop Garden (B) and put pressure on incoming CN team members.
- A full squad plus one other player should all jump in the AMTRAC and head towards the Gas Station (D). Taking the Gas Station (D) allows the controlling team access to another MRAP. Controlling these off the start can likely be the deciding factor of the match.
- Two different squads should each have two players drive the Quad Bike all the way to the Park (E). Even though this control point is closer to the CN base, the US team should focus on delaying the CN team from capturing the Park (E). The longer you can delay them the better.
- Players who decide to take the two MRAPs should both split up. One should head to the center and drop squad members off at the bottom of the Rooftop Garden (B) so they can help the team members that are parachuting out of the UH1Y-Venom. The other MRAP should take the north side of the map to check if the CN team is trying to send any flankers around the back wall.

BASE ASSETS

NAME	Quad Bike	MRAP	LAV-25	RHIB	PWC	AH-6J Little Bird	UH-1Y Venom
QUANTITY	2	2	2	2	2	1	1

CN BASE

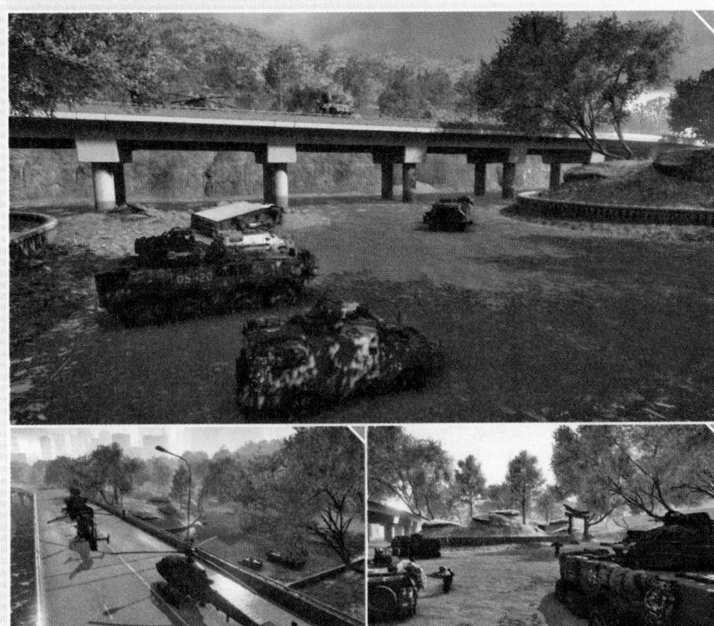

- The CN base is located on the far-east side opposite of the US team. Like the US base there are plenty of vehicles at the start of the game, so the initial push will be very important. A few players should immediately go on foot towards the Park (E) for some easy points seeing as it is nearest the CN base.
- Two air vehicles are at the base: the Z-11W and the Z-9 Haitun. The Z-9 Haitun should be filled up with five players and head straight towards the Rooftop Garden (B) and Shanty Town (C). The rooftops will play a huge role in the game so take control quickly. The pilot of the Z-11W should continue west past the Rooftop Garden (B) and put pressure on incoming US team members from the Garage (A).
- A full squad plus one other player should all jump in the ZBD-09 and head towards the Gas Station (D). Taking the Gas Station (D) allows the controlling team access to another ZBD-09. Controlling these will be very important.
- Two different squads should each have two players drive the Quad Bike all the way to the Garage (A). Even though this control point is closer to the US base, the CN team should focus on delaying the US team from capturing the Garage (A). The longer you can delay them the better, and there is plenty of cover once in the Garage (A).
- Players who decide to take the two ZFB-05s should both head in the same direction. Rolling in a pack can prove very useful, especially if an enemy vehicle is roaming the map on its own. The suggested path would be towards the Gas Station (D) to stop the US team from getting the other ZBD-09.

BASE ASSETS

NAME	Quad Bike	ZFB-05	ZBD-09	RHIB	PWC	Z-11W	Z-9 Haitun
QUANTITY	2	2	2	2	2	1	1

A: GARAGE

- This control point lies near the US base and is located within a four-story parking garage.
- The Garage (A) has a few stairwells that lead to each floor and can prove difficult for the defending team. Place players on the second level of the stairwell to get the surprise attack on the enemy if they come in from below.
- Ground vehicles can enter this Garage (A), but are extremely vulnerable. Defend with a squad composition of assault and support. The assault class can smoke the area, allowing the support players to get close enough to the vehicles to plant C4.
- When attacking, if your team makes it into this area, don't worry about capturing this point so fast. It might turn into a slugfest. So if one or two players remain alive, wait it out a bit and have squad teammates spawn up before going in for the capture.
- The top level of the Garage (A) is accessible to helicopters—not a big deal as you can hear when these get close. Be aware of the players parachuting in for a sneaky capture.

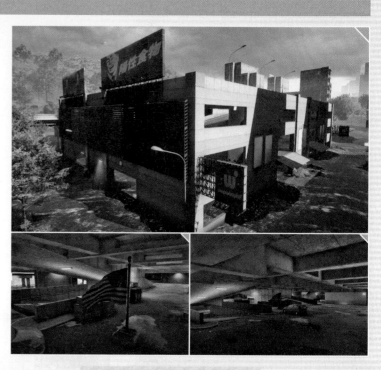

CONTROL POINT ASSETS

US CONTROL	CN CONTROL
RHIB (1)	RHIB (1)
MRAP (1)	ZFB-05 (1)

B: ROOFTOP GARDEN

- Much like Shanty Town (C), this control point lies on a roof as well. This area is important to control as it gives players access to higher ground that allows easy fire towards Shanty Town (C).
- This area holds many shacks, making it very easy to defend once captured. Have one or two players hide within until the right moment presents itself to launch a surprise attack.
- When attacking, sneak into one of the shacks to allow squad members to spawn up and then make a strong push to capture this control point.
- Near the flagpole is a bamboo walkway/staircase that leads to the top of another roof. This roof is a great location for a sniper or a support player that will lay constant rounds towards Rooftop Garden (B) or Shanty Town (C) if the enemy makes it that close.
- When the map is flooded, be sure to maintain this control point along with Shanty Town (C). The raised water level will make getting to these points much more difficult and extremely noticeable when traveling with water vehicles. It can also be very time consuming for the enemy to travel to this point.

PRO TIP: STRONGSIDE

Place a Radio Beacon at this control point on the outside bottom of the building (facing the levee). This area isn't patrolled often so you'll have a close easy spawn point near the center of the map for you and your squad. This will keep you in the action constantly!

CONTROL POINT ASSETS

US CONTROL	CN CONTROL
RCB-90 (1)	DV-15 (1)

C: SHANTY TOWN

- This control point lies on the rooftop with many shacks around it. The area promotes a lot of close-quarter combat. The only vehicles to worry about up here are helicopters.
- This rooftop is connected with many others. Some of the paths lead towards Rooftop Garden (B), so be prepared to shoot from roof to roof in this classic shootout.
- This control point can be captured easily from behind the flagpole as players can clearly see the only two directions enemies can enter from.
- There are many ledges around this area that can be used as getaways or sneaky attack routes. Be sure to brush up on your parkour skills as there are many cool jumps to do.
- There are a few stairwells that lead to the top along with bamboo walkways. Locate and study these paths as they could prove helpful.

PRO TIP: STRONGSIDE

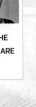

I like to play as the Recon class and place a T-UGS in the stairwell below this control point or on top of the roof in one of the many shacks to alert me exactly where the enemies are around me if I am making an attack up or down.

CONTROL POINT ASSETS

US CONTROL	CN CONTROL
RHIB (1)	RHIB (1)

D: GAS STATION

- Isolated from the rest of the map, this control point is located south from Rooftop Garden (B) and Shanty Town (C). Players must pass through the underpass or fly in with a helicopter before reaching this control point.
- Teams who capture this control point gain access to a mobile AA vehicle. This comes in handy for shooting down the enemy team's helicopters.
- There is a market inside this control point. Players can hide inside to surprise attack an enemy at close range. The market is a perfect place for a stakeout or ice cold drink if the squad needs to cool down.
- Gaining access to the highway nearby could prove useful as well, but beware—there isn't much cover. Use this position to lay fire from above once in a while to confuse the enemy about your location.
- The gas tanks are explosive, but hold off on blowing these up immediately. Hopefully the enemy isn't paying attention and doesn't know that bullets make gas tanks go BOOM! You'll take down an enemy with much entertainment.

PRO TIP: STRONGSIDE

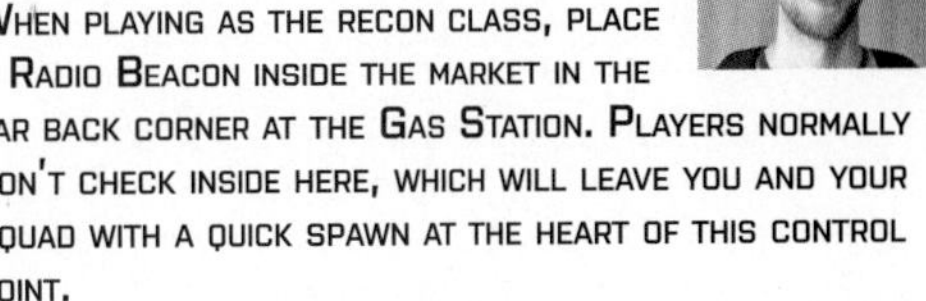

When playing as the Recon class, place a Radio Beacon inside the market in the far back corner at the Gas Station. Players normally don't check inside here, which will leave you and your squad with a quick spawn at the heart of this control point.

CONTROL POINT ASSETS

US CONTROL	CN CONTROL
LAV-AD (1)	Type 95 AA (1)

E: PARK

- This control point lies in the middle of a Chinese park. A statue lies close to the flagpole and the area has many trees.
- Within the Park (E) there are hills that allow players to gain ground on those who try to capture this control point. Use these hills to peek in the control point and drop down for cover.
- This control point favors the CN team as it is close to their home base, so it will be tricky for the US to neutralize and capture. The best time for the US team to make an attempt for this control point will be if the US team controls Rooftop Garden (B) and Shanty Town (C) or the CN team has control of Rooftop Garden (B) and Shanty Town (C) and the US team can flank to turn the tide of the match.
- If the map is flooded, you can be quite annoying and contest this control point by swimming underwater near the capture zone, since you can't been seen beneath the dark water. Come up for air when needed, but then drop back into the water to stay hidden.
- Place T-UGS near the entrance of the Park (E) to alert your team when enemies are coming in to capture the control point.

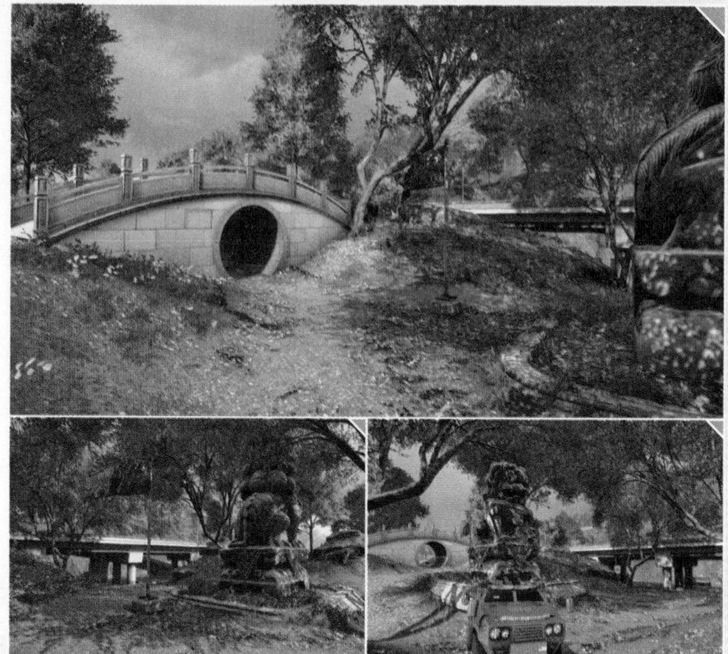

CONTROL POINT ASSETS

US CONTROL	CN CONTROL
RHIB (1)	RHIB (1)
MRAP (1)	ZFB-05 (1)

CONQUEST SMALL

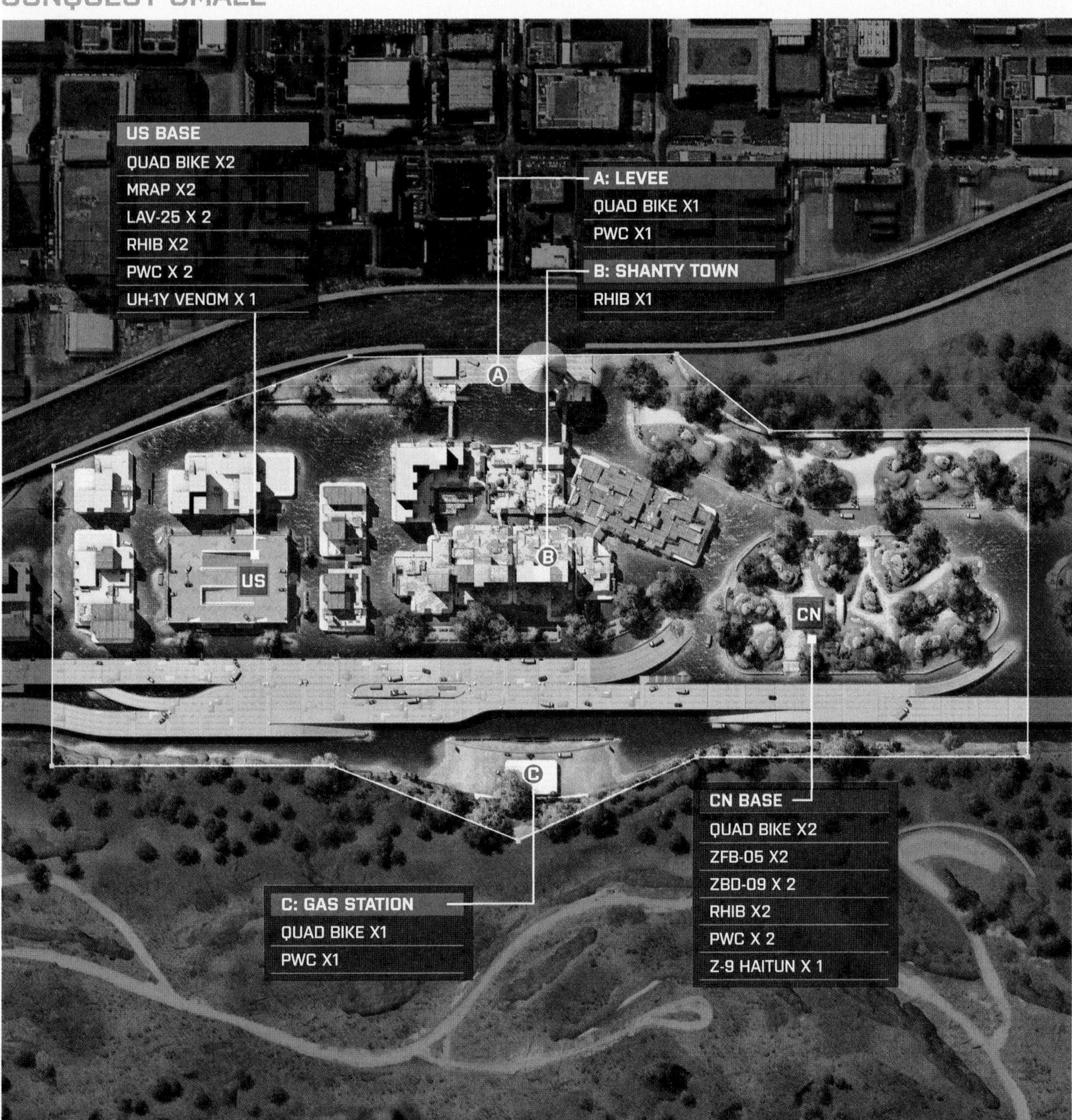

RECOMMENDED SQUAD COMPOSITION:

Flood Zone is a medium-scale Conquest Small match with a variation of ground and water vehicles. The US team starts on the west side of the map in the Garage while the opposing CN team starts on the east in the Park. This match will contain three control points. The team to capture two control points first will commence ticket drain to the other team. Control points Levee (A), Shanty Town (B), and Gas Station (C) stand between both bases. Being a map with only three control points, both the US team and CN team should only focus on defending two control points. The US team should lock down both Levee (A) and Shanty Town (B). The CN team should aim to control the same two control points as the US team. These two control points will be the most important flags throughout the entire game. First, the team who captures the flag at Shanty Town (B) will allow their Commander to call in a Tomahawk Cruise Missile at the click of a button. What makes this area even more crucial is that players can guard the Levee (A) from the top of the building near Shanty Town (B). The opposing team will always have to clear out the top of the buildings in order to gain control of the Levee (A), but this is an uphill battle as the controlling team will be laying down fire making it difficult to reach Shanty Town (B). Both the US and CN team can capture all three points if they want, the Gas Station (C) can be used as a distraction forcing the other team to neutralize so their tickets wont bleed out so quickly. Prepare for a fast paced map as an organized team can quickly claim victory.

US BASE

- The US base is located on the west side of the map in the Garage.
- At this base you'll have a good amount of vehicles to use in taking control of this map. This map has a Levolution that floods the entire map. When Levolution is activated, air vehicles will be your best bet to travel quickly.
- Immediately send a helicopter towards Shanty Town (B) to take over this control point early. This flag is the most important since it lays in-between Levee (A) and Gas Station(C). Shanty Town (B) will be a high traffic area throughout the entire game. Place Radio Beacons within Shanty Town (B) or Rooftop Garden to keep your team in the action and put pressure on the enemy. Using T-UGS around the Rooftop Garden and Shanty Town (B) will give you a huge advantage when enemies are approaching.
- Be sure to take up every seat in the MRAP as it can hold a total of 6 players. Having an engineer in one of the seats can be extremely effective when an attacking enemy vehicle engages. They won't know what hit them as the engineer repairs the MRAP from within to score a solid amount of points.
- Send a fully loaded MRAP towards the Levee (A) to capture this flag early. A few players should exit the MRAP immediately once near the Levee (A) and make their way up the stairway below the Rooftop Garden which will be a power position since it has an overview of Shanty Town (B) and the Levee(A).
- Use the light vehicles to rush a few players towards the Gas Station(C). Also place a Radio Beacon inside the store of the Gas Station to have a good spawn if you lose or are losing the control point.

BASE ASSETS

NAME	Quad Bike	MRAP	RHIB	PWC	LAV-25	UH1Y-Venom
QUANTITY	2x	2x	2x	2x	1x	1

CN BASE

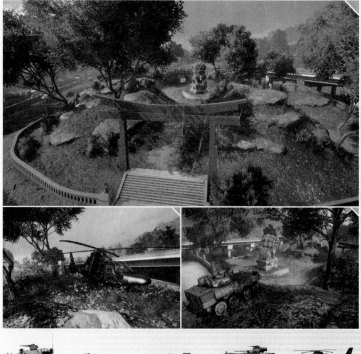

- The CN base is located on the east side of the map in the Park. This base spawns with many vehicles, take advantage of these by packing engineers inside to repair them and outlast the enemy's vehicles.
- Immediately send a helicopter towards Shanty Town (B) to take over this control point early. This flag is the most important since it lays in-between Levee (A) and Gas Station(C). Shanty Town (B) will be a high traffic area throughout the entire game. Place Radio Beacons within Shanty Town (B) or Rooftop Garden to keep your team in the action and put pressure on the enemy. Using T-UGS around the Rooftop Garden and Shanty Town (B) will give you a huge advantage when enemies are approaching.
- This map has a Levolution that floods the entire map. When Levolution is activated, water vehicles and air vehicles are your best friend. You don't want to get caught swimming with no cover as you'll be taken out quite easily.
- Send a your IFV towards the Gas Station(C) or Levee(A) and fill up every seat in the vehicle as it can hold a total of 6 players. Having an engineer in one of the seats can be extremely effective when an attacking enemy vehicle engages. They won't know what hit them as the engineer repairs the ZBD-09 from within. Remember, two engineers are always better than one.
- Use the light vehicles to rush a few players towards the Gas Station(C). Also place a Radio Beacon inside the store of the Gas Station (C) to have a good spawn if you are losing the control point.

BASE ASSETS

NAME	Quad Bike	ZFB-05	RHIB	PWC	ZBD-09	Z-9 Haitun
QUANTITY	2x	2x	2x	2x	1x	1x

A: LEVEE

> This flag is located on the north side of the map south of the destructible levee. When controlled a light vehicle spawns here. Controlling this flag will give your commander Infantry Scan.

> This control point has a wide capture and contest radius. When capturing sit on the furthest northeast position of the levee to capture the point with much cover.

> When defending or attacking this flag, send teammates to the Rooftop Garden to have a complete overview of the Levee (A) area; this position on the map is a power position for your team. The Rooftop Garden also over looks Shanty Town (B) making the Rooftop Garden the most important position in this game mode.

> When the levee is destroyed the flag stays in the same position and a light water vehicle spawns here. This area becomes flooded with water making travel to and from this flag much more difficult.

> Once controlling this flag don't stay near the area as you're extremely exposed from many angles. Make your way towards another flag or use the cover on the east side of the Levee (A) to camp out.

CONTROL POINT ASSETS

US CONTROL	CN CONTROL
Quad Bike (1)	Quad Bike (1)
PWC (1)	PWC (1)

B: SHANTY TOWN

> This control point lies on the rooftop with many shacks around it. The area promotes a lot of close quarter combat. Land vehicles will not be able to reach this area but helicopter will be a threat along with enemy infantry.

> This rooftop is connected with many others and some of the paths lead towards Rooftop Garden so be prepared to shoot from roof to roof in this classic shoot out. Be sure to have medium ranged weapons to fight in this range.

> This control point can be captured easily from behind the flagpole as players can easily see the only two directions enemies can enter from. Also equip a shotgun or Shorty 12G for the close quarter combat in the stairways and room to room combat underneath this flag.

> There are many ledges around this area that can be used as getaway or sneaky attack routes. There are a few stairwells that lead to the top along with bamboo walkways. Locate and study these paths as they could prove helpful. Be sure to brush up on your parkour skills as there are many cool jumps to do.

> This is the most important control point since it lies in-between Gas Station(C) and Levee(A). You're able to defend Shanty Town(B) from a higher point at the Rooftop Garden and it also allows your team to defend the Levee (A) from above as well. Be sure to defend this objective throughout the entire game. It will be the key to your victory.

CONTROL POINT ASSETS

US CONTROL	CN CONTROL
RHIB (1)	RHIB (1)

C: GAS STATION

- Isolated from the rest of the map, this control point is located south from Shanty Town (B). Players must pass through the underpass or fly in with a helicopter before reaching this control point.
- Teams who capture this flag gain access to a light vehicle. This vehicle should be used to rush towards the lower levels of Shanty Town (B). This will set you up for a sneaky attack if the enemies are in control of Shanty Town (B).
- This control point has a store inside the Gas Station (C) which players can hide inside to surprise attack an enemy at close range. As the recon class, place a Radio Beacon inside the store in the far back corner giving your squad quick spawns at this location if the control point is being captured by the enemies.
- When attacking this control point use helicopters, AFVs, and IFVs to overrun the area. With the helicopter your able to land on the roof of the Gas Station(C) to capture this point but beware the roof can explode if the fuel tanks are shot.
- The fuel tanks are explosive but hold off on blowing these up immediately. You can use these to take down enemies on foot or in a vehicle if they are in the blast radius. This will ensure you a few delightfully entertaining kills.

CONTROL POINT ASSETS

US CONTROL	RU CONTROL
Quad Bike (1)	Quad Bike (1)
PWC (1)	PWC (1)

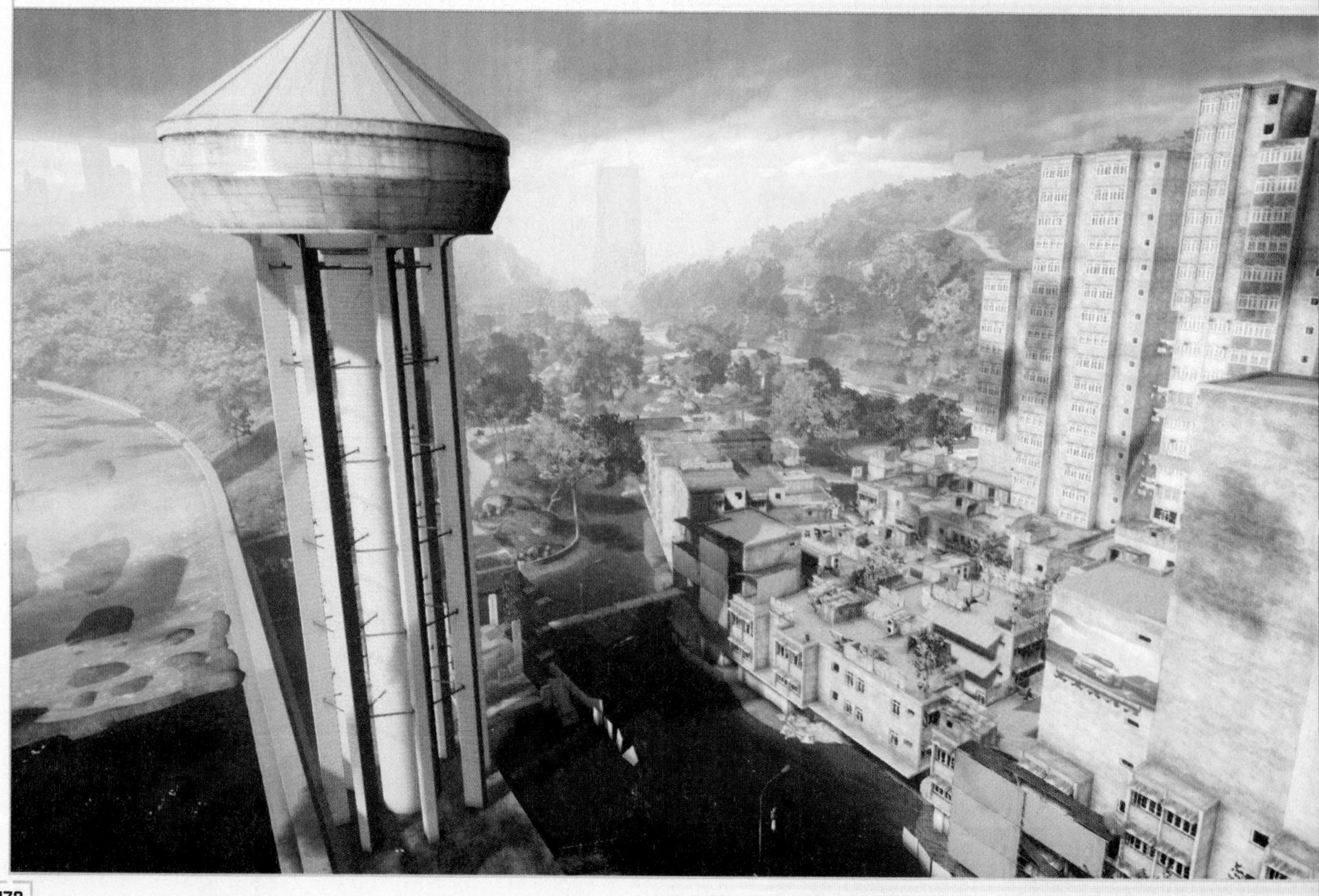

RUSH

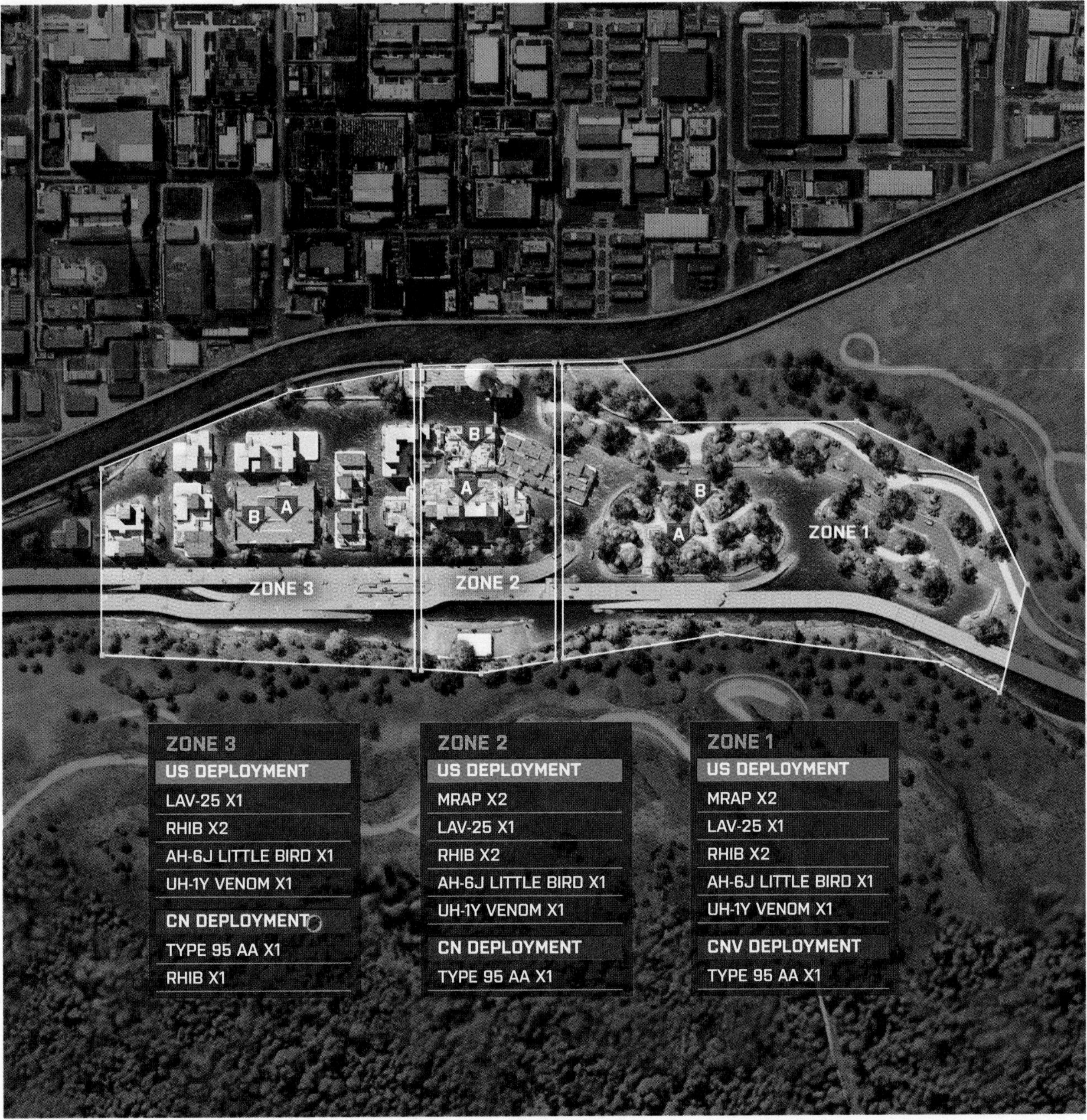

This is an exciting map to play Rush. The US team objective is to take out six M-COM stations spread throughout three different zones. The zones go from Park, to the Shanty Town/Rooftop Garden, and finally the Garage. The US team is stacked with plenty of vehicles off the start, including an AH-6J Little Bird that can be deadly in the right hands. The pilot will provide a lot of air support to allow infantry units to plant the M-COM stations across the first two zones, but the third zone becomes tricky as the M-COM stations are located inside the Garage. The CN team has their work cut out for them, starting only with a Type 95 AA while facing off against the US team's AH-6J Little Bird, two LAV-25s, and two RHIBs. If that fails, it is highly recommended to have a heavy engineer-based squad composition to defend against all the vehicles the US team has at their disposal. If the CN team is pushed all way back to the Garage in the third and final zone, don't give up! This Garage calls for a lot of close-quarter combat and the US team's vehicles will be almost useless.

ZONE 1: PARK

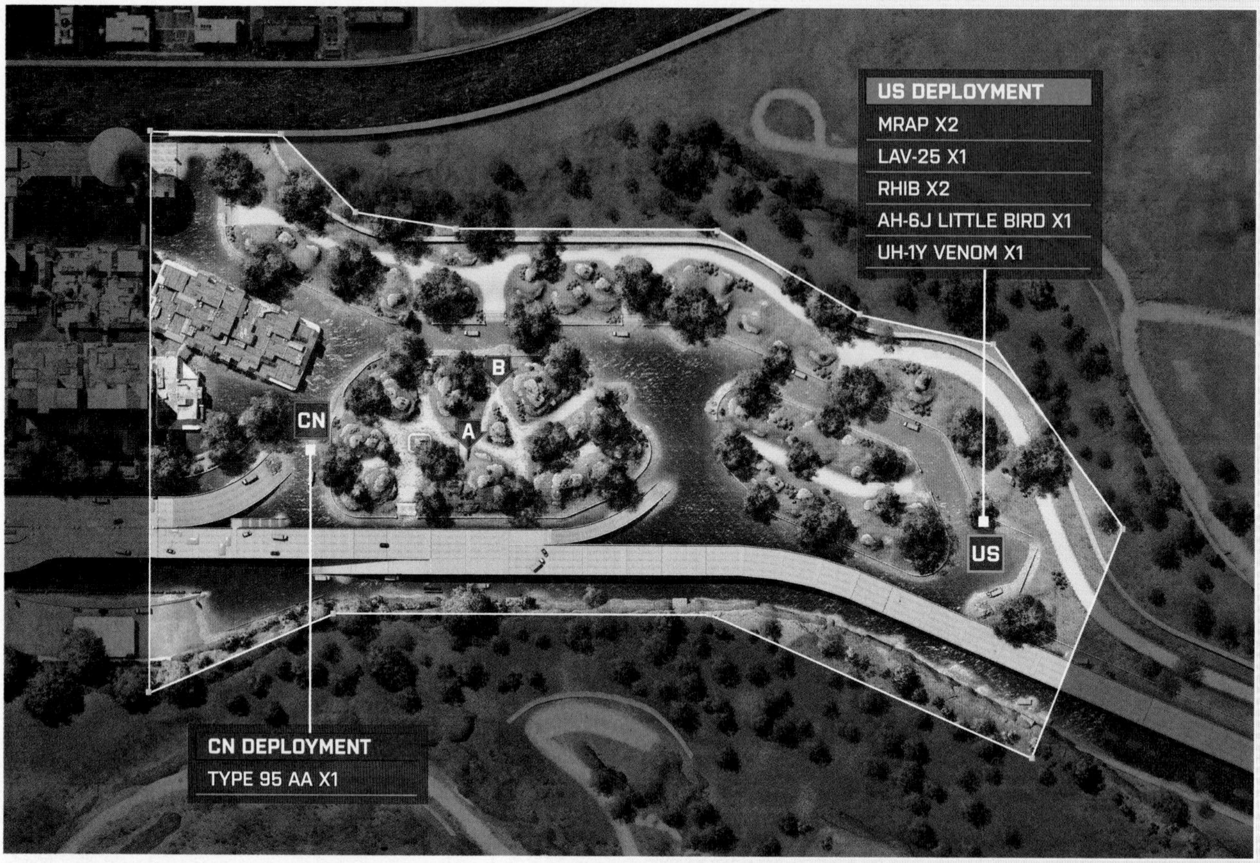

US DEPLOYMENT
MRAP X2
LAV-25 X1
RHIB X2
AH-6J LITTLE BIRD X1
UH-1Y VENOM X1

B
A
CN
US

CN DEPLOYMENT
TYPE 95 AA X1

US DEPLOYMENT

RECOMMENDED SQUAD COMPOSITION:

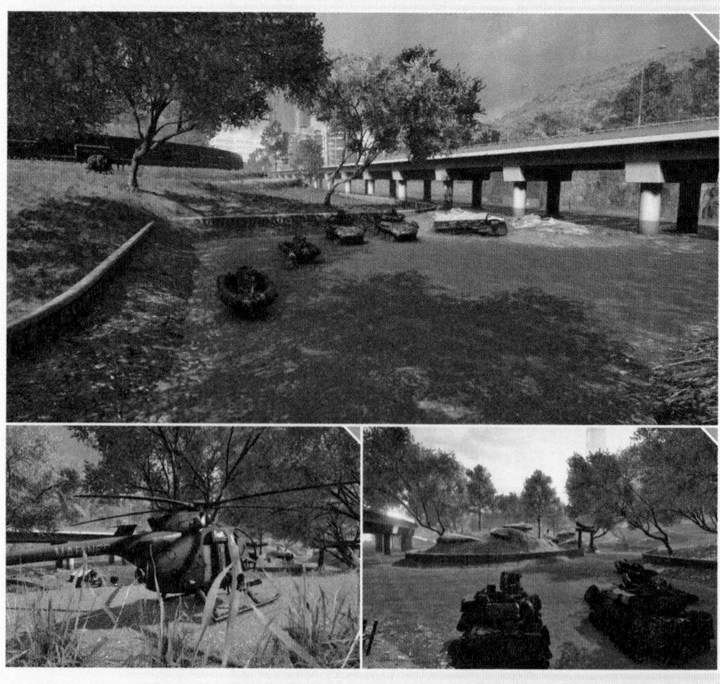

- The US team spawns at the eastern side of the map. The base starts with two LAV-25s, two RHIBs, and one AH-6J Little Bird. The opposing team starts with only a Type 95 AA. Knowing this you'll want to take out the enemy's AA with engineers and IFVs before flying in with the Little Bird. Also, having a few engineers on the team will greatly help in taking down the Type 95 AA quickly.
- When advancing towards the Park, use the rocky hills for cover to make your way closer to the M-COM stations. Send other infantry north and south of the park to have other points of attack.
- The US base also spawns two RHIBs with machine guns attached. These boats don't have much cover and leave players exposed to enemy infantry fire. Use these boats mostly for quick transport.
- For easier arming, keep the IFVs near the M-COM stations. Watch out for engineers as they will be firing many rockets to stop the IFVs. Have an engineer as a passenger to hop in and out to recover quickly from the hits you'll be taking from the enemy engineer rocket launchers.
- For a possible quick arm, at the start of the match, load up the IFVs with infantry and follow the path towards M-COM Station A. All passengers except for one should unload within the rocky hills and watch for incoming infantry and engineers. Then have both IFVs go in close near M-COM Station A, shielding the M-COM station from the north and south. The last passenger should unload from the vehicle and plant a charge. The two IFVs should cover and shield their teammate for a safe and quick arm. You can also use the AH-6J Little Bird for a distraction, but beware of the enemy's AA.

DEPLOYMENT AREA ASSETS

NAME	MRAP	LAV-25	RHIB	UH-1Y Venom	AH-6J Little Bird
QUANTITY	2	1	2	1	1

CN DEPLOYMENT

RECOMMENDED SQUAD COMPOSITION:

- The CN team spawns just east of a highway entrance. On the ramp of the highway entrance, one Type 95 AA spawns at the start of the game. Aside from that, it is a mad dash sprint to the east towards both M-COM stations.
- The CN team is outnumbered in vehicles when it comes to defending Zone 1. With only one Type 95 AA available, its main mission is to stay alive and take out the US team's AH-6J Little Bird. Be sure to have engineers near the Type 95 AA to repair it and grab some easy points.
- Be sure to have a handful of engineers head to the bridge west of M-COM Station A. This bridge will provide enough cover to be able to rocket the two LAV-25s the US team has.
- The recon and support class can also do a lot of damage to the US team. This first zone is located in a Park; the recon players will be camouflaged when prone and should lead to some easy kills. The benefit of both of these classes is C4 in case they have to aid the engineers in taking out the US team's LAV-25s.
- Be sure to send squads both to the northeast and southeast part of the map to gain multiple defending angles. The CN team should focus on having their other forces in the center around M-COM Station A while the squads on the outskirts of the map spot incoming enemies.

DEPLOYMENT AREA ASSETS

NAME	Type 95 AA
QUANTITY	1

M-COM STATION A

- M-COM Station A is just northeast of the bridge in the middle-east side of the Park surrounded by rocky hills.
- The defenders should focus on having engineers on the bridge to take out incoming vehicles. This bridge provides great cover when it is time to reload. A few other engineers and support class should be east of M-COM Station A to put initial damage on the US team's vehicles.
- This station is out in the open and doesn't have much cover when arming. The attackers should clear this open area out around the objective and watch the perimeter before making an arm. Attackers should place themselves atop the hills for a great vantage point above the enemies. The hills also provide cover when being shot from a distance.
- Just north and south of the park are the outskirts of the map. These outskirts provide great sniping positions for recon players.
- Tread carefully throughout the trails in the park. These trails are very open from many positions in the park so attackers be warned.

M-COM STATION B

- This M-COM Station is located southeast of the bridge in the Park and parallel to M-COM station A. Much like M-COM Station A, there are many rocks, hills, and trees that can be used for cover around the Park.
- Having multiple squads spread out around the hills is the ideal strategy for both attacking and defending.
- When defending, lay C4 behind the M-COM station for a quick stop kill on an enemy trying to arm the station. Make sure a defender is spotting the attackers to know when to detonate the C4.
- The recon class becomes super effective for the defending team. Be sure to throw T-UGS in close proximity to M-COM Station B which will be able to detect enemies once in range.
- When attacking use the bridge for a higher attack point. Be sure to clear the perimeter since this station is easily seen around its entire radius.

ZONE 2: SHANTY TOWN/ROOFTOP GARDEN

US DEPLOYMENT
MRAP X2
LAV-25 X1
RHIB X2
AH-6J LITTLE BIRD X1
UH-1Y VENOM X1

B
CN
A
US

CN DEPLOYMENT
TYPE 95 AA X1

US DEPLOYMENT

RECOMMENDED SQUAD COMPOSITION:

- The US base is now located in the west, among the remains of the M-COM stations in the Park. Here they have access to two LAV-25s, two RHIBs, and an AH-6J Little Bird, which spawns back in the previous deployment area. The CN base spawns again with only a Type 95 AA.
- The M-COM stations are located atop the rooftops. Land vehicles won't be of much use up here. This is where the AH 6J Little Bird comes into play. The Little Bird will be able to take out some enemies while also distracting the enemy infantry and making for a great decoy to let friendly infantry make their way up the stairways to the rooftops. The CN team still has a Type 95 AA and will be using the engineer class as well with the FIM-92 Stinger. Fly carefully with the AH-6J Little Bird using the buildings and alleys to drop down and recover damage taken to the helicopter.
- The M-COM stations are much farther away from the US base in this zone. You'll want to have a squad member play as the recon class and use the Radio Beacon for better spawning near the M-COM stations. Be sure to place the Radio Beacon in a safe spot where it won't be detected and destroyed by the enemy.
- It will be extremely hard to arm either station with the defending team overlooking every move you make. Before attempting to arm either station, take over the rooftops to make for an easier arm at both M-COM stations.
- The assault and support classes will be most effective on this zone. There will be many close-to mid-range battles ahead of you with little vehicle presence on the rooftops. Be sure to equip a Shorty 12G for the close-quarter battles.

DEPLOYMENT AREA ASSETS

NAME	MRAP	LAV-25	RHIB	UH-1Y Venom	AH-6J Little Bird
QUANTITY	2	1	2	1	1

CN DEPLOYMENT

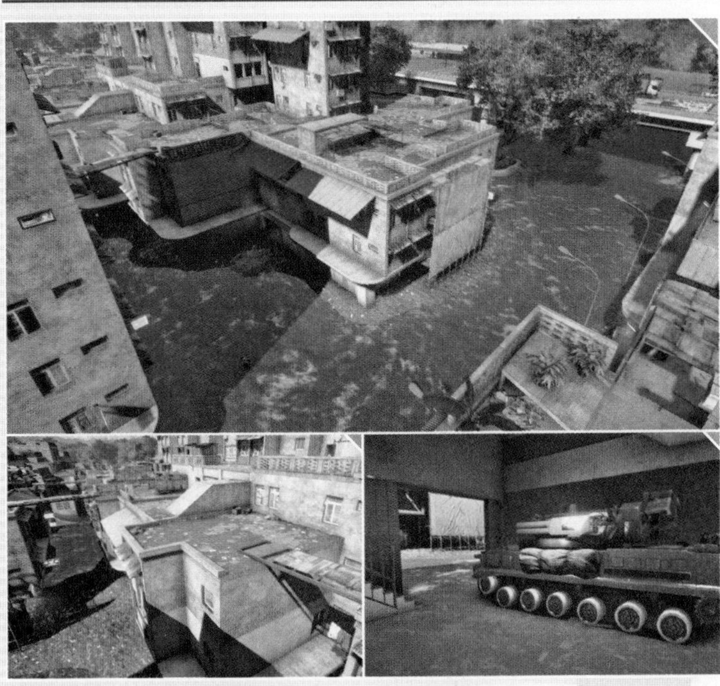

RECOMMENDED SQUAD COMPOSITION:

- After CN team loses their first base in Zone 1, they are pushed back to the rooftops. The benefit of spawning up here is that it will take some time for the US team to reach them. This allows the CN team to establish a perfect setup.
- These rooftops have many great sniping positions. Recon class becomes very effective here, either throwing down T-UGS or marking vehicles with the PLD. Also, they can pick off the enemy infantry making their way towards the M-COM stations.
- Another Type 95 AA spawns around the deployment area. If used effectively, the driver and gunner can shed many tickets of the attacking team. It is highly suggested to have engineers equipped with MK153 SMAW on the rooftops to the east to provide cover when the Type 95 AA comes in contact with the US team's LAV-25s and AH-6J Little Bird.
- There are many ways to access the rooftops from the ground, but the first way the CN team should stop is the US team's AH-6J Little Bird. Have engineers equipped with FIM-92 Stingers to make light work of this bird.
- The US team's ground vehicles will become almost useless for this zone. Be sure to go with a close-quarter squad composition as you will be fighting from roof to roof. Classes with C4 and M18 Claymores will prove useful.

DEPLOYMENT AREA ASSETS

NAME	Type 95 AA
QUANTITY	1

M-COM STATION A

- M-COM Station A is located on the roof in Shanty Town in a shack against the building. This M-COM station has a bunch of little shacks for defenders to hide in with close-quarter weapons like shotguns. These defenders will be able to pick off any attackers who managed to make their way to the top.
- With all the rooftops at the CN team's disposal, the CN team should have players as the recon class. The recon players can get great vantage points and easily pick off ground units before the US team makes it towards the building's entrance. Recon players can also set T-UGS in the staircases. This allows them to snipe and let their squads know if enemies made it in.
- When defending, if the US team's AH-6J Little Bird is down, most of the fighting will occur in the stairwells and the man-made bamboo ramp south of M-COM Station A. If the defending team makes it to this area, be sure to switch to close-quarter classes. The support class will be a wise pick, especially with the suppression effect from their LMGs.
- When attacking, this will be a tough station to take over. The US base is at a lower point in the map and the players will need to work their way up onto the rooftops. Use the AH-6J Little Bird for easy drop off on top of the roof while picking off the enemies out in the open.
- This M-COM station has a back entrance from the southwest side of the building. You are able to run across the tent hanging from the side of the building and jump over the railing wall to land in Shanty Town. This can be used by the attackers to either sneak attack from behind the defending team or be used by the defending team as a cover position to watch M-COM Station A.

PRO TIP: STRONGSIDE

Since M-COM Station A is inside a shack, when defending place C4 on the roof or the back wall of the inside of the shack for an easy kill to stop the enemy from arming the station. Players will rarely look to see if C4 is placed.

M-COM STATION B

- This station is located north of M-COM Station A in between a stack of crates and a shack. This location has many wooden bridges leading to it from rooftop to rooftop.
- The only access to this M-COM station are the many wooden bridges from rooftop to rooftop and a stairwell.
- When defending, hold the Rooftop Garden area for a good overview of the bridges leading to this M-COM station. Holding this area will make it hard for the attacking team to arm at this location.
- When attacking, take over the Rooftop Garden area by making your way up through the few stairways you have access to from below.
- North of M-COM Station B is the highest reachable roof by foot. This rooftop has a great overview of both M-COM stations in this zone. Equipping a squad with medium-range weapons to ward off nearby enemies while one recon player snipes is a suggested defensive tactic.

ZONE 3: GARAGE

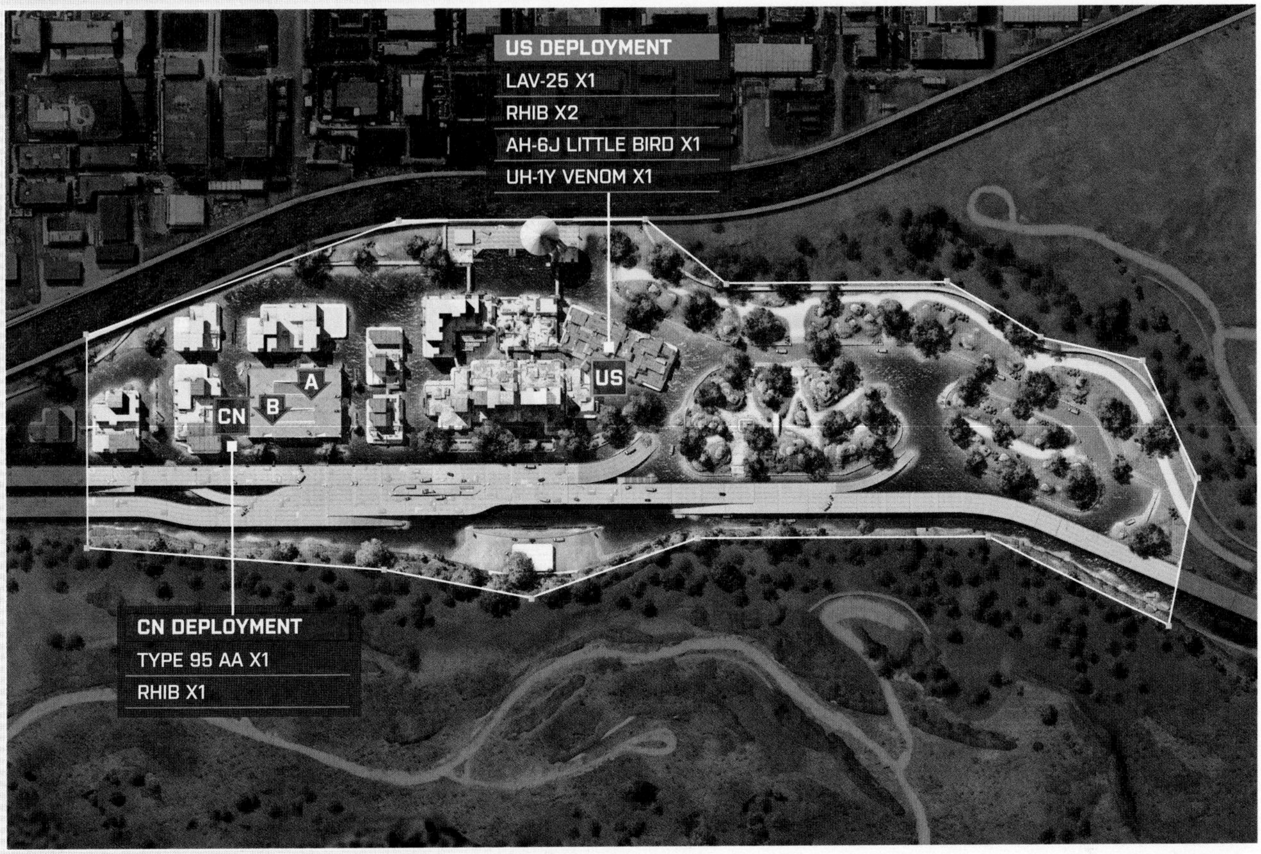

US DEPLOYMENT
LAV-25 X1
RHIB X2
AH-6J LITTLE BIRD X1
UH-1Y VENOM X1

A
B
CN
US

CN DEPLOYMENT
TYPE 95 AA X1
RHIB X1

US DEPLOYMENT

RECOMMENDED SQUAD COMPOSITION:

- After destroying the second set of objectives, the US base shifts to the Shanty Town/Rooftop Garden area, northeast of the new M-COM stations. Deploying down in the alleyway will again be two LAV-25 and two RHIBs. These boats are useless unless Levolution is activated. The AH-6J Little Bird still spawns back at its original spawn point from Zone 1. The CN team has a Type 95 AA again, but it spawns within the Garage, making it useful only if it is on the top level of the Garage.
- Again, this base is far away from the M-COM stations. The recon class will be of use to lay a Radio Beacon hidden among the buildings for spawns closer to the arm sites.
- The M-COMs are placed within the Garage on levels two and three. These will be the most difficult to arm since the enemy spawns are very close to the M-COM stations. When first advancing into the Garage, expect the enemy team to be posted up and ready for attack.
- Use the AH-6J Little Bird to parachute teammates on top of the roof to attack from multiple angles. As the recon class, it would be ideal to place a Radio Beacon and T-UGS on top of the garage. Hold down the top of the Garage while squad members and teammates make their way in from the lower level of the Garage.
- Use the two LAV-25s to push into the lower level of the Garage, but keep your eyes peeled for players with classes that use C4 or M15 AT Mines across the ground. The Garage is an extremely close-range area for vehicles, but will prove helpful if used correctly.

DEPLOYMENT AREA ASSETS

NAME	LAV-25	RHIB	UH-1Y Venom	AH-6J Little Bird
QUANTITY	1	2	1	1

CN DEPLOYMENT

RECOMMENDED SQUAD COMPOSITION:

- This is the final stand for the CN team as their base has now been pushed behind the Garage. This Garage contains four floors. The first three are inside the Garage and the fourth is open to incoming US team helicopters.
- Inside the Garage there are a few staircases that also give players access to each floor. It is suggested to have squads spread out at different ones to stop any incoming flanks.
- If the map is still not flooded, the US team will be able to bring their ground vehicles inside, so have engineers on deck.
- The CN team is granted one more Type 95 AA to help take down the US team's AH-6J Little Bird. The driver can also use the Type 95 AA to stay inside and guard both M-COM stations.
- Much of the fighting will be occurring inside the Garage unless the CN team is able to create a perimeter east of the Garage in attempt to drain as many US team tickets as possible.

DEPLOYMENT AREA ASSETS

NAME	Type 95 AA	RHIB
QUANTITY	1	1

M-COM STATION A

- M-COM Station A stands on the second floor of the Garage. The CN team has a Type 95 AA that spawns right near the station.
- The CN team is outnumbered once again when it comes to vehicles. A good defending strategy would be to keep the Type 95 AA inside the Garage while the engineers of the CN team lay M15 AT Mines around every entrance to the Garage. That should turn the tide.
- When attacking, the US team will want to have at least one recon class in every squad. The distance between the US deployment zone and the M-COM stations is far. Save some time and plant Radio Beacons near the M-COM stations to shorten the distance after spawning.
- Attackers should first attempt to surround the Garage with their vehicles and continuously fire rounds inside to suppress the CN team within. The recon class has a useful gadget called the MAV. Fly this within the Garage to spot the CN team so the ground US team members don't go in blind.
- Also, use the stairways on the north and south side of the garage for another point of attack. The main road in the Garage will be heavily guarded.

M-COM STATION B

- M-COM Station B is located on the third floor of the Garage, one level higher than M-COM Station A. This is the final M-COM station. This station has easy access from the roof.
- Much like M-COM Station A, the stairwells lead to the third floor. Utilize the stairways for means of travel instead of running in the open paths from level to level in the Garage.
- When attacking, the US team can take advantage of the AH-6J Little Bird. Squadmates can be dropped off at the top of the Garage or parachute in while the pilot lays down some cover. Once there are US team members on the roof, they can easily pinch from both directions to get the easy plant on M-COM Station B.
- When defending, the team should be aware of the US team's helicopter. The CN team should force their attackers to always come through the bottom of the Garage as opposed to the roof and bottom of the Garage. Be sure to have a squad defending the roof of the Garage when needed.
- If the map is flooded because the levee was destroyed, the CN team should have a much easier time defending this M-COM station. The US team will have to make moves, but with the right AH-6J Little Bird pilot, distractions can be made to allow US team members to make it inside the Garage.

OBLITERATION

RECOMMENDED SQUAD COMPOSITION:

- The CN team protects their three targets located in and around the Garage.
- The US team has to defend the three targets located in the Park region of the map.
- The bomb is found near the Rooftop Garden. Position a squad on top of one of the taller buildings to allow your team to swiftly grab the bomb.
- For both teams, their center target has many stationary weapons to defend against waves of attackers.
- There are plenty of vehicles that spawn at each team's base. Be sure to return to base and utilize them as they assist in moving around the map.

DEFUSE

RECOMMENDED SQUAD COMPOSITION:

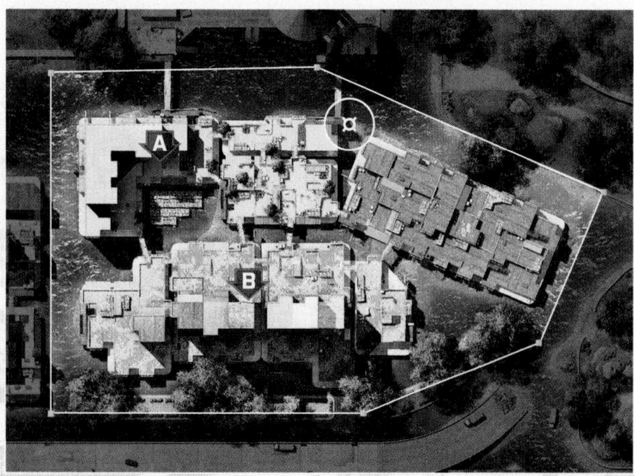

- On this map, players run around the center area between the Park and Garage. The CN team spawns west of both Laptops while the US team spawns near the destroyable levee.
- Laptop A is found in a wooden shack west of the Rooftop Garden. Defenders can camp in these shacks and surprise the attacking team.
- Laptop B is located west of Shanty Town, also found in a wooden shack. Attackers can throw grenades to expose camping defenders.
- The CN team's best strategy is to build a perimeter around the Rooftop Garden. There are two platforms that are raised higher than rest of the roofs and give clear line of sights of both objectives. Have at least one player on each platform with one or two assault class troops near Laptop B to surprise invading attackers.
- When attacking, use the inside of the building to move from building to building and to provide cover. Your safest bet is to reach the rooftops by taking the staircase that leads to the Shanty Town. This area provides an angle to take down the defenders in the high area. A player can hide in the Rooftop Garden building and flank to the top when the rest of the US squads begin engaging.

DOMINATION

RECOMMENDED SQUAD COMPOSITION:

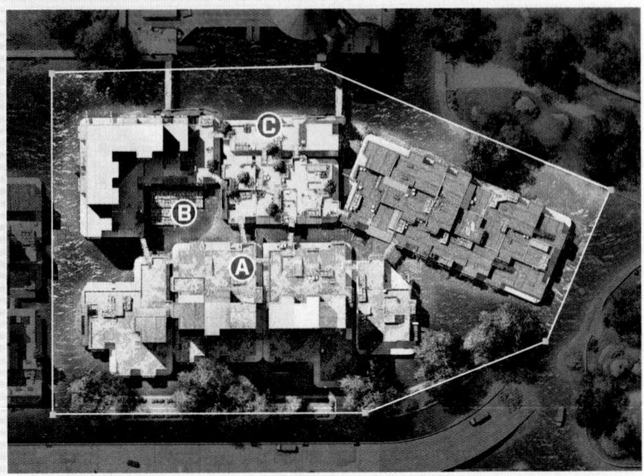

- The three control points are the Shanty Town (A), Marketplace (B), Rooftop Garden (C).
- Southwest of the Rooftop Garden (C) is a USAS-12 battle pickup. With all the shacks and obstacles on the roof, this is the perfect close-quarter weapon.
- The Rooftop Garden (C) is the best objective to control. It overviews the two other control points and provides the most cover due to the height of the building.
- Shanty Town (A) is the best location to combine T-UGS and shotguns. Wait around the corners and catch your opponent by surprise.
- Controlling the Marketplace (B) and the Rooftop Garden (C) is a good strategy. Your squad can set up a good defense perimeter on the rooftops, stopping attackers from capturing the Rooftop Garden (C). The height of the rooftops allows you to easily wipe out an enemy that goes for the Marketplace (B).

SQUAD DEATHMATCH

RECOMMENDED SQUAD COMPOSITION:

- Constant action is waiting for you on the rooftops of this map; aim to control the high ground the entire time.
- With the IFV located on the ground, players will probably avoid using it as most of the action occurs inside the buildings and the rooftops.
- The inside buildings of this map can be just as effective as the rooftops if your team does not have control. Patrol the stairways and pick off enemies sneaking inside.
- The Rooftop Garden offers more protection as there are plenty of wooden shacks to hide in. Have a shotgun ready to drop an approaching enemy quickly.
- Flanking through the stairwells is a very efficient way to regain control of the rooftops. Be sure to use one of the stairwells farthest from the action to avoid surprise attacks.

TEAM DEATHMATCH

RECOMMENDED SQUAD COMPOSITION:

- In Team Deathmatch, the action is centered on top of the many rooftops of this map, making for many firefights from roof to roof.
- Equip shotguns, utilize many of the wooden shacks around the roof, and punish unaware enemies running carelessly around the map.
- An organized team can set up a solid defensive perimeter on top of one of the two tallest buildings. The roof of either building provides a great overview of the map. One building only has one way up while the other has two ladders up. Watch these carefully.
- Study the map carefully so you can efficiently move around. This allows you to develop advanced flanks and perfect getaways when in a pinch.
- Control the high ground is the best strategy—try to remain up top at all times. You are able to spot enemies running down low. Place Claymores around stairwells.

ALPHA SQUAD: IMPRESSIONS

MABOOZA

Golmud Railway reminds me of the massive landscapes in Armored Kill from *Battlefield 3*. This is a map clearly designed for massive tank battles. Transportation is key as you don't want to be stuck on foot, sprinting from one location to the next. Wait for a vehicle to spawn or request a ride from a teammate before hoofing it.

STRONGSIDE

I really like the addition of the moving Train control point in Conquest, which makes this control point one of the most valuable to obtain. This is an awesome new concept in Conquest Large and Small. I'll rush towards the Train at the beginning of the match to secure this flag and escort it back towards our base. I hope to see more mobile control points in the future for Battlefield.

WALSHY

When I first played on this map I immediately noticed how massive it was and the high amount of vehicle presence it had. The vehicle combat on this map is amazing. You'll find me fighting in a tank, jet, or helicopter when I have the chance to get the victory.

FLAMESWORD

When I first played this map, I enjoyed taking advantage of the speedy light vehicles. These fast vehicles allowed me to harass the opposing team as I moved from each objective, either neutralizing or capturing them. I would just do laps around the map, annoying them the entire game.

ELUMNITE

When I first played on this map I had to jump into an attack jet and fly across the vast amount of territory. I love the features on this map with the IEDs, where you can remotely control bombs lying on the map and explode any vehicles that ride near them.

GOLMUD RAILWAY

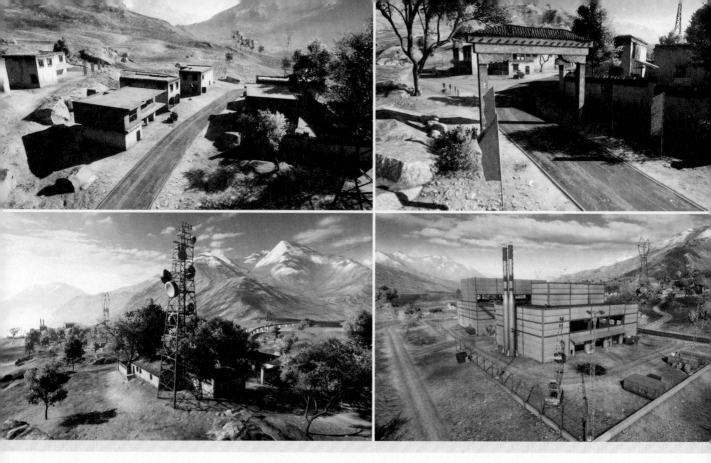

 GOLMUD RAILWAY

LEVOLUTION MOMENTS

WHAT IS IT?

A control point, atop a Train, moves towards the controlling team's base along the railroad tracks. In addition, IEDs are placed in strategic areas throughout the map, creating massive explosions capable of taking out anything within its blast radius.

HOW IS IT TRIGGERED?

The Train moves towards the home base of the team in control of its flag. IED explosions are triggered by shooting them with an explosive weapon or detonating them individually from control consoles placed around the map—follow the wires leading from the IEDs to the corresponding control consoles.

HOW IS GAMEPLAY IMPACTED?

The Train control point moves towards the team controlling its flag, making it easier to control throughout the game when it is placed near your home base. This makes it extremely hard for the opposing team to recapture it. The Train also has mounted weapons to use against enemies. The IEDs have a large blast radius and cause craters in the environment, to be used as cover for both infantry and vehicles. These explosions can take out any ground vehicle as well as damage nearby structures.

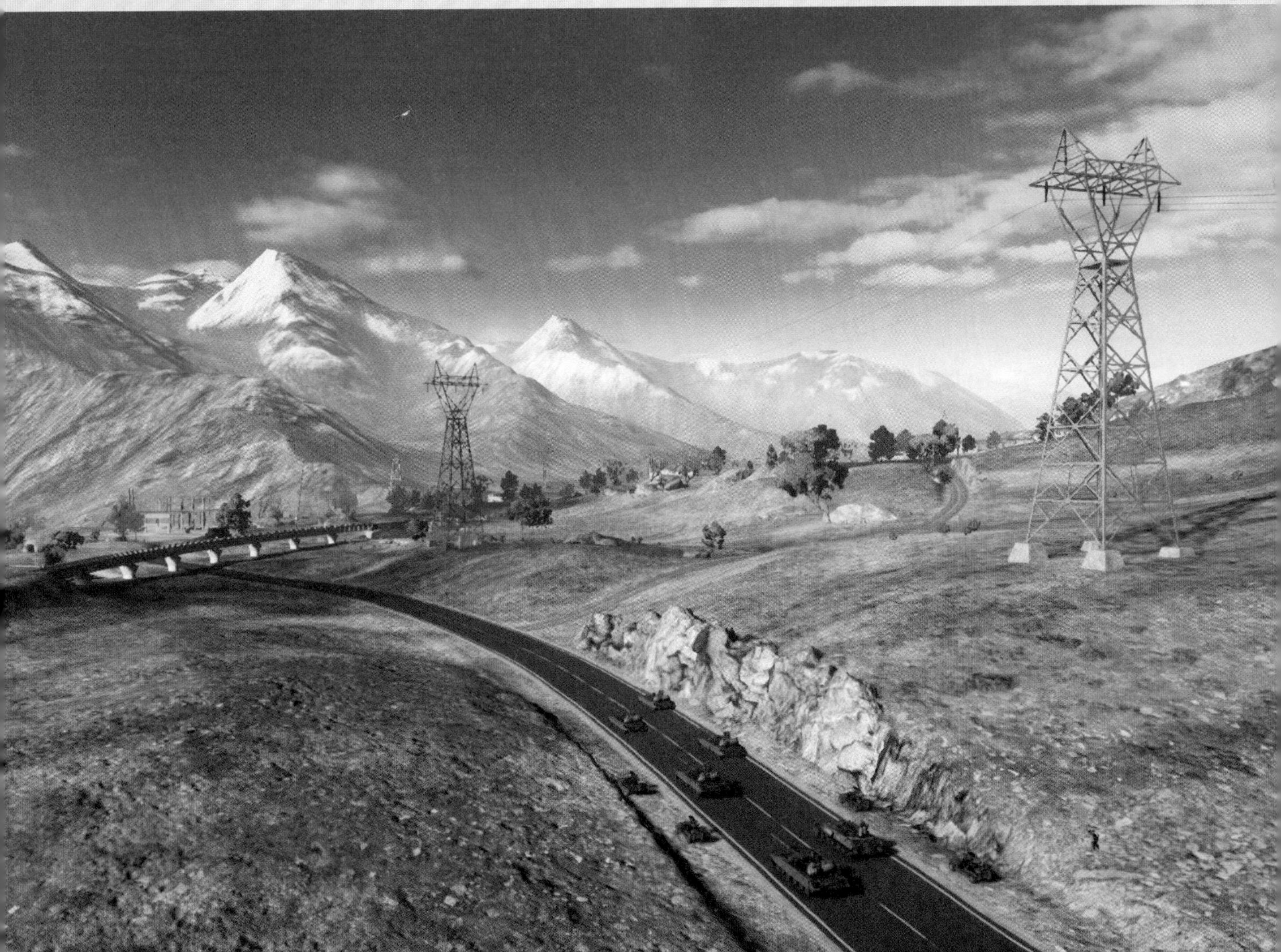

CONQUEST LARGE

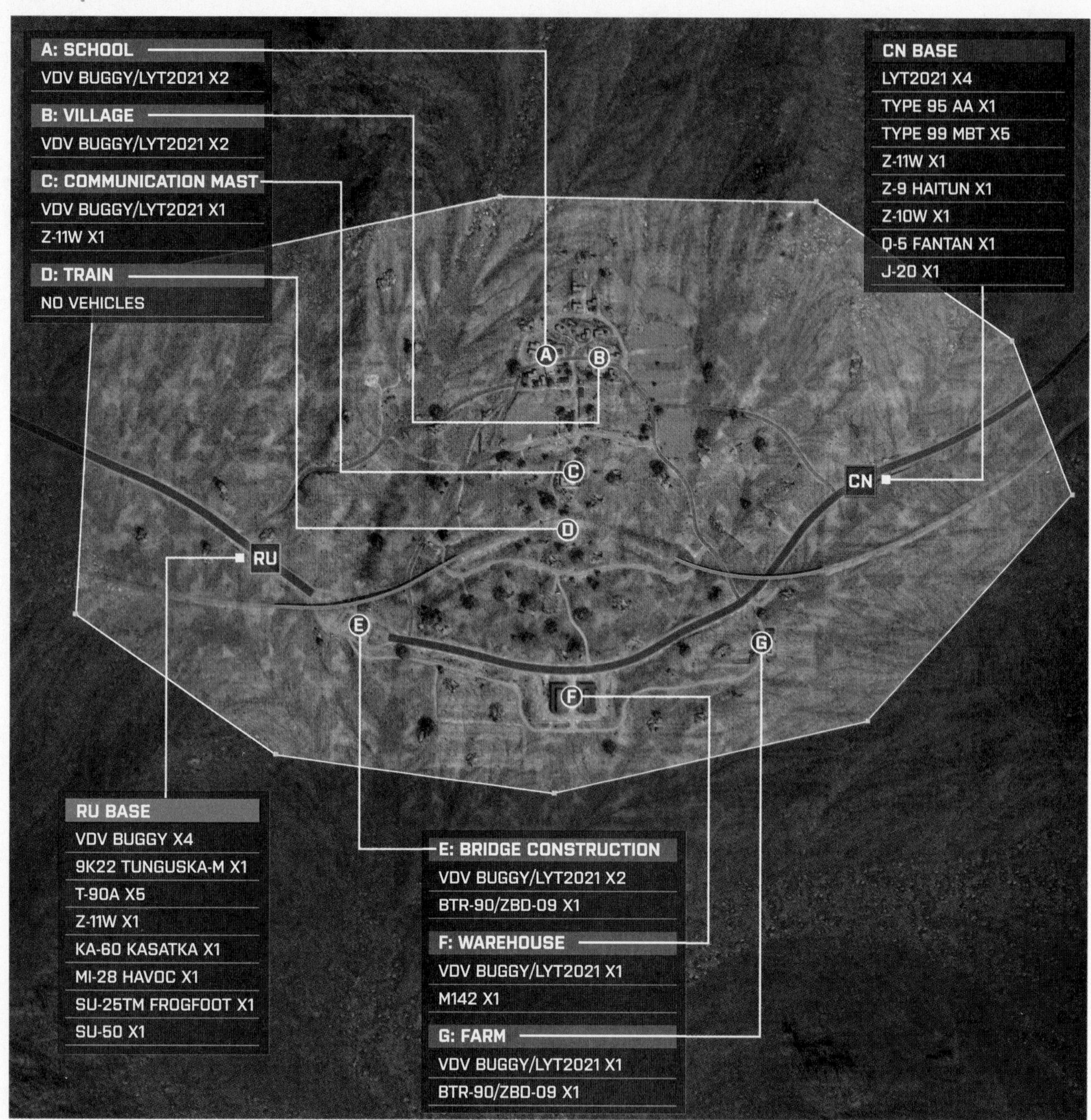

RECOMMENDED SQUAD COMPOSITION:

Prepare yourself to play on the largest map throughout the entire game! In this remote desert land, both the RU and CN team are stocked with an assortment of vehicles back at base—tanks, anti-air, jets, and more! Be prepared for non-stop explosions as squads will need to consist largely of engineers to tackle the constant waves of vehicles. This Conquest Large adds two more control points compared to the standard Conquest mode: Bridge Construction (E) and Farm (G). With the two new control points, there are now seven in all! The RU team will want to capture Bridge Construction (E) while the CN team captures the Farm (G); these two objectives are near each team's respective base. After that, both teams can implement two different strategies. One strategy will be capturing the School (A), Village (B), Communication Mast (C), and Train (D). This strategy works really well because the Train (D) has stationary turrets, which will assist in defending the Bridge Construction (E) if playing as the RU team or the Farm (G) if playing on the CN team as the Train (D) moves near the controlling team's base. Due to the close proximity of the School (A), Village (B), and Communication Mast (C), squads can quickly aid one another. Each team has five tanks back at base, so have three around the School (A), Village (B), and Communication Mast while the other two are near the Train (D) and Bridge Construction (E) to ensure the success of this strategy. The other strategy would be to control the Train (D), Bridge Construction (E), Warehouse (F), and Farm (G). This strategy grants the commander of the team a Gunship for capturing the Warehouse (F) and allows the team's tanks to set a perimeter around the Bridge Construction (E) if playing as the CN team or around the Farm (G) when on the RU team. This forces the opposing team to only approach from their base or the north. This will be a test of your endurance, so prepare yourself.

RU BASE

- The RU base is located on the road farthest west on the map.
- This is a large map that is accommodated with many vehicles, including attack helicopters, transport helicopters, tanks, FAVs, and an IFV.
- This is an engineer-friendly map. Have a few extra on the team to repair friendlies and assist in destroying enemy vehicles.
- A squad will need to split up into two of the four VDV Buggies that deploy off the start. The light vehicle with three passengers will drop one player off at the Construction Site (E) for an easy capture while continuing their way with the other light vehicles towards the Warehouse (F). The Warehouse (F) unlocks a Gunship for your team commander, so send a few tanks towards this control point to solidify the capture.
- The other team will most likely meet you head-on at the Warehouse (F), allowing for some easy captures at the other control points. Take full use of the transport and scout helicopters and drop squadmates around the School (A), Village (B), and Communication Mast (C). Have the attack helicopter escort these helicopters and provide air support as the pilot then heads towards the Warehouse (F) to assist in destroying the CN team's tanks.

BASE ASSETS

NAME	VDV Buggy	T-90A	9K22 Tunguska-M	KA-60 Kasatka	Z-11W	Mi-28 Havoc	SU-25TM Frogfoot	SU-50
QUANTITY	4	5	1	1	1	1	1	1

CN BASE

- Located on the far eastern side of the map, this base is littered with almost every choice of vehicle available to the CN army.
- Even though this map is massive, do not neglect your slower tanks as these are a force to be reckoned with once you arrive at the northern control points of School (A) and Village (B).
- Send your fastest vehicles to the Train (D) so that you can send this movable objective on the tracks back towards your base, which will be easier to defend. Early control of this objective usually means you keep it the rest of the game.
- Be sure to have squads equipped with many engineers and recon classes early on for this map. Until you start nearing the north and south sides of the map, the wide open areas and vehicles will be the main forms of combat that you will want to focus on.
- Always spot every vehicle and enemy you can. With this map being so large, you never know what angle another one of your teammates might have. This is a great way to rack up points and help out your helicopters and jets in the air.

BASE ASSETS

NAME	LYT2021	Type 99 MBT	Type 95 AA	Z-9 Haitun	Z-11W	Z-10W	Q-5 Fantan	J-20
QUANTITY	4	5	1	1	1	1	1	1

A: SCHOOL

- This objective is located on the north side of the map, west of the Village (B).
- If on foot, use the many buildings for cover to capture this control point. Beware, these buildings can all be destroyed by explosives, so keep on the move and never stay inside one building.
- The buildings surrounding this control point can all be destroyed fairly easily.
- Light vehicles spawn at this control point. Use these to quickly rush over towards nearby control points.
- The Village (B) is extremely close to the School (A). Use tanks to take charge of these two control points, shifting between the two on the path connecting the two objectives.
- If the surrounding buildings are taken down, the tanks will rule this area as there is minimal cover for ground infantry.

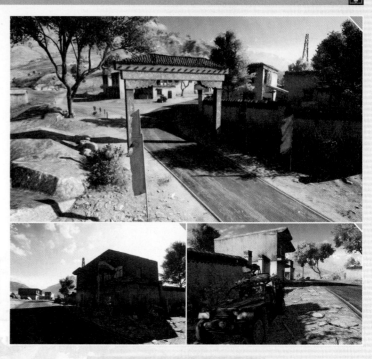

PRO TIP: WALSHY

HIDE A RADIO BEACON IN ONE OF THE MANY HOUSES TO THE NORTH OF THE SCHOOL (A) AND THE VILLAGE (B). IF YOU EVER LOSE THESE CONTROL POINTS, INSTEAD OF DRIVING OR RUNNING ACROSS THE OPEN FIELDS, YOU CAN USE THIS RADIO BEACON FOR A PERFECT FLANK THAT THE ENEMY WILL NEVER EXPECT.

CONTROL POINT ASSETS

RU CONTROL	CN CONTROL
VDV Buggy (2)	LYT2021 (2)

B: VILLAGE

- The Village (B) is east of the School (A) and is enclosed by destructible buildings.
- Capturing this flag will add light vehicles for the controlling team. These vehicles will assist in traveling to other control points at a quicker rate.
- The Village (B) is stationed with a handful of stationary turrets and launchers. These will assist when defending against vehicles.
- The houses in the Village (B) allow players to contest and capture this objective. Use this to your advantage and move from house to house to confuse your opponent.
- Recon players will play a huge role when capturing this control point. Throw Motion Sensors to pick up any defenders hiding in the area.

CONTROL POINT ASSETS

RU CONTROL	CN CONTROL
VDV Buggy (2)	LYT2021 (2)

C: COMMUNICATION MAST

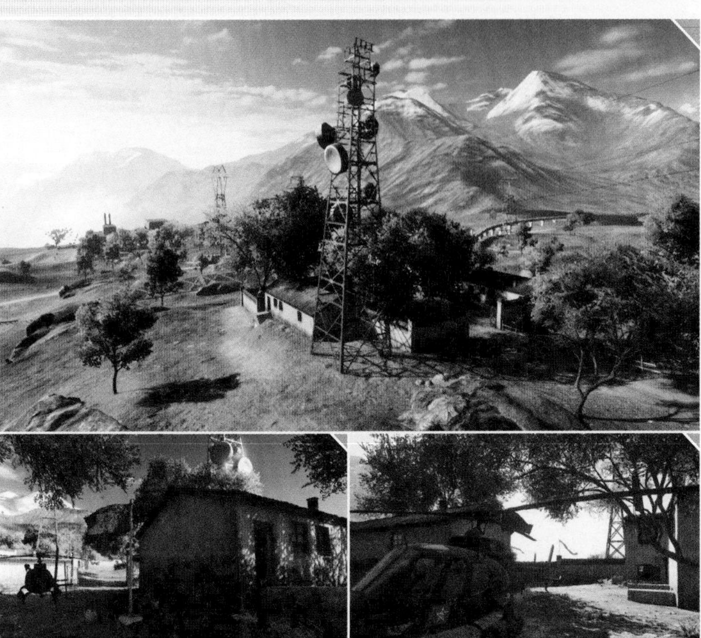

- This control point is located in the center of the map, where most of the main battle will take place.
- A light vehicle and a transport helicopter are the two vehicles that will spawn for your team when this point is first controlled. These two vehicles are super helpful to travel to the next control points.
- This flag will be the hardest control point to hold mainly because of its location on this map. Both teams will look to hold this flag as it is very close to the Village (B) and the School (A).
- While defending this control point, your team will have many options on how to go about keeping the other team from capturing it. There are small buildings everywhere, which will be very good for recon and engineer class. They can hide inside any of the buildings and, with clear vision in every direction, they can spot incoming enemies and act accordingly.
- When attacking this control point, your team is going to want to synchronize an attack with a mix of tanks and transport helicopters to overwhelm the area and quickly capture the flag.

CONTROL POINT ASSETS

RU CONTROL	CN CONTROL
VDV Buggy (1)	LYT2021 (1)
Z-11W (1)	Z-11W (1)

D: TRAIN

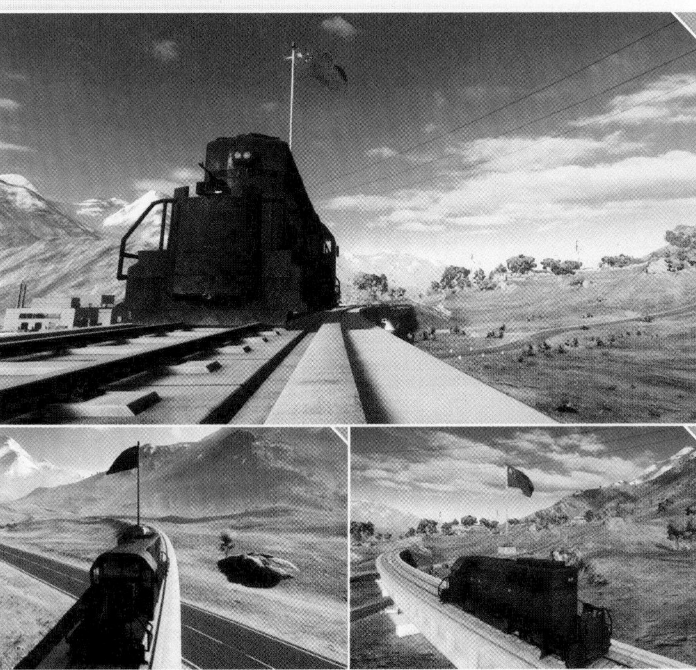

- This control point is located just south of the Communication Mast (C) towards the middle of the map, but this can vary based on the fact that it moves while players are aboard it.
- The Train (D) itself is a vehicle with two machine gun turrets in the front and back that can be used to defend it.
- The unique feature of this control point for this game type is that the Train (D) will move towards either team's base depending on which team gains control of it first. This will most likely be one of the first points that teams go for based on that sole fact, and having it move near your deployment base is an added advantage.
- Attacking the control point will be very risky. There is relatively no cover and it is very close to the enemy base, so it is imperative that your team makes getting this flag a priority. Tons of units will need to hold off whatever forces the defending team throws at you.
- When defending, have a few vehicles posted around the area close by so your team will be able to watch this point whenever there is a threat of attack. Recon classes can very easily take out any enemies trying to take this control point.

PRO TIP: STRONGSIDE

Grab a helicopter or jet to immediately rush and secure the Train (D) at the start of the game. Once this control point is captured, the Train (D) will slowly move towards your team's base. Cover the Train (D) from enemies. Once your team has this control point near to your deployment base, the enemies will have a hard time taking control of it.

E: BRIDGE CONSTRUCTION

- The Bridge Construction (E) is just southeast of the RU base. The area holds an unfinished trail rail attachment.
- Whichever team captures this objective will add an IFV and a light vehicle to their arsenal of vehicles.
- This control point is near the RU base, making it an easy capture for them. The CN team will want to approach this later in the game when the RU team lets down their defense.
- Teams will look to utilize their light vehicles and harass the team in control of this objective. The dirt roads along the side will allow you to neutralize and capture this control point. When the opposing team retreats to defend the flag, take advantage of the light vehicle's speed and move towards another objective.
- A squad with engineers can set up a defense perimeter with mines to destroy enemy vehicles when near.

CONTROL POINT ASSETS

RU CONTROL	CN CONTROL
BTR-90 (1)	ZBD-09 (1)

F: WAREHOUSE

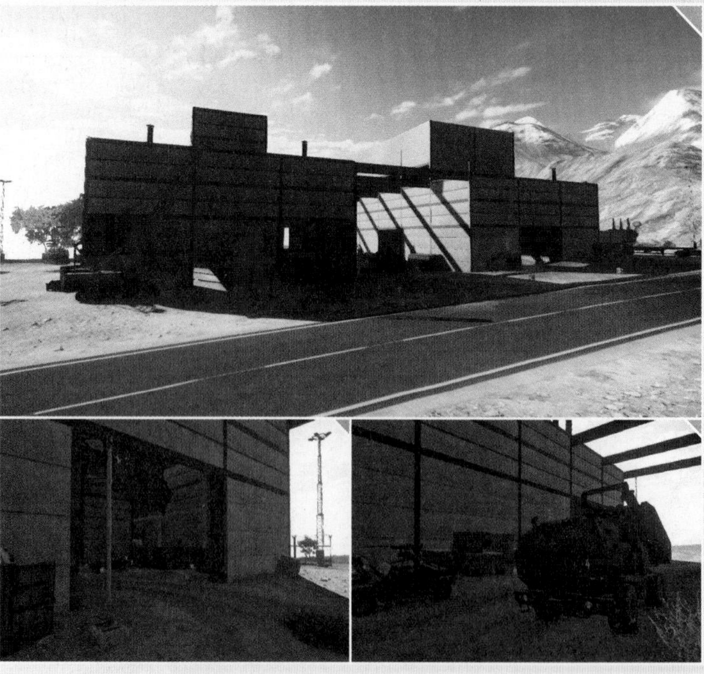

- This control point is located on the far south end of the map. This objective is placed equal distance from both the RU base and CN base.
- This objective is surrounded by two buildings. Use the ladders on the south side of these buildings to reach the rooftops. These rooftops will provide a great distant overview to spot incoming enemy vehicles. The engineer class will be most useful to stop vehicles in their tracks before reaching this control point.
- An M142 spawns at this objective. Use the gunner seat to provide cover fire for teammates farther across the map.
- Controlling this flag will be extremely important since your commander acquires the Gunship. With this massive map and the immense amount of vehicle presence on this map, you'll want this Gunship to unload on enemy vehicles and ground infantry.
- Use your team's helicopters to quickly gain control of the control point from the rooftops of the buildings.

PRO TIP: FLAMESWORD

I enjoy taking advantage of the light vehicles on this map. Many players like to rush the Warehouse (F) off the start to gain access to the Gunship for their commander and team. I enjoy using the speed of the light vehicles to capture the undefended control points and patrol the map as I harass enemies.

CONTROL POINT ASSETS

RU CONTROL	CN CONTROL
VDV Buggy (1)	LYT2021 (1)
M142 (1)	M142 (1)

G: FARM

- This control point is located on the southeast side of the map secluded by wide open plains and fields in every direction. The flag itself is positioned in the center of a three farmhouse complex that has only two narrow entrances for vehicles.
- Upon capture, an IFV spawns here. Take this vehicle to push over and capture the Warehouse (F), which will allow your commander to deploy the Gunship for your team.
- When defending this control point, have a squad comprised of recon and engineer classes. You need your recon members to pick off enemy infantry running in the open fields and your engineer players to effectively be able to deal with incoming vehicles.
- When attacking this objective with any vehicle, do not push it inside the complex. You will be surrounded and extremely vulnerable to enemy engineers and C4.
- There are two interactive consoles nearby that explode two sets of IEDs. When you are the RU team, use the detonation kit 70 meters away, because it will explode any CN vehicles on the dirt road to the north of the Farm (G). When you are the CN team, use the detonation kit further west, which will dispose of any unsuspecting RU vehicles on the paved road to the west.

CONTROL POINT ASSETS

RU CONTROL	CN CONTROL
VDV Buggy (1)	LYT2021 (1)
BTR-90 (1)	ZBD-09 (1)

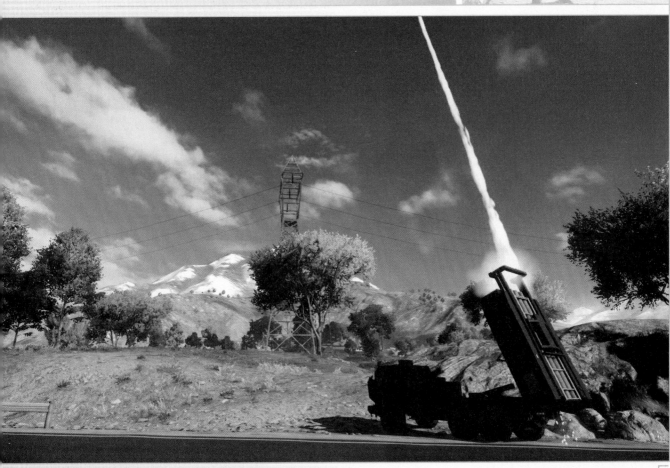

CONQUEST SMALL

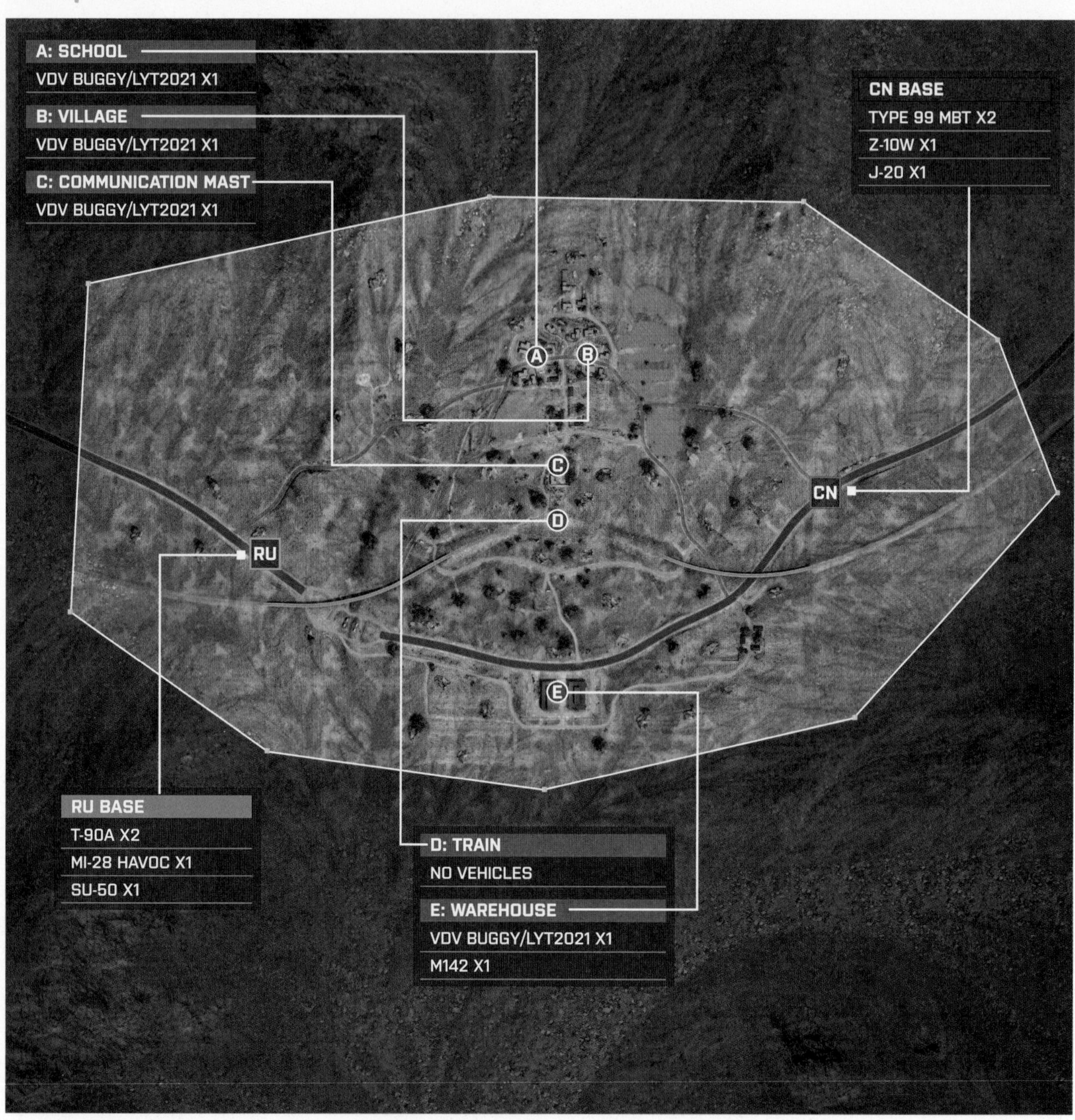

RECOMMENDED SQUAD COMPOSITION:

In this remote desert area, players will be faced with five control points. The five control points scattered around the map are the School (A), Village (B), Communication Mast (C), Train (D), and Warehouse (E). This standard mode of Conquest will test your endurance as each team will need three control points in order to bleed the opposing team's tickets. The way these control points are laid out allows for two different strategies for both teams. One strategy will be to capture the School (A), Village (B), and Communication Mast (C), as they are all in close proximity of each other. The benefit of this strategy is that players can respond quickly to teammates when needed and can establish a defense perimeter with the tank placed in the center of the three control points. These three control points also provide light vehicles for the controlling team, giving much more maneuverability. The controlling team can use the speed of these light vehicles to swiftly move around the map while picking off enemies caught on foot. The second strategy would be for teams to capture the Communication Mast (C), Train (D), and Warehouse (E). The pros of this strategy are that the Train (D) will move near the controlling team's base, making it hard for the opponent to recapture, and the Warehouse (E) allows the commander of the controlling team to call in a Gunship. This Gunship is very powerful and will aid when defending the Communication Mast (C). Both strategies offer their pros and cons, but will surely lead your team to victory.

RU BASE

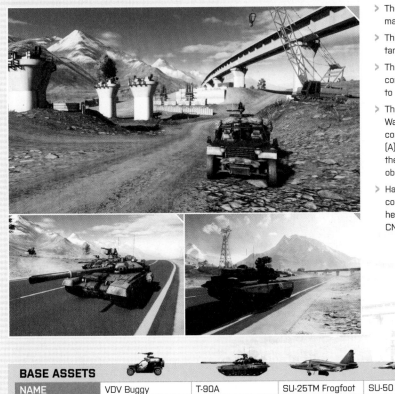

- The RU base is located on the road farthest west on the map.
- This is a large map with a solid mix of attack helicopters, tanks, and light vehicles.
- The Warehouse (E) unlocks a Gunship for your team commander, so send a few tanks towards this control point to solidify the capture.
- The other team will most likely meet you head-on at the Warehouse (E), allowing for some easy captures at the other control points. Send your light vehicle towards the School (A) or Village (B). If the opposing team is only focusing on the Warehouse (E), your team will easily capture these objectives.
- Have the attack helicopter provide air support over the three control points in the center. Once captured, the pilot can head towards the Warehouse (F) to assist in destroying the CN team's tanks.

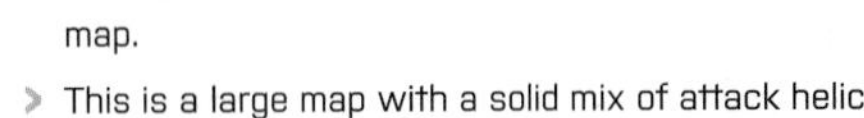

BASE ASSETS

NAME	VDV Buggy	T-90A	SU-25TM Frogfoot	SU-50
QUANTITY	2	2	1	1

CN BASE

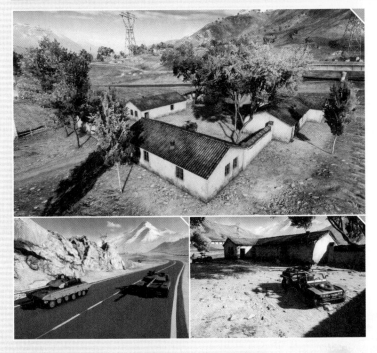

- Located on the far eastern side of the map, you can either spawn in one of the tanks or an aircraft, or you can forward spawn at the Farm on the southeast side of the map.
- Even though this map is massive, do not neglect your slower tanks as these are a force to be reckoned with once you arrive at the northern flags, School (A) and Village (B).
- Send your light vehicles to the Train (D) so that you can send this movable objective on the tracks back towards your base where it is easier to defend. Early control of this objective usually keeps it under your control the rest of the game.
- Be sure to have squads with engineers and recon early on for this map. Until you start nearing the north and south sides of the map, the wide open areas and vehicles will be the main forms of combat that you will want to focus on.
- Always spot every vehicle and enemy you can. With this map being so large, you never know what angle another one of your teammates might have. This is a great way to rack up points and help out your helicopters and jets in the air.
- Hide a Radio Beacon in one of the many houses to the north of the School (A) and Village (B). If you ever lose control of these objectives, instead of driving or running across the open areas, you can use this Radio Beacon for a perfect flank spawn that the enemy will never expect.

BASE ASSETS

NAME	LYT2021	Type 99 MBT	Q-5 Fantan	J-20
QUANTITY	2	2	1	1

A: SCHOOL

- This objective is located on the north side of the map, west of the Village (B).
- If on foot, use the many buildings for cover to capture this point. Beware, these building can all be destroyed by explosives, so keep on the move and never stay inside one building.
- The buildings surrounding this control point can all be destroyed fairly easily.
- Light vehicles spawn at this control point. Use these to quickly rush over towards nearby control points.
- The Village (B) is extremely close to the School (A). Use tanks to take charge of these two control points, shifting between the two on the path connecting the two objectives.
- If the surrounding buildings are taken down, the tanks will rule this area as there is minimal cover for ground infantry.

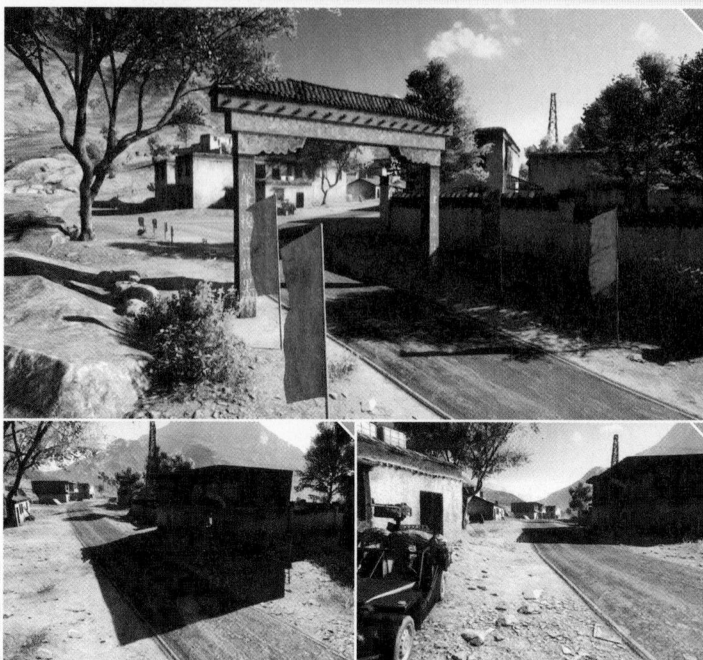

CONTROL POINT ASSETS

RU CONTROL	CN CONTROL
VDV Buggy (1)	LYT2021 (1)

B: VILLAGE

- The Village (B) is east of the School (A) and is enclosed by destructible buildings.
- Capturing this flag will add light vehicles for the controlling team. These light vehicles will assist in traveling to other control points at a quicker rate.
- The Village (B) is stationed with a handful of stationary turrets and launchers. These will assist when defending against vehicles.
- The houses in the Village (B) allow players to contest and capture this objective. Use this to your advantage and move from house to house to confuse your opponent.
- Recon players will play a huge role when capturing this control point. Throw Motion Sensors to pick up any defenders hiding in the area.

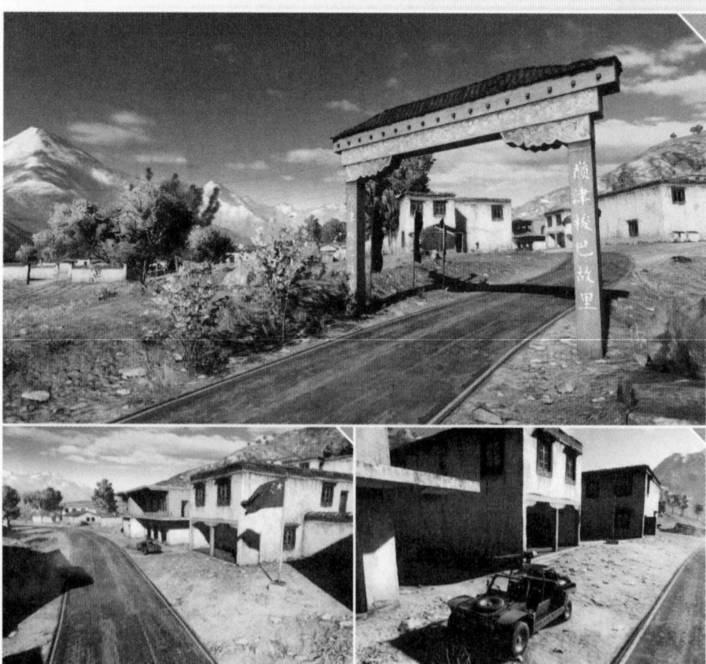

PRO TIP: ELUMNITE

Activating IEDs can be a great way to stop a pursuing tank and completely destroy the area around the explosion, even taking down some buildings in the blast radius. Timing is everything. Make sure to use these wisely, and try not to make a mess.

CONTROL POINT ASSETS

RU CONTROL	CN CONTROL
VDV Buggy (1)	LYT2021 (1)

C: COMMUNICATION MAST

- This control point is located in the center of the map, where most of the main battle will take place.
- A light vehicle spawns here when the control point is captured by either team. These vehicles are super helpful to travel to the surrounding control points.
- This flag will be the hardest control point to hold mainly because of its location on this map. Both teams will look to hold this point as it is very close to the Village (B) and the School (A).
- While defending this control point, your team will have many options on how to keep the other team from capturing it. There are small buildings everywhere that are very good for recon and engineer class. They can hide inside any of the buildings and, with clear vision in every direction, they can spot incoming enemies and act accordingly.
- When attacking this control point, your team is going to want to synchronize an attack with a mix of infantry and tanks to overwhelm the area and quickly capture the flag.

CONTROL POINT ASSETS

RU CONTROL	CN CONTROL
VDV Buggy (1)	LYT2021 (1)

D: TRAIN

- This control point is located just south of Communication Mast (C) towards the middle of the map, but this can vary based on the fact that it moves while players are aboard it.
- The Train (D) itself is a vehicle with two machine gun turrets in the front and back that can be used to defend it.
- The unique feature of this control point for this game type is that the Train (D) will move towards either team's base depending on which team gains control of it first. This will most likely be one of the first points that teams go for based on that sole fact, and having it move near your deployment base is an added advantage.
- Attacking the control point will be very risky. There is relatively no cover and you will be very close to the enemy base, so it is imperative that your team makes getting this control point a priority. Tons of units will need to hold off whatever forces the defending team throws at you.
- When defending, have a few vehicles posted around the area close by so your team is able to watch this point whenever there is a threat of attack. Recon classes can very easily take out any enemies trying to take this control point.

E: WAREHOUSE

- This control point is located on the far south end of the map. This objective is placed equal distance from both the RU base and CN base.
- This objective is surrounded by two buildings. Use the ladders on the south side of these buildings to reach the rooftops. These rooftops will provide a great distant overview for incoming enemy vehicles. The engineer class is most useful to stop vehicles in their tracks before they reach this control point.
- A light vehicle and M142 spawns here for each team. Use the M142 to hammer distant control points, supporting your team from long range.
- Controlling this flag is extremely important since your commander will acquire the Gunship. With this massive map and the immense amount of vehicle presence on this map, you'll want this Gunship to unload on enemy vehicles and ground infantry.
- Maintain possession of the control point by posting recon troops on the rooftops. From here they'll have a clear view of the rest of the map.

CONTROL POINT ASSETS

RU CONTROL	CN CONTROL
VDV Buggy (1)	LYT2021 (1)
M142 (1)	M142 (1)

RUSH

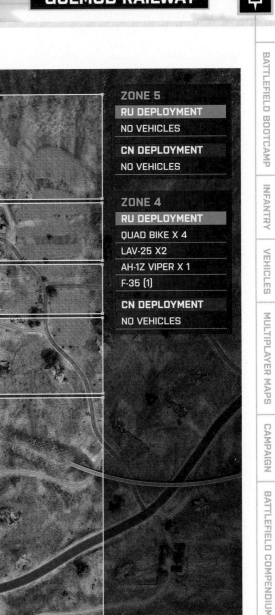

In this uphill battle, the RU team must advance past the train tracks through five different zones. Both the RU and CN team are close to equal footing when it comes to vehicles. As the RU team advances the vehicle count decreases until both teams have none to use in the last zone. The RU deployment zone is located in the Warehouse at the start of the game, and they must make their way to the train tracks to arm the objectives in the first zone. As the RU team succeeds in their advance, they will pass the Communication Mast, School, and Village, and find themselves in the last zone north of the Village. Engineers will be needed for the RU team to stay at an advantage with their vehicle count by constantly repairing the damaged tanks. The CN team has stationary weapons to aid in defending the five different zones with a tank or two as well. Defenders should take advantage of the M15 AT mines and plant them around the area to catch the attacking vehicles by surprise. The last zone provides neither team vehicles. This puts the defending team at an advantage. If you are playing as the CN team and are pushed back to this zone, take advantage of the building's roofs and send recon players to the top to snipe the attackers approaching from the south.

ZONE 1: TRAIN

CN DEPLOYMENT
TYPE 99 MBT X2

CN

A

B

RU DEPLOYMENT
VDV BUGGY X3
T-90A X3
Z-11W X1

RU

RU DEPLOYMENT

RECOMMENDED SQUAD COMPOSITION: 

- This deployment area is located directly south of the M-COM stations. The RU deployment area has a hilly plain with scattered rock structures that the enemies will surely be using as cover to ambush you.
- The dirt road that leads north to the M-COM stations is the most dangerous path for your T-90As. Push your tanks in the fields to the east and west of this dirt road to avoid being surrounded and destroyed.
- You will need a well-balanced squad with a member of every single class for this initial push. Be prepared to encounter close-range fights, tanks, and enemies sniping in the distance.
- Clear out both sides of the train tracks before attempting to arm the M-COM stations. Enemies posted on the east and west sides of the tracks have a clear view of the objectives, so be sure not to walk into a crossfire.
- One hundred meters west of M-COM Station A is a drainage pipe on the south side of the train tracks that is ideal for hiding a Radio Beacon. This will allow your squad to spawn close to the action in a flanking position.

DEPLOYMENT AREA ASSETS

NAME	VDV Buggy	T-90A	Z-11W
QUANTITY	3	3	1

CN DEPLOYMENT

RECOMMENDED SQUAD COMPOSITION: 

- This deployment area is north of both M-COM stations and spawns with two tanks.
- Take the tanks either southwest or southeast toward the objectives to have a better view of what you need to defend.
- The enemy spawns with three T-90As, one scout helicopter, and three light vehicles. Your team will be outnumbered by vehicles. Have your squad play as engineers to even the playing field.
- The M-COM stations are placed behind the train. You'll need to set up your defense to the south in front of the M-COM stations to stop the attackers from getting near the objectives.
- Place recon class players sniping from near the deployment to watch the south hill leading over to the objectives. Enemy infantry will be traveling here towards the objectives.

DEPLOYMENT AREA ASSETS

NAME	Type 99 MBT
QUANTITY	2

M-COM STATION A

- M-COM Station A is located on the southern part of the map next to the Train.
- Two Type 99 MBTs spawn for the CN team at deployment, which can be used to patrol the area around M-COM Station A.
- When attacking, it's best to clear the area out as much as possible before going in for the arm. Coming in to this battle, your team should have a good mix of tanks and helicopters push in at the same time.
- Attackers should look for a safe area to place a Radio Beacon to keep teammates spawning close to the battle to keep up the pressure.
- When defending, have a recon and a support class make their way to a location with a great angle of M-COM Station A, so they can easily stop any enemies attempting to arm.

M-COM STATION B

- M-COM Station B is attached to a train holding a nuclear missile casing, south of the CN deployment area and north of the RU deployment area.
- The train is in the middle of the ditch, requiring players to hike up before rushing down.
- When attacking, the RU team must be cautious of the stationary turrets south of the CN deployment that lay heavy fire down the hill.
- The RU team will want to send their tanks north of the objective, providing cover for the arm and stopping the defenders from succeeding in disarming the objective.
- Defenders should mount the multiple stationary turrets. This will distract the RU team, allowing the CN tanks to flank the attackers from the east and west, pinching them in the ditch and leading to some easy points.

ZONE 2: COMMUNICATION MAST

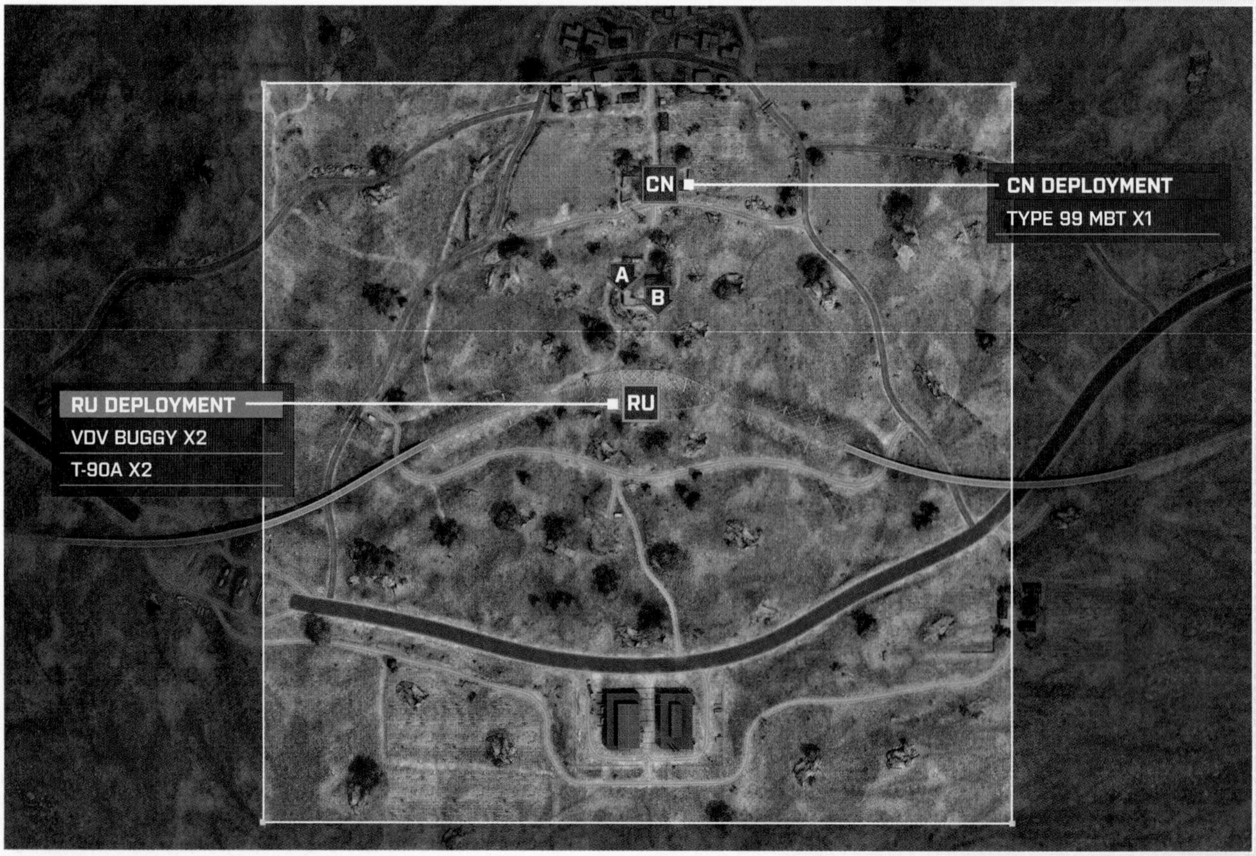

CN

A

B

RU

CN DEPLOYMENT

TYPE 99 MBT X1

RU DEPLOYMENT

VDV BUGGY X2

T-90A X2

RU DEPLOYMENT

RECOMMENDED SQUAD COMPOSITION:

- The RU deployment area is now located just south of the recently destroyed M-COM stations. However, your vehicles still spawn in the back of your Zone 1 deployment area.
- The two M-COM stations are located in the Communication Mast where you will have non-stop close-range combat. Equip your favorite shotgun or M26 assault gadget to take control of this area.
- Push your tanks up the east side of the hill. This way you can avoid the HJ-8 Launcher on the west edge and will be able to safely flank around to the north entrance of the Communication Mast without being ambushed.
- The large boulders 40 meters south of the M-COM stations is a safe location to regroup with your entire team and make your organized push into the Communication Mast.
- With only one enemy tank to worry about, you do not need many engineers for this zone, since it will mostly consist of infantry vs. infantry combat.

DEPLOYMENT AREA ASSETS

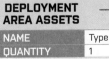

NAME	VDV Buggy	T-90A
QUANTITY	2	2

CN DEPLOYMENT

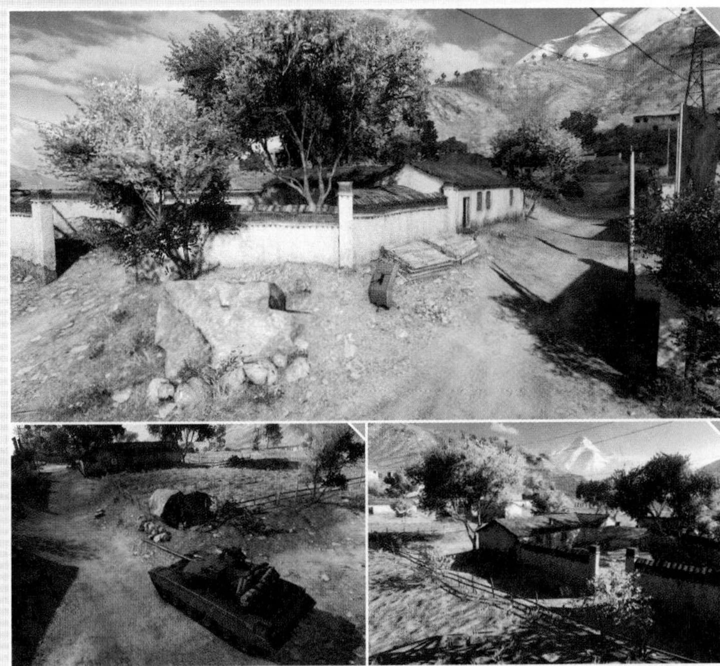

RECOMMENDED SQUAD COMPOSITION: 

- The deployment area is now moved further north and the M-COM stations are now placed where the CN team deployed for Zone 1.
- There are many buildings surrounding the objectives. Use the rooftop of the building south of M-COM Station A for a vantage point to take out infantry coming from the south.
- The deployment area only spawns with one tank, so you'll be outnumbered with vehicles once again. Have a few players play as the engineer class to assist the CN team's tank.
- Place a T-UGS inside the buildings nearest the objectives to alert you and your squad when the enemy is near the objective and attempting to arm.

DEPLOYMENT AREA ASSETS

NAME	Type 99 MBT
QUANTITY	1

M-COM STATION A

- M-COM Station A is located to the north of the train tracks and up a hill. There are a few buildings covering the area that the defenders can take refuge inside to protect the station.
- One Type 99 MBT is available for the CN team. This tank should circle the small town to take out any infiltrators that are roaming around the area.
- There are a few stationary launchers and .50Cal turrets located up the hill before M-COM Station A. These need to be used to take out any vehicles making their way towards this station.
- When attacking, the first main focus should be to regroup and take out the launchers and .50Cal turrets. This will make climbing up the hill much easier when the defending team isn't raining down so much fire.
- Defenders are posted everywhere inside the buildings near M-COM Station A, so have the tanks fire at the walls of these buildings. All of the buildings are very weak to begin with, so they can be destroyed, thus exposing any enemy snipers.

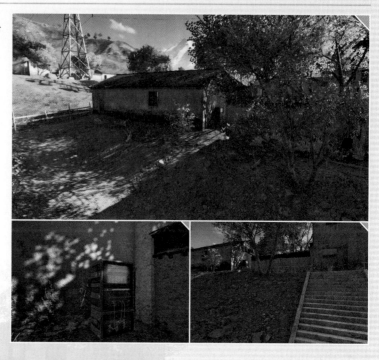

M-COM STATION B

- The objective sits at the bottom of the stairs of a building within the Communication Mast area.
- The M-COM station is enclosed by a cement wall. When defending, stay clear of the cement wall since attackers can easily destroy the wall and inflict damage on you if you are near the wall.
- The building to the west of the objective has a staircase that leads to the roof. Defending snipers can take advantage of this spot and pick off attacking infantry players.
- When attacking, try to clear out the building to the west of the M-COM station. On the second floor of this building is a window that lets you watch the objective. This is a great spot to stop defenders from disarming the objective.
- The RU team has a couple of tanks back at their deployment area. Move these near the M-COM station and provide constant fire to the buildings, forcing the defenders to relocate.

ZONE 3: HILLSIDE

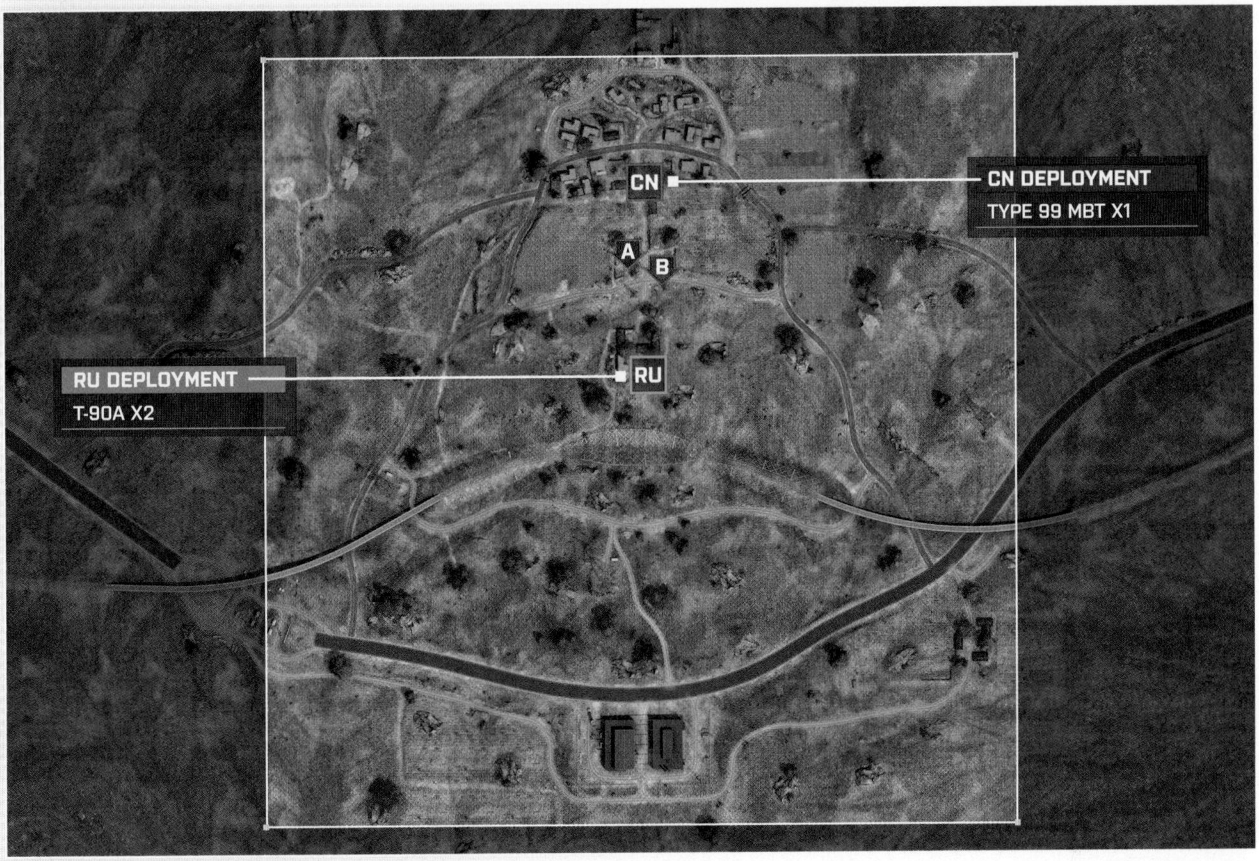

CN

CN DEPLOYMENT

TYPE 99 MBT X1

A

B

RU DEPLOYMENT

T-90A X2

RU

RU DEPLOYMENT

RECOMMENDED SQUAD COMPOSITION: 

- Once again, the RU deployment area is located downhill to the south of the new M-COM stations.
- Now the only vehicles you have at your disposal are two tanks placed at the southwest and southeast corners of the map. They are quite a distance away but, as always, a great asset once you bring them to the front lines.
- Try to group up your T-90As so they can back each other up and double-team the enemy tank. Don't get caught in a one-on-one duel when another friendly tank is available to join the fight.
- The buildings that house the M-COM stations can easily be destroyed. If you have your tank near, take down the walls so you can cover your squad while they arm the charge.
- Since the buildings near the M-COM stations crumble so fast, have your best mid-range support or assault class ready in this area. You don't want to be caught out in the open with a shotgun when there is no cover for you to get next to your enemy.

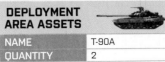

DEPLOYMENT AREA ASSETS 

NAME	T-90A
QUANTITY	2

CN DEPLOYMENT

RECOMMENDED SQUAD COMPOSITION:

- The location of the deployment area is pushed north and the M-COM stations are located to the south. This deployment area only spawns one tank.
- The enemy team has two tanks, so again be sure to have multiple engineers in your squad to assist the CN team's tank.
- Send players out to the east and west to flank around the incoming enemies. Also send players south through the center of the map. This will trap the enemies in the center of your team, taking out many tickets.
- Lay mines on the roads east and west because enemy tanks are sure to pass through the roads.

DEPLOYMENT AREA ASSETS

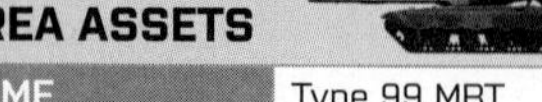

NAME	Type 99 MBT
QUANTITY	1

M-COM STATION A

- M-COM Station A is located right outside of a small one-level building that looks like it could crumble at any time and has little to no cover.
- Again with few vehicles, the CN team will have to manage with the tank that they do have in the most efficient way. Have an engineer board with a teammate so they can make necessary repairs on the tank.
- When attacking, there are two T-90As your team can use in the fight now. Have the tanks distract the defender's main force and send a different squad to the far west of M-COM Station A. Once this is done, have a few support and assault classes make their way towards the station. This should make gaining some control a bit easier with the defenders.
- Defenders should take advantage of the IEDs in the cornfield to the west of the M-COM station. With perfect timing you can take out enemies sneaking around for a flank and blow them up.
- When defending, your squad will need to equip a few engineers and a support class to make up for the lack of vehicle presence on your team.

M-COM STATION B

- M-COM Station B in Zone 3 is located north of the Communication Mast.
- The area has little cover with one building surrounded by a cement fence.
- The attacking team will send a tank along the road to the east. Have defending engineers rig the road with mines to easily stop the tank in its tracks. Be sure to fire rockets at the attacking tank, distracting it from noticing the mines.
- If the cement walls are destroyed, the defending team can plant C4 around the objective and observe it from a distance. Once they see attackers are close, detonate the C4 and then move in to wipe out the remaining players.
- The RU team can get the full use of the T-90A and fire rounds from a distance, destroying all buildings and walls from afar. This will allow attacking infantry players to easily move in and go for an arm.

ZONE 4: SCHOOL/VILLAGE

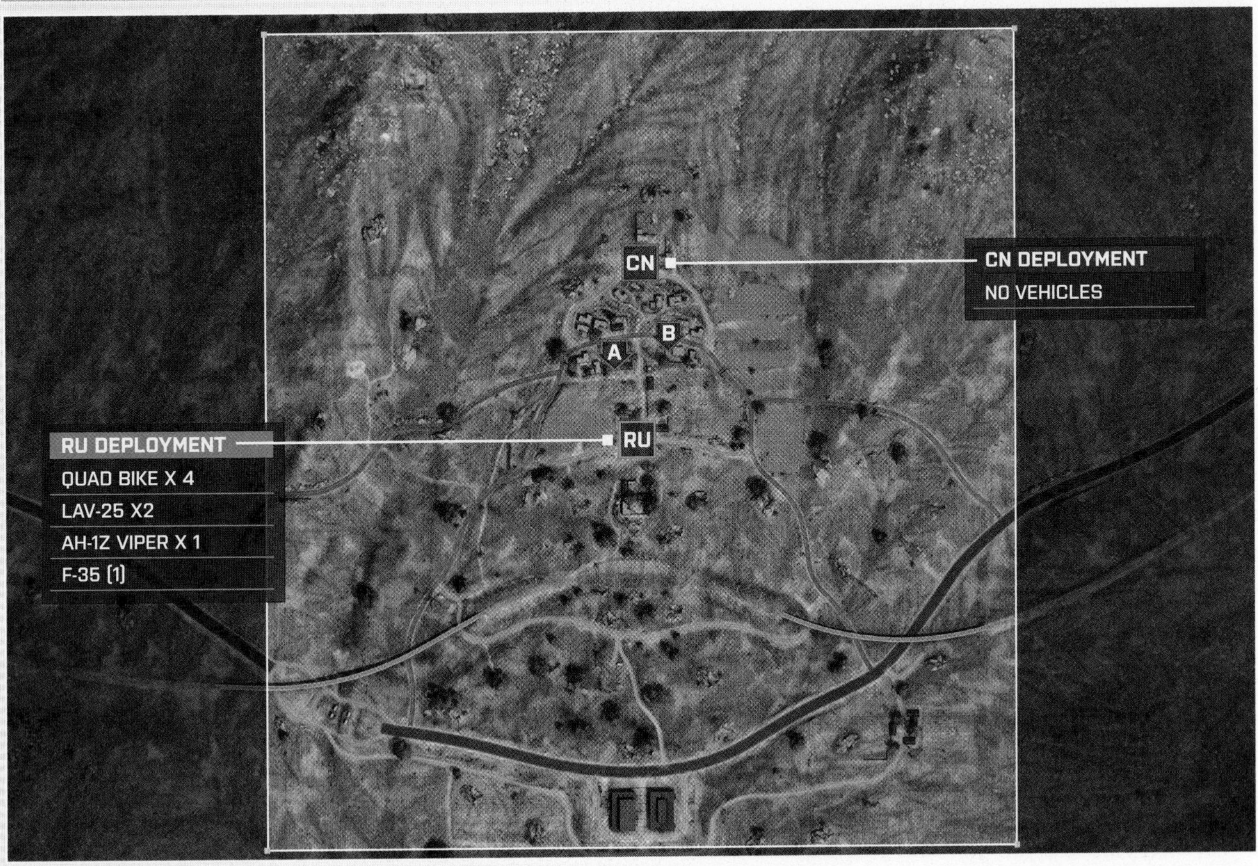

CN DEPLOYMENT
NO VEHICLES

CN
A
B
RU

RU DEPLOYMENT
QUAD BIKE X 4
LAV-25 X2
AH-1Z VIPER X 1
F-35 (1)

RU DEPLOYMENT

RECOMMENDED SQUAD COMPOSITION:

- After successfully arming both objectives in the last zone, the RU deployment area is now pushed farther into the heart of the map and is located north of the Communication Mast.
- The attackers lose the advantage of their tanks and now only have two light vehicles to use. Take advantage of these vehicles' speed to quickly reach the objectives.
- The opposing team will set a defense perimeter on top of the buildings located in the Village area. Use engineers to take these buildings down, allowing your team to breach the area.
- Flank the Village from the east and west, utilizing the perimeter roads. This is the best way to catch the defenders in a demoralizing crossfire.
- A recon player can take advantage of obstacles in between the RU deployment and M-COM stations. These provide great cover that allows you to snipe defenders.

DEPLOYMENT AREA ASSETS 

NAME	VDV Buggy
QUANTITY	2

CN DEPLOYMENT

RECOMMENDED SQUAD COMPOSITION:

- The deployment area is located even farther north again. No vehicles spawn at this deployment area. The enemies spawn with only a light vehicle.
- With the lack of vehicle presence, don't think the engineer won't be put to good use. The rockets in the engineer class will prove useful for blowing holes through buildings.
- On the roof of the building north of M-COM Station A take the recon class. You'll have a great overview and vantage point of all incoming enemy infantry towards both M-COM stations. This area also provides great cover. The sniper rifles will prove to be very useful at this location.
- The buildings around the M-COM stations have access to the rooftop buildings; take advantage of these for vantage points and overviews.
- Place T-UGS in the buildings around the M-COM stations to be alerted when enemies are approaching. With the high amount of buildings, you're sure to pick off a few enemies.

M-COM STATION A

- This M-COM station is located in between a cluster of buildings at the middle of an alleyway just northwest on the map.
- There are no vehicles on this map, so prepare for an all-out battle as just infantry units. There are so many buildings to hide in and for great angles to protect M-COM Station A.
- Attackers are going to want to focus a few squads on checking buildings and clearing them out before arming M-COM Station A. Have some assault and support classes work together to do this.
- As a defender picking the recon class, there is a building just south of M-COM Station A with a great line of sight where you can then take out any enemies wandering around the area.
- To the far northwest behind a large rock there is an IED detonator. This can take out a whole group of enemies, including the adjacent building. A recon unit should be stationed here to watch this whole location and protect it.

M-COM STATION B

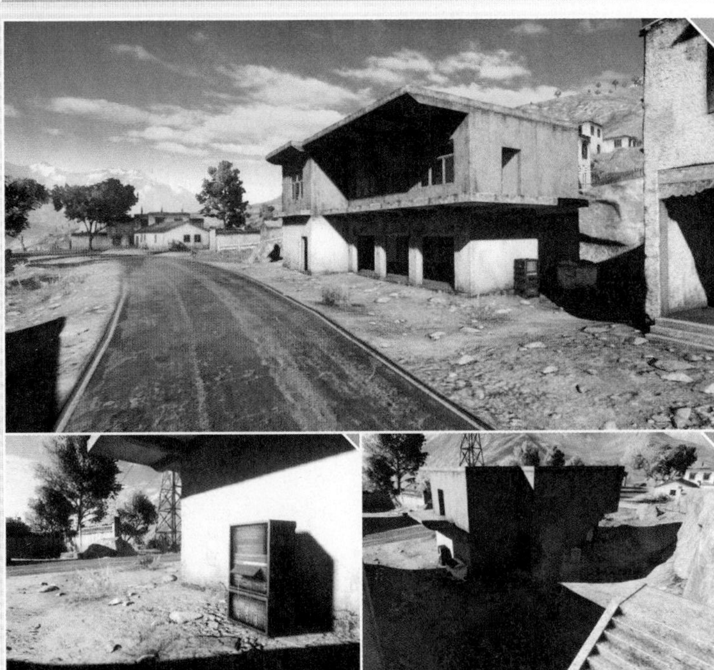

- This objective is located in the Village outside of one of the buildings near a steel dumpster.
- The attacking team now only has a light vehicle, allowing defenders to form squads specialized in close-quarter combat.
- Defenders have multiple rooftops to choose from. Spread each squad out to different rooftops and work with each other to stop the attackers approaching from the south.
- Attackers are at a disadvantage because of the line of sights that are provided from the buildings for the defending team. Take advantage at how frail these buildings are and have engineers rocket them from a distance.
- The RU team is able to move in freely once they destroy most of the buildings and walls in the area. The attackers can take full use of their light vehicle and harass players due to the vehicle's speed. While this is happening, a squad can easily flank the area and arm the M-COM station.

ZONE 5: NORTH VILLAGE

CN DEPLOYMENT
NO VEHICLES

RU DEPLOYMENT
NO VEHICLES

CN
A
B
US

RU DEPLOYMENT

RECOMMENDED SQUAD COMPOSITION:

- Located to the south of both M-COM stations, the RU deployment once again is without vehicles. Load up your best anti-infantry classes for this final push.
- When making your move, do not run up the dirt road in the center. Weave your way in and out of the buildings along the east and west sides to avoid giving the enemy an easy kill.
- With no vehicles and so many fragile buildings, instead of having too many engineers, load up as an assault class and equip your M320 HE. This will allow you to blow holes in the buildings with a single shot to take away enemy cover and make new paths for your squad.
- With so many buildings to clear out on your way to the M-COM stations, make sure to have at least two members of your squad as the assault class. These brief short-range encounters are the best time to get revives with the Defibrillator and save your team some precious tickets.
- Beware of the stationary .50Cals located near the M-COM stations. The two best ways to deal with these massive threats are flanking them from the side since they can't turn very far or killing the enemy by using splash damage from explosives such as the engineer's rocket launchers.

CN DEPLOYMENT

RECOMMENDED SQUAD COMPOSITION:

- This is the last zone and the CN deployment area is pushed to the farthest north spot of the map. You and your squad will have a few seconds to begin setting up your defenses since the RU team deploys farther away than the CN deployment.
- Absolutely no vehicles spawn for either the CN team or RU team. This will make for much close-quarter combat in this north Village.
- Watch for enemies approaching for a flank from the east and west. Use this higher position of the hill to your advantage by looking across the open areas south of these objectives.
- The building west of M-COM Station B has access to the roof. This position overlooks M-COM Station A. Use this position to stop enemies from arming and pick off players attacking from the south. Drop in the stairway if taking enemy fire to stay alive and keep a good squad spawn.
- With the recon class, make your way to the farthest northeast position on the map near the dead zone. Equip the sniper rifle and go prone to hide your location. This position is useful to watch M-COM Station B. You'll be able to snipe any enemies that try to arm.

M-COM STATION A

- M-COM Station A is located to the farthest point to the north, right outside and surrounded by three buildings.
- No vehicles are in this zone, so defenders need to make full use of all the remaining buildings and use the rooftops with .50Cals for a defensive position.
- Defenders are going to want to stay alive within the buildings to keep a good squad spawn and use the rooftops to keep a good watch over the objectives. Many of the buildings oversee both objectives. Stay alive on the rooftops to stop the enemy while they arm the objective.
- Attackers will need to destroy the buildings to uncover the defender's position. Have teammates play as an engineer class and have them equip the RPG to blow through walls of buildings. A grenade launcher and C4 work extremely well too.

M-COM STATION B

- M-COM Station B is located in the north Village. This area consists of three buildings and the objective is outside the eastern building.
- All three buildings provide a .50Cal to mount. These provide a shield to make the gunner a hard target to take out. Unload your ammunition and suppress the enemy as long as you can.
- These buildings provide a great view of the map. Take full use of this when defending; send one or two support classes equipped with LMGs to the top and let the bullets fly.
- When attacking, have engineers rocket the building from afar to startle the defenders inside. Destroying this building will leave defenders with less cover and let your team arm the M-COM station with ease.
- The RU team must be aware of snipers hiding north of the objectives. When prone, these defending snipers blend in so well that you will not be able to react until it is too late. Throw smokes on the M-COM station to reduce visibility.

OBLITERATION

RECOMMENDED SQUAD COMPOSITION:

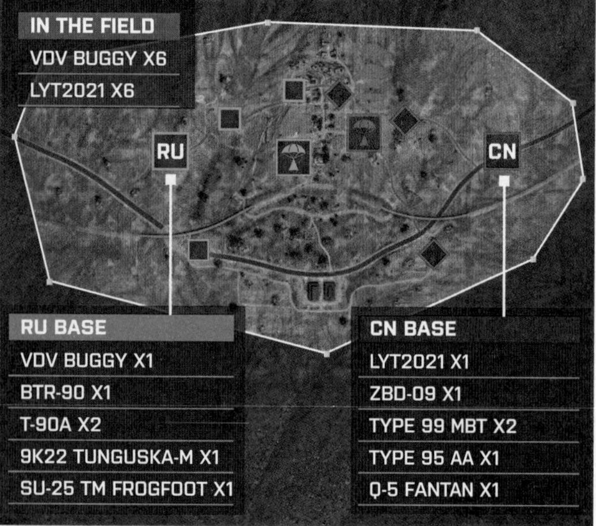

- Two of the CN targets are found east of the Village on the north side of the map and the third is found near the Farm.
- One of the RU targets is found in the Bridge Construction area and the other two are located around the west side of the Village.
- Players will find the bomb spawning near the Communication Mast. Establish a defense perimeter close by, allowing your team to easily pick up the bomb.
- This is a really large map, so be sure to utilize the vehicles at your base and scattered around the map to travel to each objective. The light vehicles are perfect for moving around the bomb carrier.
- Engineers are your best friend on this map for both destroying and repairing vehicles. Plant M15 AT mines throughout the map to destroy roaming vehicles.

DEFUSE

RECOMMENDED SQUAD COMPOSITION:

- This battle takes place within the Village and School area. The RU team spawns near the western entrance while the CN team spawns between two buildings in the east side of the Village.
- Laptop A is found between the two buildings in the eastern part of the Village. Defenders can hide in buildings and easily ambush their opponent.
- Laptop B is found in the classroom in the western part of the School area. Defenders will plant C4 and Claymores around, so when playing as the RU team, tread carefully.
- The CN team should make their way to the various rooftops of the buildings. These provide the best angles to watch the objectives.
- The RU team should have Smoke Grenades equipped. This makes the defenders on the roof useless and forces them to drop down, leading to an easy arm. Have a few squad members stay back and pick off these defenders who drop. Buildings are destroyable, so use them to your advantage.

DOMINATION

RECOMMENDED SQUAD COMPOSITION:

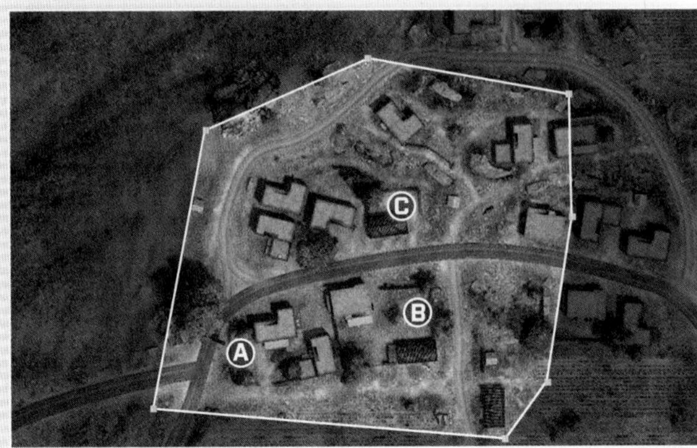

- The three control points on this map are the Backyard (A), School (B), and Hillside (C).
- Equip the M320 for the assault class. This allows you to destroy walls and quickly storm through them towards your opponent.
- Take advantage of roofs. They present the best angles to fire upon your enemies.
- Each objective has a small capture radius; plant C4 to take out an enemy attempting to capture an objective. If you see a control point being captured by the enemy, let them feel the pain.
- Your best strategy is to capture both the Backyard (A) and the School (B). These objectives are both on the south side of the map. This forces the opposing team to only attack from the north.

SQUAD DEATHMATCH

RECOMMENDED SQUAD COMPOSITION:

- This Squad Deathmatch is restricted to the village north of the original map.
- Squads will want to control the rooftops of the various village buildings. These provide the greatest lines of sights.
- The IFV on this map plays a huge role. All the buildings are destructible, so the IFV can shoot or ram through them with enough speed.
- Have extra engineers on your team to aid in destroying the IFV if the opposing squad controls it or to repair it if your squad gains control.
- Place T-UGS around various corners of the map to detect enemies. This will alert your team to the location of all the firefights occurring.

TEAM DEATHMATCH

RECOMMENDED SQUAD COMPOSITION:

- In this Team Deathmatch, prepare for a Wild, Wild West shootout. Have your trigger finger ready in this remote village.
- Take advantage of the rooftops. These provide great fire angles and cover when fighting enemies on the ground.
- Buildings are destructible, so if you trap the enemy in a building, bring the walls down with grenades and launchers.
- The buildings provide a lot of mobility with exceptional cover. Learn how to move from building to building when being chased to leave your enemy in the dust.
- Defend a corner of the map, forcing the enemies to come from fewer directions. The northeast corner is a preferred spot to hold.

ALPHA SQUAD: IMPRESSIONS

MABOOZA

Hainan Resort consists of several islands separated by narrow waterways. This has made me rethink the effectiveness of amphibious craft for moving my squad around the map. Whether using a speedy RHIB or well-armed IFV, these narrow channels are just as effective as roads and offer sneaky routes ideal for flanking enemy positions.

STRONGSIDE

On this map I really enjoyed playing as the commander in Conquest Large. Many of the control points are in an open area so I was able to utilize the Cruise Missile and take out many enemies while my team moved in to take over a control point. This led us to an easy and quick victory.

WALSHY

The first time I played this map I spent 99% of my time at the Hotel. I loved the choice of sitting on top of the Hotel roof sniping people across the map, or sitting up there with one of the assault class and parachuting down to kill the enemies that were trying to capture the objective.

FLAMESWORD

The first time I played this map I was blown away how phenomenal it looked. I have never played a game where the water looked so clear. I enjoyed maneuvering around the map with the PWC, as it allowed me to catch enemies by surprise. Overall it is an amazing balanced map that leads to a good time.

ELUMNITE

This is a beautiful map with a very realistic feel of an ideal place for relaxation. Only this Hotel isn't for a vacation, but gives you the feeling of what else can I destroy? Since I like explosives catch me blowing up the Hotel...with you inside it!

HAINAN RESORT

HAINAN RESORT

LEVOLUTION MOMENTS

WHAT IS IT?

Create your own inferno by setting fire to the oil spills scattered across the map. The left and right wings of the Hotel can be destroyed and collapse independently.

HOW IS IT TRIGGERED?

Use explosives (like grenades) to ignite the oil spills. Target the walls on the first floor of the Hotel with explosive weapons to collapse the separate wings.

HOW IS GAMEPLAY IMPACTED?

Collapsed portions of the Hotel are inaccessible and the fires from the oil pools create hazards for infantry while spewing out black smoke, temporarily reducing visibility.

CONQUEST LARGE

RECOMMENDED SQUAD COMPOSITION:

The Conquest Large variant of Hainan Resort is fairly larger sized than the standard Conquest version. Players will notice that two new control points are added to the map: Tennis Courts (B) and Bungalows (E). With five flags up for grabs, each team must try to hold at least three to begin bleeding the opposing team's tickets. The US team's best strategy will be to capture the Marina (A), the Tennis Courts (B), and the Hotel (C). The US team will want to establish a perimeter around the Hotel (B); recon players can snipe from the roof of the Hotel (B), giving them a view of the entire map while friendly vehicles maintain pressure on the enemy towards the west. The CN team, on the other hand, will want to capture the Bungalows (E), the Freighter (D), and the Hotel (C). Much like the US team, the CN team should have a couple of recon players sniping at the top of the Hotel (B) roof. The CN team will want their air vehicles to put pressure around the Marina (A) and the Tennis Courts (B) while the friendly IFVs wait for US team members to get near the Hotel (C). The Hotel (C) will be a critical flag to control throughout the game as it gives the controlling team's commander a Cruise Missile; this baby packs some serious heat. As both teams will be focusing on capturing the Hotel (B), if the fighting in the center of the map becomes too heated, consider flanking through the roads to the north with light vehicles or by water on the south side with light water vehicles. These control points will be near the opposing team's base, but that doesn't mean they are impossible to capture as their defense lines will be weaker. Either team will only need three control points to win, but if the opportunity presents a fourth control point, then by all means capture it.

US BASE

- The US base is located along the shoreline in the southeastern part of the map.
- A long journey awaits you to the nearest control point if you choose to go by foot. Take advantage of the multiple FAVs at base and head north towards the Tennis Courts (B).
- The team can deploy in an attack and stealth jet back at base. These will provide great air support and aid when destroying the opponent's ground, air, and water vehicles.
- There are few light water vehicles and a powerful RCB-90 that spawns in the water. Be unpredictable and head northwest to initiate a fight with the opposing team at the Freighter (D). Have the passengers of the light water vehicles disembark on the island to provide infantry support as well.
- Have a squad fill up the seats of the AH-6J Little Bird and immediately head to the Hotel (C). Drop the passengers onto the roof and set up a perimeter, allowing your team to move in for the capture.

BASE ASSETS

NAME	M1161 ITV	LAV-25	RHIB	RCB-90	AH-6J Little Bird	A-10 Warthog	F-35
QUANTITY	3	2	2	1	1	1	1

CN BASE

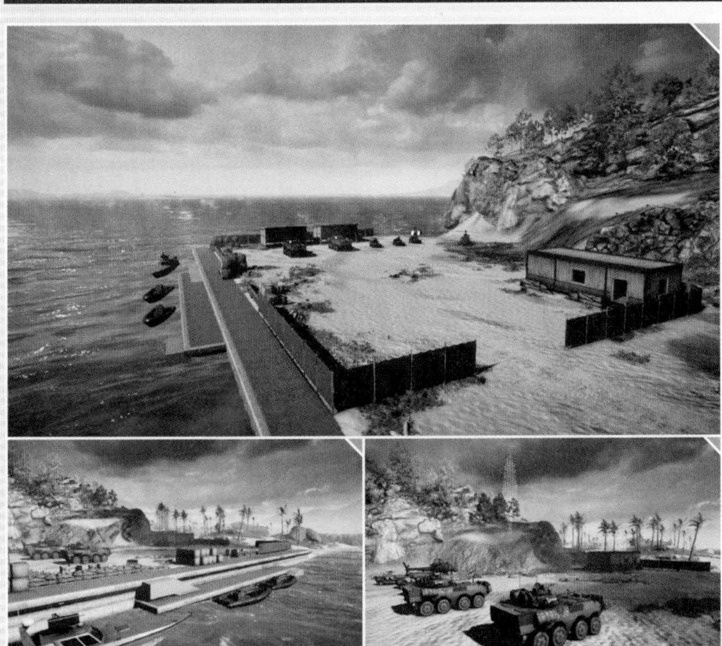

- The CN base is located at the northeast edge of the map. With this base being such a great distance away from every control point, be sure to take one of the many vehicles at the CN deployment.
- Make your way across this map via land, water, or air. Hiking on foot will take too much time and be very inefficient.
- You want to send all your land vehicles towards the Hotel (C) so you can secure the Cruise Missile for your commander. This will be the most valuable control point to obtain throughout the match.
- The best way to control the center of this map is to hold the roof above the Hotel (C). Be sure to keep your domination on this roof by eliminating any aircraft or troops trying to sneak up via the two elevator doors.
- Patrol your DV-15 outside of the Marina (A) and the Freighter (D). Avoid going in the narrow waterways around the Tennis Courts (B) and the Bungalows (E) where this strong boat can easily get taken down by enemy engineers.

BASE ASSETS

NAME	LYT2021	ZBD-09	RHIB	DV-15	Z-11W	Q-5 Fantan	J-20
QUANTITY	3	2	2	1	1	1	1

A: MARINA

- The Marina (A) control point is positioned northwest of the US base. On the west side is a cafe that views the ocean to the west.
- Once captured, the controlling team acquires a PWC and a light vehicle.
- Along the north side of the Marina (A) stands a .50Cal that will assist against attacking watercraft.
- Recon players can get to the roof and snipe enemies heading south of the Freighter (D). This will delay the opponent from reaching the Hotel (C).
- The best routes to capture this control point are by water. Take advantage of the water vehicles that spawn at each base when going for the capture.

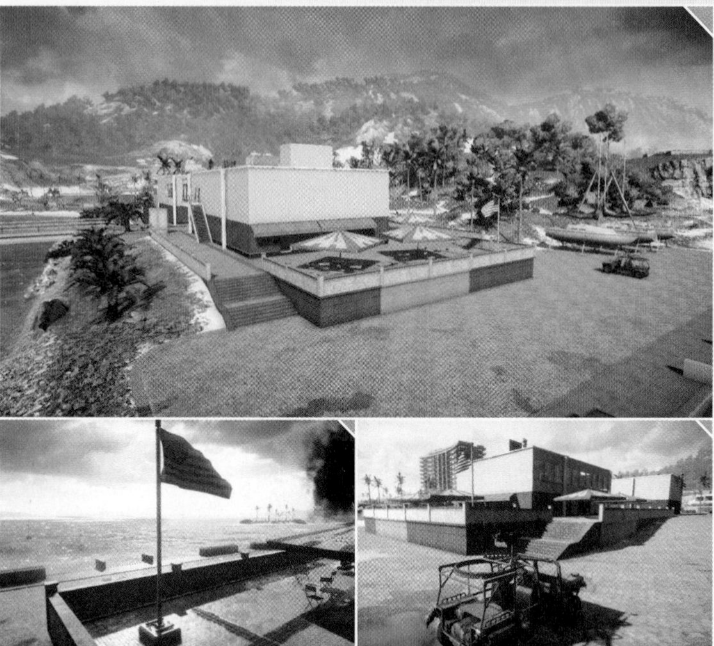

CONTROL POINT ASSETS

US CONTROL	CN CONTROL
M1161 ITV (1)	LYT2021 (1)
PWC (1)	PWC (1)

B: TENNIS COURTS

- This control point is located towards the eastern part of the map. This flag has relatively no cover by the flag except the large building east of the control point.
- A light vehicle and PWC spawn on this control point. The PWC should be used to transport to the next control point quickly.
- When defending, have a recon class player go to the second floor of the building behind the Tennis Courts (B) and snipe enemy infantry as they approach. You will even want to have some engineers here to help take out any aircraft that make their way here.
- When attacking, look to take out the main building east of the control point and take out any defenders positioned inside it.
- When defending, use the building east of the control point to set up your defenses. Also send squad members west of this control point to have an unexpected point of attack.

CONTROL POINT ASSETS

US CONTROL	CN CONTROL
M1161 ITV (1)	LYT2021 (1)
PWC (1)	PWC (1)

C: HOTEL

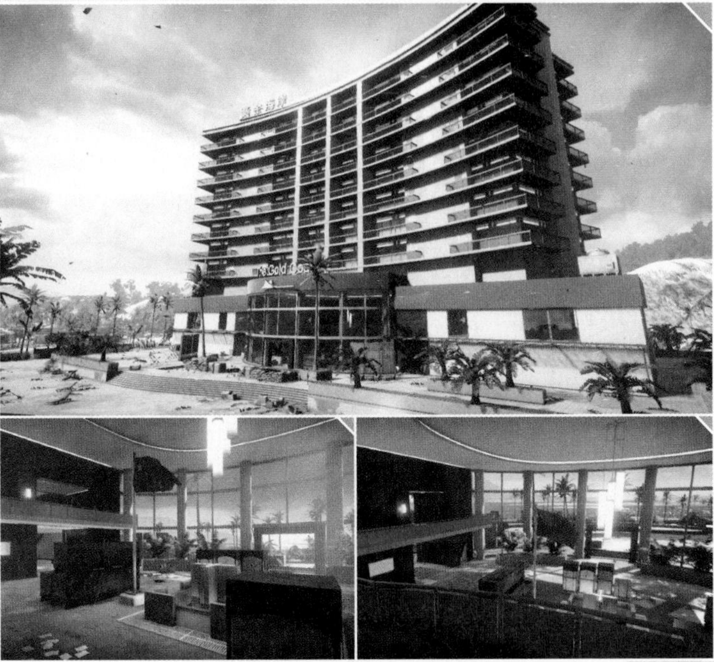

- This control point is located in the middle of map inside the lobby of the Hotel (C). This tall building has three floors, with the third one only accessible by using the elevator to reach the rooftop.
- In addition to the light vehicles, both teams get a mobile AA unit here, ideal for controlling air traffic in the center of the map.
- When attacking, drop off teammates on the roof. These teammates should make their way down the elevator for an attack as other teammates parachute down to attack from multiple directions.
- Utilize the elevator to the rooftop of the Hotel (C). This position is a great vantage point to have over your enemies. Spot enemies from afar with the recon class to aid your teammates by letting them know where enemies are attacking from.
- Take control of the second floor to have the advantage over enemies coming into the building. Keep moving while controlling this level and check the many stairways and ramps leading up to the second level. T-UGS will come in handy in this close-quarter area.

PRO TIP: STRONGSIDE

MAKE YOUR WAY UP THE ELEVATORS TO THE TOP OF THE BUILDING. YOU'LL HAVE AN INCREDIBLE OVERVIEW OF THE ENTIRE MAP. YOU'LL WANT TO CHOOSE THE RECON CLASS AND SNIPE AWAY! PLACE A CLAYMORE IN FRONT OF ONE OF THE ELEVATORS FACING THE INSIDE OF THE ELEVATOR. THE TRIP WIRES SHOULD SHOOT INTO THE ELEVATOR, MAKING IT TRIGGER AS SOON AS THE ELEVATOR OPENS WITH THE ENEMY INSIDE.

CONTROL POINT ASSETS

US CONTROL	CN CONTROL
M1161 ITV (1)	LYT2021 (1)
LAV-AD (1)	Type 95 AA (1)

D: FREIGHTER

- This flag is located on the east island of the map inside a crashed ship.
- When controlling the flag, you gain control of a light vehicle and a PWC.
- Use a helicopter to drop players off on the top of the crashed ship. Play as the recon class and equip a sniper rifle. You'll have an overview of incoming enemies from the Hotel (C) and the Bungalows (E). You can also capture the control point from on top of this ship.
- Utilize water vehicles when capturing this flag from the water and defending the flag from other incoming enemy vehicles.
- When defending, use the crates around the crashed ship as cover from incoming enemies.

CONTROL POINT ASSETS

US CONTROL	CN CONTROL
M1161 ITV (1)	LYT2021 (1)
PWC (1)	PWC (1)

E: BUNGALOWS

- This objective is located towards the northern boundary and consists of five identical cabanas connected by wooden docks.
- Like most maps, the important battles take place in the center. Be sure to immediately get back in the action with one of the light vehicles that spawns at this location.
- This is a multi-faceted battle when fighting for this control point due to the four different directions of attack. Vehicles can attack from the road to the north, watercraft can attack from the surrounding water, and ground troops can attack from the cabanas or below the docks that hold these buildings up.
- When attacking this area with vehicles, the buildings only provide temporary cover fire—an explosive round can easily reveal the enemies trying to hide inside.
- When defending this objective, be sure to have a squad heavily composed of engineers or use the HJ-8 Launcher. You will most likely encounter vehicles driving all the way to this location; rarely will infantry make the long run or swim to this area. Be sure to eliminate loaded light water vehicles before the enemy can disperse around the objective.

CONTROL POINT ASSETS

US CONTROL	CN CONTROL
M1161 ITV (1)	LYT2021 (1)
RHIB (1)	RHIB (1)

PRO TIP: WALSHY

NEAR THE BUNGALOWS, I LIKE TO PLAY AS THE SUPPORT CLASS AND USE THE M224 MORTAR FROM A DISTANCE AS UNSUSPECTING ENEMIES ARE RUNNING THROUGH THE HUTS. BUT DON'T LINGER NEAR THE MORTAR UNLESS YOU HAVE A TEAMMATE PROTECTING YOU. OTHERWISE PLACE THE MORTAR, AND THEN OPERATE IT REMOTELY.

CONQUEST SMALL

RECOMMENDED SQUAD COMPOSITION:

In this Conquest game variant, players will be looking at a total of three control points: the Marina (A), the Hotel (B), and the Freighter (C). These control points are spread out evenly, so players will find a mix of naval warfare around the Marina (A) and the Freighter (C). Meanwhile the Hotel (B) will display a ton of infantry members infiltrating there while encountering incoming fire from an IFV and enemy helicopters. The US team's best strategy will be to capture the Marina (A) and the Hotel (B). Once these two control points are captured, the CN team's tickets will slowly begin counting down. The US team will want to establish a perimeter around the Hotel (B). Recon players can snipe on the roof of the Hotel (B), giving them a view of the entire map while friendly vehicles maintain pressure on the enemy towards the west. The CN team, on the other hand, will want to capture the Freighter (C) and the Hotel (B). Much like the US team, the CN team should have a couple of recon players sniping at the top of the Hotel (B) roof. The CN team will want their air vehicles to put pressure around the Marina (A) while the friendly IFV waits for US team members to get near the Hotel (B). The Hotel (B) will be a critical flag to control throughout the game as it gives the controlling team's commander a Cruise Missile; this baby packs a punch.

US BASE

- The US base is located along the shoreline in the southeastern part of the map.
- Take advantage of the multiple light vehicles at base and head north towards the Hotel (B). This will be the most important objective to control throughout the game since it lies equal distance from both bases.
- The team can deploy in an attack jet back at the base. This will provide great air support and aid when destroying the opponent's ground, air, and water vehicles.
- There are a few RHIBs that spawn in the water. Be unpredictable and head northwest to initiate a fight with the opposing team at the Hotel (B). Have the passengers of the RHIBs disembark on the island to provide infantry support as well.
- Send a squad in the LAV-25 towards the Hotel (B) to punish the incoming enemy infantry. Delay them as long as possible to allow your teammates to come in from behind to capture the Hotel (B).

BASE ASSETS

NAME	M1161 ITV	LAV-AD	RHIB	AH-6J Little Bird	A-10 Warthog
QUANTITY	1	1	2	1	1

CN BASE

- The CN base is located at the northeast edge of the map. With the base being a great distance away from every control point, make sure to travel with one of the many vehicles at the CN deployment.
- Make your way across this map via land, water, or air.
- You want to send all your land vehicles towards the Hotel (B) so you can secure the Cruise Missile for your commander. As always, be sure to spot enemy vehicles so your attack jet can help you take them out.
- The best way to control the center of this map is to hold the roof above the Hotel (B). Hold control here on this roof by eliminating any aircraft or troops trying to sneak up via the two elevator doors. T-UGS work extremely well near the elevators.
- With no attack boats on this map, flanks from the water are going to be extremely powerful and unexpected. Load up your squad in a light water vehicle and flank all the way over to the Marina (A) when the enemy is focused on the center of the map.

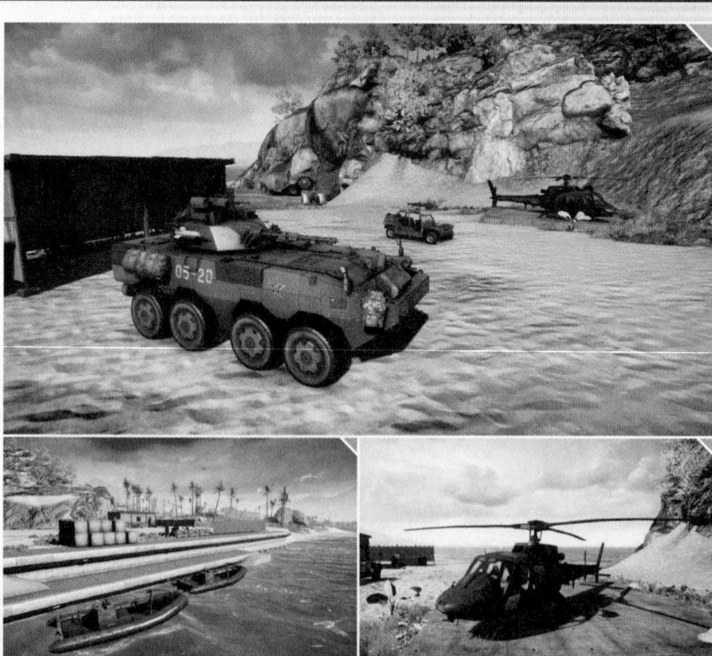

BASE ASSETS

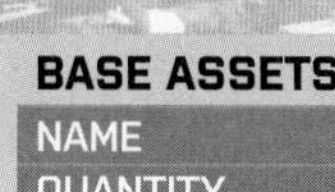

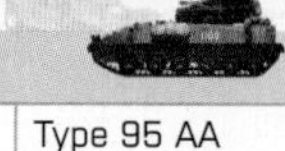

NAME	LYT2021	Type 95 AA	RHIB	Z-11W	Q-5 Fantan
QUANTITY	1	1	2	1	1

A: MARINA

CONTROL POINT ASSETS

US CONTROL	CN CONTROL
RHIB (1)	RHIB (1)

- The Marina (A) control point is positioned northwest of the US base. On the west side is a cafe that views the ocean to the west.
- Once captured, the controlling team acquires a RHIB.
- Along the north side of the Marina (A) stands a .50Cal that will assist against attacking watercraft.
- Recon players can get to the top of the roof and snipe enemies heading south of the Freighter (C). This will delay the opponent from reaching the Hotel (B). The rooftops of these two buildings north of the Marina (A) will be very useful in controlling this objective. The roofs give you an overview of enemies approaching from the Hotel (B), making it easy to pick off the enemy infantry. Also, Radio Beacons inside these buildings will keep you spawning in this area if you or your squad are taken down.
- The best routes to capture this control point are by water. Take advantage of the water vehicles when going for the capture.

PRO TIP: ELUMNITE

JUMPING IN A RHIB AND TAKING MORE OF THE WATER ROUTES WILL BE A LOT SAFER THAN MOVING ON LAND TO TAKE OVER CONTROL POINTS. EVEN THOUGH IT MAY TAKE LONGER TO REACH THESE POINTS, YOUR TEAM WILL RUN INTO LESS RESISTANCE.

B: HOTEL

CONTROL POINT ASSETS

US CONTROL	CN CONTROL
M1161 ITV (1)	LYT2021 (1)

- This control point is located in the middle of map within the lobby of the Hotel (C). This tall building has three floors with the third one only accessible by using the elevator to reach the rooftop.
- No vehicles spawn here, so most of the fighting will be done inside and in close proximity of the Hotel (C).
- When attacking, drop off teammates on the roof. These teammates should make their way down the elevator for an attack as other teammates parachute down to attack from multiple directions.
- Utilize the elevator get to the rooftop of the Hotel (C). This position is a great vantage point to have over your enemies. Spot enemies from afar with the recon class to aid your teammates and let them know where enemies are attacking from.
- Take control of the second floor to have the advantage over enemies coming into the building. Keep moving while controlling this level and check the many stairways and ramps leading up to the second level. T-UGS will come in handy in this close-quarter area.

BATTLEFIELD BOOTCAMP | INFANTRY | VEHICLES | MULTIPLAYER MAPS | CAMPAIGN | BATTLEFIELD COMPENDIUM

C: FREIGHTER

- This flag is located on the east island of the map inside a crashed ship.
- When controlling the flag you gain control of a RHIB.
- Use a helicopter to drop players off on the top of the crashed ship. Play as the recon class and equip the sniper; you'll have an overview of enemies coming from the Hotel (B). You can also capture the control point from on top of this ship.
- Utilize water vehicles when capturing this flag from the water and defending the flag from other incoming enemy vehicles.
- When defending, use the crates around the crashed ship as cover from incoming enemies.

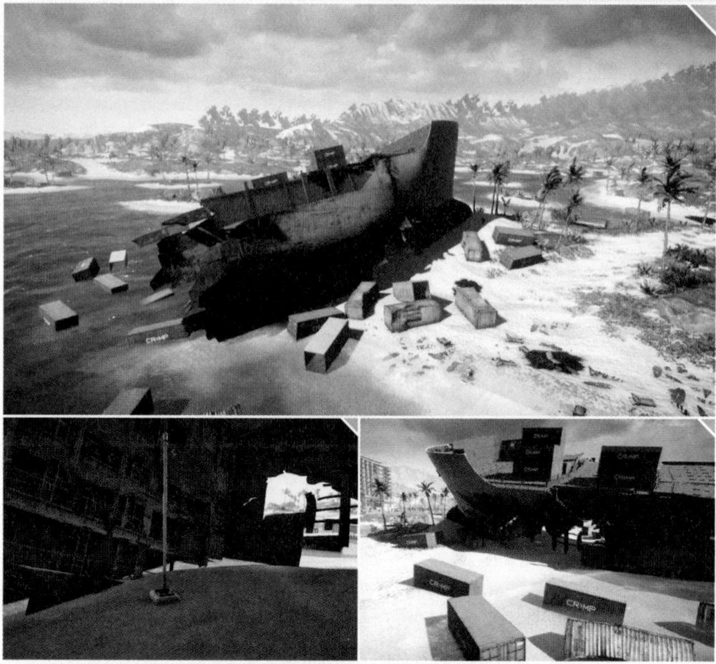

PRO TIP: FLAMESWORD

THIS IS ONE OF MY FAVORITE MAPS BECAUSE OF ALL THE COVER YOU GET FROM THE SCENERY. I LIKE TO DRAW ENEMY VEHICLES NEAR AS I GO PRONE AND WATCH CAREFULLY. WHEN THE OPPORTUNITY PRESENTS ITSELF, I GET CLOSE, THROW C4 ON AN ENEMY VEHICLE, AND WATCH IT GO BOOM! IT MIGHT TAKE A WHILE, BUT IT IS TOTALLY WORTH IT.

CONTROL POINT ASSETS

US CONTROL	CN CONTROL
RHIB (1)	RHIB (1)

RUSH

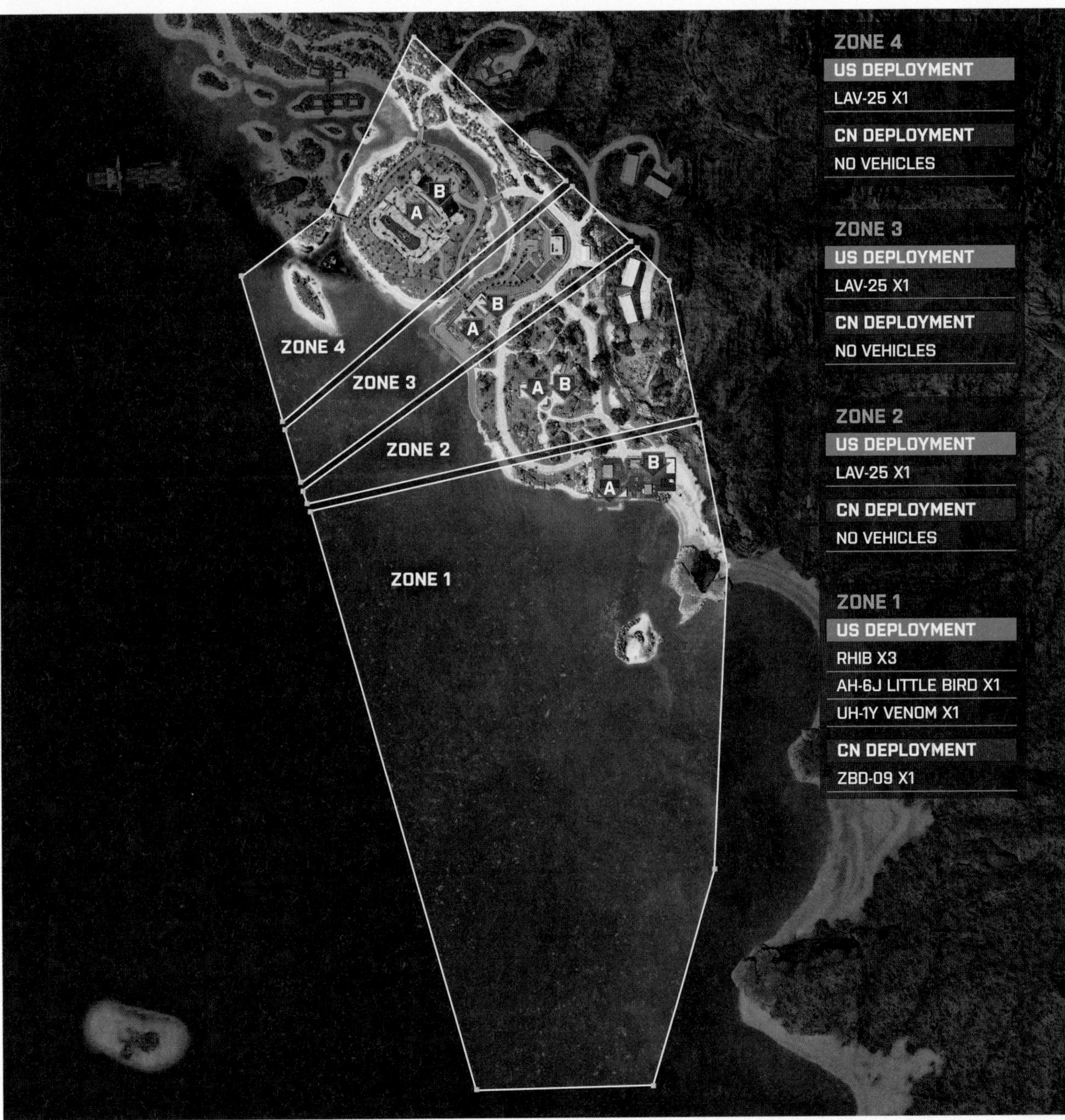

In this Rush variant, the US will start on an aircraft carrier and they are required to push through four guarded zones during their assault. The fight starts at the south end of the map on the Dockyard before the US team can make their way past the Hilltop, across the Marina, and into the Hotel. The US team is at an advantage as they have the majority of the vehicles in each zone, while the CN team only has an IFV in Zones 1 and 2. The US team must strategically plan out the routes of these vehicles or else they can fall prey to the CN team's traps and engineers. The US vehicles will play a huge role when advancing from zone to zone, so be sure to have squads consisting largely of engineers to constantly repair these vehicles. Despite the CN team being outnumbered in the vehicle count, they do have stationary weapons throughout each zone to deal with the US vehicles. Combine these stationary weapons and squads mainly consisting of engineers. The CN team will force the US team to fight by land, giving them the best chance to stop the US team's advance.

ZONE 1: DOCKYARD

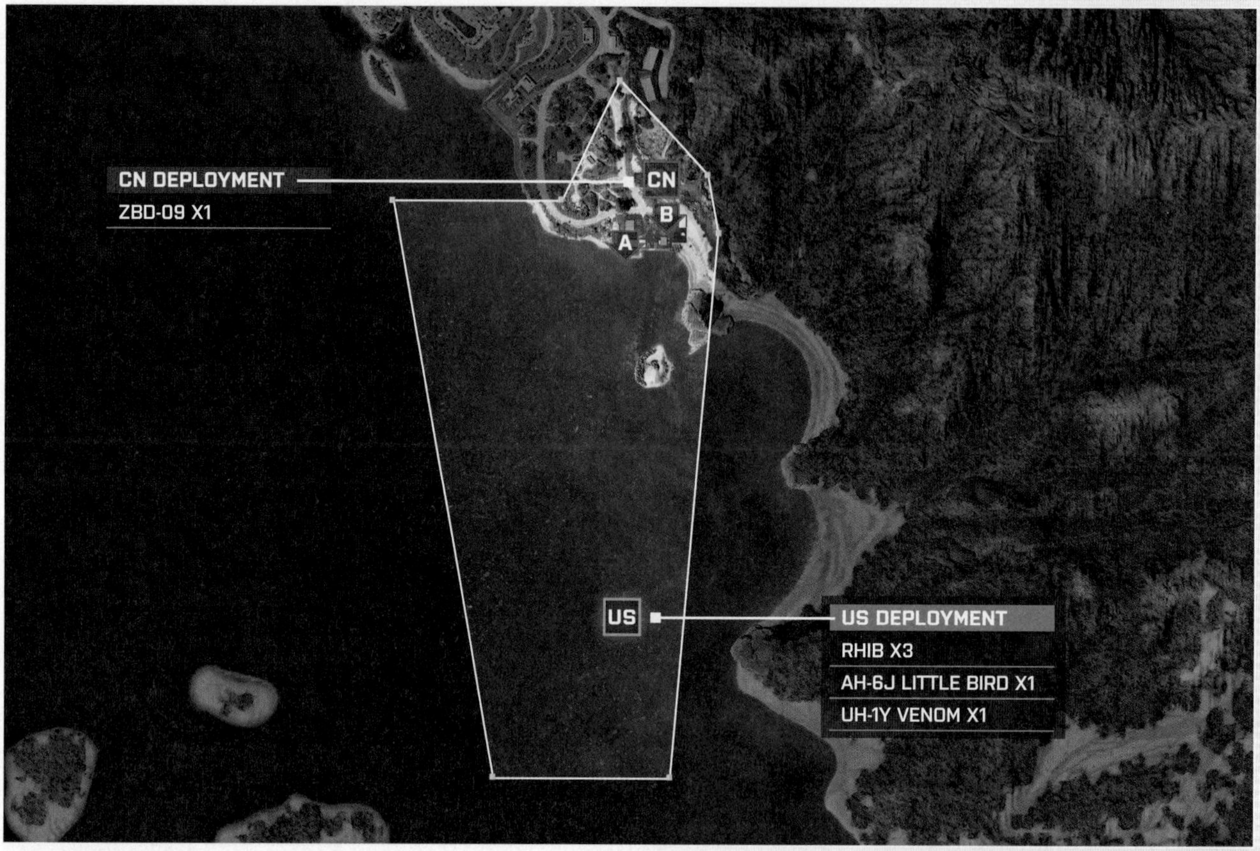

CN DEPLOYMENT
ZBD-09 X1

CN
A
B
US

US DEPLOYMENT
RHIB X3
AH-6J LITTLE BIRD X1
UH-1Y VENOM X1

US DEPLOYMENT

RECOMMENDED SQUAD COMPOSITION:

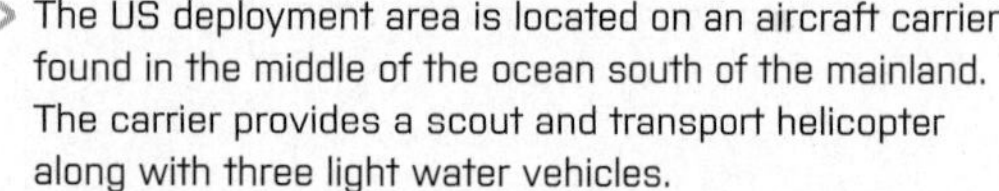

- The US deployment area is located on an aircraft carrier found in the middle of the ocean south of the mainland. The carrier provides a scout and transport helicopter along with three light water vehicles.
- Players will want to board these vehicles to make it towards the M-COM stations. If not, you will be looking at a long swim to shore.
- The scout helicopter will need to put constant pressure on the defenders, allowing your transport helicopter and RHIBs to deliver infantry units to shore.
- North of the carrier is a small island that will be a great spot for recon players to snipe from. There is a line of stationary weapons posted on the dock of the mainland—the recon player will be a huge asset in taking these defenders out. Once on the island, throw down a Radio Beacon. You don't want your teammates to take that same dreadful swim, so spawn them as close to the action as you can.
- Having a recon class in each squad will be beneficial as it is suggested to throw Radio Beacons down every chance you get to avoid swimming or waiting for a vehicle to respawn in the deployment zone.

DEPLOYMENT AREA ASSETS

NAME	RHIB	UH-1Y Venom	AH-6J Little Bird
QUANTITY	3	1	1

CN DEPLOYMENT

RECOMMENDED SQUAD COMPOSITION:

- The CN deployment area is only a few meters north of M-COM Station A, giving the defenders a chance to establish a defensive perimeter before the US attackers arrive.
- One vehicle spawns at this deployment—a ZBD-09. Use this vehicle wisely as it will serve your team by providing greater cover when capturing the objectives.
- Rush the turrets and launchers at the start of your spawn. You may be able to take out the transport helicopters dropping near the docks, and cut down the enemy pressure.
- The small storage buildings provide excellent hiding spots, ideal for ambushing attacking troops who have reached the store.
- Have a few engineers take out any of the attacker's vehicles, forcing them to come by land. Use the ZBD-09 to clean up these attackers easily around the whole area.

DEPLOYMENT AREA ASSETS

NAME	ZBD-09
QUANTITY	1

M-COM STATION A

- M-COM Station A is located on the Dockyard in the southern part of map. The station is covered by two shipping crates under a shed.
- Defending the M-COM station with the very few vehicles will be tough. With only a ZBD-09, your team is going to want some engineer classes to equip Stingers or IGLAs. This first engagement will be very important and determine the flow of the battle for this zone.
- When attacking M-COM Station A, it is imperative that your team makes a solid first attack. Losing vehicles will force the team to swim, so place a Radio Beacon southeast of this objective.
- When successful in making it to land, attackers are going to want to use the assault class to revive any fallen teammates. If you have a made this far, M-COM Station A will be yours for the taking.
- Defenders should take full advantage of the .50Cals and HJ-8 Launchers to stop the first wave of attackers.

M-COM STATION B

- M-COM Station B is located in the northeastern corner of the Dockyard. The objective is in an open warehouse with many items inside and out that will provide great cover.
- The warehouse walls are all destroyable. Both attackers and defenders can use this to their advantage. Defenders can destroy walls, making it easier to watch, and the attackers can destroy the walls to reveal defenders inside.
- Just south of the open warehouse are four explosive tanks. Defenders can draw in the attacking team and, once they are near, set them off with an explosive, easily wiping out the attacking squad.
- The pier south of the M-COM station has a stationary launcher that defenders will use to assist in destroying incoming vehicles. Make the attackers' vehicles useless, forcing them to engage by land.
- The attacking team will want at least one recon class per squad. It is a long swim from the US deployment zone, so place Radio Beacons in concealed areas, allowing you to spawn teammates near the action.

ZONE 2: HILLTOP

CN DEPLOYMENT
NO VEHICLES

US DEPLOYMENT
LAV-25 X1

US DEPLOYMENT

RECOMMENDED SQUAD COMPOSITION:

- After succeeding in arming both M-COM stations in Zone 1, the US deployment zone is now moved to the Dockyard.
- The vehicle count is downgraded in this zone. The US team will only have an LAV-25 at their disposal, but it comes in handy for hammering the Hilltop while the infantry advance.
- A squad can perform a successful flank by driving the light water vehicle west of the Hilltop right before the dead zone. This will make you unpredictable, as the CN team will not expect you to take such a risky play.
- The enemy has a line of stationary turrets waiting for you at the top of the hill. Be sure to have smoke grenades equipped and blind the stationary turrets' vision, making them useless. Players equipped with IRNV scopes will excel in this guerilla warfare.
- The safest path to the top of the hill will be following the main road and heading north at the fork. The defenders' stationary turrets will be unable to a get a clear sight on you. Let two squads take this path. Have one branch out along the grassy hill, gaining cover from the rocky and grassy area. Meanwhile, have other squad follow the road the whole way up and control the hill north of M-COM Station B, providing suppressive fire.

DEPLOYMENT AREA ASSETS

NAME	LAV-25
QUANTITY	1

CN DEPLOYMENT

RECOMMENDED SQUAD COMPOSITION: 

- This deployment is located north of the M-COM stations within the forest area.
- Your team does not spawn with any vehicles, and the US team spawns with only one LAV-25, but don't underestimate it. The LAV-25 poses a serious threat, so be ready to have your engineers knock it out with rockets and mines.
- Send a squad west of M-COM Station A. You'll want to place yourself behind the missile launchers behind the sandbags. This position will be extremely important to protect M-COM Station A.
- Send another squad south of M-COM Station A to the top of the hill with boxes surrounding the area. The boxes can be used for great cover. This area overlooks the US deployment and where the US team has to travel to make their way to the objectives. Having the vantage point here will prove useful in holding back the enemy. Also, watch for enemy flankers from the southwest trail leading north of your location.
- Northeast of M-COM Station B is another Hilltop overlooking the US deployment and the routes they need to travel to attack the objectives. When at the Hilltop you'll also be able to cover your teammates on the Hilltop south of M-COM Station A.

M-COM STATION A

- M-COM Station A is located just south of the CN deployment, in between a truck and a satellite dish with boxes covering the area.
- Use the turrets posted in this area to defend the objective.
- Defenders strategically have the high ground and have to use it by placing recon units on the hills and sniping the attackers on foot.
- When attacking, use the area to the far west to send a squad to flank and create additional pressure to the objective.
- When flanking as the attacker, drop a Radio Beacon down to keep the attack coming from multiple directions. This will keep the enemy flustered with nowhere to run and hide.

M-COM STATION B

- This objective is inside a trailer east of M-COM Station A. The entire trailer is destructible, so beware.
- Defenders can plant Claymores at the two entrances of the trailer to stop any attackers who successfully snuck through your perimeter.
- East of the M-COM station is a hill that grants players a bird's eye view of both objectives. Recon players can plant T-UGS in the grassy area while sniping attackers who approach from the east road.
- Attackers will have to strategically work with their squad to reach the top of the hill. Throw smoke grenades around the hill to evade the defenders' sights. Follow the east road while a sniper covers you from a distance.
- If following the eastern road proves to be difficult, attackers should fight from the west in a sweep attempt to arm both M-COM stations. The XM25 Airburst will prove effective as the defenders will be taking cover at the various cement blocks and sandbags at the top of the hill.

ZONE 3: MARINA

CN

CN DEPLOYMENT

NO VEHICLES

B

A

US DEPLOYMENT

LAV-25 X1

US

US DEPLOYMENT

RECOMMENDED SQUAD COMPOSITION:

- In Zone 3, the Marina, the US deployment is moved forward to the Hilltop.
- The Hilltop provides you line of sights to the roof of the buildings near the objectives. Be sure to punish the CN team if they make their way up here to snipe by picking them off first with your recon players.
- When approaching the Marina, the US team will have an LAV-25, which can approach from the land or by water. The LAV-25 should be focused on taking out the CN team's ZBD-09.
- Fill the seats of the LAV-25 to the max and head north along the shoreline. You will be able to support land units by forcing the defenders away from the shore. Being an engineer as a passenger will keep the LAV-25 alive and score you some easy points.
- The LAV-25 will greatly assist in arming the M-COM stations. Players can choose to either drive it through land or attack by water. Coordinate with your team which objective you want to arm first to decide which direction to come from. The LAV-25 can also just run rampant and distract the defenders, allowing you or a teammate to flank past enemy lines.

DEPLOYMENT AREA ASSETS

NAME	LAV-25
QUANTITY	1

CN DEPLOYMENT

RECOMMENDED SQUAD COMPOSITION:

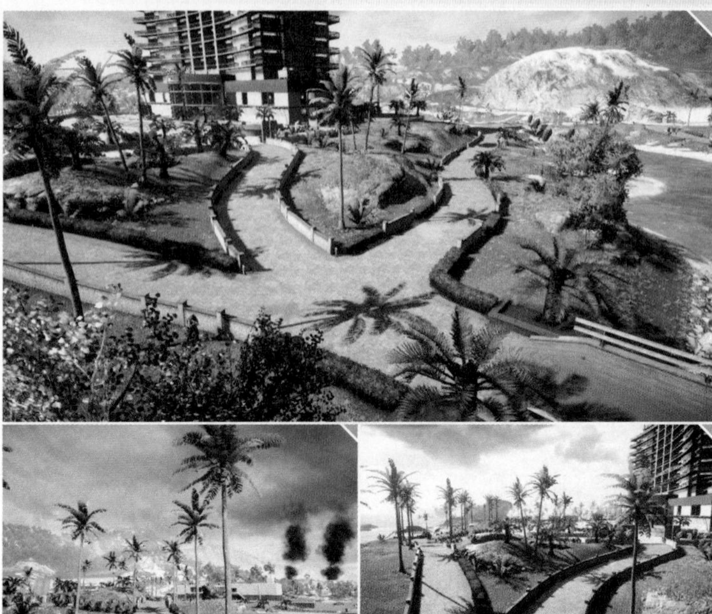

- This deployment is now pushed back northwest of the objectives. A ZBD-09 spawns here, ideal for countering the US team's LAV-25. Pack a few engineers in your squad to take out the LAV-25.
- The M-COM stations are placed in the Marina, but players are able to travel on the far east side of the map to flank around. Keep a close watch for these enemy flankers, because they could aid in arming the objective.
- Send a squad east of M-COM Station A. You'll find a cement fence surrounding the area. Use the cement fence for cover and to peek and shoot over to take down the enemies approaching from the south and southeast.
- Send a squad into the second floor of the building northeast of M-COM Station A to have a better overview of enemies approaching from the south and southeast. This area will be good for the recon class to snipe the enemies from afar.
- Send a few players to the roof of the building east of M-COM Station B. You'll have an incredible overview of incoming enemies to the east and south. Stay near the staircase as you'll need to drop down for cover if the enemy spots you.

DEPLOYMENT AREA ASSETS

NAME	ZBD-09
QUANTITY	1

M-COM STATION A

- M-COM Station A is located on the south side of the large Marina building, just around the corner from the other objective.
- There are no vehicles that spawn in for the defenders, making this a very hard zone as far as firepower. By peering out the building's windows, engineers can target approaching enemy vehicles.
- When attacking this station, shoot the building with any explosives to expose enemies inside.
- When defending, it will also be smart to move to the roof of the Marina building by using the recon class. Have teammates spot the enemies for you to make it easier to pick them off.
- The assault class will need to equip a M320 HE to blow away walls and get rid of any leftover cover the enemies could use.

M-COM STATION B

- This objective is located in the building east of M-COM Station A underneath the sky bridge connecting both buildings.
- When arming the objective, the US team will need to watch the bridge to the north as the CN team will deploy there and try to stop you.
- Just east, in front of the building, lies a stationary launcher. This will aid defenders when the US team's LAV-25 approaches.
- Defenders have access to the rooftops, and snipers can pick off attackers running down the hill. Watch out for attacking snipers from the Hilltop.
- The building is completely destructible; both teams can use this to their advantage. Defenders will have an easier time watching the objective, but less cover to hide from the US team's LAV-25.

ZONE 4: HOTEL

CN
CN DEPLOYMENT
NO VEHICLES
B
A
US
US DEPLOYMENT
LAV-25 X1

US DEPLOYMENT

RECOMMENDED SQUAD COMPOSITION:

- In this final zone, the US deployment is moved into the Marina. The team will head north as they try to arm the M-COM stations in the Hotel.
- The team once again has a LAV-25, perfect for making the push toward the Hotel.
- The CN team has a perimeter of stationary weapons guarding all angles from the sea. Have a recon player ready to use headshots against the defenders mounting these stationary weapons. This will allow your vehicles to take minimal damage when approaching the hotel.
- Have squads spread out around the Hotel, giving your team more angles of attack and a better percentage when going in for the arm.
- A squad should fill up the LAV-25 and drop squad members east of the Hotel entrance. Have one squad member be a recon player to drop a Radio Beacon, providing a spawn point that will catch the defenders off guard and allow you to flank. During this all, the LAV-25 driver and gunner will be creating mayhem for the CN team, allowing the flanking squad to swiftly enter the Hotel.

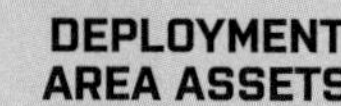

DEPLOYMENT AREA ASSETS

NAME	LAV-25
QUANTITY	1

CN DEPLOYMENT

RECOMMENDED SQUAD COMPOSITION:

- This is the last deployment and it is located northwest of the objectives. Again the CN team isn't given a vehicle while the US team has a LAV-25, so have a squad with a few engineers to take it out.
- Immediately send squads towards the Hotel to set up your defenses before the US team is able to push forward. Defending the Hotel is the key to winning in this last zone.
- Place a squad on the second level of the Hotel to have the vantage point over M-COM Station A. Also place Radio Beacons hidden throughout the second-floor rooms to keep your squad spawning in the Hotel.
- Place players around the elevators on the second floor near M-COM Station B. This position will allow you to defend both objectives.
- You'll also want a squad roaming around inside and outside level one of the Hotel. The enemies will be sneaking around, trying to make their way up to the second floor. These players will mostly likely die at some point, but have the Radio Beacon inside the Hotel to keep the defenses up.

M-COM STATION A

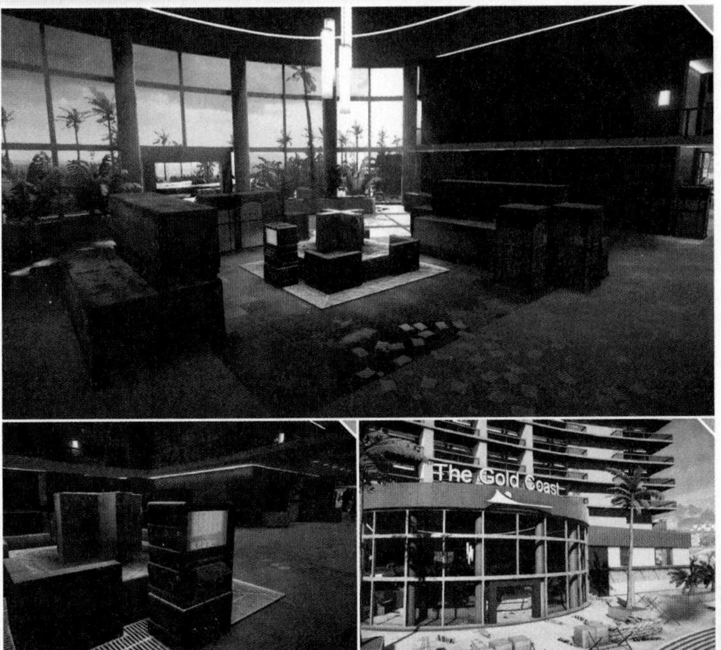

- M-COM Station A is located in the main lobby of the Hotel. This station has a few boxes and crates protecting it.
- Defenders have no vehicles at this zone, so look to just defend from the Hotel area. There are plenty of angles to shoot from, with four different ways to enter into this building.
- Attackers will use this opportunity to gain control over the surrounding perimeter with the light water vehicles and the LAV-25 and will keep the enemy pinned down towards the back of the Hotel.
- Attackers going in from the air will need to drop a smoke grenade using the M320 SMK. In this area at M-COM Station A, have support class lay down suppressive fire down while the assault class goes prone within the smoke.
- Defenders should position support troops on the second floor, overlooking the lobby. From here they can quickly respond to incursions on any part of the hotel.

M-COM STATION B

- This M-COM station is located on the second floor of the Hotel above the main entrance.
- There are only two ways to initially get to the second floor—staircases located in both wings of the Hotel. Defenders should position themselves on the second floor, watching over these two staircases.
- Outside of the Hotel are four destructible poles. Once destroyed, the glass overhangs will drop, creating new routes to the second floor of the Hotel. Attackers will use this to breach the Hotel, so defenders will need to keep a close eye on these areas.
- Attackers may want to delay before pushing into the Hotel. Both wings of the Hotel are destructible. This will force the defenders to only defend from one area of the second floor, making them an easier target.
- Defenders should have a squad outside of the Hotel, mounting the stationary weapons spread around the Hotel. These will aid in suppressing the attackers and help when destroying the enemy LAV-25.

OBLITERATION

RECOMMENDED SQUAD COMPOSITION:

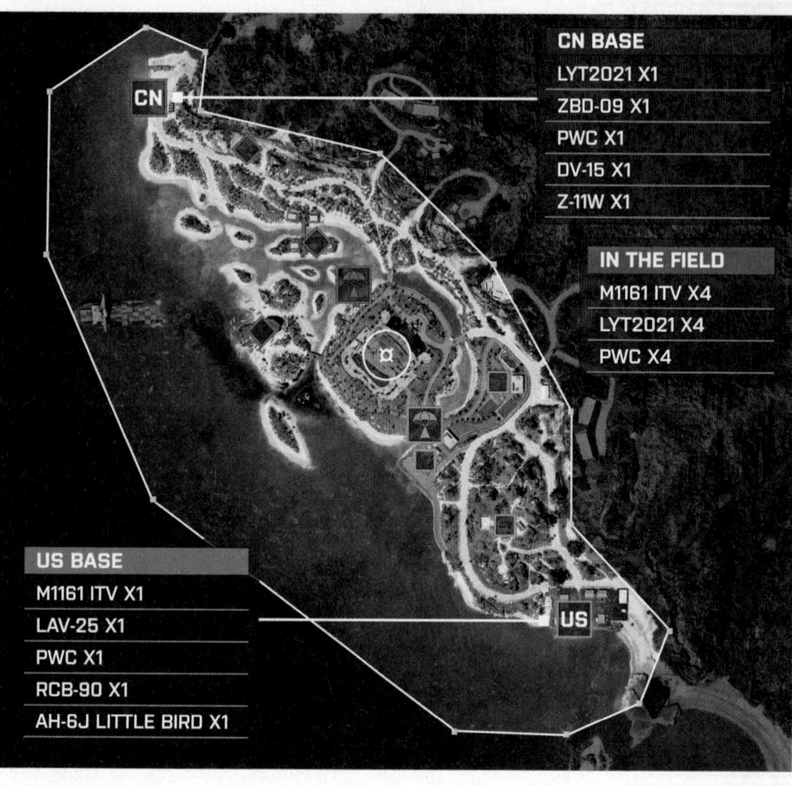

- The US team needs to guard the targets around the Bungalows and Freighter area.
- The CN team needs to set up a perimeter to guard the objectives around the Marina area.
- The Hotel is the location of the bomb. A well-organized squad can establish a defense line, allowing teammates to move in and grab the bomb.
- Both teams should utilize their IFV to transport the bomb carrier. The IFV can also push into enemy territory and clear out enemies before the bomb carrier moves in.
- Have an extra recon player on your squad. Players can snipe on top of the Hotel, picking off the opposing team's squads. Place Radio Beacons here to spawn teammates into the action.

DEFUSE

RECOMMENDED SQUAD COMPOSITION:

- This confrontation between the US and CN teams takes place at the Hotel. The US team spawns on the shore to the south and the CN team deploys in front of the main entrance of the Hotel.
- Laptop A is located in the corner of the Conference room located in the west wing. This open space makes it easier for the attacking team to arm.
- Laptop B is positioned on the second floor of the Bar located in the east wing. Defenders can crouch behind the counter in the Bar.
- The CN team should set up a perimeter on the second floor of the Hotel. This second floor provides all the defensive line of sights you will need to stop the attacking team.
- The attacking US team should destroy the pillars holding the glass overhangs around the Hotel. The defenders are on the second floor, and this allows you to breach the Hotel from the outside instead of just running in and being shot from above.

DOMINATION

RECOMMENDED SQUAD COMPOSITION:

- The three control points on this map are the Bar (A), Conference (B), and Parking Lot (C).
- A M32 MGL is north of the Bar (A) between the second floor elevators. This battle pickup helps control the Parking Lot (C) as you watch from second level.
- Always watch objectives from above once captured. This puts you in a better position than fighting from the ground.
- There are destructible pillars around the Hotel that create new entrances into the Bar (A) and Conference (B).
- Use Smoke Grenades near the Parking Lot (C) since this is the most vulnerable position when capturing.

SQUAD DEATHMATCH

RECOMMENDED SQUAD COMPOSITION:

- Prepare for constant guerilla warfare the entire match as squads battle in the desert jungle area near the Bungalows.
- Snipers enjoy getting to the top of the few hills as they are camouflaged from enemies, giving them all the time they need to snipe.
- Recon players can also snipe from the Bungalows and take cover in the various rooms in the area.
- The tall brush allows engineers to drop M15 AT mines that appear hidden to incoming enemy IFVs.
- Move with your squad throughout the entire game as you can catch a few opposing players by themselves, giving you easy points.

TEAM DEATHMATCH

RECOMMENDED SQUAD COMPOSITION:

- Prepare yourself for an explosive Team Deathmatch game mode. Players are fighting outside near the pool, inside the Hotel, and even on some rooftops.
- Defending the pool area with a recon player sniping near the southwest shore allows total control of this area. Be sure to use the cement fence for cover.
- The second floor of the Hotel is a safer location as it does not force your team to expose themselves. There are a few battle pickups in the Hotel—utilize these correctly and the enemy will never make it through the front or pool doors.
- Throw down Radio Beacons inside of the Hotel to allow your team to constantly spawn within.
- The front of the Hotel has a lot of tall brush and a cement barricade near the dead zone of the map. If your team has the lead, this area is great to hold as it forces the enemy to approach from one direction.

ALPHA SQUAD: IMPRESSIONS

MABOOZA

The horseshoe layout of this map reminds me of Wake Islet. As a result, expect plenty of long-range sniper duels between Data Central, the Islet, and the Living Quarters. Equipping a sniper rifle with a Range Finder and high-powered scope can help take all the guesswork out of lining up these epic shots.

STRONGSIDE

If you play me online you'll probably find me playing Domination on this map. The layout for this game mode is incredible. I'll be placing T-UGS and Radio Beacons hidden throughout the buildings and have my shotgun attachment for the assault class ready to pump you full of lead.

WALSHY

When playing Lancang Dam for the first time, I loved how I was able to take so many different routes around the map. I'm always a big fan of flanking and getting behind the enemy, and this map allowed me to be sneaky multiple times without the enemy knowing which way I was coming from.

FLAMESWORD

This is an awesome map that promotes both infantry and vehicle battles. The Islet is an open area that provides views for many vehicle battles, both air and water. I prefer the north side of the map, where the Power Station and the Research Facility are located. These buildings provide a lot of cover and promote close-quarter combat, which is my favorite.

ELUMNITE

Lancang Dam has a great mix of land and water combat. This allows both teams to use the Islet in the middle of the map, giving either team a clear path from their bases. The buildings at the control points are amazing locations to hold up inside using the staircases to ambush enemy infantry.

LANCANG DAM

LANCANG DAM

LEVOLUTION MOMENTS

WHAT IS IT?

A dam crumbles and falls into the playable area.

HOW IS IT TRIGGERED?

Damage the dam with missiles, rockets, and other explosive munitions. Aim for the cracked area at the top of the dam.

HOW IS GAMEPLAY IMPACTED?

The visibility is reduced throughout the map, a battle pickup is removed, electricity in the area is turned off, and the terrain is altered at the base of the dam.

OMEFI

綜合大樓

CONQUEST LARGE

RECOMMENDED SQUAD COMPOSITION:

The area that lies past the dam overflow is the site of this intense land and sea battle as the RU and CN teams fight for control of the map. The location of the RU base on the southwest side of the dam puts them potentially at an advantage with the Islet (C) as a shield for cover, while the CN base is found in the southeast direction from the dam. If the RU team manages to capture the Islet (C), they have a clear shot at opponents exiting the CN base. But this works both ways, giving the CN team the same advantage if they hold the Islet (C). For the CN team, they should capture the Living Quarters (E), the Research Facility (D), and the Islet (C). Both teams will be looking to capture and defend the Islet (C) the entire game as it grants the controlling team's commander a Gunship that can solidify a team's victory from the very beginning of the game. The RU team will look to rush the Islet (C) with the attack boat, which will provide enough cover for the team's watercraft to breach the Islet (C). The CN team will need to send all their water vehicles towards the Islet (C) as well, but send in the attack helicopter to aid in the fight. As long as your team controls three control points, the opponent's tickets will begin dropping, leading to your team's victory.

RU BASE

- The RU base is positioned at the northwest point of the map bordering a bay of water to the east. The two nearest control points are the Islet (C) and Data Central (A). Be sure to catch a ride in the vehicles that spawn at the base or you are looking at a long hike or swim to these control points.
- The RU base has a large collection of vehicles that spawn here. Immediately fill up the RHIBs east of the base and head northeast towards the Islet (C). This control point grants access to the Gunship when playing with Commander mode, so send the DV-15 that is located south of the base to provide some heavy duty cover for infantry members who are capturing the Islet (C).
- Members of a squad should take full use of the Mi-28 Havoc. This is a powerful attack helicopter that will provide great air support for the players capturing the flag on the Islet (C).
- There are two T-90As and two BTR-90s at the base. These two MBTs and IFVs will play a huge role when capturing and defending the Power Station (B) and the Research Facility (D).
- The closest control point on ground to the RU base is Data Central (A). This will be an easy capture off the start. The players in the two VDV Buggies can drop off their side passengers to capture this control point while the driver and gunner continue along the road towards the Power Station (B). The speed of these light vehicles will allow your team to start the game off with two early control points.

BASE ASSETS

NAME	VDV Buggy	BTR-90	T-90A	9K22 Tunguska-M	RHIB	DV-15	Z-11W	Mi-28 Havoc	SU-50	SU-25TM Frogfoot
QUANTITY	2	2	2	1	2	1	1	1	2	1

CN BASE

- The CN base is located on the southeastern point of the map bordering a bay of water to its west. The two nearest control points are the Islet (C) and the Living Quarters (E). Be sure to catch a ride in the vehicles that spawn at the base or you are looking at a long run or swim to these control points.
- The CN base has a variety of vehicles that spawn here. Immediately fill up the RHIBs west of the base and head northwest towards the Islet (C). This control point grants access to the Gunship when playing with Commander mode. It is also a great idea to send the DV-15, which is located south of the base, to provide some heavy duty cover for infantry members who are capturing the Islet (C).
- Two members of a squad should make full use of the Z-10W. This is a powerful attack helicopter that will provide great air support for the players capturing the flag on the Islet (C).
- There are two Type 99 MBTs and two ZBD-09s at the base. These two MBTs and IFVs will play a huge role when capturing and defending the Research Facility (D) and the Power Station (B).
- The closest control point by ground to the CN base is the Living Quarters (E). This will be an easy capture off the start. The players in the two LYT2021s can drop off their side passengers to capture this control point while the driver and gunner continue along the road towards the Research Facility (D). The speed of the LYT2021s will allow your team to start the game off with two early control points.

BASE ASSETS

NAME	LYT2021	ZBD-09	Type 99 MBT	Type 95 AA	RHIB	DV-15	Z-11W	Z-10W	J-20	Q-5 Fantan
QUANTITY	2	2	2	1	2	1	1	1	2	1

A: DATA CENTRAL

- Located on the west side of the map, this control point is surrounded by three buildings that provide great cover to hide and capture the flag. All three of these buildings' layouts are nearly identical with two entrances to the second floor and only one set of stairs to get on top of the roof.
- Once this control point is captured, a RHIB and a light vehicle spawn. It is a long run to the Power Station (B) or swim to the Islet (C). Be sure to take advantage of the vehicles that spawn here to make your next move.
- It is important to spread out in the area. Don't be content holding only one of the buildings. The team that controls the majority will have a huge advantage with cover and angles to pin down the enemies that are in the area.
- When attacking this control point, even if you have a vehicle, you are going to need to clear out the buildings to make sure the opponent does not continually spawn in the area and contest the flag.
- When defending this control point, it is crucial to have at least one engineer in your squad that can poke out and eliminate any enemy vehicles that dare to get near your squad, which has cover from three different buildings.

CONTROL POINT ASSETS

RU CONTROL	CN CONTROL
VDV Buggy (1)	LYT2021 (1)
RHIB (1)	RHIB (1)

B: POWER STATION

- This flag is located on the northwest side of the map between two buildings with a walkway that connects the buildings. There are two main routes with a clear line of sight to this control point: one from the southwest road and the other from the east road.
- Once the control point is captured, two FAV vehicles spawn in between the buildings and can be used to reach the Research Facility (D) quickly.
- Take full advantage of the walkway and its windows as it gives you protection and can be used to survey the area for incoming enemies.
- Take advantage of this open control point with IFVs and MBTs. This will make capturing and defending this control point much easier.

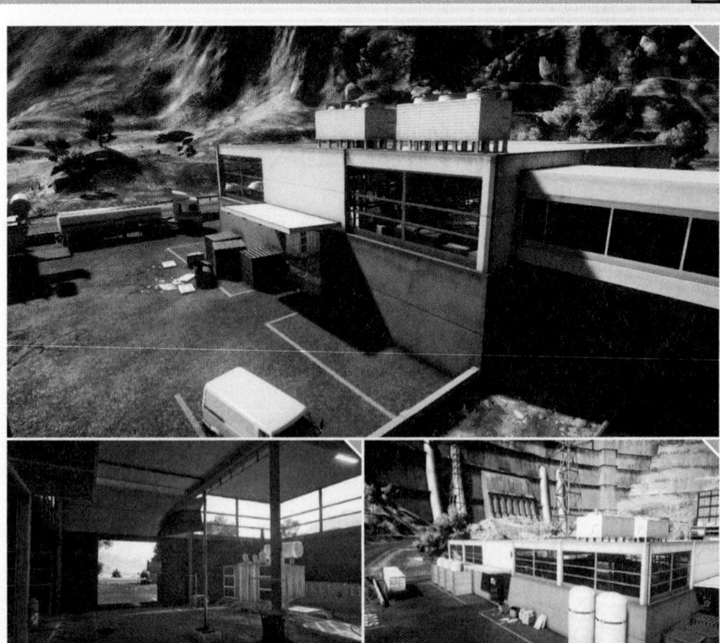

PRO TIP: ELUMNITE

VEHICLES ARE SUCH AN IMPORTANT PART OF WINNING ALMOST ANY GAMETYPE. I MAINLY USE LIGHT VEHICLES, LIKE THE VDV BUGGY AND LYT2021, TO TRAVEL FROM PLACE TO PLACE. THEY ARE HIGHLY MOBILE AND CAN OUTRUN ANY OTHER LAND VEHICLE ON THE MAP. DON'T UNDERESTIMATE THESE LIGHT VEHICLES BECAUSE OF THEIR SIZE.

CONTROL POINT ASSETS

RU CONTROL	CN CONTROL
VDV Buggy (2)	LYT2021 (2)

C: ISLET

- This control point is a remote Islet that is located in the center of the map between Data Central (A) and the Living Quarters (E). To make it over to the Islet (C), you will be required to use watercraft, helicopters, or IFVs, or go for a good old-fashioned swim.
- Once the control point is captured, two RHIBs spawn here and should be used to flank around the map. Load up your squad in one of these RHIBs and catch the enemy off guard by driving over to capture Data Central (A) or the Living Quarters (E).
- Capturing this control point will give your commander the option to deploy the Gunship. Although this flag can be difficult to control, it is well worth it since it gives your team a huge advantage.
- When attacking this control point, you must have air or water domination in order to be successful. If you prefer water combat, make sure to use the attack boat from your deployment spawn. If you prefer air combat, you have a choice of a jet or attack helicopter from your base.
- Once this control point is captured, defending it is key since the Gunship can guarantee your team a victory. When defending, be aware of incoming attackers who may submerge underwater to try and recapture this control point just offshore of the Islet (C).

PRO TIP: FLAMESWORD

I ENJOY A GOOD GAME OF MARCO-POLO TO CAPTURE OR CONTEST THIS CONTROL POINT. THE NEW DIVING FEATURE WHEN SWIMMING ALLOWS YOU TO TAKE ADVANTAGE OF THE CAPTURING DISTANCE AND ANNOY THE ENEMY AS THEY LOOK ALL OVER FOR YOU.

CONTROL POINT ASSETS

RU CONTROL	CN CONTROL
RHIB (2)	RHIB (2)

D: RESEARCH FACILITY

- This flag is located to the far north side of the map with three sturdy buildings surrounding it.
- After your team captures this point, two light vehicles spawn within this point. These can be used to transport teammates to other control points that your team needs to capture or defend.
- Look to defend this point by using all three of the buildings, which all have walkways connecting them. Place a Radio Beacon inside one of the buildings to keep a good spawn point for your squad and allow your team to constantly defend the flag.
- There are two bollard control panels located towards the southern and eastern entrance of this control point. When activating the bollards, solid poles rise up from the ground to block vehicles from reaching the inside area of the Research Facility (D).

PRO TIP: FLAMESWORD

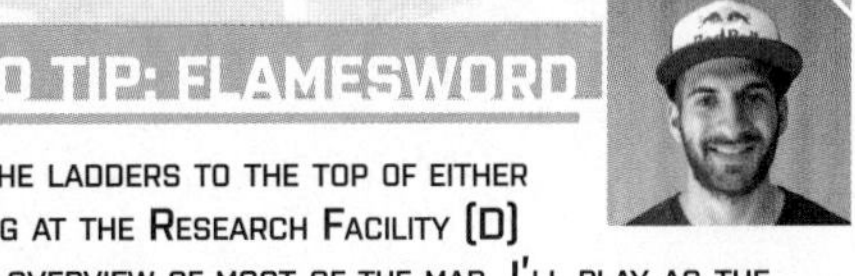

TAKE THE LADDERS TO THE TOP OF EITHER BUILDING AT THE RESEARCH FACILITY (D) FOR AN OVERVIEW OF MOST OF THE MAP. I'LL PLAY AS THE RECON CLASS TO COVER MY TEAMMATES AND SPOT ENEMIES OUT FOR THEM. ENEMY INFANTRY WILL HAVE A LONG WALK ON FOOT TO MAKE IT TO YOUR LOCATION. TAKE THEM OUT LONG RANGE BEFORE THEY HAVE A CHANCE TO ATTACK.

CONTROL POINT ASSETS

RU CONTROL	CN CONTROL
VDV Buggy (2)	LYT2021 (2)

E: LIVING QUARTERS

- Located on the east side of the map, this control point consists of two similar buildings and large, fortified concrete walls. The biggest difference in the two buildings is that the eastern building has one extra entrance to the second floor from a stairway on the back side.
- After this control point is captured, a light vehicle and RHIB both spawn. Here there are two standard choices. You can send part of your team to capture the Islet (C) while the rest of your team captures and defends the Research Facility (D). For the other option, you can completely ignore the Islet (C) and have your team completely focus on the northern part of the map by controlling both the Research Facility (D) and the Power Station (B).
- The buildings at this control point can be destroyed faster than you expect. Plan ahead by having a recon member in your squad place a Radio Beacon on the outskirts of the control point. This way if your building gets destroyed or your whole squad gets taken down, you can still spawn in the area and fight for the flag.
- When attacking this control point, attempt to take over the easternmost building first. It has one more stairwell to the second floor compared to the western building, and will allow your squad another route that you can use to surprise the enemy.
- When defending this control point, while the walls are still up these buildings provide great cover. However, these structures will crumble very quickly to explosives. Be sure to take out any threatening vehicles before it is too late and you are permanently exposed.

CONTROL POINT ASSETS

RU CONTROL	CN CONTROL
VDV Buggy (1)	LYT2021 (1)
RHIB (1)	RHIB (1)

CONQUEST SMALL

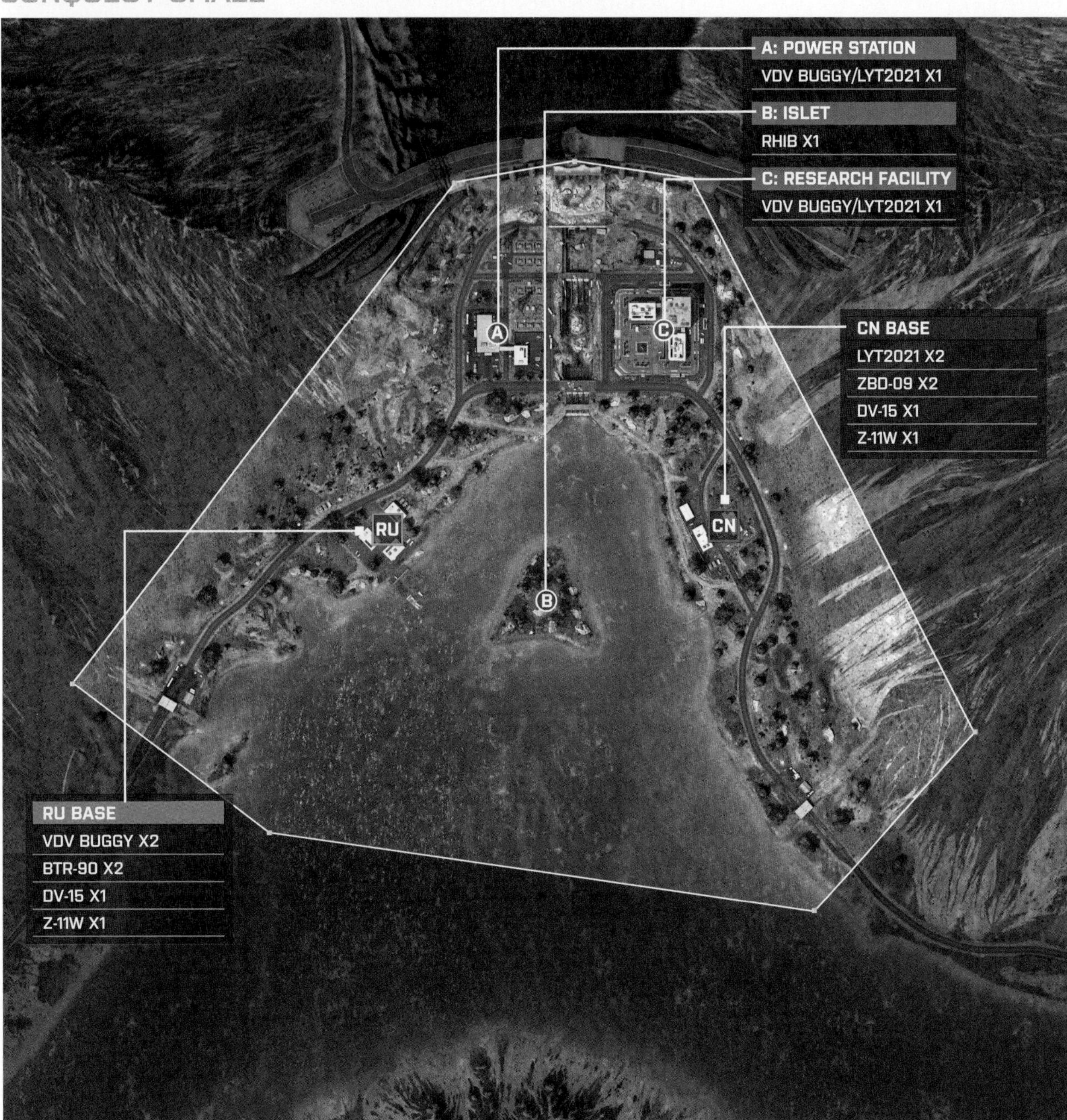

RECOMMENDED SQUAD COMPOSITION:

The area that lies past the dam overflow is the site of this intense battle between the RU and CN teams. The map will consist of three control points: the Power Station (A), the Islet (B), and the Research Facility (C). Both teams only need to capture two control points to start draining the opposing team's tickets. The RU team will be looking to take control of the Power Station (A) and the Islet (B). The CN team's best strategy will be to capture the Research Facility (C) and the Islet (B). The RU team should send every vehicle that can make it to the Islet (B) at the start of the game. The Islet (B) grants the controlling team's commander a powerful Gunship. The CN team should follow the same tactic as the RU team, as the Islet (B) will hold many battles as both teams will fight to control the Gunship. A secondary strategy that allows a team to defend against the Gunship will be to capture the Power Station (A) and the Research Facility (C). Capturing these two points, which are near each other, will provide cover from the Gunship as there are several buildings and concrete walls. This tactic is very useful as it forces the opposing team to abandon their watercrafts and fight you on equal footing.

BATTLEFIELD BOOTCAMP | INFANTRY | VEHICLES | MULTIPLAYER MAPS | CAMPAIGN | BATTLEFIELD COMPENDIUM

RU BASE

- Positioned on the west side of the map, the RU base is surrounded by a cluster of three buildings aptly called Data Central. The Islet (B) is the nearest control point, west of the base.
- The RU base has a few vehicles to choose from. The closest control point by ground to the base is the Power Station (A). The speed of the VDV Buggy will allow your team to reach and capture this control point quickly.
- A DV-15 spawns on a pier east of the base and will play a significant role when rushing towards the center to capture the Islet (B). Capturing this control point will allow the commander to have access to the Gunship.
- A squad should take control of the Z-11W and immediately head east towards the Islet (B). Members can jump out and parachute down to capture this control point. Prepare to meet head on with CN team forces.
- The two BTR-90s are able to move in water and, weighing the importance of the Gunship, these two IFVs should make their way east towards the Islet (B) to guarantee its capture.

BASE ASSETS

NAME	VDV Buggy	BTR-90	DV-15	Z-11W
QUANTITY	2	2	1	1

CN BASE

- Located on the east side of the map, the CN base consists of two similar buildings protected by large, fortified concrete walls. The Islet (B) is the nearest control point, west of the base.
- The CN base has several vehicles to choose from. The closest control point on ground to the base is the Research Facility (C). The speed of the LYT2021 will allow your team to reach and capture this control point quickly.
- A DV-15 spawns on a dock west of the base and will play a huge role when capturing the Islet (B). Capturing this control point will allow the commander to have access to the Gunship.
- Take control of the Z-11W and immediately head west towards the Islet (B). Members can jump out and parachute down to capture this control point. Prepare to meet head on with the RU team's scout helicopter.
- The two IFVs are able to move in water and, weighing the importance of the Gunship, the two IFVs should make their way west towards the Islet (B) to guarantee its capture.

BASE ASSETS

NAME	LYT2021	ZBD-09	DV-15	Z-11W
QUANTITY	2	2	1	1

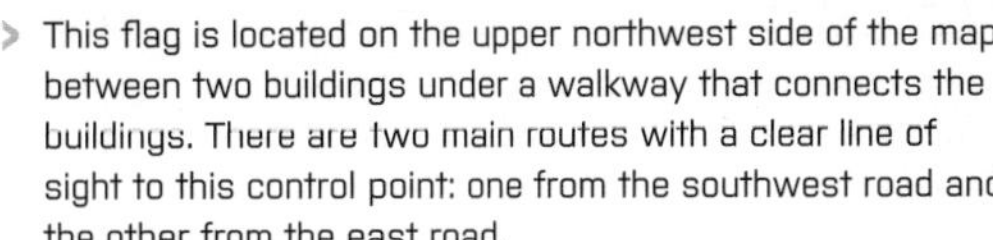

A: POWER STATION

- This flag is located on the upper northwest side of the map between two buildings under a walkway that connects the buildings. There are two main routes with a clear line of sight to this control point: one from the southwest road and the other from the east road.
- Once the control point is captured, one light vehicle spawns in between the buildings and can be used to reach the next nearest control point quickly. Use the back road to the north to make sure you avoid any enemy IFVs that are likely to be headed your way.
- Take full advantage of the walkway and its windows as it gives you protection and can be used to oversee the area for incoming enemies. Always be sure to spot the enemies to let your squad know where they are and to rack up some extra points.
- When using IFVs or light vehicles at this point be careful to not push the vehicle inside. That way, enemy players with C4 can't sneak up on you!
- The recon class should use the walkway connecting both buildings to position themselves so that they have access to the rooftop for a better vantage point. Be sure to throw down a Motion Sensor to reveal any enemies that may have slipped by.

CONTROL POINT ASSETS

RU CONTROL	CN CONTROL
VDV Buggy (1)	LYT2021 (1)

B: ISLET

- This control point is a remote Islet that is positioned in the center of the map between the RU base and CN base. To make it over to this Islet (B), you will be required to use watercraft, helicopters, or IFVs, or go for a good old-fashioned swim.
- Upon capture of this control point, one RHIB spawns here and will allow your squad to travel back to the mainland where you can take control of the Power Station (A) or the Research Facility (C).
- Capturing this control point will give your commander the option to deploy the Gunship. This flag is out of the way, so make sure that once you do capture it, you use the Gunship to help take control of the Power Station (A) or the Research Facility (C). You can't win by only holding this single control point.
- When attacking this control point, using the attack boat is the key to victory. The second best option is to take over one of your IFVs to capture the control point and then leave right after. Always keep in mind that after you capture this control point, you want to leave if the enemy has control of both the Power Station (A) and the Research Facility (C).
- When defending this control point, your biggest threat will be the enemy's attack boat. Be sure to have engineers or your own attack boat to take it down. Lastly, make sure you have a mobile squad ready to leave if you find out your team is getting overwhelmed at the Power Station (A) or the Research Facility (C). You do not want your entire team stuck at this control point.

CONTROL POINT ASSETS

RU CONTROL	CN CONTROL
RHIB (1)	RHIB (1)

C: RESEARCH FACILITY

- This flag is located to the far north of the map with three sturdy buildings surrounding it. There are multiple spots inside the building that promote sneaky gameplay to contest or capture the control point.
- Once the control point is captured, one light vehicle spawns within this control point. This can be used to quickly rush teammates towards the Power Station (A). You should take the back road to the north so the enemy won't know you are behind them until it is too late.
- Look to defend this point by using all three of the buildings, which all have walkways connecting them. Place a Radio Beacon inside one of the buildings to keep a good spawn point for your squad, ensuring control of the Research Facility (C).
- Inside the buildings on the upper level you are able to look out the windows and oversee all oncoming enemy infantry. This is a great vantage point for the recon class to take advantage of, as the long distance allows you to sit back and snipe.
- There are two interactive control panels that raise bollards located towards the southern and eastern entrance of the control point. When activating the bollards, solid poles rise up from the ground to block vehicles from reaching the inside area of the Research Facility (C).

CONTROL POINT ASSETS

RU CONTROL	CN CONTROL
VDV Buggy (1)	LYT2021 (1)

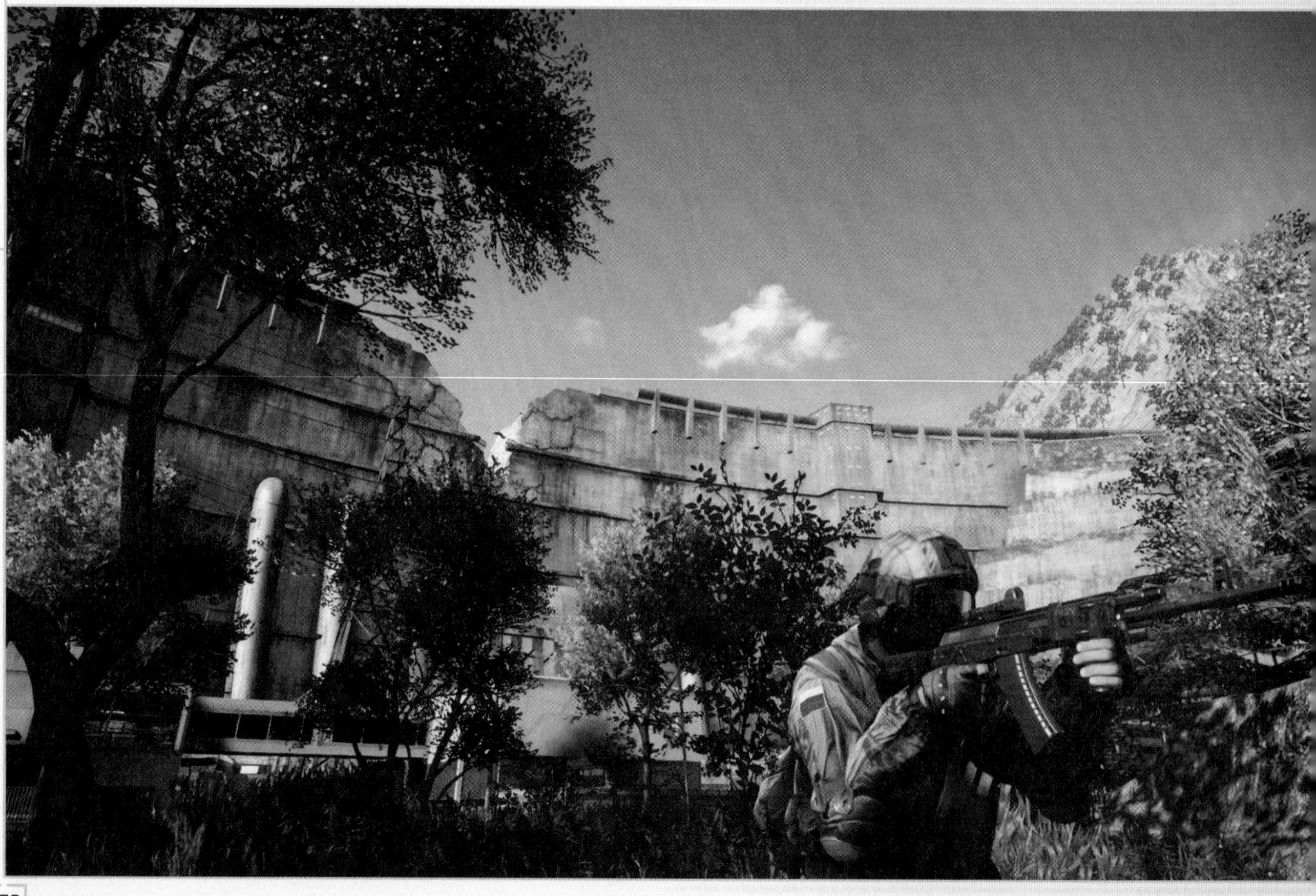

RUSH

ZONE 1

RU DEPLOYMENT
SPM-3 X2
BTR-90 X1
T-90A X1
Z-11W X1
KA-60 KASATKA X1
CN DEPLOYMENT
ZBD-09 X1
TYPE 99 MBT X1

ZONE 2

RU DEPLOYMENT
SPM-3 X2
BTR-90 X1
T-90A X1
Z-11W X1
KA-60 KASATKA X1
CN DEPLOYMENT
ZBD-09 X1
TYPE 99 MBT X1

ZONE 3

RU DEPLOYMENT
SPM-3 X2
BTR-90 X1
T-90A X1
Z-11W X1
KA-60 KASATKA X1
CN DEPLOYMENT
ZBD-09 X1
TYPE 99 MBT X1

In this Rush battle, the RU team advances through the main road of the map in a drive to destroy six M-COM stations scattered across three different zones. The attackers start in the west and eventually make it up the road towards the Data Central area. The RU team has a watercraft and two helicopters that will allow them to breach the first zone from multiple directions. The second zone will require the attackers to follow the road uphill, where defenders will be waiting with two vehicles and a handful of stationary weapons. The final zone will force the attackers to abandon their vehicles as the defending team. The CN team can activate a set of bollards around the Research Facility, stopping any attacking vehicle from breaching. The CN team has access to a Type 99 MBT throughout the duration of the game; this will assist in defending against the attacking team's infantry and vehicles. The defenders should always have an engineer on site to score some easy points by repairing the Type 99 MBT.

ZONE 1: DATA CENTRAL

CN
B
A
RU

CN DEPLOYMENT
ZBD-09 X1
TYPE 99 MBT X1

RU DEPLOYMENT
SPM-3 X2
BTR-90 X1
T-90A X1
Z-11W X1
KA-60 KASATKA X1

RU DEPLOYMENT

RECOMMENDED SQUAD COMPOSITION:

- The RU team's deployment is located to the southwest of the two M-COM stations where you have a long distance to travel before you arrive at your destination. Load up your vehicles before heading out so you don't leave a teammate behind.
- The RU deployment area spawns with every option for travel. One option is a long straight road where you can take your T-90A or SPM-3. A second option is to travel by sea with your RHIB. Your third option is to travel by air with the KA-60 Kasatka.
- Immediately send out your transport helicopter and SPM-3 to spot where the enemies are and what they are doing. These vehicles are the fastest and most expendable when compared to your valuable T-90A and KA-60 Kasatka.
- When pushing up the road, take out any enemies manning the HJ-8 Launcher, which is located near the end of the road and directly west of M-COM Station B. You'll need to have your vehicles at full health for the upcoming battles with the enemy's engineers, ZBD-09, and Type 99 MBT.
- As a squad, absolutely make sure to not have every member inside the same vehicle. The last thing you want to do is allow the enemy to kill your entire squad and force you to spawn at the RU deployment area while you leave the rest of your team outnumbered on the front line.

DEPLOYMENT AREA ASSETS

NAME	SPM-3	BTR-90	T-90A	KA-60 Kasatka	Z-11W
QUANTITY	2	1	1	1	1

CN DEPLOYMENT

RECOMMENDED SQUAD COMPOSITION:

- The CN deployment area is located between three Data Central buildings. Between these buildings is a courtyard that holds M-COM Station B.
- This deployment area is located near both M-COM stations, which allows you to set up a defensive perimeter before the RU team closes in.
- There are a couple of vehicles and stationary guns around the base. The rooftop of the building to the north holds a .50Cal. The player manning this can provide heavy support fire while spotting approaching attackers, and other squad members can make use of the HJ-8 Launcher on the ground to help against incoming vehicles.
- The vehicles at hand are the Type 99 MBT and ZBD-09—both vehicles lie north of the base. Send them along the road to encounter incoming attacks, and be sure to use the giant rocks for cover. Have engineers close by to repair these vehicles when needed.
- Have extra engineers in your squad. The attacking team has a total of six vehicles at their disposal. Engineers will be needed in order to take these out. Having players spread throughout the buildings and the pier to the west allows your team to have better angles on the RU team's attacking vehicles.

DEPLOYMENT AREA ASSETS

NAME	ZBD-09	Type 99 MBT
QUANTITY	1	1

M-COM STATION A

- This M-COM station is located southeast of M-COM Station B, and surrounded by many crates that can be used for cover. There is even a large crate to hide in, which is the one closest to M-COM Station A.
- When defending M-COM Station A, have your team take a few engineers to protect against enemy vehicles that may come from the air and water.
- When attacking M-COM Station A, your team will want to split squads up based on what type of vehicles you are using. Quickly reach M-COM Station A by using the scout helicopters and transport helicopters to drop off teammates in the area.
- Attackers should also invade this area by using watercraft vehicles to aid your teammates being dropped off by the transport helicopters.
- There is a building closest to M-COM Station A that your team is going to have to make use of. You can access this building by using a flight of stairs just outside, which will lead you to the inside and give you a great vantage point of the lake where the enemy most likely is going to attack from.

M-COM STATION B

- This M-COM station is located in between the three buildings that comprise Data Central. This spot is also the spawn point of the defending CN team.
- When defending, use the three buildings to watch over the M-COM station. On the upper level of these buildings you will have an overview of the entire area, but beware—these buildings can be destroyed fairly easily.
- When attacking this M-COM station, take over the two buildings to the south. This way you can take cover, get good spawns, and clear out any enemies that are a threat to stop you from arming.
- When defending this M-COM station, the most important location to hold is the building to the southwest. This spot allows you to keep a bird's eye view on the whole area and give you plenty of time to relocate depending on where the enemy is pushing.

PRO TIP: WALSHY

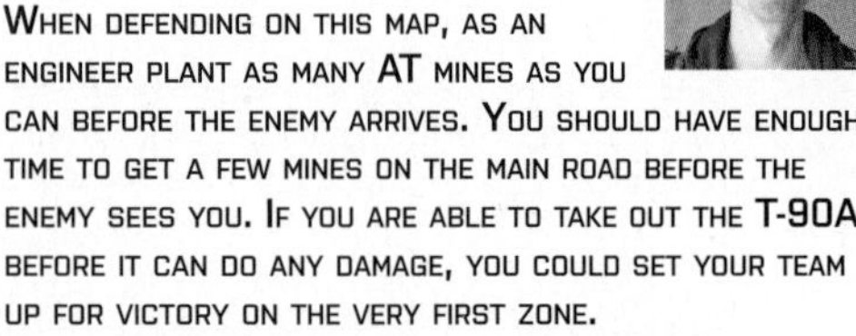

WHEN DEFENDING ON THIS MAP, AS AN ENGINEER PLANT AS MANY AT MINES AS YOU CAN BEFORE THE ENEMY ARRIVES. YOU SHOULD HAVE ENOUGH TIME TO GET A FEW MINES ON THE MAIN ROAD BEFORE THE ENEMY SEES YOU. IF YOU ARE ABLE TO TAKE OUT THE T-90A BEFORE IT CAN DO ANY DAMAGE, YOU COULD SET YOUR TEAM UP FOR VICTORY ON THE VERY FIRST ZONE.

ZONE 2: POWER STATION

CN

B

A

RU

CN DEPLOYMENT
ZBD-09 X1
TYPE 99 MBT X1

RU DEPLOYMENT
SPM-3 X2
BTR-90 X1
T-90A X1
Z-11W X1
KA-60 KASATKA X1

RU DEPLOYMENT

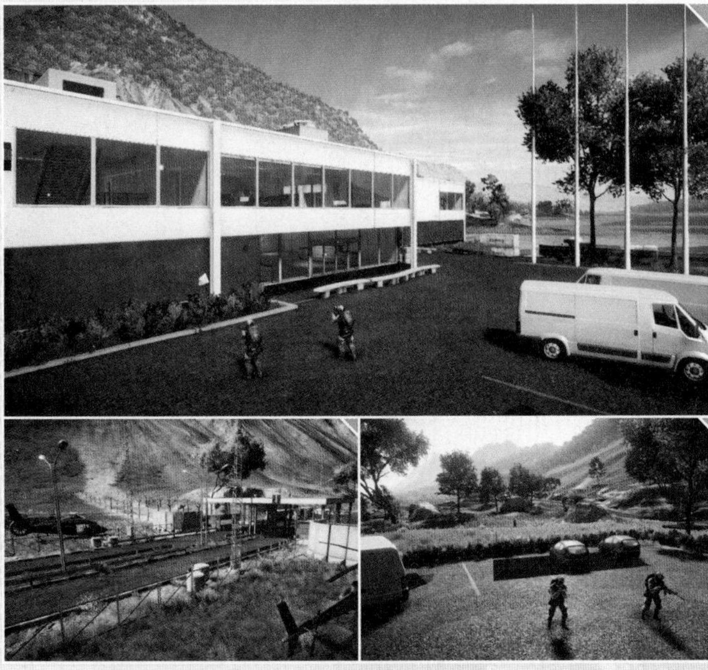

RECOMMENDED SQUAD COMPOSITION:

- The RU team's deployment area is located to the southwest of the M-COM stations, connected by a short road that eventually comes to a fork where you can go north to flank around the M-COM stations or attack them from the road that heads east.
- The RU base spawns with two options for travel. The first option is the forked road where you can take your T-90A or SPM-3. The second option is to travel by air with the KA-60 Kasatka.
- Send your SPM-3 up the north fork in the road to flank behind the Power Station and give your squad good spawns to take over the building. This also distracts the enemy team by dividing their attention into two areas instead of one.
- Use the KA-60 Kasatka to drop off your teammates on the roof above M-COM Station A. This will allow you to attack from above where the defending CN team cannot get to. Place a Radio Beacon on top of the roof to give your squad a closer spawn point for the rest of this zone.
- After taking out the enemy's only ZBD-09 and Type 99 MBT, switch your engineers to assault and support to prepare for all the close-range combat in the Power Station area.

DEPLOYMENT AREA ASSETS

NAME	SPM-3	BTR-90	T-90A	KA-60 Kasatka	Z-11W
QUANTITY	2	1	1	1	1

CN DEPLOYMENT

RECOMMENDED SQUAD COMPOSITION:

- After losing the battle in Zone 1, the CN team is pushed back. The deployment area is now located south, in front of the Power Station. The Power Station is surrounded by explosive gasoline barrels and semi trucks.
- North of the base, the CN team will find a Type 99 MBT and a ZBD-09. Being at the top of the road, the CN team will have an advantage as they wait for the RU team to push into your traps.
- In front of the Power Station lies three HJ-8 Launchers that can be used to assist the team in destroying the enemy's incoming vehicles.
- Send a squad to the building south of M-COM Station B. The roof to this building is accessible and a great spot to snipe from. This roof also provides engineers an angle to assist in destroying both ground and air vehicles.
- There is one main road that all approaching ground vehicles will have to take. Send a squad composed of engineers and support players to plant C4 and M15 AT mines all around the roads and hills to catch the attackers by surprise. Destroying the attacking vehicles early on will allow other defending squads to move south to prevent the attackers from closing in.

DEPLOYMENT AREA ASSETS

NAME	ZBD-09	Type 99 MBT
QUANTITY	1	1

M-COM STATION A

- M-COM Station A is located inside the west building of the Power Station on the second level, surrounded by wire barrels and tool crates.
- Right next to M-COM Station A is a sky bridge connecting to the building east of this station. As a defender, use the recon class and place a Radio Beacon so you can spawn your team there, allowing control of the eastern building. This will ensure that the Radio Beacon is protected and the building is defended.
- When defending M-COM Station A, have either a recon or support class drop some Claymores around the first level of the building to take out any attackers that may be infiltrating from the ground. Be sure to booby trap the stairs as well.
- Attackers can be dropped off via transport helicopters to gain roof access for the eastern building. Assault classes equipped with the Defibrillator will be useful in reviving your teammates and providing constant close-quarter combat.
- The roof of M-COM Station A provides a great overview of the map. To gain access, send a squad with a recon player or two into the opposite building, which has a staircase that allows you to position yourself on either roof. Recon players can spot and snipe incoming attackers.

M-COM STATION B

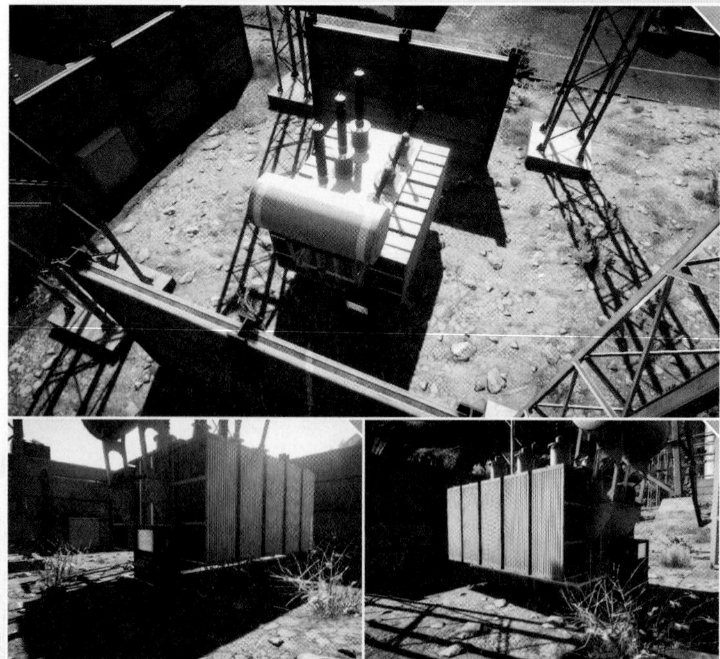

- M-COM Station B is nestled in between some concrete barriers on the northeast side of the Power Station.
- When attacking this M-COM station, if the fortified concrete walls haven't been destroyed, prepare for close-range combat around this objective.
- On the roof of the building directly south of the M-COM station, you have a perfect vantage point to stop the enemy attempting to arm this objective.
- When defending, destroy the wall to the south of the objective. This will open up the area more and make any attackers trying to arm M-COM Station B more vulnerable.
- The enemy can't push in from the east or north due to being out of bounds. So, when defending, push out to the west or south of the M-COM station. By pushing out to one of these sides, you cut the enemy's options of attack in half.

ZONE 3: RESEARCH FACILITY

RU
CN
A
B

RU DEPLOYMENT

- SPM-3 X2
- BTR-90 X1
- T-90A X1
- Z-11W X1
- KA-60 KASATKA X1

CN DEPLOYMENT

- ZBD-09 X1
- TYPE 99 MBT X1

RU DEPLOYMENT

RECOMMENDED SQUAD COMPOSITION: 

> The RU team's deployment area is located directly west of M-COM Station B with a short route to travel for your team to win the game.

> From the RU base, you have three routes by ground. Two of these routes are the roads to the north and south where you can take the T-90A, SPM-3, or BTR-90. Your other route is by foot through the outflow of the dam. Aside from the ground routes, you can fly your choice of Z-11W or KA-60 Kasatka.

> Both of these M-COM stations are located inside the buildings. You can drive over to the objectives, but you will eventually have to exit the vehicles and finish the job by hand.

> Use the KA-60 Kasatka to drop off your teammates on the roofs above both of the M-COM stations. Unlike the previous zone, the enemy can get on top of both of these rooftops, so prepare to fight for control of these areas.

> When attacking these objectives, beware of enemy T-UGS in the buildings. These buildings promote close-quarter combat. Equip your shotgun and expect enemies around every corner.

DEPLOYMENT AREA ASSETS

NAME	SPM-3	BTR-90	T-90A	KA-60 Kasatka	Z-11W
QUANTITY	2	1	1	1	1

CN DEPLOYMENT

RECOMMENDED SQUAD COMPOSITION:

- Being pushed back farther, the CN base is now located west of the Research Facility. The CN team has one last chance to stop the RU team.
- Around the Research Facility are interactive control panels that will raise a line of bollards. These bollards will stop ground vehicles from penetrating the heart of the Research Facility.
- Just north of the Research Facility, the CN team once again has a Type 99 MBT and ZBD-09 at their disposal. Be sure to always check if these vehicles are up, as they will help tremendously against the RU team's vehicles.
- The building that holds M-COM Station B has a ladder that you can climb to the top of the building. Send a squad with one or two recon players here. They will have a great overview of the map and will be able to watch M-COM Station B.
- Both M-COM stations are inside the Research Facility buildings. These buildings have many close corners, so take advantage of the M18 Claymores that both recon and support classes have. Pack your Shorty 12G to dominate these close-quarter fights.

DEPLOYMENT AREA ASSETS

NAME	ZBD-09	Type 99 MBT
QUANTITY	1	1

M-COM STATION A

- M-COM Station A is located in the northwest building in the Research Facility on the second floor in a Laboratory room.
- On the west side of the M-COM station there is a balcony. When defending, you should use the engineer class equipped with either the MBT LAW or MK153 SMAW to take out any land vehicles.
- Within this close-quarter area, use support and assault classes to defend M-COM Station A. Having an XM25 Airburst watching the staircase closest to M-COM Station A will be very effective in holding off enemy attacks. On top of watching the staircase, place T-UGS towards the top to spot enemies on your radar.
- When attacking, be sure to clear the roof of M-COM Station A. Placing a Radio Beacon or keeping a squad member alive will allow other squad members to continuously spawn, allowing for more attempts at the objective.
- When playing as the RU team, having Smoke Grenades and Flashbangs will help in getting through the defenders hidings in the stairwells.

M-COM STATION B

- When defending, use the interactive bollards to prevent the attackers from driving their vehicles next to the building. Watch for the enemy to exit a vehicle and try to deactivate the bollards to get an easy kill.
- This objective is located at the top floor of the Research Facility amongst all the medical equipment.
- When attacking this objective, take over the roof first. This way you can spawn your squad above and can control the building with the high ground advantage.
- When defending, hold the rooftop above this objective. Not only does this allow you pick off attackers running in the open outside of the building, but it also lets you surprise the enemies from above when they are inside the building.
- Besides dropping in from the roof, there are only three ways to enter the top floor of this building where the objective is located. When defending, place M18 Claymores around the narrow stairwells that lead up to the objective to pick up easy kills or to alert you when an enemy is approaching.

OBLITERATION

RECOMMENDED SQUAD COMPOSITION:

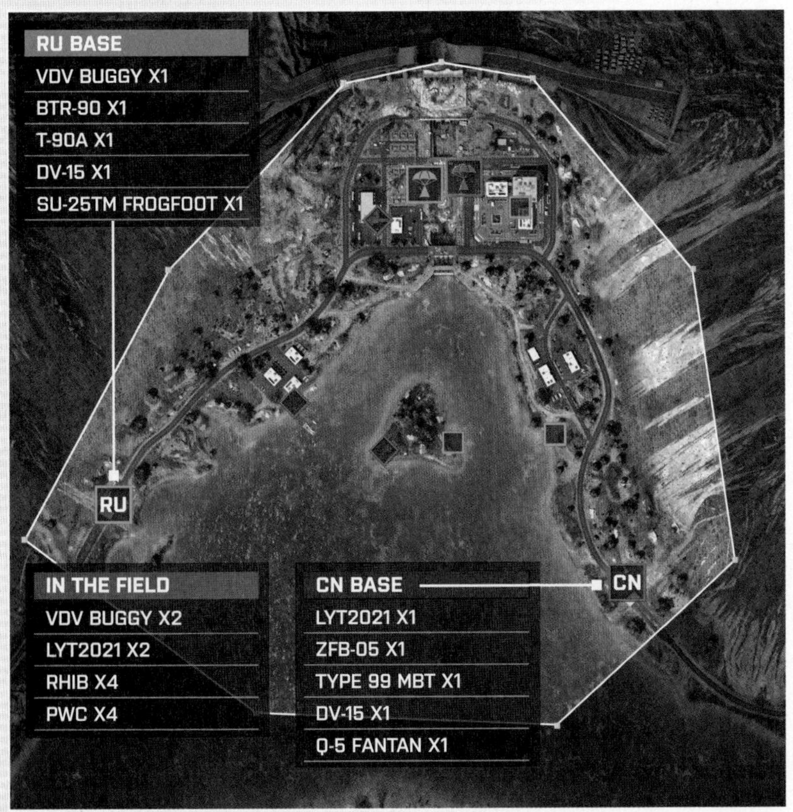

- Both teams have targets located on the Islet and on the docks nearby.
- The last CN target is found in the Research Facility and, to the west, players can find the RU team's last target.
- The bomb can be found near the main bridge above the dam overflow. Prepare for firefights across this bridge; have a recon player snipe from a distance, stopping the other team from grabbing the bomb.
- The attack boats aid both teams in defending their objectives on the Islet. Have an engineer on board to easily repair the attack boat.
- Use transport helicopters to drop off teammates behind enemy lines while the bomb carrier pushes towards a target. This leaves an opening for the bomb carrier as the opposing team has to defend two different attack waves.

DEFUSE

RECOMMENDED SQUAD COMPOSITION:

- Both teams battle throughout the Research Facility of this map. The defending CN team spawns behind the northeast building and the attacking RU team spawns southwest in front of Research Facility's main staircase.
- Laptop A is located in the second floor of the Laboratory. Attackers can flank the north side of this building and throw Smoke Grenades through the windows to the second floor, decreasing the enemy's ability to see.
- Laptop B is found in the back surveillance room of the Lobby. These walls are indestructible, so defenders can set up Claymores near the three entrances of the room.
- When attacking, be sure to avoid running through the parking lot off the start as you can easily be picked off. Instead have two players run inside of the southeastern building and take the sky bridge into the Lobby; be sure to look across where defenders might be waiting. The rest of the squad should storm through the side entrances of the Lobby to enter the surveillance room the quickest.
- When defending the Laboratory, be sure to watch the ladder on the west side—you do not want the defenders to reach the roof of the building or else they can pick you off. Stay near the sky bridge that connects to the Lobby to also watch the other objective.

DOMINATION

RECOMMENDED SQUAD COMPOSITION:

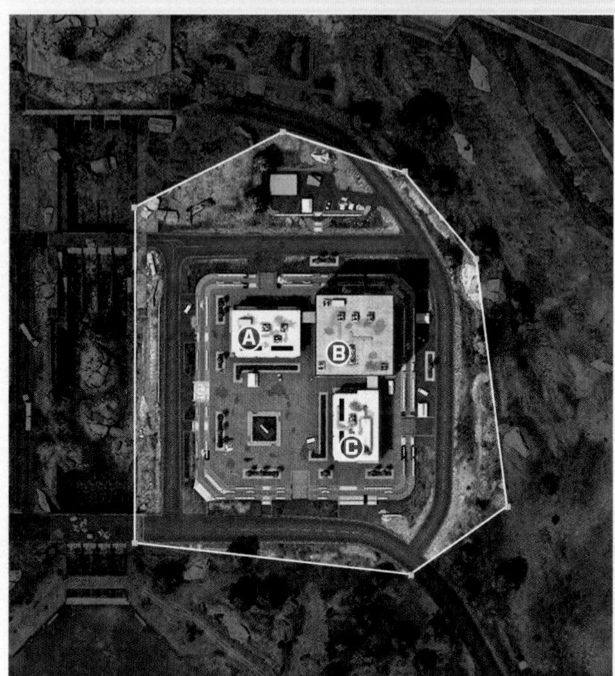

- Get the high ground and patrol the stairwells for easy, close-range kills with shotguns or M18 Claymores. This is extremely effective when you have T-UGS strategically placed within the buildings.
- Domination consists of three control points: Laboratory (A), Lobby (B), and Research (C). In order to drain the opponent's tickets you need to capture two control points.
- There are two approaches. Either cover the Laboratory (A) and Lobby (B), or cover Research (C) and Lobby (B). When controlling these, hold the sky bridges at the top. These provide a great view of the Lobby (B) and allow you to have the upper hand on incoming attackers.
- The Laboratory (A) and Research (C) buildings have ladders, allowing you to access their rooftops, which is ideal for defending both locations. When up top, there are glass windows that let you watch the flags from above. Have someone up here to watch the flag and keep control of this high ground to give your squad good spawns.
- If the enemy has two control points and one of these is the Lobby (B), this is a perfect opportunity to sneak around to either the Laboratory (A) or Research (C), since the enemy will expect your squad to attack the closest objective.

SQUAD DEATHMATCH

RECOMMENDED SQUAD COMPOSITION:

- The map in Squad Deathmatch is restricted to the Laboratory, Lobby, and Research rooms of the Research Facility.
- Controlling the roof of the Laboratory or the Research room gives your team amazing fire angles to shoot the enemies on the ground.
- If your team controls the IFV, be sure to roam the edges of the Research Facility. Getting too close lets an enemy run up and throw C4 on you. Avoid driving between buildings.
- Having an engineer and support class assists in destroying the IFV if one of the opposing squads takes control.
- Control the sky bridges to move from either building to the Lobby where you can shoot enemies on the floor.

TEAM DEATHMATCH

RECOMMENDED SQUAD COMPOSITION:

- This is an intense Team Deathmatch consisting of close- and medium-range gunfights around the Research Facility. The parking lot is a for sure no fly zone—do not risk running through this open area.
- The Laboratory and Research buildings both have ladders that lead to the roof. This is a safe haven for support players as they can lay suppressive fire throughout the game from above.
- The rubble from the dam provides great cover if you find yourself fighting around the northwestern part of the map. If guerilla warfare is your forte, draw enemies to this location.
- Control the sky bridges to move from either building to the Lobby where you can shoot enemies on the floor.
- Take advantage of the tinted windows to pick off enemies running from building to building or just out in the open area.

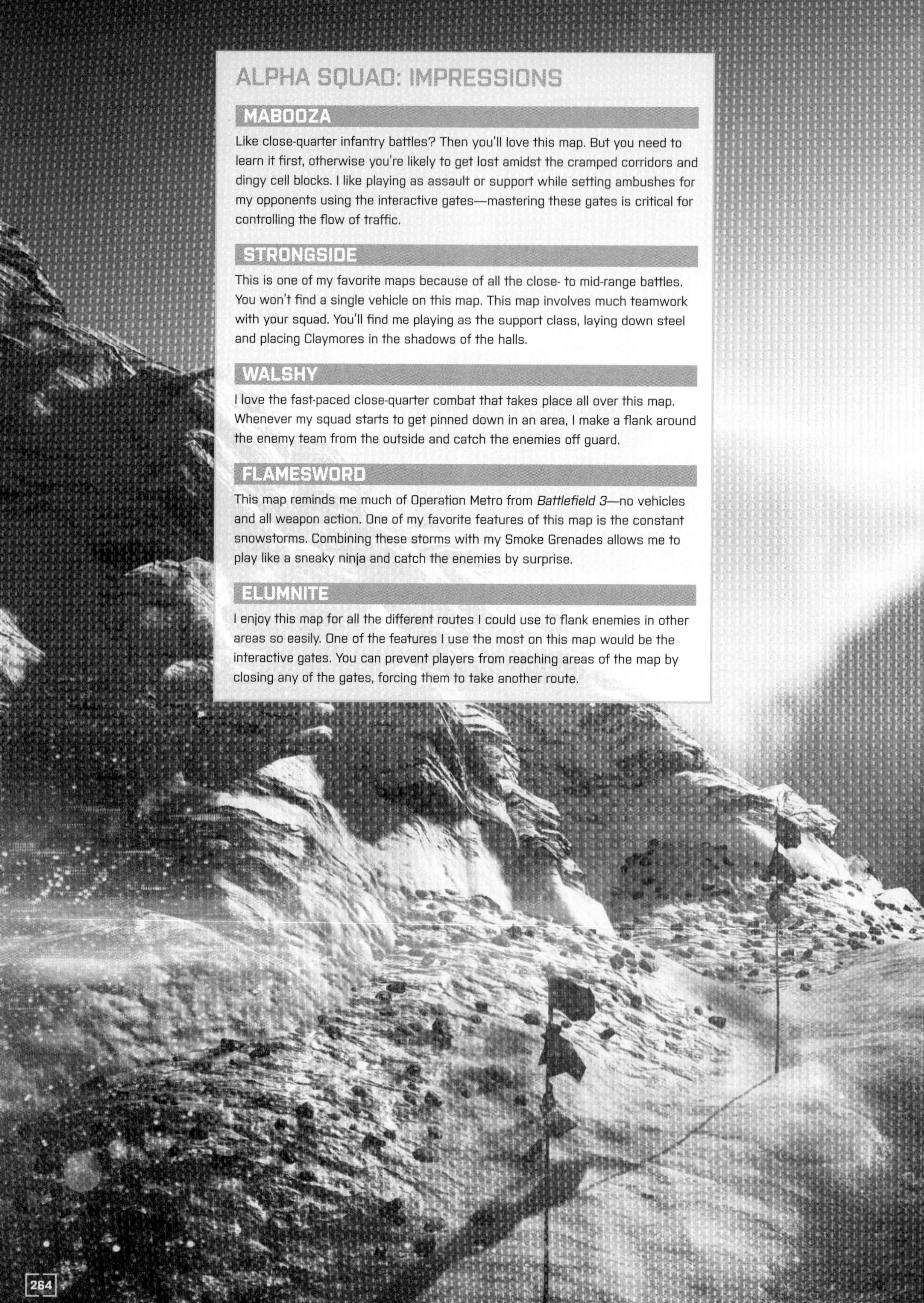

ALPHA SQUAD: IMPRESSIONS

MABOOZA

Like close-quarter infantry battles? Then you'll love this map. But you need to learn it first, otherwise you're likely to get lost amidst the cramped corridors and dingy cell blocks. I like playing as assault or support while setting ambushes for my opponents using the interactive gates—mastering these gates is critical for controlling the flow of traffic.

STRONGSIDE

This is one of my favorite maps because of all the close- to mid-range battles. You won't find a single vehicle on this map. This map involves much teamwork with your squad. You'll find me playing as the support class, laying down steel and placing Claymores in the shadows of the halls.

WALSHY

I love the fast-paced close-quarter combat that takes place all over this map. Whenever my squad starts to get pinned down in an area, I make a flank around the enemy team from the outside and catch the enemies off guard.

FLAMESWORD

This map reminds me much of Operation Metro from *Battlefield 3*—no vehicles and all weapon action. One of my favorite features of this map is the constant snowstorms. Combining these storms with my Smoke Grenades allows me to play like a sneaky ninja and catch the enemies by surprise.

ELUMNITE

I enjoy this map for all the different routes I could use to flank enemies in other areas so easily. One of the features I use the most on this map would be the interactive gates. You can prevent players from reaching areas of the map by closing any of the gates, forcing them to take another route.

OPERATION LOCKER

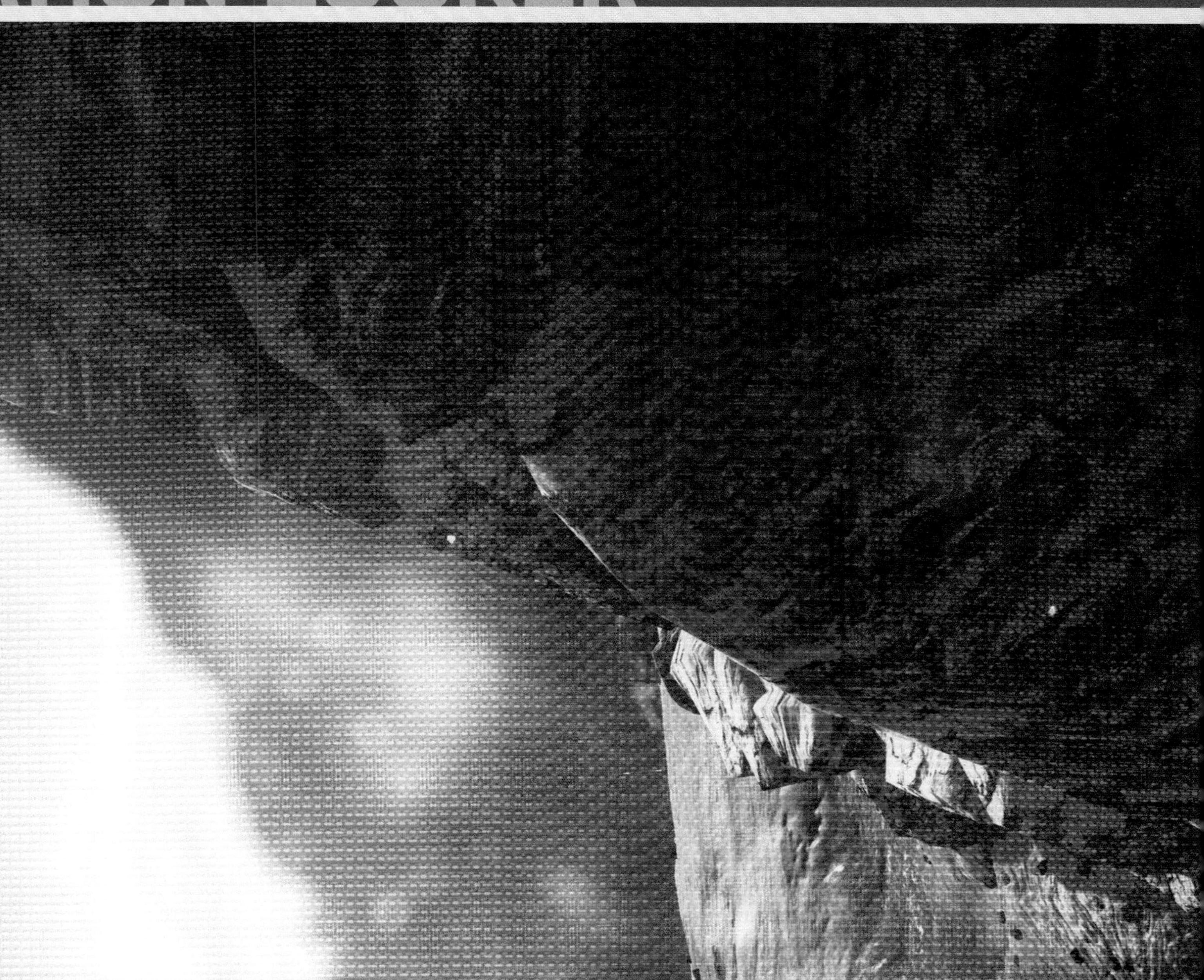

OPERATION LOCKER

LEVOLUTION MOMENTS

WHAT IS IT?

Shifting snow drifts every so often on the outside of the prison. Prison security systems allow players to lock prison gates from one entrance of the hallway. The guard tower in Panopticon crumbles.

HOW IS IT TRIGGERED?

The Panopticon tower collapses when hit with explosive weapons. To lock the prison gates, press the interaction key/button when near a gate. The blinding snowstorm outside the prison walls intensifies and calms at regular intervals.

HOW IS GAMEPLAY IMPACTED?

The prison gates block off routes in the map, forcing players to take other routes. The Panopticon guard tower has weaponry that is disabled after it's destroyed and the layout of Panopticon also changes when guard tower falls. The shifting snow at the entrances and exits of the prison make it tough to see for players in and out of the prison.

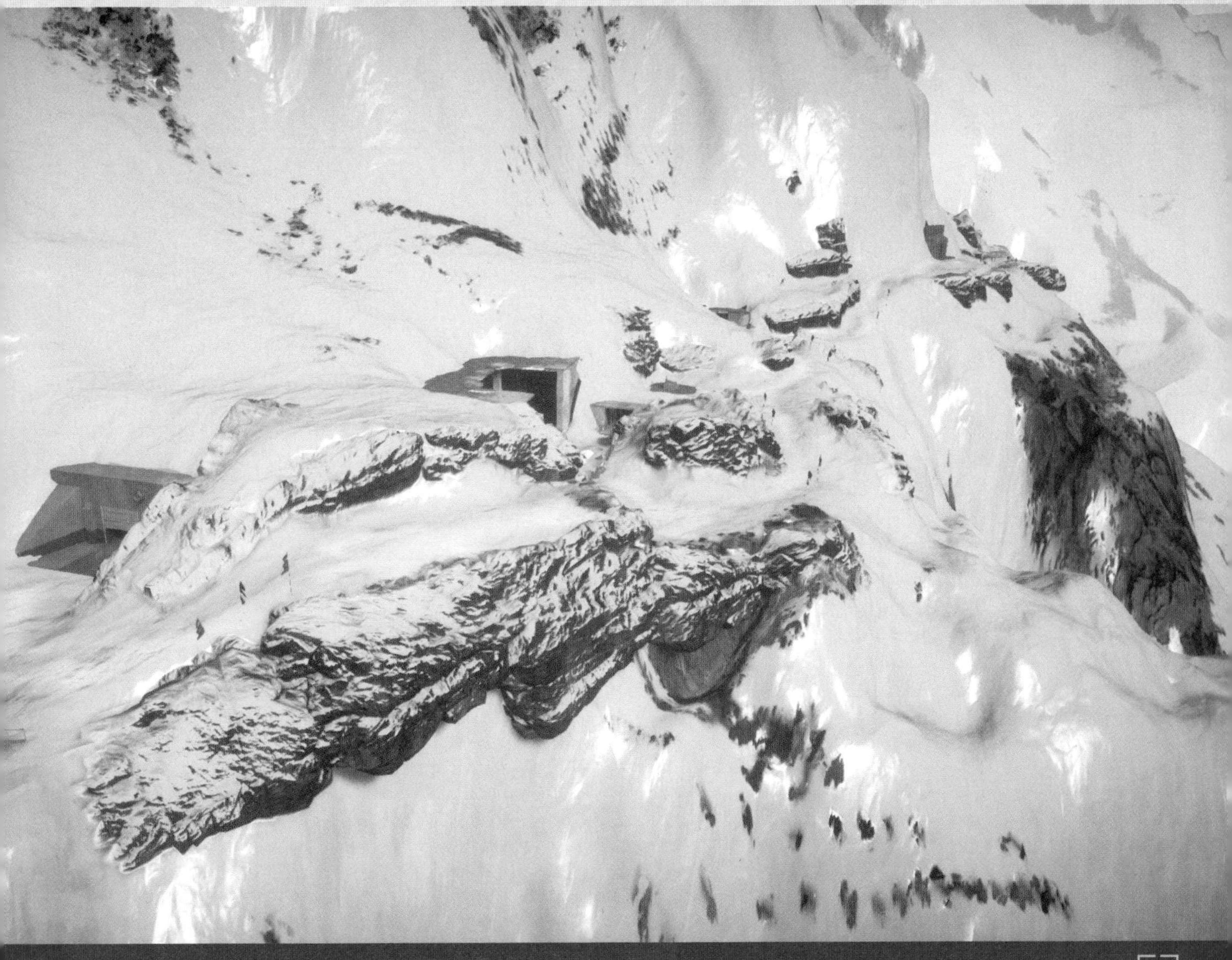

CONQUEST LARGE

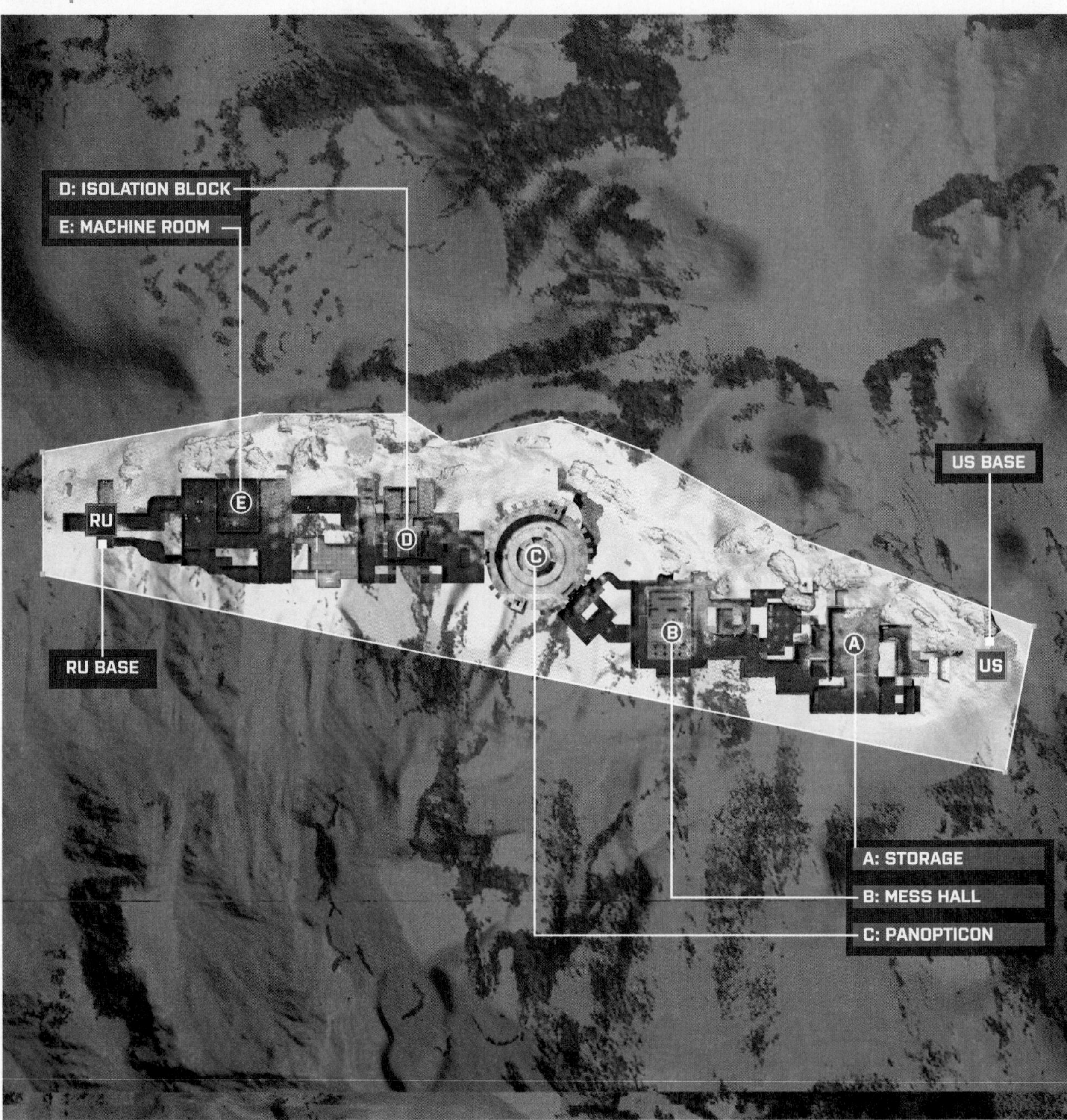

RECOMMENDED SQUAD COMPOSITION:

The 64-player variant of this map adds two more control points: Storage (A) and Machine Room (E). Like on the smaller version of Conquest, on this map there are no vehicles, so prepare for a lot of gun action now that there are 64 players. The best strategy for the US team will be to control Storage (A), Mess Hall (B), and the Panopticon (C) in the center of the map. For the RU team, the three control points they should focus on are Machine Room (E), Isolation Block (D), and the Panopticon (C). The objective will be to capture three control points to start draining the enemy's tickets. The Panopticon (C) is in the center of the map and has a guard tower that contains two .50Cals. These stationary weapons allow you to watch the two main entrances to the Panopticon (C) and provide great cover. A great tactic that can be applied in the center is having a few people throw Smoke Grenades at the two entrances to bait the enemy out for the players on the stationary turrets to pick up some easy kills. Breaking the opposing team's setup in the center will be tough. If needed, take one of the exits on the north side of the prison to run outside in the cold snowstorm. There are a bunch of entrances back into the prison located near each control point. If the center is guarded well, flank around and steal one of the other control points that are less guarded. This will create an opening to try and regain control of the center and the Panopticon (C). Three control points is all you need, but if the team is pushing the enemy, back be sure to go for that fourth control point: either the Mess Hall (B) if playing on the RU team or Isolation Block (D) if playing as the US team. This will lower the opponent's spirit and lead to an easy victory.

US BASE

- The US base is located in the east wing of the prison. There are no vehicles, so choosing the right squad composition will be critical. A lot of the combat will be infantry based, so having a few extra assault soldiers will be beneficial.
- The closest control point to the US base is Storage (A). Only a few members of a squad should capture this control point while the rest advance towards the power position in the center of the map.
- The Panopticon (C) in the center of the map will be the deciding factor for the winning team. The US team's best strategy is to capture Storage (A), Mess Hall (B), and Panopticon (C). If this is done, the other team's tickets will be drained.
- A single squad should take one of the north exits off the start and flank outside all the way to the Isolation Block (D). The RU team will have this captured before the US team reaches the Isolation Block (D), but don't worry. The real objective here is to try and force a few RU squads back to stop the neutralization. This allows the other US squads to capture Panopticon (C) with relative ease due to less resistance.
- One squad that heads to the center should go through the lower levels. Once they are under the Panopticon (C) there is a staircase that provides great angles to stop the opposing team from gaining control of the objective. At the top of the staircase is an exit leading outside. Check this area periodically for enemy flankers.

RU BASE

- The RU base is in the west wing, the opposite wing from the US team. There are no vehicles, so choosing the right squad composition will be critical. A lot of the combat will be infantry based, so having a few extra assault soldiers will be beneficial.
- The closest control point to the RU base is Machine Room (E). Only a few members of a squad should capture this control point while the rest advance towards the power position in the center of the map.
- The Panopticon (C) in the center of the map will be the deciding factor for the winning team. The RU team's best strategy is to capture Machine Room (E), Isolation Block (D), and Panopticon (C). If this is done, the other team's tickets will be drained.
- A single squad should take one of the north exits off the start and flank outside all the way to the Mess Hall (B). The US team will have this captured before the RU team reaches the Mess Hall (B), but don't worry. The main objective here is to try and force the US squads back to stop the neutralization. This will allow the RU team to capture the Panopticon (C) with less enemy infantry.
- One squad that heads to the center should go through the lower levels. Once they are under the Panopticon (C) there is a staircase that provides great angles to stop the opposing team from capturing this flag. At the top of the staircase there is an exit outside. Check this periodically for enemy flankers.

A: STORAGE

- This control point is connected with the outside and is closest to the US base. When positioned here, watch the adjacent hallways from the raised platform.
- Only a few US team members should capture this control point at the start of the game while the rest advance west towards the center.
- The raised platform provides great cover when fighting infantry units are on the ground. Be sure to hold this position when defending this control point.
- The Storage (A) area has a ton of crate shelves that players can hide behind for cover as they wait for the enemy to get close.
- Players utilizing the support or recon class can lay M18 Claymores around the halls that lead to the outside to blow up those attacking flankers.

B: MESS HALL

- This control point lies in a cafeteria hall with a few tables and a kitchen that can be used for cover. This control point favors the US team as it is near their base. The US team should have a few players capture this control point while the rest head towards the center where most of the action will take place.
- North of the Mess Hall (B) is an exit that leads outside. When defending this control point be sure to have a squad in this area to watch out for flankers.
- The kitchen is a great place to go prone and only resurface when enemies are near.
- The RU team will have a tough time capturing this control point as it is nearest the US base and should only approach if the opportunity presents itself. When going for this control point, be sure to cover the left and right flanks before rushing in blindly.
- In the center of this control point lies the USAS-12 weapon pick up. This weapon can be used effectively for offense or defense.

C: PANOPTICON

- Most of the fighting will occur here in the center of the prison. There is a small guard tower in the center with two .50Cals that can be used to watch the two main entrances.
- Using the lower levels to gain control of the Panopticon (C) can prove to be effective. Players can capture or contest this control point from underneath.
- Holding the staircase north of Panopticon (C) is key. It allows players to spread out onto the different floors in the center, creating a much stronger defensive perimeter.
- Planting the lower level entrances with C4 will result in easy kills for your team and less tickets for the opposing team.
- Smoke Grenades become super effective here, delaying the opponent from rushing in. If the opponent decides to rush blindly, the stationary turrets will make light work of them.

PRO TIP: STRONGSIDE

The stairwell in the Panopticon (C) is a great position to control this objective when playing Conquest. I'll set T-UGS near the exit at the top of the stairwell and Claymores at the bottom of the stairwell in the shadows. This allows me to focus on the top floor of the Panopticon (C) as I defend this entire area.

D: ISOLATION BLOCK

- This control point holds the prison cells for the most dangerous war criminals. This control point favors the RU team as it is near their base. The RU team should have a few players capture this control point while the rest head towards the center where most of the action will take place.
- North of the Isolation Block (D) is an exit that leads outside. When defending this control point be sure to have a squad in this area to watch out for flankers. Planting C4 around this exit will prove useful.
- Most of these holding cells are destructible, which allows players to hide inside once the cells are destroyed. This is beneficial for both defending and capturing this control point.
- Recon class users can throw T-UGS around the Isolation Cell (D), allowing players to focus on defending other areas.
- On the lower level of the Isolation Block (D) is a tiny surveillance room. A player can stay crouched in this area and only pop out when needed.

E: MACHINE ROOM

- This is the closest control point to the RU base. Only a few RU team members should capture it at the start of the game while the rest advance east towards the center.
- This area has a few explosive generators that can be used to the RU team's advantage after capturing. Have a defender watch from a distance and shoot the generator when an enemy approaches.
- The second floor of the Machine Room (E) is where players want to be. If playing as the US team, it is much easier to clean out the room from above than walking through the front door. This is also a great spot for the RU team to watch the main entrance to the Machine Room (E).
- To the north of the Machine Room (E) is another exit that leads to the outside of the map. T-UGS or C4 will help in guarding this exit.
- There are plenty of crates around the Machine Room (E) area, so use these for cover and to get the jump on enemies.

CONQUEST SMALL

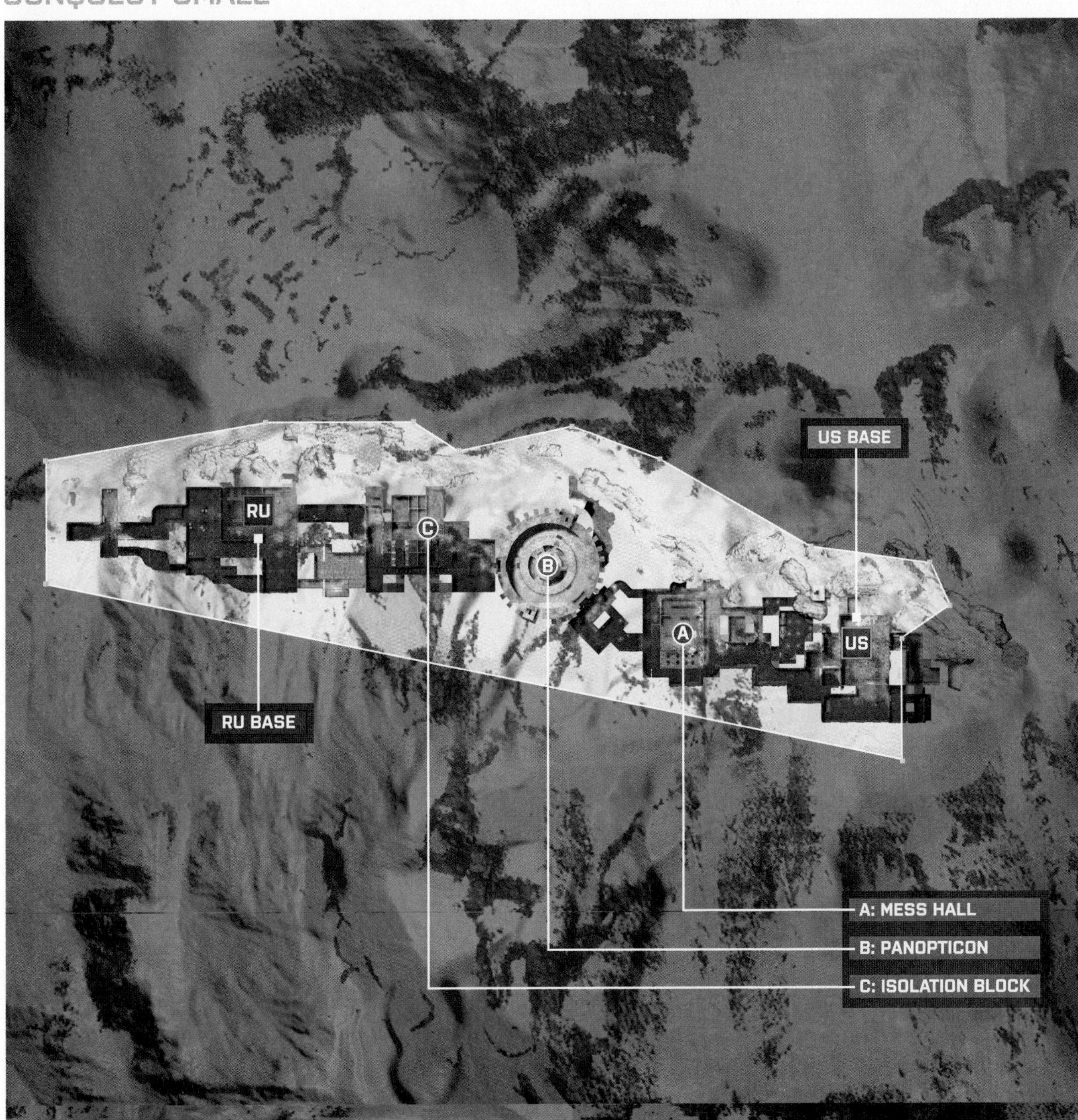

RECOMMENDED SQUAD COMPOSITION:

This map will remind many of Operation Metro from *Battlefield 3*. This is a small-scale map with no vehicles, so much of the game will rely on gun skill and positioning. The prison is isolated inside of a mountain that deals with constant snowstorms. There are three control points in Operation Locker: the Mess Hall (A), Panopticon (B), and Isolation Block (C). Both teams will be fighting to control two of these control points. The US base is located in the east wing of the prison. The best strategy for the US team will be to control both the Mess Hall (A) and Panopticon (B). On the west wing, players can find the RU base. Being such a small map, the best strategy will be to hold only two control points. For the RU team, that would be the Isolation Block (C) and the Panopticon (B). Both teams will quickly realize that the Panopticon (B) will be the determining factor of the game. The Panopticon (B) is in the center of that map and has a guard tower that contains two .50Cals. These stationary weapons allow you to watch the two main entrances to the Panopticon (B) and provide great cover. With there only being three control points, two control points is all you need to drain the opposing team's tickets. Get control of the Panopticon (B) and bunker up.

US BASE

- The US base is located in the east wing of the prison. There are no vehicles, so choosing the right squad composition will be critical. A lot of the combat will be infantry based, so having a few extra assault soldiers will be beneficial.
- The closest control point to the US base is Mess Hall (A). Only a few members of a squad should capture this control point while the rest advance towards the power position in the center of the map.
- The Panopticon (B) in the center of the map will be the deciding factor for the winning team. Taking this control point with the Mess Hall (A) will be all the US team needs to win. Be sure to send over half the team to the center off the start.
- A single squad should take one of the north exits from the start and flank outside all the way to the Isolation Block (C). The RU team will have the Isolation Block (C) captured before you reach it. The objective here is to try and force a few RU squads back to stop the neutralization, allowing the other US squads to capture Panopticon (B) with ease.
- One squad that heads to the center should go through the lower levels. Once they are under the Panopticon (B) there is a staircase that provides great angles to stop the opposing team. Be sure to lock this down by preventing enemies from entering through the lower level or the exit that leads outside.

RU BASE

- The RU base is in the west wing, the opposite wing from the US team. There are no vehicles, so choosing the right squad composition will be very important. A lot of the combat will be infantry based, so having a few extra assault soldiers will help your team tremendously.
- The closest control point to the RU base is Isolation Block (C). Only a few members of a squad should capture this control point while the rest advance towards the power position in the center of the map.
- The Panopticon (B) in the center of the map will be the deciding factor for the winning team. Controlling this point with the Isolation Block (C) will be all the RU team needs to win. Be sure to send plenty of squads to the center off the start.
- A single squad should take one of the north exits at the start and flank outside all the way to the Mess Hall (A). The objective here is to try and force the US squads back to stop the neutralization, allowing the RU team to capture the Panopticon (B) with less of a fight.
- One squad that heads to the center should go through the lower levels. Once they are under the Panopticon (B) there is a staircase that provides great angles to stop the opposing team. Be prepared to fight the US team at the bottom as well.

A: MESS HALL

- This control point lies in a cafeteria hall with a few tables and a kitchen that can be used for cover. This control point favors the US team as it is near their base. The US team should have a few players capture this control point while the rest head towards the center where most of the action will take place.
- North of the Mess Hall (A) is an exit that leads outside. When defending this control point be sure to have a squad in this area to watch out for flankers.
- The kitchen is a great place to go prone and only resurface when enemies are near.
- The RU team will have a tough time capturing this control point as it is near the US base and should only be approached if the opportunity presents itself. When going for this control point, be sure to cover the left and right flanks before rushing in blindly!
- In the center of this control point lies the USAS-12 weapon pickup. This weapon can be used effectively for offense or defense.

B: PANOPTICON

- Most of the fighting will occur here in the center of the prison. There is a guard tower in the center with two .50Cals that can be used to watch the two main entrances.
- Using the lower levels to gain control of the Panopticon (B) can prove to be effective. Players can capture or contest this control point from underneath.
- Holding the staircase north of Panopticon (B) is key! It allows players to spread out onto the different floors in the center, creating a much stronger defense perimeter.
- Planting the lower level entrances with C4 will result in an easy kill.
- Smoke Grenades become super effective here, delaying the opponent from rushing in. If the opponent decides to rush in blindly, the stationary turrets will make light work of them.

PRO TIP: WALSHY

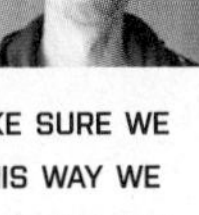

WHETHER I AM A LITTLE AHEAD OR A LITTLE BEHIND, I ALWAYS STAY SLIGHTLY SEPARATED FROM MY SQUAD ON THIS MAP TO MAKE SURE WE ALL DON'T GET TAKEN OUT AT THE SAME TIME. THIS WAY WE CAN CONTINUALLY GIVE EACH OTHER GREAT SPAWNS FOR THE ENTIRE GAME AND NEVER GIVE UP ANY GROUND THAT WE DON'T HAVE TO.

C: ISOLATION BLOCK

- This control point holds the prison cells for the most dangerous war criminals. This control point favors the RU team as it is near their base. The RU team should have a few players capture this control point while the rest head towards the center where most of the action will take place.
- North of the Isolation Block (C) is an exit that leads outside. When defending this control point, have a squad in this area to watch out for flankers. Planting C4 around this exit will prove useful.
- Most of these holding cells are destructible, which allows players to take cover inside. This is beneficial for both defending and capturing this control point.
- Recon class users can throw T-UGS around the Isolation Cell (C), allowing players to focus on defending other areas.
- On the lower level of the Isolation Block (C) is a tiny surveillance room. A player can stay crouched in this area and only pop out when needed.

RUSH

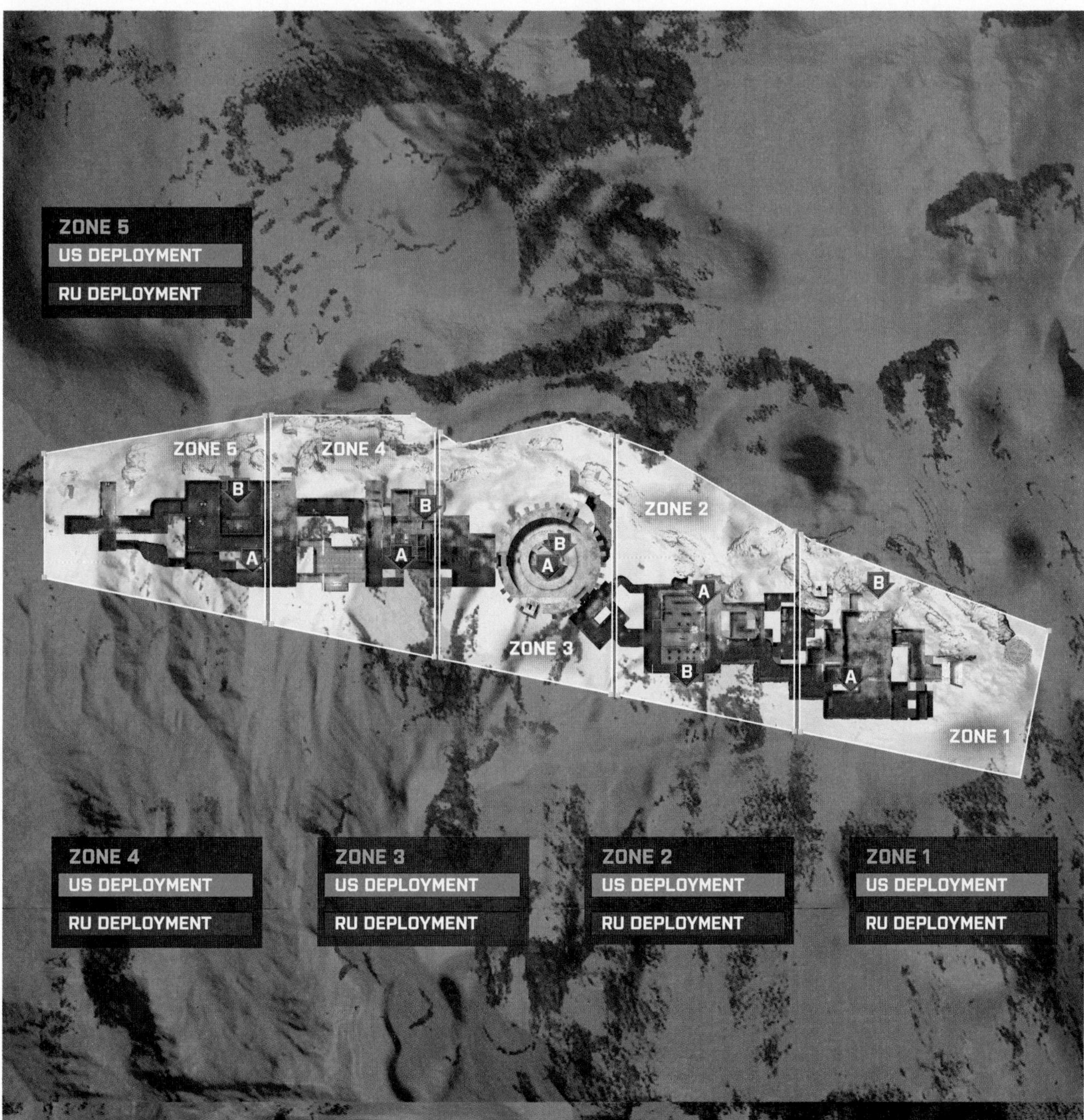

In Operation Locker, players will immediately realize that it is a run and gun game mode. With no vehicles on the map, players must rely on their gun skill and positioning to complete the objective. The US team is the attacking team in this Rush mode and has five zones to go through before claiming victory. These zones start at the east wing of the prison and move west from zone to zone until reaching the last zone in the west wing. The prison has many rooms that players should get comfortable with as players can learn a few different routes leading to each M-COM station. The defenders of this Rush mode will be the RU team. Defenders will have to worry about attacks from both inside the prison and outside. Be aware of all the weapon pickups on the map. These weapons help the RU team escape tight situations whenever the US team is pushing towards the M-COM stations.

ZONE 1: STORAGE

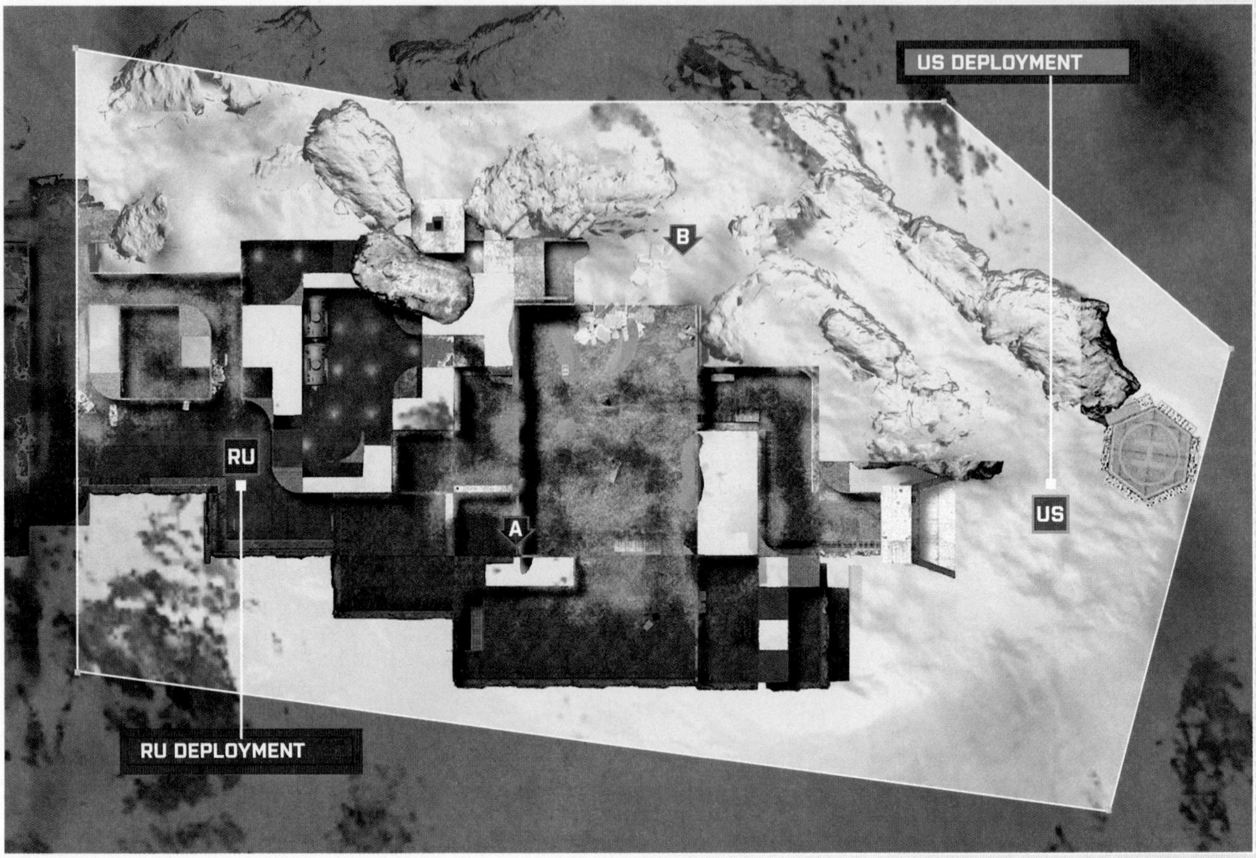

US DEPLOYMENT
B
RU
A
US
RU DEPLOYMENT

US DEPLOYMENT

RECOMMENDED SQUAD COMPOSITION:

- The US team deploys at the very east point of the map outside near a heli-pad. There are no vehicles for the US team or the RU team, so both teams' gun skills are going to be tested.
- A squad or two should follow the northwest path outside towards M-COM Station B. With Smoke Grenades attached, the US team can get a quick arm as the Smoke Grenades and snow decrease the enemy's visibility.
- Radio Beacons should be placed around the northwest path to spawn squad members closer to the battle.
- The rest of the US team should head inside the prison and flood through the inside entrances. The southwest entrance will be the toughest, but keeping the RU team there will help the other squads in arming M-COM Station B.
- The squads that run through the center entrance should focus on picking off enemies who are trying to disarm M-COM Station B and slowly make their move towards M-COM Station A.

RU DEPLOYMENT

RECOMMENDED SQUAD COMPOSITION:

- The RU team starts off inside the prison with three different paths to take. Two of the paths lead directly to M-COM Station A. On one of these paths lies a staircase that grants access to a balcony. The third path, which lies on the north side, is a hall that leads to M-COM Station B. Also in this hall is a ladder that leads outside and provides a higher vantage point to defend M-COM Station B.
- The balcony southeast of M-COM Station A will provide a great vantage point to oversee both M-COM stations. The RU team will have an open view at M-COM Station B to stop anyone who starts an arm.
- Immediately send players toward the center of the Storage area to set up your defenses quickly. This area will be a high-traffic area.
- Send some players to the north hall towards M-COM Station B to watch for oncoming US infantry from the east path in the mountain.
- Watch for US infantry attempting to close the gate east of your deployment base. This gate can only be opened and closed from the east side of the gate. When closed, this provides your team only two paths to move towards.

M-COM STATION A

- M-COM Station is located in the Storage area. There are plenty crate shelves that provide cover for both teams.
- North of M-COM Station A is a door way, past this doorway is a hall that leads to M-COM Station B if the player goes east and the RN base if the player chooses to go west.
- Southeast of M-COM Station A is a balcony that provides an overview of both M-COM Stations. At the most eastern part of this balcony lies a door way the US team can come through. Defending this area would force the US team to only approach from below.
- When attacking, be aware of the interactive gate southwest of M-COM Station A. When closing this gate it will eliminate an open path for the RN team. This will make arming A much easier as the defender has to take a longer route now.
- After arming on the attacking team, head into the doorway and wait to ambush defenders who attempt to disarm the M-COM station.

M-COM STATION B

- M-COM Station B is located outside in the icy snowstorm north of the Storage area.
- Near M-COM Station B there is a lot of debris and rocks surrounding the M-COM station. Use these for cover for either the attacking or defending team.
- When attacking, be aware of the enemies hiding in the hall west of the M-COM station. Throwing Smoke Grenades around M-COM Station B will decrease the enemy's visibility even further and allow for a sneaky arm.
- When defending, the snowstorm decreases visibility, so plant M18 Claymores around the area.

PRO TIP: FLAMESWORD

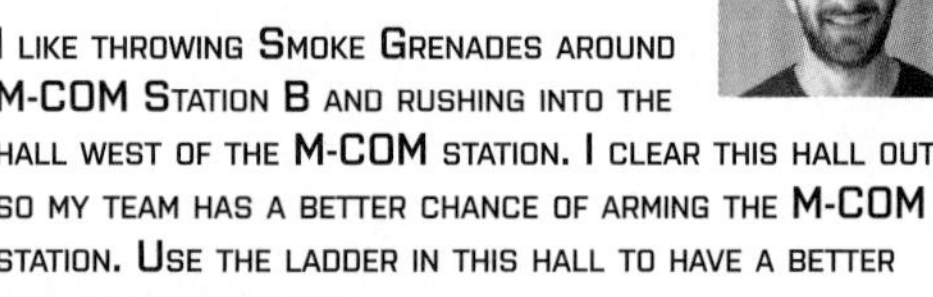

I like throwing Smoke Grenades around M-COM Station B and rushing into the hall west of the M-COM station. I clear this hall out so my team has a better chance of arming the M-COM station. Use the ladder in this hall to have a better view of the objective.

ZONE 2: MESS HALL

US DEPLOYMENT

B

RU

US

A

RU DEPLOYMENT

US DEPLOYMENT

RECOMMENDED SQUAD COMPOSITION: 

- After clearing the first zone, the US base is now moved to the Storage area.
- The assault and support classes will be ideal for this zone due to the close-quarter combat that will be encountered.
- The M-COM stations sit far west from the US base. Have squads equip a recon class to drop Radio Beacons to shorten the travel for the squad.
- Send a squad along the northwest path outside of the prison towards M-COM Station B for an unexpected point of attack.
- Have a squad head west towards M-COM Station A. Gain control of the Mess Hall before attempting to arm.

RU DEPLOYMENT

RECOMMENDED SQUAD COMPOSITION: 

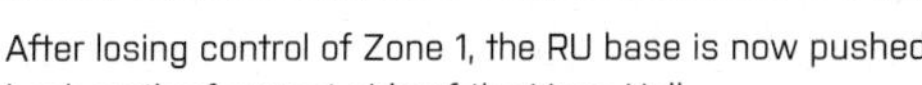

- After losing control of Zone 1, the RU base is now pushed back on the far west side of the Mess Hall.
- Much of the battles will be close-quarter ones, so have extra assault and support soldiers to withstand incoming fire.
- Be sure to grab the M32 MGL (Grenade Launcher) at the RU base. This will prove to be useful with the close-quarter combat and tight hallways.
- Send a squad to M-COM Station B and take advantage of the snowstorm by laying C4 or M18 Claymores around.
- Equip the Shorty 12G to have the upper hand when fighting in the tight halls.

M-COM STATION A

- M-COM Station A is located in the Mess Hall. The Mess Hall contains a kitchen and tables that can be used for cover.
- When defending, players can go prone in the kitchen area and resurface when enemies begin approaching.
- When defending, take advantage of the map layout. There are many corners the attackers have to pass to make their way near M-COM Station A.
- When defending, plant C4 and M18 Claymores in the dark and shadowy corners.
- When playing as the US, try to sneak through the halls on the north side and flank the enemy.

M-COM STATION B

- M-COM Station B is located in the backroom of the kitchen, just off the Mess Hall.
- This station is surrounded with food crates, attackers be prepared to deal with prone defenders who will try to catch the US attackers by surprise.
- There is a hallway to the east of the objective, defenders should be ready for incoming US attackers. Lock this hall down by planting C4 and baiting the attackers near for some easy kills.
- Defenders should push along the northeast path outside to take a few tickets from the US team before they get close. Outside also lies an elevated platform above the prison exit. When playing as the RN team, send a few players here to have the first jump on the attacking team.
- When attacking, be prepared for the Claymores the defenders have set up. There are many tight corners that the defenders will try to booby trap so be careful when hugging the wall for those tiny explosives.

PRO TIP: ELUMNITE

THERE IS LEDGE RIGHT ABOVE M-COM STATION B YOU CAN ACCESS YOURSELF, WHICH IS A GREAT HIDING SPOT, AND THE BLIZZARD GIVES YOU SOME EXTRA COVER AS WELL. LOOK FOR ME TO CAMP AROUND HERE AND PICK OFF ANY ENEMIES TRYING TO ARM THE BOMB.

ZONE 3: PANOPTICON

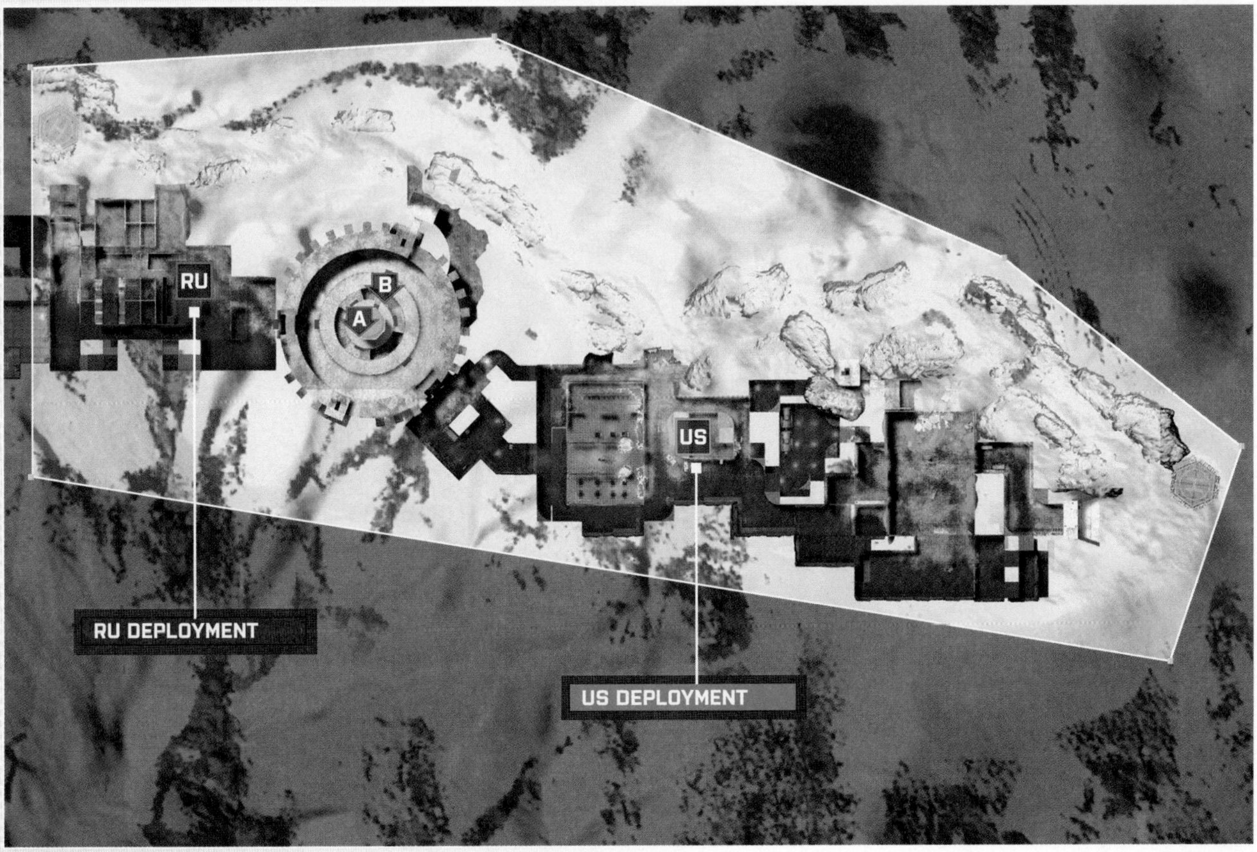

RU
B
A
US
RU DEPLOYMENT
US DEPLOYMENT

US DEPLOYMENT

RECOMMENDED SQUAD COMPOSITION: 

- After destroying both previous objectives, the US base now sits on the east of the Mess Hall.
- Deploying here will lead to a long journey to the M-COM stations. Be sure to assign a recon class to the squad to take advantage of their gadgets.
- With the base so far away, be aware that the RU team will probably already be in the center waiting for an attack.
- Send a squad along the northwest path outside to gain control before pushing into the Panopticon area in the center.
- A squad will need to head through the lower levels as quickly as possible to gain access to the basement of the stairways where M-COM Station B is located.

RU DEPLOYMENT

RECOMMENDED SQUAD COMPOSITION:

- Once Zone 2 is lost, the RU base is pushed even farther back and now lies west of the Panopticon area.
- This gives the team just enough time to get into defensive position before the attacking team makes it to the objectives.
- Squads should be spread out on the different floors in the Panopticon area to have multiple ways of attack.
- Be sure to control the stairway as it gives access to both objectives. Watch the north exit at the top of the stairs that leads outside, where incoming attackers will be.
- Support class proves its worth once again. Plant C4 around the US team's lower level entrance to stop any flankers from below.

M-COM STATION A

- This objective is located in the heart of the Panopticon, just below the watch tower on the main floor.
- The M-COM station is surrounded by a stack of sandbags on each side. If playing as the US team, go prone in this area to take cover when arming the objective.
- When defending, take the high ground to get an overview of the area and objective.
- Be sure to send a defender into the watch tower. Inside is a stationary turret that can watch the US team's main entrance into the Panopticon.
- The attacking team will need to gain control of the stairwell from the outside to ensure a safe arm of the objective.

M-COM STATION B

- This M-COM station lies in the basement under the watch tower, which can also be reached through the north stairwell.
- When playing as the RU team, setting up M18 Claymores will prove super effective due to the dark area.
- Until M-COM Station A is detonated, there are only two entrances the US team can use to gain access to the basement.
- The RU team has two choke points to lock down if M-COM Station A is still active: the tunnel underneath the objective and the entrance that leads to the top of the north stairwell. Defend the two choke points to prevent the attackers from reaching the objective.
- Attackers should have a squad set up a perimeter at the top of the stairwell entrance outside and slowly try to make their way in. Keep a squad member alive to allow downed allies to spawn near the combat. Smoke Grenades will allow for a successful push.

ZONE 4: ISOLATION BLOCK

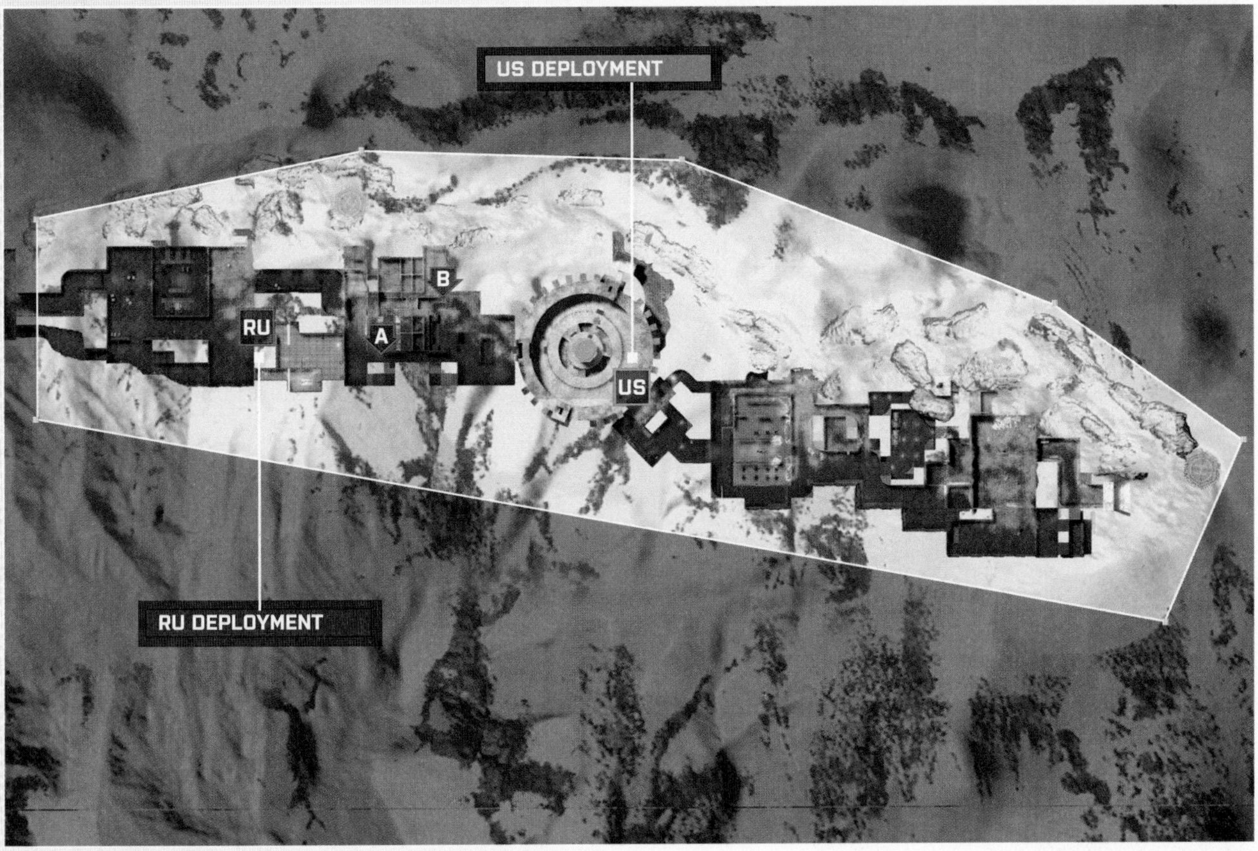

US DEPLOYMENT

B

RU

A

US

RU DEPLOYMENT

US DEPLOYMENT

RECOMMENDED SQUAD COMPOSITION:

- Succeeding once again in destroying the last zone's M-COM stations, the US base is now moved into the Panopticon.
- Once again, send a squad along the northwest path outside to reach M-COM Station B. Drop a Radio Beacon once you've made it inside the prison again. This will save players time from having to travel from the deployment spawns.
- Send a squad through the lower hall south of M-COM Station A. Tread carefully through this area as it is an extremely close-quarter combat area.
- A squad with support troops will benefit in this zone immensely! Just east of M-COM Stations A and B are crates that can be used with LMGs with Bipods to suppress the enemy.
- When moving around the dark areas near these M-COM stations, be sure to toggle off your Laser Sights. Avoid giving away the squad's position at all costs.

RU DEPLOYMENT

RECOMMENDED SQUAD COMPOSITION:

- After losing the objectives in the Panopticon, the RU team has little time to establish a setup around the new M-COM station.
- Being pushed back once again, the RU base is brought back farther west and located just east outside the Machine Room.
- Send a squad north outside of the prison to prevent any flankers from getting near M-COM Station B.
- Equip Smoke Grenades to better defend the M-COM station in these tightly closed hallways.
- Once again, take advantage of M18 Claymores and C4 by planting them in the dark area around M-COM Station A.

M-COM STATION A

- M-COM Station A is located in the lower level of the Isolation Block.
- This objective has four points of access: you can enter through three hallways and you are also able to drop down through an opening from above.
- When playing as the RU team, the upper level is a good position to guard this station. It provides a good overview of the objective. A few defenders can stay low near the stairs waiting for attackers.
- When attacking, the US team has to be cautious of defenders crouching in corners. This area has dark sections so take advantage of the Flashlight and blind those defenders waiting around corners!
- As a defender, go prone south of the objective on the stairway platform. Keep your sights down the hallway as enemies are sure to cross.

M-COM STATION B

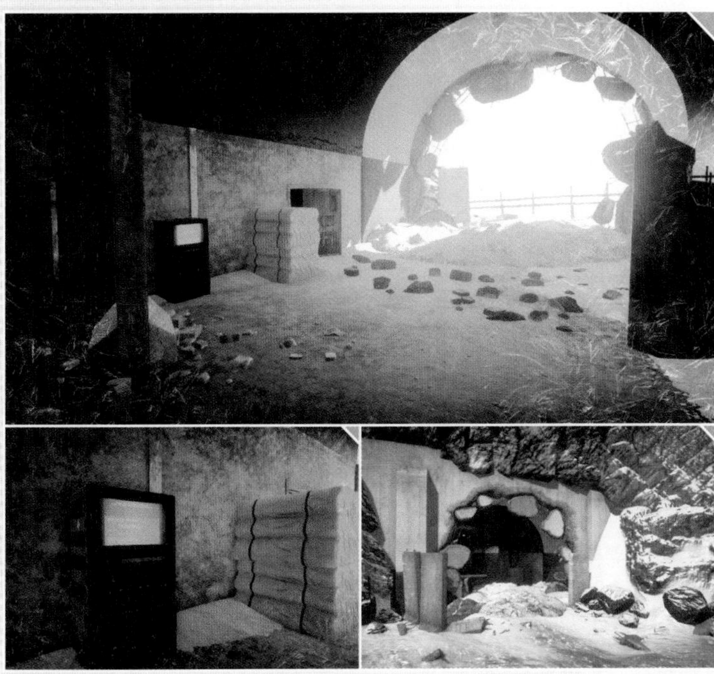

- M-COM Station B is located on the higher level of the Isolation Block towards the north exit that leads outside the prison.
- This area is heavily shielded by objects. When defending, be sure to have a good eye on the objective to keep attackers away.
- As the defending team, the safest and best strategy will be to blow up the surrounding holding cells around the objective. This will make the area more open, allowing the defenders to spot attackers.
- When attacking, follow the northwest path into the prison. Once near the objective, a huge concrete wall shields players to be able to arm the station.
- Send an attacking squad west of the objective to build a perimeter to allow another attacking squad to come in from behind and arm the station.

ZONE 5: ISOLATION BLOCK

US DEPLOYMENT
B
CN
US
A
RU DEPLOYMENT

US DEPLOYMENT

RECOMMENDED SQUAD COMPOSITION:

- Good job making it this far. This is the last zone—fight it out and the US team takes home the gold!
- The US base is now moved to the Isolation Block area. Just a bit farther west are the last two M-COM stations.
- Again, stick to sending a squad through the northwest path outside. This squad will be able to gain control of the top level of M-COM Station B.
- A squad flank through the halls south of M-COM Station A will cause a good distraction to allow the rest of the team to move in.
- When moving towards both these M-COM stations, be aware of all the explosive barrels. The defending team will surely try to bait players in.

RU DEPLOYMENT

RECOMMENDED SQUAD COMPOSITION: 

- This is the last chance to stop the enemy. The RU base is now pushed to the farthest west point of the prison.
- Spawning at the base will give little time to return to the objectives to disarm. Placing a Radio Beacon east of the M-COM stations will allow you to spawn behind the attackers, resulting in a successful flank.
- Expect the attackers to push from outside of the prison. The attackers will try to gain control above M-COM Station B. Stop them outside of the prison.
- Send a squad towards M-COM Station B and hide in the shadows for a good surprise attack.
- Being the last zone, stock up on extra assault soldiers. Reviving downed teammates will be crucial in this last stop.

M-COM STATION A

- South of the Machine Room, M-COM Station A is located on the lower level.
- This objective only has two points of access. This leaves either team hopeless if they are pushed back by the opposing team.
- This objective is surrounded by many obstacles. These obstacles can be used by both attackers and defenders for cover, but tread carefully. There are explosive containers at both ends that can easily take down multiple enemies.
- When defending, be sure to blow up the explosive containers on the west side of the objective. Afterwards, get behind the sandbags that provide great cover against attacking enemies coming from the east.
- For both attackers and defenders, Smoke Grenades prove to be very useful. This also allows attackers to push past the M-COM station to clear a path for other teammates.

M-COM STATION B

- This M-COM station is located inside the Machine Room in between two generators.
- There is an entrance from outside the prison that leads to above the Machine Room. This area will need to be watched when defending.
- Controlling the upper level of the Machine Room will be the main key when it comes to arming or defending this objective. Defending players will want to plant C4 around the exit that leads outside the prison.
- When attacking, planting a Radio Beacon outside the northwest path will allow squad members to spawn near the objective. Once the upper level is controlled, arming the objective will be easier.
- The US team should be prepared for the defending RU team to close the gate east of the objective. Try to delay this at all costs. If not, the attacking team will have fewer paths to take.

OBLITERATION

RECOMMENDED SQUAD COMPOSITION:

- The RU team must protect three targets located in close proximity of the Machine Room and the medical facility.
- The US team needs to guard the three targets just east of the Mess Hall.
- The US team should have a designated squad defending the Mess Hall area at all times to protect against invading attackers.
- The RU team should have an assigned squad positioned at the center of their three targets, allowing them to quickly move from objective to objective to prevent the US team from arming the targets.
- Both teams should move together at all times while controlling the Panopticon, granting either team map dominance. This makes it easier to defend and allows teammates to slowly push into enemy territory to arm the targets.

DEFUSE

RECOMMENDED SQUAD COMPOSITION:

- On this map, the attackers and defenders are facing each other in the Isolation Block of the prison. The US team spawns outside in the snowy storm while the RU teams spawns down low in the Isolation Block.
- Laptop A is located directly in the Isolation Block in the watch room. Nearby is a USAS-12 battle pickup; defenders who grab this are very effective in this close-quarter area.
- Laptop B is found inside one of the medical rooms of the prison. There are circuit boxes that attackers can shoot to turn off the lights. This allows them to move in undetected.
- Defenders should never move outside of the prison unless they outnumber the opposing team. Attackers will most likely be waiting on top of the higher up cliffs for lone wolf defenders attempting to flank. Don't give the attackers this opportunity; there are many holding cells that defenders can use for cover. Be sure to plant Claymores in the dark corners of the map, especially in the room of Laptop A.
- The attacking team should equip Smoke Grenades and Flashbangs. This is a very close-quarter map. Flashbangs blind defenders, allowing you to flank the enemy or to get the jump on defenders around the corner. Laptop B is closest to your deployment; destroy the walls around it to reveal camping defenders.

DOMINATION

RECOMMENDED SQUAD COMPOSITION:

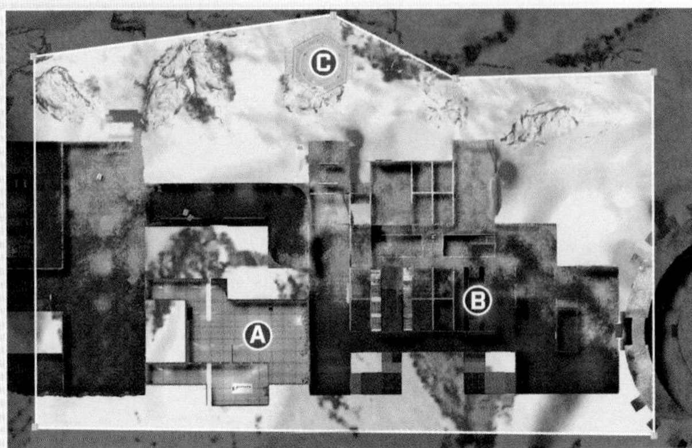

- The three control points on this map are the Infirmary (A), the Isolation Cells (B), and the Helipad (C).
- Even though this is a close-quarter map, equip medium-range weapons as there are so many open areas.
- Equip Flashbangs as there are many rooms players are moving in.
- When going to capture the Helipad (C), always capture it from underneath the platform. It is a disadvantage to capture from above as there is no cover.
- A good strategy is to take charge of the two control points inside: Infirmary (A) and the Isolation Cells (B). The third point, Helipad (C), is outside and has little to no cover.

SQUAD DEATHMATCH

RECOMMENDED SQUAD COMPOSITION:

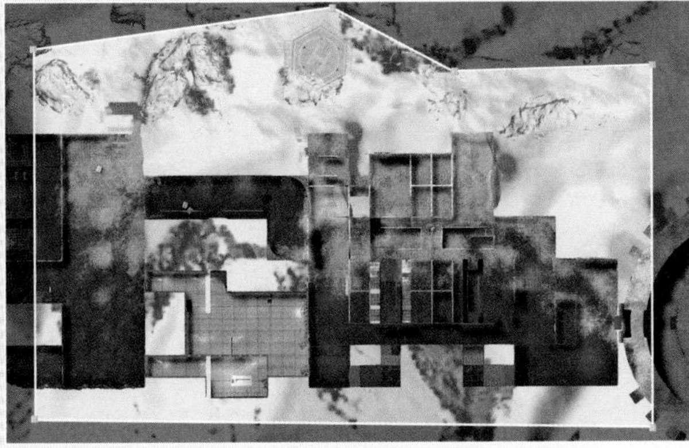

- This is a non-stop battle, so be sure that you and your squad are always moving.
- All fights consist of close-quarter combat. Shotguns prove critical as players can run into each other as soon as they turn the corner.
- You want your squad inside at all times—camping does not benefit you as this game mode is a free-for-all between three other teams.
- Placing Claymores in the dark areas surely gets you a kill or two, especially if the opposing squad is bunched up.
- An extra assault class or two is very effective as you want to heal or revive your squadmates as you and your squad fight for dominance.

TEAM DEATHMATCH

RECOMMENDED SQUAD COMPOSITION:

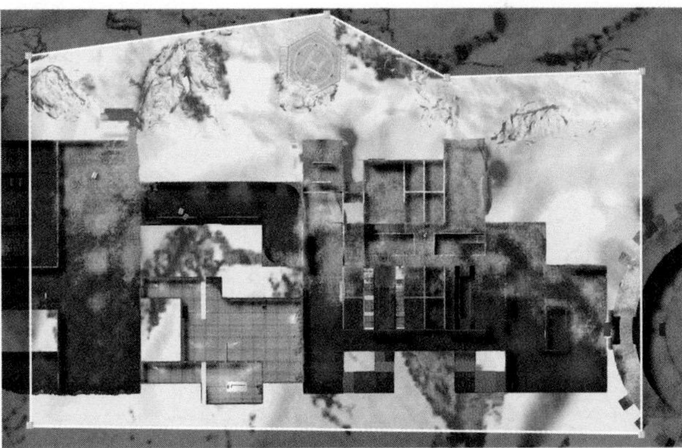

- This is one of the most fast-paced Team Deathmatch modes that you play in the game. You are pitted in constant gunfights, so don't stop moving.
- Take advantage of the new lean system against walls. Don't just blindly rush around the corner. Take a peak around before moving out.
- Flashbangs greatly assist players in this tightly spaced map. Throw them in all directions. If you get a hit marker, you know the enemy is around.
- Shotguns are a trademark of this map. There are many holding cells players can move from, making the enemy double guess their movements.
- Usually you don't want to be outside because of the little cover, but if your team has the lead that all changes. There are only three ways out of the prison, so be sure to watch these and the game is yours to take.

ALPHA SQUAD: IMPRESSIONS

MABOOZA

In Paracel Storm, naval and air units rule supreme, offering a nice change-up over other maps where land-based vehicles are so dominant. If you want to try out the new attack boats, this is the map to do it on. However, get ready for rough seas once the storm rolls in. When I'm not cruising around in an attack boat, I like to strafe opponents with the agile scout helicopters.

STRONGSIDE

Experiencing Levolution on this map is incredible—the ocean environment changes immensely, making travel and battling in the water much more difficult but so much fun. You'll find me holding the island with the Dockyard (A) and the Barracks (B) flags most of the game.

WALSHY

The very first time I played this map early on in the game, my team and I were destroyed mainly because we were running around trying to explore the islands by ourselves. However, later in the same game, I got into a DV-15 with my squad and we just controlled the center of the map. In the end, we pulled out a victory. If you enjoy water combat, you will absolutely love Paracel Storm.

FLAMESWORD

This is a large map with multiple islands in the center of an ocean. Being a large map, I enjoyed the air space that allowed me to freely travel the map with the jets that spawned back at base. Pilots will love this map as they take out infantry and vehicles from above.

ELUMNITE

Paracel Storm is absolute water warfare at its best! When I first played on this map it was like, "What island do I go to first!" Grab a few teammates and go raid one of the many little islands and do what I like to call a water drive-by.

PARACEL STORM

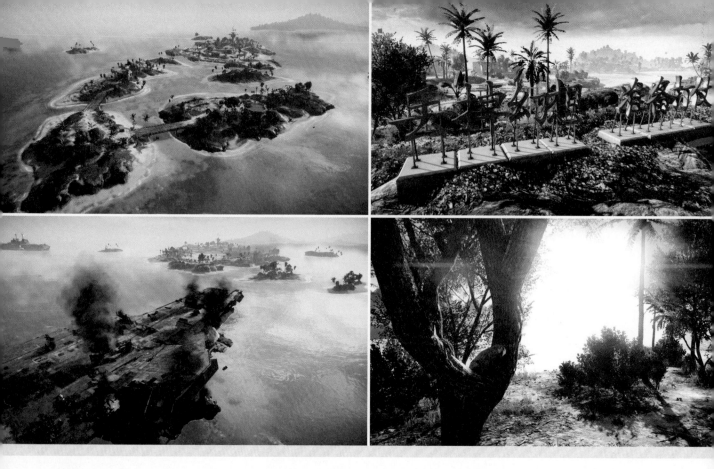

PARACEL STORM

LEVOLUTION MOMENTS

WHAT IS IT?

A large storm arises and a US destroyer ship crashes on shore, changing the playing environment.

HOW IS IT TRIGGERED?

The storm is automatically triggered based on round progression and the turbine holding the destroyer in place can be destroyed following a lightning strike. Aim for the broken/cracked area on the turbine.

HOW IS GAMEPLAY IMPACTED?

The storm increases the size of the waves, which makes boat combat more interesting and skill based. The destroyer that crashes onto shore moves the flag on Firebase Island. This also gives control over the destroyer's AA cannon to the team owning the flag as well as offers new battle pickups that spill out onto the ground.

CONQUEST LARGE

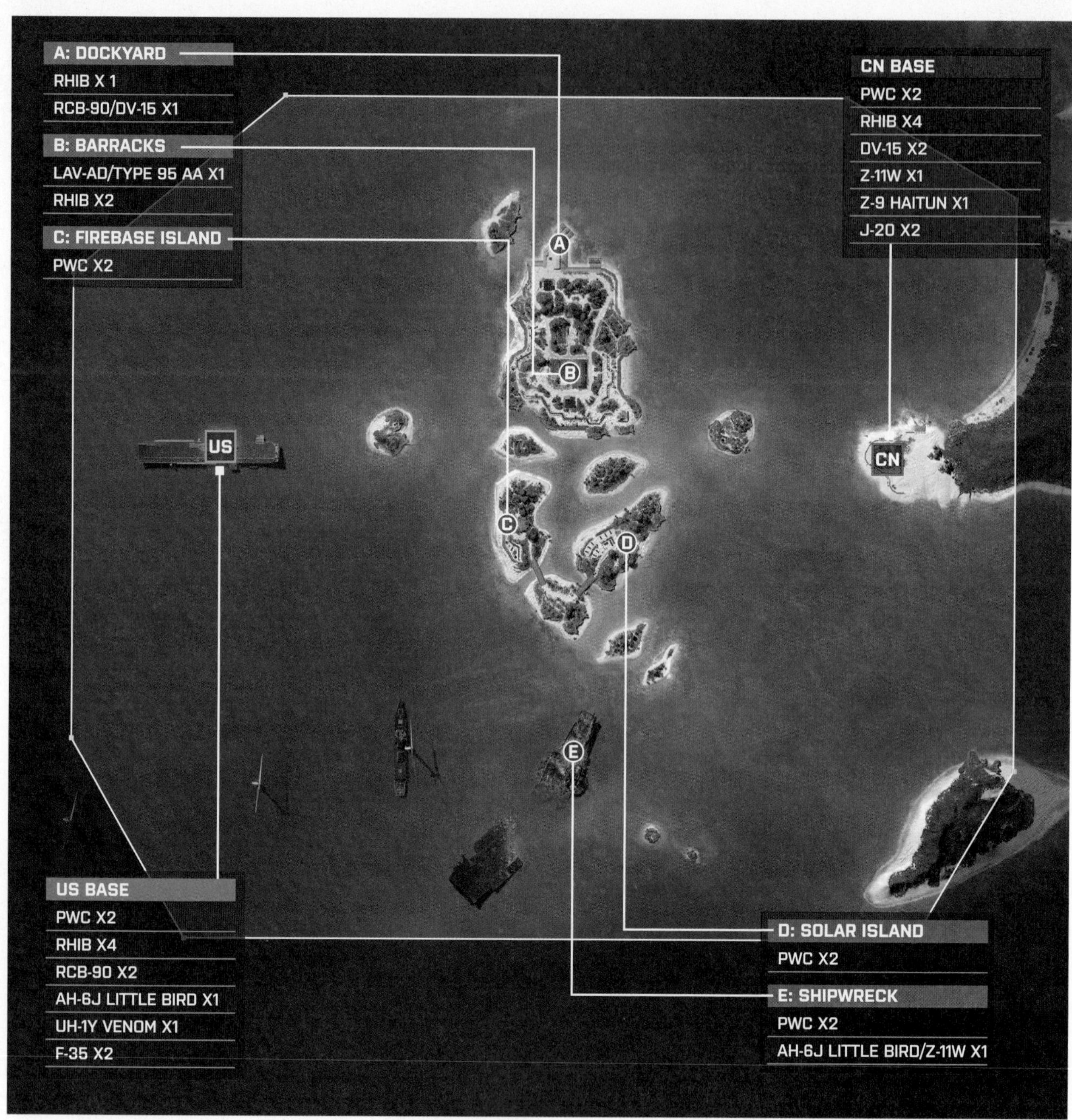

RECOMMENDED SQUAD COMPOSITION:

This is a battle of water and air superiority, with five control points lined up from north to south. The five control points the US team and CN team will be battling over are Dockyard (A), Barracks (B), Firebase Island (C), Solar Island (D), and Shipwreck (E). With five flags up for grabs, your team will need to capture three control points in order to drain the opposing team's tickets. The best strategy for the US team will be to hold the Dockyard (A), the Barracks (B), and Firebase Island (C). By building a perimeter around the Barracks (B), the US team can send players either north or south to support teammates in the Dockyard (A) and Firebase Island (C).The CN teams should try to hold the Dockyard (A), the Barracks (B), and Solar Island (D), plus the Shipwreck (E) if the US team isn't putting up much of a fight. The Shipwreck (E) is positioned on the south end of the map, but closer to the CN base. The CN team will need their attack boat to patrol the south side, warding off the US attackers as they try to flank the Solar Island (D) and push towards the Shipwreck (E). The US team can extend their defensive perimeter to capture the Shipwreck (E) as well, but defending four flags on this large map can be difficult, so be warned. Regardless of what team you are on, prepare for a mix of defending against constant vehicle attacks and close-quarter combat on one of the many islands on the map. With so many vehicles, it is suggested to have a few extra engineers to use target-locked launchers and support members to replenish the engineer's ammo.

US BASE

- The US base is on the western edge of the map, stationed atop a US aircraft carrier.
- It's a few hundred meters to shore and the US base provides plenty of vehicles—both air and water—to escort friendlies to land.
- A squad should control a RCB-90 to cover the team's light water vehicles as they head north to capture the Dockyard (A) and the Barracks (B). The light water vehicles are fast-moving watercraft that will allow you to reach these control points quickly.
- Fill every seat of the transport helicopter and head east towards Firebase Island (C) where two passengers should jump down to score an easy control point. Once the passengers are dropped, immediately head south towards the Shipwreck (E) to provide air support for the remaining squads who rushed this objective at the start.
- The CN team has a handful of vehicles as well, so stock up on engineers to aid your team in destroying the enemy's vehicles. Having engineers near squad vehicles will score you easy points as you can repair them when they take damage. Keep your squad vehicles in tip top shape as they will lead you to victory.

BASE ASSETS

NAME	PWC	RHIB	RCB-90	UH1Y-Venom	AH-6J Little Bird	F-35
QUANTITY	2	4	2	1	1	2

CN BASE

- Positioned on an island to the east, the CN base is too far from every control point by foot. It is crucial to jump in as many vehicles as you have at hand.
- Take an attack boat to any point except for the Barracks (B), where this powerful boat will be ineffective. Take your transport helicopter to drop off your squad at the Barracks (B), Firebase Island (C), or Solar Island (D) where they can effectively move around from objective to objective.
- You will encounter many vehicles throughout this map. Have three engineers in your squad the entire game to be able to deal with these threats and repair your own vehicles.
- Whatever team can utilize their stealth jets the best will be able to control the air. When flying around with a stealth jet, make sure to harass objectives all across the map. Making your presence felt in the air may urge opposing engineers to switch to Stingers or IGLAs, which are useless against your team's water vehicles. Bait them with your jet, then kill them with your boats.
- As a squad, try not to have everyone in the same vehicle. This way the enemy can't win a fight, wipe out your whole squad, and decrease your Field Upgrade progress. Being slightly split up can also guarantee that at least one of your squadmates will be able to give you a good spawn if you die.

BASE ASSETS

NAME	PWC	RHIB	DV-15	Z-9 Haitun	Z-11W	J-20
QUANTITY	2	4	2	1	1	2

A: DOCKYARD

- This control point positioned north of the cluster of islands is a loading dock that can be challenged from land or the surrounding water.
- Upon capture of this control point you have your choice of pushing by land over to the Barracks (B) or taking one of the light water vehicles that spawn and flanking around to another objective.
- On the very top of the radar tower to the south of this objective, there is a M82A3 MID sniper battle pickup. You are in a prime position to either hold back enemies running across the open area from the Barracks (B) or pick off a couple enemies before pushing over and taking the objective.
- When defending this capture point on land, be very careful because you have less cover than you think. Most of your small buildings and boxes will be nonexistent after a few rounds are fired from the enemy team.
- Beware of the mobile AA that spawns at the Barracks (B). Even though it is designed to take out air vehicles, it can make quick work of your squad that is on the ground if you don't eliminate it immediately.

PRO TIP: WALSHY

To the south of the Dockyard (A) there is a tall radar tower. With the recon class here, you can snipe and paint vehicles with your PLD for your engineers to take out the multiple watercraft that are cruising around the map.

CONTROL POINT ASSETS

US CONTROL	CN CONTROL
RHIB (1)	RHIB (1)
RCB-90 (1)	DV-15 (1)

B: BARRACKS

- This flag is located north towards the middle of the map. The Barracks (B) is covered by a small gate with a shrine next to the flag. There are also four different buildings surrounding this control point, so cover shouldn't be hard to find.
- A mobile AA unit will spawn here for your team, which will be very useful given that the enemy team's most effective way to reach this control point will be by air.
- After securing the Barracks (B) look to move towards the next closest objective which will be the Dockyard (A). This will help you keep control or regain control as you can move from objective to objective as they are both on the same island.
- When attacking this control point, have one squad make their approach by air and drop near the northern part of the Barracks (B). While doing this, have a second squad make their way towards the southern part by using some light water vehicles and attack boats.
- When defending this control point, make full use of the buildings by having a recon and engineer classes inside any of these buildings. This will assist in taking out transport helicopters and infantry units that reach this objective.

CONTROL POINT ASSETS

US CONTROL	CN CONTROL
RHIB (1)	RHIB (1)
LAV-AD (1)	Type 95 AA (1)

C: FIREBASE ISLAND

- This flag is located closest to the US base and further west of the CN base. Firebase Island's (C) biggest feature is the massive four-story building, which has a clear view of the whole island. There also is a long trench right by the flagpole that can be used for hiding from the enemy and contesting the control point.
- Levolution takes place at this control point and splits the island in half. This will completely destroy the building located here and kill any players inside and around it. Once the destroyer has run ashore, the ship's autonomous AA cannon opens fire on enemy aircraft. Keep control of this flag to maintain control of the destroyer's AA cannon.
- The PWCs spawned here will come in handy for quick travel to the nearest islands. The .50Cals on the island will help defend against incoming enemies approaching from the water.
- When attacking this control point use a stealth jet to lay down some heavy fire on the main building and do as much damage as possible. This should kill or force any recon units posted on the roof of the building to take cover, making them useless.
- When defending this control point, have engineers equipped with IGLAs or Stingers to take out any stealth jets, scout helicopters, and transport helicopters. This will limit enemies, forcing them to approach by water.

CONTROL POINT ASSETS

US CONTROL	CN CONTROL
PWC (2)	PWC (2)

D: SOLAR ISLAND

- This control point lies west of the CN base with a building surrounded by solar panels and sandbags that are used for cover.
- Upon capturing, PWCs spawn here. Use the PWCs to reach enemy control points quickly and annoy them by constantly contesting their control points.
- The island has three stationary weapons: a .50Cal and two HJ-8 Launchers. These will help teams defend against both air and water vehicles.
- This map allows you to capture and contest many of the flags from a distance in the water. When going for the capture, take advantage of this and dive underwater near the shore to confuse the enemy and buy time for your team.
- The roof of the building on the island provides a great view for recon classes to snipe from and watch the flag. This building provides great cover when attack boats or helicopters come to attack, but be careful—the building can be destroyed.

CONTROL POINT ASSETS

US CONTROL	CN CONTROL
PWC (2)	PWC (2)

PRO TIP: STRONGSIDE

A great way to pick up quick control points on this map is by driving the attack boat manned with four players. Have at least one engineer to repair the vehicle. You're able to capture most of the control points from the water's edge, so speed from one control point to another while taking out enemies.

E: SHIPWRECK

- Shipwreck (E) is a destroyed aircraft carrier found at the south tip of the map.
- The team who captures this control point will gain access to another scout helicopter. This will assist the team greatly so you can move around the map faster, as players will want to avoid swimming on this larger map.
- The team who captures the Shipwreck (E) should focus on controlling both Firebase Island (C) and Solar Island (D). These are the nearest control points to the Shipwreck (E), which allows players to react to what the enemy is doing.
- Upon capturing, PWCs appear. Infantry units should use these to head back to land to assist fellow squads in capturing and defending Firebase Island (C) and Solar Island (D).
- The destroyed aircraft carrier has an opening that leads inside of it. This is a great place for defenders to hide and take cover from attack boats and helicopters. This forces the opposing team to take the fight to the ground where you will be waiting for them.

CONTROL POINT ASSETS

US CONTROL	CN CONTROL
PWC (2)	PWC (2)
AH-6J Little Bird (1)	Z-11W (1)

CONQUEST SMALL

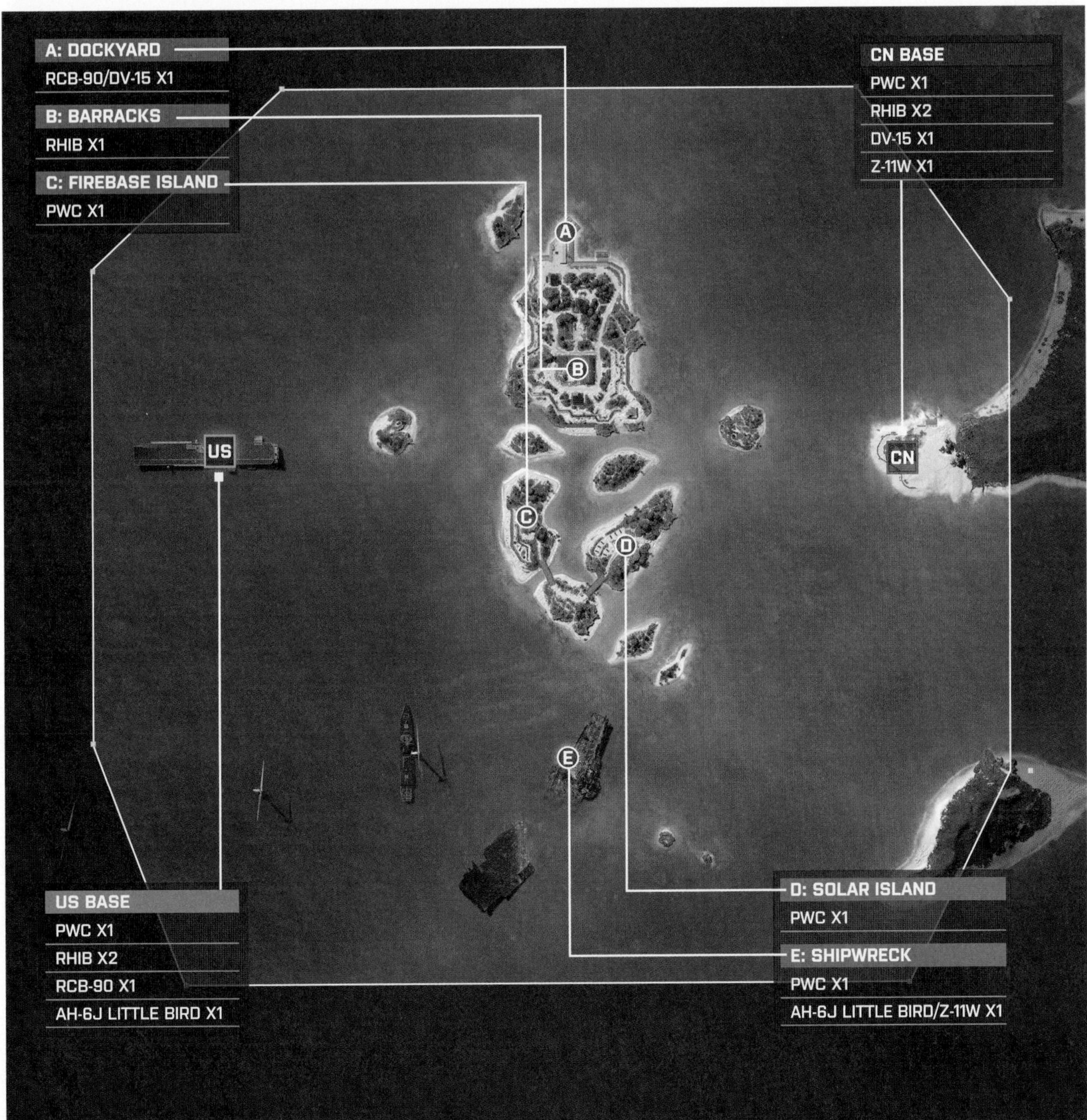

RECOMMENDED SQUAD COMPOSITION:

This is a battle of water and air superiority, with five control points lined up from north to south. The five control points the US team and CN team will be battling over are Dockyard (A), Barracks (B), Firebase Island (C), Solar Island (D), and Shipwreck (E). With five flags up for grabs, your team will need to capture three control points in order to drain the opposing team's tickets. The best strategy for the US team will be to hold the Dockyard (A), the Barracks (B), and Firebase Island (C). By building a perimeter around the Barracks (B), the US team can send players either north or south to support teammates in the Dockyard (A) and Firebase Island (C).The CN teams should try to hold the Dockyard (A), the Barracks (B), and Solar Island (D), as well as the Shipwreck (E) if the US team isn't putting up much of a fight. The Shipwreck (E) is positioned on the south end of the map, but closer to the CN base. The CN team will need their attack boat to patrol the south side, warding off the US attackers as they try to flank Solar Island (D) and push towards the Shipwreck (E). The US team can extend their defensive perimeter to capture the Shipwreck (E) as well, but defending four flags on this large map can be difficult, so be warned. Regardless of what team you are on, prepare for a mix of defending against constant vehicle attacks and close-quarter combat fighting on one of the many islands on the map. With so many vehicles, it is suggested to have a few extra engineers to use target-locked launchers and support members to replenish the engineer's ammo.

US BASE

- The US base is on the western edge of the map stationed atop a US aircraft carrier.
- It's a few hundred meters to shore and the US base provides plenty of vehicles—both air and water—to escort friendlies to land.
- A squad should control a RCB-90 to cover the team's light water vehicles as they head north to capture the Dockyard (A) and the Barracks (B). The light water vehicles are fast-moving vehicles that will allow you to reach these control points quickly.
- Fill every seat of the transport helicopter and head east towards Firebase Island (C) where two passengers should jump down to score an easy control point. Once the passengers are dropped, immediately head south towards the Shipwreck (E) to provide air support for the remaining squads who rushed this objective at the start.
- The CN team has a handful of vehicles as well, so stock up on engineers to aid your team in destroying the enemy's vehicles. Having engineers near squad vehicles will score you easy points as you can repair them when they take damage. Keep your squad vehicles in tip top shape as they will lead you to victory.

BASE ASSETS

NAME	PWC	RHIB	RCB-90	AH-6J Little Bird
QUANTITY	1	2	1	1

CN BASE

- Positioned on an island to the east, the CN base is too far from every point by foot. It is crucial to jump in as many of the vehicles at your disposal as you can.
- Take an attack boat to any point except for the Barracks (B), where this powerful boat will be ineffective. Take your transport helicopter to drop off your squad at the Barracks (B), Firebase Island (C), or Solar Island (D) where they can effectively move around from objective to objective.
- You will encounter many vehicles throughout this map. Have three engineers in your squad the entire game to be able to deal with these threats and repair your own vehicles.
- Air combat is not as big of a threat on this map. Have your engineers equipped with surface-to-surface missiles to deal with all the light water vehicles you will encounter.
- As a squad, try to all not be in the same vehicle. This way the enemy can't win a fight, wipe out your whole squad, and decrease Field Upgrade progress. Being slightly split up can also guarantee that at least one of your squadmates will be able to give you a good spawn if you die.

BASE ASSETS

NAME	PWC	RHIB	DV-15	Z-11W
QUANTITY	1	2	1	1

A: DOCKYARD

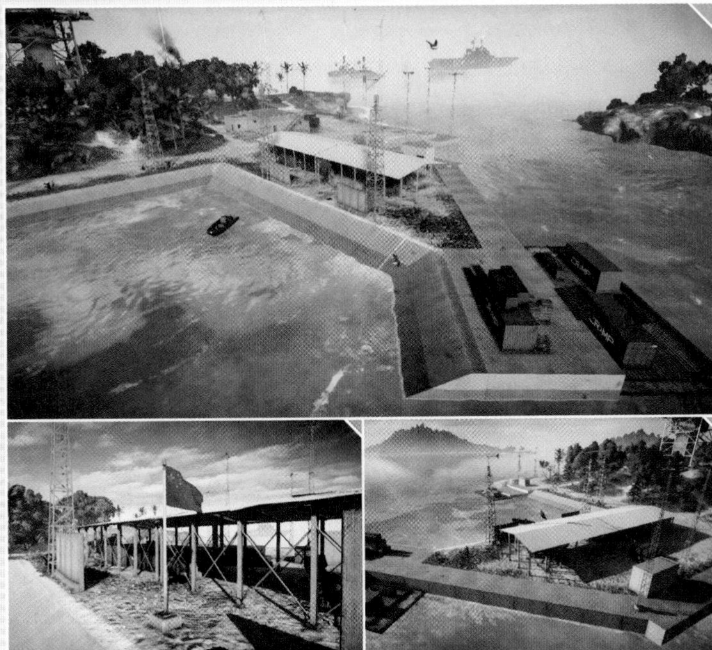

- This control point positioned north of the cluster of islands is a loading dock that can be challenged from land or the surrounding water.
- Upon capture of this control point, you have your choice of pushing by land over to the Barracks (B) or taking one of the light water vehicles that spawn and flanking around to another objective.
- On the very top of the radar building to the south of this objective, there is a M82A3 MID sniper battle pickup. You are in prime position to either hold back enemies running across the open area near the Barracks (B) or pick off a few enemies before pushing over and taking the objective.
- When defending this control point on land be very careful, because you have less cover than you think. Most of your small buildings and boxes will be nonexistent after a few rounds fired from the enemy team.

CONTROL POINT ASSETS

US CONTROL	CN CONTROL
RCB-90 (1)	DV-15 (1)

B: BARRACKS

- This flag is located north towards the middle of the map. The Barracks (B) is covered by a small gate with a shrine next to the flag. There are also four different buildings surrounding this control point, so cover shouldn't be hard to find.
- After securing the Barracks (B), look to move towards the next closest objective, which will be the Dockyard (A). This will help you keep control or regain control as you can move from objective to objective because they are both on the same island.
- When attacking this control point, have one squad make their approach by air and drop near the northern part of the Barracks (B). While doing this, have a second squad make their way towards the southern part by using some light water vehicles and attack boats.
- When defending this control point, make full use of the buildings by having a recon and engineer classes inside any of these buildings. This will assist in taking out transport helicopters and infantry units that reach this objective.

CONTROL POINT ASSETS

US CONTROL	CN CONTROL
RHIB (1)	RHIB (1)

C: FIREBASE ISLAND

- This flag is located closest to the US base and farther west of the CN base. Firebase Island's (C) biggest feature is the massive four-story building, which has a clear view of the whole island. There also is a long trench right by the flagpole that can be used for hiding from the enemy and contesting the control point.
- Levolution takes place at this control point and splits the island in half. This will completely destroy the building located here and kill any players inside and around it. Once the destroyer has run ashore, the ship's autonomous AA cannon opens fire on enemy aircraft. Keep control of this flag to maintain control of the destroyer's AA cannon.
- The PWCs come in handy for quick travel to the nearest islands. The .50Cals on the island will help defend against incoming enemies approaching from the water.
- When attacking this control point, use a stealth jet to lay down some heavy fire on the main building and do as much damage as possible. This should kill or force any recon units posted on the roof of the building to take cover, making them useless.
- When defending this control point, have engineers equipped with IGLAs or Stingers to take out any scout helicopters. This will limit enemies, forcing them to approach by water.

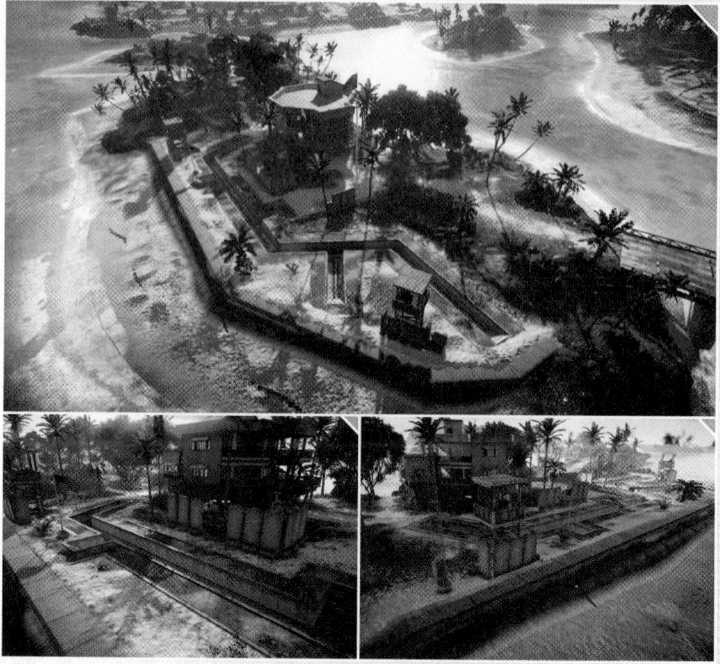

CONTROL POINT ASSETS

US CONTROL	CN CONTROL
PWC (1)	PWC (1)

D: SOLAR ISLAND

- This control point lies west of the CN base with a building surrounded by solar panels and sandbags that are used for cover.
- Upon capturing, a PWC spawns. Use the PWC to reach enemy control points quickly and annoy them by constantly contesting their control points.
- The island has three stationary weapons: a .50Cal and two HJ-8 Launchers. These will help teams defend against both air and water vehicles.
- This map allows you to capture and contest many of the flags from a distance in the water. When going for the capture, take advantage of this and dive underwater near the shore to confuse the enemy and buy time for your team.
- The roof of the building on the island provides a great view for recon classes to snipe from and watch the flag. This building provides great cover when attack boats or helicopters come to attack, but be careful—the building can be destroyed.

CONTROL POINT ASSETS

US CONTROL	CN CONTROL
PWC (1)	PWC (1)

E: SHIPWRECK

- Shipwreck (E) is a destroyed aircraft carrier found at the south tip of the map.
- The team who captures this control point will gain access to another scout helicopter. This will assist the team greatly so you can move around the map faster, as players will want to avoid swimming on this larger map.
- The team who captures the Shipwreck (E) should focus on controlling both Firebase Island (C) and Solar Island (D). These are the nearest control points to the Shipwreck (E), which allows players to react to what the enemy is doing.
- A PWC spawns here for both teams. Infantry units should use the PWC to head back to land to assist fellow squads in capturing and defending Firebase Island (C) and Solar Island (D).
- The destroyed aircraft carrier has an opening that leads inside of it. This is a great place for defenders to hide and take cover from attack boats and helicopters. This forces the opposing team to take the fight to the ground where you will be waiting for them.

CONTROL POINT ASSETS

US CONTROL	CN CONTROL
PWC (1)	PWC (1)
AH-6J Little Bird (1)	Z-11W (1)

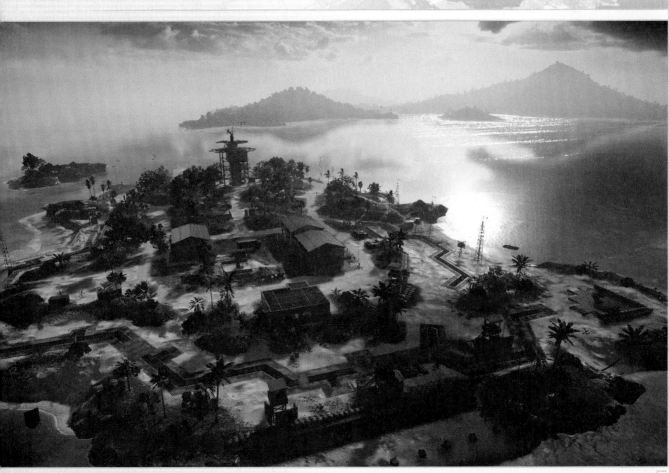

RUSH

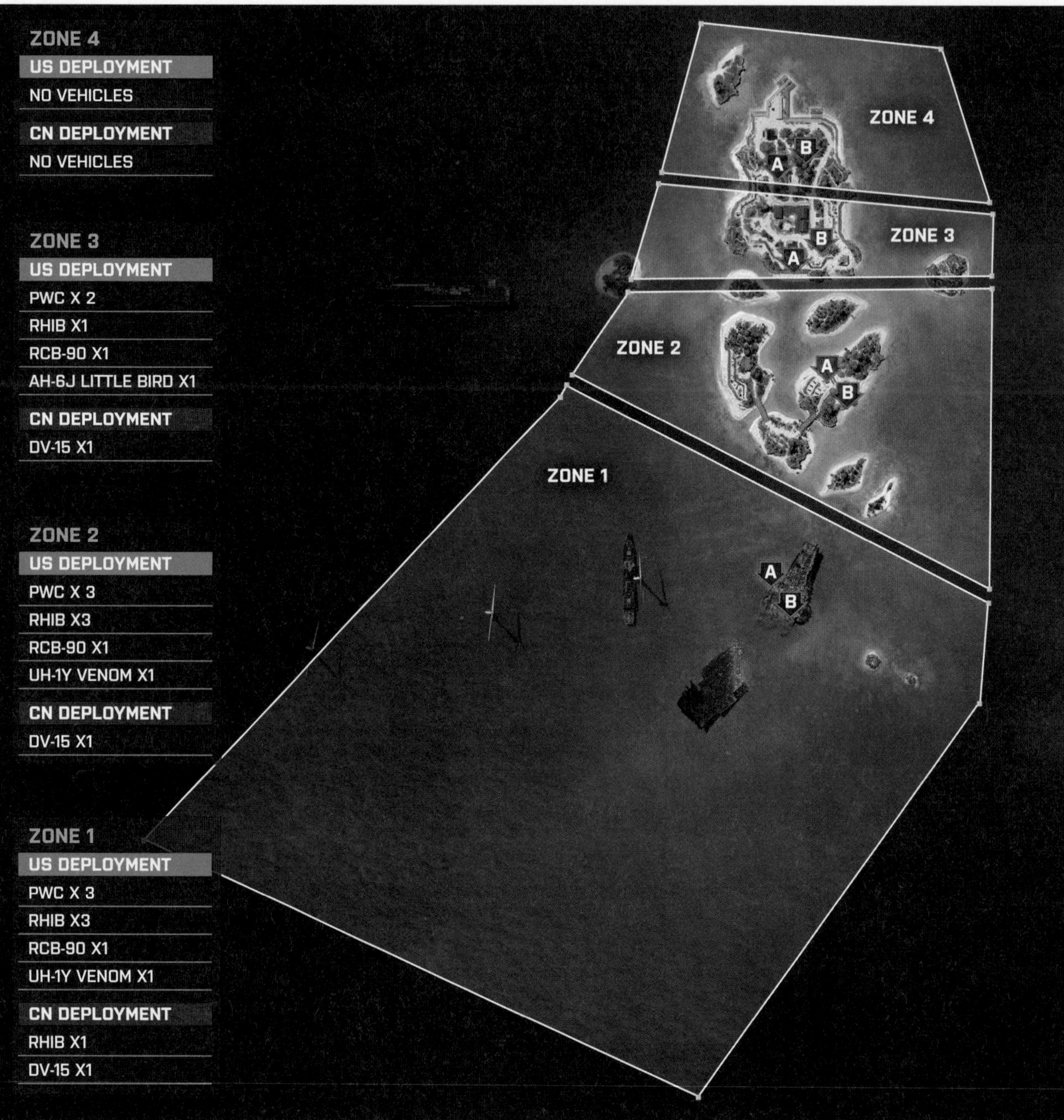

In this epic naval brawl, the US team must arm eight M-COM stations across four different zones. Both teams will be offered a variety of action, including intense attack boats duels, aerial assaults, and close-quarter infantry engagements. The US team will start on an aircraft carrier, make their way towards the Shipwreck, and proceed to Zone 4 in the Dockyard. With four zones to defend, the CN team has their work cut out for them. The CN team will have a tough time defending the objectives spread throughout the Shipwreck. Have recon players sit on the south tip of the destroyed carrier and snipe the attackers as they try to take off from their carrier. Don't get nervous if you are on the defending team and get pushed backed to Zone 3 or even Zone 4. Zone 4 is in the Dockyard with a radar tower that allows the CN team to set up a strong defensive perimeter. Attackers will have various vehicles to help complete the objective throughout the first three zones until Zone 4 in the Dockyard. Take advantage of these vehicles and then switch to close-quarter classes to successfully complete the mission.

ZONE 1: SHIPWRECK

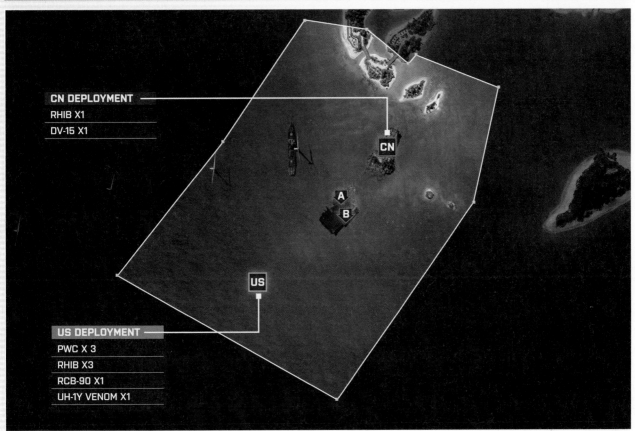

CN DEPLOYMENT
RHIB X1
DV-15 X1

CN

A

B

US

US DEPLOYMENT
PWC X 3
RHIB X3
RCB-90 X1
UH-1Y VENOM X1

US DEPLOYMENT

RECOMMENDED SQUAD COMPOSITION: 

- The US deployment is to the southwest of the half-sunk aircraft carrier where both M-COM stations are located. Wait for your entire team and make a push together. Don't leave anyone behind to swim.
- The RCB-90 is your most valuable vehicle, so send out your scout helicopter and light water vehicle ahead to spot the enemy's attack helicopter and attack boat. Eliminating these threats and keeping your RCB-90 will be one of the biggest keys to victory on this zone with all the cover fire it can provide.
- Send one of your light water vehicles to the southwestern half of the broken battleship with a recon member. This way you can have a Radio Beacon and a sniper for backup, which will allow you to spawn near the action if you die. More importantly, use your sniper and get some easy kills by picking off all the enemies near the M-COM stations that will only have mid- to close-range weapons.
- Your squad initially needs to be composed of multiple engineers to deal with all the vehicles of the defending CN team. After you make it to the battleship, switch to your best mid-range support or assault class.
- With all the early threat of vehicles, you must also be careful to not get sniped by enemy recon players on the southwest edge of the broken battleship. Take all the enemies out on this half of this ship first so they can't shoot you from behind as you try to arm the M-COM stations.

DEPLOYMENT AREA ASSETS

NAME	PWC	RHIB	RCB-90	UH-1Y Venom
QUANTITY	3	3	1	1

CN DEPLOYMENT

RECOMMENDED SQUAD COMPOSITION:

- The CN deployment is positioned on the north side of the Shipwreck that holds both M-COM stations.
- The CN team has an attack boat. This will play a huge role when stopping the attacking vehicles, which outnumber the defenders. The attack boat should stay near the destroyed aircraft carrier, allowing fellow engineers to support against nearby threats.
- Being outnumbered in vehicles, add a few extra engineers to your squad. Your team's vehicles will need all the assistance they can get when fighting the enemy.
- Send infantry units to the destroyed aircraft carrier. There is a level inside the carrier near M-COM Station B that you will use to catch the enemy by surprise if they board the destroyed aircraft carrier.
- On the south side, the tail of the carrier is tilted, providing great cover for snipers. Send a squad with a recon class or two and pick off as many attackers as you can before the enemy reaches the destroyed aircraft carrier.

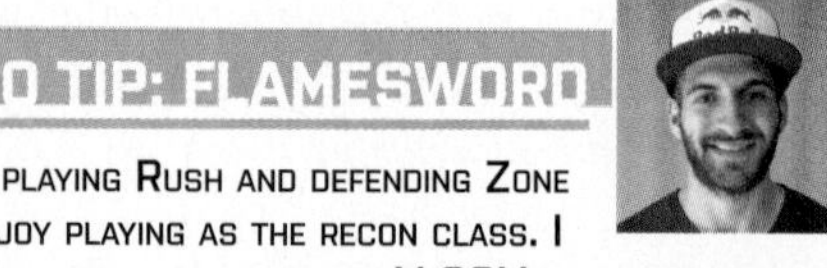

PRO TIP: FLAMESWORD

When playing Rush and defending Zone 1, I enjoy playing as the recon class. I position myself south of the M-COM stations and snipe towards the attacking team's deployment zone. I reduce the attacking team's ticket before they can even get close.

DEPLOYMENT AREA ASSETS

NAME	DV-15	RHIB
QUANTITY	1	1

M-COM STATION A

- M-COM Station A is located towards the middle of the destroyed ship, and is behind a downed transport helicopter.
- Defending for the CN team will be very hard, given that the only cover you can use is the debris scattered around the area.
- When attacking, have the scout helicopter relay information on the enemy location and numbers. This will help direct the attack boats and light water vehicles on where the weakest points of defense are and show where to make their approach.
- Since there is little to no cover for the defenders, attacking the other objective will make M-COM Station A very easy to capture by taking out remaining enemies with the scout helicopter.
- Defend M-COM Station A with a few engineers equipped with the FIM-92 Stinger to take out helicopters and the FGM-148 Javelin for attack boats.

M-COM STATION B

- This M-COM station is positioned on the south end of the shipwrecked aircraft carrier. There is much rubble and wreckage around this objective for defending this control point. This cover with prove to be very useful for the defending team.
- When defending, use this area for cover and prepare for incoming enemies unloading on the south end of the Shipwreck.
- When the attacking team takes over this area, they can use the cover to stay alive and spawn more squad members here.
- When attacking, push to get infantry onto the shipwrecked aircraft carrier. Spawning teammates here will prove to be immensely helpful. Get as many infantry units near this area as you can to gain control and capture the objective.
- When defending, take advantage of the wreckage by laying down Claymores. These Claymores will blend in with the wreckage, making them nearly impossible to detect.
- To the west and north of this M-COM station lies a underwater ramp that leads inside the carrier. This will provide incredible cover from enemy attacking helicopters. This underwater hallway also allows you to surprise the enemies arming this station.

ZONE 2: SOLAR ISLAND

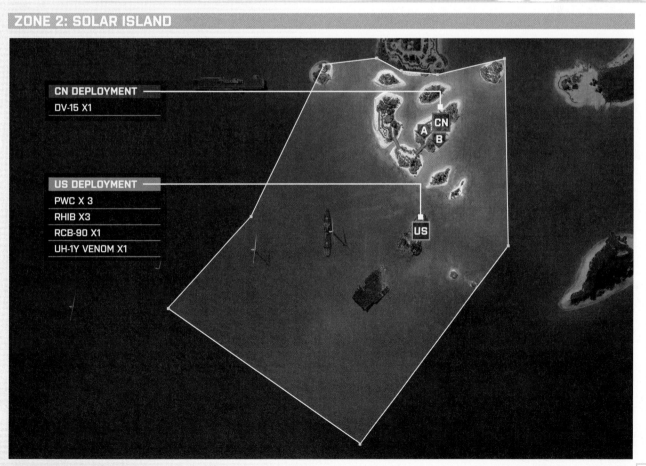

CN DEPLOYMENT

- DV-15 X1

US DEPLOYMENT

- PWC X 3
- RHIB X3
- RCB-90 X1
- UH-1Y VENOM X1

CN

A

B

US

US DEPLOYMENT

RECOMMENDED SQUAD COMPOSITION:

- You start at the same deployment location, but this time you are much farther away from the new M-COM stations that are located on the largest island to the northeast. Like last time, leave no man behind—it is too far of a swim.
- The enemy only has one attack boat. Send your RHIBs, PWCs, or scout helicopter to spot where this is located so you can take it out. Be careful when circling the islands in your watercraft. There are a few threatening HJ-8 Launchers and .50Cals that will do massive damage if they are not taken care of.
- Be sure to leave a squad member behind on the southwestern island to give cover fire and good spawns until it is safe to push up. You do not want to have your squad wiped out and force you to start all the way back at the US deployment.
- Make it a priority to first clear out the M-COM Station B building before trying to go for M-COM Station A. The enemy can easily pick you off from this building and cost you precious tickets if you don't go for this objective first.
- If the M-COM Station B building is proving difficult to take over, make sure to target the enemy's cover by destroying the walls. This will expose them and allow you to take control by getting easier kills.

DEPLOYMENT AREA ASSETS

NAME	PWC	RHIB	RCB-90	UH-1Y Venom
QUANTITY	3	3	1	1

CN DEPLOYMENT

RECOMMENDED SQUAD COMPOSITION:

- If the battle is lost on the Shipwreck, the CN deployment will be pushed back to Solar Island.
- The defender's only vehicle is an attack boat, but don't worry—Solar Island has many stationary weapons to use when warding off attacking vehicles.
- Having an engineer with the Repair Tool will allow your attack boat to put a dent in the attacking team's tickets. The engineer will also score some easy points for repairing the vehicle.
- The roof of the building located on Solar Island can be reached by taking the stairs inside. A squad composed of engineers and recon players will benefit from the multiple vantage points provided.
- The building provides cover inside. When defending, it will be easier to watch M-COM Station B from the first floor of the building. There are open windows that allow you to spot attackers who go for the arm.

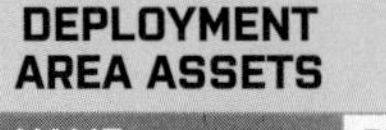

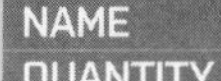

DEPLOYMENT AREA ASSETS

NAME	DV-15
QUANTITY	1

M-COM STATION A

- This station is located behind a large satellite and right next to a truck. It is completely covered by sandbags with a building to the west of M-COM Station A.
- For the CN team, vehicles will not be of much use since the only one that spawns is the DV-15. The building near M-COM Station A will be used primarily as a point of defense, giving your team plenty of angles to work with.
- When attacking M-COM Station A, have a scout helicopter to transport a few teammates to the island just south of the objective. Have another squad make their way via attack boats and light water vehicles to the west side of M-COM Station A. This will ensure that one of the two routes will be successful.
- Focus on gaining control of the building next to M-COM Station A when playing as the attacking team. Have a few assault classes infiltrate the building and clear out any remaining defenders.
- When defending M-COM Station A, use recon and engineer classes and make your way inside the building near this station. The recon class should lay down a Radio Beacon to keep teammates spawning nearby and to retain control. The engineer's main focus should be to take out any vehicles that may approach from the air or water.

M-COM STATION B

- Located on Solar Island, this objective is placed outside the east part of a building.
- When defending this objective, use the windows to have both great cover and a great view over incoming enemy boats dropping off infantry.
- When defending, beware that the building adjacent to M-COM Station B can be destroyed. Take out the incoming enemy with engineers before the attackers can accomplish this.
- The roof of the building will prove useful as it is a great vantage point to take out incoming enemies.
- When attacking this objective, take over the building adjacent to M-COM Station B. Spawn your squad here to have easy cover and control of this area.
- You can take down the building adjacent to M-COM Station B with explosives and attack boats by destroying the walls on each floor of the building. This will eliminate all cover the defenders have for this objective.

ZONE 3: BARRACKS

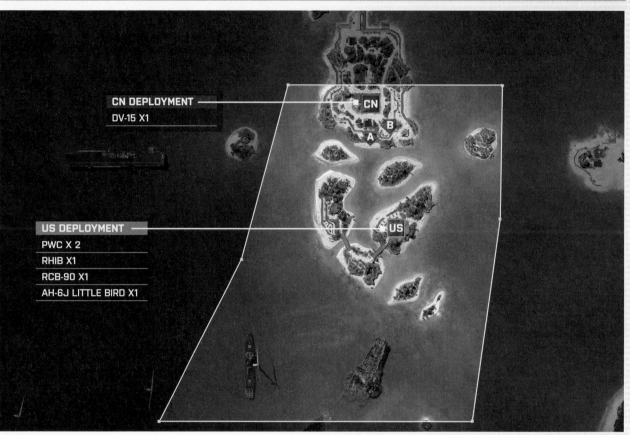

CN DEPLOYMENT
DV-15 X1

US DEPLOYMENT
PWC X 2
RHIB X1
RCB-90 X1
AH-6J LITTLE BIRD X1

CN
B
A
US

US DEPLOYMENT

RECOMMENDED SQUAD COMPOSITION:

- The US team spawns to the south of both M-COM stations. You are much closer now that you spawn in the cluster of islands, but taking one of your watercraft will still be the faster way to travel.
- The shoreline on the island with both M-COM stations is heavily armed. Take out the watchtowers and concrete blocks before landing on the beach to reduce the defender's cover.
- Be careful when running through the trenches on the beach here. The enemy team will likely place M18 Claymores in these dark, narrow areas.
- Get control of the building to the north of M-COM Station A. This will allow you to cut off enemy reinforcements, and the roof will give you a bird's eye view of the entire surrounding area.
- The enemy only has one DV-15, which is very powerful, but the majority of this zone will be fought with infantry against infantry combat. Be sure to have a couple members of your squad as the assault class so you can save some tickets by reviving each other.

DEPLOYMENT AREA ASSETS

NAME	PWC	RHIB	RCB-90	AH-6J Little Bird
QUANTITY	2	1	1	1

CN DEPLOYMENT

RECOMMENDED SQUAD COMPOSITION:

- The US team succeeded in arming the objectives in the previous zone. The CN deployment is now pushed to the Barracks located north of Solar Island.
- Both M-COM stations lie south of the CN deployment and are close to the shoreline.
- The Barracks are surrounded by .50Cals and HJ-8 Launchers. These stationary weapons will aid when defending against attacking vehicles.
- The building north of M-COM Station A is a great sniping spot. While one player snipes, the rest of the squad should push up to the trenches around the objective. This will provide great cover and the element of surprise once attackers reach the shoreline.
- Classes with C4 and Claymores can set up traps along the trenches near both objectives. East of M-COM Station B is a trench that gives a great line of sight of the objective. Use this to kill any attackers that go for quick arms.

DEPLOYMENT AREA ASSETS

NAME	DV-15
QUANTITY	1

M-COM STATION A

- M-COM Station A is located just south of the Barracks inside a trench. You can find this area riddled with .50Cals and stationary launchers.
- The CN team is going to rely heavily on these turrets and launchers to protect M-COM Station A, since the team will only have one attack boat at their disposal.
- When attacking M-COM Station A, you are going to want to split the defender's forces and focus on drawing their attention elsewhere. Have a scout helicopter make its way towards the west and have watercraft come from the south.
- Place Claymores in these trenches to pick up easy kills and alert you when the enemy is getting close to the objective. Try to clear the enemies out of these trenches before they can spawn their teammates.

PRO TIP: ELUMNITE

THE RECON CLASS IS SO INVALUABLE FOR STEALTH PURPOSES IN RUSH. I LOVE TO SNEAK AROUND AN ENEMY LOCATION AND PLACE A RADIO BEACON TOWARDS THE FARTHEST POINT OF THE WESTERN TRENCHES BEHIND A CRATE. THIS WILL KEEP MY TEAM IN THE FIGHT MUCH LONGER, KEEPING THEM CLOSE TO THE OBJECTIVES.

M-COM STATION B

- This M-COM station is located northeast of M-COM Station A on the Barracks. This objective has crates placed around it for minimal cover.
- Surrounding this objective you'll find destructible guard towers equipped with .50Cals. By taking out these towers, you'll take out the .50Cals as well.
- When defending, use the trenches east, west, and south of the objective for great cover to drop in when taking fire.
- When attacking, to take control of the building north of M-COM Station A make a flank around the east side of M-COM Station B near the beach. Once here, you can head west following the dead zone marker where the enemy will not expect you to be.
- When defending, use the roof of building west of the objective to take advantage of the higher position with the recon class to snipe any incoming infantry. This overview will provide for great position to spot incoming enemies as well.

ZONE 4: DOCKYARD

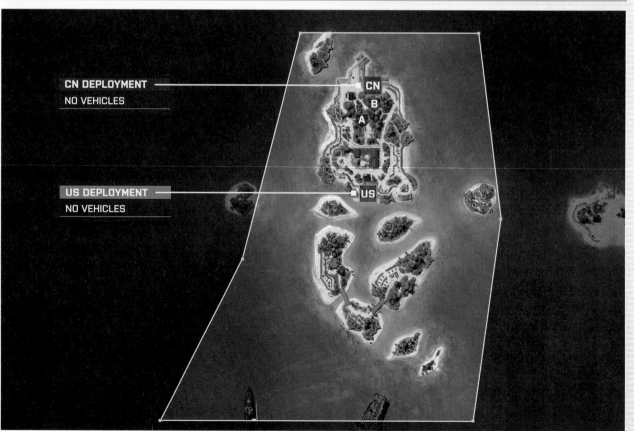

CN DEPLOYMENT
NO VEHICLES

US DEPLOYMENT
NO VEHICLES

US DEPLOYMENT

RECOMMENDED SQUAD COMPOSITION:

- For this last zone, the US deployment is directly south of both M-COM stations, which are located in a basketball court and at the base of a radar tower. M-COM Station B is the most difficult to arm.
- With no vehicles on this zone for either team, make sure to have to your squad comprised mainly of assault, recon, and support classes to eliminate the 100% infantry army that you will encounter.
- Although M-COM Station B is located at the base of the radar tower, push up the stairs and take over the tower so you can control the surrounding area. The last thing you want is to be killed over and over again from above.
- Before your team tries to push up and take the radar tower, have a recon member sit back and snipe some of the enemies that are sure to be sitting on top of the radar tower out in the open. Take your time lining up these shots; you may only get one chance before the enemy starts to be more careful.
- Flanking from the east and west sides of the island will allow your team to get behind the enemy and cut off reinforcements. Make sure a recon member of your squad places a Radio Beacon occasionally so your squad never has to spawn back at the US deployment.

CN DEPLOYMENT

RECOMMENDED SQUAD COMPOSITION:

- The attacking team has made it to the last zone and now have pushed you back to the Dockyard. This is your last chance to win the game, so bring your best skills.
- South of the base stands a radar tower. This tower provides a great overview of the map.
- There are no vehicles for the team, but a handful of stationary weapons. Use these to lay down steel and keep the attackers back.
- A squad will head up the flight of stairs to the top of the radar tower. Have two recon players providing cover from above. Players can easily watch over M-COM Station A, which sits in a basketball court just below.
- The US team has no vehicles for this last zone. Be sure to have a squad composed of short- to medium-range players. Classes with Claymores and C4 will prove useful in planting the areas around the objective. This will lead to some easy kills and less tickets for the attacking team.

M-COM STATION A

- M-COM Station A is located just north of the Barracks in a small basketball court with a few crates around it and an explosive fuel tank right outside.
- With no vehicles, once again the CN team will have to position recon classes on top of the large radar tower to spot any infantry making their way towards M-COM Station A.
- The close area around the basketball court allows the defending team to set up C4 and Claymores in close proximity of the objective.
- When attacking, destroy the fuel tanks outside of the basketball court to take out any defender prone near the objective.
- The attackers will have an easier time arming M-COM Station A by knocking down the wooden fence around the court. Combining this with Smoke Grenades will force the defenders to leave their post on the radar tower, allowing your team to move to the next objective once M-COM Station A is destroyed.

M-COM STATION B

- This objective is located on the south side at the base of the radar tower with very little cover surrounding it.
- When defending, make your way up the radar tower to utilize the recon class. Sniping from the highest point on the radar tower will give you and your squad the advantage by spotting players and picking enemies off as they move forward towards the objectives.
- When defending, place T-UGS within the radar tower to be alerted of the enemy attempting to make an arm or trying to sneak up the stairwell behind you.
- South of the objective are two .50Cals. This will prove useful to take out the enemy ground infantry traveling on the south trail leading to M-COM Station B. After getting a couple kills, relocate so you aren't a sitting target.
- When attacking, a safer route to travel would be to the east and west of M-COM Station B, following the shoreline for a long flank. This route will be lengthy but well worth it when you get behind the enemy team.

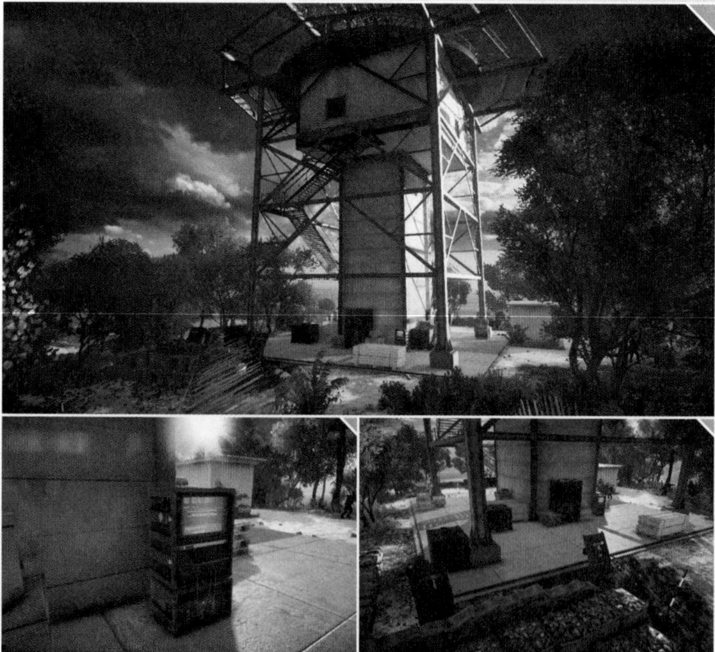

OBLITERATION

RECOMMENDED SQUAD COMPOSITION:

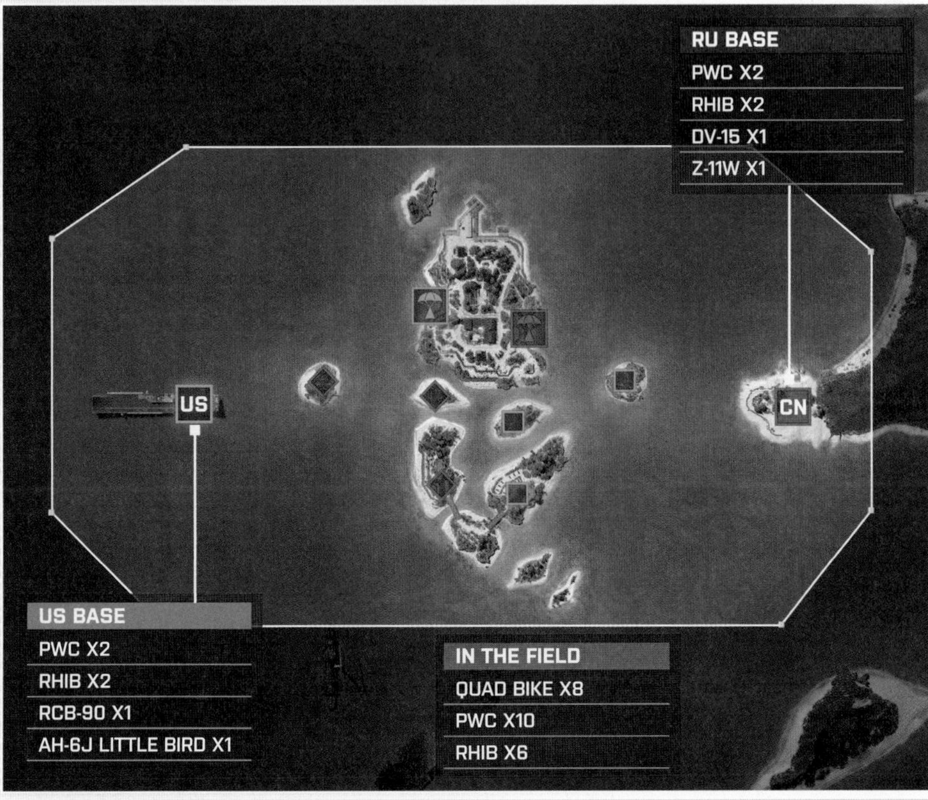

- The CN team looks to arm the three targets scattered around Firebase Island.
- The US team aims to arm the three targets around Solar Island.
- The bomb is located near the Barracks. There is a radar tower to the north. Sending recon players to the tower allows your team to control the Barracks.
- Both teams should utilize their scout helicopters to move around squad members and the bomb carrier. The helicopter also provides great defense as it can quickly move around the map.
- The attack boat is very effective when going for the arm. Bring this powerful boat near the targets and fire rounds to scatter the defenders.

DEFUSE

RECOMMENDED SQUAD COMPOSITION:

- In this Defuse match, both teams are confined to the Barracks of Paracel Storm. The US team spawns to the west of the Barracks while the CN team spawns to the east.
- Laptop A is located between the two main buildings of the Barracks. The objective has many items around for cover and an explosive tank nearby.
- Laptop B is positioned in the building to the south of the Barracks. The building has a staircase that leads to the roof, providing great firing angles and cover.
- When defending, the CN team should head into the two buildings west of their spawn point. Have your squad spread throughout both buildings; this allows you to watch both objectives. Prepare for gunfights with the attackers from the building directly west of Laptop A.
- When playing as the US team, attackers want to stick together as they go for the objectives. The best route is to take the Trenches to the south to get behind the building that holds Laptop B. The building walls are very fragile, so blow the back wall and go in for the arm.

DOMINATION

RECOMMENDED SQUAD COMPOSITION:

- The three control points on this map are the Trenches (A), Monument (B), and Court (C).
- There is a USAS-12 battle pickup north of the Monument (B). After you grab this, stick near the buildings as this is a perfect short- to medium-range shotgun.
- With the capture radius being so short, lob grenades towards an objective that is being captured. You will either kill the enemy or injure them before you rush in.
- Use the trenches to move around the map—it is a much safer route than running out in the open. Do this when the other team has superior positioning.
- The best strategy is to capture the Monument (B) and Court (C). Defend these objectives by using the building to the west to view both flags.

SQUAD DEATHMATCH

RECOMMENDED SQUAD COMPOSITION:

- This battle is set around the Barracks, which is experiencing a vicious storm.
- Squads will want to take shelter in one of the buildings. The building provides cover and allows you to look towards any direction of the map. Take cover and engage squads that are fighting other squads.
- There are a ton of explosive tanks scattered throughout the map. Shoot these when enemies are near to easily take the enemy down.
- Have an engineer in the squad to assist in taking out the IFV when it is under enemy control or repair it when your squad controls it. Use the Trenches for cover if the other squads are in control of the IFV.
- The M32 MGL battle pickup is in the center of the map. This weapon packs some heavy heat, so be sure to grab it every chance you get.

TEAM DEATHMATCH

RECOMMENDED SQUAD COMPOSITION:

- In this Team Deathmatch variant, controlling the one of the three buildings in the Barracks area is a good strategy.
- There are a handful of explosive tanks around the map. Shoot these when enemies are near for an easy kill.
- Utilize the Trenches around the map for quick getaways and possible flanks.
- Scattered around the map are shipping containers that provide great cover. Some are interactive and you can hide inside. Place a T-UGS inside to detect nearby enemies and jump out at the appropriate time.
- There are two battle pickups on the map: the USAS-12 and the M32 MGL. These weapons pack some heavy firepower, so pick them up any chance you get.

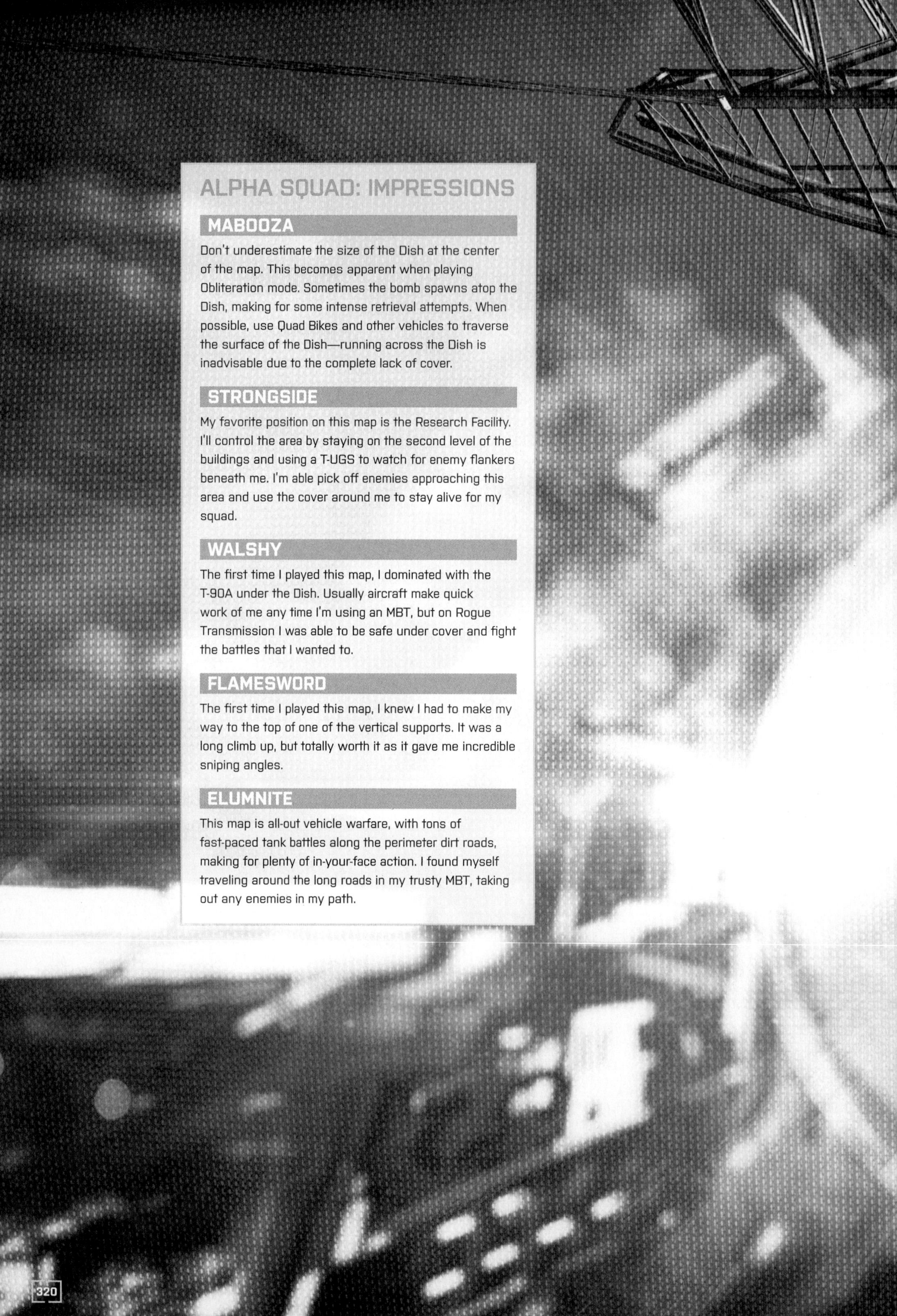

ALPHA SQUAD: IMPRESSIONS

MABOOZA

Don't underestimate the size of the Dish at the center of the map. This becomes apparent when playing Obliteration mode. Sometimes the bomb spawns atop the Dish, making for some intense retrieval attempts. When possible, use Quad Bikes and other vehicles to traverse the surface of the Dish—running across the Dish is inadvisable due to the complete lack of cover.

STRONGSIDE

My favorite position on this map is the Research Facility. I'll control the area by staying on the second level of the buildings and using a T-UGS to watch for enemy flankers beneath me. I'm able pick off enemies approaching this area and use the cover around me to stay alive for my squad.

WALSHY

The first time I played this map, I dominated with the T-90A under the Dish. Usually aircraft make quick work of me any time I'm using an MBT, but on Rogue Transmission I was able to be safe under cover and fight the battles that I wanted to.

FLAMESWORD

The first time I played this map, I knew I had to make my way to the top of one of the vertical supports. It was a long climb up, but totally worth it as it gave me incredible sniping angles.

ELUMNITE

This map is all-out vehicle warfare, with tons of fast-paced tank battles along the perimeter dirt roads, making for plenty of in-your-face action. I found myself traveling around the long roads in my trusty MBT, taking out any enemies in my path.

ROGUE TRANSMISSION

ROGUE TRANSMISSION

LEVOLUTION MOMENTS

WHAT IS IT?

The receiver of a massive radio telescope crashes down on the Dish.

HOW IS IT TRIGGERED?

Destroy the ten cables connected to the two concrete slabs using explosive weapons. These concrete slabs are located next to each team's base.

HOW IS GAMEPLAY IMPACTED?

The area beneath the Dish is reconfigured by the receiver crashing down through the Dish; a vehicle no longer spawns in this location.

CONQUEST LARGE

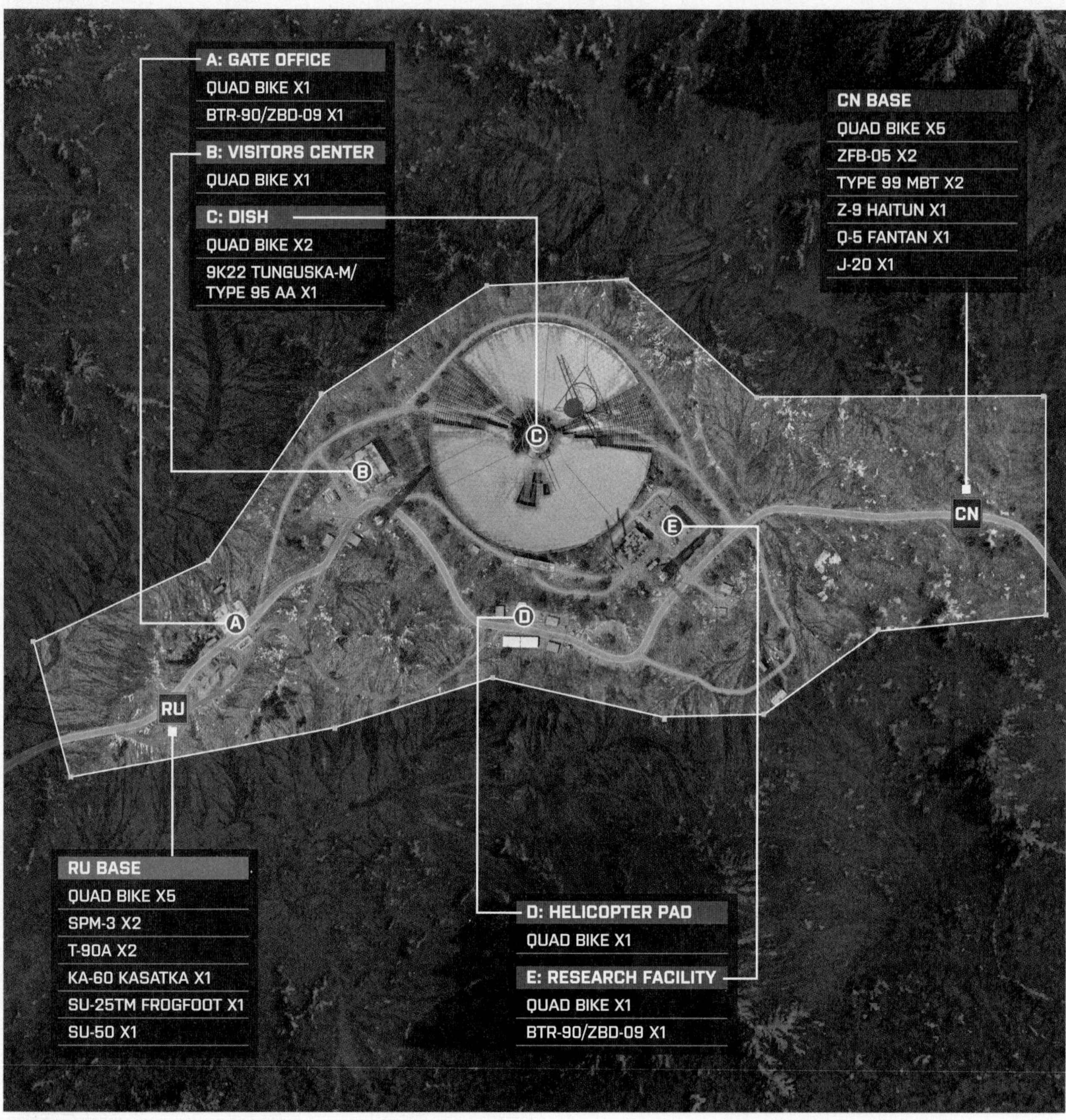

RECOMMENDED SQUAD COMPOSITION:

In Conquest Large, one more control point is added—the Gate Office (A) located east of the RU team's base. With five control points, both teams will try to capture three of the five objectives, and (if the opportunity presents itself) go for that fourth one to drain the opponent's tickets even quicker. This map has jets that, if put in the right hands, can single-handedly change the outcome of the battle, so be sure to let your best pilot take control. The RU team's best strategy will be capturing the Gate Office (A), the Visitors Center (B), and the Dish (C). On the other hand, the CN team will want to capture the Research Facility (E), the Dish (C), and the Helicopter Pad (D). Both teams benefit from the third control point they go for. The Dish (C) will grant the team's commander a Gunship that is very powerful and the Helicopter Pad (D) deploys an attack helicopter that can be a thorn in the opposing team's side. The CN team is at quite an advantage as they will be trying to defend the Dish (C) and the Helicopter Pad (D), giving them control of the Gunship and an attack helicopter. The RU team will always want to go for the less protected control point. If they let the CN team control these two objectives for too long, the game can be over before the RU team knows it. This map will have many vehicles, so have a few more engineer players in your squad to destroy the enemy's vehicles, and have a support player to replenish the engineer's ammo. If there is a chance for your team to capture a fourth control point, then go for it.

RU BASE

- The RU base is located to the southwest side of the map with numerous vehicles to choose from.
- Off the start, send your SPM-3 and T-90A towards the Dish (C). Not only is this objective extremely important to control, but your important vehicles will be safe from the enemy aircraft under this cover.
- The main points to focus on this map will be the Visitors Center (B), the Dish (C), and the Helicopter Pad (D), since every one of these points will give your commander powerful abilities.
- Your squad on this map should make slight changes depending on what the enemy is doing, but always have at least two engineers and one recon member to deal with all the vehicles and long-range battles that will take place.
- The paved road that runs through the Helicopter Pad (D) has the highest amount of traffic going through it. Have your engineers place M15 AT mines on this road to pick up easy kills on unsuspecting vehicles.

BASE ASSETS

NAME	Quad Bike	SPM-3	T-90A	KA-60 Kasatka	SU-25TM Frogfoot	SU-50
QUANTITY	5	2	2	1	1	1

CN BASE

- The starting position for the CN base is on the eastern tip of the map.
- There is a variety of vehicles at the CN base. Players will be able to choose from an arsenal of light vehicles, a couple of ZFB-05s, a Type 99 MBT, and a transport helicopter.
- The CN team can deploy in an attack jet and stealth jet back at base. These will provide great air support and aid when destroying the opponent's jets.
- The speed of the light vehicles will prove very beneficial. Take advantage of their speed and rush towards the Dish (C) or the Helicopter Pad (D). The Dish (C) grants your commander a Gunship that can turn the tide of the battle.
- Have squads enter the heavy-duty MBT and ZFB-05s and head towards the Helicopter Pad (D). Capturing this control point will let your team gain control of an attack helicopter. This helicopter is very powerful and, with the right pilot, can make the opponent pay.

▶ PRO TIP: ELUMNITE

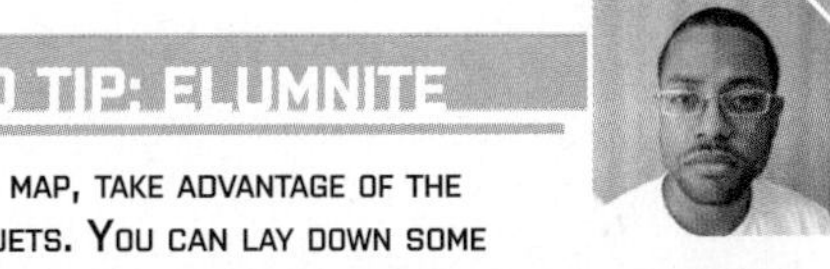

ON THIS MAP, TAKE ADVANTAGE OF THE ATTACK JETS. YOU CAN LAY DOWN SOME HEAVY COVER FIRE AND EVEN TAKE OUT SOME OF THE ENEMY VEHICLES AS WELL. MAKE SURE YOU GIVE YOURSELF ENOUGH SPACE TO CRUISE ABOVE THE WHOLE MAP TO EFFECTIVELY USE THESE JETS.

BASE ASSETS

NAME	Quad Bike	ZFB-05	Type 99 MBT	Z-9 Haitun	Q-5 Fantan	J-20
QUANTITY	5	2	2	1	1	1

A: GATE OFFICE

- This control point is located on the southwest side of the map and is connected to the RU base and the Visitors Center (B) by a two-lane road.
- Upon capture, this control point spawns an IFV and a Quad Bike. Take advantage of the size and speed of these light vehicles to quickly flank around the northern and southern dirt paths on this map.
- When defending this control point, hold the two-story shack to the west of the flag. This will give you the best view of the area.
- When attacking this control point, be careful not to push your vehicles too far into this area. There are many places for the enemies to jump out and C4 your vehicle before you can stop them.
- When attacking this control point, your squad needs to have plenty of explosives to deal with any enemy vehicles and also to take down all the destructible walls that the enemy will be hiding behind.

CONTROL POINT ASSETS

RU CONTROL	CN CONTROL
Quad Bike (1)	Quad Bike (1)
BTR-90 (1)	ZBD-09 (1)

B: VISITORS CENTER

- This control point is located west of the Dish (C) on the northern side of the map. One Quad Bike spawns at this location. Use it to rush towards the other control points.
- North of this objective you'll find a ladder leading to the top roof above this flag. This area is a great place to oversee incoming enemies from the Dish (C), the Helicopter Pad (D), and the Gate Office (A). When taking fire here, drop to the prone position to cover yourself from ground infantry.
- This control point is valuable due to your commander gaining control of the Infantry Scan. Use it to locate opponents hiding beneath the Dish.
- South of this flag is a vertical beam with a ladder reaching to the highest point of the map. When playing as the recon class, place a Radio Beacon at the top of the vertical beam to give you and your team a spawn point above the action. Parachute down and take out the enemies from the top of the vertical beam. You can snipe from this position, but it will be quite tough. When attacking, have a few teammates flank around from the trail north of the flag to catch your enemy off guard and to take over the control point easier.

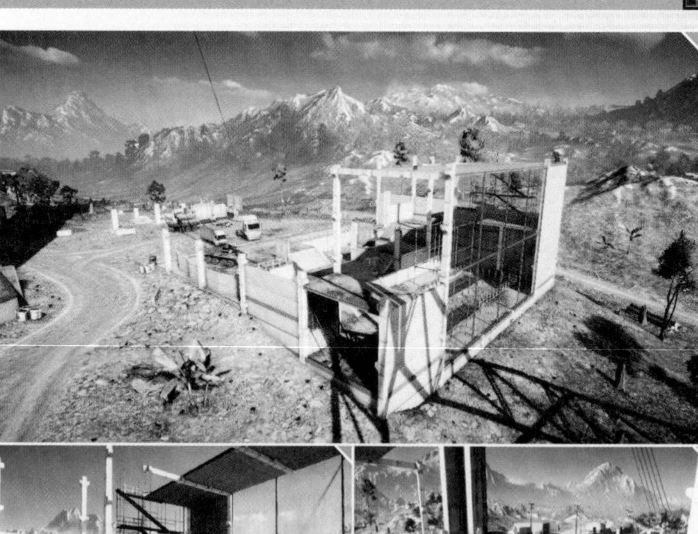

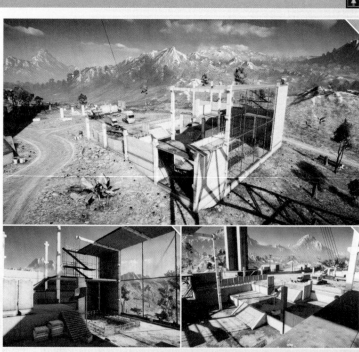

PRO TIP: WALSHY

I LOVE TAKING THE UNEXPECTED ROUTE TO THE NORTH OF THE DISH (C) ON MY QUAD BIKE. I PATROL THIS ROUTE BACK AND FORTH FROM THE VISITORS CENTER (B) TO THE RESEARCH FACILITY (E) TO CONSTANTLY THROW OFF THE ENEMY TEAM.

CONTROL POINT ASSETS

RU CONTROL	CN CONTROL
Quad Bike (1)	Quad Bike (1)

C: DISH

- The Dish (C) is located to the north of the map under a large satellite dish. The Dish (C) is the focal point of Rogue Transmission, and has an enormous amount of cover and hiding places for both teams to use to their advantage.
- Once captured, four Quad Bikes and one mobile AA vehicle will spawn near the flag for either team's use. Teams should either use the light vehicles to transport themselves to another control point or circle the area to protect this point. The mobile AA vehicle is an excellent asset for defending the Dish (C).
- The Dish (C) is one of the most important control points to capture for both teams, giving either team the use of the Gunship. The Gunship will provide much help in capturing and defending other control points.
- Defenders of this control point can use the dark area and the cluster of buildings to hide. This will make it easy to contest the flag when the attackers arrive.
- The attacking team's first goal when trying to capture this base will be to locate a safe area near a surrounding building and drop a Radio Beacon to keep the attack going.

CONTROL POINT ASSETS

RU CONTROL	CN CONTROL
Quad Bike (4)	Quad Bike (4)
9K22 Tunguska-M (1)	Type 95 AA (1)

D: HELICOPTER PAD

- The Helicopter Pad (D) is located at the most southern part of the map. Around the flag there are a few small buildings that are surrounding the area and can be used to hide and contest the flag from.
- Vehicles that spawn here when this point is captured are an attack helicopter and two Quad Bikes. Both of these vehicles will be very useful to quickly move towards any of the other close control points. In the hands of a skilled pilot and gunner, the attack helicopter can be a game changer—make an effort to capture and hold this control point to maintain access to the attack helicopter.
- Capturing the Helicopter Pad (D) gives your commander the use of Vehicle Scan. Use it to spot enemy vehicles hiding beneath the Dish.
- If defenders find themselves losing this control point, there is a building to the southeast of the flag. This is a very dark room where a recon unit can lay a Radio Beacon down and keep the team spawning there.
- When attacking this control point, use the team's MBT to destroy the buildings and expose any defenders hiding around the location attempting to contest the flag.

CONTROL POINT ASSETS

RU CONTROL	CN CONTROL
Quad Bike (2)	Quad Bike (2)
Mi-28 Havoc (1)	Z-10W (1)

E: RESEARCH FACILITY

- The Research Facility (E) is west of the CN base in a nearly finished construction site.
- Capturing this objective grants the capturing team an IFV. This vehicle will prove its worth when encountering enemy infantry under the Dish (C).
- Near the flagpole is a concrete vertical beam with a ladder attached. This is a very tall beam that grants recon players a bird's eye view of the map to snipe from.
- Next to the flag is a large shipping container that allows players to open and shut its doors. When defending, players can contest the objective by hiding inside. The attacking team will need to take you out in order to capture the control point.
- The area is surrounded with a good amount of stationary weapons; these will assist in controlling this objective throughout the entire game.

PRO TIP: STRONGSIDE

WHEN YOU HAVE SECURED THE RESEARCH FACILITY (E), MAKE YOUR WAY UP EITHER BUILDING SURROUNDING THE FLAG. PLACE A RADIO BEACON ON THE TOP FLOOR TO SPAWN YOU AND YOUR SQUAD IN THIS AREA IF YOU ARE TAKEN DOWN. ON THE TOP FLOOR OF THESE BUILDINGS YOU'LL ALSO HAVE AN EXCELLENT VIEW OF INCOMING ENEMIES.

CONTROL POINT ASSETS

RU CONTROL	CN CONTROL
Quad Bike (1)	Quad Bike (1)
BTR-90 (1)	ZBD-09 (1)

CONQUEST SMALL

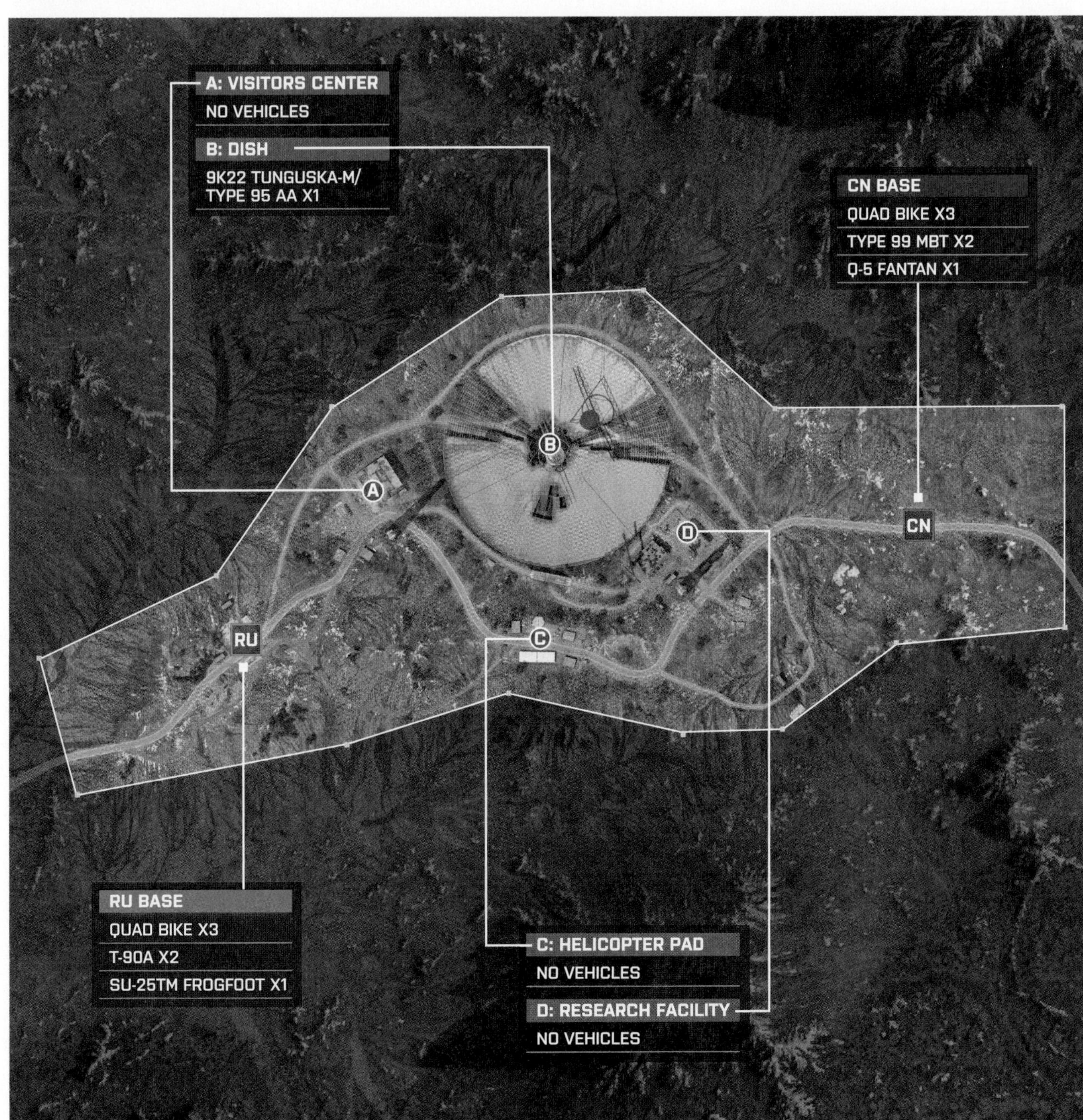

RECOMMENDED SQUAD COMPOSITION:

In this vehicle-friendly map, a large satellite dish sits in the center of the map. Above the satellite dish is a dome held by wires attached to three vertical beams. Both teams will be looking at four control points: Visitors Center (A), Dish (B), Helicopter Pad (C), and Research Facility (D). The RU team's best strategy will be to capture the Visitors Center (A), the Dish (B), and the Helicopter Pad (C). On the other hand, the CN team will want to capture the Research Facility (D), the Dish (B), and the Helicopter Pad (C). The Helicopter Pad (C) will be a control point fought over throughout the duration of the match. The team who captures this flag will gain access to an attack helicopter. In the right hands, this attack helicopter will put the opposing team into chaos. Another control point both teams will fight over will be the Dish (B). Capturing this flag will grant your commander access to the Gunship. The RU team will have an easy time capturing the Visitors Center (A), so send two squadmates towards the Dish (B). These players will relay information to the RU team and let them know which control point the rest of the team should go for. The CN team should capture the Helicopter Pad (C) after capturing the Research Facility (D).The Research Facility (D) provides great cover if the opposing team does get access to the Gunship. Besides the cover, the CN team will also add an attack helicopter to their arsenal of vehicles. Prepare to load up on extra engineers, as this map will consist of both teams warding off each other's vehicles.

RU BASE

- The RU base is located to the southwest side of the map at the Gate Office with a handful of vehicles to choose from.
- Off the start, send your SPM-3 and T-90A towards the Dish (B). Not only is this objective extremely important to control, but your important vehicles will be safe from the enemy aircraft under this cover.
- The main points to focus on this map will be the Visitors Center (A), the Dish (B), and the Helicopter Pad (C), since every one of these points will give your commander powerful abilities.
- Your squad on this map should make slight changes depending on what the enemy is doing. But always be sure to have at least two engineers and one recon member to deal with all the vehicles and long-range battles that will take place.
- The paved road that runs through the Helicopter Pad (C) has the highest amount of traffic going through it. Be sure your engineers place M15 AT mines on this road to pick up easy kills on unsuspecting vehicles.

BASE ASSETS

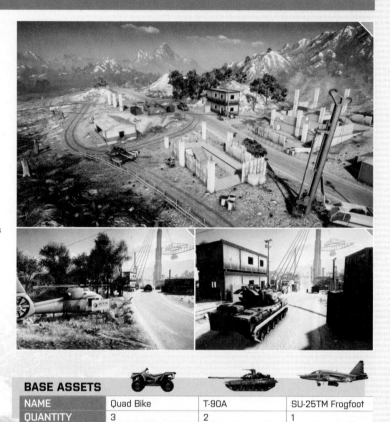

NAME	Quad Bike	T-90A	SU-25TM Frogfoot
QUANTITY	3	2	1

CN BASE

- The starting position for the CN team is on the eastern tip of the map.
- There is a variety of vehicles at the CN base. Players will be able to choose from a set of Quad Bikes, a ZFB-05, a Type 99 MBT, a Type 95 AA, and a transport helicopter.
- The CN team can deploy in an attack jet back at base. This jet will provide great air support and aid when destroying the opponent's jet and helicopters.
- The speed of the Quad Bikes will prove to be very beneficial. Take advantage of their speed and rush towards the Dish (B) or the Helicopter Pad (C). The Dish (B) grants your commander a Gunship that can turn the tide of the battle.
- Have squads enter the heavy-duty MBT and ZFB-05 and head towards the Helicopter Pad (C). Capturing this control point will let your team gain control of an attack helicopter. This helicopter is very powerful and, with the right pilot, can make the opponent pay.

BASE ASSETS

NAME	Quad Bike	Type 99 MBT	Q-5 Fantan
QUANTITY	3	2	1

A: VISITORS CENTER

- This control point is located west of the Dish (B) on the northern side of the map.
- North of this objective you'll find a ladder leading to the top roof above this flag. This area is a great place to oversee incoming enemies from the Dish (B) and the Helicopter Pad (C). When being shot at, drop to the prone position to cover yourself from ground infantry.
- This control point is valuable due to your commander gaining control of the Infantry Scan. Use it to locate enemy troops hiding beneath the Dish.
- South of this flag is a vertical beam with a ladder reaching to the highest point of the map. When playing as the recon class, place a Radio Beacon at the top of the vertical beam to give you and your team a spawn point above the action. Parachute down and take out the enemies. You can snipe from this position, but it will be quite tough.
- When attacking, have a few teammates flank around from the trail north of the flag to catch your enemy off guard and take over the control point easier.

PRO TIP: FLAMESWORD

WHEN PLAYING THIS MAP, YOU'LL CATCH ME SNIPING ON TOP OF ONE OF THE VERTICAL BEAMS. IT'S A LONG WAY UP, BUT TOTALLY WORTH IT. I LIKE SETTING A RADIO BEACON ON TOP IN CASE AN ENEMY PICKS ME OFF. I THEN PARACHUTE RIGHT BACK IN AND GET MY REVENGE.

B: DISH

- The Dish (B) is located to the north of the map under a large satellite. The Dish (B) is the focal point of Rogue Transmission, and has an enormous amount of cover and hiding places for both teams to use to their advantage.
- Once this control point is captured, a mobile AA vehicle will spawn near the flag for teams to use. The mobile AA vehicle is an excellent asset for defending this flag. However, it can also be used to shoot down the enemy's attack jet.
- The Dish (B) is one of the most important control points to capture for both teams, giving them use of the Gunship. This, in turn, from this point will help every other base in securing points on the map.
- Defenders here can utilize the shadows among the cluster of buildings to hide, which will make it easy to contest the flag when the attackers arrive.
- The attacking team's first goal when trying to capture this base will be to locate a safe area near the flag and drop a Radio Beacon to keep the attack going.

CONTROL POINT ASSETS

RU CONTROL	CN CONTROL
9K22 Tunguska-M (1)	Type 95 AA (1)

C: HELICOPTER PAD

- This flag is located at the most southern part of the map. Around this flag there are a few small buildings that are surrounding the area and can be used to hide and contest the flag.
- An attack helicopter and Quad Bikes spawn here. Both of these vehicles will be very useful in quickly moving towards any of the other close control points. In the hands of a skilled pilot and gunner, the attack helicopter can be a game changer—make an effort to capture and hold this control point to maintain access to the attack helicopter.
- If defenders find themselves losing this control point, there is a building to the southeast of the flag. This is a very dark room where a recon unit can lay a Radio Beacon down and keep the team spawning there.
- When attacking this point when the team is capturing, use your MBT to destroy the buildings to expose any defenders hiding around the location attempting to contest the flag.

CONTROL POINT ASSETS

RU CONTROL	CN CONTROL
Quad Bike (1)	Quad Bike (1)
Mi-28 Havoc (1)	Z-10W (1)

D: RESEARCH FACILITY

- The Research Facility (D) is west of the CN base. The facility has yet to be completed and is in the middle of a construction site.
- Near the flagpole is a concrete vertical beam with a ladder attached. This is a very tall beam that grants recon players a bird's eye view of the map to snipe from.
- Next to the flagpole is a large shipping container that allows players to open and shut its doors. When defending, players can contest the objective by hiding inside. The attacking team will need to take you out in order to capture the control point.
- The area is surrounded with a good amount of stationary weapons; these will assist in controlling this objective throughout the entire game.
- Capturing this control point gives your commander access to the Vehicle Scan. This will notify your whole team of what vehicles the enemy is using and where they are going.

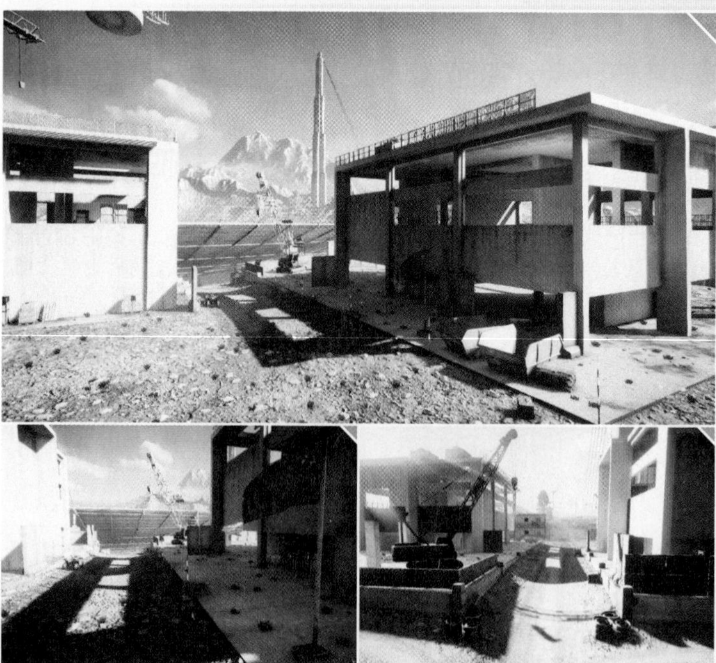

RUSH

In this Rush battle, the RU attacking team will make their way through four different zones in an attempt to destroy a total of eight M-COM stations. The attackers will begin at the start of the road west of the map and head east to the Gate Office for the first zone. The defending CN team will have one .50Cal to deal with the various light vehicles. The RU team has an HJ-8 Launcher to deal with the incoming BTR-90. The defenders are at a disadvantage in this zone, but with the proper teamwork can stop the attackers here. If the attackers do succeed in making it to the next few zones, the defenders will have a harder time as the attackers gain more vehicles. Zone 3 and Zone 4 are the defending team's time to shine as they gain vehicles of their own to tackle the RU team's vehicles. Defenders should have engineers on deck to plant M15 AT mines and rockets to take care of attacking vehicles.

ZONE 1: GATE OFFICE

RU DEPLOYMENT
RU DEPLOYMENT
QUAD BIKE X3
BTR-90 X1

CN DEPLOYMENT
NO VEHICLES

CN
B
A
RU

RU DEPLOYMENT

RECOMMENDED SQUAD COMPOSITION: 

- The RU deployment is located at a dead end position in the southwest part of the map. When heading east, the main road splits into two and provides an off-road path.
- The RU team will spawn with one IFV and four light vehicles. These light vehicles will be a great asset due to their speed.
- It is about 250 meters from the deployment zone to the M-COM stations, so be sure to catch a ride in the IFV or light vehicle, otherwise you'll be looking at a long hike. If you do find yourself on foot, be sure to run on the outskirts and not the main road. You will be concealed in all the tall grass, bushes, and trees.
- Have your best driver take control of the IFV and have them navigate through both objectives. Drop players off at M-COM Station A and make timely sweeps through both objectives. The enemy will be flustered as they only have two stationary weapons to defend against vehicles.
- A lot of the fighting will be close- to medium-range battles, so be sure to have a few extra assault players. These players will be able to revive each other safely as the grassy area camouflages downed teammates, allowing you to go prone as you revive them. This will score you easy points and allow your team to keep the pressure on the CN team.

DEPLOYMENT AREA ASSETS

NAME	Quad Bike	BTR-90
QUANTITY	3	1

CN DEPLOYMENT

RECOMMENDED SQUAD COMPOSITION:

- This deployment area is located northeast of the objectives. The CN team will have a good amount of time to set up their defenses due to the RU deployment being located about 300 meters southwest of the objectives.
- Send a group of engineers towards the southwest fence to take out incoming enemy vehicles. The RU base spawns with four light vehicles and a BTR-90. The CN team should use mines and rockets to keep the BTR-90 from rushing the objectives.
- Send another squad to the crates west of M-COM Station B. This area has great cover and can be used to pick off incoming enemies on the main road to the west. The main road to the west and along the main road to the north and south are the only routes for the RU team to take. Set up your defense and don't let the RU team pass.
- Send a few players towards the nearest hilltop southwest of M-COM Station B. The player at this position will need to watch the enemies flanking from the northwest. This position also has an incredible vantage point over the main road to southwest, ideal for recon troops to monitor the RU team's movements.
- The building containing M-COM Station A can be destroyed. Destroy this building for an easier time defending against enemies attempting to arm the objective.

M-COM STATION A

- This M-COM station is located toward the south of the map inside an open building just to the right of the main road.
- No vehicles spawn for the CN team, but there are two stationary turrets—a .50Cal and a HJ-8 Launcher— which can be used to defend in this first zone.
- Defenders need to work together and watch two roads at this zone. Engineers have to be used to be able to successfully stop the enemy from arming at the station. Have your team equip the mines and rocket launchers to stop the enemy's IFVs.
- Attackers have two paths to M-COM Station A. One is a dirt road that leads right by M-COM Station A, and is on a very exposed side of the station as well. Attackers should split squads up and send the bulk of the force up the main road.
- Have the other squad composed of engineers travel down the dirt road. This way your team can avoid the launcher placed in the small building.

M-COM STATION B

- M-COM Station B is located northwest of M-COM Station A. This objective is in the middle of an office that construction workers have just started working on.
- South of the M-COM station is a two-level trailer that has a stationary launcher that will aid defenders in damaging and destroying incoming vehicles.
- Defenders can plant M15 AT mines and M2 SLAMs across the main road. The main focus of the RU team's IFV will be on the incoming rockets from the defenders, so they won't notice the M15 AT mines and M2 SLAMs across the path.
- When attacking, follow the dead zone to the west as you make your way north towards the objective. The tall grass, bushes, and trees will provide you camouflage. This path also grants you the highest view in this hill terrain. Take out defending snipers as they will use this hill as well.
- North of the objective is another two-story trailer. Position troops on the second floor. They will be able to spot any attackers trying to flank all the way around.

ZONE 2: VISITORS CENTER

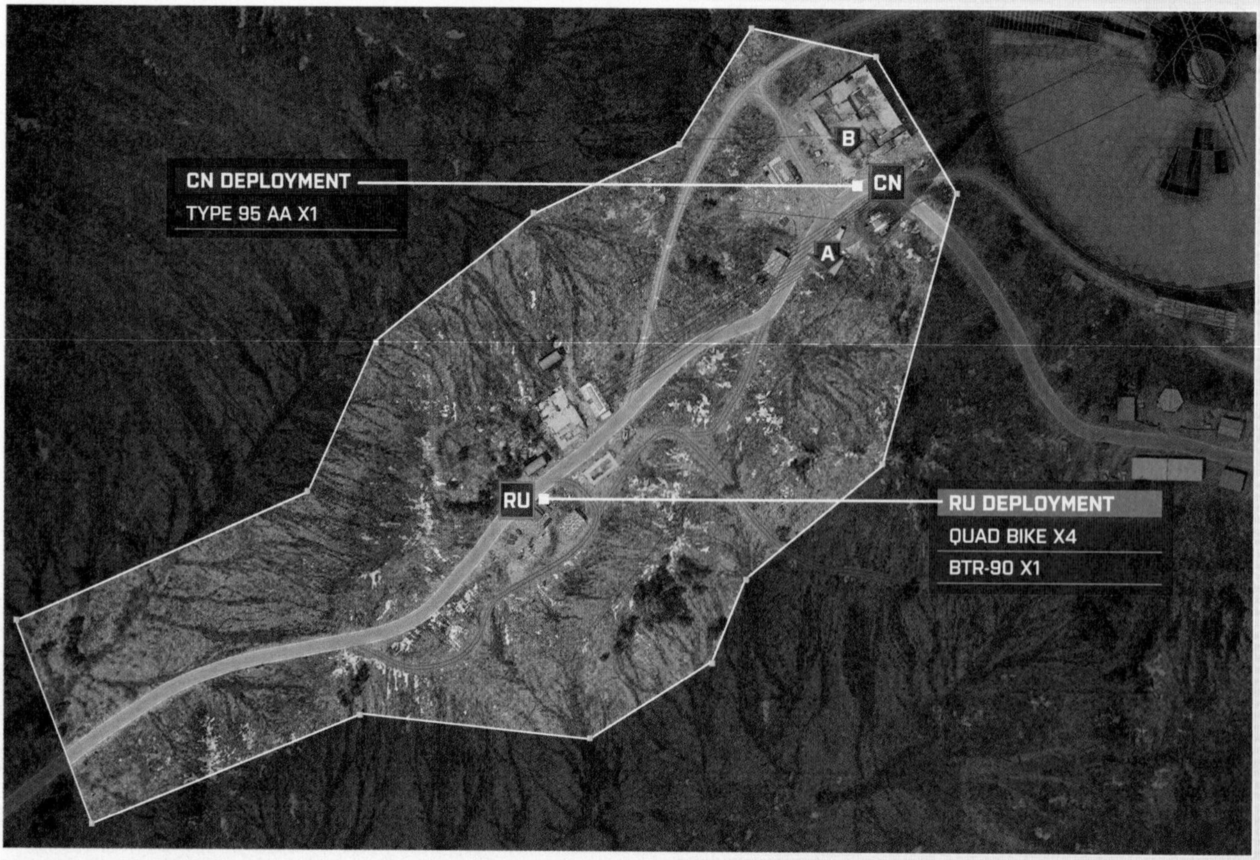

B

CN DEPLOYMENT

TYPE 95 AA X1

CN

A

RU

RU DEPLOYMENT

QUAD BIKE X4

BTR-90 X1

RU DEPLOYMENT

RECOMMENDED SQUAD COMPOSITION:

- After a successful sweep of Zone 1, the RU deployment is moved north to the Gate Office.
- The RU team maintains the same vehicles from Zone 1.
- Have a pair of the Quad Bikes travel along the northwest dirt path and flank the defenders around M-COM Station B. These vehicles will allow you to drop off the backseat passenger, creating different attack paths towards M-COM Station B.
- The defenders have a Type 95 AA, a mobile anti-aircraft, to take out your Z-11W. Send in your BTR-90 to crush through the CN team's infantry on your way to destroy the Type 95 AA.

DEPLOYMENT AREA ASSETS

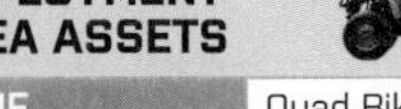

NAME	Quad Bike	BTR-90
QUANTITY	4	1

CN DEPLOYMENT

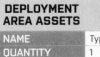

RECOMMENDED SQUAD COMPOSITION:

- This deployment area is located east of the objectives and spawns with one Type 95 AA.
- Send a couple recon soldiers on the roof of the building holding M-COM Station B. You'll have a great view of the enemies approaching from the southwest.
- Again, destroy the building holding M-COM Station A to better defend the objective and have better visibility on the enemy arming the objective.
- Equip engineers with rocket launchers to take out the enemy's IFV. Place the engineers around the building west of M-COM Station A. This building will provide cover and a great point of attack to stop the enemy's IFV before it gets near to the objectives.
- Take the Type 95 AA north of M-COM Station A to aid both M-COM stations and watch for the RU team's scout helicopter. Keep an engineer nearby to repair if needed.

DEPLOYMENT AREA ASSETS

NAME	Type 95 AA
QUANTITY	1

M-COM STATION A

- M-COM Station A is located just south of the CN deployment in dark building on the side of the main road.
- The CN team finally has a vehicle available now at the deployment location—a Type 95 AA that will take some of the stress off the engineers at this zone. Placing the Type 95 AA in between both of the M-COM stations will ensure better protection from any scout helicopters trying to transport infantry and attack the stations.
- Attackers will push up to the north and be able to take two roads once again. The main road leads straight into M-COM Station A, and the walls surrounding this objective can easily be destroyed by assault classes equipped with the M320 HE.
- When defending, there is a building to the southeast of M-COM Station A that can be used to bait the enemy in and attack from the rear when the enemy overcommits and goes for the arm. Destroy the building holding M-COM Station A so your team has a clear view of it.
- When defending, another good position is on the top level of the construction site above M-COM Station B. This position will give you a great overview of incoming enemies.

M-COM STATION B

- This objective is located north of M-COM Station A in the corner of the foundation of a building being built.
- The CN team will need an extra engineer or two in order to deal with the scout helicopter that the RU team has. Have a support player to drop ammo boxes to replenish the engineer's ammo.
- Defenders can position themselves at the top of the half-complete roof. Recon players are suggested here to pick off attacking infantry players.
- The M-COM station is in a corner. Attackers should keep an eye out for C4 placed by the CN team. Throw grenades into this corner blowing any booby trap set up.
- The attacking team's best plan of attack will be from the west. Use the light vehicles to get to this side before the defenders can set up a perimeter.

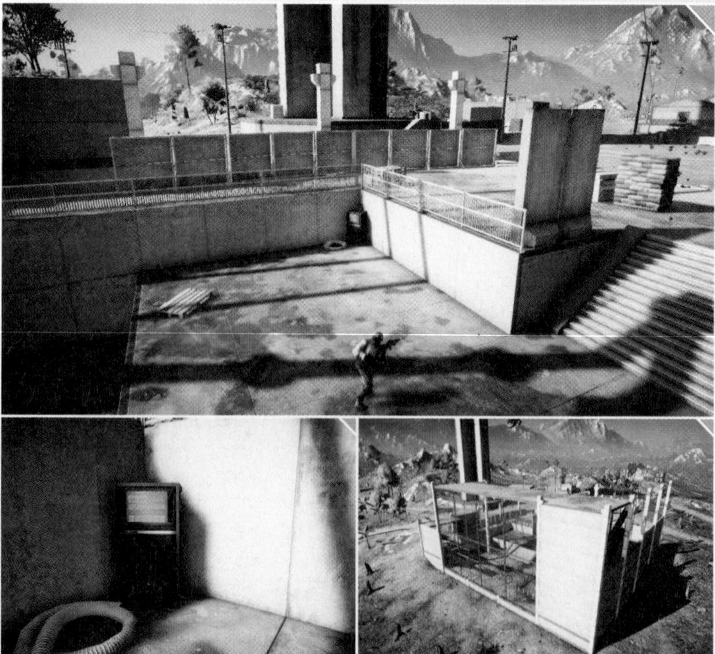

ZONE 3: DISH

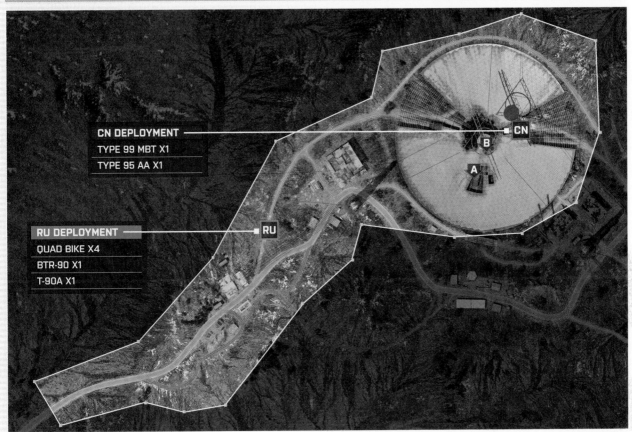

CN DEPLOYMENT
TYPE 99 MBT X1
TYPE 95 AA X1

RU DEPLOYMENT
QUAD BIKE X4
BTR-90 X1
T-90A X1

CN

RU

A

B

RU DEPLOYMENT

RECOMMENDED SQUAD COMPOSITION: 

- The new deployment zone for the RU team is now pushed even further into the CN territory and is located in the Visitors Center.
- Once again, the RU team has a good mix of vehicles, ideal for making a push on the next pair of objectives. However, the helicopters may be less effective due to the cover of the Dish.
- The BTR-90 will play a huge role in arming these M-COM stations. Proceed under the Dish and fire rounds into the distance. Try to destroy all buildings and cement walls. This allows your IFV to move in and take out the CN team's scattered infantry.
- Have players spread out with the light vehicles. Try to approach from multiple angles, pinching the enemy in the center.

DEPLOYMENT AREA ASSETS

NAME	Quad Bike	BTR-90	T-90A
QUANTITY	4	1	1

CN DEPLOYMENT

RECOMMENDED SQUAD COMPOSITION:

- Located east of the objectives, this deployment spawns with a Type 99 MBT and one Type 95 AA. The RU team deploys with a handful of vehicles.
- Use the CN team's tank wisely by keeping it back near the M-COM stations, but watch out for enemy classes holding C4. The area holding the M-COM stations is a dark area and it is hard to see every enemy moving around.
- Above M-COM Station A is an incredible position on top of the Dish to defend both objectives. You have the vantage point over the enemies and can stop any infantry attempting to arm the objective.
- M-COM Station B is located underground in a dark area. This is the perfect place for a Claymore, making it hard to see the trip wires since they will blend in with the darkness. Enemies will come running in to arm the objective and you'll easily pick the first one off with the Claymore.
- The building southwest of M-COM Station B and west of M-COM Station A will prove extremely useful as you can cover both objectives. Position yourself on the lower platform of the roof, which will give you cover when taking enemy fire, but be sure to go prone to completely cover yourself.

DEPLOYMENT AREA ASSETS

NAME	Type 99 MBT	Type 95 AA
QUANTITY	1	1

M-COM STATION A

- M-COM Station A is located under the Dish around some unfinished construction ramps just south of the deployment and M-COM Station B.
- Two vehicles that the CN can now use are the Type 99 MBT and Type 95 AA. These two vehicles will be the sole protectors of this area and both stations and can cover the Dish by circling around.
- Defenders will want to lay some M15 AT mines around the dark areas leading to M-COM Station A. These will slow the enemy's advance. But keep engineers posted nearby to mop up damaged and immobilized vehicles.
- When attacking M-COM Station A, have one squad lay down some cover fire so that a scout helicopter can drop off some support and recon class troops. Immediately place a Radio Beacon to keep your team spawning on the Dish.
- Also on the Dish there is a M32 MGL battle pickup, which the either team will have access to depending on who gets to it first. Once obtained, players can do some massive damage to buildings and vehicles.

M-COM STATION B

- This M-COM station is located in a basement of a building that has yet to be completed.
- Attackers can take their scout helicopter and parachute to the top of the Dish. In the center of the Dish is an opening that lets you drop underneath the Dish and make a dash to the objective for a quick arm.
- The attacking team will need assistance from their MBT. Have it slowly move near the objective as it shoots off rounds from a distance, destroying all items the defenders can use for cover.
- The CN team will need a few extra engineers. Have them plant M15 AT mines around the area. The area is dark, so the attackers will not be able to spot them.
- Southwest is a building that will be extremely useful as it allows defenders to watch both M-COM stations. Position yourself on the lower platform of the roof as it will give you cover, especially if you go prone.

ZONE 4: RESEARCH FACILITY

RN DEPLOYMENT
QUAD BIKE X4
BTR-90 X1
T-90A X1

RU

A

B

CN

CN DEPLOYMENT
TYPE 99 MBT X1
TYPE 95 AA X1

RU DEPLOYMENT

RECOMMENDED SQUAD COMPOSITION:

- The final deployment zone is located underneath the Dish. One last push and the victory goes to you and your team.
- In this Rush mode, the RU team is rewarded for successfully moving through each zone. The team has the exact same vehicles as in Zone 3.
- The last zone is in the Research Facility. Fill up your team's helicopters and drop the passengers off on the roof of the building that holds M-COM Station A. This is the only way to get on top and it provides a great view of the objectives. Drop a Radio Beacon for constant spawns.
- Be sure to keep an eye on the vertical beam. It has a ladder that leads to the top of it, and the opposing team might try to get a sniper up there to pick off your teammates.
- Have an extra engineer in your squad. The CN team still has Mobile Anti-Aircraft and two IFVs, which could put a damper on your team's tickets. Take these out and force the CN team to fight you gun to gun.

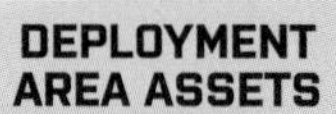

NAME	Quad Bike	BTR-90	T-90A
QUANTITY	4	1	1

CN DEPLOYMENT

RECOMMENDED SQUAD COMPOSITION:

- This is the last zone and the CN deployment is located on the southeast of the map, offering the same vehicles as the previous zone. Equip a few engineers on your squad to help counter the great amount of vehicles the RU team has.
- Send a squad to the top level of the building northwest of M-COM Station B. This position will give you a great overview of the enemies approaching the objectives from the northwest. Choose the recon class and place T-UGS on the upper level to be alerted when enemies are approaching from the lower level.
- Destroy M-COM Station B's trailer walls with explosives to make it easier to see and stop the enemies attempting to arm the objective.
- Send players to the top level of the building containing M-COM Station A. This will also provide a great overview of incoming enemies from the northwest. Equip engineers to take out the vehicles and a recon class to place a T-UGS and Radio Beacon on the top level of this building.
- Use the Type 95 MBT and Type 95 AA near these objectives to assist the engineers in taking out the enemy vehicles approaching from the northwest.

DEPLOYMENT AREA ASSETS

NAME	Type 99 MBT	Type 95 AA
QUANTITY	1	1

M-COM STATION A

- M-COM Station A is located at the bottom of a large construction building by a staircase.
- With this being the last zone for the defenders, the CN team gets a new mix of tank and stealth jet vehicles to protect M-COM Station A. With these vehicles at your disposal, the defending team will be on equal footing.
- When defending, have a few players go to the mid and top level and snipe enemy assault units from this vantage point.
- Attackers have a cluster of vehicles to evenly match the defenders at this point. Striking from the air first will be the most efficient way of disposing of the defender's snipers.
- The attacker's BTR-90s will need to have a few engineers and assault class soldiers for a direct fight, taking out the rest of the defender's land vehicles to clear a path to the M-COM station so it can be armed.

M-COM STATION B

- This M-COM station is in the corner on the second level of a two-level trailer, south of M-COM Station A.
- Attackers should make their way to the north or west roof of the objective. To gain access to this roof, the attackers will need to fly their scout helicopter and drop off its passengers. Once on top, attackers have many angles to take down the CN team.
- The RU team will need to be cautious of the CN team's vehicles; have a few extra engineers to destroy them. The area will then be vehicle-free, allowing the attackers to move more freely around the area.
- When defending, blowing up the walls of the second level of the trailer will make it a lot easier to defend. Plant C4 on the second level and watch from a distance. Detonate the C4 when attackers make it near the M-COM station.
- On the second level of the building to the west, defenders will be able to watch M-COM Station B. On the west side of the building, defenders can also spray enemies from above as they try to make their way out of the Dish.

OBLITERATION

RECOMMENDED SQUAD COMPOSITION:

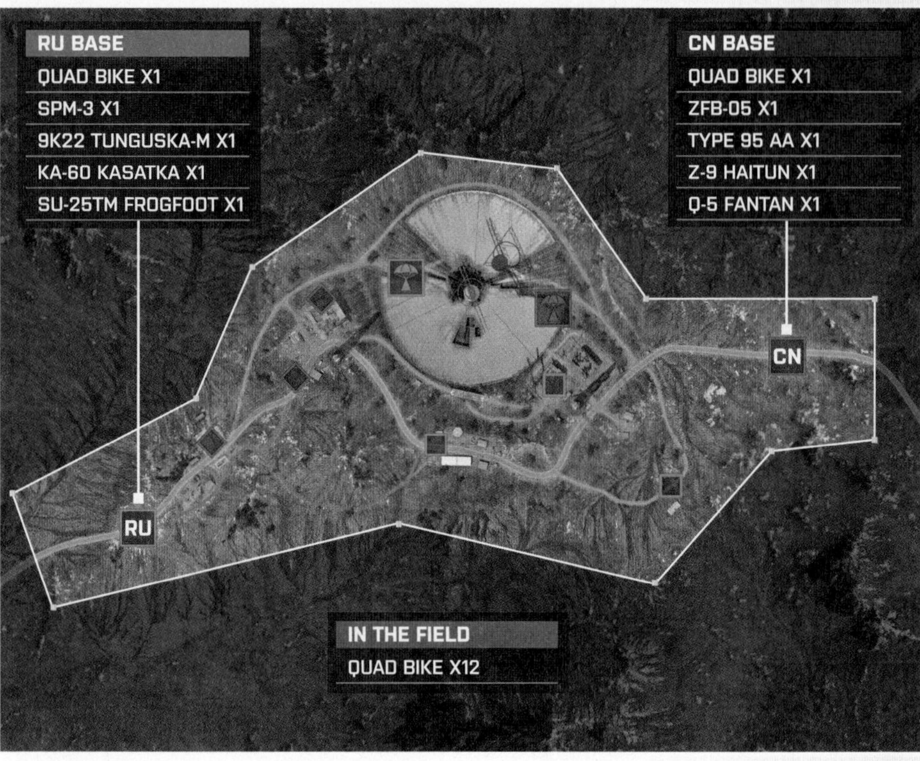

- Around the Helicopter Pad and Research Facility, the CN team has to protect their targets.
- The Gate Office and Visitors Center are the locations of the US team's targets.
- The bomb spawns under the Dish. Take advantage of the speed of the light vehicles to reach this area off the start.
- The map is very large, so transport bomb carriers around the outskirts of the maps to safely reach the enemy's targets.
- The air vehicles play a huge role in the game. The attack jet provides great air support as the transport helicopters move players around the map quickly.

DEFUSE

RECOMMENDED SQUAD COMPOSITION:

- Players attempt to arm the objectives in the Research Facility of this map. The attacking RU team spawns on the southern road and the defending CN team spawns near the northern tip of the map.
- Laptop A is in a corner on the second floor of the building to the west of the map. Attackers need to tread carefully in this area as the defenders have better firing angles.
- Laptop B is outside the two trailers found on the east of the map. Defenders can use the ladder at the back of the trailer to reach the top and provide cover from above.
- Attackers should head northwest around the building that holds Laptop A. When heading this way, look east to pick off any defender running in the open. Lock down the building and go for the arm or slowly pick off the defenders one kill at a time.
- Defenders want to get control of the building south of their deployment. The building provides an overview of both objectives. This building provides all sorts of cover and is a safe haven for the CN team.

DOMINATION

RECOMMENDED SQUAD COMPOSITION:

- The three control points on this map are Construction (A), Tower (B), and Storage (C).
- Be sure to grab the two battle pickups on the map as they are very powerful and will save your primary gun ammo.
- Having the engineer's rockets is a great gadget to equip on this map because of all the destructible walls. Destroying walls reveals the location of your enemies and leaves them vulnerable.
- Construction (A) only has two ways to get in, making it easy to defend. This is the most important control point since you can oversee the other objectives and control the entire map from there.
- Your best strategy is to capture Construction (A) and Storage (C). These two points provide the best cover and only allow the opponent to come from a few entrances. You are able to shoot from building to building, making it difficult for the opposing team to fight back.

SQUAD DEATHMATCH

RECOMMENDED SQUAD COMPOSITION:

- In this Squad Deathmatch, squads constantly battle for control of the north and west buildings as those buildings provide the best overview of the map.
- You want to avoid running through the middle of the map or the players in the north and west buildings will make mincemeat of you.
- You can easily protect this building to the north by destroying the inside walls, creating new angles to fire upon the enemy.
- The north building has a M32 MGL battle pickup that assists in warding enemy squads away, giving your squad complete control of the building.
- The vertical support can be used for cover as you peek towards the center of the map to pick off opposing squads battling each other.

TEAM DEATHMATCH

RECOMMENDED SQUAD COMPOSITION:

- When playing on a full server, avoid running through the middle of the map or the players in the various buildings will punish you.
- Control the stairwells inside of the buildings with Claymores and C4; a dedicated player can watch as well to make sure no enemy makes it up.
- The team that defends the building on the north side is rewarded the battle pickup on the second level. This M32 MGL can destroy the opposite building's walls, revealing the enemies behind them.
- You can easily protect this building to the north by destroying the inside walls, creating new angles to fire upon the enemy.
- If your team has the lead, an organized team can establish a perimeter south of the vertical support. Have a player hide near the vertical support near the bulldozer while the rest of the players hide behind the crates and dumpsters scattered around. The player hiding behind the support should only pop out when an enemy is fighting one of your teammates, giving the enemy no time to react to your ambush.

ALPHA SQUAD: IMPRESSIONS

MABOOZA

While the toppling Skyscraper is the main Levolution event on this map, don't overlook other ways to give your team a tactical advantage. Raise the bollards north of the Skyscraper to control the flow of traffic along the bridges. Or close the shutters in the Arcade to prevent infantry incursions from the east.

STRONGSIDE

The first time seeing the Levolution on this map when the Skyscraper topples to the ground, my jaw hit the floor. I was speechless. I enjoyed skydiving off the roof of the Skyscraper as the building crumbled down. DICE spared no detail with this incredible Levolution.

WALSHY

When I first played this map, I found myself in Rush heaven. I loved fighting through the five different zones to win this game. Nothing was sweeter than my final arm on the objective outside the Foodcourt to claim victory.

FLAMESWORD

Seeing as the support class is my favorite class, I couldn't contain my excitement as I noticed the amount of buildings on the map when I played for the first time. I love moving around this map like a ninja and throwing C4 on vehicles not paying attention while using the various buildings for cover.

ELUMNITE

Playing Siege of Shanghai, the tall buildings were instantly the first thing drawing my attention. There are many rooftops to post up on top of and rain fire down on your enemies. Look for me to be hiding on the roof above the Metro control point, sniping everyone in the area.

SIEGE OF SHANGHAI

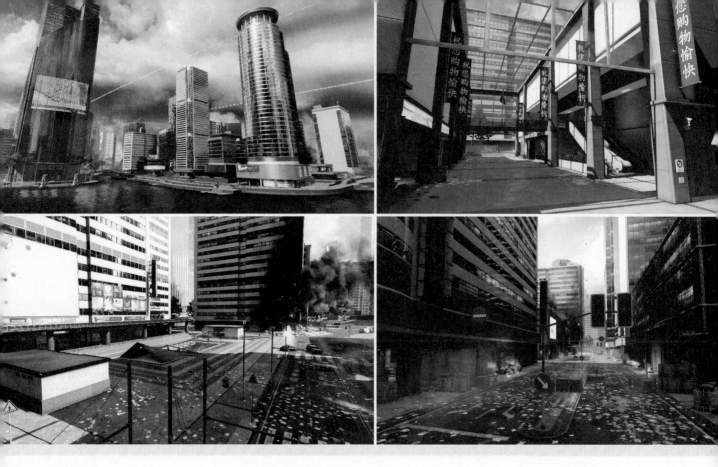

SIEGE OF SHANGHAI

LEVOLUTION MOMENTS

WHAT IS IT?

The Skyscraper crumbles down into the bay, creating a new control point: Ruins. Bollards can be raised to block vehicle traffic near the bridges to the north of the Skyscraper.

HOW IS IT TRIGGERED?

Using explosives, destroy the four cracked pillars facing the bay on the ground level under the Skyscraper. Interact with the control panels next to the bridges to raise and lower the bollards.

HOW IS GAMEPLAY IMPACTED?

The Skyscraper crashes down and the area is now called Ruins. Dust and ash float through the air lowering visibility. When the bollards are raised, no vehicles can cross the bridges.

CONQUEST LARGE

RECOMMENDED SQUAD COMPOSITION:

In the heart of Shanghai and this Conquest Large variant, there are five control points. Both the US and CN team will look to ultimately capture and defend three control points. The team with three control points will begin bleeding the opposing team's tickets until they are left with none. The US team's best strategy will be to capture the Garage (A), Metro (B), and Skyscraper (C). The CN team, on the other hand, will need to capture the Foodcourt (E), Arcade (D), and Skyscraper (C) to successfully bleed the US team's tickets. The main battle will go down around the Skyscraper (C) as the controlling team is rewarded a Cruise Missile that the team's commander can call in. Both teams have access to an attack helicopter back at their bases and, in the right hands, it can become very lethal. Have your best players fly the attack helicopter patrolling the skies and providing constant air support. Always return back to base to use one of the many vehicles that spawn as you do not want to be caught moving by foot on this large-scale map.

US BASE

- The US base is positioned in the southwest part of the city. To the east of the base, US players can see battle cruisers firing missiles into the distance.
- The US team will spawn with a few ground vehicles and two helicopters on top of the building to the east. These helicopters can only be used if deployed in them.
- It is a long run to reach the control points scattered around the map. Be sure to always return to base to see if vehicles have spawned. There are two tanks that you do not want sitting back at base; make full use of these every chance you get.
- The nearest control point to the base is Garage (A). This is an easy capture off the beginning of the game so only a few members of a squad need to stay here to secure this objective.
- A group of two should take control of the AH-1Z Viper at the base and escort the transport helicopter towards the Skyscraper (C). Capturing this control point will give your commander the ability to drop Cruise Missiles towards designated targets.

BASE ASSETS

NAME	MRAP	LAV-25	M1 Abrams	PWC	UH-1Y Venom	AH-1Z Viper
QUANTITY	1	1	2	2	1	1

CN BASE

- Located on the east side of the map, the CN base has multiple vehicles at your disposal. Just make sure to not push up too far ahead of your team. You only need three points to start draining enemy tickets.
- Send your fastest vehicles towards Skyscraper (C) so you can get control of the objective and so your commander can use the Cruise Missile.
- When driving your tanks towards the center of the map, you will run into the enemy's vehicles around the base of the Skyscraper (C). Immediately, destroy the vertical concrete pillars on the opposing bridge to the east. This will eliminate all the cover for the enemy vehicles and make them much easier to hit.
- You will be able to reach Arcade (D) before the enemy team, and when you acquire this objective it gives your commander the Infantry Scan ability. Make sure your commander uses the Infantry Scan as soon as possible so you can see where the enemy is headed at the start of the match.
- With so many powerful vehicles on this map, you will want to regularly look back at the CN base to see if there are any attack helicopters or tanks that you can bring up to the front line for your team.

BASE ASSETS

NAME	ZFB-05	ZBD-09	Type 99 MBT	PWC	Z-9 Haitun	Z-10W
QUANTITY	1	1	2	2	1	1

A: GARAGE

- The Garage (A) is located northeast of the US base. The flag stands at the top of a parking garage between both residential buildings.
- These residential buildings have stairs that lead to both levels of the parking garage. When capturing this control point, scan these halls for defending enemies.
- Capturing this control point spawns a tank for your team. This map promotes vehicle gameplay, so the more tanks you have, the better.
- When defending this control point, there is a HJ-8 Launcher on the second level of the parking garage. This will help defend against incoming ground vehicles.
- Most of the action will happen towards the center of map near the Skyscraper (C). Have a recon player plant a T-UGS in a corner of the parking garage. This will let you push up towards the action, only having to return to the Garage (A) once an enemy is detected.

CONTROL POINT ASSETS

US CONTROL	CN CONTROL
M1 Abrams (1)	Type 99 MBT (1)

B: METRO

- Located in the northwest sector, this subway station has three main entrances, all providing quick access to the flag. But exercise caution where entering through any of the entrances, as defending opponents may be hiding in the darkness, waiting to ambush your squad. Deploy Motion Sensors to detect any defenders before rushing toward the flag.
- There are two unique features to this control point, which can affect it in a few different ways. First is the unfinished pillar. When C4 is placed on the pillar, detonating it will cause the above ground to collapse. A new entrance is created if successful.
- The second feature is to activate the shutters, which are located at the bottom west of the control point. This will seal off a few places, but they can be opened back up if reactivated. This would also be a great place to contest the objective.
- When attacking this control point, either team will want to have a recon class to throw Motion Sensors to locate enemies hiding around the lower level. Once done, this makes cleaning up the area easy.
- Defenders will want to place Claymores around the staircases to take out any wandering enemies attempting to take control of this objective.

PRO TIP: FLAMESWORD

THIS IS A HEAVY VEHICLE-BASED MAP WHEN PLAYING CQL. ONE OF MY FAVORITE TACTICS IS JUMPING OFF THE SKYSCRAPER AND THROWING C4 TOWARDS THE VEHICLES BELOW. AS I DEPLOY MY PARACHUTE I JUST WATCH THE FIREWORKS AS I SLOWLY DRIFT DOWN.

CONTROL POINT ASSETS

US CONTROL	CN CONTROL
MRAP (1)	ZFB-05 (1)

C: SKYSCRAPER

- This objective is positioned on the center north area of the map. The control point is equal distance to both bases and is at the very top of the Skyscraper. This flag also grants your commander the Cruise Missile, making this flag very important to control throughout the entire game.
- A rocket launcher and sniper rifle spawn on the roof of this building. Use these to take down incoming helicopter and enemy infantry across the map.
- When attacking, use helicopters to quickly drop off teammates on the roof to infiltrate the area.
- This control point is extremely tough to control since the building can be taken down from the base by explosives. When controlling this point, have a few teammates patrol the base of this building to stop the enemy from taking down the building.

PRO TIP: STRONGSIDE

In the Skyscraper (C), near the elevators, place down a T-UGS. This will alert you when players are approaching up the two elevators on your side. Work with a teammate to mimic what you're doing at the other set of elevators to hold this control point. Engineers should also be present to take out incoming enemy helicopters.

CONTROL POINT ASSETS

US CONTROL	CN CONTROL
MRAP (1)	ZFB-05 (1)

C: RUINS

- This flag moves down to the ground level when the building is destroyed. This area is surrounded by rubble that can be used as great cover.
- When the flag is controlled, you gain use of an attack boat. The attack boat's weapons provide great fire support, perfect for mowing down incoming infantry.
- A HVM-2 battle pickup spawns in the area of this flag. Use this to take down enemy helicopters dropping off enemy infantry.
- When defending or attacking use the rubble to hide yourself within the control point. This flag has a large capture radius and can be contested from many areas.
- This flag still grants your commander the Cruise Missile and will still be a valuable control point.

CONTROL POINT ASSETS

US CONTROL	CN CONTROL
RCB-90 (1)	DV-15 (1)

D: ARCADE

- This control point is located towards the northeastern part of the map on the second floor. The Arcade (D) has many access areas, but two main entrances coming from the north and south. There is also an elevator that will give you roof access.
- Once captured, two Armored Fighting Vehicles become available and will be used to defend or transport players to other control points. Since this flag is very accessible, either team can patrol the area very effectively by circling the objective.
- There are many corners to hide in and contest this control point, so use this to your team's advantage as much as possible. In this control point there is a button to close the shutters and block that entrance off from the enemy.
- When attacking this flag, the roof has many windows, making air attacks very effective by using transport helicopters to drop players off and raid the objective from the sky.

CONTROL POINT ASSETS

US CONTROL	CN CONTROL
MRAP (1)	ZFB-05 (1)

E: FOODCOURT

- This control point is located in the southeastern edge of this city amongst a variety of stores that provide limited cover for anyone in the area. The stores to the south of the control point provide the best cover.
- There is a staircase leading up to the rooftop patio overlooking the flag. But if you can't reach the staircase, blast the pillar on the southeast corner, making the glass overhang collapse, forming a ramp. If you are planning to hold this area down, place a T-UGS near the stairs so enemies will not be able to sneak up on you.
- If you are outnumbered at this objective, buy time for your squad and team to come help you by hiding below inside the stores to the south of this control point.
- When driving vehicles to and from this control point, two roads connect this objective to the Arcade (D). If you are the CN team, be sure to use the road to the east as it will provide more cover and the element of surprise as you push towards the Arcade (D). If you are the US team, make sure to use the west road so you don't have any opportunities to get your vehicle ambushed from enemies hiding in the side streets.
- When defending this control point, have an engineer place mines on the two roads leading up to this objective. If you are on the US team, place the mines on the eastern roads. Or if you are the CN team, placing the mines on the roads to the northeast and northwest will allow your squad to hold back any vehicles while you regroup and prepare to push out of this control point.

CONTROL POINT ASSETS

US CONTROL	CN CONTROL
M1 Abrams (1)	Type 99 MBT (1)

CONQUEST SMALL

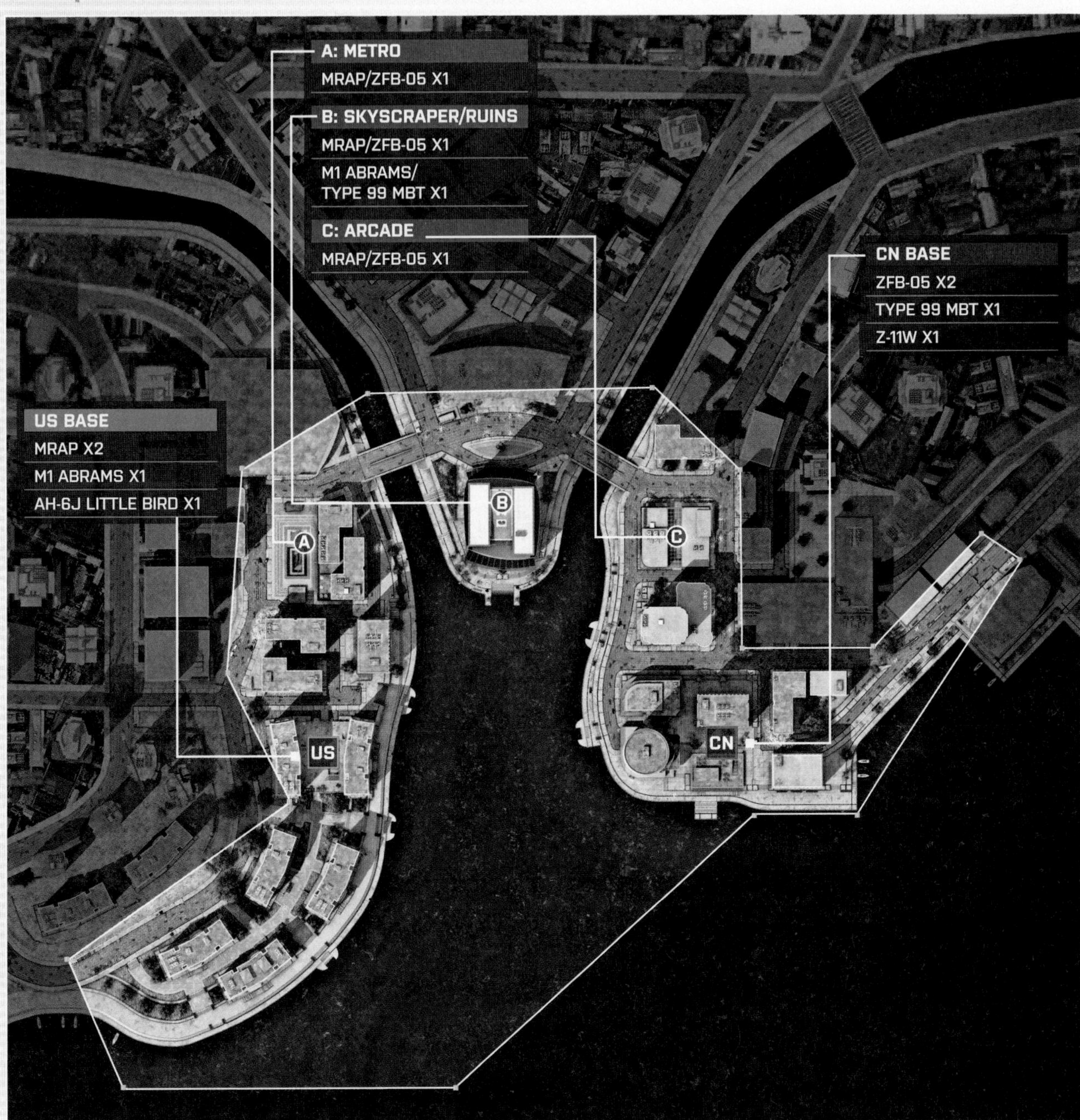

RECOMMENDED SQUAD COMPOSITION:

This battle takes place in the business district and streets of Shanghai. The US team takes on the CN team in a fight to capture two control points out of a total of three on the map. The three control points on the map are the Metro (A), the Skyscraper (B), and the Arcade (C). The US base is positioned in the Garage, and the best strategy is to capture and defend the Metro (A) and the Skyscraper (B). The CN team's base is found around the Foodcourt and they should capture the Arcade (C) and Skyscraper (B). The Metro (A) and Arcade (C) both have elevators that lead to the top of their buildings; these high vantage points provide great firing angles for recon snipers. The main battle will go down around the Skyscraper (B) as the controlling team is rewarded a Cruise Missile that the team's commander can call in. The Skyscraper (B) is easily defended from the roof once controlled, but be warned—the building can collapse, so have a squad set a perimeter on the ground level to defeat incoming infantry. If the Skyscraper (B) does collapse, be prepared to fight through the leftover debris as the control point now turns to Ruins (B). This map will provide constant action, so brace yourself.

US BASE

- The Garage is the location of the US base in this Conquest mode. Both residential buildings have stairs that lead to both levels of the parking garage.
- The US base spawns many vehicles. Use these immediately to start your push towards the Metro (A) nearest your base and the Skyscraper (B).
- The scout helicopter can only be accessed through the deploy screen. A squad should fill up this helicopter and head towards the Skyscraper (B). Capturing this point will allow your commander to have a Cruise Missile.
- The nearest control point to the base is Metro (A). This is an easy capture off the beginning of the game, so only a couple squad members need to stay here to capture it while the rest of the US team fights for the Skyscraper (B).
- A very useful class on this map is the recon class. This map has many buildings you have to make your way through, which can cause you to get caught by surprise. A recon player can fly around an MAV and spot enemies; this will let your squad know where the enemies are.

BASE ASSETS

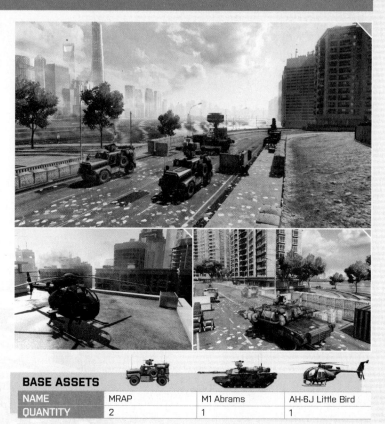

NAME	MRAP	M1 Abrams	AH-6J Little Bird
QUANTITY	2	1	1

CN BASE

- Located on the southeast side of the map, the CN base has a few vehicles at your disposal. Make sure to not push up too far ahead of your team past the Skyscraper (B) and carelessly lose one of your vehicles.
- Send your fastest vehicles towards the Skyscraper (B) so you can get control of the objective and your commander can use the Cruise Missile.
- When driving your tank towards the center of the map, you will run into the enemy's vehicles around the base of the Skyscraper (B). Immediately destroy the vertical concrete pillars on the opposing bridge to the east. This will eliminate all the cover for the enemy vehicles and make them much easier to hit.
- You will be able to reach the Arcade (C) before the enemy team, and when you acquire this objective it gives your commander the Infantry Scan ability. Make sure your commander uses the Infantry Scan as soon as possible so you can see where the enemy is headed at the start of the match.
- Every control point on this map gives the commander an asset. Be aware of what your team has and what the enemy has. For example if the enemy has Metro (A), their commander will have a vehicle scan, which will prepare the US team for any sort of vehicle flank you might attempt.

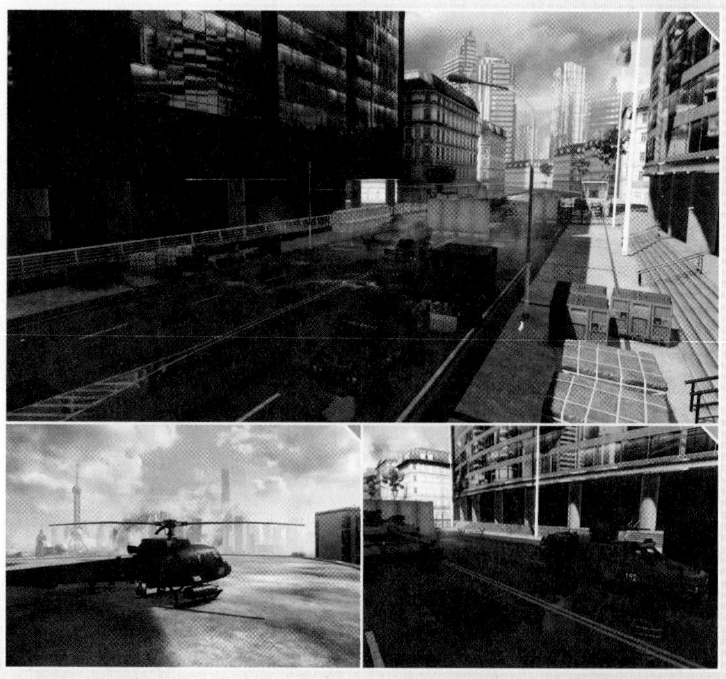

BASE ASSETS

NAME	ZFB-05	Type 99 MBT	Z-11W
QUANTITY	2	1	1

A: METRO

- Located in the northwest sector, this subway station has three main entrances, all providing quick access to the flag. But exercise caution when entering through any of the entrances, as defending opponents may be hiding in the darkness, waiting to ambush your squad. Deploy Motion Sensors to detect any defenders before rushing toward the flag.
- There are two unique features to this control point, which can affect it in a few different ways. First is the unfinished pillar. When C4 is placed on the pillar, detonating it will cause the above ground to collapse. A new entrance will be created if the detonation is successful.
- The second feature would be to activate the shutters, which are located at the bottom west of the control point. This will seal off a few places, but they can be opened back up if reactivated. This would also be a great place to contest the objective.
- When attacking this control point, either team will want to have a recon class to throw Motion Sensors to locate enemies hiding around the lower level. Once done, this will make cleaning up the area easy.
- Defenders will want to place Claymores around the staircases to take out any wandering enemies attempting to take control of this objective.

CONTROL POINT ASSETS

US CONTROL	CN CONTROL
MRAP (1)	ZFB-05 (1)

B: SKYSCRAPER

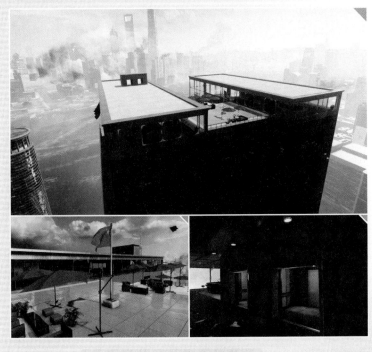

- This objective is positioned on the center north area of the map. The control point is equal distance to both bases and is at the very top of the Skyscraper. This flag also grants your commander the Cruise Missile, making this flag very important to control throughout the entire game.
- A rocket launcher and sniper rifle spawn on the roof of this building. Use these to take down incoming helicopter and enemy infantry across the map.
- When attacking, use helicopters to quickly drop off teammates on the roof to infiltrate the area.
- When defending, a squad should have a few engineers to take out enemy helicopters, and other teammates should watch the elevators. Use T-UGS at the top of the elevators to alert you when enemies come up the elevators. The elevators are placed on the east and west side of the building.
- This control point will be extremely tough to control since the building can be taken down from the base by explosives. When controlling this control point, have a few teammates patrol the base of this building to stop the enemy from taking down the building.

CONTROL POINT ASSETS

US CONTROL	CN CONTROL
MRAP (1)	ZFB-05 (1)

PRO TIP: WALSHY

The bridges north of the Skyscraper (B) are where the majority of vehicle battles take place. Be sure to load up these areas with explosives such as M15 AT mines and M2 SLAMs. Also, don't forget to raise the bollards.

B: RUINS

- This flag moves down to the ground level when the building is destroyed. This area is surrounded by rubble that can be used as great cover.
- When the flag is controlled, you gain control of an attack boat. The attack boat's weapons provide great fire support, perfect for mowing down incoming infantry.
- A HVM-2 battle pickup spawns in the area of this flag. Use this to take down enemy helicopters dropping off enemy infantry.
- When defending or attacking, use the rubble to hide yourself within the control point. This flag has a large capture radius and can be contested from many areas.
- This flag still grants your commander the Cruise Missile and will still be a valuable control point.

CONTROL POINT ASSETS

US CONTROL	CN CONTROL
M1 Abrams (1)	Type 99 MBT (1)

C: ARCADE

- This control point is located towards the northeastern part of the map on the second floor. The Arcade (C) has many access areas, but two main entrances coming from the north and south. There is also an elevator that will give you roof access.
- Once captured, an Armored Fighting Vehicle will become available and should be used to defend or transport players to other control points. Since this flag is very accessible, either team can patrol the area very effectively by circling the objective.
- There are many corners to hide in and contest this control point, so use this to your team's advantage as much as possible. In this control point, there is a button to close the shutters and block that entrance off from the enemy.
- When attacking this flag, the roof has many windows, making air attacks very effective by using transport helicopters to drop players off and raid the objective from the sky.

CONTROL POINT ASSETS

US CONTROL	CN CONTROL
MRAP (1)	ZFB-05 (1)

RUSH

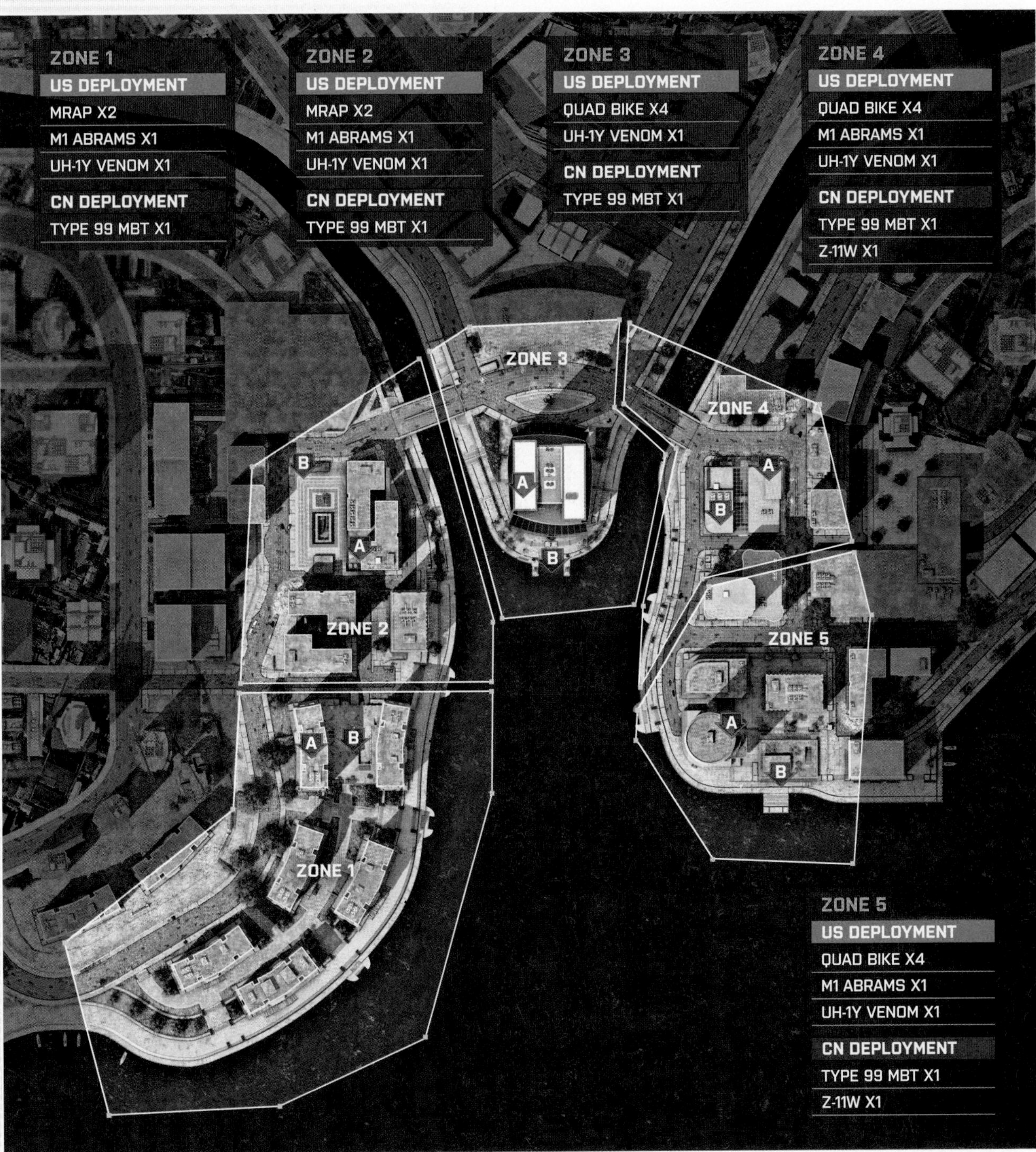

In this intense and heated battle, the US team will make their way through the heart of Shanghai as they attempt to advance through five different zones. Despite the US team having a couple of vehicles, a lot the fighting is infantry-based as the M-COM stations are found inside the buildings and structures of their respective zones. The US team will begin their attack on the Garage where the CN team has an assortment of stationary weapons to defend against the US vehicles. The US vehicles should coordinate accordingly as M15 AT mines can be found scattered throughout the roads, planted by the defending CN team. If the US team succeeds in their advance, the CN team will eventually fall back to the Foodcourt where they have one more chance to hold off the attackers. With infinite tickets for the defenders and five zones to fight in, the US team is looking at a battle of stamina.

ZONE 1: GARAGE

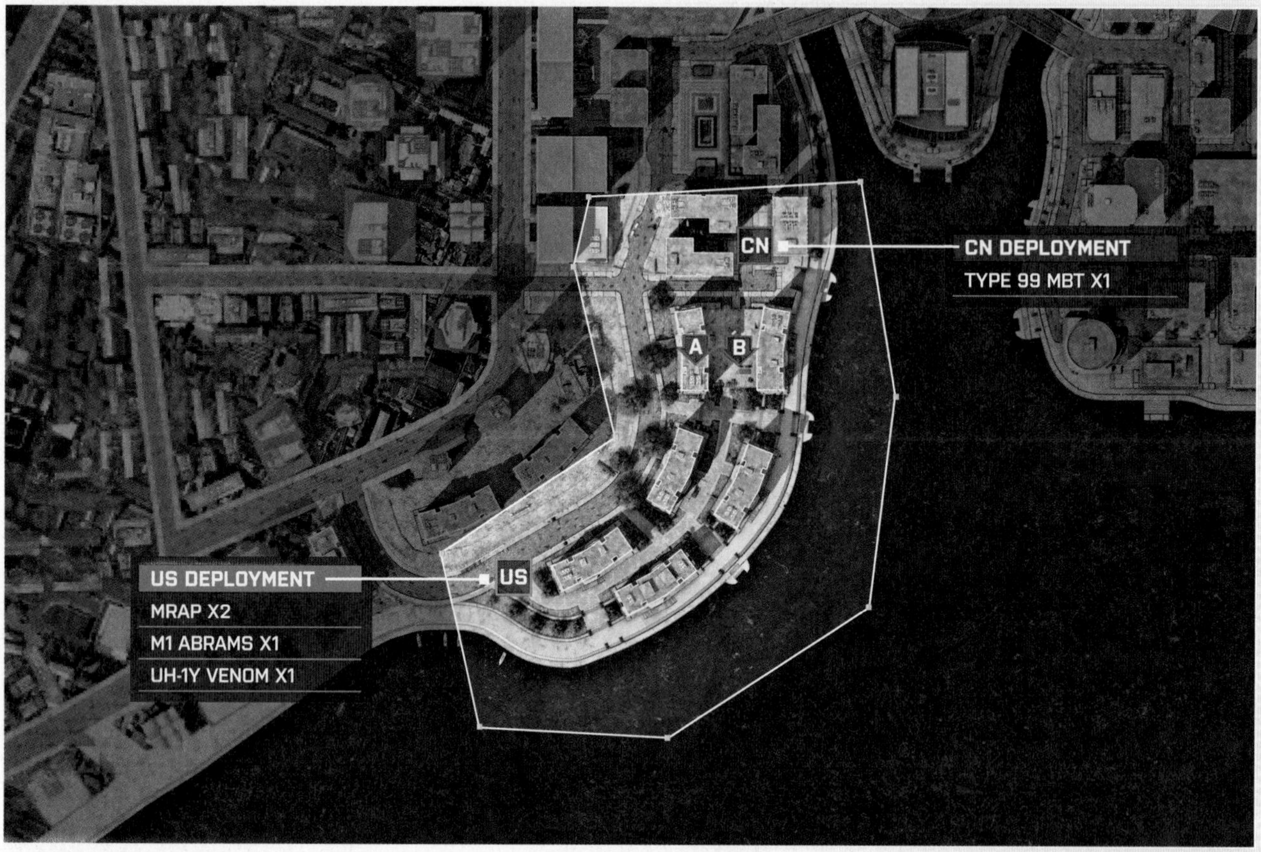

CN
CN DEPLOYMENT
TYPE 99 MBT X1

A
B

US
US DEPLOYMENT
MRAP X2
M1 ABRAMS X1
UH-1Y VENOM X1

US DEPLOYMENT

RECOMMENDED SQUAD COMPOSITION: 

- The US base is located to the southwest of the M-COM stations and is connected by a wide four-lane road. With this open road, out here you should easily be able to avoid being ambushed by enemy engineers.
- Since the road is open and you are unlikely to run into mines, the biggest threats to your M1 Abrams are the opponent's tank, engineers, and HJ-8 Launcher on the northwest side of the M-COM stations. Make sure to have a couple engineers in your squad to repair your M1 Abrams and help take out the opponent's tank.
- You have your choice of three transport vehicles and one tank. Make sure your tank clears the way for your MRAPs to safely drop off its passengers.
- Have your transport helicopter drop off your squad on top of the Garage to help get control of it. There are six ways to get on top of the garage, but a successful helicopter drop is crucial to getting control of this hectic area.
- On the south side of the Garage are two stationary .50Cals. Don't advance directly to the garage from the south. Instead, use the buildings to the southeast and southwest for cover, avoiding the .50Cals.

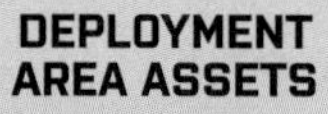

DEPLOYMENT AREA ASSETS

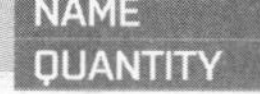

NAME	MRAP	M1 Abrams	UH1-Y Venom
QUANTITY	2	1	1

CN DEPLOYMENT

RECOMMENDED SQUAD COMPOSITION:

- In Zone 1, the CN deployment is in between the Garage and Metro.
- The CN team gets one vehicle, a Type 99 MBT, to defend against four vehicles from the attacking team. Be sure to have an engineer close by to repair any damage your vehicle may take.
- Send a squad south of the Garage. This location has fortified concrete walls and sandbags for cover, so proceed with caution. Have engineers in the squad to rocket incoming vehicles, stopping them in their tracks.
- The attacking team has a few ground vehicles off the start. Head to the main road west of the Garage and plant it with mines. Players can also throw Smoke Grenades over the mines, decreasing the enemy's visibility as they drive over the explosives.
- A squad will need to set a perimeter on top of the parking garage around M-COM Station B. This top floor has two .50Cals that can be used to ward off enemy ground and air vehicles. There are six entrances to the top, so spread your squad out to cover the entrances.

DEPLOYMENT AREA ASSETS

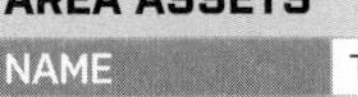

NAME	Type 99 MBT
QUANTITY	1

M-COM STATION A

- M-COM Station A is located inside of a parking garage on the main floor, and it is in a corner with virtually no cover.
- There are no vehicles, so defending this point will be very difficult given the location of M-COM Station A. The defending team is going to want to use mostly support and engineer classes. C4 and Claymores can be effectively used in this close space as enemy vehicles make their way inside. Engineers are going to want to equip M15 AT mines and lay them all around the area to prevent enemy vehicles from over running M-COM Station A.
- Defenders can also blow away the walls surrounding M-COM Station A and expose it for a better view to prevent attackers from arming.
- When attacking, make good use of the M1 Abrams that spawns at the US deployment to start your main push. Also be sure to have some engineer classes follow in case any vehicles need repairing. Have the engineers scout for land mines on the road to ensure safe routes to M-COM Station A.
- When attackers are going for the arm, Smoke Grenades will be incredibly useful in lowering vision for defenders and getting a sneaky arm.

M-COM STATION B

- This is located in the heart of the Garage—on the top level in between two vans.
- There are six entrances to this upper level of the Garage. These will all be the focal points to watch when defending.
- When defending, you're able to watch multiple entrances from situated positions. Have your squad watch these six entrances. Place T-UGS in certain areas to have multiple entrances watched.
- When attacking, deploy players from the helicopter to the upper level on the Garage while sending ground infantry through the many entrances. This will be a tough push to make but once you've taken down the defenders you'll have a clear path to the objective.
- When attacking, bring your tank up through the bottom of the Garage to assist in arming this objective.

ZONE 2: METRO

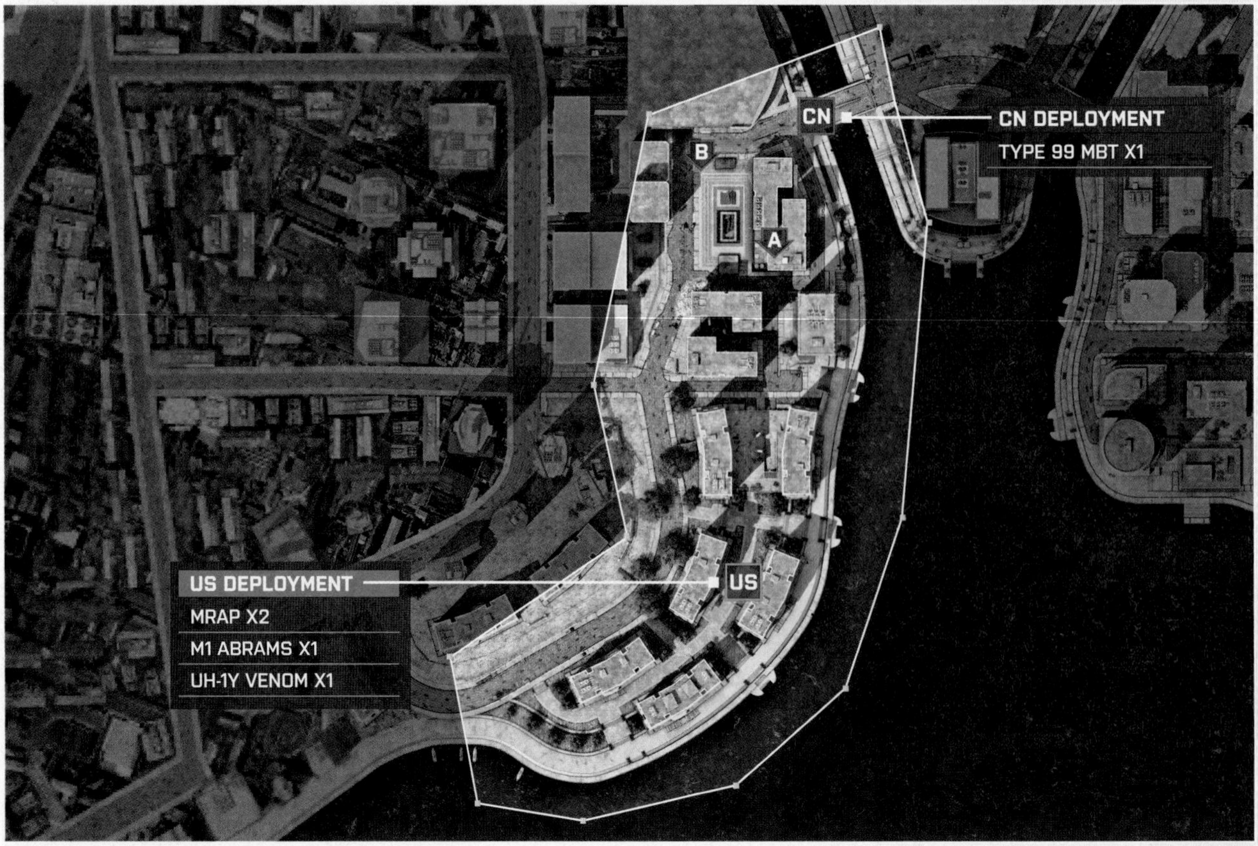

CN DEPLOYMENT
TYPE 99 MBT X1

US DEPLOYMENT
MRAP X2
M1 ABRAMS X1
UH-1Y VENOM X1

US DEPLOYMENT

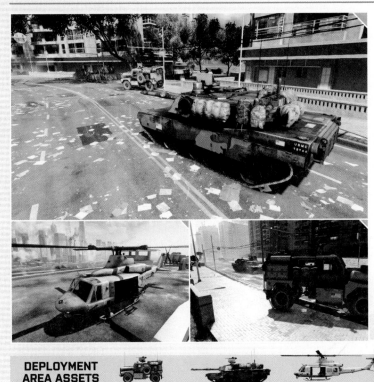

RECOMMENDED SQUAD COMPOSITION:

- The US deployment is located directly to the south of both M-COM stations where you can either take the wide road or walk by foot, weaving between the buildings.
- Beware of enemy snipers on top of the building to the east of M-COM Station A. Go up the elevator to the top of this building to flank any potential enemies and to get a perfect view of the entire top of the Metro area.
- Don't send your entire team through the front entrance near M-COM Station A. Instead, send your squad to the north where there are two more stairwells to go down and flank behind M-COM Station B.
- Place a Radio Beacon hidden above to the northwest of M-COM Station B. The enemy will rarely check this area and you can continue to give your team great spawns for this rest of this zone.
- If the enemy is hiding below near the M-COM stations, send a recon member of your squad to toss Motion Sensors in the area before pushing in to reveal exactly where they are hiding.

DEPLOYMENT AREA ASSETS

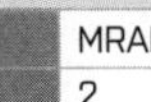
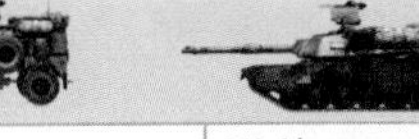
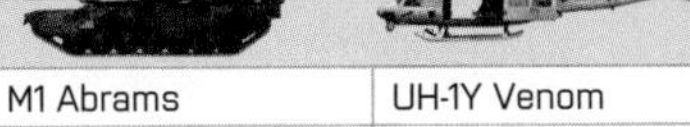

NAME	MRAP	M1 Abrams	UH-1Y Venom
QUANTITY	2	1	1

CN DEPLOYMENT

RECOMMENDED SQUAD COMPOSITION:

- After losing the fight in Zone 1, the CN deployment is pushed back near the Metro.
- Much like Zone 1, the CN team gets another Type 99 MBT to defend against enemy vehicles and infantry.
- East of M-COM Station A is an elevator that leads to the top of the building. Send a squad with recon and engineer classes to the top. Recon players can snipe approaching attackers while the engineers will focus on targeting vehicles.
- A squad of support and assault classes can shoot the pillar east of M-COM Station A to knock down a balcony. This balcony now acts as a ramp that leads to two .50Cals that over watch the objective.
- A squad composed of short-range players will prove to be super effective near M-COM Station B as there are only four entrances to this underground area. A fifth entrance can open if the pillars north of this objective are destroyed, causing the road above to cave in.

PRO TIP: ELUMNITE

THERE ARE GLASS OVERHANGS AROUND SHANGHAI THAT CAN BE USED TO REACH HIDDEN AREAS AND GAIN A HEIGHT ADVANTAGE. THERE IS A PILLAR THAT HOLDS UP THE STRUCTURE, SO USE EITHER C4 OR A GRENADE TO DESTROY IT. THIS CAUSES PART OF THE OVERHANG TO BREAK AND TURN INTO A RAMP FOR YOU TO CLIMB UP ON.

DEPLOYMENT AREA ASSETS

NAME	Type 99 MBT
QUANTITY	1

M-COM STATION A

- M-COM Station A is located down the first flight of stairs of Metro, right across from M-COM Station B. This area will be heavily guarded with mostly recon classes.
- There is only one vehicle that spawns for the defenders. The Type 99 MBT is located in the northern part of the CN deployment and there are a several .50Cal turrets and AT Launchers to help protect both of the M-COM stations.
- When attacking, use the UH-1Y Venom to transport a few support and recon classes to the roof of the eastern part of M-COM Station A. Attackers can then use the elevator to reach the ground floor for a safer route. Have your team then place a Radio Beacon on the roof of the building to keep your team spawning close to the area.
- When defending, if your team gets overwhelmed, then fall back under to the Metro's lower levels. Defenders will still have perfect vision of M-COM Station A from here.
- The defending team should utilize T-UGS Motion Sensors to alert them to attackers approaching from above.

M-COM STATION B

- This objective is located on the north side of the Metro underground. This objective is placed behind a counter. When attacking, go prone when arming the objective to have much cover from incoming enemies.
- When defending, watch the enemies pushing from the south in the underground tunnel. Beware of enemies flanking, which are able to enter from the north entrance of the Metro.
- With this objective being underground, defenders will want to stay below and watch for attackers sneaking into the few entrances. There are only four entrances to this objective.
- The underground Metro area is close-mid range. Pack your assault and support class to have the advantage on your enemies.
- The ceiling above this area can be used to drop in for an attack or be used for a vantage point to kill the awaiting defender below.

ZONE 3: RUINS

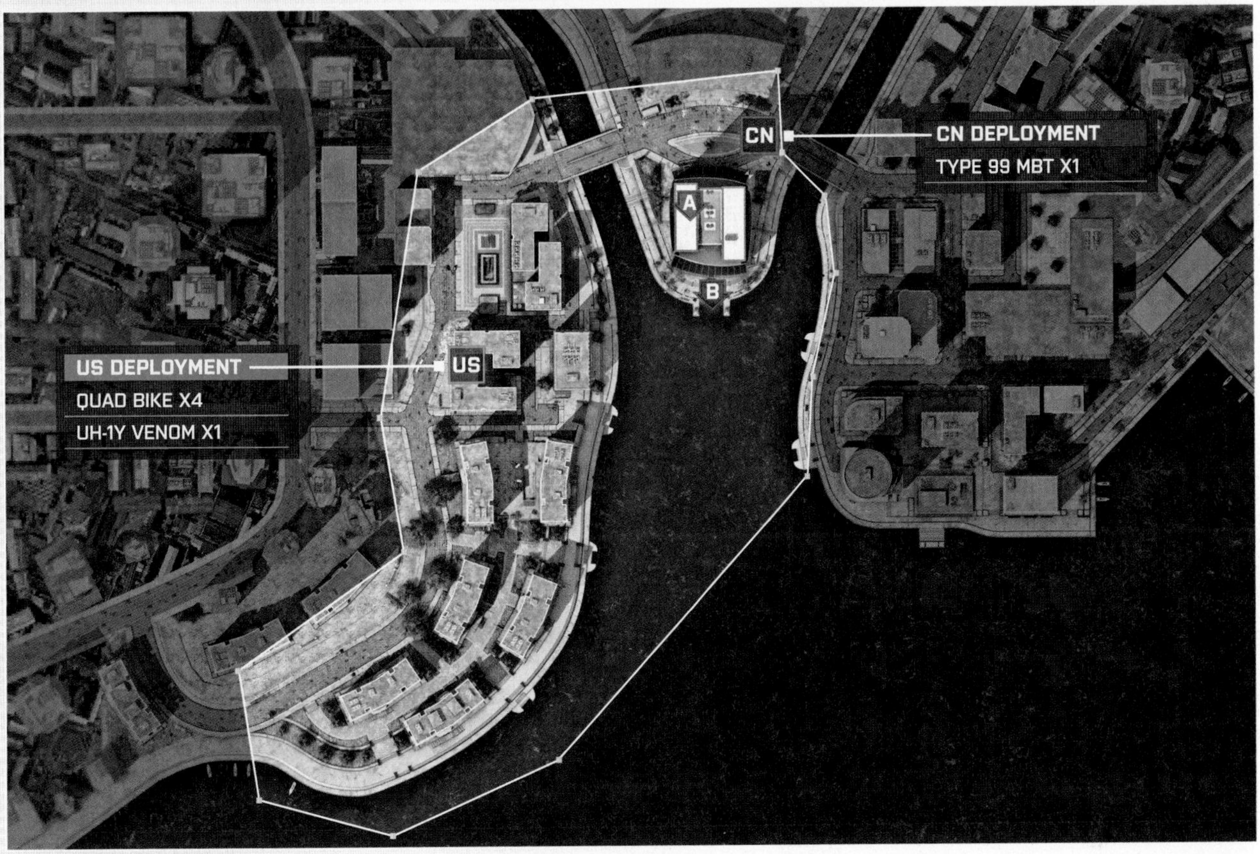

CN DEPLOYMENT
TYPE 99 MBT X1

US DEPLOYMENT
QUAD BIKE X4
UH-1Y VENOM X1

US DEPLOYMENT

RECOMMENDED SQUAD COMPOSITION: 

- Upon the start of the zone, the Skyscraper collapses and your goal is to arm the two M-COM stations located in the rubble to the northeast of the US deployment.
- For vehicles, you now only have four Quad Bikes and the UH-1Y Venom. Keep an engineer on board the transport helicopter to conduct repairs while circling the objectives and raining down fire with the miniguns.
- The Quad Bikes won't do you much good crawling through the rubble, so move in on foot to maintain better control while advancing through the debris field.
- Dust kicked up by the Skyscraper's collapse makes visibility difficult. Add to the haze by deploying smoke around the objectives.
- Once you reach the rubble around the M-COM stations, be sure to equip an explosive gadget such as the assault's M320 HE. This will allow you to get easy kills with all the small hills and rubble to explode these grenades off of.

DEPLOYMENT AREA ASSETS  

NAME	Quad Bike	UH-1Y Venom
QUANTITY	4	1

CN DEPLOYMENT

RECOMMENDED SQUAD COMPOSITION:

- The CN deployment is now pushed behind the destroyed Skyscraper, surrounded by all the wreckage.
- The team gets a Type 99 MBT. Due to the rubble caused by the destroyed Skyscraper, you are only able to patrol the streets as opposed to defending the M-COM station up close.
- The debris will force the attacking team to get out of their ground vehicles, making most of the action in this area close quarter.
- Be aware of the enemy's transport helicopter. There are buildings where the enemy can drop off recon players, which will ultimately be a thorn in your side. Stock up on engineers and don't let this helicopter fly around.
- The debris allows for C4 and Claymore classes to booby trap both M-COM stations. Combine these with Motion Sensors to ambush incoming attackers.

DEPLOYMENT AREA ASSETS

NAME	Type 99 MBT
QUANTITY	1

M-COM STATION A

- M-COM Station A is located northeast in the Ruins of the Skyscraper. M-COM Station A is only protected by a few pillars left by the Skyscraper, which can be used as some cover.
- A Type 99 MBT is the only vehicle that the defenders have at their disposal to protect M-COM Station A. Have this tank stick near M-COM Station A to help take out any attackers that are on foot.
- When attacking, make your way from the north side of the objective and have a few teammates split up going southeast and southwest towards the objective. This will help in taking over M-COM Station A.
- Have at least one teammate take position towards the far north of Skyscraper. Have squad members spawn here to keep the pressure on a different area.

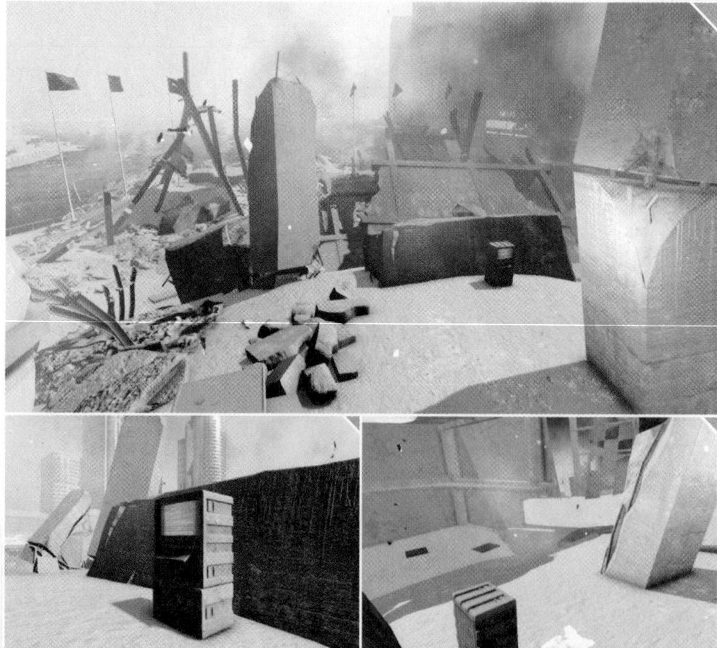

M-COM STATION B

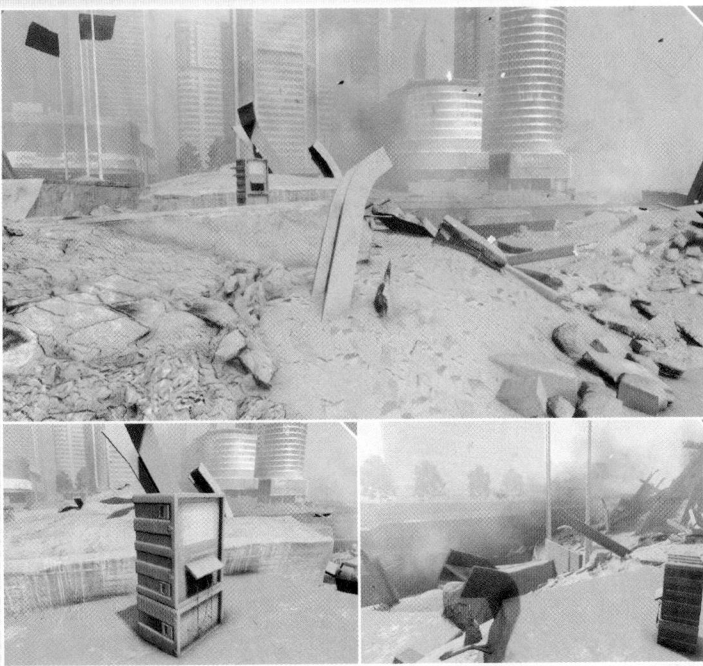

- This M-COM station is located on the south side of the Skyscraper rubble.
- This objective is surrounded by extreme amounts of rubble. Players should use all this rubble for cover when defending or attacking.
- When defending, watch the enemies traveling in light water vehicles towards the south side of M-COM Station B. Otherwise they'll be sure to spawn their squad on the wreckage and easily take over.
- North of this objective lies a slanted cement wall. At the farthest south tip of this wall you're able to have an incredible overview watching this M-COM station.
- Just north of the objective, there is a M32 MGL battle pickup. This pickup provides a heavy punch and does heavy damage in close quarters. Draw attackers in and then let them feel the pain.

ZONE 4: ARCADE

US DEPLOYMENT
QUAD BIKE X4
M1 ABRAMS X1
UH-1Y VENOM X1

US

A B

CN

CN DEPLOYMENT
TYPE 99 MBT X1
Z-11W X1

US DEPLOYMENT

RECOMMENDED SQUAD COMPOSITION:

- The US deployment is located to the northwest of the M-COM stations, connected by a short bridge.
- Beware of snipers and engineers sitting on top of the roof of the Arcade. To counter this, have a recon member of your own sit on your side of the bridge, ready to pick off enemies who peek over the edge.
- You will want to use your transport helicopter or the elevator under M-COM Station B to get up on the roof to clear out the enemies.
- M-COM Station B is nearly impossible to arm unless you clear out the roof. Be sure to take care of this before attacking inside the building.

DEPLOYMENT AREA ASSETS

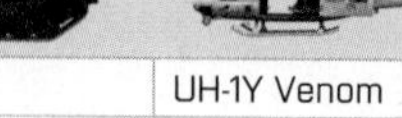

NAME	Quad Bike	M1 Abrams	UH-1Y Venom
QUANTITY	4	1	1

CN DEPLOYMENT

RECOMMENDED SQUAD COMPOSITION:

- After losing the fight at the Skyscraper, the CN team is pushed back even farther, and now their deployment is set up at the Foodcourt.
- The defenders only have one tank and a scout helicopter, giving them a good chance to stand up against the US team's transport helicopter and tank.
- Head north towards the Arcade, which holds both M-COM stations. Send a squad into M-COM Station A and close the shutters. This will force the attackers to come from one direction when they try to arm the objective.
- Two players should take control of the MBT and head towards the bridge north of the Arcade. Most of the attackers will come from this direction, allowing you to get easy points and kills. Have an engineer close by to repair the tank when needed.
- West of the Arcade are a couple of stationary weapons. As most of the enemies will approach the objectives from this direction, man the stationary weapons and lay steel.

DEPLOYMENT AREA ASSETS

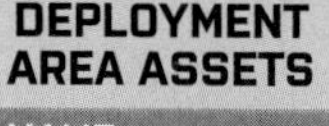

NAME	Type 99 MBT	Z-11W
QUANTITY	1	1

M-COM STATION A

- M-COM Station A is located in the eastern part of the Arcade building on the first floor.
- There is one Type 99 MBT that can be used to defend the outer region of M-COM Station A.
- Defenders can close the shutters and block off the eastern entrance to M-COM Station A. This will only leave one way to enter this area, making defending M-COM Station A much easier for your team.
- Attackers will make good use of the UH-1Y Venom for airstrikes above the roof of M-COM Station A. This will be a much better point of attack, and with less resistance.
- The recon class is useful here to place T-UGS. This is a high-traffic area—having the advantage of knowing where your opponent is will be incredibly useful.

M-COM STATION B

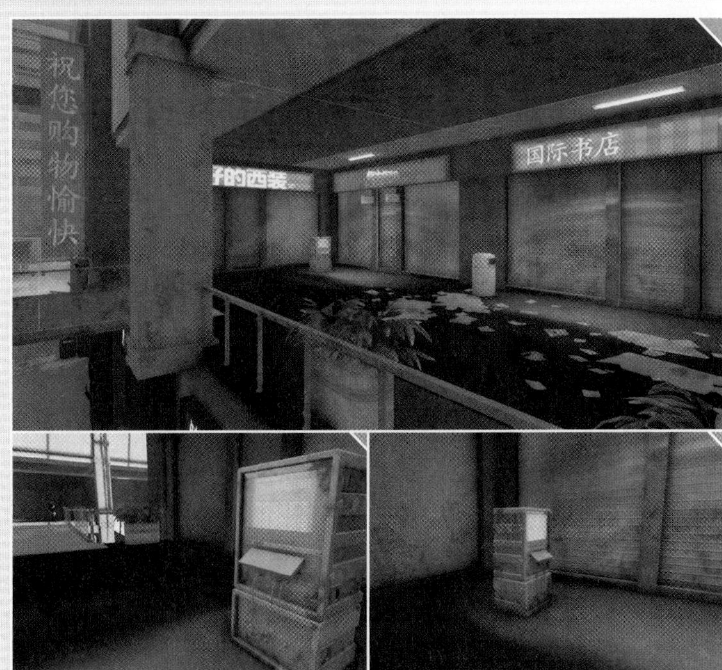

- This M-COM station is located in the upper-west level of the Arcade.
- This objective only has two staircases leading to it. It is also possible to drop down from the roof.
- When attacking, make a push to get on the roof by going to the elevator in the lower-northwest section of the building. This will give you a vantage point over the defending players and a chance to distract them. This allows your teammates to push in from ground level much easier.
- When defending, be sure to hold down the rooftop, as this will provide much use in stopping the attackers trying to arm the objective. You're able to see the M-COM station from a position on the roof.
- When defending or attacking, place a radio beacon on the roof to constantly get a spawn near the objective. Place T-UGS on the roof to have the jump on your enemies approaching this area.

ZONE 5: FOODCOURT

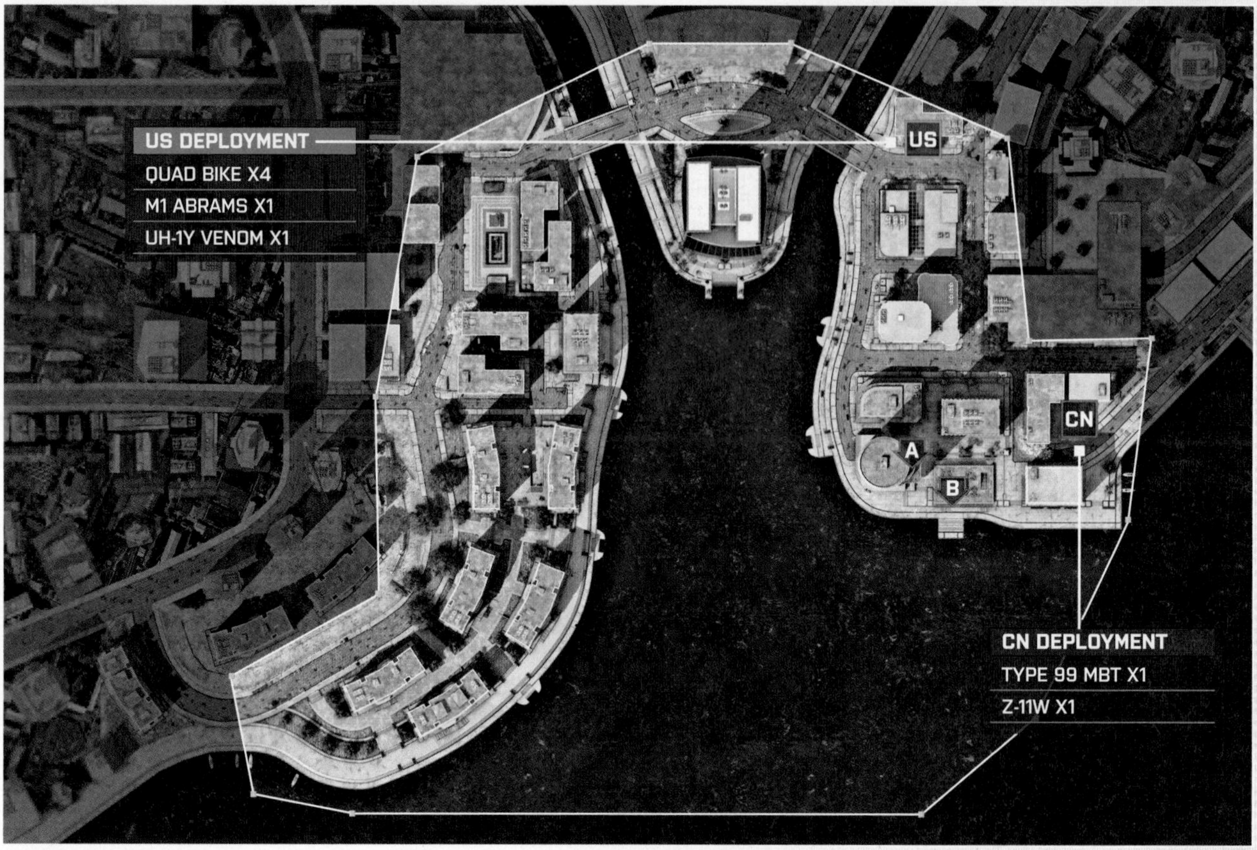

US DEPLOYMENT
QUAD BIKE X4
M1 ABRAMS X1
UH-1Y VENOM X1

US

A

B

CN

CN DEPLOYMENT
TYPE 99 MBT X1
Z-11W X1

US DEPLOYMENT

RECOMMENDED SQUAD COMPOSITION: 

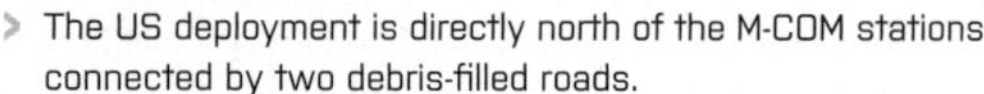

- The US deployment is directly north of the M-COM stations, connected by two debris-filled roads.
- Push your M1 Abrams through the western road, since it is a little more open and this way you can avoid any ambushes that might take place.
- The enemy once again only has a single MBT. Be sure to have only two engineers at the most to help take their MBT down. The rest of your squad needs to be assault, recon, or support to take care of all the infantry that you will encounter.
- You need to clear out the roof above M-COM Station A before trying to arm M-COM Station B. A great way to flank this point is to destroy the pillar on the southeast corner of the building so that you have another ramp up to the roof where you can catch the enemy off guard.

DEPLOYMENT AREA ASSETS 

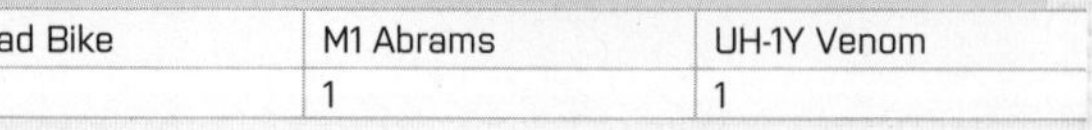

NAME	Quad Bike	M1 Abrams	UH-1Y Venom
QUANTITY	4	1	1

CN DEPLOYMENT

RECOMMENDED SQUAD COMPOSITION:

- The CN deployment is now located northeast of the M-COM stations.
- In your final stand against the US team, the CN team once again has the Type 99 MBT to help defend.
- The objectives are a few hundred meters away from the CN deployment. Have recon players drop Radio Beacons to avoid making that long run towards the objectives.
- There are multiple stationary weapons that allow you to suppress the enemy and keep them at bay. Have players move towards the attackers while the stationary weapons are providing cover.

DEPLOYMENT AREA ASSETS

NAME	Type 99 MBT	Z-11W
QUANTITY	1	1

M-COM STATION A

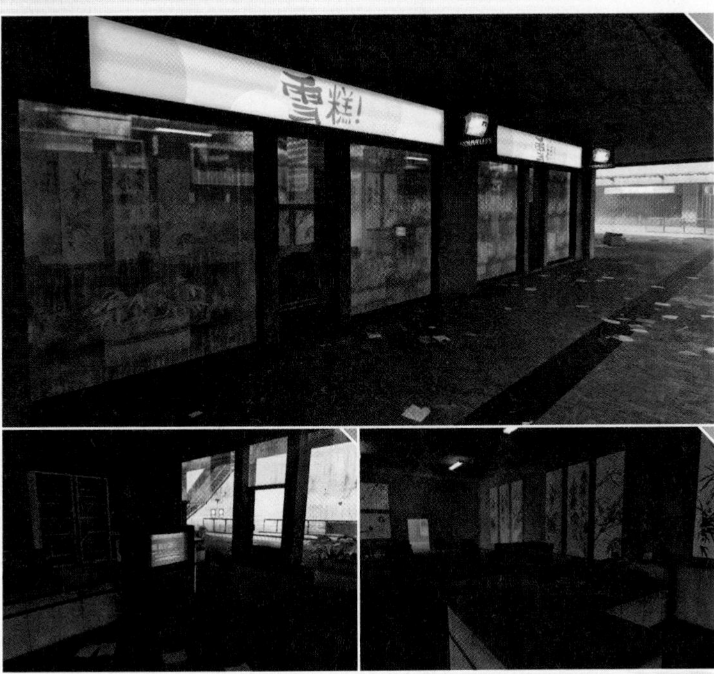

- This M-COM station is positioned on the south end inside the Foodcourt.
- When defending, the CN team should position their MBT in an angle to fire towards the enemy while taking cover from the Foodcourt building.
- Attackers should be aware of the pillars holding the glass overhangs outside of the objective. These will open a new way to gain entrance to the Foodcourt.
- There are a handful of stationary weapons for the defenders to use when defending against attacking waves. Throwing Medic Bags on the players mounted on these stationary weapons will keep them alive longer.
- When attacking, be sure to have Motion Sensors equipped and lob them into the Foodcourt. This will reveal the location of the defenders hiding inside, allowing you and your team to clear the area with ease.

M-COM STATION B

- This M-COM station is located on the west side of the Foodcourt and has minimal cover.
- When attacking this objective, completely clear out the enemies before you attempt to arm the objective. This objective is in a very open position and is easily seen from many directions.
- When defending, find an angle to snipe from as this objective can be seen from a distance. This allows other teammates to put pressure on the attacking team.
- When attacking, using the M320 SMK and Smoke Grenades can decrease the enemy's visibility, allowing you and your team to sneak into the Foodcourt.

OBLITERATION

RECOMMENDED SQUAD COMPOSITION:

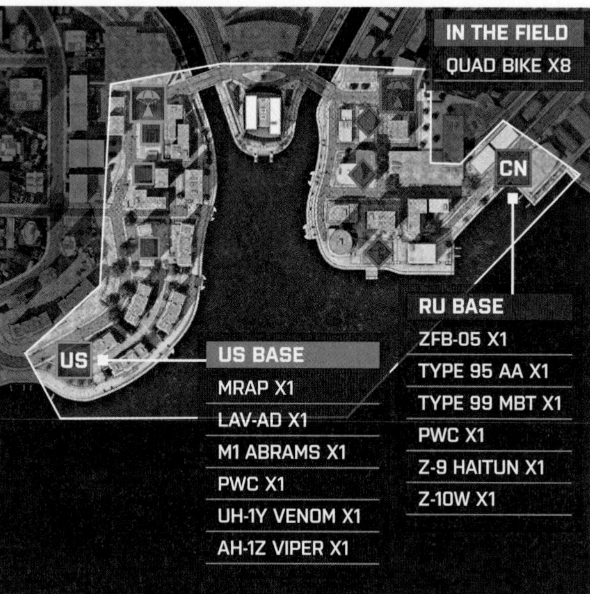

- The targets for the US team are positioned north to south between the Metro and Garage.
- The CN team guards the targets south of the Arcade and inside the Foodcourt.
- The bomb is located north of the Skyscraper in front of the building's statue.
- Have a few engineers in your squad as this a vehicle-friendly map. Place mines around the map to destroy the ground vehicles.
- Both teams will need to control the air space by using their attack helicopter and look to destroy the transport helicopters to force the enemy team to only maneuver on land.

DEFUSE

RECOMMENDED SQUAD COMPOSITION:

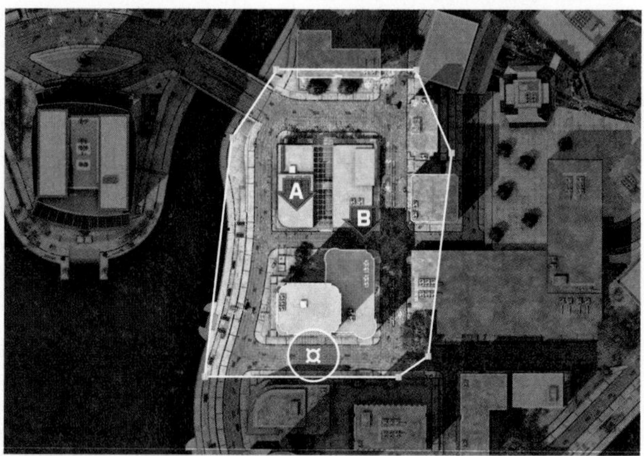

- The location of this Defuse map is in the Arcade area of the map. The attacking team US team spawns north of the Foodcourt and the defending CN team spawns south of the Arcade.
- Laptop A is located in the south restaurant of the Arcade. The back room of the restaurant leads to an elevator that grants you access to the roof.
- Laptop B is inside the car dealership inside the Arcade. There is an interaction that raises and lowers the shutters of the room.
- When defending, be sure to lower the shutters, forcing the attackers to take another approach. If they try to breach the shutters with explosives, it will give up their position, allowing you to counterattack.
- The attacking team won't be able to just storm in and flank around the west side of the Arcade. Here you can either force your way into the back room of the restaurant with Laptop A and clear out enemies or take the ladder above the glass overhang to reach the roof. When taking the back room, be prepared for defenders guarding the elevator and objective. If you take the ladder, you will have an overview of the Arcade to locate enemies.

DOMINATION

RECOMMENDED SQUAD COMPOSITION:

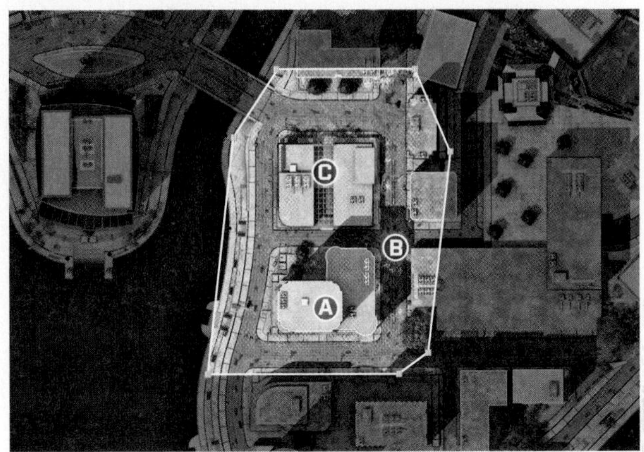

- The three control points on this map are the Storefronts (A), Wreckage (B), and the Arcade (C).
- Close the shutters to defend the Arcade (C). This forces the opposing team to come through the center of the building, making it an easier area to defend.
- Use the elevator to get on top of the Arcade (C). The roof of this building allows you to watch the Wreckage (B) from a bird's eye view.
- Storefronts (A) is a close-range area, so be sure to equip your favorite shotgun to deal with enemies coming around the corners.
- The best and safest strategy to lead you to victory is to capture Wreckage (B) and the Arcade (C). These flags are in close proximity, allowing you to react to squad commands at a whim.

SQUAD DEATHMATCH

RECOMMENDED SQUAD COMPOSITION:

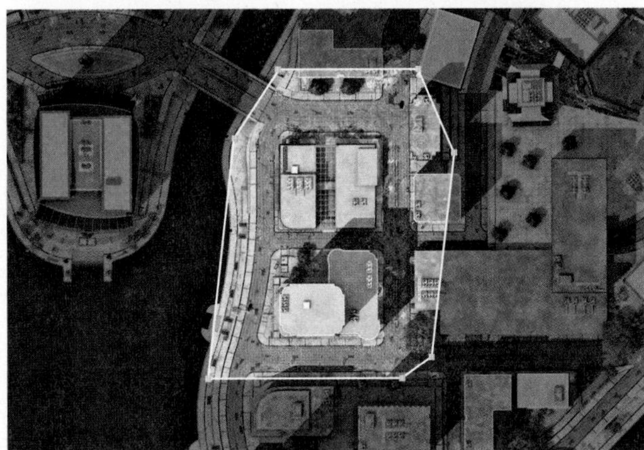

- This game mode revolves entirely around the Arcade building.
- Use the roof of the Arcade to have a vantage point over the enemies on the ground and inside the building. Place a T-UGS on the roof to have the advantage over the enemies underneath you.
- Keep control of the roof, but be aware that there are two ways to access the roof: by elevator and by the ladder on the west side of the building.
- South of the Arcade is a steel pillar holding a glass overhang. Knock this pillar down and walk up and follow it to the end. Players can use medium- to long-range weapons to fire at enemies in the middle of the Arcade. Your squad can ambush the players who try to hunt you down.
- Control the second level of the Arcade; this keeps you near all the action and lets you rack up kills.

TEAM DEATHMATCH

RECOMMENDED SQUAD COMPOSITION:

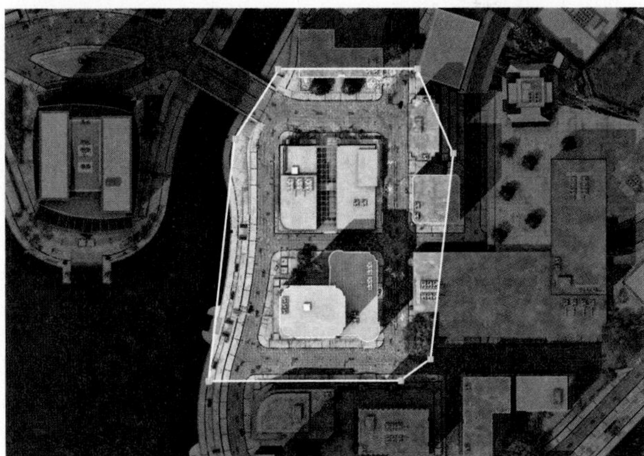

- Prepare to battle around a restaurant, clothing stores, and a car shop in this shopping plaza.
- In the car shop, there is a switch that raises and lowers the shutters. This assists you when defending this area, as the enemies only have a few directions to come from.
- The restaurant has a back room with an elevator that leads to the roof. The roof has an open ceiling, allowing you to shoot down towards your enemies.
- Avoid running through the middle of the plaza as enemies are posted on the second floor, waiting for players to make mistakes.
- Be sure to plant T-UGS in the corners of the plaza to detect nearby enemies. This allows you to get the jump on the enemy.

ALPHA SQUAD: IMPRESSIONS

MABOOZA

Regardless of the game mode, much of the fighting centers around the factory facility in the center of the map. Be ready for some intense infantry combat between the Manufacturing and Assembly buildings, particularly within the underground tunnel connecting the two structures—shotguns and PDWs are deadly down here. But don't neglect the surrounding areas either. My default class is the engineer, especially if enemy armor is on the prowl.

STRONGSIDE

One of my favorite positions is on top of the Assembly and Manufacturing buildings. It's a great place to utilize the recon class for sniping. This position has an incredible overview to pick off incoming enemies. Place a Radio Beacon on the roof, giving you and your squad a spawn point at the center of the action. Levolution creates an entirely new environment between these buildings, opening a new entrance to the tunnels beneath, ideal for staging surprise attacks or a sneaky getaway!

WALSHY

I love the battles that take place at the factory in the middle of this map. This map seems to have the perfect balance of times when vehicles are necessary and when you need to go on foot to get the job done.

FLAMESWORD

This is a beautiful map, featuring a factory facility surrounded by a vast forest. You'll find me running around as the support class. The map has so many ways to flank enemies and drop C4 on them. The Train Yard is my favorite spot, but don't be surprised if you see me parachuting towards the factory in the middle to join all the close-quarter combat with my LMG!

ELUMNITE

The assault and engineer classes are my choice for this map. Or if playing as support or recon, laying C4 and Claymores in the tunnels helps stop enemies from capturing objectives. The Bunker is my favorite place to hide when the generator has been shot to turn the lights off. This dark interior is where I like to pick off players who come looking for me—using the IRNV or FLIR optics gives me a distinct advantage.

ZAVOD 311

ZAVOD 311

LEVOLUTION MOMENTS

WHAT IS IT?

A big smoke stack falls down over the central area and opens up new paths.

HOW IS IT TRIGGERED?

There is a countdown timer that can be toggled in the Manufacturing building. The warhead blows up when the timer reaches zero.

HOW IS GAMEPLAY IMPACTED?

The area between Assembly and Manufacturing becomes almost impossible to traverse with vehicles. Geometry around the two areas changes by opening up routes and closing others. It is possible to access the tunnel below from up above. Tread carefully where the warhead has exploded because you can be injured by the radiation field now surrounding the area.

CONQUEST LARGE

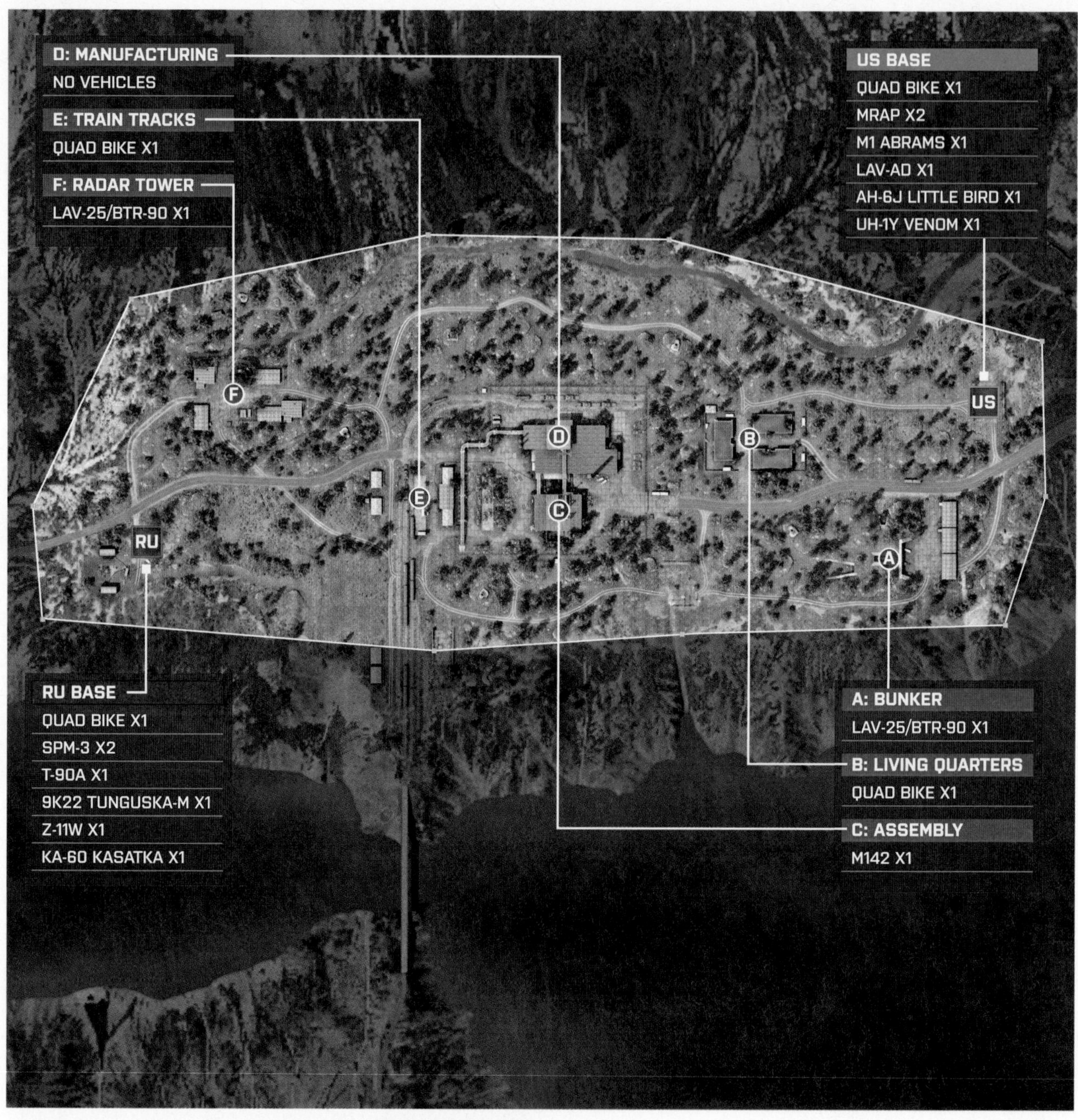

RECOMMENDED SQUAD COMPOSITION:

Compared to Conquest Small, the 64-player variant of the map adds two new control points: the Bunker (A) located near the RU base and the Radar Tower (F) located by the US base. The best strategy for the US team is to capture the Radar Tower (F), Train Tracks (E), Manufacturing (D), and Assembly (C). On the other side of the coin, the RU team wants to hold the Bunker (A), Living Quarters (B), Assembly (C), and Manufacturing (D). Both Assembly (C) and Manufacturing (D) have ladders that lead to the top of their buildings. These are great spots to fight the opposing team as you can spot them from afar and have the advantage due to the high ground. As the map size increases, so does the number of vehicles spawning at both bases, and additional vehicles spawn depending on what control points you capture. It is highly important for the team to continually bring the vehicles from the bases to the center. Usually, only one or two players are needed for capturing the closest control point to each base, but now the Bunker (A) spawns a BTR-90 for the RU team and Radar Tower (F) spawns a LAV-25 for the US team. These vehicles can turn the tide to the initial battle that goes down for control of Assembly (C) and Manufacturing (D). With an attack helicopter added in now, you can apply pressure to the opposing team's spawn. Controlling the center is the overall gameplan once again, but if the US team can get control of the Living Quarters (B), they can drain a lot of RU tickets. This applies for the RU team as well if they take over the Train Tracks (E). Flank along the edge of the forest; if the center is being guarded heavily, be sure to jump on the Quad Bikes and flank around to take either the Bunker (A) if playing as the US team or Radar Tower (F) if playing as the RU team. Just neutralizing these locations helps your team make a push to gain control of the center.

US BASE

- Stack the MRAPs with as many members as possible. Head towards Assembly (C) and Manufacturing (D) and work together to capture these flags early in the game.
- Have a few teammates ride the Quad Bikes all the way to the Bunker (A) in order to force the opposing team to come back and defend. The players who flank here should attempt to stay alive as long as possible. The fewer enemies the team has to fight at Assembly (C) and Manufacturing (D) makes it that much easier to capture them.
- Any units on foot should head for the Radar Tower (F) and Train Tracks (E). Send less towards the Train Tracks (E) because once the Radar Tower (F) is captured, an LAV-25 spawns, allowing them to catch up. Once both are captured, head towards Assembly (C) and Manufacturing (D).
- Air superiority is important. Keep the team's birds alive and have a few engineers ready to take out RU team's air vehicles. Use the team's scout helicopter to put pressure on the opposing team's spawn.
- Team members on foot should be engineers for the initial push in order to take out enemy vehicles. A couple players should use the recon class and take advantage of sniping atop of the Radar Tower (F).

BASE ASSETS

NAME	M1 Abrams	MRAP	LAV-AD	Quad Bike	AH-6J Little Bird	UH1Y-Venom
QUANTITY	1	2	1	1	1	1

RU BASE

- Stack the SPM-3s with as many members as possible! Head towards Assembly (C) and Manufacturing (D) and work together to capture these points early in the game.
- Have a few teammates ride the Quad Bikes all the way to the Radar Tower (F) in order to force the opposing team to come back and defend. The players who flank here should attempt to stay alive as long as possible. The fewer enemies the team has to fight at Assembly (C) and Manufacturing (D) makes it that much easier to capture them.
- Any units on foot should head for the Bunker (A) and Living Quarters (B). Send less towards the Living Quarters (B) because once the Bunker (A) is captured, a BTR-90 spawns, allowing them to catch up. Once both are captured, head towards Assembly (C) and Manufacturing (D).
- Air superiority is important. Keep the team's birds alive and have a few engineers ready to take out US team's air vehicles. Use the team's attack helicopter to put pressure on the opposing team's spawn.
- Team members on foot should be engineers for the initial push in order to take out enemy vehicles.

BASE ASSETS

NAME	T-90A	SPM-3	9K22 Tunguska-M	Quad Bike	Z-11W	KA-60 Kasatka
QUANTITY	1	2	1	1	1	1

A: BUNKER

- Capturing this point as the US team is a handful since the RU team base borders it very closely. If you are able to sneak around, allowing the RU players to pass isn't a bad idea. Capturing will force the RU team to decide if they want to come back and defend or continue their push towards the center.
- The name of the control point is no joke: it is a Bunker with a total of four entrances. Inside there is a generator that can be interacted with.
- This interaction causes a laser motion detector at three of the four entrances. The alarm will sound regardless of whether friend or foe cross its path. To avoid this, use the drop-down entrance on the top of the Bunker because it does not have a laser motion detector. Once inside the Bunker, head for the bottom level and take out the generator by either shooting it or pressing the action button. Taking out the generator will turn off all the lights and lasers, which provides plenty of hiding spots to take out enemies in the Bunker. This is a great strategy when outnumbered and you need a place to hide in the shadows. Keep in mind, the generator can still be reactivated.
- As most of the fighting is done in the Bunker, be sure the squad specializes in close-quarter combat. This requires a well-trained squad to get the job done.
- A tank can lay heavy fire through the main entrance, so stay away from it if you are the US team when capturing this control point.

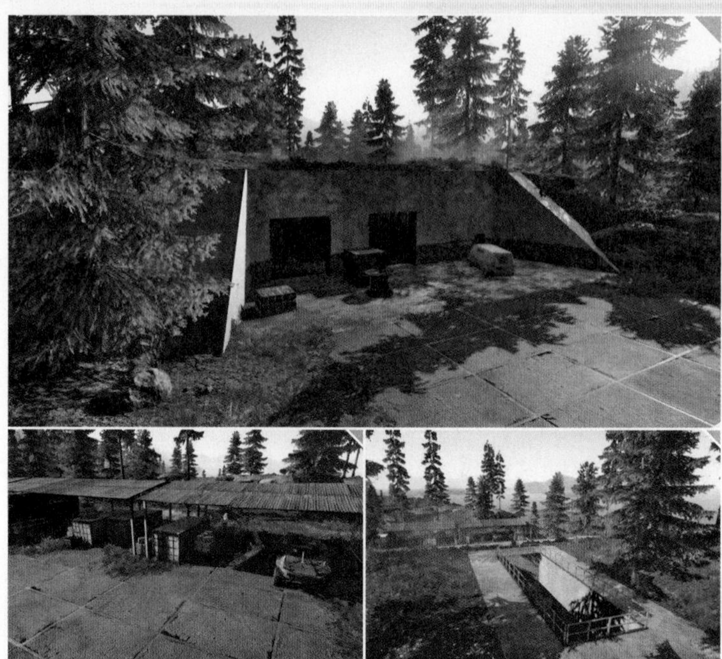

CONTROL POINT ASSETS

US CONTROL	RU CONTROL
LAV-25 (1)	BTR-90 (1)

B: LIVING QUARTERS

- This control point is surrounded by three homes/buildings that promote close-quarter combat, both for the attackers and defenders.
- These buildings are all destructible. If the team feels it would be easier to defend with them gone, then by all means let them fall!
- When defending, move from building to building, never allowing the enemy to pinpoint your location. There are many windows and stairs to keep the opponent guessing where you're at.
- The area is a decent size, which is fenced in by four concrete walls forming a square around the three homes/buildings.
- Vehicles can capture this control point, but be aware engineers could be hiding between the buildings and fire off easy rocket launcher strikes.

CONTROL POINT ASSETS

US CONTROL	RU CONTROL
Quad Bike (1)	Quad Bike (1)

C: ASSEMBLY

CONTROL POINT ASSETS

US CONTROL	RU CONTROL
M142 (1)	M142 (1)

- Beneath this point lies a tunnel that leads to Manufacturing (D). This tunnel can also be used to hide and wait for the enemy to come down for a surprise attack.
- The flagpole has a half-built tank beside it, making it a great place for cover when capturing. Be wary—the wall to the tank's side is destructible, so be ready to move if you hear explosions outside the building.
- Under the flagpole there lies an underground room. Infantry units can also capture this point from underneath. There are four stairways giving access to the upper level.
- On the opposite side of the tank, there are many bushes beginning to grow into the building. This a useful spot to surprise the enemy as most people will stick near the tank by the flagpole. Outside there is a M142. This vehicle contains six missiles that you can aim through a mini computer screen inside the vehicle.

PRO TIP: STRONGSIDE

Playing as the Recon class I'll climb up the ladders to the highest point of this building to snipe enemies making their way to the center of the map from either east or west. I'll place a Radio Beacon down before I parachute down to take out enemies within Assembly.

D: MANUFACTURING

- Inside there are two interactions. One is a generator that starts an array of compactor-like manufacturing machines. These machines will instantly kill a player who walks under it when it is coming down. The other interaction is a computer that causes Levolution.
- The tunnel from Assembly (C) connects these two buildings. There are two entrances to this tunnel: one from the inside of the building and the other outside. Entrances/exits allow for great escape routes.
- The building also has a ladder that leads to the roof. The roof is a great sniping spot, but close the hatch atop the ladder to prevent enemy troops from sneaking upon you. Consider placing a Radio Beacon on the roof to give your squad a spawn point at the center of the action.

PRO TIP: STRONGSIDE

In this factory I'll make my way up one of the manufacturing machine ladders to have a bird's eye view over the area. Enemies don't expect a player to be up in the rafters, giving you the jump on them. While up here I'll stay prone/crouched to appear less visible too.

E: TRAIN TRACKS

- This is a very wide area with a lot of bushes and broken-down tanks for cover. These tanks provide cover for you to sneak and flank around the enemy.
- One of the boxcars has an interactive feature. You can open the doors to the boxcar and be concealed within. This boxcar is indestructible, so if there are nearby tanks, be sure to make it inside. Going up against the wall also allows you to capture or contest the control point.
- Players specializing in close-quarter combat are suggested for this area, whether they are capturing or defending due to the large amount of surroundings.
- Having an engineer for the US team at the start is very useful. It is an easy point to capture for one or two players. Although this control point is close to the US base, the US team should be prepared for early-round RU vehicle attacks. As few as two US engineers posted at this control point can capture the flag and deter RU attacks. Vehicles can capture this point, but they are extremely vulnerable due to all the bushes, surroundings, and interactive train. Make them pay for their mistake, with mines or C4.

CONTROL POINT ASSETS

US CONTROL	RU CONTROL
Quad Bike (1)	Quad Bike (1)

F: RADAR TOWER

- This control point is near the US base, which makes it difficult for the RU team to capture. If the RU team decides to flank off the beginning to get to this control point, wait for the US team to move a bit away from the control point before capturing. The RU team should force the US team to make a decision: continue going for Assembly (C) and Manufacturing (D) or come back and stop the RU team from capturing the Radar Tower (F).
- This tower is a great spot for a sniper. A single sniper can hold this point for a long time. If the sniper is on the US team, the sniper can look towards the center and spot or pick off the enemy one by one.
- If the sniper is on the RU team, it means the team has control of the map, and now the sniper can target the US team.
- If playing as the RU team, getting to the top of the tower is critical. Being able to plant a Radio Beacon at the top can be the reason the team is successful in capturing the Radar Tower (F).
- An LAV-25 spawns here after the US team has captured the Radar Tower (F). This makes the point important to capture immediately because the US team wants as many vehicles as possible at the center near Assembly (C) and Manufacturing (D).

CONTROL POINT ASSETS

US CONTROL	RU CONTROL
LAV-25 (1)	BTR-90 (1)

CONQUEST SMALL

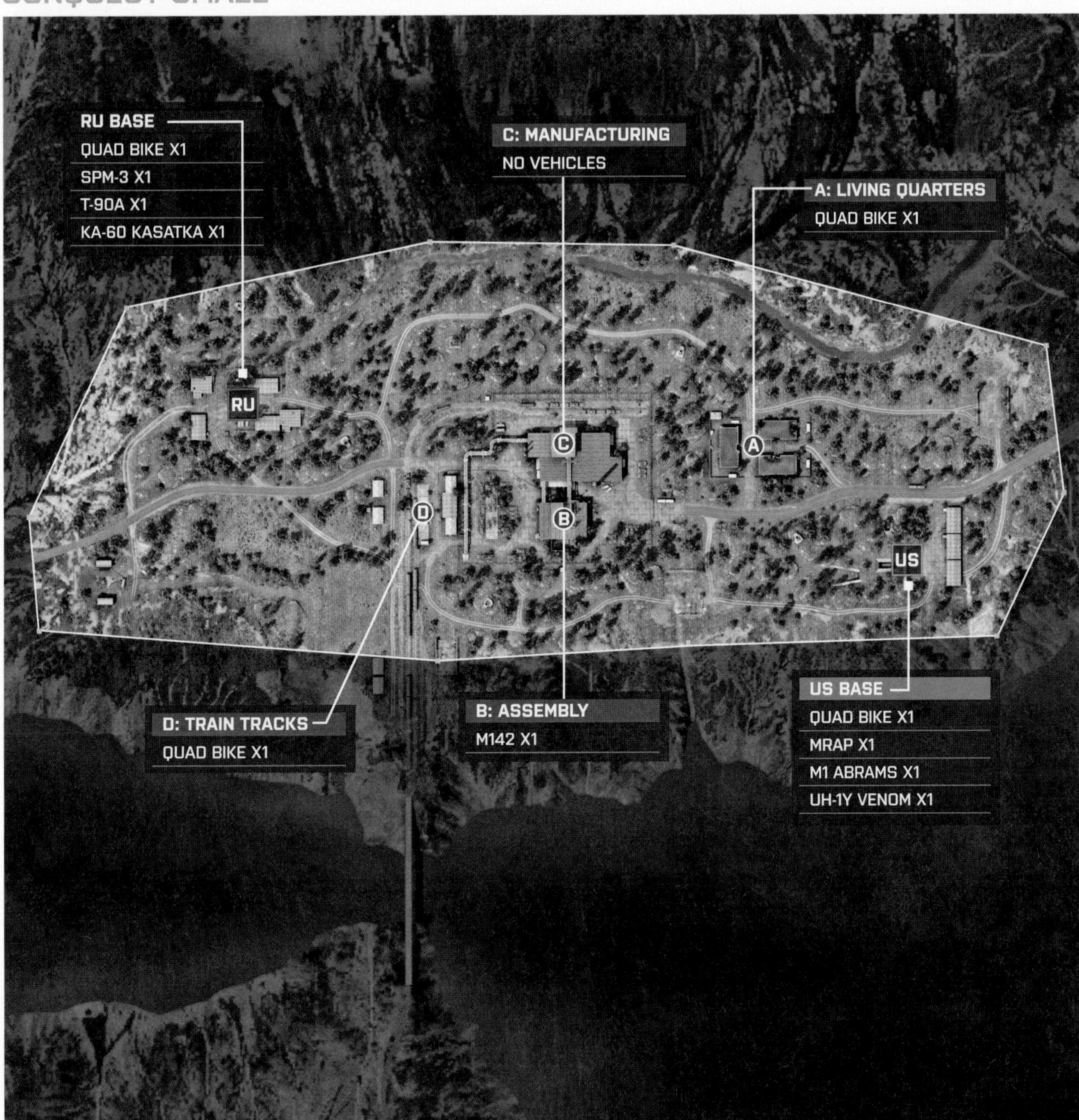

RECOMMENDED SQUAD COMPOSITION:

In this isolated forest, within which lies an old abandoned tank manufacturing facility, both the US and RU teams fight for control of the Assembly (B) and Manufacturing (C) warehouses in the center of the map. There are four controls points, meaning the best strategy is to hold three control points to begin draining the enemy's tickets. For the US team, holding the Train Tracks (D), Manufacturing (C), and Assembly (B) is the team's safest bet. On the other side, the RU team wants to control Living Quarters (A), Assembly (B), and Manufacturing (C). Once control is taken of the center bunker up around these points, both Assembly (B) and Manufacturing (C) have ladders that lead to the top of their buildings. These are great spots to fight the opposing team as you can spot them from afar and have the advantage due to the high ground. A set squad should wait on the floor as there is an underground tunnel that connects both points allowing your team to react to enemies at either point quickly. Also, be sure to have the team's tank between Assembly (B) and Manufacturing (C); it will help tremendously against waves of enemies. Flank along the perimeter of the forest so if the center is being guarded heavily, be sure to jump on the Quad Bikes and flank around to take either the Living Quarters (A) if playing as the US team or Train Tracks (D) if playing as the RU team. On the flipside, if the center is controlled well and the team can make a push for the fourth and final control point, then by all means charge ahead! This is a fairly large map, so be sure to make use of the vehicles that spawn back at the team base.

US BASE

- Stack the MRAP with as many members as possible. Head towards Assembly (B) and Manufacturing (C) and work together to capture them early in the game.
- Have a few teammates ride the Quad Bikes all the way to Living Quarters (A) in order to force the opposing team to come back and defend. The players who flank here should attempt to stay alive as long as possible. The fewer enemies the team has to fight at Assembly (B) and Manufacturing (C) makes it that much easier to capture.
- Any units on foot should head for the Train Tracks (D). Have one or two stay until the point is captured and then continue towards Assembly (B) and Manufacturing (C).
- Air superiority is important. Keep the team's birds alive and have a few engineers ready to take out RU team's air vehicles.
- Team members on foot should be engineers for the initial push in order to take out enemy vehicles.

BASE ASSETS

NAME	M1 Abrams	MRAP	Quad Bike	UH1Y Venom
QUANTITY	1	1	1	1

RU BASE

- Stack the ZFB-05 with as many members as possible. Head towards Assembly (B) and Manufacturing (C) and work together to capture these points early in the game.
- Have a few teammates ride the Quad Bikes all the way to the Train Tracks (D) in order to force the opposing team to come back and defend. The players who flank here should attempt to stay alive as long as possible. The fewer enemies the team has to fight at Assembly (B) and Manufacturing (C) makes it that much easier to capture.
- Any units on foot should head for the Living Quarters (A). Have one or two stay until the point is captured and then continue towards Assembly (B) and Manufacturing (C).
- Air superiority is important. Keep the team's birds alive and have a few engineers ready to take out the US team's air vehicles.
- Team members on foot should be engineers for the initial push in order to take out enemy vehicles.

BASE ASSETS

NAME	Type 99 MBT	ZFB-05	Quad Bike	Z-9 Haitun
QUANTITY	1	1	1	1

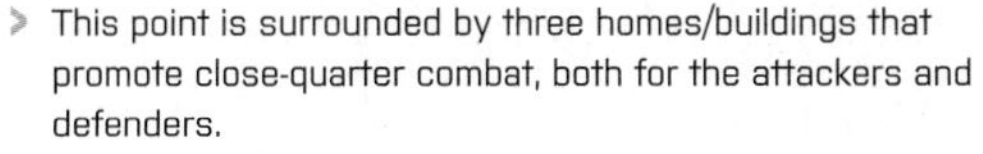

A: LIVING QUARTERS

- This point is surrounded by three homes/buildings that promote close-quarter combat, both for the attackers and defenders.
- The area is a decent size, which is fenced in by four concrete walls forming a square around the three homes/ buildings.
- When defending, move from building to building, never allowing the enemy to pinpoint your location.
- These buildings are all destroyable. If the team feels it would be easier to defend with them gone, then by all means let them fall!
- Capturing this point as the US team is a handful since the RU base borders it very closely. If you are able to sneak around, allowing the RU players to pass isn't a bad idea. Capturing will force the RU team to decide if they want to come back and defend or continue their push towards the center.

CONTROL POINT ASSETS

US CONTROL	RU CONTROL
Quad Bike (1)	Quad Bike (1)

B: ASSEMBLY

- Beneath this point lies a tunnel that leads to the Train Tracks (D). This tunnel can also be used to hide and wait for the enemy to come down for a surprise attack.
- The flagpole has a half-built tank beside it, making it a great place for cover when capturing. Be wary, the wall to the tank's side is destroyable, so be ready to move if you hear explosions outside the building.
- Under the flagpole there lies an underground room. Infantry units can also capture this point from underneath. There are four stairways giving access to the upper level.
- Outside this building a ladder leads to the roof. At the highest point there is a hatch. You can close this hatch, stopping enemies from gaining access. Planting a Radio Beacon at the top with the recon class can prove very useful. It is a great sniping spot and area to spawn teammates.
- On the opposite side of the tank, there are many bushes beginning to grow into the building. This a useful spot to surprise the enemy as most people will stick near the tank by the flagpole.

PRO TIP: FLAMESWORD

When I defend Assembly in either Conquest game mode, there are four ramps here I utilize. I hide underneath these ramps and contest the control point. Once an enemy comes into view, I'll shoot them in the ankles and watch them fall. I like to switch from ramp to ramp to confuse my opponent.

CONTROL POINT ASSETS

US CONTROL	RU CONTROL
M142 (1)	M142 (1)

C: MANUFACTURING

- Inside there are two interactions. One is a generator that starts an array of compactor-like manufacturing machines. These machines will instantly kill a player who walks under it when it is coming down. The other interaction is a computer that causes Levolution.
- You can capture or contest the control point from atop the machine closest to the flag. This gives you higher ground within the building, which makes spotting enemies inside easier.
- The tunnel from Manufacturing (C) connects these two buildings. There are two entrances to this tunnel—one from the inside of the building and the other outside. Entrances/exits allow for great escape routes.
- The building also has a ladder that leads to the roof. The roof is a great sniping spot, but close the hatch atop the ladder to prevent enemy troops from sneaking up on you. Consider placing a Radio Beacon on the roof to give your squad a spawn point at the center of the action.
- Outside there is a M142. This vehicle contains six missiles that you can aim through a mini computer screen inside the vehicle.

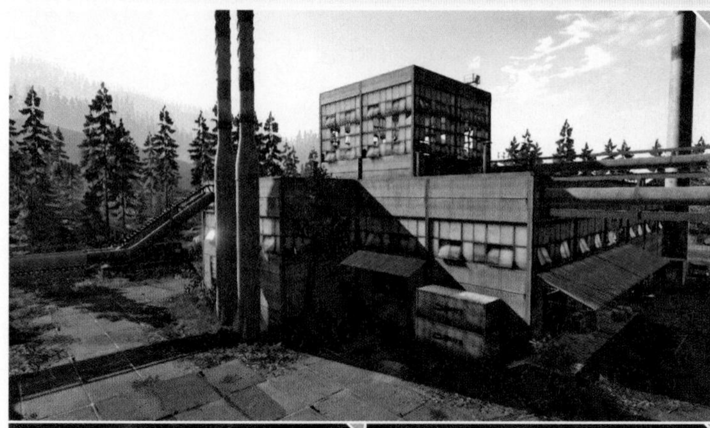

D: TRAIN TRACKS

- A very wide area with a lot of bushes and broken-down tanks for cover. These tanks provide cover for you to sneak and flank around the area.
- This control point is near the US base, which makes it difficult for the RU team to capture. If the RU team decided to flank off the beginning of the game to get to this point, wait for the US to move a bit away from the location before capturing. The RU members should force the US team to make a decision: continue going for Assembly (B) and Manufacturing (C) or come back and stop the RU team from capturing the Train Tracks (D).
- One of the boxcars has an interactive feature. You can open the doors to the boxcar and conceal yourself within. This boxcar is indestructible so if there are nearby tanks, be sure to make it inside. Going up against the wall also allows the player to capture or contest the control point.
- Players specializing in close-quarter combat are suggested for this area, whether they are capturing or defending.
- Having an engineer for the US team at the start is very useful. It is an easy point to capture for one or two players. Although this control point is close to the US base, the US team should be prepared for early-round RU vehicle attacks. As few as two US engineers posted at this control point can capture the flag and deter RU attacks.

CONTROL POINT ASSETS

US CONTROL	RU CONTROL
Quad Bike (1)	Quad Bike (1)

RUSH

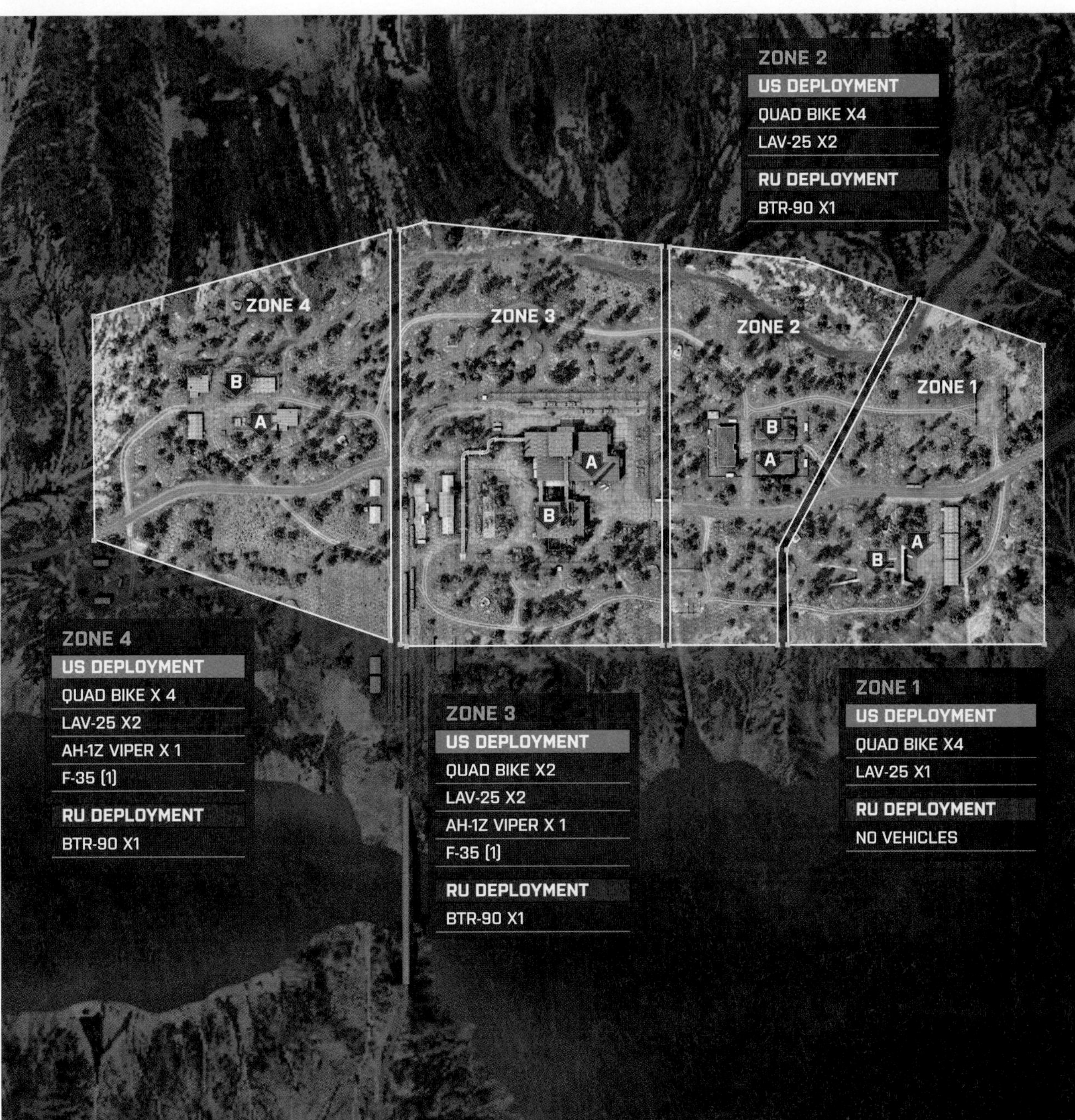

In Rush, the RU attackers attempt to arm two M-COM stations at each of the four diverse zones that the US defenders have to protect at all costs. This map offers few vehicles, especially for the US defenders, and is sure to be a favorite for those who prefer good old-fashioned infantry vs infantry combat. One recurring theme you will see throughout this map is how the RU attackers will have to traverse across open fields and roads, just to have the range of the fighting completely change to close-quarter combat. It is generally not safe for the few vehicles the RU team controls to be attacking in such a close-quarter area, so be sure to pack an engineer with your driver and watch out for C4. With four zones to hold off the attacking RU team, the US team's key to victory will be finding the perfect balance of classes to take out the small amount of vehicles that RU team will most certainly push up with, all while having enough anti-infantry firepower to hold the majority of ground units that constantly will be making their way towards the M-COM stations.

ZONE 1: BUNKER

US DEPLOYMENT
QUAD BIKE X4
LAV-25 X1

RU DEPLOYMENT
NO VEHICLES

US
A
B
RU

US DEPLOYMENT

RECOMMENDED SQUAD COMPOSITION: 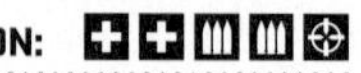

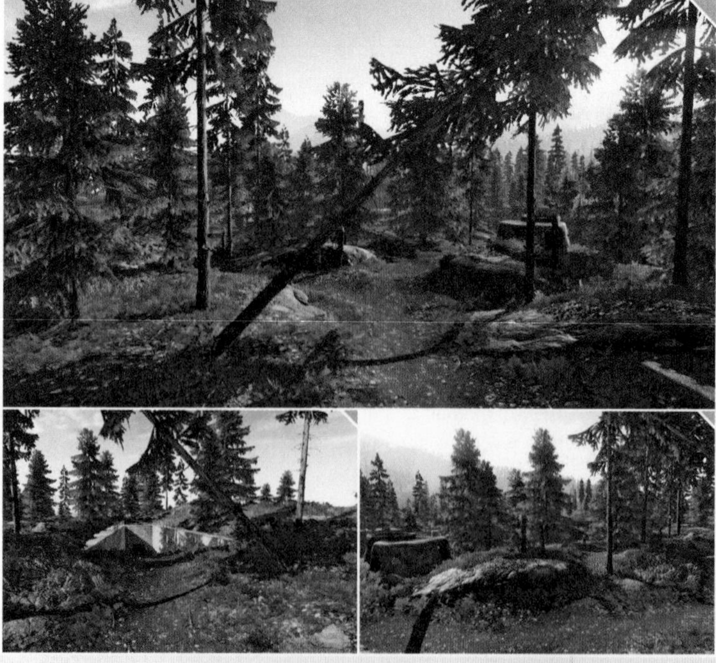

- With few vehicles in this zone and a long, open road from the RU deployment, you can comfortably use a long-range class such as recon to start off this game and hopefully take away some easy tickets before the enemy gets close to the M-COM stations.
- It is fine to spread out near the M-COM stations and even further north of M-COM Station A, but as soon as the RU team gets in closer to the Bunker, you immediately have to react and also move back closer to the M-COM stations.
- Getting above M-COM Station B is a very strong area because you have options on where you want to go. You can attack from above, drop in the building and move in from ground level, or (if you are feeling lucky) make a flank to the north or south to try and catch the RU attackers off guard.
- Although there are few vehicles here, that does not mean that explosives are entirely useless! Feel free to set up some C4 and Claymores to get some easy kills on unsuspecting RU attackers who are moving up too fast for their own good.
- Support class is a great compliment to any squad in this zone. It will give other US defenders the Ammo Boxes they need to lay down more mines and throw more grenades—not to mention the anti-infantry firepower you need for the attacking RU team that consists of 100% infantry units!

DEPLOYMENT AREA ASSETS

NAME	Quad Bike	LAV-25
QUANTITY	4	1

RU DEPLOYMENT

RECOMMENDED SQUAD COMPOSITION:

- This deployment is located closer to M-COM Station A than the US deployment. Make a dash for M-COM Station A and push the US infantry back into the Bunker to quickly set the charge at M-COM Station A.
- Vehicles do not spawn at either the RU or the US deployment. That makes this first zone a close-quarter to mid-range battle with little long-distance recon sniping.
- Support and assault classes will be used mostly in this first deployment for an initial push from RU deployment since vehicles are obsolete on this zone. When pushing off the start, have squads split up and approach from two or three angles. Think of the flying V! Brute squads push down the center to gain attention of the enemy while the squads on the outside try to infiltrate swiftly.
- M-COM Station A will be the easier station to arm, so try to force the defender back into the bunker so RU attackers can gain access to the roof of the bunker. This will be a power position from which you will be able to arm M-COM Station B.
- Be sure to have one recon class per squad, and have them drop Radio Beacons in close proximity to the Bunker. This will allow squad members to spawn closer to the action as opposed to running the long distance from the deployment spawn.

M-COM STATION A

- Smoke grenades will be vital to arm this station if the defenders are on top of the Bunker laying heavy fire as the RU attackers approach. Smoke grenades can be the very reason why the plant is set. This goes for the defenders as well; it allows for the US team to fight near M-COM Station A.

- On this first zone, using the assault class would be a likely choice when attacking M-COM Station A. There are no vehicles to worry about, so this point should be the easiest to get with an all-out push from the team. The only down side to this would be that the defenders have cover from the Bunker. Plan the team's push carefully at the beginning to force the defenders out of the Bunker.
- M-COM Station A is located right outside of the Bunker, which is near a non-usable van. Be sure to blow this van up immediately or save it until the team arms the station. This could lead to an easy kill when the US team goes for the disarm or an easy kill for the US team when the RU team goes for the plant.
- Once this station is armed, be sure to spread around the area with a few players near just in case the defenders drop smoke grenades and try for a sneaky disarm. There are a few spots outside the Bunker's main entrance that allows you to watch the station from afar. Apply assault and recon classes to pick off the disarmers. You could even take out the other team by laying some C4 around the front entrance of the Bunker to stop them from pushing out.
- As the defending team, try to establish a defensive line between M-COM Station A and the RU deployment area. The recon class comes in handy to pick off the RU team as they make their run across the open land towards M-COM Station A. Try to take as many tickets as you can before they arrive near M-COM Station A. If the team gets pushed back, holding the top of the Bunker is the safest bet for a better line of sight.

M-COM STATION B

- When defending, be sure that some of your squad members are spread out around this area, that way you can always ensure a good close spawn in case you or some of your squadmates die.
- If defending and your team is getting surrounded, don't be afraid to push out back of the west side of the base and get control of the top and around M-COM Station B. The front eastern entrance will be a death trap if the RU team has already destroyed M-COM Station A. Try to go out of the northern or western exit if you want to spread out.
- If you are the defending US team and want to pull a sneaky one-time play, you have to push over here early and sit in the garage to the east of M-COM Station B. Wait until you see at least two enemies before going for the kills to make this play worthwhile, otherwise you will only get one kill and the enemy will see where you are hiding.
- When defending this position, you don't always need to have the interactive generator on. Sometimes it can be better left off so you can hide in the shadows and catch the attackers off guard.
- When attacking this station, make sure to get control of the top of the base. Not only can you push in from multiple angles, but you can also cut off US reinforcements from the west.
- As the attacking RU team, when you eventually make it inside the base, secure the area first. There are very likely to be more US defenders inside, so make sure to clear them all out to ensure you get the arm and good spawns for your team.

ZONE 2: LIVING QUARTERS

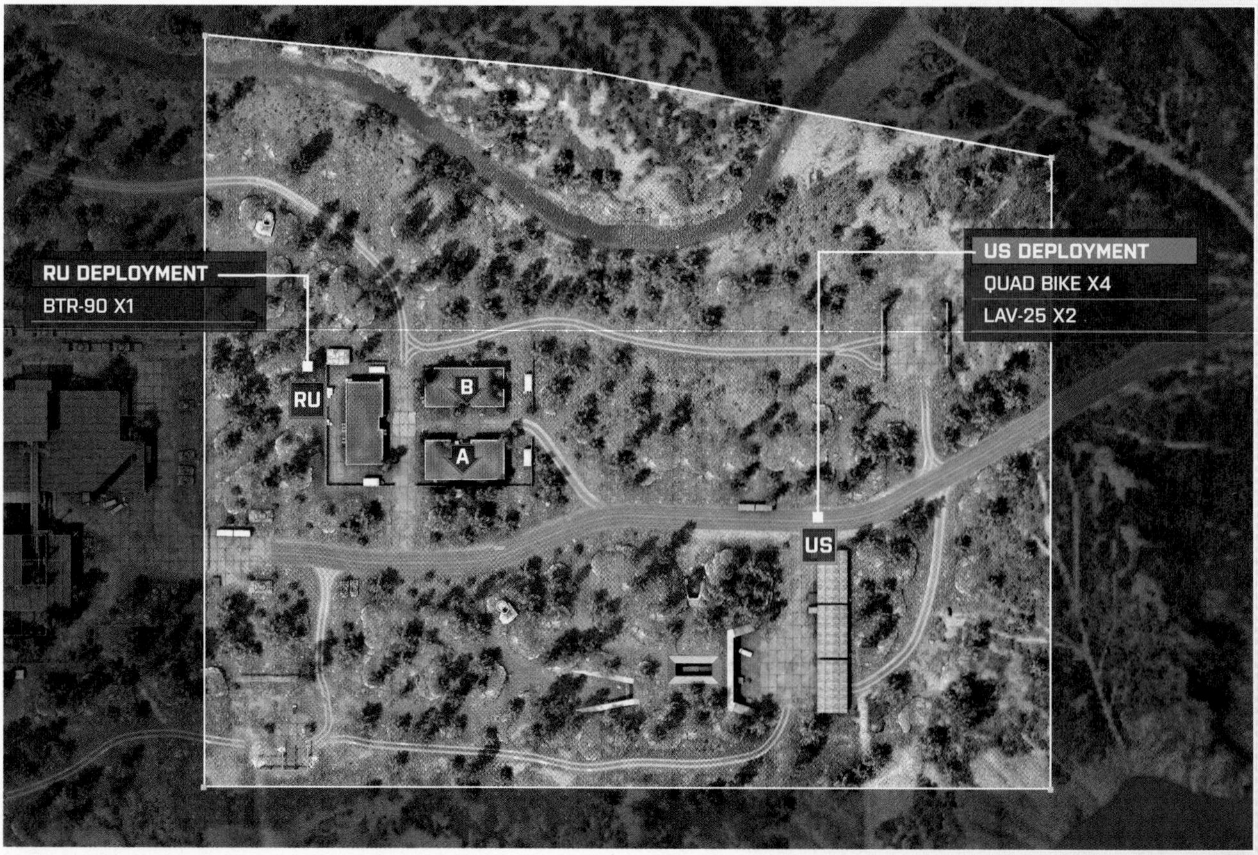

RU DEPLOYMENT
BTR-90 X1

US DEPLOYMENT
QUAD BIKE X4
LAV-25 X2

RU
B
A
US

US DEPLOYMENT

RECOMMENDED SQUAD COMPOSITION:

- Now you have a M1 Abrams to work with. If you do get in vehicle-to-vehicle combat, make sure to take out the BTR-90 first. The SPM-3 is not as much of a threat to your thick armor. Ideally you want to hide the location of your tank until you know where the enemy BTR-90 is.
- Secure the area around both M-COM stations, and expect troops to try and sneak closer directly to the east of the stations.
- The easiest way to win this zone early on will be to spot and take out the enemy vehicles, that way your M1 Abrams can safely patrol the area.
- The building will naturally be destroyed by all the attacks over time. Don't be afraid to blow up walls in order to give you another line of sight on a M-COM station. You don't always have to leave your own buildings intact.
- The building to the west isn't as crucial to hold as it is to keep away from the attacking RU team. If the enemy controls this building, they effectively cut off your reinforcements and can attack the M-COM stations from two different fronts.

DEPLOYMENT AREA ASSETS

NAME	Quad Bike	LAV-25
QUANTITY	4	2

RU DEPLOYMENT

RECOMMENDED SQUAD COMPOSITION:

- Now with control of the Bunker, the RU team has more of a base to work with and a few vehicles at their disposal. This deployment has plenty of vantage points and places to attack from. Utilize the recon, engineer, and assault classes here on out for this next station.
- Split up the attack from your new base by sending some infantry to attack from the north of M-COM Stations A and B. Send in your team's vehicles through the east or south entrance, but have engineers ready for the US tank.
- Be sure to stack the SPM-3 with as many people as it holds. Drop teammates off around the concrete fences that box the Living Quarters in. Destroying the walls will help arming stations from different angles.
- Have a squad member play as the engineer and hop in the BTR-90 to jump out and repair when needed. The BTR-90 should be focusing on keeping the defenders busy so the RU team's infantry can sneak in quietly.
- Again, the recon class is important for Radio Beacons. Spawning closer to the M-COM stations is better than running by foot or waiting at the Bunker for a vehicle to spawn.

DEPLOYMENT AREA ASSETS

NAME	BTR-90
QUANTITY	1

M-COM STATION A

- This station is located in the building across from M-COM Station B. This is a station for infantry units both on the defending and attacking team since a lot of the fighting will happen inside the building. Both sides can also take advantage of blowing up the building. This will make it a little harder to plant, but if the bomb is planted already, this makes it easier to watch the disarm. For the defenders, it gives more visibility of the station so it is easier to defend.
- At this point the attackers should be using the engineer and recon class. It will make the job way easier by taking out the stationary launchers that will be looking to take out any vehicles coming towards them. Engineers on your team should be ready to take out an enemy tank that could cause heavy damage to your team if left alone.
- Defenders should man the M220 TOW Launchers in order to stop the attackers' SPM-3 from dropping enemies close to the stations while also destroying their BTR-90 as, if left alone, it could do a lot of damage to the defenders.
- The defending team now has access to an M1 Abrams. If used properly, it can be the very reason why the attackers are wiped out in Zone 2. A good strategy to apply is to move the tank forward and trap the attackers in their base. Play smart though—once it has taken damage retreat back to the Living Quarters and get repaired by a teammate. Repairing a damaged tank is a surefire way for a friendly engineer to score some easy points.
- Attackers should take advantage of the SPM-3 that spawns to deliver teammates near the entrance of the Living Quarters. If the buildings are not blown up, try getting medium- to long-range fighters on top to shoot the defenders at their spawn once the team has pushed up from behind and taken control.

M-COM STATION B

- The important part about guarding this station is to watch the flank from the north, that way you can limit the angles the attacking RU team can push in the area from.
- If the building is still standing attach a shotgun to your loadout. You'll be able to sneak around inside the buildings and pick off the enemy in close-quarter combat. If the building is destroyed, swap to a mid-range weapon for longer-range combat around the demolished building.
- When attacking this station, try and secure the building to the west. This will allow your team to attack the M-COM station from multiple angles and cut off the reinforcements for the defending US team. This also allows you to use the western M220 TOW Launcher if there is the M1 Abrams nearby.
- As the defending team, at the start of this zone push out east, while leaving one member of your squad back at the M-COM station. This member of the squad will create a good spawn if you are killed. The goal is to try and catch RU members off guard in the field for easy ticket drain. At worst, you are picked off, but then you're able to spawn on the squad member that safely stayed back.
- As the attacking team, have a couple extra engineers to take out the defenders' M1 Abrams. Afterwards you can freely move up your vehicles and secure the area around M-COM Station B.

ZONE 3: ASSEMBLY/MANUFACTURING

US DEPLOYMENT
QUAD BIKE X2
LAV-25 X2
AH-1Z VIPER X 1
F-35 (1)

A
B
US
RU

RU DEPLOYMENT
BTR-90 X1

US DEPLOYMENT

RECOMMENDED SQUAD COMPOSITION: 

- This is a recon's time to shine. Get way up on top of the building above M-COM Station A so you can snipe from above. Be quick though—this will only work early on while the attackers are further away. Once they get up close, you won't have any good angles to snipe from up here.
- Controlling the top of the map is most important. Once you start to lose control of the ground level, feel free to retreat down low to the tunnels so you can spawn your squad and safely move back and forth between the M-COM stations.
- Once again you have a M1 Abrams at your disposal—use it very carefully. There aren't any great spots to be fully safe and effective with this vehicle. Work with your squad and react to what the enemy is doing.
- There aren't many options for the attacking RU vehicles to drive up. Prepare by setting land mines on the main road to the east of M-COM Station B.
- While the road is the main way for vehicles to push up, the fence to the east/northeast of M-COM Station A is where you can expect infantry to try and sneak up. Find them out here in the open before they can slip into the buildings and spawn their squadmates.

DEPLOYMENT AREA ASSETS

NAME	Quad Bike	LAV-25	AH-1Z Viper	F-35
QUANTITY	2	2	1	1

RU DEPLOYMENT

RECOMMENDED SQUAD COMPOSITION:

- Same deployment as Zone 2, making the IFV as crucial as ever for countering the US team's vehicles.
- Rounding up a group of teammates in a few of the vehicles at this stage will be the best thing, but do this while a tank is in front for the extra cover. The tank will catch the enemy's attention and allow the SPM-3 to drop off players around both M-COM stations. The BTR-90 should follow the SPM-3 to give it cover and allow the members to jump out safely to take the chosen M-COM station.
- Given the ample distance between the deployment area and the M-COM stations, the RU team has several flanking opportunities. The ground units flanking should pick the opposite M-COM station that the players in the vehicles went to. This gives a wide amount of attack options to go on.
- If the team finds itself not being able to push from the deployment zone, have squad members wait at the Living Quarters before pushing up. Attacking with the entire squad/team will be much easier on this zone.
- Be sure to always spawn back at your base when the vehicles respawn.

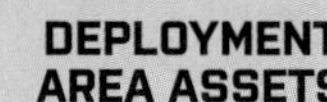

DEPLOYMENT AREA ASSETS

NAME	BTR-90
QUANTITY	1

M-COM STATION A

- As a defender it is important to gain control of the roof of the building. Keep a lookout on the back entrance to the tunnel. There may be an enemy attempting to sneak around. On top of the Manufacturing building there is a ladder that gives the defenders access to the roof where snipers will have a great vantage point to pick off any enemies on foot.
- The M1 Abrams in this area will not be as effective because of all the big crates, but there are some good spots along the middle of the buildings and along the sides of them for some great angles. You will most likely be stationary with the M1 Abrams around this station because of low mobility. Cover the outside tunnel and access to the roof with the M1 Abrams.
- As an attacker, gain control of the rooftop and place a Radio Beacon to spawn within the action. It is vital to spawn near M-COM Station A to help your team to set the charge. You can also drop in from the roof with your squad for a surprise attack to set the charge.
- With this area now in your control, your team is going rely on tanks to lay down huge fire on both M-COM stations to help give the team room to push.
- The long tunnel connecting both objectives is a likely hot spot for both teams. Be prepared to encounter C4, Claymores, and LMG-equipped support troops laying down fire from fixed positions.
- Check corners in the manufacturing rooms before just rushing in to go for the arm. There is almost always going to be someone hiding around a wall in this area!

M-COM STATION B

- As an attacker, one of the longest unexpected flanks to this M-COM station can be made all the way from the northeast side of the M-COM Station A building where a set of stairs can take you down in a tunnel to go stealthily underneath the defenders. This will allow you to give your squad great spawns and catch the defending US team completely by surprise.
- On defense, one of the best ways to use the M1 Abrams is to circle around M-COM Station B so that the enemy engineers will get frustrated by the tank not always being within striking distance. This will give your team time to spot enemies instead of sitting out in the open waiting to be hit.
- When attacking, be careful of immediately pushing through the eastern garage entrance. US defenders will most certainly be watching this spot. Instead, push around to the south where you can flank and not be expected.
- When attacking, carefully move up your vehicles but do not drive the vehicle inside the building. You will be extremely vulnerable to engineers and C4 explosives from every direction. You are better off staying outside the eastern garage door where you can lay down cover fire for your squad and back up if you see an incoming infantry unit.
- When defending, feel free to poke out and fight out the front garage entrance as long as you have other squadmates safely hidden in the underground tunnel watching the flank. Your goal should be to make the enemy waste as many tickets as possible while they approach.

ZONE 4: RADAR TOWER

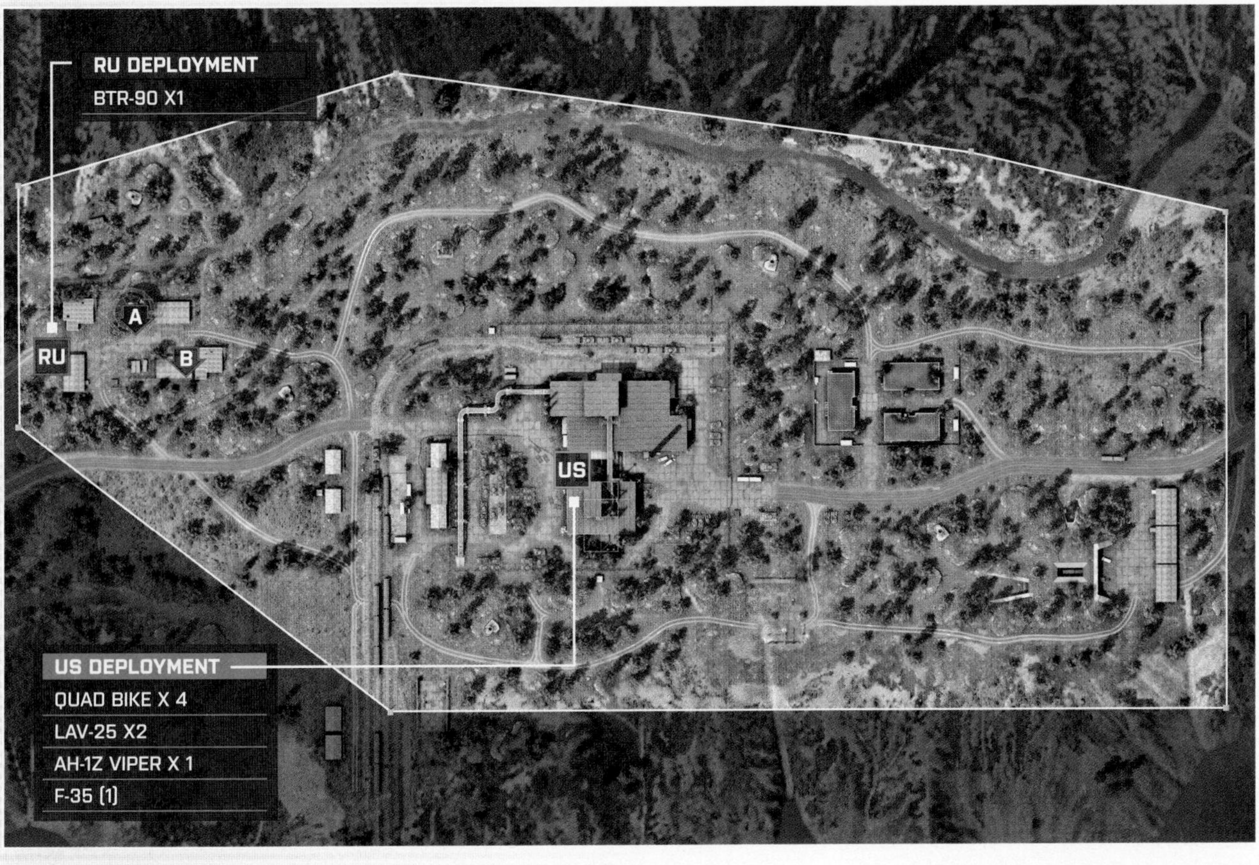

RU DEPLOYMENT

BTR-90 X1

A

B

RU

US

US DEPLOYMENT

QUAD BIKE X 4

LAV-25 X2

AH-1Z VIPER X 1

F-35 (1)

US DEPLOYMENT

RECOMMENDED SQUAD COMPOSITION:

- Last chance to stop them here, and unfortunately one of the M-COM stations doesn't have the greatest cover. It is absolutely crucial that you make a stand before your base so you can drain as many tickets as possible before the enemy reaches the M-COM stations.
- Not only is M-COM Station A hard to defend, but this time the attackers have three vehicles! You are going to have to heavily rely on engineers to successfully keep the RU vehicles at bay. Right away take to the hills and set up an ambush with your squad to take down an unsuspecting enemy vehicle.
- Work with your team, and once they have put some damage into an enemy vehicle push up with your M1 Abrams to try and take the enemy vehicle down. The enemy has two vehicles that pose a danger to you. Don't move in to attack unless you have the advantage.
- With the long road from the RU team spawn, be sure to set up more vehicle traps. Land mines on a narrow path are always a great way to rack up easy kills on some careless drivers.
- Get a recon on top of the M-COM Station B building to snipe and spot enemy vehicles. You want to do this sooner rather than later because once the enemy gets too close, it is much more difficult to snipe at such an extremely close angle.

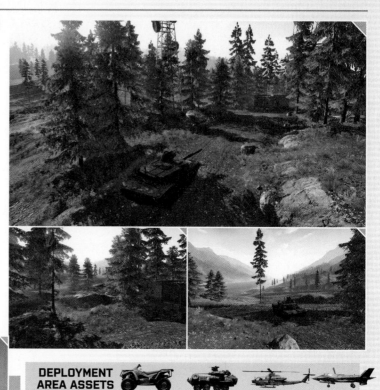

PRO TIP: FLAMESWORD

I LIKE TO SNIPE FROM THE TOP OF THE RADAR TOWER. I'LL GET EASY POINTS FOR SPOTTING AND TAKING DOWN ENEMIES FROM AFAR.

DEPLOYMENT AREA ASSETS

NAME	Quad Bike	LAV-25	AH-1Z Viper	F-35
QUANTITY	4	2	1	1

RU DEPLOYMENT

RECOMMENDED SQUAD COMPOSITION:

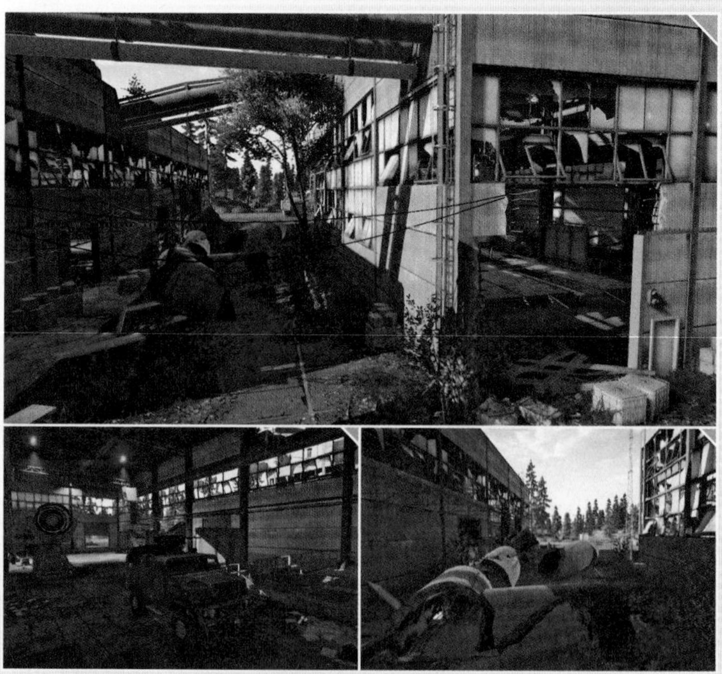

- With control of this deployment zone the RU team will have everything the team needs with space, cover, angles and vehicles to use for this last attack.
- Usually you would want more teammates pushing toward the M-COM stations. However, it's imperative to post a few snipers on these rooftops to cover the Radar Tower, where US defenders are likely to have their own snipers posted. Pick off the defending snipers while teammates rush upstairs to plant a charge on M-COM Station B.
- The rusty, disabled tanks outside the deployment zone offer excellent cover while advancing toward the Radar Station. Alternatively, sneak through the forest on the perimeter in an attempt to reach the M-COM stations without being detected. There are a bunch of disabled tanks right outside of the base that assault classes can use as cover while making their push.
- Once again, use the vehicles at the deployment zone. Always stack the SPM-3 with as many people as possible and continuously drop them off near the front of M-COM Station A.
- With the M1 Abrams and BTR-90 you'll have the upper hand against the US M1 Abrams. Apply heavy fire towards M-COM Station B to keep the enemy down. Suppression fire is the key to arm both M-COM Stations A and B.

DEPLOYMENT AREA ASSETS

NAME	BTR-90
QUANTITY	1

M-COM STATION A

- The Radar Tower is a sniper haven because it is up so high. Snipers will be able to spot anything and should be able to do massive damage to incoming enemies. This makes it a tough station to capture. Tanks will have to draw most of the fire away from ground infantry.
- Within this station there is a building with some cover from the tower where M-COM Station B is located, so your team is going to want to take out any snipers that you see before you go for the arm.
- Be on the lookout for an enemy tank coming from the deployment base, because you will need to take it out very quickly before they damage the building where M-COM Station A is. When or if this happens, it will be very easy for snipers to protect this station with how exposed it will be.
- Any vehicles (such as tanks) that you send should go on the main road around to the southern area to attract as much fire as possible away from the arming squad.

M-COM STATION B

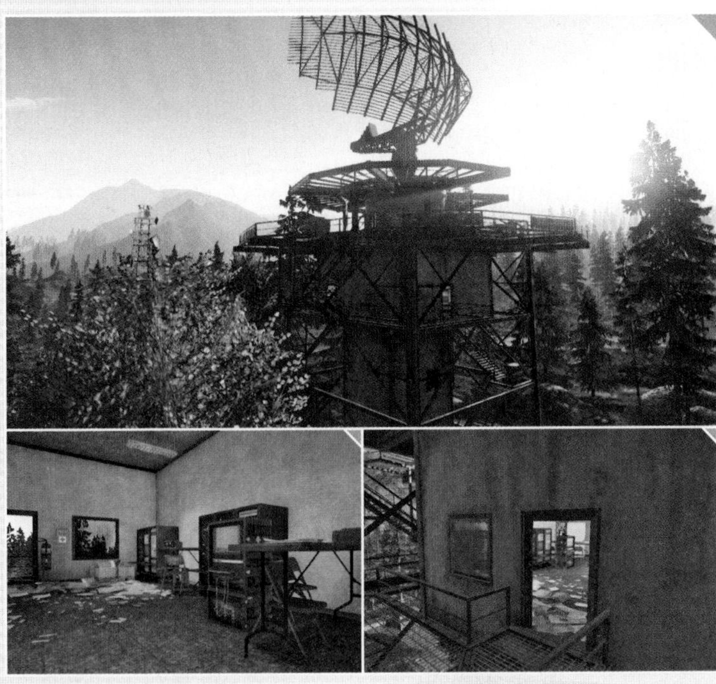

- When defending this M-COM station, make sure to not let an enemy up the final stairwell. Prepare to spam the stairwell with grenades/Flashbangs to help clear it out. Also placing a Claymore is good to notify you when the enemy is making its way up the stairwell. The reason you want to hold the attackers off at the stairwell is because once they make it out of the stairwell and into the M-COM room, they can spread out and start spawning inside. You want to keep them spawning from afar or on the stairwell out of the tower.
- When defending, support is a must-have class inside the building. The Ammo Boxes are crucial so your team can grenade and Flashbang before clearing out the stairwell.
- When defending, if the enemy breaks through into the M-COM room, run up to the roof right away so you can buy time for your squad to spawn on you. If you lose all your spawn points in the building, it is going to be much more difficult to take back control.
- When attacking, make your way up the stairwell and don't stop pushing until you have control of the roof. Don't allow the defenders to spawn up above you after taking control of the Radar Tower.
- When attacking, taking control of the Radar Tower from the stairwell can be very difficult by yourself. Have squadmates throw grenades or lay cover fire from below into the M-COM room.

OBLITERATION

RECOMMENDED SQUAD COMPOSITION:

- The US team guards the target around the Train Tracks and the other two targets near the Radar Tower.
- The RU team should establish a perimeter to defend the targets around the Living Quarters and the Bunker.
- The bomb spawns near the Manufacturing building.
- Teams want to take advantage of the tanks that spawn at both bases. Move these near the center of the map and patrol the Manufacturing and Assembly buildings.
- The perimeter of the map provides great cover for vehicles. The bomb carrier should board the IFV as the driver delivers the carrier from target to target. The tank leads the way to provide extra firepower.

DEFUSE

RECOMMENDED SQUAD COMPOSITION:

- In this intense battle, the RU team find themselves spawning north of the Manufacturing building. South of the Assembly building is the spawn point for the US team.
- Laptop A is located in the underground tunnel that connects the Manufacturing building with the Assembly building. This objective is easily reached by the attacking team.
- Laptop B is found in between the many disabled tanks located west of the Assembly building. Defenders have many different disabled tanks to use for cover; if defending, be sure to use this to your advantage.
- The RU team has a quicker route to Laptop A. Have two players rush to the bottom and chuck a Frag and Smoke Grenade across to hold the defenders back. The other three players can flank around the east side of the Assembly building to ambush the defenders.
- At the start of the defenders' spawn have at least one defender climb the ladder located directly towards the north of the spawn point. This gives your team a great vantage point of the tank graveyard where Laptop B lies.

DOMINATION

RECOMMENDED SQUAD COMPOSITION:

- The three control points on this map are Assembly (A), Tanks (B), and Manufacturing (C).
- Place C4 around your control point while you push for a new one. When you see the enemy team neutralizing your point, detonate and watch your kill feed!
- With how fast paced this game is, Claymores are great to place around the map since enemies are moving from control point to control point often. Placing Claymores in narrow, high-traffic areas, such as a tunnel, doorway, hallway, or around a corner, is highly effective.
- Play as the recon class and use the spawn beacon to spawn closer to a captured flag. Place the beacon in shrubs and away from high-traffic areas so the beacon is not destroyed easily.
- A very good strategy is to capture Assembly (A) and Tanks (B). Both Assembly (A) and Manufacturing (C) have ladders that lead to the top of their buildings, but Assembly (A) is easier to defend since it has fewer entrances. Get a player to the top and then focus on the opposing team just running in the open as they try to exit the Manufacturing (C) building. The player on the roof is able to watch Tanks (B) the entire game, allowing the rest of the squad to defend Assembly (C) from below.

SQUAD DEATHMATCH

RECOMMENDED SQUAD COMPOSITION:

- On this map, Squad Deathmatch is confined to the Manufacturing and Assembly buildings. Controlling the IFV greatly increases your squad's chance of winning.
- The Manufacturing and Assembly buildings both have ladders to give your squad superior firing angles. At the roof you are able to pick up easy kills on the players spawning around the perimeter of the map.
- The pressing machines in the Manufacturing building have ladders to climb to the top of them. This is another good position to have an overview of the incoming enemies inside the Manufacturing building.
- When spawning, immediately look to the rooftops to spot any enemies attempting to kill you when you spawn.
- Use the tunnel connecting the Manufacturing and Assembly buildings to easily sneak from building to building to pick up easy kills.

TEAM DEATHMATCH

RECOMMENDED SQUAD COMPOSITION:

- In this Team Deathmatch game variant, players are fighting around the Manufacturing and Assembly buildings.
- Both buildings have ladders that lead to the roof. Be sure to make your way up for superior firing angles.
- Near the southwest tip of the map is a walkway near the tank graveyard. If you walk towards the center of this walkway and go prone, you have great cover allowing recon players to snipe.
- In the Manufacturing building, take the ladders connected to the interactive pressing machines. This is a great position to defend this building. Be sure to turn on the generator to make these pressing machines work, stopping the enemies from hiding underneath you.
- Take advantage of the underground tunnel to quickly move from north to south and catch your opponents off guard. There is a battle pick up in this passageway—be sure to grab it.

CAMPAIGN

To ensure you have the latest and most up to date information for the Campaign we're covering it fully at www.PrimGames.com/BF4 with a complete video walkthrough including all collectible locations.

SINGLE-PLAYER

"The world is on the brink of chaos, China is the tinderbox, and you and your squad are the inadvertent spark that could ignite a global conflict. As Sergeant Daniel Recker, you play as a member of an elite group of unlikely heroes known as Tombstone squad, navigating the turmoil around you as you fight to save the final hope for peace."

The *Battlefield 4* single-player campaign takes you on an intense, dramatic, emotional journey. Herein is the help you need to find all of the unlockables hidden throughout the campaign. However for more details and in-depth videos, use the code to access your free digital guide via www.PrimaGames.com/BF4.

ASSIGNMENTS AND SCORING

Many of the single-player assignments are based on your score for that level. These points are awarded in a similar manner as in multiplayer. Completing assignments in each level will unlock a number of things within the game, including dog tags, weapons, and achievements!

See below for a complete breakdown on how you can gain points during the game:

EVENT NAME	POINTS	DESCRIPTION
Enemy Down	100	Kill an enemy.
Headshot	25	Score a headshot.
Multi Kill	Kills x 100	Kill 2 or more enemies. This is in addition to the normal points for kills.
Melee	25	Kill an enemy with the knife. In addition to the normal kill points.
Adrenaline Kill	50	Get a kill while having below 31% health.
Kill Streak	50	Kill an enemy within 3 seconds of another kill.
Squad Kills	50	Squad AI kills another AI.

DOG TAGS

Dog tags to be found throughout the campaign, but you'll need to take your time and look carefully to find them. You can only get dog tags by finding them in the level or by getting one of three endings.

▶ TIP

Visually you should look for a knife stuck in walls with dog tags hanging from them. You will find them in areas that make it seem like they fit the environment and with the context of the scene, but it's not always obvious.

▶ NOTE

Please reference the eGuide for images/videos of exact locations for all dog tags throughout each level.

Once found, the dog tags will be unlocked in the dog tags screen. Dog tags found in single-player can be used in your multiplayer profile.

WEAPONS AND ACCESSORIES

As you progress through the game you will encounter a number of different weapons, each level having its own selection for you to find. There are four ways that you can find a weapon:

1. **STARTING WEAPON**
2. **DROPPED BY AN ENEMY**
3. **PLACED IN THE LEVEL (EXPLORATION)**
4. **AS AN UNLOCK UNIQUE TO THAT LEVEL**

As you find weapons, they will be added to your personal Weapon Crate. This crate is persistent, once you acquire a weapon it will be in the box from then on for you to choose to use.

At the start of the game your 'default' weapon, the MK11 MOD 0, will be available in your crate.

▶ TIP

In reference point #3. You may have to go off the beaten path to find some weapons, but they will be placed in ways that make sense. In the hands of a dead sniper, in a downed helicopter, or on a weapon rack, for instance.

▶ NOTE

Please reference the eGuide for images/videos of exact locations for each weapon in the individual levels.

BAKU

ASSIGNMENTS:

NAME	CRITERIA	UNLOCK
Bronze score	1500pts	CZ-805
Silver score	4000pts	UTS-15
Gold score	6000pts	SVD-12
TOMBSTONE ACTUAL	Complete Baku	MP412 REX (Multiplayer)

Dog Tags:

Nice Play: On a board during movement tutorial (obvious first reward)

One Way Trip: Over the C4 tutorial room. Player needs to find a way to jump over the hole.

Sergeant Dunn: Inside the crashed helicopter on the Dunn is Down scene.

WEAPONS:

WEAPON	TYPE	ACQUIRED THROUGH	NATIONALITY	OPTICS	BARREL	ACCESSORIES	UNDERBARREL	AUXILIRY	AMMO TYPES
SCAR-H	Assault Rifle	Starting	Belgium	EOTech(US) Holo	—	Laser Pointer	—	—	—
M39 EMR	DMR	Exploration	USA	ACOG(US) 4x	Heavy	Laser Pointer	Bipod	—	—
MG4	LMG	Exploration	Germany	RX01(US) RDS	Muzzle Brake	Magnifier(x3)RDS/Holo	Bipod	—	—
CBJ-MS	PDW	Exploration	Sweden	—	Muzzle Brake	Tactical Light	—	—	—
CZ-805	Assault Rifle	Bronze Score	Czech Republic	Kobra(RU)RDS	—	Magnifier(x3) RDS/Holo	Vertical Grip	—	—
UTS-15	Shotgun	Silver Score	USA	RX01(US) RDS	Muzzle Brake	—	—	—	Buck
SVD-12	DMR	Gold Score	Russia	PSO-1(RU) 4x	—	—	Angled Grip	—	—
AK-12	Assault Rifle	Enemy	Russia	PKA-S(RU) Holo	Heavy	Magnifier(x3) RDS/Holo	Folding Grip	—	—

SHANGHAI

ASSIGNMENTS:

NAME	CRITERIA	UNLOCK
Bronze score	3000pts	FAMAS
Silver score	7000pts	SG553
Gold score	10000pts	SCOUT ELITE

Dog Tags:

One Man Riot: On a door in a dead end in back street transit.

Going Up: Over the elevator at the beginning of Lobby Assault.

Business Casual: In the calm back alley after the tank chase.

WEAPONS:

WEAPON	TYPE	ACQUIRED THROUGH	NATIONALITY	OPTICS	BARREL	ACCESSORIES	UNDERBARREL	AUXILIRY	AMMO TYPES
UMP-45	PDW	Starting	Germany	RX01(US) RDS	Heavy	—	Angled Grip	—	—
MP412 REX	Pistol	Starting	Russia	RMR (US)	Heavy	—	—	—	—
RFB	DMR	Exploration	USA	ACOG(US) 4x	Flash Supressor	Canted Ironsights	Bipod	—	—
QBS-09	Shotgun	Exploration	China	Tru Brite(CH) Holo	—	Flashlight	—	—	Buck
FAMAS	Assault Rifle	Bronze Score	France	RX01(US) RDS	Compensator	Flashlight	Potato Grip	—	—
SG553	Carbine	Silver Score	Switzerland	RX01(US) RDS	Heavy	Magnifier(x3) RDS/ Holo	—	—	—
Scout Elite	Sniper Rifle	Gold Score	Austria	CL6x (X6) (CH)	Flash Suppressor	Canted Irongsights	—	Straight Pull Bolt	—
JS2	PDW	Enemy	China	Coyote(CH) RDS	Heavy	Laser Pointer	—	—	—
HAWK 12G	Shotgun	Enemy	China	—	—	Flashlight	—	—	Buck
QBZ-95-1	Assault Rifle	Enemy	China	Tru Brite(CH) Holo	Compensator	Magnifier(x3) RDS/ Holo	—	—	—

SOUTH CHINA SEA

ASSIGNMENTS:

NAME	CRITERIA	UNLOCK
Bronze score	4000pts	M4A1
Silver score	6000pts	MX4
Gold score	10000pts	USAS-12

Dog Tags:

Carcharodon: Inside a cabin during the move to medbay.

Lord of the Waves: In a rubble pile during the swimming tutorial.

Agent Kovic: Inside a crashed helicopter during the helicopter boss fight.

WEAPONS:

WEAPON	TYPE	ACQUIRED THROUGH	NATIONALITY	OPTICS	BARREL	ACCESSORIES	UNDERBARREL	AUXILIRY	AMMO TYPES
SCAR-H	Assault Rifle	Starting	Belgium	EOTech(US) Holo	—	Laser Pointer	—	—	—
MP412 REX	Pistol	Starting	Russia	RMR (US)	Heavy	—	—	—	—
P90	PDW	Exploration	Belgium	Tru Brite (CH) Holo	Heavy	Tribeam	—	—	—
U-100 MKS	LMG	Exploration	Singapore	CP1 Prismatic(CH)3.4x	—	—	Bipod	—	—
SPAS-12	Shotgun	Exploration	Italy	—	Full Choke (Wide)	PEQ-15 (Combo)	—	—	Buck
M4A1	Carbine	Bronze Score	USA	—	Muzzle Brake	Laser Pointer	Ergo Grip	—	—
MX4	PDW	Silver Score	Italy	Kobra(RU) RDS	Heavy	—	Stubby Grip	—	—
USAS-12	Shotgun	Gold Score	South Korea	Coyote(CH) RDS	Compensator	Canted Irongsight	Ergo Grip	—	Slug
Type 88 LMG	LMG	Enemy	China	CP1 Prismatic(CH) 3.4x	Heavy	—	Bipod	—	—

SINGAPORE

ASSIGNMENTS:

NAME	CRITERIA	UNLOCK
Bronze score	11000pts	SAR-21
Silver score	15000pts	QBB-95
Gold score	19000pts	M82A3

Dog Tags:

Horizontal Rain: On a stranded boat on the beach.

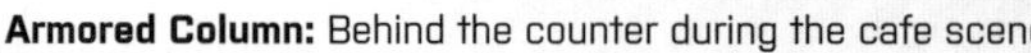

Armored Column: Behind the counter during the cafe scene.

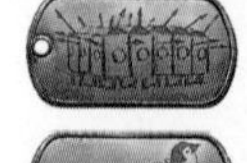

Grounded: On the door of the exploding plane. The dog tag is pretty obvious but needs tactics to be reached. You must sneak and run to the wing as soon as you are discovered, avoiding fire and reaching the dog tag before the wing is destroyed.

WEAPONS:

WEAPON	TYPE	ACQUIRED THROUGH	NATIONALITY	OPTICS	BARREL	ACCESSORIES	UNDERBARREL	AUXILIRY	AMMO TYPES
SCAR-H	Assault Rifle	Starting	Belgium	EOTech(US) Holo	—	Laser Pointer	—	—	—
MP412 REX	Pistol	Starting	Russia	RMR (US)	Heavy	—	—	—	—
SCAR-H SV	DMR	Exploration	USA	ACOG	Flash Suppressor	—	Bipod	—	—
M240B	LMG	Exploration	USA	EOTech(US) Holo	Muzzle Brake	—	Bipod	—	—
M16A3	Assault Rifle	Exploration	USA	EOTech(US) Holo	Muzzle Brake	Magnifier(x3) RDS/Holo	—	—	—
SAR-21	Assault Rifle	Bronze Score	Singapore	Coyote(CH) RDS	Heavy	Magnifier(x3) RDS/Holo	—	—	—
QBB-95	LMG	Silver Score	China	CP1 Prismatic(CH) 3.4x	—	Laser Pointer	—	—	—
M82A3	Sniper Rifle	Gold Score	USA	Ballistic Scope (x40)	Muzzle Brake	STORM	—	Bipod	—
FY-J5	Sniper Rifle	Enemy	China	Visionking(x20) (CH)	Flash Suppressor	—	—	Straight Pull Bolt	—

KUNLUN MOUNTAINS

ASSIGNMENTS:

NAME	CRITERIA	UNLOCK
Bronze score	5000pts	G36C
Silver score	7000pts	AUG A3
Gold score	11000pts	CZ-3A1
Fang of the Underworld	Complete Kunlun Mountains	Shive (Multiplayer)

Dog Tags:

Cage Fighter: In a cell during breakout.

Freedom at any Cost: Inside the loading bay, on an electrical box on the second floor.

Shaw-shanked Redemption: Under the tram platform in the tram bridge encounter.

WEAPONS:

WEAPON	TYPE	ACQUIRED THROUGH	NATIONALITY	OPTICS	BARREL	ACCESSORIES	UNDERBARREL	AUXILIRY	AMMO TYPES
308-RECON	Sniper Rifle	Exploration	USA	Rifle Scope (x8)	—	Variable Zoom (x14)	—	Bipod	—
G36C	Carbine	Bronze Score	Germany	—	Muzzle Brake	Tribeam	Potato Grip	—	—
AUG A3	Assault Rifle	Silver Score	Austria	EOTech(US) Holo	—	Magnifier(x3) RDS/Holo	Ergo Grip	—	—
CZ-3A1	PDW	Gold Score	Czech Republic	RX01(US) RDS	PBS-4 Silencer (RU)	Canted Ironsights	—	—	—

TASHGAR

ASSIGNMENTS:

NAME	CRITERIA	UNLOCK
Bronze score	5000pts	M416
Silver score	10000pts	M1014
Gold score	14000pts	QBU-88
A Trapped Wolf Will	Complete Tashgar	Machete (Multiplayer)

Dog Tags:

Destruction Enthusiast: Inside a destructible truck during the bridge encounter.

Upstream Swimmer: After the helicopter encounter, you must jump from the walkway to the highest container and then another jump to the container with the dog tag.

WEAPONS:

WEAPON	TYPE	ACQUIRED THROUGH	NATIONALITY	OPTICS	BARREL	ACCESSORIES	UNDERBARREL	AUXILIRY	AMMO TYPES
SCAR-H	Assault Rifle	Starting	Belgium	EOTech(US) Holo	—	Laser Pointer	—	—	—
MP12 REX	Pistol	Starting	Russia	RMR (US)	Heavy	—	—	—	—
A-91	Carbine	Exploration	Russia	PKA-S(RU) Holo	Compensator	Magnifier(x3) RDS/ Holo	—	—	—
M249	LMG	Exploration	USA	M145(US) 3.4x	—	Laser Pointer	—	—	—
AEK-971	Assault Rifle	Exploration	Russia	PKA-S(RU) Holo	Heavy	Magnifier(x3) RDS/ Holo	Potato Grip	—	—
M416	Assault Rifle	Bronze Score	Germany	RX01(US) RDS	Heavy	Magnifier(x3) RDS/ Holo	—	—	—
M1014	Shotgun	Silver Score	USA	EOTech(US) Holo	Compensator	—	—	—	Buck
QBU-88	DMR	Gold Score	China	Compact (CH) 4x	Compensator	—	—	—	—
PP-2000	PDW	Enemy	Russia	Kobra(RU) RDS	—	Laser Pointer	—	—	—

WEAPONS (CONTINUED)

WEAPON	TYPE	ACQUIRED THROUGH	NATIONALITY	OPTICS	BARREL	ACCESSORIES	UNDERBARREL	AUXILIRY	AMMO TYPES
SAIGA-12K	Shotgun	Enemy	Russia	PKA-S(RU) Holo	Mod Choke (Narrow)	Flashlight	—	—	Buck
PKP PECHENEG	LMG	Enemy	Russia	—	—	—	Bipod	—	—
SV-98	Sniper Rifle	Enemy	Russia	PKS 07 (x7) (RU)	—	—	—	Straight Pull Bolt	—

SUEZ

ASSIGNMENTS:

NAME	CRITERIA	UNLOCK
Bronze score	3000pts	870 MCS
Silver score	4000pts	ACE 52 CQB
Gold score	5000pts	PDW-R
To Valhalla	Sacrifice the Valkyrie	QBZ-95-1 (Multiplayer)
Peace maker	Sacrifice Hannah at the end	P90 (Multiplayer)
Final Duty	Sacrifice Irish at the end	M249 (Multiplayer)

Dog Tags:

Rebel: On the back of a plane during the flight deck encounter. You need to go on top of the plane from the propeller to reach it.

Fleet Guardian: On a bed during the medbay scene.

WEAPONS:

WEAPON	TYPE	ACQUIRED THROUGH	NATIONALITY	OPTICS	BARREL	ACCESSORIES	UNDERBARREL	AUXILIRY	AMMO TYPES
SCAR-H	Assault Rifle	Starting	Belgium	EOTech(US) Holo	—	Laser Pointer	—	—	—
MP412 REX	Pistol	Starting	Russia	RMR (US)	Heavy	—	—	—	—
AK5C	Carbine	Exploration	Sweden	EOTech(US) Holo	Heavy	Magnifier(x3) RDS/Holo	—	—	—
870 MCS	Shotgun	Bronze Score	USA	—	Compensator	—	—	—	Buck
ACE 52 CQB	Carbine	Silver Score	Israel	Kobra(RU) RDS	—	Magnifier(x3) RDS/Holo	Angled Grip	—	—
PDW-R	PDW	Gold Score	USA	EOTech(US) Holo	Heavy	PEQ-15 (Combo)	—	—	—

ACHIEVEMENTS

Achievements are tied to fun events in that are not always based on the skill of the player, but rather key events or milestones within the game.

	NAME	DESCRIPTION
	Fishing in Baku	Complete the Baku
	Wolves in Sheep's Clothing	Complete Shanghai
	The Fall of a Titan	Complete South China Sea
	Braving the Storm	Complete Singapore
	Dead by Dawn	Complete Kunlun Mountains
	Antediluvian	Complete Tashgar
	Guns at Dawn	Complete Suez
	Dunn's Pride	Get 7000 score on Baku
	A One Man Riot	Get 11000 score on Shanghai
	Terror of the Deep	Get 11000 score on South China Sea
	Stormbringer	Get 20000 score on Singapore
	Gladiator	Get 12000 score on Kunlun Mountains
	Demolition Man	Get 15000 score on Tashgar
	Guardian of the Fleet	Get 6000 score on Suez
	Fish	Complete the campaign on any difficulty.
	Wolf	Complete the campaign on medium or hard
	Tombstone	Complete the campaign on hard
	Recon	Find 28 collectibles in the campaign
	Above and Beyond the Call	Unlock all assignments in the campaign

	NAME	DESCRIPTION
	Full Arsenal	Unlock all assignments and collectibles
	Stumbled Over It	Find 3 collectibles in the campaign
	It Was on the Way...	Find 6 collectibles in the campaign
	Took a Casual Look Around	Find 9 collectibles in the campaign
	Done Some Searching	Find 12 collectibles in the campaign
	Methodical Search	Find 15 collectibles in the campaign
	No Stone Left Unturned	Find 18 collectibles in the campaign
	Every Nook and Cranny	Find 21 collectibles in the campaign
	Well Placed	Get 10 kills on Baku with C4
	Wrecker	Get 10 multi-kills on Shanghai
	Blood Wake	Get 30 headshots on South China Sea
	War Turtle	Get 15 kills with the RPG in Singapore
	Shawshank	Get 5 kills with the shiv in Kunlun Mountains
	Infiltrator	Get 10 adrenaline kills on Tashgar
	For Tombstone	Let the Valkyrie be destroyed
	For the People	Sacrifice Irish to save the Valkyrie
	For the Cause	Sacrifice Hannah to save the Valkyrie
	Patience is a Virtue	Get all 3 endings

BATTLEFIELD BOOTCAMP | INFANTRY | VEHICLES | MULTIPLAYER MAPS | CAMPAIGN | BATTLEFIELD COMPENDIUM

BATTLEFIELD COMPENDIUM

MULTIPLAYER SCORING

EVENT	POINTS	DESCRIPTION
COMBAT		
Enemy Down	100	Kill an enemy.
Assist as Kill	75+	Assists over 75 also count as kills.
Suppression Assist	10	Enemy is killed while you suppress them.
Payback	50	Kill your most recent killer.
Dog Tag Payback	100	Take the dog tags of your most recent killer.
Kill Streak Stopped	TBD	Stop an enemy's killing spree of 4 or more.
Comeback	TBD	Die 4 (or more) times in a row and then score a kill.
Headshot Bonus	25	Score a headshot.
Avenger Bonus	25	Kill an enemy that recently killed a teammate.
Savior Bonus	25	Kill an enemy that's currently damaging a teammate.
Driver Bonus	25	Passenger performs a kill or disables/ destroys a vehicle.
Driver Spawn Bonus	25	A teammate spawned in the vehicle you're driving.
Spot Bonus	25	Target spotted by you is killed/disabled/ destroyed.
Multi Kill	200+	Kill 2 or more opponents within .8 seconds of each other.
Equipment Destroyed	25	Destroy an enemy MAV, T-UGS, Radio Beacon, Motion Mine, or SOFLAM.
Squad Wiped	50	Kill last member of a squad.
Roadkill Bonus	25	Drive over an enemy and kill them.
HVT Bonus	50	Kill an enemy while being marked as HVT by the enemy commander.
HVT Killed	100	Kill the HVT marked by your commander.
Melee Bonus	25	Kill an enemy with your knife.
VEHICLE COMBAT		
Vehicle Hit	TBD	Damage an enemy vehicle. Score = amount of damage inflicted on enemy vehicle.
Mobility Critical	50	Damage a vehicle until it gets slowed movement and steering.
Mobility Kill Bonus	25	Damage the vehicle so it gets immobilized.
Vehicle Disabled	50	Disable a vehicle so it catches fire.
Vehicle Destroyed	100	Destroy a vehicle.
Vehicle Destroy Assist	TBD	Assist in destroying a vehicle. Score = amount of damage inflicted on enemy vehicle.
SQUAD		
Squad Assist as Kill	75+	Assists over 75 also count as kills.
Squad Suppression Assist	20	Enemy is killed by your squadmate while you suppress.
Squad Avenger Bonus	50	Kill an enemy that recently killed a squadmate.
Squad Savior Bonus	50	Kill an enemy that's currently damaging a squadmate.
Squad Spot Bonus	50	A squadmate kills an enemy/vehicle that you spotted.
Squad Spawn	25	A squadmate spawns on you.
Last Man Spawn	50	A squadmate spawns on you when you're the last man.
Squad Revive	125	Revive a squadmate.
Squad Heal	15	Heal a squadmate.
Squad Repair	15	Repair a vehicle operated by a squadmate.
Squad Resupply	15	Resupply a squadmate.
Squad Order Bonus	50	Score a kill or temaplay action in the order area designated by your squad leader.
Squad Order Followed	25	Follow a capture/M-COM order issued by your squad leader or commander.
Squad Target Vehicle Hit	75	A squadmate damages a vehicle you have designated.
Squad Target Vehicle Destroyed	125	A squadmate destroys a vehicle you have designated.
Squad Vehicle Kill Assist	50	When a vehicle kill is performed, every squadmate in vehicle earns points.

EVENT	POINTS	DESCRIPTION
GAME MODE		
Capturing Flag	10	Awarded while within enemy flag's capture radius.
Flag Neutralized	100	Participate in a flag neutralize.
Flag Captured	150	Capture a flag.
Flag Defense	25	Awarded when killing enemies in a friendly flag area.
Flag Possession	TBD	Your team holds the majority of flags.
M-COM Armed	10	Arm an M-COM station.
M-COM Disarmed	200	Disarm an M-COM station.
M-COM Destroyed	400	Destroy an M-COM station.
M-COM Defense	50	Kill an enemy while they're arming or disarming an M-COM station.
Bomb Pickup	100	Pick up the bomb in Obliteration mode.
Bomb Carrier Killed	50	Kill the bomb carrier.
Bomb Delivered	500	Transport bomb to target area.
Bomb Deliver Assist	50	Awarded to team when bomb is delivered to target area, minus the bomb carrier.
Bomb Possession	50	Your team holds the bomb.
Domination Capture	100	Capture a flag in Domination mode.
Domination Defense	10	Kill an enemy near an enemy flag.
Domination Lockdown	10	Your team hold all the flags.
CLASSES		
Heal	10	Heal a teammate
Revive	100	Revive a teammate
Repair	10	Repair a vehicle occupied by a teammate.
Resupply	10	Resupply a teammate.
Marksman Bonus	50+	Perform a headshot with a sniper rifle greater than 50 meters. Score = distance to target.
Radio Beacon Spawn	25	A squadmate spawns on your Radio Beacon.
Motion Sensor Assist	10	Enemy is killed in vicinity of your Motion Sensor or T-UGS.
Target Vehicle Marked	25	Designate an enemy vehicle with a laser designator.
Target Vehicle Hit	50	A teammate damages a vehicle you have designated.
Target Vehicle Destroyed	100	A teammate destroys a vehicle you have designated.
COMMANDER		
Commander Order Accepted	10	A squad leader has accepted your order.
Supply Drop Used	10	A teammate uses your supply drop.
Vehicle Drop Used	10	A teammate has entered your vehicle drop for the first time.
Cruise Missile Launched	50	Launch a Cruise Missile attack.
Gunship Deployed	50	Deploy a friendly Gunship.
Squad Reinforced	25	Reinforce a squad. Reduce their respawn time and make them immune to Squad Wipe.
Scan Bonus	25	Teammate kills an enemy spotted by a UAV or Infantry/Vehicle Scan.
EMP Bonus	25	Enemy unit is killed/disabled/destroyed while being jammed by EMP UAV.
HVT Marked	50	Mark a highlighted enemy unit on a kill streak for your team.
HVT Eliminated	TBD	Marked HVT is killed. Score varies based on enemy's kill streak.
Early Warning Issued	50	Deploy an Early Warning.
Unanimous Support	50	No mutiny votes against you.
Gunship Kill Assist	10	Teammate performs a kill with the Gunship you deployed.

ACHIEVEMENTS

IMAGE	NAME	DESCRIPTION	GAMERSCORE	TROPHY
CAMPAIGN				
	Fishing in Baku	Complete the Baku	20	Bronze
	Wolves in sheep's clothing	Complete Shanghai	20	Bronze
	The fall of a Titan	Complete South China Sea	20	Bronze
	Braving the storm	Complete Singapore	20	Bronze
	Dead by dawn	Complete Kunlun Mountains	20	Bronze
	Antediluvian	Complete Tashgar	20	Bronze
	Guns at dawn	Complete Suez	20	Bronze
	Dunn's pride	Get 7,000 Score on Baku	25	Silver
	A one man riot	Get 11,000 Score on Shanghai	25	Silver
	Terror of the deep	Get 11,000 Score on South China Sea	25	Silver
	Storm bringer	Get 20,000 Score on Singapore	25	Silver
	Gladiator	Get 12,000 Score on Kunlun Mountains	25	Silver
	Demolition man	Get 15,000 Score on Tashgar	25	Silver
	Guardian of the fleet	Get 60,000 Score on Suez	25	Silver
	Fish	Complete the campaign on any difficulty	20	Bronze
	Wolf	Complete the campaignon medium or hard	25	Silver
	Tombstone	Complete the campaign on hard	25	Silver
	Recon	Find 28 collectables in the campaign	65	Gold
	Above and beyond the call	Unlock all assignments in the campaign	25	Silver
	Full arsenal	Unlock all assignments and collecatbles	65	Gold
	Stumbled over it	Find 3 collectables in the campaign	20	Bronze
	It was on the way...	Find 6 collectables in the campaign	20	Bronze

IMAGE	NAME	DESCRIPTION	GAMERSCORE	TROPHY
	Took a casual look around	Find 9 collectables in the campaign	20	Bronze
	Done some searching	Find 12 collectables in the campaign	20	Bronze
	Methodical seach	Find 15 collectables in the campaign	20	Bronze
	No stone left unturned	Find 18 collectables in the campaign	20	Bronze
	Every nook and cranny	Find 21 collectables in the campaign	20	Bronze
	Well Placed	Get 10 kills on Baku with C4	20	Bronze
	Wrecker	Get 10 multi-kills on Shanghai	20	Bronze
	Blood wake	Get 30 headshots on South China Sea	20	Bronze
	War Turtle	Get 15 kills with the RPG in Singapore	20	Bronze
	Shawshank	Get 5 kills with the Shiv in Kunlun Mountains	20	Bronze
	Infiltrator	Get 10 adrenaline kills on Tashgar	20	Bronze
	For Tombstone	Let the Valkyrie be destroyed	20	Bronze
	For the People	Sacrifice Irish to save the Valkyrie	20	Bronze
	For the Cause	Sacrifice Hannah to save the Valkyrie	20	Bronze
	Patience is a Virtue	Get all 3 endings	20	Silver
MULTIPLAYER				
	Turn Around...	Perform 5 dog tag kills in Multiplayer	10	Bronze
	Won Them All	Win one round in each of the 7 game modes in Multiplayer	10	Bronze
	.45 Old School	Perform 45 kills with the M1911 handgun in Multiplayer	25	Silver
	Bomb Squad	Deliver 5 bombs in Obliteration in Multiplayer	25	Silver
	Call me Sir	Reach Captain rank (rank 25) in Multiplayer	50	Gold
PS3/PS4 EXCLUSIVE				
	Platinum	Earn all trophies	N/A	Platinum

RANKS

NAME	POINTS
1. Private First Class	5,700
2. Private First Class II	18,600
3. Private First Class III	37,000
4. Private First Class IV	61,000
5. Private First Class V	88,000
6. Lance Corporal	121,000
7. Lance Corporal II	157,000
8. Lance Corporal III	197,000
9. Lance Corporal IV	240,000
10. Lance Corporal V	287,000
11. Corporal	338,000
12. Corporal II	392,000
13. Corporal III	449,000
14. Corporal IV	509,000
15. Corporal V	572,000
16. Sergeant	639,000
17. Sergeant II	708,000
18. Sergeant III	780,000
19. Sergeant IV	856,000
20. Sergeant V	933,000
21. Staff Sergeant	1,014,000
22. Staff Sergeant II	1,098,000
23. Staff Sergeant III	1,184,000
24. Staff Sergeant IV	1,273,000
25. Staff Sergeant V	1,364,000
26. Gunnery Sergeant	1,458,000
27. Gunnery Sergeant II	1,555,000
28. Gunnery Sergeant III	1,654,000
29. Gunnery Sergeant IV	1,756,000
30. Gunnery Sergeant V	1,860,000
31. Master Sergeant	1,966,000
32. Master Sergeant II	2,080,000
33. Master Sergeant III	2,194,000

NAME	POINTS
34. Master Sergeant IV	2,308,000
35. Master Sergeant V	2,422,000
36. First Sergeant	2,540,000
37. First Sergeant II	2,660,000
38. First Sergeant III	2,780,000
39. First Sergeant IV	2,910,000
40. First Sergeant V	3,040,000
41. Master Gunnery Sergeant	3,170,000
42. Master Gunnery Sergeant II	3,300,000
43. Master Gunnery Sergeant III	3,430,000
44. Master Gunnery Sergeant IV	3,570,000
45. Master Gunnery Sergeant V	3,710,000
46. Sergeant Major	3,850,000
47. Sergeant Major II	3,990,000
48. Sergeant Major III	4,130,000
49. Sergeant Major IV	4,280,000
50. Sergeant Major V	4,430,000
51. Warrant Officer One	4,580,000
52. Warrant Officer One II	4,740,000
53. Warrant Officer One III	4,900,000
54. Warrant Officer One IV	5,060,000
55. Warrant Officer One V	5,220,000
56. Chief Warrant Officer Two	5,380,000
57. Chief Warrant Officer Two II	5,540,000
58. Chief Warrant Officer Two III	5,700,000
59. Chief Warrant Officer Two IV	5,870,000
60. Chief Warrant Officer Two V	6,040,000
61. Chief Warrant Officer Three	6,210,000
62. Chief Warrant Officer Three II	6,390,000
63. Chief Warrant Officer Three III	6,570,000
64. Chief Warrant Officer Three IV	6,750,000
65. Chief Warrant Officer Three V	6,930,000
66. Chief Warrant Officer Four	7,110,000
67. Chief Warrant Officer Four II	7,290,000

NAME	POINTS
68. Chief Warrant Officer Four III	7,480,000
69. Chief Warrant Officer Four IV	7,670,000
70. Chief Warrant Officer Four V	7,860,000
71. Chief Warrant Officer Five	8,050,000
72. Chief Warrant Officer Five II	8,240,000
73. Chief Warrant Officer Five III	8,430,000
74. Chief Warrant Officer Five IV	8,630,000
75. Chief Warrant Officer Five V	8,830,000
76. Second Lieutenant	9,030,000
77. Second Lieutenant II	9,230,000
78. Second Lieutenant III	9,440,000
79. Second Lieutenant IV	9,650,000
80. Second Lieutenant V	9,860,000
81. First Lieutenant	10,070,000
82. First Lieutenant II	10,280,000
83. First Lieutenant III	10,490,000
84. First Lieutenant IV	10,710,000
85. First Lieutenant V	10,930,000
86. Captain	11,150,000
87. Captain II	11,370,000
88. Captain III	11,590,000
89. Captain IV	11,810,000
90. Captain V	12,040,000
91. Major	12,270,000
92. Major II	12,500,000
93. Major III	12,730,000
94. Major IV	12,960,000
95. Major V	13,200,000
96. Lieutenant Colonel	13,440,000
97. Lieutenant Colonel II	13,680,000
98. Lieutenant Colonel III	13,920,000
99. Lieutenant Colonel IV	14,160,000
100. Colonel	14,400,000

ASSIGNMENTS

IMAGE	NAME	POINTS	CRITERIA 1	CRITERIA 2	CRITERIA 3	CRITERIA 4	REWARD
BRONZE							
	Assault Combat Basic	500	Rank 10 (Lance Corporal V)	7 kills with a Assault riffle	11 Heals with Medkit	—	Assault Combat Basic Dog Tag
	Engineer Combat Basic	500	Rank 10 (Lance Corporal V)	7 kills with a Carbine	16 Repairs with repair tool	—	Engineer Combat Basic Dog Tag
	Recon Combat Basic	500	Rank 10 (Lance Corporal V)	7 kills with Sniper rifle	4 squad member spawn on you	—	Recon Combat Basic Dog Tag
	Support Combat Basic	500	Rank 10 (Lance Corporal V)	7 kills with Light Machine Gun	16 Resupplies from ammo box	—	Support Combat Basic Dog Tag
	Land Vehicles Basic	500	Rank 10 (Lance Corporal V)	In a round, kill 7 enemies with Land Vehicles	Destroy 25 vehicles with Land Vehicles	—	Land Vehicles Basic Dog Tag
	Air Vehicles Basic	500	Rank 10 (Lance Corporal V)	In a round, kill 7 enemies with Air Vehicles	Destroy 25 vehicles with Air Vehicles	—	Air Vehicles Basic Dog Tag
	Marine Vehicles Basic	500	Rank 10 (Lance Corporal V)	5 kills with marine vehicles	Marine Vehicle Ribbon x 10	—	Marine Vehicles Basic Dog Tag
	Carbine Basic	500	Rank 20 (Sergeant V)	7 kills with a Carbine	Carbine Ribbon x 10	—	Carbine Basic Dog Tag
	PDW Basic	500	Rank 20 (Sergeant V)	7 kills with a PDW	Personal Defense Weapon Ribbon x 10	—	PDW Basic Dog Tag
	Shotgun Basic	500	Rank 20 (Sergeant V)	7 kills with a Shotgun	Shotgun Ribbon x 10	—	Shotgun Basic Dog Tag
	Conqueror	500	Rank 20 (Sergeant V)	Capture 20 flags.	Conquest Ribbon x 10	—	Conqueror Dog Tag
	Rusher	500	Rank 20 (Sergeant V)	M-COM Attacker Ribbon x 10	Rush Ribbon x 10	—	Rusher Dog Tag
	Obliterator	500	Rank 20 (Sergeant V)	Pick up 20 bombs.	Obliteration Ribbon x 10	—	Obliterator Dog Tag
	By My Command	500	Rank 20 (Sergeant V)	Commander Leadership Ribbon x 10	Commander Resupply Ribbon x 10	—	By My Command Dog Tag
	Blade Runner	500	Rank 20 (Sergeant V)	5 kills with the knife	Melee Ribbon x 10	—	Blade Runner Dog Tag
SILVER							
	Assault Combat Veteran	1,000	Assault Combat Basic	8 kills with a Assault riffle	12 Heals with Medkit	—	Crimson Woodland Weapon Paint
	Engineer Combat Veteran	1,000	Engineer Combat Basic	8 kills with a Carbine	17 Repairs with repair tool	—	TTsKO Blue Weapon Paint
	Recon Combat Veteran	1,000	Recon Combat Basic	8 kills with Sniper rifle	5 squad member spawn on you	—	Duckweed Weapon Paint
	Support Combat Veteran	1,000	Support Combat Basic	8 kills with Light Machine Gun	17 Resupplies from ammo box	—	Green Underbrush Weapon Paint
	Land Vehicles Veteran	1,000	Land Vehicles Basic	In a round, kill 10 enemies with Land Vehicles	Destroy 50 vehicles with Land Vehicles	—	Black Shark Vehicle Paint
	Air Vehicles Veteran	1,000	Air Vehicles Basic	In a round, kill 10 enemies with Air Vehicles	Destroy 50 vehicles with Air Vehicles	—	Flanker Vehicle Paint
	Marine Vehicles Veteran	1,000	Marine Vehicles Basic	6 kills with marine vehicles	Marine Vehicle Ribbon x 20	—	Blue Sky Vehicle Paint
	Carbine Veteran	1,000	Carbine Basic	8 kills with a Carbine	Carbine Ribbon x 20	—	Ripple Weapon Paint
	PDW Veteran	1,000	PDW Basic	8 kills with a PDW	Personal Defense Weapon Ribbon x 20	—	Ink Blotch Weapon Paint
	Shotgun Veteran	1,000	Shotgun Basic	8 kills with a Shotgun	Shotgun Ribbon x 20	—	Blue Tiget Weapon Paint
	Tin Foil Hat	1,000	Rank 50 (Sergeant Major V)	Commander Surveilance Ribbon x 10	Obtain 30 EMP Bonuses as Commander	Spotting Ribbon x 20	Tin Foil Hat Dog Tag
	We'll Meet Again	1,000	Rank 50 (Sergeant Major V)	Launch 100 Tomahawks	Deploy 50 Early Warnings	—	We'll Meet Again Dog Tag
	Leave No Man Behind	1,000	Rank 50 (Sergeant Major V)	Obtain 25 Squad Savior bonuses	Obtain 25 Squad Avenger bonuses	Perform 50 Squad Revives	Leave No Man Behind Dog Tag
	Wrecking Ball	1,000	Rank 50 (Sergeant Major V)	Obtain 25 Mobility Critical Hits	—	Obtain 50 Catastrophic Kill bonuses	Wrecking Ball Dog Tag
	Stealth Assassin	1,000	Blade Runner	Obtain 20 Dog Tags	Melee Ribbon x 20	—	Stealth Assassin Dog Tag
GOLD							
	Assault Combat Expert	5,000	Assault Combat Veteran	Receive 10 Assault RifleRibbons	Receive 50 Medkit Ribbons.	200 kills with assault rifles	ACE 23 Assault Rifle
	Engineer Combat Expert	5,000	Engineer Combat Veteran	Receive 10 CarbineRibbons	Receive 50 Repair Tool Ribbons.	200 kills with carbines	UMP-9 PDW
	Recon Combat Expert	5,000	Recon Combat Veteran	Receive 10 Sniper RifleRibbons	Receive 50 Marksman Ribbons.	200 kills with sniper rifles	FY-JS Sniper Rifle
	Support Combat Expert	5,000	Support Combat Veteran	Receive 10 Light Machine Gun Ribbons	Receive 50 Ammo Ribbons.	200 kills with light machine guns	RPK-12 LMG
	Offensive Commander	5,000	By My Command	Kill 30 enemies with the Cruise Missiles	Designate 10 High Value Targets	Deploy 50 Gunships	Offensive Commander Dog Tag

ASSIGNMENTS, CONTINUED

IMAGE	NAME	POINTS	CRITERIA 1	CRITERIA 2	CRITERIA 3	CRITERIA 4	REWARD
	Hitman	5,000	Rank 100 (Colonel)	Wipe 10 squads	Get 5 Kill streak stopped	Kill 3 Commander designated High Value Targets	Hitman Dog Tag
	Land Warrior	5,000	Rank 100 (Colonel)	Obtain 1 Main Battle Tank Medal	Obtain 1 Infantry Fighting Vehicle Medal	Destroy 1 Helicopter with Main Battle Tanks.	Land Warrior Dog Tag
	Air Warrior	5,000	Rank 100 (Colonel)	Obtain 1 Attack Helicopter Medal	Obtain 1 Jet Fighter Medal	Destroy 5 Jets with Attack Helicopters.	Air Warrior Dog Tag
	Taxi Driver	5,000	Rank 100 (Colonel)	In a round, obtain 10 driver spawn bonuses	Obtain 30 driver bonuses	Obtain 10 squad vehicle kill assist	Taxi Driver Dog Tag
	Wall of Shotgun	5,000	Rank 100 (Colonel)	Perform 50 kills with the DBV-12	Perform 50 kills with the M26 MASS	Perform 50 kills with the Serbu Shorty	Wall of Shotgun Dog Tag
	Swedish Steel	5,000	Rank 100 (Colonel)	Perform 100 kills with the AK5D carbine	Perform 50 headshots with the AK5D carbine	Perform 100 kills with the CBJ-MS PDW	Swedish Steel Dog Tag
	Made in China	5,000	Rank 100 (Colonel)	Perform 50 headshots with the QBU-88 DMR	Perform 100 kills with the QBS-09 shotgun	Perform 50 kills with the QBZ-92 handgun	Made in China Dog Tag
	From Russia With Lead	5,000	Rank 100 (Colonel)	Perform 50 headshots with the SKS DMR	Perform 100 kills with the A-91 carbine	Perform 50 kills with the MP412 REX handgun	From Russia With Lead Dog Tag
	American Classics	5,000	Rank 100 (Colonel)	Perform 50 headshots with the M39 DMR	Perform 100 kills with the M4A1 carbine	Perform 50 kills with the .44 Magnum handgun	American Classics Dog Tag
	Melee Expert	5,000	Stealth Assassin	In a life, perform 3 kills with the knife	Melee Ribbon x 50	—	Melee Expert Dog Tag

RIBBONS

IMAGE	NAME	POINTS	CRITERIA
	Kill Assist Ribbon	500	Perform 5 kill assists.
	Anti Vehicle Ribbon	500	Destroy 2 vehicles.
	Squad Wipe Ribbon	500	Receive 2 squad wipes.
	Headshot Ribbon	500	Receive 3 headshots.
	Avenger Ribbon	500	Perform 2 avenger kills.
	Savior Ribbon	500	Perform 2 savior kills.
	Spotting Ribbon	500	Perform 4 spot bonuses.
	Ace Squad Ribbon	500	Be part of the best squad.
	MVP Ribbon	500	Receive the highest combat score.
	Handgun Ribbon	500	Kill 4 enemies with handguns.
	Assault Rifle Ribbon	500	Kill 6 enemies with assault rifles.
	Carbine Ribbon	500	Kill 6 enemies with carbines.
	Sniper Rifle Ribbon	500	Kill 6 enemies with sniper rifles.
	Light Machine Gun Ribbon	500	Kill 6 enemies with light machine guns.
	Designated Marksman Rifle Ribbon	500	Kill 6 enemies with designated marksman rifles.
	Personal Defense Weapon Ribbon	500	Kill 6 enemies with personal defense weapons.
	Shotgun Ribbon	500	Kill 6 enemies with shotguns.
	Melee Ribbon	500	Kill 4 enemies with the knife.
	Infantry Fighting Vehicle Ribbon	500	Kill 5 enemies with infantry fighting vehicles.
	Main Battle Tank Ribbon	500	Kill 5 enemies with main battle tanks.
	Anti Air Tank Ribbon	500	Kill 4 enemies with anti air tanks.
	Scout Helicopter Ribbon	500	Kill 5 enemies with scout helicopters.
	Attack Helicopter Ribbon	500	Kill 5 enemies with attack helicopters.

IMAGE	NAME	POINTS	CRITERIA
	Jet Fighter Ribbon	500	Kill 5 enemies with jet fighters.
	Marine Vehicle Ribbon	500	Kill 4 enemies with marine vehicles.
	Flag Capture Ribbon	500	Capture 2 flags in Conquest.
	M-COM Attacker Ribbon	500	Arm 2 M-COMs in Rush.
	Bomb Delivery Ribbon	500	Deliver 1 bomb in Obliteration.
	Conquest Ribbon	500	Win a Conquest round.
	Rush Ribbon	500	Win a Rush round.
	Team Deathmatch Ribbon	500	Win a Team Deathmatch round.
	Squad Deathmatch Ribbon	500	Win a Squad Deathmatch round.
	Obliteration Ribbon	500	Win an Obliteration round.
	Elimination Ribbon	500	Win a Elimination round.
	Domination Ribbon	500	Win a Domination round.
	Medkit Ribbon	500	Perform 8 heals with the medkit.
	Defibrilator Ribbon	500	Perform 5 revives with the defibrilator.
	Repair Tool Ribbon	500	Perform 8 repairs with the repair tool.
	Exceptional Marksman Headshot Ribbon	500	Achieve a headshot with the distance of 250m.
	Radio Beacon Spawn Ribbon	500	Have 3 squad spawns on you.
	Ammo Ribbon	500	Perform 8 resupplies with the ammo box.
	Commander Surveilance Ribbon	500	Obtain 10 scan bonuses as commander.
	Commander Resupply Ribbon	500	Obtain 10 supply crate uses as commander.
	Commander Leadership Ribbon	500	Receive 10 orders accepted as commander.
	Commander Gunship Ribbon	500	Deploy 2 Gunships as commander.

MEDALS

IMAGE	NAME	POINTS	CRITERIA
COMBAT			
	Kill Assist Medal	5,000	Receive 50 Kill Assist Ribbons.
	Anti Vehicle Medal	5,000	Receive 50 Anti Vehicle Ribbons.
	Squad Wipe Medal	5,000	Receive 50 Squad Wipe Ribbons.
	Headshot Medal	5,000	Receive 50 Headshot Ribbons.
	Avenger Medal	5,000	Receive 50 Avenger Ribbons.
	Savior Medal	5,000	Receive 50 Savior Ribbons.
	Spotting Medal	5,000	Receive 50 Spotting Ribbons.
	Ace Squad Medal	5,000	Receive 50 Ace Squad Ribbons.
	MVP Medal	5,000	Receive 50 MVP Ribbons.
WEAPONS			
	Handgun Medal	5,000	Receive 50 Handgun Ribbons.
	Assault Rifle Medal	5,000	Receive 50 Assault Rifle Ribbons.
	Carbine Medal	5,000	Receive 50 Carbine Ribbons.
	Sniper Rifle Medal	5,000	Receive 50 Sniper Rifle Ribbons.
	Light Machine Gun Medal	5,000	Receive 50 Light Machine Gun Ribbons.
	Designated Marksman Rifle Medal	5,000	Receive 50 Designated Marksman Rifle Ribbons.
	Personal Defense Weapon Medal	5,000	Receive 50 Personal Defense Weapon Ribbons.
	Shotgun Medal	5,000	Receive 50 Shotgun Ribbons.
	Melee Medal	5,000	Receive 50 Melee Ribbons.
VEHICLES			
	Infantry Fighting Vehicle Medal	5,000	Receive 50 Infantry Fighting Vehicle Ribbons.
	Main Battle Tank Medal	5,000	Receive 50 Main Battle Tank Ribbons.
	Anti Air Tank Medal	5,000	Receive 50 Anti Air Tank Ribbons.
	Scout Helicopter Medal	5,000	Receive 50 Scout Helicopter Ribbons.
	Attack Helicopter Medal	5,000	Receive 50 Attack Helicopter Ribbons.
	Jet Fighter Medal	5,000	Receive 50 Jet Fighter Ribbons.
	Marine Vehicle Medal	5,000	Receive 50 Marine Vehicle Ribbons.

IMAGE	NAME	POINTS	CRITERIA
GAME MODE			
	Flag Capture Medal	5,000	Receive 50 Flag Capture Ribbons.
	M-COM Attacker Medal	5,000	Receive 50 M-COM Attacker Ribbons.
	Bomb Delivery Medal	5,000	Receive 50 Bomb Delivery Ribbons.
	Conquest Medal	1,000	Receive 50 Conquest Ribbons.
	Rush Medal	1,000	Receive 50 Rush Ribbons.
	Team Deathmatch Medal	1,000	Receive 50 Team Deathmatch Ribbons.
	Squad Deathmatch Medal	1,000	Receive 50 Squad Deathmatch Ribbons.
	Obliteration Medal	1,000	Receive 50 Obliteration Ribbons.
	Squad Annihilation Medal	1,000	Receive 50 Squad Annihilation Ribbons.
	Domination Medal	1,000	Receive 50 Domination Ribbons.
CLASSES			
	Medkit Medal	5,000	Receive 50 Medkit Ribbons.
	Defibrilator Medal	5,000	Receive 50 Defibrilator Ribbons.
	Repair Tool Medal	5,000	Receive 50 Repair Tool Ribbons.
	Marksman Medal	5,000	Receive 50 Marksman Ribbons.
	Radio Beacon Spawn Medal	5,000	Receive 50 Radio Beacon Spawn Ribbons.
	Ammo Medal	5,000	Receive 50 Ammo Ribbons.
COMMANDER			
	Commander Surveilance Medal	5,000	Receive 50 Commander Surveilance Ribbons.
	Commander Resupply Medal	5,000	Receive 50 Commander Leadership Ribbons.
	Commander Leadership Medal	5,000	Receive 50 Commander Resupply Ribbons.
	Commander Gunship Medal	5,000	Receive 50 Commander Gunship Ribbons.